CARS IN THE UK

Volume Two: 1971 to 1995

CARS IN THE UK

A survey of all British-built and

officially imported cars available

in the United Kingdom since 1945

Volume Two: 1971 to 1995

GRAHAM ROBSON

MRP

MOTOR RACING PUBLICATIONS LTD
Unit 6, The Pilton Estate, 46 Pitlake, Croydon CR0 3RY, England

First published 1997

British Library Cataloguing in Publication Data

Robson, Graham, 1936–
    Cars in the UK : a survey of all British-built and officially imported cars available in the UK since 1945
    Vol. 2: 1971 to 1995
    1. Automobiles – Great Britain
    I. Title
    338.7'629222'0941

ISBN 1899870164

Typeset by Richard Clark, Penzance
Printed in Great Britain by
Hartnolls Ltd, Bodmin, Cornwall

Contents:

Introduction

How many times have you searched for a car's top speed, then not known how much it cost? Or looked for an engine size, but not known what was the car's top speed? Wondered which Ferrari was fastest? Which car was made over the longest period? Or tried to equate length with weight, and body options – and failed? That's right – often, and so have I.

This book, I hope, will solve all – or at least most of – your problems, for it sets out to list, summarize and describe every production car made, or sold, in the UK from 1971 to the end of 1995. A companion volume covers the period 1945 to 1970.

Because I have a large library at home, I know I am very lucky, but I've always been irritated by the lack of an all-can-do book to save me the hours of digging around for information. Some time ago, more than 40 years after I bought my first motoring magazine, I decided to do something about it.

CARS in the UK sets out to provide you with all the facts, without any flowery opinions – and hopefully without any prejudice. There are tens of thousands of 'what's, 'when's, 'how fast's and 'how much's in these pages – and I hope I have covered every production car sold in the UK. Because of the way sales and prices have changed so radically over the years, I have also included tables to help you work out what is cheap by 1970 standards – or costly by 1945 standards.

When I first approached my publisher, John Blunsden, he thought I was about to propose yet another 'Centenary Book' (for the book was likely to appear for the first time in the British motor industry's centenary year, 1996), but when he saw that my intention was to cover only the post-Second World War period, but to do so in great detail, he became enthusiastic.

Originally, the intention had been to produce one vast volume covering the first 50 postwar years, but as the project progressed we both realized that if it were to do every subject justice, such a book would almost certainly be a lot too large for the reader to handle comfortably, as well as colossally expensive. We therefore decided to cover the same period in two matching volumes, to be published in quick succession, which would neatly and tidily split at the end of 1970, making this volume the second part of my 50 postwar years survey.

Ground rules

From the very first day that work started on this project, I was determined to conform to carefully selected rules as regards content and structure, and subject to my informants/information being correct, here they are:

Firstly, I decided to treat the subject by calendar year rather than by individual make, so that the way the UK motoring scene developed and changed could be seen more clearly.

I also decided to describe new cars in the year in which they were officially revealed, which was not necessarily the year in which they went on sale. As far as British cars were concerned, it usually was, but many overseas cars were announced a year (or even more, in some cases) before they were first sold in the UK. (Naturally, this means that there is a slight overlap between 1970, where Volume I ended, and 1971, where this Volume begins, but I am sure the reader will understand the necessity for this.)

I have included, by family, every basic car, whether British or imported, which has been sold in the UK fully built-up, by a factory or import concessionaire since the beginning of 1971. Any cars missed must have slipped into these islands undetected by either newspapers or motoring magazines – in which case they deserve their place in the shadows!

As far as possible I have tried to sift out what I call the 'Motor Show Specials', which appeared, flared briefly, but were never heard of again, and were probably never sold to customers. How many French Hotchkiss or Russian Zaporozhet cars, for example, survived after Earls Court's doors finally closed?

I have omitted cars made in the UK which were sold entirely for export – the DeLorean DMC-12 being a perfect example. Nor have I included 'grey imports' (ie personal imports, such as some 1990s exotica), or the import of one-offs.

Also, I have omitted cars which were only ever sold as do-it-yourself kits – which explains why there is no Lotus 6, or Duttons, or several other marques.

Where engine options were available, I have only included those which were ever listed for sale on British-market cars. In particular, cars imported from Japan or Europe were often sold in the UK with only a limited proportion of the home-market engine ranges.

I decided to include as much data as possible in a massive specification chart, which has been trimmed only insofar as I have only quoted the length of the shortest derivative, and the lightest weight, and only the price of the car when introduced: otherwise, the chart would have been quite unwieldy. For cars launched before the end of 1970, and made for many years afterwards, I have included every derivative: the first-generation Porsche 911, which was built from 1964 to 1989, is an example of this.

(If a particular feature is missing from the specification chart, please forgive me – there simply wasn't space for anything more!)

Controversially, I decided to include the most believable set of production figures in every case: you would be amazed how these seem to change, over the years, and from authority to authority.

Lastly, I accepted that I was most certainly fallible, and that inevitably and inadvertently there would be a few omissions. However, I am not blessed with second sight, and if I could find no record of a particular car in my researches, it has not been included!

On this occasion, I hope I may be allowed to end by quoting that great personality, Sir Winston Churchill, who once wrote:

'Writing a book is an adventure. To begin with it is a toy and an amusement. Then it becomes a mistress, then it becomes a tyrant. The last phase is that just as you are about to be reconciled to your servitude, you kill the monster and fling him to the public.'

I know what he meant, for in writing this book I went through all those phases. Here it is, then – a monster which I am delighted to have defeated.

GRAHAM ROBSON
Burton Bradstock
June 1996

Acknowledgements

If I tried to write down every name, publication, source and influence which has gone into the preparation of this book, it would be a colossal Appendix all on its own.

Everything I have ever read, written, learned, or observed has helped, in one way or another, to provide the facts listed here. Which means that I would like to thank:

Every editor who has helped to produce 50 years of motoring magazines since 1945.

Every publisher who has commissioned a motoring book during the same period – British, European or North American.

Every industry press officer, past and present, here or overseas, who has provided facts, figures and other reference material.

Every club enthusiast, individual and fully-paid-up car 'buff' who has helped me over many years.

Because they all provided paper, reams of it, this proves something that my wife has always complained about – that I rarely throw anything away!

GRAHAM ROBSON

1945 to 1970

As detailed in Volume I...

As I have already explained in the Introduction, my plan to cover 50 post-war years of the British motoring scene has matured into two Volumes. In Volume 1, I have covered the evolution of the British motoring scene from 1945 to 1970, from which point this book takes over.

Volume 1 covers a particularly fascinating period, for in 1945 the British motor industry really had to start again from scratch, while its customers were anxious to return to peacetime motoring conditions as rapidly as possible. So what were the most important developments in those early postwar years?

The market

In 1945, the time taken for factories to be converted from producing tanks, guns, aero-engines and aircraft into assembly lines for private cars meant that a huge waiting list for new cars soon built up.

Until the early 1950s it was usual for a private motorist to have to wait years for his order to be met – and even then he might be offered an alternative on a 'take it or leave it' basis. It was not until about 1955 that an orderly market developed, when manufacturers once again had to go out and *sell* rather than merely take orders.

Fortunately for the car-makers, Britain's standard of living rose almost without pause in the 1950s and 1960s, which meant that many more people could afford to buy cars – and did so. In Britain, annual sales of new cars rocketed from 135,000 in 1950 to 820,000 in 1960 and 1,127,000 in 1970 – a leap of more than 800 per cent in 20 years.

New roads, new restrictions

By 1970 there was both good and bad news for motorists. Britain's motorway network was expanding rapidly, but an overall speed limit was in force. In 1945, there had been no British motorways and no overall limit!

After the war, existing roads were badly neglected, many of them having been battered by overuse from heavy military traffic. Although successive Governments promised new roads, there was no action to back up the hot air until the mid-1950s. By that time, congestion on many so-called trunk roads had become unacceptable.

Britain's first stretch of motorway – the M6 around Preston – was opened in December 1958, and the St Albans–Coventry stretch of the M1 came a year later. New motorways appeared rapidly after that, major sections of the M2, M3, M4, M5, M6 and M62 in England all being opened to traffic by 1970, and central Scotland also getting its share of new highways. At the same time, the A1 Great North Road was progressively transformed into a dual-carriageway highway.

Drivers of fast cars could enjoy truly rapid travel on those new roads until the end of 1965, when a 70mph overall limit was applied on totally specious evidence. In spite of promises that it was only an experimental limit, it has never been lifted.

Petrol supplies and rationing

Private motoring – motoring for pleasure – had been banned from 1942, but a tiny basic petrol ration was allowed from 1945. The allowance was withdrawn completely in 1947–48, but then reinstated until May 1950, when rationing suddenly came to an end. But it was reimposed for several months in 1956–57 (a direct consequence of the Suez War of 1956), after which supplies were once again unrestricted.

The only available 'Pool' petrol was of truly execrable quality (rated at about 72 octane) until 1953, when branded petrol of a much higher octane rating finally returned.

Taxation on car prices

Today's car prices may be a lot too high, but they would be a whole lot higher if early postwar taxation levels still applied.

Immediately after the war, all car prices were subjected to purchase tax (the predecessor of Value Added Tax), which began at 33⅓ per cent in 1945, but rose to 66⅔ per cent in the early 1950s. After that, tax levels gradually came down, but there was still a long way to go when the 1970s opened, purchase tax still being levied at 36⅔ per cent.

British car-makers – the old order changeth...

Immediately after the war, the British motor industry was dominated by the Big Six, but by 1970 they had contracted to the Big Four, only one of which remained in British ownership.

In 1945, the battle for leadership was between Austin and the Nuffield Organisation (Morris, MG, Riley and Wolseley), with Ford in third place, the Rootes Group (Hillman/Humber/Sunbeam-Talbot) behind them, followed by Standard and Vauxhall. Only Ford and Vauxhall were American-owned.

By 1970, British Leyland had evolved, incorporating Austin, Nuffield, Standard and several minor marques. Ford and Vauxhall had expanded considerably, while Chrysler United Kingdom had taken over from the Rootes Group.

British Leyland still held market leadership in 1970, but Ford was closing in fast and would take over the No 1 spot during the 1970s.

British Leyland – megalomania gone wrong

Although British Leyland still led the British market in 1970, the edifice was already tottering. A series of mergers – forced or otherwise – had never been followed by rationalization. This is how the empire had been built up:

** Austin merged with the Nuffield Organisation in 1952 to form BMC. This brought Austin, Morris, MG, Riley and Wolseley together. Princess and Vanden Plas marques were invented by this group.

** Leyland (the truck-maker) took over Standard-Triumph in 1961.

** Rover bought Alvis in 1965.

** BMC merged with Jaguar (who already owned Daimler) in 1966. There was a new holding company called British Motor Holdings (BMH).

** Leyland absorbed Rover in 1967. This brought Triumph and Rover together.

** British Leyland was formed in 1968 by the merger of Leyland with BMH. Leyland bosses, staff and policies became dominant. The immediate result was that British Leyland controlled the following car marques:

Austin
Austin-Healey
Daimler
Jaguar
Land-Rover
MG
Morris
Princess
Riley
Rover
Triumph
Wolseley

– and the dormant trademarks of Alvis and Lanchester.

British Leyland also now controlled these truck-makers:

AEC
Albion
Austin
BMC
Guy
Leyland
Morris Commercial
Scammell

– but it would all go wrong within five years…

Imported cars

At the end of the war, 'Great Britain plc' was deeply in debt to the rest of the world. In order to begin paying off these debts, the Government urged British industry to 'export or die', and at the same time all car imports were effectively banned by imposing on them extremely difficult regulations and high taxation.

By the end of 1950, only 3,749 foreign cars had been imported in five years: by the mid-1990s more than 3,000 imported cars were being sold in Britain every day!

Although import restrictions were abandoned in the early 1950s, it took a long time for overseas manufacturers to establish their UK market. Even by the end of 1960, the import market share was still only 7 per cent, but it would be 14 per cent in 1970 – and the import explosion was about to begin.

Japanese cars

Looking back from an era when the number of cars imported from Japan is restricted by the gentlemen's agreement of a quota, and when three large factories are assembling Japanese cars in the UK, it is difficult to remember that there were *no* Japanese car imports until 1965, and that the first determined assault on the British market did not come (from Datsun) until the end of the 1960s.

British car-making gurus made the same mistake as their motorcycle counterparts – taking an instant dislike to Japanese products of the period and being dismissive of their quality and market appeal. But the customer thought differently, and Japanese car sales would mushroom in the 1970s.

Technical innovations

The traditional car layout of the 1930s – front-engine/rear-drive, separate chassis – was swept aside by the 1950s and a further revolution took place in the 1960s.

After the war, almost every newly-designed mass-market car was built around a unit-construction body/chassis unit. In Europe, though not in the UK, there was also a rush to design cars with the engine over the driving wheels. At first these were rear-engined layouts: the VW Beetle, really a car of the 1930s, but much-delayed because of the war, was the first to set the trend, but the Renault 4CV and the Fiat 600 soon followed.

Front-wheel-drive cars like the DKWs, Saabs and Citroen 2CVs all made their mark by the 1950s, but it was the Citroen DS19, followed by the amazing BMC Mini and the Renault 4, which really made the market sit up and take notice. By the end of the decade it was clear that front-wheel drive had won the battle over rear-mounted engines, while all-independent suspension became the norm.

Except for Volkswagen and Fiat (with the 500), few manufacturers persevered with air-cooled engines, while new water-cooled engines became more powerful. Overhead-camshaft engines were common by 1970, twin-cams were moving downmarket, while the first four-valves-per-cylinder engines had also appeared.

Automatic transmission was still a comparative rarity among European cars, though it had become a widely quoted option on cars with engines as small as 1.5 litres.

Four-wheel drive for private cars was known, but still expensive, so after Europe's first 4x4 private car (the Jensen FF of 1966) there would be no further advances until the 1980s.

Disc brakes and radial-ply tyres were two important innovations in the 1950s: both are now normal fittings on even the smallest of microcars.

Fuel injection, on the other hand, was an expensive rarity which only gained a fingerhold in the 1960s, the limitation of exhaust emissions did not begin until the late 1960s, and no-one yet seemed to be worried about aerodynamic drag.

Bubblecars

As a direct reaction to low living standards, fuel crises and fuel rationing, a series of very small, very light and very basically-equipped bubblecars appeared in the 1950s and lasted until the 1960s. In almost every case these put operating economy, light weight and basic equipment ahead of any luxury.

Popular for a time, such machines disappeared as soon as European prosperity could shrug them off. One is reminded of the cyclecar boom of the 1920s – the bubblecars were right for the time, but have been derided ever since.

Now read on…

1971

The 'pecking order' in the British motor industry continued unchanged for another year, though British Leyland's dominance was already in question. Although racked by strikes and the arrival of mundane new models, it still held on tenuously to its lead. In 1969 it had taken 40.25 per cent of the market, in 1970 38.12 per cent, before recovering to 39.8 per cent in 1971. Hit hard by a nine-week strike, Ford slipped back that year, but in the course of the next few years would gradually overhaul British Leyland.

In 1971, in fact, Ford's long strike reduced their market share to just 16 per cent in the first half of the year, while British Leyland were in heaven with a share of 41.33 per cent, but all this changed later in the season as Ford deliveries soared. For the fourth year in succession, incidentally, BLMC's front-wheel-drive Austin-Morris 1100/1300 was the country's best-selling car.

Imports, meanwhile, surged upwards, reaching no less than 281,037 in 1971, or 21 per cent of the market, but this was only a prelude to what was to follow.

In Britain, decimal currency was officially introduced in February 1971, thus laying to rest the age-old pounds, shillings and pence system. Because there were now fewer pence in the pound – 100 instead of 240 – it was anticipated that traders might look for bigger price rises, and sure enough they did so.

At this time petrol cost around 33.5 to 36.5 pence per gallon – which means that it would rise by more than 700 per cent over the next quarter-century.

A change in the political atmosphere became more obvious in July when, for the first time in eight years, the purchase tax levied on cars was *reduced* – from 36⅔ to 30 per cent – and at the same time all hire purchase controls were abandoned. There was an immediate upsurge in demand, which resulted in more cars being made and sold in the latter part of the year – this trend becoming more visible in 1972.

As a result of the reduction in purchase tax, there were price savings ranging from about £35 on a BLMC Mini Clubman, through £47 on a Hillman Avenger and £54 on a Vauxhall

Victor to £70 on a Triumph 2000 and no less than £441 on a Rolls-Royce Silver Shadow. It was the fillip the British motor industry thought it deserved – but in fact the main beneficiaries were to be the importers of foreign cars, sales of which soared.

The British road-building programme was still booming ahead. Apart from the opening of many new bypasses and stretches of dual carriageway, the M6 motorway was opened all the way from Birmingham to the Scottish border, and M5 was completed from Birmingham to Bristol, with extensions into Devon already being constructed. With these openings, the first 1,000 miles of the planned British motorway network were completed.

New models

Alfa Romeo: The most important new Alfa Romeo since the Giulietta was first seen in November, when the front-wheel-drive Alfasud became the star of the Turin motor show. In every way the Alfasud was a new venture for the Italian company. Not only was it a small/medium-sized front-wheel-drive car, but it had an overhead-camshaft flat-four engine (of 1.1 litres on the first cars) and it would be built in a brand new factory close to Naples.

It was a brave effort by the Italian company, although experience would show that there was much to be improved on the Alfasud – in particular, it was prone to early rusting, while its handling was so good that it deserved larger and more powerful engines. Sales began in 1972, but the first British deliveries were delayed until summer of 1973.

Mid-way through the year a new 1,962cc version of the familiar twin-cam four-cylinder engine was announced to replace the 1750 versions. At a stroke Alfa Romeo was therefore able to announce the new 2000 saloon, the 2000GTV coupe and the 2000 spider.

Bentley: *(See Rolls-Royce, below.)*

BMW: After a 3-litre version of the company's modern overhead-camshaft six-cylinder engine was developed, it was used progressively to upgrade BMW's saloons and coupes. First in carburetted 180bhp guise, and before the end of the year in fuel-injected

200bhp form, it was found in new cars like the 3.0S and Si saloons, along with the 3.0CS and 3.0CSi coupes.

The most powerful of all the 2002 derivatives – the 2002Tii – was finally announced, five years after the original 1600 type had gone on sale. The sturdy 2-litre engine had been given Kugelfischer fuel injection and was rated at 130bhp. At a price of £2,295 this was a spirited performer, which not only sold well, but also performed well on the race track.

The 2000 Touring was a three-door estate car version of the 2002, but BMW had an aversion to the word 'estate', and for the next 25 years would never use it on their cars.

Clan: The Crusader was a smart, though short-lived car (launched in 1971 but dead by 1974), which was built in a factory at Washington New Town, County Durham. Designed by Paul Haussauer, a one-time Lotus development engineer, the Crusader was a rear-engined two-seater sports coupe, with a glassfibre monocoque (not unlike the Lotus Elite of the 1950s in concept), and used Sunbeam Imp Sport/Stiletto running gear – engine, transmission, front and rear suspensions. The handling was remarkably good, and there was a 100mph top speed, but even when sold in kit form this was quite a costly little car.

Datsun: A new-generation Type 160B/180B Bluebird was announced in Japan and initially went on sale in the USA. This was effectively the 'Cortina' of the vast Datsun-Nissan range, though the 160B/180B was a much more advanced car than the Ford, being equipped with all-independent suspension, and an even wider choice of body styles, including a coupe. UK deliveries would begin in 1972, with a choice of 1.6 and 1.8-litre overhead-cam engines.

UK deliveries of 100A Cherry models – Datsun's first front-wheel-drive car – began in the UK in the middle of the year.

De Tomaso: British sales would not begin for another year or so, but the big four-seater Deauville (almost a Jaguar XJ6 lookalike with De Tomaso's own engineering and Ford V8 power) went on sale, having been previewed at the Turin motor show of 1970.

Ferrari: The 365GTC/4, of which 500 would be built, was a short-lived successor to the 365GTC *and* the 365GT 2+2 models. Under the swoopy two-door 2+2-seater body style was the same general chassis layout as the Daytona's, with the engine up front. In this application the 4.4-litre V12 engine produced 340bhp, and the top speed was over 150mph.

The prototype mid-engined flat-12 Berlinetta Boxer was previewed at the Turin show, styled by Pininfarina, but this single car was shown only as a riposte to the latest mid-engined cars from Lamborghini and Maserati which were already available. Although prototypes were seen at motor shows in 1972, there would be no deliveries for at least two years.

Fiat: The new 127 model, introduced in April, would eventually take over from the 850 range, and was new in every respect except for the engine. The 850 had been rear-engined, whereas the 127 had a transversely-mounted front engine driving the front wheels.

One size smaller than the 128, the 127 was destined for a long life, but in its initial form it used a 47bhp/903cc version of the 850's well-known four-cylinder engine. Here was another car which looked as if it should be a hatch-back but (initially at least) was not, for there were two-door and four-door saloons only. Unlike the 128, the 127 had MacPherson-strut suspension geometry all round, but Fiat still stayed faithful to its transverse leaf-spring suspension at the rear.

The 128 Sport Coupe was unveiled at the Turin show, this being a straight-forward fastback body atop the 128 platform, with a choice of 1.1-litre or 1.3-litre engines. British sales began in 1972.

The 124 Special T went on sale in the UK. This was a combination of the 124's four-door saloon style, with an 80bhp/1,438cc version of the 125's twin-cam engine.

The sleek Pininfarina-styled 130 Coupe was introduced. Except that its V6 engine was upgraded to 3.2 litres, this car was mechanically similar to the rather mundane 130 saloon, but it had a large and extremely smart two-door four-seater body style. British sales of this attractive model would begin in mid-1972.

Ford: The GT70 of January 1971 was a stillborn prototype, originally intended for production as a 'homologation special' for rallying. It was a mid-engined two-seater coupe with a steel-perimeter/platform-floor chassis-frame and a glassfibre body, along with all-independent suspension and four-wheel disc brakes.

Initially a whole range of engines from Ford-Europe was being considered, the most suitable pair being the 1.6-litre Cosworth BDA and the 2.6-litre Ford-Germany RS2600 unit. The car was further developed in 1971 and 1972, but was destined never to be put on sale.

The 3-litre 'Essex' V6 engine fitted to Capris was considerably revised, enabling it to breathe better, rev higher, produce better torque and have 138bhp instead of 128bhp. This change of specification was never applied to the current Zodiacs because they were shortly due to be dropped in favour of new models (*see 1972 for details of the Granada*).

The Escort Sport arrived in October, being a combination of Mexico/RS1600 bodyshell and chassis, but with 72bhp 1.3-litre Escort GT running gear.

Jaguar: The long-awaited V12 engine finally appeared, not, as had been expected, in the XJ saloon, but powering the latest E-type, the Series III. Compared with the six-cylinder SII, all SIIIs, whether open or closed, were built on the longer (105in) wheelbase. To make space for the 272bhp V12, the multi-tubular front structure had been redesigned, while there was a larger front grille opening for the radiator and extensions over the wheelarches to cover the fatter wheels and tyres.

Although the cabin was little changed, in open form it was a lot more roomy than before, and the V12 engine was even more flexible than the old XK unit. No more six-cylinder E-types would be built, but this V12 model would be produced until the end of 1974.

The engine was a 5.3-litre 60-degree unit, with aluminium cylinder block and heads. There were two valves per cylinder in single-overhead-camshaft heads, and carburation was by four Zenith-Stromberg units mounted outboard of the camshaft covers. Although its 5,343cc displacement was not increased until the 1990s, it was destined for a very successful life in

various Jaguar and Daimler models for around 25 years.

Jensen: The Interceptor/FF range advanced to become Series III in October (though the FF would shortly be withdrawn altogether). Changes included the use of the latest detoxed 6.3-litre engines from Chrysler, new-type alloy road wheels and a much-revised interior.

At the same time a limited-production SP (Special Performance) model was introduced with a 385bhp (gross) 7.2-litre Chrysler engine.

Jensen-Healey: The existence of this project, but not its actual name, was revealed in October 1971 when Lotus showed a road-going 140bhp version of its new 16-valve 2-litre four-cylinder engine and made the preliminary announcement. The car itself, however, would not be introduced until the spring of 1972.

Lada: European-market deliveries of this Russian-built car, previewed in 1970, finally began. The new car was really a heavy-duty Russian version of the Fiat 124, but with a new 1.2-litre single-overhead-camshaft four-cylinder engine. There were no frills, and the price was low.

Lamborghini: A prototype of the mid-mounted V12-engined Countach was displayed at the Geneva motor show, but production was still more than two years away. Eventually the Countach would take over from the Miura.

Compared with the Miura, the Countach was technically very different, for it had a longitudinally-mounted engine. On the prototype this was a 5-litre unit, though the first production cars would have a 3.9-litre version.

Lancia: Following the upgrades and facelifts already given to the Fulvia and the Flavia coupes, Lancia now applied the same treatment to the Flavia saloon, giving it the latest version of the 2-litre engine and renaming it the Lancia 2000. The basic four-door saloon structure and mechanical layout were as before, but the nose and tail styles were much smoother.

Land-Rover: The famous 4x4 advanced to become Series III, with the same basic leaf-sprung chassis and choice of engines as before, but with modified exterior styling, a new facia/instrument board and many detail improvements.

Lotus: The existing Elan and Elan Plus 2 models were given much more powerful (126bhp) versions of the 1,558cc twin-cam engine, the cars becoming known as Elan Sprint and Elan Plus 2S 130. Although this change was advertised as a 25 per cent improvement in power, it was actually rather less than this, as road test figures later confirmed – probably no more than an extra 8–10bhp.

In October, the Europa was also upgraded with a 105bhp version of the Lotus-Ford twin-cam engine and renamed Europa Twin-Cam. At the same time the rear-quarter sail panels were cut down.

Marcos: The Wiltshire company survived receivership and carried on building the same coupes as before for a few months, but only in Ford 3-litre V6 guise. The unsuccessful Mantis was dropped.

Maserati: The mid-engined Bora was revealed with a four-overhead-camshaft V8 engine, and styling by ItalDesign. Clearly this was meant to be a competitor to the Lamborghini Miura, and it instantly made the Ferrari range (which had no mid-engined large cars) look out of date.

Mercedes-Benz: The new W107 range of sports tourers began their career in April with the launch of the 350SL model. Taking over directly from the 280SL, a family which had been built for eight years, the W107 in all its derivatives would be produced for the next two decades.

The basis of the design was a sturdy new monocoque structure with coil-spring independent suspension all round and power by the latest 3.5-litre V8 engine. As with the previous SL range, there was a choice of soft-top or hardtop bodies, the removable hardtop being very sturdy but well engineered, so that it could turn the 350SL into almost a two-seater saloon when fitted.

By the time W107 assembly ended, there would have been two wheelbase lengths for two-seater or 2+2 SLC

types, and the V8 engine (up to 5.6 litres) would also have been joined by six-cylinder power units in what was to become a very complex range.

The German company also continued to mix-and-match engines and bodies with the launch of the 280SE 3.5 and 280SEL 3.5 saloons, an obvious combination of new V8 engine with existing four-door saloon shells.

Morris: The Marina, launched in April, was the first major new Austin-Morris model to have been developed under British Leyland control. It had depressingly conventional engineering, little flair and not much attraction except for its low prices and service costs, being clearly aimed at the Cortina/Victor/Hunter fleet market which the former BMC company had ignored for years. At British Leyland it was a replacement for both the old Morris Minor and the 12-year-old Morris Oxford.

Marinas were sold as two-door coupes or four-door saloons, both based on the same unit-construction steel platform, and there was a choice of A-series 1.3-litre and B-series 1.8-litre single and twin-carburettor engines. The front suspension was the torsion-bar layout fitted to the Morris Minor since its inception in 1948, and at first there were serious criticisms of the heavy understeer which this seemed to promote on these cars.

Opel: In what was a very quiet year for the West German company, the ageing Kadett (it would disappear in 1973) was given the option of a larger (1.2-litre) version of the small engine, this also becoming the base engine in the Rallye Kadett.

Porsche: The 911 range advanced a stage further with the launch of 2.4-litre (actually 2,341cc) versions of all cars for the 1972 model year. Although there was more power and torque than before, a general lowering of compression ratios allowed the rear-engined coupes to run in the USA on lead-free fuel.

Renault: One year after the 12 saloon had been introduced, Renault now revealed the 15/17 range of coupes, which used the same basic body/chassis platform, suspension systems and front-engine/front-wheel-drive

layout, though with two variations of a new two-door coupe body.

The basic 15 used a 60bhp version of the 12's 1,289cc engine and had a body style with much glass along the flanks, while the 15TS used the same body, but a 90bhp version of the Renault 16's 1,565cc engine.

Both the 17s – 17TL and 17TS – used a 1,565cc engine, one with 90bhp, the other with fuel injection and 108bhp. The Renault 17TS had four-wheel disc brakes, and all 17s had a different cabin, with less glass area along the sides. UK deliveries would begin in July 1972.

Automatic transmission became optional on 16 and 16TS models.

Rolls-Royce: Although the parent company struck major financial problems and had to be rescued by the Government (see under Industrial developments), the car division carried on unscathed.

In February, the new Corniche models (coupe and convertible, with Rolls-Royce or Bentley badges) arrived. These were lightly-modified versions of the Mulliner, Park Ward models which had been on sale for the last few years, but the 6.75-litre V8 engines had 10 per cent more power than before.

Rover: To satisfy great demand, the 3500S was introduced – a manual-transmission version of the compact-bodied 3500, which was still only available with automatic transmission.

Toyota: Quietly and without fanfare, the old-type Crown was dropped, to be replaced by a new-style Crown 2600, which used a Granada-size body style and 2.6-litre overhead-camshaft engine.

Triumph: The new overhead-camshaft Dolomite was ready and in the wings, but its launch was twice postponed because of the serious disruption caused by industrial strife within British Leyland.

The only Triumph innovation of the year was the addition of a more powerful (65bhp) version of the 1.5-litre engine in the front-wheel-drive 1500 model.

TVR: Initially for sale only to the USA, but with some supplies eventually reaching the UK in 1971, the 2500 was yet another variation on a familiar theme, this time with a 'detoxed' 105bhp version of the Triumph TR6 engine.

There was also the short-lived 1300 model, visually and technically the same as all other current TVRs, except that it was powered by a 75bhp/1.3-litre Triumph Spitfire engine. It was a commercial failure.

Vauxhall: The new Firenza, introduced in May, was a rather half-hearted response to Ford's ultra-successful Capri. Firenzas were effectively two-door coupe versions of the latest Vivas, and were available with the same range of 1.2-litre and 1.6-litre engines, plus the 2-litre engine previously found in Viva GTs and also used in the current Victor models. The 1.1-litre version was built for only a few months before being upgraded in line with the 1972-model Vivas (see below).

Only one year after the new Viva HC range had been introduced, it was improved by the fitment of a larger (1,256cc) version of Vauxhall's small four-cylinder engine. There were significant power and torque increases, this being the final capacity change for an engine which had been introduced in 1963.

Volga: In a totally vain hope of expanding the market for Russian cars, the large, heavy and totally undistinguished M24 model was put on to the British market. Here was a car as large as a Ford Zodiac or a Vauxhall Cresta, but with a four-cylinder engine, no automatic transmission option, drum brakes all round and a solid rear axle.

This was a rock-solid, but awful car, which stood no chance of success in the UK, except in Embassy hands.

Volvo: Ten years after it had gone on sale as a sports coupe, Volvo redesigned the 1800 as a 'sporting estate', using the same basic packaging as seen in the Reliant Scimitar. There was no performance increase, but this prolonged the life of the range by another two years.

The big 3-litre 160-series cars were given a boost by the introduction of the 164E model, which had Bosch fuel injection and 160bhp.

Industrial developments

In February Rolls-Royce went into receivership with large debts, and had to be rescued by Government finance. Although the car division was solvent, the much larger aero-engine side of the business had been seriously hit by development problems with its new RB211 gas turbine unit. Eventually, Government help enabled the entire business to carry on, and the cars side continued to prosper.

Following a disastrous experience in selling cars to North America (including being hampered by a prolonged dock strike), Marcos also had to call in the receiver. But within weeks the business was revived, in a more modest form, by the Rob Walker Group. The awful Mantis did not survive this upheaval, but traditional Marcos coupes continued in production for a time.

Early in the year Aston Martin dropped the DB6 Mk 2, so the fine twin-cam six-cylinder engine first seen in 1958 was also discontinued. Parts and rebuild expertise have been available ever since.

Triumph finally dropped the Herald and Vitesse models after a successful and (finally) profitable 12-year career. The sporting derivatives – Spitfire and GT6 – remained in production.

The four-wheel-drive Jensen FF dropped out of production at the end of the year, which meant that there would be no more European-built 4x4 private cars until 1980, when the sensational Audi Quattro arrived.

Technical developments

In the USA, what was always known as the Muskie Bill became law. This was anti-pollution legislation applying to the engines of new cars, which required the emissions of their engines to be reduced to only 5 per cent of the current value by 1976.

This was originally thought to be an impossible target, though in fact it was achieved by the world's industry. However, the expense involved was so high that it would drive many of the world's car-makers out of the US market.

Even at this stage, airbags were being developed and actively canvassed for fitment in US-made cars. Development and reliability problems persisted for many years, however, and such bags would not be fitted in large quantities until more than 20 years later.

1972

With a Government set on helter-skelter economic expansion, the rate of purchase tax levied on new cars was reduced for the second time in less than a year – from 30 to 25 per cent. This change came in the Budget in March, and typical reductions were £23 for a Mini 850, £36 for a Hillman Avenger GL and £413 for a Rolls-Royce Corniche.

Along with other relaxations in credit restrictions and taxation, this caused an exciting boom in British car production and sales. Even though the industry suffered from a number of stupid and unnecessary unofficial strikes, it produced no fewer than 1,971,311 cars in 1972, an outright record that has never been beaten: output, in fact, would halve by the end of the 1970s.

UK car registrations totalled 1.7 million, which was another new record that would not be beaten until 1983 – and most importantly, 450,000 of them (26 per cent) were of imported machines.

One very significant change was that Datsun overhauled Volkswagen in the imported-car pecking order – with every sign that it would soon be challenging the likes of Fiat and Renault.

Many years after it had first been proposed, the motorway network through the Midlands was finally completed. When the final link of M6, through Birmingham, was opened in May, it gave a continuous stretch of M6 from the M1 to north of Carlisle, all tying up with the M5, which stretched from Birmingham to the south of Bristol.

After a decade of faithful service, the British Air Ferries Carvair aircraft, which carried thousands of motorists to and from the Continent, was supplanted by the bigger and more modern Britannia-based CL44 aircraft – but the fashion for travelling by air was already on the wane.

New models

Alfa Romeo: Less than a year after the Alfasud had been launched (and at a time when it was only just going into production), the state-controlled Italian company introduced another important new car – the Alfetta.

Although the well-known twin-cam four-cylinder engine – this time in 1.8-litre form – was retained, almost everything else about this car was new. The Alfetta was a four-door monocoque saloon, rather bigger than the Giulia-based 2000, with a radically different layout, having the clutch/gearbox/final-drive unit at the rear. Independent front suspension was by longitudinal torsion bars, Jaguar-style, while there was coil spring and de Dion suspension at the rear.

This was the first of a whole new family of medium-sized Alfas to be launched during the next decade – more Alfettas, similar but smaller Giuliettas and several smart coupes. All would be well-liked as drivers' cars, but all suffered from early and excessive corrosion. Alfa's descent into quality disrepute, which peaked in the 1980s, had begun.

Yet another reshuffle of cars and engines led to the launch of the GT Junior 1.6 in June, this effectively being a return to the original Giulia Sprint GT of 1963, though with a more powerful engine; it replaced sales of the 1300GT.

Audi: The first of a new family of front-engined, front-wheel-drive cars was revealed in July, the new 80 range. Except for its general layout, with the engine mounted in line and ahead of the line of the front wheels, the new 80 was totally different from any previous car in the Audi-NSU-VW range. The engine was a new water-cooled overhead-valve four-cylinder unit, which would be used in many other Audis and VWs in the years ahead.

Within a year the Audi 80 would be joined by the VW Passat, which was based on the same design, and a new dynasty was well and truly founded.

Austin: The 2200 model, launched in March, was really an 1800 into which a new straight-six overhead-camshaft engine of 2.2 litres had somehow been shoehorned into the transverse-engine layout of this front-wheel-drive car. The engine, coded E6, was really one-and-a-half Austin Maxi units, and had already been seen in BLMC cars being built in Australia. At the same time, near-identical Morris 2200 and Wolseley Six models were also unveiled.

Later in the year the Maxi was upgraded, with the introduction of a new 1750HL type, which had a twin-SU engine and 95bhp, offering a 100mph-plus top speed.

BMW: The original 5-series cars were introduced in September, coinciding with the staging of the Olympic Games in Munich. There was a new, rather stockily-styled, four-door saloon monocoque, with an initial choice of carburetted or fuel-injected four-cylinder 2-litre overhead-camshaft engines (520 and 520i), but the range would expand and grow in complexity in the coming years, firstly with the addition of a six-cylinder engine option (525).

The chassis was a development of that already being used for the 1600/2002 types, with MacPherson-strut front suspension and semi-trailing-link rear suspension. British deliveries would begin in the spring of 1973.

Another new model was announced, specifically with motorsport in mind and the need to homologate special parts: the 3-litre coupe was upgraded to become the 3.0CSL model, having a slightly enlarged engine of 3,003cc (which meant that the works race team could then enlarge the engine much further if they so wished) and aluminium instead of steel body skin panels. Although the original 3.0CSL was a glamorous machine, it was by no means as practical as it should have been, for the body panels proved to be vulnerable to even minor accident damage.

Citroen: Fuel injection appeared on two new versions of existing cars. The DS23 was a new (and, as it turned out, final) edition of the long-running 'Goddess' range, this now having a 2,347cc version of the four-cylinder engine, in 115bhp (carburetted) or 130bhp (Bosch injected) form, along with the five-speed gearbox of the SM coupe.

There was also a 178bhp fuel-injected version of the 2.7-litre SM coupe, which took over from the original carburetted type.

In the autumn, a 1,220cc version of the flat-four engine was fitted to the medium-sized GS saloon, with 60bhp instead of the 55bhp of the original 1-litre type, and with a lot more medium-range torque.

Daf: By facelifting the 55, giving it de Dion instead of swing-axle rear suspension, and providing equipment changes, Daf produced the 66 model.

Daimler: The V12-engined Double Six model, a Jaguar XJ12 clone, was introduced in July (see *Jaguar, below*). A few weeks later a longer-wheelbase Vanden Plas version of this model was introduced, the longer wheelbase gradually being added to other Daimlers and Jaguars of this increasingly complex range.

Datsun: The 160B/180B Bluebird models, which had been previewed in 1971, went on UK sale in May.

There was an additional Cherry model at the Earls Court motor show, which would go on sale in the UK in January 1973, this having an enlarged, 69bhp/1.2-litre version of the engine.

The Type C200 Laurel range was also new to the UK in the autumn of 1972, this being a larger car than the new Bluebird (and with a totally different unit-construction style), along with a four-cylinder 2-litre overhead-camshaft engine which had not previously been seen in the UK, where sales would begin in 1973.

At the end of the year, the 240C (which had only been on sale for 18 months) was replaced by a 2.6-litre version known as the 260C. Datsun's range was getting wider, and more complicated, very rapidly indeed.

Ferrari: This year's major new arrival was the 365GT4 2+2, which was a four-seater saloon and the effective replacement for the 365GT 2+2 which had been dropped in 1971. Naturally it was a front V12-engined car, this particular machine having a 340bhp twin-cam-per-bank unit of 4.4 litres. This car and its descendants – the 400GT and later types – would be built in gradually decreasing numbers until the end of the 1980s.

Fiat: This was an amazingly productive year for Fiat for new models. Commercially, the most important was the arrival of the tiny new 126, which took over from the extremely successful old 500D, which had been on sale for more than a decade. British deliveries began in the summer of 1973.

Like the old 500, the 126 was a rear-engined marginal-motoring four-seater saloon, only 10 feet long, but without the passenger space of the similar-sized BL Mini. The twin-cylinder air-cooled engine was a 23bhp/594cc

development of that previously used in the 500.

Because it was trendy to do so, some motorists chose 126s over the equivalent Minis, but in the UK there was really no contest as the Mini could swallow more payload and was significantly faster. Even so, well over 2 million 126s would be produced in the next two decades.

To take over from the 125, Fiat introduced the 132 saloon in May, this being a slightly larger but somewhat less distinguished and sporty model. There was a choice of twin-cam four-cylinder engines – 1,592cc and 1,756cc – both being new developments of the twin-cam theme which had been new in 1966.

Not only were four-speed and five-speed manual gearboxes available, but for the first time on a Fiat of this size there was an automatic transmission option. British sales began in January 1973.

At the end of the year, the smart little mid-engined X1/9 sportscar made its entrance. Styled by Bertone (which also built the two-seater structures), the original X1/9 used a 128 Rally power pack (see *below*), mounted immediately behind the cabin. The rigid roof panel could be removed, either to be left in the garage, or stowed in the front boot. There were two stowage boots – one up front ahead of the footwell, the other in the tail, above and behind the transaxle.

Even though this was clearly destined to be a very popular car, there were no official UK imports of right-hand-drive versions until the autumn of 1976 – four years after launch.

Beginning their expansion of the 128 range, Fiat added a 67bhp/1.3-litre engine, calling this model a 128 Rally.

The 3.2-litre 130 executive saloon, complete with automatic transmission, went on sale in the UK, priced at £3,818, to be joined a few weeks later by a £5,257 coupe derivative.

At the end of the summer, Fiat also reshuffled the 124 range, adding a 1.6-litre twin-cam engine to the Special T (instead of the 1.4-litre twin-cam), giving the 124 Sport Coupe a front-end facelift and offering both that and the Sport Spider with the latest 1.6-litre and 1.8-litre engines so recently introduced for the 132 saloon.

At the same time the limited-production 124 Abarth Rally, a 128bhp

'homologation special' version of the Spider, with glassfibre panels and a permanent hardtop, was also put on sale, though all cars had left-hand drive, and they were never officially marketed in the UK.

Ford: A new range of Consul/Granada models took over from the Zephyr/Zodiac range which had been in production since 1966. The new models were made both in West Germany and in the UK, using a brand-new monocoque and a wide choice of engines. For the British market there was a 2-litre V4, along with V6s of 2.5 and 3 litres.

Unlike the old Zephyrs/Zodiacs, the new cars had a new type of all-independent suspension (coil springs and wishbones being used at the front) and they reverted to rear-wheel drum brakes. Only four-door saloons were available at first, but estate cars followed shortly afterwards.

In October the Capri received its mid-life update, with a new dashboard and a reshuffle of engines. The old-type 1.6-litre Kent engines were dropped and replaced by new-type overhead-camshaft Pinto engines.

For 1973 there was a trim-and-equipment reshuffle of Mexico and RS1600 saloons, but more important was the arrival of an aluminium cylinder block for the 16-valve BDA engine which powered the RS1600. There were no power or torque changes, but there was a significant weight reduction – and the ability for the cylinder block to be enlarged to give a full 2-litre capacity for motorsport purposes.

Gilbern: One final upgrade was given to the Genie/Invader series – which dated from 1966 – with the launch of the Mk III in September. Although this car was said to have its glassfibre body built from entirely new moulds, and to have fresh styling, it was really no more than a facelifted Invader Mk II

Hillman: The Hunter range was thoroughly revised in March. Although existing 1.5-litre and 1.7-litre engines were retained, there was a good deal of reshuffling of model names, power outputs and equipment levels, along with a new facia design and grille.

A new Hunter GLS model was launched, this basically being a Hunter

GT, but fitted with the twin Weber-carburetted Rapier H120 engine, and with a modified version of the four-headlamp Humber Sceptre nose. The suspension had been reworked, and in fact this became a very capable car which enjoyed some limited success in British touring car races.

At the same time an estate car version of the Avenger was put on sale, while the limited-production Avenger Tiger was previewed in March, this model having a specially-redeveloped 1.5-litre Avenger GT engine, complete with twin dual-choke Weber carburettors and special manifolding.

Honda: The original transverse-engined Civic was introduced in Japan, this being the first of a developing family which has subsequently sold in millions. It fell neatly into the Supermini class at first, and like all Japanese cars of the day, it sold well in the UK because of low prices and high levels of equipment.

The first Civic had a 1.2-litre overhead-camshaft engine, and was built in two-door saloon and three-door hatchback forms. It would be seen at the British motor show in October, and UK sales would begin in mid-1973.

By the mid-1990s, more than 10 million Civics in various guises and shapes would have been built.

Jaguar: The long-awaited V12-engined saloon – the XJ12 – was put on sale in July, a launch which was instantly crippled by a strike at the factory. The XJ bodyshell had always been designed with this engine in mind. Nevertheless, the 5.3-litre 60-degree V12 was a tight fit under the bonnet and heat dissipation was a problem – so much so that there was a thermostatic cooling fan for the battery.

There were virtually no styling changes from the six cylinder-engined XJ6, while the rest of the chassis needed little upgrading to cope with the 265bhp/150mph performance. Longer-wheelbase versions of the XJ6 and XJ12 saloons soon followed, these eventually becoming the standard bodyshells for later models of a long-running family.

Jensen-Healey: The long-forecast new sportscar from Jensen arrived in March, though deliveries did not begin until July. Although it looked attractive,

technically this new car was a bit of a mongrel. The unit-construction bodyshell was powered by the 140bhp/2-litre version of Lotus' new 16-valve twin-cam engine, backed by a Rootes/Chrysler Rapier H120 gearbox, while the suspensions and steering were from the latest Vauxhall Viva/Firenza models.

Jensen planned to make 100 sportscars a week – but the demand never developed and less than 11,000 Jensen-Healeys would be built in total before assembly ended in the winter of 1975/76.

Lada: The Fiat 124-based Lada was finally confirmed as in production and on sale, though its initial title was the totally unmemorable Shiguli Vaz 2102.

Lancia: The most important Lancia for a decade appeared in October with the arrival of the Beta saloons. These were the first new models to have been developed by Lancia under Fiat ownership, and were clearly intended to be made and sold in much higher numbers than any previous Lancia.

To save on development and capital expenditure, the Beta used the Fiat twin-cam engine which was already being employed in several other Fiat models, but this time it was mounted sideways and drove the front wheels through a brand-new five-speed transmission.

There were 1.4, 1.6 and 1.8-litre versions of the engine at first – but the range would become much more complicated than that in the years to come! All-independent suspension was by MacPherson struts at each corner, and although the six-light style looked as if it might be a hatchback, this was in fact a four-door saloon. Several other derivatives, including Coupes, Spiders and even an HPE (similar to the Reliant Scimitar GTE package) model would follow in the next two or three years.

The front-wheel-drive (ex-Flavia) 2000 range was improved yet again with the use of a fuel-injected 125bhp version of the engine.

Lotus: From October, the Elan Plus 2S model was given the option of a newly-developed five-speed gearbox. This was intended for use in a new generation of Lotus models, which would appear in the spring of 1974.

Only a year after the Europa had been relaunched with Lotus' own twin-cam engine, it was once again upgraded, this time to become the Europa Special, complete with a 126bhp/1,558cc engine and a new type of five-speed gearbox. The Europa Twin-Cam was dropped to make way for this model.

Maserati: The Italian company pulled a big surprise in the autumn with the announcement of the Merak, which was effectively a smaller-engined Bora with more cabin space.

The Merak's engine was a 3-litre version of the 90-degree V6 already being used in the Citroen SM, and being smaller than the Bora's V8, it allowed the cabin bulkhead to be moved backwards and a pair of (quite useless) '+2' seats to be fitted.

Also announced at this time was the very smart Khamsin two-seater coupe, which not only used a 4.9-litre version of the famous V8 engine, but was the first front-engined Maserati to be equipped with independent rear suspension.

Mazda: A pair of new saloons – the 818 with a 1.3-litre four-cylinder engine, and the RX3, which was the same car but with a much more powerful twin-rotor Wankel engine of 2-litre equivalent capacity – widened the range considerably.

Except for the RX3's rotary engine, these were very conventional front-engine/rear-drive cars, with MacPherson-strut front suspension and a solid rear axle. There was a big price differential between the two types – the 818 was listed at £1,199 and the RX3 at £1,525.

Mercedes-Benz: A new twin-overhead-cam 2.75-litre six-cylinder engine was unveiled in April, this initially being built in 160bhp carburetted or 185bhp fuel-injected form. It was intended to take over from the venerable single-cam 2.8-litre engine which had been in production for some years. At first it appeared in new 280E saloon and 280CE coupe models, which went on sale in the UK in August, but other uses would unfold in the years ahead.

To complement these changes, the single cam-engined 250 was upgraded to become the 250 2.8, with a 2,778cc version of the old-type six-cylinder engine offering 130bhp and more torque.

The most important Mercedes-Benz launch of the year, however, was of a new generation of S-class saloons to replace those which had been running since 1965.

These big cars had every feature one would expect from Stuttgart, and there was a wide choice of engines including the newly-launched twin-cam 'six', and modern 3.5-litre V8s, a 4.5-litre derivative of the V8 following early in 1973.

Instead of the swing-axle rear suspension of the earlier S-class, the new versions had semi-trailing arms and coil springs, and there were four-wheel disc brakes, all these features having been previewed in the 350SL/SLC sports coupes which had been on the market since 1971, although UK deliveries were to be delayed until the spring of 1973. The 350SLC – a longer-wheelbase 2+2 coupe version of the 350SL sports roadster, went on sale at £7,395.

MG: The Midget was changed in several details, most noticeably with what are now known as the 'round wheel-arches' at the rear, along with Rostyle road wheels, a style that would last only until the autumn of 1974.

Morgan: For 1973, the V8-engined Plus 8 was made available with the latest all-synchromesh Rover four-cylinder gearbox instead of the old-style separately-positioned Moss gearbox which had been fitted to other Morgan cars for so many years.

Morris: (For 2200 details, see Austin, above.)

An estate car derivative was added to the Marina range.

Opel: A new range of Rekords, which shared the same floorpan and basic suspensions as the new-generation Victor (see below) were launched in January. These were conventionally-engineered medium/large cars, and for the British market were only available with the 1.9-litre cam-in-head engine (in continental Europe, smaller engines, and eventually diesels, were also available).

Shortly, a new range of Commodores went on sale. As before, these were six cylinder-engined ver-

sions of the Rekord, with a choice of 115bhp or 130bhp 2.5-litre power units. In the autumn the Commodore range grew further with the launch of the 2.8-litre GS/E model, the engine of which produced 160bhp.

Panther: The first J72 sportscars, pseudo-SS100 lookalikes (they were *not* replicas), went on sale and found a small market among people with more money to spare than taste.

Although it looked somewhat like the SS100 of the 1930s, the J72 had a tubular chassis-frame, beam front and rear axles, a Jaguar XK 3.8-litre engine and a hand-built aluminium-panelled two-seater bodyshell. Like the SS100, the J72's acceleration was astonishing, but the aerodynamics were so awful that the top speed was a mere 114mph. A 4.2-litre version of this car would soon follow and, in later years, even a few V12-engined versions would be built.

Peugeot: The 104, revealed in October, represented yet another massive investment for Peugeot. Not only was this a transverse-engined/front-wheel-drive car, with a new and rather plain five-door bodyshell and all-independent suspension, but it was also the first showing of a new family of small overhead-camshaft Peugeot engines. The engine was laid back at an angle of 72 degrees in the chassis, which meant that the transmission was in the sump (Mini-style), but the final-drive unit was under the cylinder block.

Porsche: Although the mainstream 911 models were only changed in detail during the year, there was a new 2.7-litre Carrera RS, a lightweight with more power and a more specialized track-bred nature than ever before. This 210bhp machine immediately became everyone's favourite Porsche, and it seems to have retained that title through into the mid-1990s.

Reliant: The slow-selling Rebel model was made a little more brisk by the fitment of a 748cc engine in place of the 700cc unit it had used for the past few years.

Renault: The new 5 hatchback appeared in February, being a modernized restatement of the Renault 16's front-wheel-drive layout, with the in-

line engine behind the line of the front wheels and the transmission ahead of it: the Renault 12, of course, had its engine mounted ahead of the line of the wheels.

At first the well-known 845cc and 956cc engines were fitted, though many other engine types and sizes would be used in future years. A novel feature, the gearchange lever sprouted through a hole in the facia panel. Front and rear suspension was by torsion bars.

Adding to the front-wheel-drive 12 saloon range, from October there was also the 12TS model, which used a 60bhp version of the latest 1.3-litre engine.

Saab: The first 2 litre-engined 99 models went on sale in the UK in mid-summer, these using Saab's own-manufacture version of the Triumph overhead-camshaft engine.

Simca: The 1100 Special became even more special in April when it was given a larger 75bhp/1,294cc version of the four-cylinder engine.

Also available in the UK from the same period was the 1000 Rallye 1, with the same engine, although it was mounted in the rear of this car.

Skoda: Although it had been on sale in Europe for some years, the S110R coupe was finally launched in the UK, this being a two-door fastback version of the well-known S100/S110 saloons, equipped with the most powerful (54bhp/1.1-litre) version of the rear-mounted engine.

Toyota: Like its worldwide rival, Nissan/Datsun, Toyota was expanding its range as fast as possible. In the UK the latest Corona – called the 2000 Mk II – took over from the Corona 1900 of 1969–72. A little larger than the ousted car, with coil-spring suspension of its rear axle beam, it had a larger and more powerful (113bhp/1,968cc) engine, though several other engines were available in other markets. Toyota customers, however, had little time to get used to this car, as it would be displaced by the next-generation Corona in three years' time.

Triumph: After several delays, the new Dolomite (later to be known as the Dolomite 1850) was finally put on sale in January. This car, as expected, was an amalgam of Triumph 1500 four-door shell, chassis and transmission, with the 1.85-litre version of the overhead-camshaft engine which was already being supplied to Saab.

The interior had been retrimmed, and the car was more completely equipped than the 1500. With a top speed of around 100mph, this was an attractive proposition, even though the basic body style was now more than six years old.

TVR: A new M-series chassis was introduced to replace the one which had been developed progressively over the previous 10 years (it had originated with the Grantura III of 1962). This used the same basic multi-tubular/backbone chassis layout, and it was immediately made available in 1600M, 2500M and 3000M guises, with Ford Capri GT, Triumph and Ford Granada engines respectively.

Vauxhall: The fifth-generation (FE) Victor models appeared in March, sharing their entire floorpans and suspensions with the latest Opel Rekord, but having their own unique four-door saloon and estate car superstructures.

By comparison with the earlier (FD) Victors, the wheelbase was longer and there was more cabin space, the overhead-camshaft engines had been enlarged – to 1.8 and 2.3 litres – while there was also a 3.3-litre Ventora-engined derivative called the Victor 3300SL. The VX4/90 continued, as did the top-of-the-range 3.3-litre Ventora.

From the spring of the year, the enlarged (1.8-litre and 2.3-litre) overhead-camshaft engines were made available in Viva models and in the Firenza coupes.

Volkswagen: The final major change was made to the Beetle when the 1302S, with its MacPherson-strut front-end, became the 1303S by the addition of a curved windscreen and many other detail changes to the body style.

The 411 gave way to the 412, with a front-end facelift and a series of trim and equipment improvements.

VW-Porsche: The six cylinder-engined 914/6 having been dropped some time earlier, the four-cylinder version of this mid-engined sports coupe was upgraded in the autumn to become the 914SC, complete with a 2-litre version of the VW-produced engine.

This model would then carry on, selling only slowly in the UK, but much better in the USA, until the end of 1975, when it was replaced by the new front-engined 924.

Wolseley: (For 'Six' details, see Austin 2200, above.)

Industrial developments

British Leyland moved again to make sense of its sprawling empire, merging Rover with Triumph, setting up a central management structure, and ensuring that only one new model (the Rover SD1) took over from the ageing Rover 2000 and Triumph 2000 ranges.

Chrysler completed its purchase of the one-time Rootes Group, renamed Chrysler United Kingdom Ltd, by acquiring the final 12 per cent of voting stock.

Aston Martin was sold by the David Brown Corporation to Company Developments Ltd, which subsequently proved to be more interested in stripping out excess land and selling it than introducing new models. The Company Developments regime would last for less than three years.

In West Germany, the VW Beetle passed the Ford Model T's domestic USA production record of 15,007,003 cars in February. By the mid-1990s the Beetle was still in production – in Brazil and Mexico – with production close to the 22 million mark.

Jaguar chairman Sir William Lyons announced his retirement (he was 70 years old), F R W 'Lofty' England becoming his successor. Sir William had been 'Mr Jaguar' since he founded the marque, and all cars except the E-type had been styled under his personal direction.

In Sweden, Saab began making their own 2-litre four-cylinder engine, which was not a stretched version of the Triumph-built unit previously used in 99 models, but an almost total redesign using the same basic dimensions. This engine, with periodic updates, would be used in various Saab models until the 1990s.

During the year when Ford unveiled a new series of large saloons (the Consul/Granada range), Vauxhall left this sector completely after announcing the end of the long-running Cresta/Viscount range. It would be some years before new Vauxhalls again entered this sector – with rebadged Opels.

National Motor Museum

With the opening of a large, brand new and industry-funded building at Beaulieu, the Montagu Motor Museum was transformed into the National Motor Museum. Designed by Leonard Massaneh & Partners, the new building incorporated access for an overhead monorail – which would not be built for some years – was on two levels, and had a large built-in workshop for restoration projects.

UK car sales in 1972

After this record year for car sales, the SMMT released the following league table of individual makers' achievements:

British Leyland	542,440
Ford	401,994
Chrysler UK	153,765
Vauxhall	147,172
Renault	60,242
Volkswagen	52,686
Fiat	47,606
Chrysler (France)/Simca	34,121
Datsun	30,197
Volvo	19,911

– other interesting statistics included Toyota, at 13,526 in 15th place, BMW with 8,918 in 18th place and Mercedes-Benz with 5,017 in 21st place.

Technical developments

Mercedes-Benz signalled a new trend, which was for more twin-overhead-camshaft engines to take over from older single-cam types in middle and upper-middle size cars.

Lancia, too, joined in by using twin-cams in its new Beta range, this confirming what Fiat had already started with the same basic design a few years earlier.

1973

This was the year in which many drivers thought that their motoring lives were about to be hit hard and permanently. Soon after Israel attacked the Arab countries in October, in what became known as the Yom Kippur war, the Arabs turned off the taps in the oil refineries, and suddenly there were grave shortages.

Because North America had already become a large-scale oil importer, it could not eliminate shortages, and for a time there was a real threat of rationing. The British authorities moved swiftly, printing and issuing 16 million ration books (and, as it transpired, storing them for many years after the crisis was over). This and the later imposition of an overall speed limit of 50mph (even on motorways) was claimed to have reduced the consumption of petrol, and rationing was never imposed – but it had been close!

Inflation, in any case, was on the way up. Prices rose by 16 per cent during the year – the first time since the war that inflation had exceeded 10 per cent – and worse was to come. Because inflation feeds on inflation, wage demands also shot up, one result being that car prices began to soar.

It was a measure of the general gloom that afflicted British drivers at this time that the Earls Court Motor Show attendance was at its lowest for many years.

Great Britain officially joined the EEC, or Common Market, on January 1, committed to building up its trade with European nations (which automatically meant reducing it with the old Empire countries). As a consequence, car sales to countries such as Australia, South Africa and New Zealand slumped.

In the same year, British and French Governments agreed that a Channel Tunnel was a necessity, and preliminary work started from each end of the alignment, although economic difficulties would soon bring it to a halt again!

Once again this was a year in which Britain's motor industry was wracked with unofficial strikes. The industrial atmosphere, in general, was sour, and before the end of the year the threat of a full-blooded miners' strike led to compulsory short-time working across the whole of British business.

One of the most significant shifts in British car sales was the continuing rise of Datsun. In 1971 only 6,000 cars had been sold in the UK, but this rose to 30,200 in 1972 and to around 50,000 in 1973. It would not be long before Datsun sales were approaching those of Chrysler-UK, which was one reason for the British Government eventually imposing a 'voluntary' limit on the number of Japanese cars which could be sold in the UK.

The issue and reissue of car and driving licences was centralized with the opening of the DVLC operation at Swansea.

New models

AC: The first prototype of a mid-engined, Ford 3-litre-powered two-seater sports coupe was shown at the Earls Court Motor Show, but it was nowhere nearly ready for sale. After what must be one of the longest gestation periods ever, first deliveries of this car would eventually be made in 1978/79!

Austin: Although British Leyland had high hopes for its new Allegro, introduced in May, it soon became the 'Lemon of the Decade'. As an intended replacement for the long-running 1100/1300 models, it was not as smart, did not handle as well, and certainly did not sell as well.

The theory, at least, was well-tested because under the rather bulboid body, which had a more roomy cabin than the ousted models, there was a transverse-engine/front-drive layout and all-independent suspension.

Two types of engine were on offer – 1,098cc and 1,275cc A-series units, both ex-1100/1300, and 1,485cc/1,748cc E-series units (with five-speed transmission), both ex-Austin Maxi. The suspension medium was new, too – Hydragas instead of Hydrolastic, where high-pressure inert gas replaced the hollow rubber convolute of Hydrolastic systems – though the soft ride and rudimentary self-levelling features remained.

It was the details of this car which grated so much – particularly the bizarre Quartic steering wheel, which was more square than round and was hated by almost everyone except British Leyland management.

Yet although few people ever seemed to have a good word for the Allegro, it stayed in production until 1983, by which time 642,350 of all types had been produced.

BMW: The German manufacturer was unlucky. Just weeks before the Energy Crisis erupted, making high-performance cars unfashionable for a time, three new fast BMWs were launched. All had a limited life!

The 3.0CSL was upgraded, with what is now known as the 'Batmobile' aerodynamic kit, which included a big rear spoiler, and at the same time the engine was enlarged to 206bhp/3,153cc.

The 2002 Turbo was Europe's first turbocharged production car, and had been developed and refined from the works racecars of recent years. This was an evolution of the 2002Tii, having a 170bhp turbocharged version of the 2-litre engine, and coming with a large front chin spoiler and wheelarch extension flares. It would only be made in left-hand drive, though a limited number were sold in the UK in 1974.

The 525 was a logical extension of the new 520 range, in which the existing six-cylinder 2.5-litre engine (developing 145bhp) had been squeezed into the engine bay of the new 5-series bodyshell.

Finally, there was the new 3.3L, which was a stretched version of the existing big BMW saloon. The wheelbase and overall length were approximately 4in longer than in standard cars (the increase being intended to give more rear seat space) and the 3,295cc version of the six-cylinder overhead-cam engine developed 190bhp.

Caterham: The Seven S4 of May 1973 was no more than a rebadged Lotus Seven, following the takeover of all production and assembly rights by Caterham Cars.

The previously obsolete Seven S3 would soon be revived as the Caterham Seven, and this car has been in production, in constantly-developing form, ever since.

Chrysler-France: The French-built Chrysler 180 had never been a success, and the additional 1973 version, a 2-litre, with 1,981cc engine and automatic transmission as standard, was little better. Although this model would stagger on until 1980, it lacked any further improvement by Chrysler-Europe; for the last few years of its life it would be assembled in Spain.

Citroen: The new Ami Super was a classic example of 'new wine in old bottle', for it featured the 1-litre flat-four GS unit in the existing Ami 8 structure, which was normally powered by a 602cc flat-twin. Described inaccurately as Citroen's Mini-Cooper, it was nevertheless the fastest car yet built on this old-style (2CV-based) front-wheel-drive chassis.

Daf: The Dutch manufacturer continued to squeeze every possible model out of its single basic design. For 1974 the 66 Marathon was given a 1.3-litre/57bhp version of the Renault engine. During 1974 this engine would also become available on other 66 models.

Daimler: The Sovereign and Double Six models became Series II in the autumn, and a two-door coupe model was previewed – see *Jaguar* for details.

Datsun: The new 120Y Sunny range of saloon, coupe and estate car replaced the old-style 1200 Sunny in the autumn of the year. Like the earlier model, this was a front-engined, rear-wheel-drive design with solid beam axle rear suspension. Except that the equipment level was higher than on most equivalent cars, the new Sunny had little other than low prices to recommend it.

Fleshing-out its already large range even more, Datsun launched a new series of Type 710 Violet models in Japan in February, though UK sales would not begin until the autumn of the year.

Third up in size and pecking order after the Cherry and Sunny, the Violet slotted in beneath the Bluebird, the Type 710 being a conventionally-engineered front-engine/rear-drive car with a beam rear axle, 1.4-litre or 1.6-litre overhead-camshaft engines, and a choice of transmissions. Like most Datsuns of this period, it was no beauty.

The 240GT Skyline – larger than the Laurel, smaller than the 260C – filled in yet another tiny gap in Datsun's burgeoning range. Powered by a 130bhp version of the 2.4-litre engine used in the 240Z sports coupe, it had a totally conventional chassis, and sold

only in small numbers in the UK.

Dino (Ferrari): In October there were sensations in Italy, for not only was the much-loved Dino 246 displaced by a larger type of Dino 308, but it had a new 2.9-litre 90-degree four-cam V8 engine instead of the charismatic V6, it was a longer and heavier 2+2-seater instead of a pure two-seater, and the body style was by Bertone.

This was a controversial new approach, for which Ferrari received a great deal of criticism – for a replacement two-seater (the Dino 308GTB) would not be unveiled until 1975.

Ford: The Escort 1300E was a limited-edition version of the 1300GT/1300 Sport, complete with a more upmarket interior and special paint jobs, including a rather lurid purple. Technically insignificant, it immediately built up a following, and in later years took on minor collectors' car status.

The Escort RS2000 appeared in July 1973, being the third Advanced Vehicle Operations model to go into production at South Ockendon. Once again based on the Escort Twin-Cam/RS1600 structure, the RS2000 used a 100bhp version of the 2-litre overhead-camshaft Pinto engine, together with a Cortina-type (German-sourced) gearbox. All early production was reserved for German customers, with UK deliveries beginning in October.

In October, in a traditional mid-life revamp, the Cortina range received a front-end facelift and a smart and much less 'American' facia style, while the overhead-camshaft Pinto engine finally displaced the old overhead-valve 1.6-litre Kent unit. At the same time a new top-of-the-range Cortina, the lushly-trimmed 2000E, was introduced, the obvious intention being to recapture the reputation of the old-type 1600E (Mk II) model: the tactic failed.

The Capri RS3100 made a brief appearance in November, though its career would be over in about four months. Developed as the base car for Ford to go touring car racing with a more powerful engine in 1974, the RS3100 used a 148bhp/3.1-litre version of the existing 60-degree V6 engine, along with most of the (German) Capri RS2600's chassis settings, and was also equipped with a large

transverse rear spoiler on the bootlid.

As with the BMW 2002 Turbo, the RS3100 arrived at the wrong time. In addition, it was to be rendered visually obsolete by the Capri Mk II in March 1974. Although only 500 needed to be built for sporting homologation, Ford struggled to sell 200 such cars – but homologation was achieved anyway!

Hillman: In March, Chrysler-UK introduced two-door versions of the entire Avenger range. This, however, was only a prelude to what was planned for October, when the entire range was upgraded. Out went the original 1.25-litre and 1.5-litre engines, and in came enlarged versions, measuring 1,295cc and 1,599cc. For the first time there was to be a GT version of the smaller engine, which produced 69bhp, while the 1.6-litre GT/GLS type produced 81bhp.

Jaguar: The XJ6 and XJ12 became Series II, with few mechanical changes, but a front-end styling facelift and many equipment improvements. The front bumper was raised, the grille and other air inlets were modified to suit, and there was a totally new and much simplified facia style.

For the time being, normal and longer-wheelbase four-door saloons were still available (though this range would soon settle on the longer wheelbase).

Smart two-door XJ6C and XJ12C coupe models were previewed (with Daimler equivalents), but the cars were not yet ready for sale. It was altogether typical of British Leyland that such new models were shown before they could be purchased! There would be no deliveries until the spring of 1975.

Lamborghini: The fabulous mid-mounted V12-engined Countach, previewed as long ago as 1971, finally went into production, displacing the well-loved Miura. Not only was the Countach extremely fast, even in its original 4-litre form, with a top speed of at least 170mph, but it had unique 'coleopter' doors, which swing straight up and forward when opened, rather than sideways, this being a neat and effective halfway house between conventional and gullwing operation.

Lancia: Production of the fabulous

mid-engined Stratos two-seater 'homologation special' began in the summer/autumn, though there were never any official sales to British customers. Even so, a goodly number of the approximately 500 cars built eventually found homes in Britain.

Short, wide and with very twitchy handling, the Stratos was designed as a potential World and European rally-winning car, which it was for the rest of the decade, its entire engine/five-speed transaxle package having being lifted from the now-obsolete Ferrari Dino 246 model. Standard road cars had 190bhp, though fully-prepared rally car units could usually produce 270–290bhp with great reliability.

Leyland: Although the big Rover V8-powered P76 four-door saloon, which was newly available as built in Australia, was previewed in the UK, when it was announced that it would be sold through up to 20 selected dealerships, this scheme was abandoned almost at once, and as far as is known no UK deliveries were ever made.

Matra-Simca: Later known purely as a Matra, the new Bagheera was a smart mid-engined sports coupe with the interesting feature of three-abreast seating in a none-too-wide cabin. Packaged rather like the better-known Fiat X1/9, the Bagheera used the engine/transmission pack from the 1.3-litre Simca 1100 Special, and its 84bhp gave it a useful top speed of around 100mph.

Because of the three-abreast seating, it was not economically possible for Matra to build right-hand-drive Bagheeras, but a few left-hand-drive types were sold in the UK over the next few years.

Mercedes-Benz: New 4.5-litre versions of the existing V8 engine were made available in the 450SL, SLC, SE and SEL models, and in each case the existing 350 types continued.

In what was a quiet autumn by its own hyperactive standards, the company announced a reshuffle to its existing smaller W114/W115 range of cars. An oversquare 2,307cc engine replaced the 2,197cc engine previously used, and at the same time an enlarged 2,404cc four-cylinder diesel engine was added to the range of power units available.

MG: The MGB GT V8, complete with a 137bhp version of the light-alloy Rover 3.5-litre V8 engine, went on sale in August. Developed in direct response to specials which Ken Costello had been producing for a couple of years, this was by far the best high-powered derivative of the MGB ever developed, with a 125mph top speed.

Commercially, however, it would be a failure, as only 2,591 such cars were to be sold in the next three years. British Leyland made several basic mistakes – it was only a home-market car, it was never sold as an open roadster, and it always carried too high a price. The excuse about there being a shortage of Rover engines was nonsense. Actually this was a botched project from start to finish. What a pity.

Opel: A completely new range of Kadett models – saloons, estates and coupes – appeared in August, these being the T-Cars which later formed the basis for several other General Motors models in different parts of the world (including, in the UK, the Vauxhall Chevette of 1975).

The new Kadett had a brand-new platform, with conventional front-engine/rear-drive layout, coil-spring front suspension and a rear axle located by coil springs and radius arms. All UK-market cars (from the end of 1973) used 1.2-litre engines, though both smaller and larger engines would follow in future years.

A 2.8-litre version of the six-cylinder engine became optional on Commodore models.

Porsche: For 1974, every version of the 911 was fitted with the 2.7-litre flat-six engine, rated at between 150bhp and 210bhp. Style changes included the fitting of USA-mandatory '5mph' bumpers as standard, which increased the length, and there was a larger fuel tank.

Renault: The 16TX, launched in October, was a top-of-the-range development of the front-wheel-drive 16 hatchback, this time with a 93bhp/1.65-litre version of the engine and a five-speed transmission. British sales began in May 1975.

Rover: After a 10-year life, the 2000 range was finally uprated in October to become the 2200, complete with 98bhp and 115bhp 2,205cc versions of the overhead-camshaft four-cylinder engine.

Saab: The latest version of the still-evolving 99 range was the 110bhp EMS type, which had a fuel-injected version of the 2-litre engine.

Triumph: The new Dolomite Sprint was the final upgrading of the Dolomite range, using the same well-trimmed four-door saloon body and suspensions as the existing Dolomite 1850, but having a new 16-valve single-overhead-cam 2-litre version of the modern slant-four engine. The single camshaft operated inlet valves directly by inverted tappets, and the exhaust valves by long rockers and inverted tappets.

This engine, which produced a very torquey 127bhp, was mated to the massive TR6/Stag-type gearbox, and although overdrive was an optional extra most cars were ordered with this valuable feature.

Except that it had a rather upright eight-year-old body style, the Dolomite Sprint was at least the equal, in performance terms, of similar 2-litre saloons from Alfa Romeo and BMW, and the works racecars eventually proved just how fast and capable the car could be.

After only eight years, the front-wheel-drive 1300/1300TC/1500 model family was finally discontinued, with the front-drive 1500 being dropped in favour of a new 1500TC. This model could most simply be described as a 1.5-litre pushrod-engined version of the modern Dolomite 1850, or a rear-wheel-drive version of the previous front-drive 1500, or even as a better-trimmed, furnished and equipped version of the Toledo. The result, though, was that Triumph was now producing rear-wheel-drive Toledos, 1500TCs, Dolomite 1850s and Dolomite Sprints!

To bring it into line with the Spitfire, the GT6 was given the smaller car's swing-spring rear suspension instead of the lower-wishbone layout which had been such a success in the previous four years. This, in fact, was to be the GT6's last year, for it was dropped at the end of 1973.

Vauxhall: For 1974, the company simplified its complex range of Vivas, keeping that name only for the cars produced with 1,256cc engines. Those with 1.8-litre and 2.3-litre overhead-camshaft engines were driven upmarket, with more fully-equipped interiors, four-headlamp noses and Rostyle wheels, and were renamed Magnums. The old-type Firenza coupe range was also rejigged, the 1.26-litre version being dropped and the others being renamed Magnum coupes.

At the same time the VX4/90 was reworked, with a more powerful, 116bhp, engine, and a top speed which was genuinely more than 100mph (whereas other VX4/90s had struggled to reach that figure).

On the eve of the motor show, the latest Firenza coupe, complete with a new front-end style which included a slanting panel which instantly gained the nickname 'Droopsnoot', and with a 131bhp version of the 2.3-litre overhead-camshaft engine and a five-speed ZF gearbox, was previewed. It was not yet ready to go on sale, and before being dropped in 1975 only 204 examples would be made.

Volkswagen: The new front-wheel-drive Passat, which was revealed in June, was based very closely on the layout of the Audi 80 (VW, of course, owned Audi), but with different rear-end styling.

Like the Audi 80, the Passat had a choice of 1.3-litre and 1.5-litre in-line front-mounted four-cylinder engines, with front-wheel drive. The fastback six-window style looked as if it was a hatchback, but (like the Lancia Beta, which was almost its contemporary) it was actually a four-door saloon – the hatchback derivative would follow in 1975.

Forgetting the K70, which was really no more than a mildy reworked NSU model, the Passat was the first of an entirely new type of VW – front-engined, with water-cooling and front-wheel drive – and several more new VW families would be introduced in the next two years.

The K70 itself was facelifted early in the year, with a new four-headlamp nose and slightly softer front-end styling, though without mechanical improvements. Later in the year a more powerful version, the K70LS, appeared, this having a 1.8-litre version of the engine and a top speed of over 100mph.

Volvo: The Swedish company moved firmly down the path to building ultra-safe cars, sometimes in the face of the pundits' derision. For 1974, massive new bumpers, several inches proud of the panelwork, were added to allow the cars to meet new USA regulations requiring damage-proof panelling in 5mph accidents.

Industrial developments

At British Leyland, behind-the-scenes battles led managing director George Turnbull to retire (almost immediately he would be head-hunted to set up the Hyundai car-making operation in South Korea), while John Barber became Lord Stokes' heir apparent.

Volvo took a 33 per cent stake in Daf during the winter of 1972/73, and it soon became clear that they were looking to take control in the next few years. For the time being, though, production of belt-driven Daf cars carried on unchanged.

Ford decided to build a major new car assembly factory in Spain. This was the start of the front-wheel-drive Fiesta project, though the new car would not be launched until 1976.

Two years after the traumatic financial crisis which caused Rolls-Royce to be rescued by the Government, the Cars Division was floated off into private hands, with David Plastow as managing director. Shares were sold at 90p each, which valued Rolls-Royce Motors at £38.4 millions.

This was the year in which Caterham Cars took over the rights and all assembly facilities for the Lotus Seven range. Starting with the Lotus Seven S4, but soon reverting to the S3, Caterham expanded sales of an already-popular car, and more than 20 years later, by the mid-1990s, more Sevens were being built than ever before.

Clan, the plucky little maker of sports coupes based in Washington, County Durham, was forced out of business, one of several small car-makers crippled by the imposition of VAT. Gilbern would not be far behind, and Ginetta also wobbled for some time.

Taxation changes

As a direct result of Britain joining the Common Market, from April 1 the old purchase tax system was dropped in favour of a new Value Added Tax (VAT).

On cars, the final rate of purchase tax had been 25 per cent (having been reduced to this level in March 1972), which was levied on the wholesale price and was equivalent to about 21 per cent of the retail price.

The new taxation comprised two imposts – a 10 per cent Special Car Tax on the wholesale value of the car, and 10 per cent VAT on the retail value (including the 10 per cent SCT!). The overall result was that after SCT + VAT had been introduced, taxation amounted to about 19.3 per cent. This meant an overall price reduction of £17 per £1,000 – trivial, but nonetheless welcome. Such reductions, incidentally, were almost immediately swallowed up by galloping inflation, which saw car prices being increased every three months at this time.

Incidentally, this innovation signalled the death-knell of the kit-car. Previously, cars sold as 'build-them-yourself' kits were free of taxation, but now VAT was payable on all parts, whether assembled into cars or not.

Technical developments

In many ways, the arrival of the Bosch K-Jetronic fuel-injection system was the most significant launch of 1973, for it would be mass-produced, at a sensible price, to equip many European cars in the years ahead.

Bosch had developed K-Jetronic with continuous mechanical metering, which could be applied to engines of all sizes and layouts.

Soaring production finally made radial-ply tyres as cheap to build as cross-plies. British manufacturers which hitherto had resisted fitting radials on cost grounds soon changed their approach. From January 1973, for instance, Ford announced that it had standardized radial-ply tyres on all except its very cheapest 'fleet' Escorts – and even they fell into line soon afterwards. The demise of the cross-ply tyre came swiftly, and by the mid-1970s it was rare to find a new car on them.

British Leyland's Allegro was the first car to use Hydragas suspension, a further development of the Hydrolastic system (see 1962). High-pressure gas took the place of rubber as the main suspension medium.

1974

For British motorists, this was a year dominated by politics. As a direct consequence of the miners' strike, there was a change of Government following a General Election in February. Once the Labour party took control, it approved many absurdly inflationary pay settlements and inflation itself breached the 20 per cent per annum barrier by the end of the year, making this the worst year since the war for rising prices; official figures show that prices rose by 24 per cent. The following two comparisons tell their own story:

On January 1, a Mini 1000 cost £836, and on December 31, it cost £1,184. On January 1, an MGB cost £1,471, but this had risen to £1,939 by the end of the year.

The financial situation was made worse by the imposition of 10 per cent VAT on petrol from March, which inevitably led to a fall in demand for cars and motoring services.

This, Government policies, and the effects of the huge increase in crude oil prices imposed by the OPEC countries, meant that petrol rocketed from 42p/gallon in January to 74p/gallon at the end of the year. Naturally, there were dire predictions from the doom merchants of the limited worldwide reserves of oil left for consumption, which subsequently have proved totally wrong. In every year since 1973/74, more oil has been discovered than has been consumed!

The Chancellor, however, having second thoughts in the middle of the year, presented a mini-Budget (one of many which would take place in the next few years), in which the standard VAT rate was reduced from 10 to 8 per cent. This had a marginal effect on the price of petrol (around 1p a gallon), while the retail price of new cars fell by around £17 for a Mini to about £100 for a Jaguar XJ12.

As oil embargoes were withdrawn during the spring and oil supplies gradually returned to normal (though at much higher prices!), there was widespread criticism (and abuse) of the 50mph 'energy-saving' speed limit, many motorists suggesting that they should be allowed to go faster when coasting!

The limit was eventually rescinded in mid-May 1974, but this was only a temporary respite. On December 16, a limit of 50mph on single-carriageway roads, 60mph on dual carriageways and 70mph on motorways came into force, but the lower limits came in for a great deal of abuse – both vocally and in fact – by the vast majority of drivers and they would not persist for very long.

Demand for cars slumped all round the world, the British experience being typical. Compared with 1973, 400,000 fewer cars were sold in the UK, 200,000 fewer were produced, and 125,000 fewer imported cars were sold. Things would be even worse in 1975 – the Energy Crisis had been a real culture shock.

This was one reason why, having made £51.3 million profit in 1973, British Leyland hit major financial problems. Its UK market share slipped inexorably away, and in the all-important peak August selling period (when the 'new letter' was phased in) Ford took over market leadership for the first time.

Even Fiat, one of Europe's largest car-makers, made a loss for the first time in many years and cut back its new model programme drastically. Many years later the company admitted that it had thought the great car boom was over...

With the opening of the Avon Bridge, to the west of Bristol, a further stretch of M5 was completed, this stretching the total usable length of M5 and M6 from Bridgwater to Carlisle, more than 300 miles.

Although safety belts (for front seats) were compulsory fitments to all British cars, it was not yet compulsory to wear them. In 1974, the Government introduced legislation which would enforce wearing, but this would not become law for some time.

The cars-by-air market to Europe finally collapsed as more motorists turned to hovercraft and larger, quicker, ferries. Well before the end of the year, British Air Ferries revealed that its sales had dropped by 50 per cent in comparison with its 1973 figures, which in turn had been well down on 1972. Although BAF retained four routes from Southend – to Basle, Le Touquet, Ostend and Rotterdam – the slump continued and the service was doomed.

New models

Alfa Romeo: The Alfetta GT coupe appeared in May, being an extremely smart 2+2 hatchback derivative of the modern front-engine/rear-transmission Alfetta design. Built on the same platform as the Alfetta saloon, it used the latest version of the 1.8-litre twin-cam engine, was styled by Giugiaro/ItalDesign, and had a top speed of more than 110mph.

Right-hand-drive versions of the V8-engined Montreal became available for the first time, but relatively few were sold in the UK, and this model would be dropped altogether in 1977.

Aston Martin: Although the company itself was in dire financial trouble and went into suspended animation in the winter of 1974/75, there was one new model – in October the long-delayed Lagonda four-door saloon car was shown. This was based on a much longer wheelbase version of the Aston Martin V8's platform, together with its V8 engine and running gear, but with a more spacious cabin.

Audi: The 80 range had already been on sale in the UK since March 1973, but a new version, the 100bhp/1.6-litre 80GT, was added to the lists in August 1974.

The new small 50 model appeared in September, complete with transverse engine and front-wheel drive. It was a forerunner of the still-secret VW Polo, but was never sold in the UK.

Austin: In September there were two additional Allegro models, the 1750 Sport and HL types, both of which had a twin-carburettor 1,748cc engine developing 90bhp.

BMW: Eight years after the big-selling 02-series had gone on sale, originally as a 1.6-litre car, this engine size was reintroduced to the British market. Badged as the 1602, the new model used an 85bhp/1,573cc version of the famous four-cylinder overhead-camshaft engine, but had simplified equipment and effectively became BMW's economy-conscious entry-level model once again.

Citroen: Some 19 years after the big DS range had appeared, Citroen was finally ready to launch its eventual successor, the equally-advanced CX range of five-seater/four-door saloons.

The CXs retained the lengthy wheelbases, front-wheel drive and ingenious (and highly effective) hydropneumatic suspension of the DS, but this time the engines were transversely mounted, driving through new gearbox/final-drive units, which were closely based on those used in Lancia Betas, for this had been a joint development effort.

UK-market deliveries of the 2-litre-engined CX2000 began in September 1974, though the first deliveries of the larger and more powerful CX2200 were delayed for another year. This range would gradually take on more engine, transmission and body options, and would be on sale for more than a decade.

As a result of the launch of this CX family in the UK, the last old-type DS deliveries were to be made in the spring/summer of 1975.

Years after it had been dropped from the British market, the 2CV returned again in the autumn of 1974, this time as the 2CV6, with (by 2CV standards) a vastly more powerful (29bhp/602cc) version of the old flat-twin engine. At £830 in the winter of 1974/75 it was the cheapest car on the British market. Trendies, the impecunious and Francophiles all loved the 'Tin Snail', which would once again have a long and honourable UK career before being killed off in 1990.

Colt: These Mitsubishi-manufactured cars (which would revert to their proper name in the early 1980s), went on sale in the UK at the end of 1974. There were two ranges, both with front-engine/rear-drive family saloon/estate layouts, and with overhead-cam four-cylinder engines.

The Colt Lancer (Mitsubishi Lancer in other countries) was a 1.4/1.6-litre machine of Escort size, while the Galant (of which a coupe version was also available) had a choice of 1.6 or 2-litre engines.

Daf: The 46 model, introduced at the end of the year, was yet another reshuffling of existing resources. It was a development of the 44 model (34bhp/844cc aircooled engine), with the de Dion rear suspension and transaxle of the more powerful 66 model. UK sales began in 1975.

Datsun: A new-generation Cherry – the Cherry F-11 series – was announced in Japan in October, which meant that British deliveries were sure to start in 1975. Somewhat larger than the original type of Cherry, it would be available in 1-litre and 1.2-litre forms, but there were no mechanical innovations, and the style was strictly Oriental.

The 260Z 2+2 model, introduced early in the year, was a longer-wheelbase, 2+2-seater version of the already successful 260Z two-seater.

In a further gap-filling move into its already complex range, the 160J coupe arrived, being a 1.6-litre-engined version of the 140J Violet with a two-door coupe body style.

Ferrari: During the winter of 1973/74, the first deliveries of the mid-engined 365GT/4 BB (Berlinetta Boxer) were made. This Ferrari supercar took over from the well-loved front-engined Daytona, and its basic chassis layout, including the magnificent flat-12 engine, would still be in use in revised Ferraris of the mid-1990s.

Previewed at the 1971 Turin motor show as a non-functioning prototype, the Boxer had since been redeveloped. The style, by Pininfarina, was a larger version of what would soon become familiar on the Dino 308GTB, while the layout – in which the flat-12 engine actually sat above the five-speed transmission, thus drawing criticism about the height of the car's centre of gravity – was unique.

Fiat: In October, the 124 saloon/estate range was retired after eight successful years, to be replaced by the new 131 models. The new car was conventionally engineered, with a beam rear axle, and was longer but no wider, and initially was fitted with a choice of 1,297cc and 1,585cc pushrod ohv engines, both being simple enlargements of those previously used in the 124 range. For the time being there was no twin-overhead-camshaft engine option, though this would follow shortly.

After less than two years on the market, the slow-selling 132 received its first facelift. This included lowering the sill line of the side and rear windows (thus increasing the glass area), giving the GLS a new grille, and slightly boosting the power output of 1.8-litre models.

The new 128 Special combined the existing 128 style with a more powerful 60bhp/1.3-litre engine.

Ford: So brave in marketing terms in those days, Ford was the first big car-maker to launch a major new model in the depths of the Energy Crisis – the Capri II.

Although it retained the same basic body/chassis platform and suspensions of the earlier range, the Capri II had a completely new superstructure and 'glasshouse'. Not only was there more space inside the cabin (nevertheless this was still only an 'almost four-seater') but the rounded style also incorporated a hatchback. As before there was a choice of 1.3, 1.6, 2 and 3-litre engines (the 1.6 and 2-litre types being the latest overhead-cam Pinto units), though there were far fewer trim and equipment packs than before.

Ford advertised this as 'the once in a lifetime car'. This basic shape of Capri would remain on the market until 1986, a 12-year run.

In the middle of the year, the Granada Ghia coupe – a two-door fastback derivative of the Granada saloon – was added to the range. In the UK this was available in 2-litre (four-cylinder) or 3-litre (V6-engined) form, but only in top-of-the-range Ghia trim.

Hyundai: The prototype of the first Korean-built car, a front-engine/rear-drive car called the Pony, was revealed in October. It used Mitsubishi engines and had been styled in Europe by ItalDesign.

George Turnbull was directing the project, but at launch time he made it clear that British sales would not begin for some years, which eventually turned out to be 1982.

Jensen: Nearly eight years after the big Interceptor coupe model had been launched, Jensen finally added a 7.2-litre convertible version to the range.

Jensen-Healey: In December, what is now usually called the Jensen-Healey Mk II appeared. It looked the same as before, but was fitted with a five-speed Getrag gearbox, a new facia and '5mph' crash-resistant bumpers.

Lada: The first UK deliveries of this

Russian-built and much modified version of the Fiat 124 were made.

Lancia: In March a new Beta Coupe was introduced, using a shortened version of the modern front-wheel-drive Beta saloon's platform, but with a smart 2+2-seater coupe body style. At first it was available in 108bhp/1.6-litre and 120bhp/1.8-litre forms, but many other derivatives of this Fiat twin cam-engined car would appear in due course.

Lotus: After several weeks' delay, during which colour adverts appeared in Sunday newspapers before the car had been launched, the first new-generation Lotus, the Elite, was finally introduced. This was an altogether larger and more expensive type than previous Lotus road cars, being a front-engined 2+2-seater hatchback/sports coupe, powered by a 160bhp version of the new 16-valve Type 907 2-litre Lotus engine.

As expected, there was a steel backbone chassis-frame, all-independent suspension, a five-speed transmission and four-wheel disc brakes, the smart body being made from glassfibre.

Mazda: The 1000 and 1300 models were derivatives of the old 1200, with dumpy styling, more economy and a distinct lack of character. Even so, they stayed in Mazda's UK-market range for another three years.

In May, the Cortina-sized 929 made its bow in the UK, this in effect being the 1.8-litre piston-engined version of the Wankel-engined RX4. Available as a saloon, coupe or estate car, it expanded this Japanese car-maker's range even further.

Mercedes-Benz: Reflecting the changes many car-makers had to rush through to provide more economical cars, the German company revealed smaller-engined 280SL and 280SLC models, these being the first of this family to use the modern 185bhp straight-six engine instead of a V8.

However, although these cars went on sale in Germany and other markets in mid-1974, they would not be introduced to the UK until 1980 – six years later!

At the opposite end of the performance scale was the introduction of an inline five-cylinder 3-litre diesel engine, rated at 80bhp, for fitment to the 240D model. Initially called a 240D 3.0, it went on sale in the UK in September 1976 badged as the 300D.

MG: British Leyland faced a great deal of criticism for the style changes made to Midgets and MGBs at motor show time in October, in both cases to meet the latest USA crash and damage-protection regulations. The Midget was given vast black polyurethane bumpers, and reverted to the older square rear wheelarch style, while the MGB received similar black bumpers and a considerably increased ride height.

Although there were no mechanical changes to the MGB, the Midget became Midget 1500, complete with a 65bhp 1,493cc engine and gearbox from the Triumph Spitfire. Diehard MG enthusiasts were appalled, but at least these were genuine horsepower, and made this the first 100mph Midget of all time.

To rationalize on bodyshells, the home market-only MGB GT V8 also inherited the same black bumper style, though there were no British regulations which required it.

Opel: The Commodore range was expanded from the autumn, when the fuel-injected 160bhp/2.8-litre version was added to the range.

A limited-production turbocharged Manta coupe was introduced in October, this car having a very short life. The 1.9-litre engine produced 156bhp, the conversion work having been completed by the British Broadspeed concern. To keep the price down, this model was actually a British-built conversion on cars which had been assembled in Germany, delivered to the UK and sold to a customer, and were already registered.

Panther: Continuing its policy of offering pastiche body styles hiding modern Jaguar-based running gear, the massive De Ville was new in October. The 123in-wheelbase tubular chassis was special, but the V12 engine, automatic transmission and coil-spring independent suspension were all pure Jaguar XJ12. A 4.2-litre six-cylinder Jaguar XK engine was also made optional.

The style was meant to remind people of the 1920s-shape Bugatti Royale, but was far too vulgar to be convincing.

Few were sold in the UK – in fact only 60 were sold in all during the next few years.

Peugeot: Still expanding its 504 range, even after six years, the French company introduced a diesel version, this having the 1,948cc XD88 power unit which produced 56bhp. At the same time the brake specification was downgraded, to disc-front and drum-rear. Naturally this was the slowest of any 504 type, but it was also much the most economical.

The Pininfarina-inspired 504 coupe and cabriolet models were given the new PRV 2.66-litre V6 engine from October, which produced 136bhp and gave them a near-120mph top speed. A limited number of these cars were sold in the UK, but always to special order, so rarity value is now guaranteed.

Polski-Fiat: Later known as FSO cars, these were derivatives of Fiats and built by the state-owned car factory in Poland.

The 125P was previewed in the UK in October 1974, with deliveries beginning in April 1975. As this was basically an old-type Fiat 125, but fitted with the even older-type Fiat 1500 four-cylinder engine from the early 1960s, its main attraction was a low price. The 125Ps never built up any sort of image, except for their low cost.

Porsche: To the joy and astonishment of all 911 lovers, the German company previewed a turbocharged version of the car. Known internally as the 930, it was always badged as 911 Turbo. The first type, which would go on sale throughout the world during 1975, had a 260bhp/3-litre version of the air-cooled flat-six engine, allied to a four-speed gearbox.

To keep the handling and stability in check at high speeds, there was a new-type whale-tail rear spoiler and much wider-rimmed wheels/tyres which required extra flaring of the wheelarches.

Seat: To be marketed in the UK as a Fiat car, the Seat 133 (introduced in Spain in April, but not on UK sale until 1975) was a strange Italian-Spanish hybrid with engineering links to the 1960s, but modern styling.

The platform and layout were almost

pure Fiat 850, with a rear-mounted/
rear-drive 34bhp/843cc four-cylinder
engine, but the two-door/four-seater
cabin was new. This was a stubby little
car, in marketing terms falling between
the 126 and 127 models, but apart
from a potentially low price it was
never likely to appeal to British customers, and it was only to be on the
British market from May 1975 to February 1976.

Toyota: Like many other car-makers,
Toyota wanted to have a super-economy
car in its range. In October, therefore,
the small, old-fashioned, front-engine/
rear-drive Publica 1000, with 45bhp/
993cc, was added to the range. It had
already been on sale in Japan and
other territories since 1972, but it held
little appeal in the UK. The cabin was
very cramped, and the Publica was
only ever available in two-door saloon
form. The introductory price of £1,158
was just about its only attraction.

The Celica 1600GT was a top-of-
the-range addition to this popular sports
coupe, with Toyota's new four-cylinder
twin-overhead-camshaft engine. The
1600ST, with its overhead-valve engine,
continued.

Triumph: The 2500TC appeared in
May, this being a 2.5-litre-engined
version of the existing 2000 model,
complete with twin Zenith-Stromberg
carburettors and 99bhp.

The final derivative of the Spitfire
sportscar – the 1500 – was unveiled in
November as a 1975 model. Like cars
which had been on sale in the USA for
some time, the 1500 had a 1,493cc
engine rated at 71bhp in the UK,
which made it more powerful than the
same type of engine which had just
been adopted for the MG Midget. At
the same time a new type of all-
synchromesh gearbox (also used in the
Morris Marina and Toledo/1500 models) was standardized.

Vanden Plas: As expected, a Vanden
Plas derivative of the Austin Allegro
was developed, this time a 1500
based on the 1.5-litre overhead
camshaft-engined Allegro 1500. As
with the old-type 1300, which it displaced, there were no mechanical
changes, though there was a new
Vanden Plas-type front grille (though
not nearly as elegantly placed as in the
old car), and a completely retrimmed

and refurnished interior.

Final assembly was at the Vanden
Plas factory in North London, and there
was a hefty price premium for this sort
of exclusivity – the VDP Princess 1500
cost £1,950.

Volkswagen: The Scirocco coupe,
introduced in March, was the first of an
extremely successful new family of
front-wheel-drive cars, which rapidly
helped VW to shed its age-old Beetle
image.

The Scirocco's platform was based
very closely on that of the Golf (see
below) which followed a few months
later, but it had a smart Giugiaro-
styled 2+2-seater coupe/hatchback
body style. For sale in the UK there was
an 85bhp/1.5-litre engine, which
guaranteed a top speed of more than
100mph. As with the previous VW
Karmann-Ghia model, the Scirocco
was built in its entirety by Karmann,
instead of by Volkswagen. British deliveries began in September.

The Golf, a commercially much
more important car than the Scirocco
which preceded it, was finally unveiled
in June 1974, immediately became the
car which would push the long-running
Beetle out of Germany, and started
selling in very large quantities. Along
with the Scirocco, it used a completely
new platform, with front-wheel drive
and a choice of transverse four-cylinder
engines, along with a new type of
'end-on' four-speed all-synchromesh
gearbox.

The chubby style, by ItalDesign, was
available in three-door or five-door
hatchback forms, totally different in
shape, character and marketing
approach from the Beetle which it
would soon replace. By any standards
it was a most significant car, and
would sell by the million before being
replaced by the Golf II in 1983. A Golf
III would follow in the early 1990s, by
which time this had become the sec-
ond-fastest selling VW of all time.

Volvo: After a lengthy gap without
introducing important new models,
Volvo revealed the new 240/260 family. Although these had new front-end
styles, their structures were obviously
direct modifications of the 140/160
series, which had sold so well in recent
years.

There were two new engines in what
was already a comprehensive range.

Instead of the old pushrod engine of
the 144GL, the 244GL used a new
overhead-camshaft 2,127cc four-
cylinder unit. All 264/265 models
(saloons or estates) used the brand-
new 90-degree 2,664cc V6 engine,
which had been developed as a joint
project with Renault and Peugeot. This
unit would soon find a home in new
French cars, and 20 years later would
still be used in a variety of models.

Industrial developments

As its market share ebbed away and its
industrial relations drifted ever more
towards mindless anarchy, British Leyland's finances went from precarious
to calamitous during the autumn, and
by the end of the year the Corporation
had approached the Government for
support. The final collapse into near-
bankruptcy was swift, and reconstruc-
tion was needed early in 1975.

In May 1974 George Turnbull, who
resigned from British Leyland in 1973,
was revealed as the man who would
guide Hyundai, the Korean industrial
concern, towards developing and
marketing its first car. Although this
would be unveiled well before the end
of 1974, badged as a Pony, it would
not go on British sale until 1982 – and
by this time Turnbull would have moved
on to another top-level appointment.

In December, enthusiasts were
appalled to hear that Ford proposed to
close down its specialist Advanced
Vehicle Operations factory at South
Ockendon, where high-performance
Escorts like the RS1600, RS2000 and
Mexico had been manufactured since
1970. In spite of protests, the closure
went ahead, the last cars leaving the
plant early in 1975.

In the autumn Volvo made an
agreed takeover bid for the Dutch car-
maker Daf, and almost immediately
set about converting the Born factory
into another Volvo plant. The first
change would be to retitle the Daf 66
as the Volvo 66, which occurred in
autumn 1975, while the first new
'Volvo-Daf' would follow in 1976.

During the year Peugeot began a
merger process with Citroen – this
being placarded as an agreed mar-
riage, but in fact was the result of the
intention of Citroen's major shareholder (Michelin) to unload its loss-

making investment in the car company. The takeover would be finalized in 1976, when Peugeot took 90 per cent of Citroen's share capital.

Even though Aston Martin had been a rich man's toy for some years, every successive owner had eventually tired of funding the losses. William Willson's Company Developments concern followed the familiar path, and having failed to get Government support, decided to walk away from its crumbling investment. Production was suspended early in 1975.

Technical developments

Although there was nothing new in its layout, the arrival of the transverse-engined, front-wheel-drive VW Golf was tremendously significant. Volkswagen, it seemed, had abandoned rear-engined cars for good, which meant that such layouts were surely doomed. Rear-engined Hillman Imps would also disappear in 1976, after which only Fiat, with the 126, and

Skoda, with the still to be announced Estelle, remained faithful to the rear-engine concept.

General Motors began offering steering wheel airbags as optional extras from January 1974 – but in spite of the earnest hot air talked by many safety campaigners, demand was so far almost non-existent.

At the end of the year Wartburg was forced out of the British and all other European Economic Community markets because its two-stroke engine could no longer meet emissions standards.

Men of Influence

Ferruccio Lamborghini

Most of the legends surrounding Ferruccio Lamborghini, the founder of the Lamborghini sportscar business, are true. This self-made millionaire did, indeed, only decide to start the business because he had one too many rows with Enzo Ferrari – and was determined to beat the old zealot at his own game. Not only that, but when he walked away from his business in 1974, he seemed to have lost all interest in it.

Born near Ferrara, in Italy, in 1916, the young Lamborghini returned from the Second World War to set up a business converting surplus military vehicles into makeshift farm machinery. From there he built up a business which made newly-designed Lamborghini tractors in the 1950s, soon following it with a heating and air-conditioning enterprise.

Having bought, run and been insulting about his own Ferrari, he set up Automobili Ferruccio Lamborghini in 1963, building a brand new factory at Sant'Agata Bolognese, not far from Bologna, and inspiring the birth of a four-overhead-camshaft V12-engined GT supercar. He was 37 years old, and the general opinion was that this was a foolhardy venture.

By drawing in expertise from Giotto Bizzarrini (engines), Franco Scaglione (body style), Giampaolo

Dallara (chassis and structures) and finally Bertone (styling and body construction), his new cars soon built their reputation and began to challenge Ferrari's credibility.

By the late 1960s Lamborghini had installed good managers to run his tractor and heating/ventilation businesses, enabling him to concentrate on running the fledgling car business. After the 350GT there was the revolutionary mid-V12-engined Miura, the impressive four-seater Espada, and finally the smaller mid-V8-engined Urraco.

Early in the 1970s Ferruccio Lamborghini inspired the birth of the mid-engined Countach, but by 1974, with the Energy Crisis affecting the sales of all supercars, he was tiring of business. His other businesses had already been sold, he had ceded 51 per cent of Automobili Ferruccio Lamborghini in 1972, and in 1974 he walked away from it entirely by selling his remaining stock: he was still only 58 years old.

For the next decade Lamborghini staggered from crisis to crisis, but the founder was well clear of it all. Having retired to his vineyard in Panicarola, southwards towards Rome, he was aloof from the upheavals and was never tempted to return to the motor industry.

1975

Because this was Britain's worst-ever postwar year for inflation (prices rose by more than 24 per cent during the year, and wages by 27 per cent to compensate), the price of cars continued to rocket, demand sagged, and the entire industry was cast into post-Energy Crisis gloom. Had we known it, this would be the worst point in a decade during which prices would rise in total by more than 360 per cent! Amazingly, though, petrol prices rose very little during the year – on average by just 2p per gallon.

British Leyland officially passed into state ownership in April. The National Enterprise Board's ludicrously over-optimistic Ryder Report was published, Sir Don (later Lord) Ryder became the company's chairman, and the Government agreed to pump in £1,400 million to stabilize its position.

Although UK car sales dropped to a mere 1.2 million (well down on the peak of 1.7 million which had been reached three years earlier) sales of imported cars continued to increase inexorably, and British manufacturers' fury was turned on the Japanese. Datsun, in particular, had carved out a large market share, immediately behind the British Big Four and sometimes among them. Market penetration reached 40 per cent at times, and over the whole year it settled at 37 per cent, easily the highest figure so far recorded.

North Sea oil began to flow into British refineries at last, though there was no prospect of this causing fuel prices to fall. The first deliveries were made in June from the Argyll field by a tanker 'cab rank' system, then in November the first piped supplies came ashore (via a 127-mile system) at the Grangemouth refinery in Scotland. From this moment on, Britain's reliance on imported (in particular Middle East) oil supplies began to decrease, the country actually becoming self-sufficient in the early 1980s.

Work on the Channel Tunnel, which had been started in 1973/74, was halted in January. Although France was content to carry on funding its contributions, the new British Government could, or would not finance its completion.

During the year, a law to make the use of safety belts in the front seats of cars became compulsory. Surprisingly, there was little resistance to this sensible development, except for the few blinkered souls who talked airily of preferring to be thrown clear in an accident.

Inflation continued to rage, and during the year the last sub-£1,000 new car (the Lada 1200) was sold – by the end of the year the same car cost £1,199.

New models

Austin: From March until September there was a new range of Austin 1800/2200 models, but these were then renamed Princess (see under Princess for details).

Two years after its launch, and after a long period of derision, the weird Quartic steering wheel of the Allegro was abandoned, all future models being supplied with a conventional round steering wheel. An estate version of the car appeared at the same time.

BMW: In June a brand new small/medium-sized car, the 3-series, took over from the long-running 02-series, which had been on the market since 1966. Still only available as a two-door saloon at first, and with a very similar engine/transmission/driveline combination as before, the 3-series was set to becoming a best-selling BMW.

At first there would be four different four-cylinder engines – 1.6, 1.8 and 2-litre (carburettor) plus a fuel-injected 2-litre, though six-cylinder versions would follow, and a brand-new and smaller six-cylinder engine was also planned. UK sales were scheduled to start in 1976.

Even so, the old-type car was still being made in limited numbers. In October, the 1502 took over from the 1602 in Britain, with a lower power output of 75bhp and simplified equipment.

During the spring, two new versions of the rapidly-expanding 5-series range appeared on the British market. The 518 became the entry-level model, complete with 1.8-litre four-cylinder engine, and the 528 used a 2.8-litre version of the established six-cylinder unit. UK sales began in April.

BMW also introduced the 3.0L, which was effectively a 3-litre version of the slow-selling 3.3L. Although it remained on the market for the next three years, very few were sold.

Bristol: For the first time since 1969 there was a new shape and a new model from this tiny maker of hand-built cars. The 412, introduced in May, used the familiar Bristol chassis and a 6.6-litre version of the Chrysler V8 engine, but it was fitted with a rather angular convertible body, which included a rigid roll-over 'Targa' bar above and behind the front seats.

Chrysler-France: A few years earlier, the new front-wheel-drive Alpine hatchback would have been badged as a Simca, for this is from where it was mainly developed. Much of the concept work, however, had been completed in Britain by Chrysler-UK (ex-Rootes) engineers. Using the same basic transverse engine/transmission as the existing 1100, this was a rather larger five-door, five-seater package, similar in size to the Austin Maxi/Renault 16.

The torsion-bar independent front suspension and trailing-arm rear suspension was all new, as was the stretched engine size of 1,442cc, which was one of the alternatives.

Citroen: The GX range, new in 1970, kept on expanding. The GSX-2 of February 1975 had a more powerful 1.2-litre engine, giving 65 instead of 60bhp, but it was expensive at £1,729.

Colt: The latest new model from this Mitsubishi marque was the Celeste coupe, introduced late in the year and based on the Lancer (smaller-type saloon) floorpan, but fitted with the 1.6-litre or 2-litre overhead-camshaft engine from the Galant. Eventually there would be three versions, two of them with a five-speed gearbox and a 100mph-plus top speed.

At the same time Colt also launched the Galant 2000GTO coupe (nice name, but with scarcely the performance to match) as a top-of-the-range addition to the series.

Daf: Soon after Volvo took over the business, it decided to run down the Daf name and build up the Volvo name instead. From August/September 1975, therefore, the existing Daf 66 was rebadged as a Volvo 66, without significant change. Older-model Dafs – the 44 and newly-marketed 46 – retained their badges, but would be dropped completely in 1976.

Daimler: (For new models, see under Jaguar, below.)

Datsun: The familiar Laurel was modified in March with a new 115bhp/2-litre six-cylinder engine as an option to the existing 100bhp/ 2-litre four-cylinder unit.

Ferrari: In October the true replacement for the much-loved Dino 246GT appeared, this being the Pininfarina-styled 308GTB two-seater. Unlike the Bertone-shaped GT4 which had already been on sale for two years, the GTB reverted to the wheelbase and chassis of the old Dino 246GT, used the modern 2.9-litre 90-degree V8 engine, and rediscovered all the performance, poise and panache of the old car. Surprisingly, most of the bodywork of this new car was in glassfibre – the first time that this material had ever been used on a Ferrari production car.

Fiat: The 128 coupe, which had only been in production for four years, gave way to the 128 3P in mid-year. The new car's platform, front-end style and engine/transmission package were as before, but there was a new type of cabin with a lift-up hatchback (hence the new model name – 3P = three porte, or doors). First UK deliveries were made at the end of the year.

Ford: In January the Mk II Escort took over from the seven-year-old Mk I. Based on the same platform as the last of the Mk Is, the Mk II had a more angular and slightly more spacious style than before, but was mechanically unadventurous.

There was a wide choice of engines – 1100, 1300, 1300 Sport and 1600 – and trim packs ranged from Standard (meaning plain, for fleet markets) to the top-of-the-range Ghia.

In July the new Escort range was extended further with the launch of the much cheaper 1100 Popular – £1,299 instead of £1,529 for the 1100L – in which there was a less powerful (41bhp) engine, cross-ply tyres, drum brakes all round and simplified trim and equipment.

With the death of the Mk I Escorts, all the sporting RS models were killed off for the time being – which meant no Mexicos, RS2000s or RS1600s. Early in the year, though, prototypes of a new RS1800 (to be put on sale during the year) and a new beaky-nosed RS2000 (for January 1976) were shown.

The 1.8-litre BDA-engined RS1800 – similar to the RS1600 except for its new style and slightly larger engine – went on sale in June in strictly hand-built quantities.

The first Capri S model (with firmed-up suspension and cast-alloy wheels) was shown at Geneva in March as a limited edition, but would soon become a mainstream model.

In a very early sneak preview, the existence of a new, small 'Bobcat' supermini project was revealed. But this car was not due for launch until 1976, when of course it would be badged as a Fiesta.

Jaguar: The XJ-S coupe, a 2+2-seater V12-engined car, arrived in September. Although it took over as Jaguar's most sporting model, it could not replace the obsolete E-type in enthusiasts' hearts as it was a much larger, bulkier and more Grand Touring type of car.

The XJ-S was based on a shorter-wheelbase (102in) version of the well-known XJ12 platform, chassis and running gear, complete with all-independent suspension and an amazingly supple ride/handling combination. The fuel-injected 5.3-litre V12 engine was rated at 285bhp, and there was a choice of manual or automatic transmission; the manual-transmission cars were always rare, and the option was abandoned before the end of the 1970s.

The style was always controversial, for it featured larger oval headlamps (though for the USA, pairs of round headlamps were substituted – UK buyers were jealous!), and there were 'flying buttress' or sail panels between the rear corners of the cabin roof and the rear wings.

This was a 150mph-plus machine which, in spite of its appearance, was aerodynamically more efficient than the old E-type: such is progress…

From May, the entire Jaguar-Daimler XJ6/XJ12 range was revised, though these were still called Series II machines. All four-door saloons were

now being built on the longer wheelbase first seen as an option in 1972.

For the first time since 1968/69, a 3.4-litre version of the XK engine returned to the range for Daimler and Jaguar saloons. This time it was rated at 161bhp (DIN), but it was much more powerful than the so-called 160bhp engine originally offered at the end of the 1940s!

The two-door coupe model finally went into production – either in 4.2-litre/six-cylinder or 5.3-litre/V12 form. This car was built on the original shorter wheelbase, and was always more costly than its equivalent four-door saloon, which might explain the limited sales of the type.

The V12 engine was modified and improved, being fuelled by Bosch-Lucas fuel injection, and henceforth rated at 285bhp – 35bhp up on the original V12 rating of 1972.

Jensen: The new GT model, launched in July, was no more than a GTE/ HPE/sporting estate version of the Jensen-Healey sportscar, which continued in production. Mechanically the same as the Mk II Jensen-Healey, it was about 100lb heavier than the open version, and had +2 seating added in what was a far from spacious cabin.

Lamborghini: A new 3-litre version of the mid-engined Urraco went on sale in the UK in August.

Lancia: Adding further to the Beta range, the Beta HPE was a high-performance estate car which followed the lines of the Reliant Scimitar GTE and the Volvo 1800ES (which was out of production by this time). The HPE used the Beta saloon's length of platform, and was immediately available with a 1.6-litre version of the twin-cam engine, though several alternative engines would follow in the years ahead.

The Beta spider, an open-top version of the short-wheelbase coupe, was also introduced in mid-year.

The mid-engined Monte Carlo coupe was an exciting new concept for Lancia. Originally planned by Fiat to be a Fiat, effectively a bigger-brother for the X1/9, it shared the same basic layout. There was a brand-new unit-construction steel shell, with the Beta saloon's type of engine/transmission mounted behind the two-seater cabin and driving the rear wheels. This car used a 1,995cc version of the twin-cam engine and a top speed of 120mph was claimed.

Later in the year the original Beta 1400 saloon was dropped in favour of the even smaller-engined Beta 1300; the new engine was a 1,297cc/82bhp version of the twin-cam design. Shortly, too, 2-litre versions of the Beta saloon, coupe and spider were added.

Just to confuse historians, though, the 1.8-litre engine was then adopted for the USA-market Monte Carlo, where it was called a Scorpion!

Lotus: At motor show time, in October, the prototype of the new Esprit mid-engined two-seater coupe was shown. This was premature, as testing and tooling had not yet been completed and first deliveries would not be made until the middle of 1976.

In many ways the Esprit was a grown-up Europa, for it had a backbone chassis-frame, mid-mounted engine and two-seater accommodation. It was all-new, however – longer in the wheelbase and wider, powered by the 160bhp/2-litre Type 907 16-valve Lotus four-cylinder engine, and covered by a Giugiaro/ItalDesign body in glassfibre.

The Eclat fastback coupe, which appeared in October, was virtually the same car as the modern Elite (1974-vintage), though with a coupe instead of a hatchback cabin, and (originally, at least) a rather more simplified specification which included a four-speed instead of a five-speed gearbox and steel instead of cast-alloy wheels. Automatic transmission became an option on the Elite, but few such cars were produced.

Mazda: The first 616 appeared in Britain in mid-year, though it had already been on sale in Japan for some years. Fitted with a 75bhp/1,586cc four-cylinder engine, it was the successor to the 1600/1800 models and had utterly conventional engineering.

Mercedes-Benz: Seven years after the generation of medium-size saloons went on sale, Mercedes-Benz finally made the smallest-engined version, the four-cylinder 95bhp/1,988cc 200, available in the UK.

The 450SEL 6.9 took over from the obsolete 300SEL 6.3 as a brutally powerful, massive and ultra-fast flagship for the S-class range. The engine was an enlarged version of the original 6.3-litre, and there was a new type of self-levelling hydropneumatic suspension. Although 7,380 of these cars would be sold in the next five years, they were far too expensive to buy and run for all but the most profligate of tycoons.

Morris: From March until September, there was a new range of 1800/2200 models, but these were then renamed Princess. *(For details, see the Princess entry.)*

Opel: The most important new models of the year – new-generation Ascona saloons and Manta coupes – were introduced in August. These replaced the first-generation Ascona/Manta types, which had been running since 1970, and were slightly larger, with smoother styling. Two-door and four-door saloons were available, while the Manta was much more of a fastback than the original type had been.

The front-engine/rear-drive running gear, which comprised the same ranges of engines and transmissions as before, was familiar, but this time the Manta was significantly more roomy inside. The range of Asconas started with a 1.2-litre, but this version was never marketed in the UK.

This new generation of Opels was doubly significant for British motorists, for it also formed the basis of a new type of Vauxhall – the Cavalier – which was launched only a few months later *(see under Vauxhall for details)*.

Later in the year the Rekord models were given enlarged (nearly 2-litre) versions of the four-cylinder engine, which helped keep them ahead of the new-generation Asconas. At the same time a 2.1-litre diesel engine option was added to the Ascona range.

A new economy version of the Kadett, with a 40bhp/993cc engine, went on sale in April, and in the autumn, the Kadett GT/E arrived, intended not only as a flagship Kadett, but also as the basis for a rally car. All GT/Es used the fastback two-seater coupe body style, and were fitted with a 105bhp version of the 1.9-litre cam-in-head engine. Initially, it was said, UK imports would be of left-hand-drive cars, and only to special order.

Peugeot: The large new 604 was previewed at Geneva in March, but did not actually go on European sale until mid-summer, the first British deliveries following in the autumn. Powered by the new PRV 2,664cc V6 engine, the 604 had nondescript styling and all-independent suspension.

Although it was as well-built and refined as Peugeot customers always expected, the 604 never seemed to have much charisma, and it sold only steadily in the UK.

With an eye to the economy-first trend fashionable in Europe, the 1.8-litre engine was reintroduced for the 504 model as an alternative to the 2-litre unit standardized a few years previously.

Porsche: The new 924 was previewed in November (though production did not begin until early 1976). This new sports coupe, which had started life as a VW-badged project, was Porsche's first front-engined car, and its first car with a water-cooled engine.

Designed to replace the 914SC, which was dropped to make way for it, and to sell much more cheaply than the 911 range, the 924 used mainly Audi and VW components in a smoothly-detailed 2+2 coupe shell. The 125bhp/2-litre engine helped produce a top speed of around 125mph, and the gearbox was in unit with the chassis-mounted differential at the rear.

The 924 was the first of a large family of cars which Porsche would build in the next two decades. Even 20 years later, in the mid-1990s, the 968 was a direct descendant of the 924 model.

Princess: British Leyland turned this previous model name into a marque name in September by rebadging the ADO71 Austin/Morris/Wolseley cars which had been introduced in March. Each of them had a slightly different and individual front style, but shared common sheet metal bodywork and mechanical layout.

The cars were direct replacements for the BMC 1800/2200 range which had been on sale since 1966. Like those, the new ADO71 types were large, transverse-engined, front-wheel-drive cars, this time with surprisingly graceful wedge-nosed four-door saloon styles.

As before, there was a choice of 1.8-litre/four-cylinder or 2.2-litre/six-cylinder engines, with manual or automatic transmission, but the Allegro-type Hydragas suspension replaced the older-type Hydrolastic of previous cars.

The Wolseley was only sold in six-cylinder form, the Austin and Morris types both having a choice of engines. When rebadged, there were four models – 1800, 1800HL, 2200HL and 2200HLS.

Crayford almost immediately showed a hatchback conversion of this car, but the factory hatchback type, badged Austin Ambassador, would not go on sale until 1982, nearly seven years later.

Reliant: Although the latest Scimitar GTE SE6, which was introduced in October, looked very similar to the old SE5, its body had been chopped in half (lengthways *and* sideways across the cabin), the result being a physically longer, wider and more roomy car on a new longer/wider chassis-frame. As before, the GTE was powered by a Ford 3-litre V6 engine, and the performance was virtually the same.

At the same time a new little Kitten four-seater/two-door saloon, with glass-fibre body, took over from the Rebel. As before, the Kitten was really a four-wheeler equivalent of the current three-wheeler which, in this case, was the now-notorious Robin. The Reliant engine had been further enlarged to 848cc, giving 40bhp.

Although the Kitten was larger, faster and no less economical than the ubiquitous Mini, it was also rather more costly, and did not sell very quickly.

Renault: The all-new front-wheel-drive 30 hatchback appeared in February, though the first British deliveries were delayed until October. Looking rather like a larger and smoother-styled version of the 16, the 30 used the latest PRV V6 engine of 2,664cc.

The new car featured a five-door hatchback cabin, all-independent suspension by coil springs, and the in-line engine located well ahead of the line of the front wheels. This was the first in a family of cars which would eventually include four-cylinder engines, which were the true successors to the successful 16 range.

Just before the end of the year, in fact, the new 20 model was revealed in France, using the structure, suspension and front-wheel-drive layout of the 30, but with the 90bhp/1,647cc engine of the Renault 16TX. British sales would begin towards the end of 1976.

Rolls-Royce: The two-door four-seater Camargue was introduced in March. Based on the platform of the existing Silver Shadow saloon, the car had been styled by Pininfarina. It offered less space than the Silver Shadow, had styling of which many Rolls-Royce enthusiasts disapproved, and was very expensive – at £29,250 – when launched.

Toyota: The Corolla 30 – the newly-styled and slightly larger version of the previous Corolla (which carried on for a time) went on sale in the UK. Still very conventionally engineered, with front-engine/rear-drive and a beam rear axle, the Corolla 30 sold in huge numbers all round the world.

A new-generation Crown 2600 went on UK sale in May. Using the same platform and 2.6-litre overhead-cam six-cylinder engine as the previous Crown model, it was a Granada-sized car with a more squared-up cabin style.

In October a new 2000 model (called a Corona 2000 in other markets) went on sale, effectively as a replacement for the Corona Mk II of 1972–75. Like that car, it was conventionally engineered, with a 2-litre overhead-camshaft engine and a leaf-sprung axle.

There were advances and regressions – a five-speed instead of a four-speed gearbox, but a shorter wheelbase and less interior space than before. The style was squared-up, rather like that of the latest Crown 2600.

The Land Cruiser 4x4 vehicle, already long-established in other countries, was put on sale in the UK in mid-year. With its 135bhp/4.2-litre engine, separate ladder-type chassis, and beam axles sprung on leaf springs, this was a massive and rugged machine, functional rather than refined. At £4,178 when introduced, it was expensive, and functionally it represented Land-Rover rather than Range Rover competition.

Triumph: The new TR7 sportscar was unveiled in January, though for the first 18 months all production was earmarked for delivery to the USA.

The TR7 was totally different from the TR6, which continued in production for the time being. Based on a new unit-construction shell, with a wedge-nose body style, it was only available as a two-seater fixed-head coupe. The engine was an enlarged (2-litre) version of the Dolomite 1850 overhead-cam unit, while the four-speed gearbox and beam rear axle came from the same car. MacPherson-strut front suspension and coil spring/radius arm location of the rear end were all totally different from the old-type TR6. The TR7 would eventually go on sale in the UK in mid-1976.

In a final rejig of the long-running 2000 Mk II range, the fuel-injected 2.5PI was dropped and a new version, with twin SU carburettors and 106bhp, took over. At the same time the power output of the 2000 was increased from 84 to 91bhp (DIN), and an anti-roll bar was added to the front suspension.

TVR: The small Blackpool-based company became the first British firm to announce a turbocharged engine. The Ford V6 engine was turbocharged by Broadspeed and produced 230bhp, and was offered as a conversion on the 3000M and its later descendants, but only 63 would be made.

Vauxhall: The Chevette, introduced in March, was an interesting amalgam of Vauxhall and Opel hardware. The basic front-engine/rear-drive platform was lifted from the 1973-vintage Opel Kadett, as was the cabin (which was the same as the Kadett City, a model not sold in the UK), but the engine and transmission were from the latest Viva and there was a unique droop-snoot nose.

Cheaper and smaller than the Viva, which was in a different size and price class, the Chevette was a three-door four-seater hatchback which would sell in large numbers in the next few years.

In the autumn there was another important new Vauxhall, the original Cavalier, which was a rebadged and slightly modified new-generation Opel Ascona/Manta. Visually, the main difference was that all Cavaliers had the Manta-type nose, with sloping beak and squared-up headlamps.

For some reason Vauxhall was diffident about this new model, and there was virtually no pre-launch activity or description in the motoring press –

things have changed a lot since then!

Volkswagen: The new small Polo hatchback, a transverse-engined front-wheel-drive car with a choice of 895cc or 1,093cc engines, was launched in March – and was almost identical to the Audi 50 which had first been seen in October 1974. British sales began in February 1976.

The most exciting new front-wheel-drive VW of the year, however, was the GTi, which was the first European-market Golf to use fuel injection. With 110bhp from its slightly enlarged (1.6-litre) engine, and with very sporty roadholding, this was the first of what would become known as the 'hot hatch' models.

After only two years, the Passat style was altered significantly by being given a hatchback option.

In the UK, at least, the legendary Beetle was on the way towards retirement. Once Polo and Golf deliveries had built up, all except the basic Beetle 1200L saloon were dropped. Except that convertibles would be reintroduced in 1976, this was almost the end for VW's rear-engined air-cooled cars.

Volvo: The Volvo 66, introduced to the UK in August, was only a new model because of its badges, for this was the Daf 66 under a different name.

Wolseley: A new front-wheel-drive 2200 Six was marketed from March to August, when Wolseley production closed down for the last time. The Wolseley Six was carried on, however, as a rebadged top-of-the-range Princess. (For further details, see the Princess entry.)

Industrial developments

Following its financial collapse in December 1974/January 1975, British Leyland officially passed into Government control in April, with Sir Don (later Lord) Ryder of the newly-fledged National Enterprise Board as its chairman. Lord Stokes and John Barber were both ousted from the management team, as was Geoffrey Robinson (who had been running Jaguar), while Alex Park became the new managing director.

Later in the year Chrysler-UK also struck serious financial problems, with its British market share slipping to only 7 per cent, its only reasonably modern car being the five-year-old Avenger, which resulted in Chrysler-USA (which was also making losses) threatening to close down the business unless it received substantial aid from the Government.

This time there was no question of the Government taking control, or taking an equity stake, but there was agreement for the company to be slimmed down, involving 7,000 job losses, and to fund losses and provide loans. Imp and Hunter ranges were to be withdrawn, the Avenger lines were to be moved to Linwood, and new models (which Chrysler could not otherwise afford to fund) would follow at Ryton. The final deal was not signed off until the first weeks of 1976.

After a period of suspended animation (virtually no cars were produced in the first half of the year), Aston Martin was bought by Peter Sprague, of National Semi-Conductors, and George Minden, for £1.05 million. Laid-off workers were recalled, and limited production of cars was resumed almost at once.

Jensen, on the other hand, staggered towards a final crisis. Hit hard by the Energy Crisis, when demand for its V8 cars had slumped, it had petitioned the British Government for aid, but without success, and in the end Kjell Qvale called in the receiver in September. Production staggered on for a time, but eventually the factory was closed

down during the early months of 1976.

Over in Italy, too, Maserati closed down for a time when Citroen withdrew its investment, but the company was eventually rescued by Alejandro de Tomaso.

Technical developments

Airbags, which had been a $138 option on new General Motors cars in the USA, were dropped from the lists during the 1975 model year. GM stated that there was 'massive public indifference' – and that only 6,000 units had been sold in the 18 months from January 1974.

After years of testing, sometimes in the floodlight of rallying, Dunlop put the Denovo 'run-flat' tyre on to the market. This was a tubeless design which, when punctured, remained on the wheel rim, and could be used for a further 100 miles, if not driven at more than 50mph, before being changed.

The problem, of course, was cost, for even on the tiny Fiat 126 the extra cost was £43 – about 4 per cent of the total price. The vast majority of motorists were ready to put up with the occasional inconvenience of immediately having to change a punctured tyre, so this innovation fell by the wayside a few years later.

Officially, the last Jaguar E-type was made early in the year, though later evidence suggested that it been part-completed before the end of 1974. This brought the E-type's career to a close after 14 years.

The Wolseley marque was finally abandoned by British Leyland in September, after the new 18/22 series had been in production for only a few months.

After nearly 20 years, the Citroen DS range was finally killed off, to be replaced by the new CX range. A total of 1,415,719 DS cars had been built.

In Italy, Iso closed its doors. Although its cars had always been very fast, most wealthy drivers had proved reluctant to buy supercars powered by Detroit-built V8s – originally Chevrolet and latterly Ford products.

1976

Britain's MPs finally voted to approve the compulsory wearing of front-seat safety belts in March, but there would still be a considerable delay before this became law as the House of Lords threw out the legislation at one point. At the end of the year the Government conceded that it would be difficult to get the law on to statute books before the end of 1977, and this was not actually achieved.

On the other hand, the same legislators were very swift to extend the so-called fuel-saving speed limits of 50mph on single-carriageway roads and 60mph on non-motorway dual-carriageways into 1977.

The Government produced its first proposals for taxing the drivers of company cars because they were deemed to be receiving 'benefit in kind'. This new type of taxation was to be graded according to the size of the car's engine, and was bound to affect the sales of larger-engined cars. The tax was due to come into force in 1977. Hated from the first day, it would become ever more oppressive in the years ahead, regardless of the political colour of the Government.

Original proposals were drastically changed in mid-summer and different rates were later applied to cars under 1.3 litres, under 1.8 litres and over 1.8 litres; 1.3 litre-engined cars were already commonplace, of course, but during the next few years there would be a burgeoning of what became known as 'tax break models' with 1.8-litre engines.

In view of the continuing high inflation in Britain (in 1976 it was 16 per cent – considerably lower than in previous years, but still far too high), it was remarkable that petrol prices remained largely unchanged during the year. Even though the Chancellor increased the tax from 22.5p to 30p/gallon in his April Budget, by the end of 1976, petrol pump prices had settled at between 78p and 83p per gallon.

(In 1976 more than 20 per cent of all oil consumed in the UK came from North Sea sources, this percentage being set to leap further in the next few years.)

As inflation was gradually reduced,

so car sales in Britain increased and, compared with 1975, an extra 100,000 machines were sold. Sales of imports rushed ahead, and for the first time they almost equalled the number of British cars being exported – something which would have been unthinkable only five years or so earlier.

As sales of imported cars continued to rise (by year-end they accounted for 40.8 per cent of the market), there were growing calls for quota limits to be applied, particularly to Japanese products. These were targetted for criticism because Japan was making it so difficult for cars to be imported into Japan from Europe, but despite the barrage of criticism in the years which followed, the 'sales to Japan' question was never properly resolved.

In the USA, GM built its last Cadillac convertible in April, and it was thought at the time that the age of the open-top American car was over. New and pending crash and safety legislation had forced such cars out of existence, it was said. However, this was *not* to prove a permanent change, for none of the proposed legislation was ever enacted, and convertibles would eventually return in the 1980s.

Britain's motorway network continued to evolve, with the completion of the M62 across the north of England, from the outskirts of Liverpool to the approaches to Hull.

Taking one's car to the Continent by air – a service so bravely introduced by Silver City in 1948 – came to end in October when British Air Ferries' Carvairs were finally withdrawn. Patronage had been falling steadily for some years, the Carvairs were worn out, and no suitable replacements were available.

New models

Alfa Romeo: Continuing their famous game of mix-and-match, the company fleshed-out the Alfetta coupe range by introducing 1.6 and 2-litre versions, while dropping the original 1.8-litre type. There were no significant style changes.

At the same time the Alfetta 1800 saloon was dropped, as was the popular 2000GTV coupe.

The popular front-wheel-drive Alfasud range continued to expand, notably with the launch of the very pretty 2+2

hatchback Sprint coupe, and with the addition of five-speed gearboxes to certain models. For the next few years the Alfasud range would expand, interbreed and become almost impossibly complex for all but Alfa enthusiasts to understand.

Aston Martin: A new-generation Lagonda four-door four-seater saloon appeared in October, though the first deliveries would not be made until 1978. Styled by William Towns, the new car was a sharp-edged and rugged derivation of the Aston Martin V8 on a much longer (115in) wheelbase. One much-lauded feature of the prototype (which was actually downgraded before production began) was an advanced electronic dashboard/instrument display.

Audi: In mid-summer the new 100 range appeared, this being the first time Audi had altered its large-size saloon shapes in eight years. As expected, the new 100 used a mixture of new-type Audi/VW and old-type Audi four-cylinder engines, but it sprang a real surprise by launching an in-line *five*-cylinder unit based on the modern VW/Audi four-cylinder design.

Five-cylinder engines were not technologically new (Mercedes-Benz had recently introduced a diesel 'five' for its passenger cars), but this was the first private-car application.

In all other respects, the new-generation 100 was conventional, with an in-line/front-wheel-drive layout and a neat six-light body style.

Still stretching its 80 range after four years, the company added the 110bhp/1.6-litre 80GTE derivative in the spring.

BMW: The new 6-series coupe, which went on sale in the spring, was a replacement for the long-running 2500/2800/3.0CS coupe line. Larger, heavier and with more space in the closed cabin, the first of these cars was called 633CSi, and had a 200bhp/3.2-litre version of the well-known six-cylinder engine.

The unit-construction shell was all-new, but the underpinnings – engine, transmission and front and rear suspensions were all developed versions of other BMW 'parts bin' items, some from the established 5-series saloons, and newer items destined to be shared with the still-secret 7-series models.

Bristol: The long-running 411 model was finally discontinued, to be replaced in October by the new fastback Type 603. This used the familiar chassis, suspension layout and running gear, including Chrysler V8 engines, of the older cars.

The 603 offered a choice of two engines – the 603S used a 5.9-litre Chrysler V8, the 603E (E for Economy? – Bristol never admitted to anything...) a 5.2-litre V8. All cars were equipped with Chrysler Torqueflite automatic transmission.

Chrysler-UK: In the spring the company announced that it intended to assemble the French front-wheel-drive Alpine at the ex-Rootes Ryton-on-Dunsmore factory. British-built Alpines started to roll off the lines in August.

From the start of the 1977 model year – in August 1976 – the Chrysler badge was applied to all surviving Hillman models from the Avenger range. At the same time the Avenger was given a facelift, with a smoother nose and a new facia/instrument panel based on that of the new Alpine.

Citroen: For 1977, a 2.2-litre diesel engine was added to the big front-wheel-drive CX range, and at the same time a 2.4-litre petrol-engined car was previewed. UK-market deliveries began before the end of the year.

Colt: The original Lancer and Galant ranges were augmented from October by a larger Sigma model. This was a conventional front-engine/rear-drive saloon with a choice of 1.6 and 2-litre four-cylinder 'balancer' engines.

Colt also added to the Lancer range by importing a 1.2-litre version of the existing car.

Datsun: Although the FII version of the Cherry had been launched in Japan in 1974, first UK deliveries were not made until the autumn of 1976, and not all the body derivatives of the new range were available at first.

A new-generation 160B/180B Bluebird range was announced in Japan, with UK sales due to begin in 1977. Looking broadly the same as before, with a choice of 1.6 or 1.8-litre engines, the new model was slightly larger, with more cabin space.

Changes to the 140J/160J Violet models were mainly confined to cosmetic improvements around the tail, though a five-speed gearbox became standard on the 160J.

DeLorean: The first non-running prototype was shown of a rear-engined coupe which ex-GM vice-president John DeLorean was determined to put on sale, somewhere in the world. It would be two more years before he made a notorious deal with the British Government to build the cars in Northern Ireland, and five years before the first cars were ready for delivery.

Ferrari: Only two years after it first went on sale, the flat 12-engined Boxer was upgraded with a 4.9-litre/360bhp power unit, becoming the more flexible, practical (and expensive!) BB512 Boxer.

Similarly, Ferrari's only conventional saloon was also up-gunned in the autumn with a 340bhp V12 4.8-litre engine, to become the 400GT.

Fiat: The X1/9 sportscar was shown at the Earls Court Motor Show in right-hand-drive form, nearly four years after the original car had been revealed, but even so, the first deliveries to British customers would not take place until early 1977.

Ford: The all-new Fiesta was revealed in mid-summer from assembly plants in Spain, Germany and Dagenham in the UK. This was Ford's first transverse-engine, front-wheel-drive car, a hatchback with few mechanical innovations. For Ford, however, it was a major investment, as the company had previously ignored the 'supermini' market sector.

Technically, the Fiesta was unadventurous, for it had overhead-valve engines, a four-speed transmission and beam-axle rear suspension. All cars until 1989 would have a three-door hatchback body.

It was an extremely busy year for Ford. A new type of (Ford-Germany) Taunus had appeared in the spring, and only weeks after the Fiesta had been introduced, a new Mk IV Cortina was put on the market. Logically enough, the Mk IV Cortina was very closely based on the Taunus design.

As expected, this was not just one new model, but an entire family. The platform, suspensions and general running gear were as used in late-model Mk III Cortinas, but there was a different superstructure/cabin, with more squared-up lines. Two-door and four-door saloons and five-door estate cars were available, with 1.3, 1.6 and 2-litre engines and a wide choice of trim and equipment packs.

Two new Mk II RS Escorts – the RS Mexico and the RS2000 – went on sale in January, though these cars were assembled in Germany (at Saarlouis) rather than in the UK, like the first-generation RS Escorts.

Both cars were developments of the previous RS2000, though the later Mk II shell was used. The RS Mexico used a 95bhp/1.6-litre version of the overhead-cam Pinto engine, and looked like any other Escort. The RS2000, on the other hand, had a 110bhp version of the 2-litre Pinto unit, with an elongated 'beaky nose' front style.

Because the RS2000 was a near-110mph car, and almost as rapid as the very limited-production Escort RS1800, it sold very well indeed for the next five years.

With economy in mind, the Capri 1300, Cortina 1300 and Granada 2000 'base' model were all given less-powerful/lower-revving versions of their engines. Although Ford marketed these changes strenuously, they proved unpopular and within a couple of years had been pushed into the background.

Hillman: From August the Hillman Avenger disappeared, being replaced by a revamped car badged as a Chrysler.

Honda: The first Accord hatchback coupe, with a transversely-mounted 1.6-litre engine, went on sale in Japan and the USA during the year and was shown at Earls Court in October, though British deliveries would not begin until 1977. Compared with the Civic, this was an altogether larger, and more gracefully-styled car, and was additional to the range.

Lada: Expansion of the range of Russian-built models so closely based on Fiat 124s continued in May, when Satra Motors introduced the first of the Lada 1500 models, with a 75bhp/1,452cc version of the existing overhead-camshaft engine. A four-headlamp nose confused everyone, for when fitted with it this car looked remarkably like the Fiat 125, which had become obsolete in 1972.

Lamborghini: Now that the Countach had gone on sale, the company concentrated on its other models. Still struggling with the development of the Urraco, which had never sold as well as hoped, Lamborghini also announced the Silhouette version, which was really a much-modified Urraco with a removable roof panel, flared wheel-arches and an uprated version of the 3-litre V8 engine. Few of these cars were sold, and only a handful arrived in the UK.

Lancia: In March the last 'Lancia-Lancia' of all – the Gamma – was unveiled. Thereafter, all new Lancia models would effectively be much-modified Fiats and would use Fiat hardware and components.

Like other current Lancias, the Gamma was a front-wheel-drive car, but it was a large five-seater with a new 2.5-litre flat-four engine, a five-speed gearbox, all-independent suspension, and styling by Pininfarina. Only a few months later (see below) the Gamma would be seen to have a remarkable resemblance, in size and general proportions, to the new Rover 3500 SD1.

At the same time as the saloon, Lancia also previewed an extremely elegant two-door coupe version, also with Pininfarina styling, and with some proportions rather like that of the Fiat 130 coupe. In both cases, British sales did not begin until 1978.

The mid-engined Monte Carlo, which had been announced in 1975, finally went on UK sale towards the end of 1976.

Mercedes-Benz: The W123 range appeared in January, taking over from the extremely successful W114/W115 family of medium-sized saloons, which had been on sale for the previous eight years.

Although there was a completely new unit-construction bodyshell, and there was a reshuffle of existing four, five and six-cylinder petrol and diesel engines from 2 to 3 litres, the mixture was very much as before.

The styling was broadly similar to the older cars', but sufficiently different if you were a Mercedes-Benz watcher. The W114/W115 cars had used vertically stacked headlamps, whereas the new W123 type used horizontally-paired lamps. The wheelbase had been stretched by 2 inches, and the cabin was slightly wider than before. UK sales began before the end of the year, and a smart two-door/four-seater coupe version of this new range was previewed in the autumn.

MG: The MGB GT V8 coupe was dropped in mid-summer, after extremely low sales over the previous year.

Morgan: The much-admired Plus 8 was improved by the fitment of a new-type Rover five-speed gearbox.

Moskvich: Because the Lada had become such a success, causing British sales to dwindle, the Moskvich marque was withdrawn from the UK market at the end of the year.

Panther: The new Lima, a much smaller and less specialized car than Panther had been used to building, was revealed in the autumn. Like other Panthers, in styling it was 1930s-type pastiche, but the underpan, engine, transmission and suspensions (all Vauxhall Magnum 2300) were thoroughly modern.

The open two-seater style featured free-standing headlamps, but at least it had wind-up door windows, which were actually MG Midget assemblies. The main body was made from glass-fibre.

Peugeot: From mid-summer, ready for 1977, the French company re-shuffled its range. The long-running 204 models were dropped, the smaller end of the market now being covered by 104 and 304 types.

The 104 was modified from saloon to hatchback style, and offered with a choice of 954cc or 1,124cc engines. At the same time the stubby, short-wheelbase 104ZS coupe was put on sale in the UK.

Renault: The most important new Renault of the year was the front-wheel-drive 14 hatchback, which appeared in May. Not only was it Renault's first transverse-engined car, it was the first (and only) model to use a Peugeot-derived four-cylinder engine, actually a modified version of that used in 104s.

The 14 was always a rather hump-backed design, sometimes described as a rather swollen Renault 5, with a conventional (by Renault standards) all-independent suspension. As in the Peugeot, though, the transverse engine lay back at an angle of 72 degrees, the gearbox being below the crank-shaft, with the final-drive unit behind that (and therefore underneath the steeply angled cylinder block).

The front-wheel-drive 15/17 coupe range was facelifted in April and reduced to only two models – 15GTL and 17TS; the fastest and best-specified model, the 17 Gordini, was dropped at this stage.

The latest cars were given a new and rather more squared-up nose and there were changes to the cabin style, both inside and out.

The 5GTL, though simple enough in concept, was an interesting attempt to produce a more economical car. The already-proven front-drive 5 model was given a larger (1.3-litre) engine, but this was in a modest state of tune, and the gearing was much higher than on other 5s.

Rover: In July the new V8-engined SD1 3500 model appeared. This big, graceful, five-door hatchback model effectively replaced the old P6B type (the P5B range had died three years earlier). Although unknown at the time, a new range of six-cylinder engines was being developed, and Rover made it clear that SD1 would eventually take over from all old Rover P6 and Triumph 2000/2500 models.

Except for its light-alloy V8 engine, which Rover had already been using for nine years, the 3500 was new from end to end. Not only was the 110.5in wheelbase platform totally fresh, but there was a new five-speed manual transmission and heavy-duty rear axle, and most surprisingly the rear suspension comprised a beam axle, coil springs, trailing arms and a Watts linkage. Sales began at once, the car being even faster than expected, but within months the first complaints about low build quality were heard.

Saab: In the autumn the first 99 Turbo was introduced in Sweden. This was to be Europe's first turbocharged family car (the Porsche 911 Turbo and the TVR Turbo were both out-and-out sportscars). With 145bhp from its 2-litre engine, this was a rapid and remarkably civilized 120mph car.

Skoda: The first new model from Czechoslovakia since the mid-1960s, the rear-engined Estelle was previewed in the autumn, though the British concessionaires would not be able to deliver cars until spring 1977.

Using much of the same running gear as the old models, thus ensuring a rearward weight bias, the latest Skoda was a neat but very simply equipped four-door saloon, whose handling immediately came in for a great deal of criticism.

Triumph: The TR7, which had been revealed and put on sale in the USA in January 1975, finally entered the British market in May with its 2-litre engine rated at 105bhp. At this stage the TR7 had a four-speed gearbox, but it was known that a five-speed box and an automatic transmission option were both on the way. These were introduced to UK-market cars towards the end of the year – then withdrawn because of supply difficulties and subsequently reintroduced. British Leyland was like that in those days...

The Toledo/1500/Dolomite range was reshuffled in March, a more logical range of 'Dolomites' – 1300, 1500, 1500HL, 1850 and Sprint – taking over. Mechanically there were no changes, but all cars now shared the existing long-nose/long-tail four-door saloon shell, the old short-tail Toledo shell having been dropped.

TVR: An addition to the range from October, the Taimar was a hatchback derivative of the 3000M; both types would continue in production until the end of the 1970s.

Vauxhall: Only four years after it had been launched, the FE-series Victor was facelifted and renamed the VX. Without styling changes, therefore, Victors became VX1800s and VX2300s. The VX4/90 disappeared from the range for a time, and all the six-cylinder derivatives were dropped as well.

Both the 1.8 and 2.3-litre overhead-cam engines had been modified to produce more power and torque, but otherwise there were no major mechanical changes. To identify the latest cars they were given new and more 'American' front grilles, whose aperture was derived from the old Ventora, a car which had been killed

off. Thus modified, the VX models would be built until 1978.

The Chevette range, new in 1975, advanced several stages further with a notchback saloon and later an estate car joining the original hatchback. Apart from its nose style, the saloon and estate car shells were identical to those of the current Opel Kadett.

Using the three-door hatchback shell from the normal Chevette, Vauxhall installed a 2.3-litre twin-cam 16-valve version of the VX/Magnum 2300 engine, backing it by a Getrag five-speed gearbox and a heavy-duty rear axle.

Volkswagen: The first of the 110bhp/1.6-litre fuel-injected Golf GTi and Scirocco coupe models were unveiled in June. Not only were these the fastest VWs up to that time, but their handling was quite outstanding by previous VW standards.

Even though it had been in production for 41 years, the Beetle refused to die in Britain. The cabriolet model, which had always been produced for VW by Karmann, was reintroduced, this time using the largest and most powerful 1.6-litre version of the air-cooled engine.

Volvo: The 343 saloon, unveiled in February, was the first real fruit of Volvo's takeover of Daf in 1974. Originally conceived as a larger Daf (the name Daf 77 was often rumoured), it was eventually completed as a Volvo, and its descendants would run on, as the 340/360 family, until 1991.

The 343 was larger than the 66, which continued. Mechanically there was much continuity with the past, for the front-mounted 1.4-litre was from Renault, and there was a rear-mounted belt-drive automatic transmission and de Dion rear suspension, as found on the Daf 66. UK deliveries began in the autumn.

Industrial developments

British Leyland announced that it was planning to turn the Triumph Canley/Fletchamstead plant into a gigantic engine and transmission production plant – and that car assembly lines would be closed down to make space for this. It was one of several grandiose

plans which came to nothing, for BL was increasingly affected by strikes over pay, and would lose so much more money in years to come that such investment became impossible.

It wasn't all bad news, though, for in June Rover built the millionth Land-Rover, which was in greater demand than ever before.

As part of the Chrysler-Europe shake-up, Imp assembly ended in Scotland, being replaced by Avenger assembly from Ryton, while the new front-wheel-drive Chrysler Alpine (actually a Simca masquerading under the Chrysler name) went into production at Ryton.

Jensen finally stopped building cars in the spring (officially in May, though only a tiny number had been produced in earlier weeks) as the receiver abandoned hope of getting an acceptable offer for the ailing company. Not even a consortium which included ex-BLMC managing director John Barber and Donald Healey himself could raise the money needed to carry on.

VW finally decided to build an assembly plant in the USA, where specially-modified versions of the Golf, called the Rabbit, would be produced from 1977.

Quietly and without fuss, in the middle of the year Triumph built the last of the separate-chassis TRs – a TR6 destined for the USA. The TR line had been founded in 1953, when the original TR2 went into production; the one remaining TR – the TR7 – was an entirely different type of unit-construction sports coupe.

The Saab 95/96/V4 range was finally dropped from the UK market, though production would continue in Saab's Finnish factory for some years to come.

The Enfield electric car project was finally abandoned after only 108 examples had been made. The Electricity Board had originally bought 61 such machines, and almost all the others had been sold to electricity-producing or selling organizations at home and abroad. Only six cars, it seems, were ever sold to true private owners.

British Leyland – the long slide...

British Leyland had lost ground nearly every year after it was set up in 1968.

State rescue in 1975 did nothing to stop the rot – in fact the loss of market share intensified.

I have assembled British Leyland's nominal market share in the years before its foundation by adding in the Rover-Triumph figures. Here is how the Corporation's UK market share eroded between 1965 and 1979:

Calendar year	UK market share (%)
1965	44.5
1966	45.2
1967	40.7
1968 (First 'official' BLMC year)	40.6
1969	40.2
1970	38.1
1971	40.2
1972	33.1
1973	31.9
1974	32.7
1975 (First 'State-owned' year)	30.9
1976	28.2
1977	24.3
1978	23.5
1979	19.6

The slide continued during the 1980s.

Technical developments

Turbocharging, though not new, finally got a grip on family cars with the launch of the Saab 99 Turbo. This was the start of a revolution which continued for the next generation.

Turbocharged engines were found in powerful military aircraft during the Second World War, and in massive truck diesel engines in the 1950s and 1960s. The first automotive application was in selected General Motors models in the early 1960s, the first European *production* car was the BMW 2002 Turbo of 1973, and the first Porsche 911 Turbo came in 1975.

From time to time in the next 20 years the turbocharger was prematurely written-off as unnecessary and too expensive. Four-valves-per-cylinder were regularly written up as a replacement for turbocharged engines, but this trend never took off. In the 1990s, as in the 1980s, turbos (especially matched to diesel engines) seemed to be everywhere.

European Car of the Year

To British Leyland's great joy, the new Rover 3500 (SD1) was awarded the increasingly prestigious European Car of the Year prize for 1976, ahead of rivals like the Ford Fiesta, the Audi 100 and the Renault 14.

As always, the award was made on technical and styling merit. The jury could have had no knowledge of the way that quality problems would intervene and how in consequence this car's reputation would sag in future years.

Men of Influence

Lord Ryder

Totally unknown to the British motorist before his name hit the headlines in the wake of the British Leyland crisis, and a man who speedily dropped out of sight after a few years, Sir Don (later Lord) Ryder was a hard-working businessman who never made any secret of his left-leaning politics.

Famously feted by Fleet Street for the insanely long hours he seemed to put in at the office – he probably vied with Lew (later Lord) Grade for his early starts, for he always seemed to arrive at Grosvenor Gardens before the cleaners clocked on – he had been appointed as an industrial adviser to Prime Minister Harold Wilson soon after the Labour Government came to power in February 1974.

Heading up the activities of the new National Enterprise Board (which was later accused of being a blanket organization seeking to influence, control and later nationalize many of Britain's key industries), Sir Don was the obvious personality to be asked to report on British Leyland's prospects after this ramshackle organization appealed for Government support at the end of 1974.

As is now notoriously well-known, the Ryder Report (which leaned heavily on strategy documents which the original British Leyland management team was considering) proposed the nationalization of British Leyland and the capital expenditure of no less than £1.264 billion. In a crazy demonstration of megalomania, the Report proposed total centralization of the business (Soviet-style?).

The Government, in accepting the Report's recommendations, saw Lord Stokes and John Barber ousted, and although Sir Don (who was soon ennobled) never had an executive role at the nationalized British Leyland, chief executive Alex Park had to clear every major decision with him before it could be enacted.

Nevertheless, as British Leyland sunk ever further into a strike-torn, inefficiently managed quagmire, the media moved in, always probing, criticizing and demanding answers. Only two years after his influence had first become obvious, Lord Ryder resigned from the NEB in the summer of 1977 and rapidly disappeared from public gaze.

As far as British Leyland was concerned, his epitaph was to turn a bankrupt privately-owned colossus into an even more bankrupt nationalized concern, for which no-one remembers him fondly.

1977

In spite of a further slight reduction in the rate of inflation, down to about 16 per cent, British car-makers still raised their prices every 90 days (the shortest interval allowed by Government legislation). This meant that even though the basic rate of income tax was reduced from 35 to 33 per cent in the Budget in March, demand for cars was still restricted, and overall sales continued to stagnate at around the 1.3 million mark.

British Leyland's problems redoubled (see under Industrial developments), a result of lost production being lost sales. Consequently, Ford became UK market leaders, a position which they have never since lost.

The surge in sales of imported cars continued, and for the first time their market share exceeded 50 per cent – 52 per cent, to be exact. That figure, however, needs explanation. Not only did it reflect buyers' increasing disdain for British Leyland and its workforce, it was also aided by increasing numbers of Ford and Vauxhall products, nominally British, being built in Belgium, West Germany or Spain, where labour relations were better and productivity higher.

For the first time since 1947 there was no official motor show at Earls Court. Like several other European organizers, the SMMT had decided to mount a biennial show (the previous one being in 1976), and to move it to the newly-built National Exhibition Centre (NEC) on the eastern outskirts of Birmingham.

In place of the traditional London motor show, another show called Motorfair, nominally only supported by dealers (though there seemed to be a lot of manufacturer support behind the scenes…), was held at Earls Court.

After a great deal of wavering, and downright reluctance, the Government finally raised Britain's overall speed limits after agreeing that the fuel supply emergency of 1973/74 was over. From May the limits were raised to 60mph on single-carriageway roads and 70mph on dual carriageways and motorways – where they have stayed ever since. Petrol prices were raised in the Budget, but Parliament threw out that impost later in the summer, which meant that petrol prices in the Home Counties were still hovering around the 80p/gallon mark by year-end.

When the Exeter bypass was opened in May, the M5 motorway was finally completed, giving an unbroken length of dual carriageway from Plymouth to the outskirts of Glasgow. Unhappily, the Government's seemingly unending financial problems resulted in major cutbacks in road building at this time – there were even suggestions that completion of the M25 (five short sections of which had recently come into use – the first of all being eastwards from the A1(M) at South Mimms) should be abandoned!

New models

Alfa Romeo: The most important new model of the year was the new-generation Giulietta four-seater saloon, which arrived at the very end of the year. Although this was clearly a new style, rather angular but distinctive, it used the same platform, suspensions and front-engine/rear-transmission layout of the modern Alfetta.

The original version to be sold in the UK (from late 1978) used a 1.6-litre version of the famous twin-cam engine, though 1.8-litre and eventually 2-litre types would also arrive.

Following up what had been done for the Alfetta coupe in 1976, early in 1977 the company also introduced an Alfetta 2000 saloon.

Aston Martin: The Vantage version of the existing V8 model was revealed, with a claimed 40 per cent increase in peak power, though since Aston Martin had ceased quoting power figures the enthusiasts were never told the horsepower.

Except that the front grille was blanked-off (most of the air, it seemed, had always entered the V8's engine bay from beneath the car!), and a rear spoiler and bigger front-end spoiler were fitted, there were virtually no style changes. The new car had a claimed top speed of around 170mph – and acceleration to match.

Audi: The new Avant, introduced in September, was really a five-door semi-estate/hatchback version of the latest 100 range, but sufficiently different in character to constitute an extra model range. As with the 100, these were front-wheel-drive cars with four or five-cylinder engines.

Bentley: (See under Rolls-Royce, below.)

BMW: The original-generation 7-series range was introduced in May, taking over from BMW's old 3-litre and 3.3-litre saloons. The basic layout of the new four-door saloons was familiar, for like other BMWs they retained MacPherson-strut front suspension and semi-trailing arm independent rear suspension. Similarly, there was a choice of 2.8, 3.0 and 3.2-litre six-cylinder engines, as seen on many other BMWs in the past decade or so. This big new BMW flagship would be built until the mid-1980s.

For the first time since 1968, BMW showed a new range of engines. The first of a new six-cylinder range – a 122bhp/2-litre unit – was fitted to the 320 for 1978 in place of the old 2-litre 'four', along with a 143bhp/2.3-litre version in the new 323 model.

Early prototypes of a mid-engined supercar, later to be named M1, were seen on test in Europe. Lamborghini had been contracted to develop and build a limited production run, but this arrangement later collapsed when Lamborghini struck financial problems.

Chrysler: Less than two years after the British Government offered financial assistance to persuade Chrysler to keep its UK operations in being, the company revealed the new Sunbeam hatchback range. This car used a shortened version of the Avenger's platform and suspensions, but there was a new superstructure, with a three-door hatchback style. Three engine sizes were available – the 1.3 and 1.6-litre being virtually unchanged Avenger types, while there was also a 930cc-engined car, using an enlarged version of the Hillman Imp's (rear-mounted and installed at 45 degrees) alloy unit, though in this case positioned upright at the front of the car.

Other 'new' models in the autumn were the final derivatives of the Hunter which, until the summer of 1977, had been badged as a Hillman. There were no technical changes.

Chrysler-France: For sale early in 1978, the new five-door Horizon hatchback appeared at the end of the year, being a replacement for the old Simca 1100 design. Under the skin it used a 1.1 or 1.3-litre version of the long-established 1100/Chrysler Alpine front-wheel-drive engine and transmission pack.

The Horizon would have a very long career, being assembled not only in France, Spain and at Ryton in the UK, but also in the USA, where it carried Dodge Omni and Plymouth Horizon badges.

British deliveries began late in 1978 – actually *after* Chrysler had agreed to sell the business to Peugeot.

Citroen: The CX range of big front-wheel-drive saloons continued to expand. From May, Citroen added a new flagship, with a 128bhp fuel-injected version of the existing 2.4-litre four-cylinder engine allied to a five-speed gearbox.

Finally recognizing that the entry-level GS model was underpowered, Citroen increased the engine size from 1,015 to 1,130cc for 1978.

Colt: The first front-wheel-drive (Mitsubishi) model was previewed in Japan before the end of the year. More details would be available when UK deliveries began in 1979.

Daihatsu: The Japanese company, which had not been represented in Britain since a brief foray in the mid-1960s, launched a new front-wheel-drive hatchback in Japan which went on sale in the UK in 1979. Called Charade, the new car was unique at the time in having a transversely-mounted *three*-cylinder engine.

Daimler: (See under Jaguar, below.)

Datsun: There was really no end to the new models pouring out of the Japanese company at this time. In February, new-generation Laurel models appeared, then in June the rebodied Bluebirds, which had been seen in Japan the previous year, finally went on sale in the UK. In those days, one medium-sized Datsun looked much like another, and only the dealers really seemed to know what all the different type numbers and horsepower ratings actually meant!

In November, the Sunny range was renovated into a fourth-generation,

still with 1.2-litre (and the Violet's 1.4-litre) engines on the established platform, but with an all-new family of body styles going on sale in Japan. This was to be the last of the front-engine/rear-drive Sunny generations, UK deliveries starting in August 1978.

Then, in December, Datsun-UK started selling the latest-generation Violet range, these being available with 1.4 and 1.6-litre engines. In fact they were the last of the very ordinarily-specified Violets (which had beam rear axles and were nicknamed 'Violents'), for the Sunny range below them was growing larger with every revision, a true replacement being the Stanza of the early 1980s.

Ferrari: For the rich and sporting-minded, Ferrari started importing the 308GTS, a Targa-topped version of the mid-engined two-seater 308 model. This style, modified and with larger engines, would remain in the Ferrari range for some years to follow.

Fiat: The front-wheel-drive 127 was redesigned, though its basic structure and layout were retained. As an addition to the existing overhead-valve 907cc engine, a Brazilian-built overhead-cam engine of 1,049cc, which produced 50bhp, was added to the range, and there was a new front-end style.

To improve the 126's performance (though it would still be a slow car...) the engine was enlarged to 652cc in August.

More than four years after production began, right-hand-drive versions of the mid-engined X1/9 sports coupe model began in the UK, at £2,997.

Still puzzled as to why its 132 saloon was not selling well, Fiat introduced a torquey 112bhp/2-litre version as an addition to the range. It was needed, because assembly of the larger and more powerful 130 models had just ended. In Britain, the old 1.6 and 1.8-litre types were dropped when the 2-litre car arrived.

Ford: The new-generation Granada arrived in September, being a direct replacement for the original-shape Granadas of the 1972–77 period.

Although the new car rode on the same platform and suspensions as the original type, there was a brand-new, squared-up, four-door saloon shell (and an estate car derivative), all these

cars now being assembled in Germany.

The old Ford-UK V6 engines had been dropped, the new Granada's line-up being 2-litre four-cylinder, 2.3 and 2.8-litre Ford-Germany V6s and a Peugeot diesel. For the first time, too, there was a fuel-injected V6 engine, the 2.8-litre car being rated at 160bhp.

The front-wheel-drive Fiesta, probably Ford's most important new UK arrival for many years, went on sale in Britain in February 1977. At first there were six models in the range, with a choice of 957cc or 1,117cc pushrod overhead-valve engines.

From September, 66bhp/1.3-litre Kent-engined versions of the car, known as Fiesta 1300S or 1300 Ghia, also went on sale.

A new version of the Cortina was added to the range for the 1978 model year, using a 108bhp/2.3-litre version of the Ford-Germany V6 engine.

The Escort RS1800, which had been a very slow seller, was quietly dropped during the year.

Hillman: This famous British name was finally dropped in the autumn, when the Hunters (which were assembled in Ireland in the last stages of their career) were renamed Chryslers.

Jaguar: Towards the end of the year, the range of two-door coupe models – six-cylinder or V12, Jaguar or Daimler-badged – were discontinued. They had been on sale since 1975, but had sold slowly and were getting in the way of rationalization within the company.

Jeep: The American Motors import company had been in disarray in the UK for some years, but under new control by TKM, bravely announced that it was to import more examples of the CJ-7 model in the next few years. In the end, though, very few such 4x4 vehicles were brought in – the impression being that more arrived as personal imports.

Lada: In the autumn the Russian carmaker added further derivatives of the basic saloon/estate car range, there now being a 1.3-litre version to add to the 1.2 and 1.5-litre models which continued in production.

The first 4x4 Niva was previewed in Russia at this time, though sales of this short, high, stiffly-sprung and uncompromising off-road machine would not begin until 1979.

Lancia: The mid-engined 2-litre Monte Carlo sports coupe finally went on UK sale in April. This 120bhp machine, a larger statement of the Fiat X1/9's layout, was available as a fixed-head coupe, or a removable-top (Targa) spider, prices starting at £5,927.

From mid-year, a new 1.3-litre version of the Beta Coupe, with 82bhp and priced at £3,643, was added to the company's front-wheel-drive range.

Matra: *(See under Simca, below.)*

Mazda: The first-generation 323 model, a front-engine/rear-drive car sold only as a hatchback, appeared in mid-1977, with a choice of 1.0 or 1.3-litre pushrod engines and a solid rear axle. In effect this was the last of the conventional Mazdas, for a transverse-engined/front-wheel-drive 323 would follow in only three years' time.

Mercedes-Benz: The company's first estate car, based on the W123 series, was unveiled in the spring, with world-wide deliveries due to begin before the end of the year, right-hand-drive cars being scheduled for launch in 1978.

Two-door coupe versions of the same W123 range were also announced in 1977, these being previewed at the Geneva motor show in March.

Expansion of the SL/SLC sporting cars continued with the launch of a limited-production 450SLC 5.0 model: this had a 240bhp/5-litre version of the V8 engine, which had an aluminium instead of cast-iron cylinder block, while the bodywork was lightened by the use of aluminium door and bonnet panels.

Opel: More than five years after the last major change, Opel introduced a new-generation range of Rekords, these being conventional front-engine/rear-drive cars, slightly larger and better equipped than the old types.

Home-market Rekords were available with a choice of five different petrol and diesel engines (and there would be more in the next few years), but in the beginning (from early 1978), UK buyers were offered only the 1.9-litre petrol or 2.05-litre diesel engines.

Shortly, the Commodore was also replaced, and as expected the new car was a 2.5-litre six-cylinder version of the Rekord.

Only weeks later, Opel then previewed a new range of large cars to replace the Diplomats, which had never been sold in the UK. These were large, square-styled, but handsome six-cylinder cars to be called Senator (saloon) and Monza (two-door four-seater fastback). More details – including those of Vauxhall-badged cars to be called Royales – would follow in 1978 when the cars actually went on sale.

Panther: The Motorfair exhibition in October revealed the Panther Six, a remarkably ugly, but technically interesting *six*-wheeler convertible with twinned front wheels. Power was by a mid-mounted turbocharged 8.2-litre Cadillac V8 engine. Panther claimed 600bhp, but no-one believed them as the car was not complete, and it was suspected that the engine had never even been introduced to a test-bed. Only this one car was ever produced.

Peugeot: The new 305 range was introduced just before the end of the year as an eventual replacement for the long-running 204 range and using quite a number of 204 features.

As usual for this size of Peugeot, there were transverse-mounted engines, front-wheel drive and all-independent suspension. The original model was offered with 1,290cc (204-type) or 1,472cc (enlarged 204-type) overhead-camshaft petrol engines, a 1.55-litre diesel eventually being added to the range. Although there was little cause for excitement about the style or performance of the 305, it would remain in production for 11 years and sell in very large numbers indeed.

The 504, which had been on sale in the UK for eight years, continued to be changed and improved. From March there was the option of a 70bhp/2.3-litre diesel engine, which was an enlarged version of the early 2.1-litre design.

Porsche: The 928, which was previewed in March, was an all-new front-engined car which had been intended to take over from the rear-engined 911 in due course, although this would never happen.

In design terms – it was conceived even before the smaller 924 (which reached the market ahead of it) – the 928 was the company's first front-engined car, its first with a watercooled engine, and its first to have V8 power. Bulbous, smoothly detailed and technically advanced, the 928 started life with a 240bhp/4.5-litre engine, a choice of manual or fully-automatic (Mercedes-Benz) transmission, and technically fascinating rear suspension details.

The 928 sold steadily rather than sensationally, and although it would be developed and improved and remain in production for two decades, by the end of the 1980s it had become an almost-forgotten model.

Later in the year, the 911 range, which had reached its 14th birthday, was updated, its base engine being enlarged from 2.7 to 3 litres and the Turbo from 260bhp/3 litres to 300bhp/3.3 litres.

The first UK deliveries of 924s took place in the spring, more than a year after the car had been launched in Germany.

Renault: A third version of the front-wheel-drive 20/30 models, the 20TS, went on sale during the year, fitted with a brand-new 2-litre four-cylinder single-overhead-camshaft engine, this being the third of the famous co-operative engine designs developed between Renault and Peugeot in the 1970s.

The engine, originally rated at 110bhp/1,995cc in the 20TS, would find use in a variety of Renault and Peugeot models, latterly at 2,165cc, in the 1980s.

Rolls-Royce: Early in the year, the 11-year-old Silver Shadow range was given a mechanical freshen-up, featuring rack-and-pinion steering, revised front suspension details and with automatic air conditioning as standard equipment.

The longer-wheelbase version of this car was renamed Silver Wraith II and was thereafter marketed as a separate model. All the mechanical changes were simultaneously applied to Corniche, Camargue and all equivalent Bentley models.

Rover: Later than hoped, the six-cylinder 2300/2600 models were added to the original 3500 model, with power outputs of 123bhp and 136bhp. The engine was an all-new overhead-cam 'six' which had been designed by

Triumph, originally for use in a Triumph 2000 replacement which was cancelled, and it was backed by four-speed and five-speed derivatives of the latest 3500 gearbox.

Simca: In co-operation with Matra (which already built Bagheeras using Simca running gear), the new Rancho estate car was introduced in March. Sometimes unkindly called a poseur's Range Rover, the Rancho was based on the platform, front end and front-wheel-drive running gear of the Simca 1100, the engine being the 1,442cc size already employed in the Chrysler Alpine. Its high-roof three-door style in glassfibre was somewhat like that of the Range Rover, but much smaller.

Although the Rancho looked as if it should have been an off-roader, it was nothing of the sort, as it only had front-wheel drive, and no four-wheel-drive version was ever developed.

Years after it had been launched, the three-abreast mid-engined Bagheera coupe was finally made available in the UK in limited numbers.

Skoda: The new-shape rear-engined Estelle (previewed in 1976) went on sale in Britain in May. At the time Skoda let it be known that a front-engined/front-drive version of this model was already under development and would appear before the end of the 1970s. But either this was a blatant lie, or the project was abandoned, for no such front-engined derivative was ever put on sale.

The handling and build quality of the original cars was very poor, so much so that Britain's *Motor* magazine wrote a critique headed: 'Why we wouldn't buy a Skoda Estelle', stating that the handling was: '...in our opinion, so poor that, under certain conditions, it can become dangerous...'

With the arrival of the Estelle in the UK, all old models except the rakish S110R coupe were dropped.

Subaru: At the end of the year, the first British imports were made of this Japanese marque, its engine a front-mounted 1.6-litre flat-four, normally with front-wheel drive, but with optional switchable four-wheel drive under the estate car version of this ageing Leone model.

Toyota: For the first time since 1970, Toyota made major changes to the Carina/Celica models. For the Celica, Toyota produced a newly styled machine, complete with coupe or Lift-back (hatchback) coupe styles. The new-generation Carina shared the new floorpan, but was a thoroughly conventional car. British imports of these two new cars began in 1978.

Imports of the rugged but distinctly agricultural Land Cruiser ended during the year, though this massive 4x4 carried on in production for some time.

Vauxhall: After a year off the market, the Victor/VX-based VX4/90 was reintroduced, this time with a 116bhp version of the 2.3-litre overhead-cam engine and a five-speed Getrag gearbox as standard.

Starting early in the year, the Cavalier became available as an economy special with the 58bhp/1.25-litre Viva engine instead of its usual 1.6 or 1.9-litre types. This was the slowest petrol-powered Cavalier ever put on sale, and it sold in only limited numbers.

The Chevette 2300HS saga continued throughout the year, with controversially homologated works rally cars notching up outright victories, prototypes being demonstrated to dealers and the public, but without any deliveries – yet – to customers. This story would come to a climax in 1978...

Volkswagen: As an additional model to the front-wheel-drive Polo hatchback, VW revealed the Derby two-door saloon version – structurally and functionally the same, but with a conventional booted version of the body.

This was the first of many such conversions/additions which followed over the next few years in response to customers who wanted a separate boot compartment rather than a hatchback.

In the meantime, the Golf range was reshuffled, this time with the introduction of a new 70bhp/1,460cc engine to replace the 1,588cc unit on LS and GLS models.

Industrial developments

During the year British Leyland's industrial state went from bad to worse as

relations between management and unions reached an all-time low. Even though the Austin and Morris franchises were merged at the end of the year, sales sagged alarmingly, and it was clear that the strategy and all the high hopes expressed in the Ryder Report of early 1975 had already been reduced to tatters.

In October, British Leyland's chairman, Sir Richard Dobson, felt obliged to resign following a so-called racist speech he made at a private dinner. His successor was Sir Michael Edwardes, the first really determined chairman the state-owned giant had had in three years. Edwardes soon made it clear that he intended to be an executive rather than a purely titular chairman, which meant that Alex Park was immediately obliged to step down to become executive vice-chairman – though he would shortly leave the company. In January 1978, too, Derek Whittaker, who had been managing director of Leyland Cars, also resigned. Even so, it would be some years before Sir Michael made any sense of what was a thoroughly shambolic corporation.

Two years after assembly started in Europe, Vauxhall began producing Cavaliers in Britain at the Luton factory (which hitherto had concentrated on Victor/VX and Viva types).

Reliant changed hands, with J F Nash Securities emerging as the new owners, in spite of a higher bid from a consortium which included Donald Healey and ex-British Leyland managing director John Barber.

In Sweden there was an amazing, but short-lived, proposal for the country's two largest car-makers – Volvo and Saab – to merge, but this was swiftly forgotten. Proposed in May, it was annulled in September.

George Turnbull was on the move again. Having spent three years originating the Hyundai car programme, he moved on to Iran, where (at Iran National) he was to advise the local enterprise of how to start building its own cars instead of importing kits of Chrysler (Hillman) Hunters from the British Isles.

Production of Wankel-engined NSU Ro80 models, which had only been ticking over since the early 1970s, finally came to an end, after nearly 10 years and 37,204 cars.

1978

Suggesting that perhaps the worst was now over, British inflation followed its gradual downward path, dipping below 10 per cent in February for the first time in more than five years.

Even though the country was increasingly riddled by strikes, some of them by powerful groups of public-sector workers, car sales increased considerably, hitting more than 1.6 million – a level of sales which had not been seen since the pre-Energy Crisis period of 1973. Capitalizing on British Leyland's strike-struck business, Ford became market leader with a 25.7 per cent market share.

Imports rocketed to no fewer than 800,772 cars – eight times their level a decade earlier and twice as high as in 1975. Although this market share was still just below the politically sensitive 50 per cent, there were worrying signs that the majority of private (as opposed to business) buyers were now buying imports instead of the British cars, which had such a dodgy reputation for quality problems and obsolete technology.

With Japanese car sales reaching new heights in the UK – they took up to 13 per cent of the market at times – an increasing crescendo of voices were demanding quota limits, or even a ban on imports from that continent. By mid-year it was estimated that there were more than 800,000 Japanese cars on British roads.

During the year the British Government issued 'guidance' to Japanese importers, stressing that it thought the levels were already high enough, and that Japan should loosen its restrictions on sale of British goods into that country. Before long a 'gentleman's agreement', signalling voluntary restraint – both being as near to formal agreements as was likely to be achieved – came into existence, which effectively limited the market share of Japanese imports to about 11 per cent, where it has been ever since.

This was the year in which the publication of official Government fuel efficiency figures first had to be displayed in showrooms for all new cars sold in the UK. Three figures – one simulating a cycle of urban driving, another a constant-speed test at 56mph/90kph and the third a constant 75mph/120kph – had to be shown, industry protests that these were effectively meaningless being ignored.

Although the official figures have been published ever since, they have habitually been ignored by virtually everyone. As far as the industry was concerned, carrying out and publishing these tests was always a colossal waste of money.

New models

AC: After an embarrassingly long five-year development period, the Ford mid-engined 3000ME model was finally ready for sale and the first deliveries were made at the end of the year. Unhappily, time had not been kind to this car, which was now seen as crude and expensive. Sales were always very slow indeed.

Alfa Romeo: The latest development in the front-wheel-drive Alfasud range was the Super 1300, which arrived in February. This had a larger and much-needed 68bhp/1,286cc engine and a revised facia style, and initially it sold for £2,999.

Later in the year, 1.5-litre versions of the boxer-engined Alfasud went on sale in the UK, and at the same time an intermediate 1,351cc version also became available. From this point, the Alfasud range, and the 33 types which would eventually replace it, became extremely complex and at times difficult to unravel.

Late in the year the Alfetta was up-gunned once again in the UK with the launch of a 130bhp 2000L type, with minor front-end style changes, and to follow this up, the first UK sales of the mechanically similar Giulietta were made just before the end of the year.

Aston Martin: The first new-generation four-door Lagonda saloon models were delivered, nearly two years after the prototype had been shown at the motor show. Among the many detail changes made during that period, the high-tech facia/instrument display had been simplified a little, but it was still dauntingly complex by most standards.

Prices were extremely high, starting in April 1978 at £32,620 – a massive 63 per cent more costly than the shorter two-door Aston Martin V8 coupe.

From the middle of the year, a new version of the V8, the Volante convertible, was introduced, though sales were restricted to the USA until 1979. Mechanically the same as the V8 coupe, it was Aston Martin's first open-top car since 1970, when the last of the old-type DB6 Volantes had been dropped. Soft-top operation was almost entirely automatic.

Audi: After six years, the German company was ready to launch the second-generation 80 range. Like the original type, this was a conventional front-wheel-drive car, with in-line engines ahead of the line of the front wheels.

As before, there were many structural similarities with the VW Passat – platforms and running gear were all shared – though the six-light style was uniquely detailed. The new 80 was slighter larger and heavier than the original, with a bigger cabin, and was only available in four-door saloon form.

BMW: Still developing its 6-series coupe range, BMW launched the 635CSi model in July with a 218bhp/3,453cc version of the already-famous six-cylinder engine, matched to a five-speed Getrag gearbox. This was a very fast (nearly 140mph), if rather bulky machine, but even more powerful versions would follow in the next few years.

In May, the 143bhp/2.3-litre six-cylinder 323i went on sale in the UK, this being the fastest 3-series model so far.

The mid-engined M1 project staggered from crisis to crisis. Originally BMW had planned to have the homologation run of this car produced by Lamborghini in Italy, but after that company hit financial trouble, development and production-tooling problems intensified. Eventually BMW was obliged to take the project away from Lamborghini, and production cars would subsequently be built (starting in 1979) by Baur (specialist coachbuilders) in West Germany. The definitive road car was shown in the autumn of the year, with a 24-valve twin-overhead-cam version of the famous straight-six engine.

Chrysler-UK: The 1600TI model was launched in October, this car having a 100bhp version of the conventional 1.6-litre pushrod engine. With twin dual-choke Weber carburettors, this was a close descendant of the engine used in the Avenger Tiger. Sales did not begin until the spring of 1979.

The company also announced that a twin cam-engined Sunbeam-Lotus model would be introduced in 1979.

Chrysler-Europe: The front-wheel-drive Horizon, previewed at the end of 1977, went on sale in the UK in the autumn.

Citroen: The most important new model of the year was the Visa hatchback, which was revealed in September. Intended to fill the considerable market gap between the ancient 2CV/Dyane and the GS range, the Visa was yet another idiosyncratic front-wheel-drive French car, though under the skin there were strong links with the Peugeot 104.

This five-door hatchback rode on a slightly-modified 104 chassis/platform, which featured MacPherson-strut suspension at front and rear. Although that platform was originally designed around a transversely-mounted water-cooled engine (a 954cc version was used in the Visa), the Visa version was also modified to accept a newly-developed aircooled overhead-valve flat-twin, whose general layout was like that of the existing 2CV/Dyane, though it had been stretched to 36bhp/654cc.

The Visa range would remain in production until 1989 – 11 years, during which time several larger and more powerful (Peugeot) engines would become available, along with a new corporate 1.8-litre diesel power unit, though in all that time the style was left virtually unchanged.

Although this move was more important in its native France than in the UK, Citroen was very enthusiastic about the launch in May of a larger, 2.5-litre, diesel engine for the front-wheel-drive CX model, in place of the original underpowered 2.2-litre diesel.

During the year the old Ami 8, which was a lineal descendant of the 2CV, but with different engine and body style, was dropped from the UK market.

Colt: A new type of 2-litre coupe, badged Sapporo, went on UK sale, this having the latest 'balancer' engine and being based on the underpan and running gear of the latest Sigma model.

Better known everywhere else as a Mitsubishi, the Colt Mirage went on sale in Japan, and would begin its British

career in 1979. This was Mitsubishi's first transverse-engine front-wheel-drive car, the transmission including the interesting feature of a two-ratio final-drive.

Daihatsu: The Japanese marque made an extremely tentative comeback into the British market when the new importers (TKM) introduced at short notice the high ground-clearance, F20LK 4x4 model. Smaller, lighter, slower and not nearly as rugged as the Land-Rovers with which it had to compete, the F20LK soon sank without trace.

Datsun: For the enthusiasts, the most important new Datsun of the year was the 280Z/280Z 2+2 range of sporty coupes, which went on sale in Japan and the USA and, as production of the old-type 260Z had ended, was obviously destined for the UK; sales began, in fact, in March 1979.

Compared with the 260Z, the 280Z had a 2.8-litre engine, was larger, wider, with a bigger cabin, and rather heavier. For all those reasons, it was ideally suited to the North American, but not to the British market.

A new-generation Cherry (called Pulsar in Japan) was launched into its home market but, as was normal for Japanese makes at this time, British sales would not begin for a further year.

Meantime, a new-generation Sunny range – the fourth of this genre – went on sale in the UK in August, this B310 type using the platform and running gear of the old B210 models, but with angular and slightly more spacious cabins. Still an utterly conventional front-engine/rear-drive car, the B310 was sold in the UK with a 1.2 or 1.4-litre engine. Nearly 1.8 million such cars would be produced in Japan in a four-year run.

Fiat: Having reeled in its investment programme in the aftermath of the Energy Crisis of 1973/74, the Italian giant soon regained its confidence and 1978 saw the start of a flood of new models and products.

The new Strada front-wheel-drive hatchback (which, incidentally, was called Ritmo almost everywhere else in the world) was previewed in April, but did not go on sale in the UK until March 1979.

The Strada was a modernized

restatement of Fiat's design approach to small/medium-sized hatchbacks, with a choice of transverse engines and front-wheel drive. Early cars came with a choice of 1.1, 1.3 and 1.5-litre versions of the overhead-cam 'four' as already found in 128 models, and a five-speed transmission had also been developed. Some features, like the transverse leaf spring used in the independent rear suspension, were also part of Fiat's small-car folklore!

For 1979, too, there was the 127 Sport, which combined a 70bhp version of the Brazilian-built 1.05-litre engine with a firmed-up version of the 127 hatchback's chassis

At the same point, Fiat also introduced the 131 Mirafiori Sport, which combined the 131's two-door saloon shell with a 115bhp version of the well-known Fiat 2-litre twin-cam engine and a five-speed transmission.

The medium-sized 131 Mirafiori had already been updated in the spring, and at the same time a new model, with a 96bhp version of the 1.6-litre twin-cam engine, had been introduced at that time.

The pretty little mid-engined X1/9 was also updated for 1979 with the adoption of the latest 85bhp/1.5-litre engine, and the new five-speed transmission which had been developed specifically for the new Strada.

Ford: The Capri III took over from the Capri II in March, this being no more than a facelift of the hatchback style which had already been on sale for four years.

Visually the major change was the adoption of four circular headlamps, rather than the two oblong lamps of the Capri II, and there were now five different engines ranging from a 57bhp/1.3-litre four-cylinder to a 138bhp/3-litre V6 unit. The old GT badge had been dropped, with all sporting versions now becoming known as S types.

The Escort was given a mid-range facelift for 1979, with no mechanical innovations. At the same time the slow-selling RS Mexico was dropped, and the RS2000 rejigged to be available in standard and Custom varieties.

Ford-USA: In the USA, the third-generation Mustang was introduced, this having rather angular styling with a choice of coupe or hatchback cabins. As this was much more of a European-sized car than many other American models (just as the Mustang II had been), a number would eventually be sold in the UK on a personal import basis.

FSO: The Polish company which had been assembling Fiats for some years now introduced a new five-door hatchback model called Polonez. In the course of the next few years there was considerable confusion about this car's intended name – was Polonez a model name or a marque name, and should the word Fiat appear anywhere in the title?

Technically, however, there was no confusion, for this car used the same underpan/platform, suspension and all Fiat running gear as the old-type 125P (itself a version of the even older Fiat 125), but it was covered by a rather high and narrow five-door hatchback body style. There was a choice of 1.3 and 1.5-litre engines, both being of the 1960s Fiat 1300/1500 type, and UK prices were at bargain-basement level.

Honda: The Japanese maker continued its gradual and determined move upmarket. With the Accord now on sale, it showed a new coupe model based on a shortened version of the same platform and front-wheel-drive chassis and known as the Prelude. The style was somewhat awkward and craggy, while the cabin only provided 2+2 seating. The new Prelude would not, in fact, go on sale in the UK until May 1979.

Jaguar: Very discreetly, a five-speed manual gearbox was made available for the 4.2-litre XJ6 model. The lack of fuss was not because this was a doubtful move, but because the box had been bought-in from another British Leyland company – Rover – for this was the same gearbox as used in the Rover 3500 and the Triumph TR7 sportscar.

As far as Jaguar diehards were concerned, this was the thin end of a very undesirable wedge. Neutral observers, on the other hand, saw it as sensible rationalization of British Leyland's tightly-stretched resources. However, there is confusion here, for very few indeed of these boxes seem to have been fitted before the model became Series III in 1979.

Lada: A new small 4x4 estate car, the Niva, was announced in Russia, this being a stubby, high ground-clearance, Land-Rover type machine with a rugged chassis. Powered by the latest 1.6-litre engine which was shared with the Lada saloons, its transfer box was some inches further to the rear of the main gearbox, with near-equal length front and rear propeller shafts linking the front and rear axles. British deliveries, at the bargain price of £4,098, began before the end of the year.

Meantime, from late summer, the existing saloon car range was changed yet again, this time with the addition of a 1.6-litre version of the existing model. This had a four-headlamp nose like that of the obsolete Fiat 125, though of course the main bodyshell was still a modified version of the (also obsolete) Fiat 124 saloon/estate car range. For 1979, therefore, Lada saloons were available in 1200, 1300, 1500 and 1600 types.

Lancia: Assembly of mid-engined Monte Carlo models (which were called Scorpion when sold in the USA) was suspended in 1978 and would not resume until 1980. Certain chassis problems (including a tendency for front brakes to lock on wet or slippery roads) had to be sorted, while the lacklustre performance of the USA-market cars, which only had a 1.8-litre engine, also had to be addressed. Lancia was unlucky with this model, for although it was always an attractive-looking machine, it was never as fast or as capable as it promised.

Normally the announcement of yet another car with automatic transmission would pass without comment, but in the case of Lancia's Beta, unveiled late in the year, it was news because it used a new type of British AP three-speed installation, with some parts built at a new factory in Italy and some in the UK.

Lotus: The Esprit SII arrived in August, visually facelifted with new engine bay scoops behind the doors, and with new-style Lotus alloy wheels, but with few mechanical changes.

Mazda: Only a year after NSU had written off its investment in Wankel rotary engines, Mazda confirmed that it still believed in rotary units by launching the smart new RX-7 sport coupe. This front-engined/rear-drive car was aimed squarely at the North American market at first, where it was fighting for the interest of customers who might otherwise buy Datsun 260Z/280Z types or Porsche 924s.

Although Mazda's UK importers dithered over the new model's prospects, British-market deliveries began before the end of the year when the original RX-7 had an engine nominally equivalent to 2.3 litres and producing 100bhp at first, though clearly there was much more development potential to come. Backed by a five-speed transmission, with an optional automatic (not available in the UK), this was a very promising car, but in the UK it always had to fight two demons – its high price, and the still-doubtful hearsay reputation of Wankel rotary engines.

The new-generation 626 Capella was shown late in the year, but for some bizarre reason the British importers decided to call it a Montrose! Why not a Mansfield, Manchester, Middlesborough or Macclesfield model? Perhaps the controversial choice of name was wise, for at least it made a talking point, as there was no technical innovation in a car which had a front-engine/rear-drive layout with a beam rear axle.

Mercedes-Benz: Anti-lock braking (ABS) became optional on the largest models from the end of the year, this being the culmination of a 15-year test and development programme carried out with Robert Bosch (see under Technical developments).

Midas: The first of Harold Dermott's GRP monocoque coupes was previewed, this car using the entire front and rear suspension/subframe layouts of the Mini, with Mini-Cooper engine and gearbox. In the next decade, Midas cars would progress through various derivatives until the business was fatally crippled by a disastrous factory fire.

Morris: As with the Princess marque for 1979 (see below), the Marina was redeveloped to accept the new BL O-series overhead-camshaft engine. For 1979 there was an 11-car Marina range, which used a choice of existing 1.3-litre A-series or the new 78bhp 1.7-litre single-carburettor O-series engine.

Opel: The new large-car range – Senator saloons and Monza coupes – officially went on sale in May (having been previewed at the end of 1977). Both cars were originally fitted with 2.8-litre six-cylinder engines, while the smart Monza was also available with a 3-litre injected version of Opel's big 'six'. Chassis details included independent rear suspension by semi-trailing arms and coil springs, along with four-wheel disc brakes.

Later in the year, GM badge engineering struck again, with Vauxhall Royale versions of these cars being introduced. (See under Vauxhall for more details.)

At the same time, a Commodore model was reintroduced, this being a 2.5-litre six-cylinder-engined version of the new-generation Rekord, of which British sales had only recently begun. In fact UK deliveries of this car would not begin until the end of 1980.

During the year, the well-known cam-in-head four-cylinder engine was enlarged from 1,897 to 1,979cc on selected models, including the Rekord, while the latest 2.3-litre diesel engine also became an option on the Rekord.

Later in the year a new version of the Manta, actually a coupe hatchback, also went on sale, this body soon becoming available on the Vauxhall Cavalier model.

Polonez: (See FSO for all details.)

Porsche: The latest addition to the 924 range was the 170bhp 924 Turbo, whose turbocharged 2-litre engine gave the front-engined 2+2 model a 140mph top speed.

Princess: In July the big front-wheel-drive 'Wedgie' was updated with the fitment of two new versions – 1.7 and 2-litre – of the newly-developed overhead-cam O-series four-cylinder engine, which had itself evolved from the ancient B-series. More powerful and supposedly with a much cleaner exhaust emissions performance, the O-series engine was soon to be seen in the Morris Marina, but plans to fit it to the ancient MGB (where its improved emissions performance would have been important in North America) were abandoned.

Range Rover: An overdrive became optional equipment on Range Rovers,

something which would do more to improve the heavy fuel consumption than the performance.

Renault: The 18 model, previewed in March and officially launched in April, was a major development, being an eventual replacement for the old Renault 12 saloon. Like all other medium-sized Renaults of this period, the 18 had front-wheel drive from four-cylinder engines, longitudinally-mounted, and ahead of the line of the front wheels. The style was neat but anonymous, the four-door saloon shape hiding 1.4 and 1.65-litre engines with a choice of manual or automatic transmission.

The 18, in fact, was typical of so many European cars which would be launched in the years ahead – not so much a single model as an entire model range.

The 5 Automatic, put on sale in the UK in the autumn, was a specially-developed model combining the three-door shell, Renault's latest automatic transmission and a 55bhp version of the long-stroke 1,289cc engine (which was already being used in less-powerful guise in the 5GTL type).

For British enthusiasts, the automatic option might have been boring, but the launch of the 5 Gordini on the British market was anything but that. Sold in France as the 5 Alpine since 1976, the Gordini had a 93bhp/1.4-litre engine and a five-speed transmission, which gave it a 110mph top speed, all delivered with a great deal of panache.

British sales began in the spring of 1979. Perhaps this was not as rounded or as capable a car as the VW Golf GTi, but it had a great deal of puppy-like character: Renault UK would later promote a one-make racing series for this model.

At the Paris motor show, Renault also previewed an excitingly-specified mid-engined 5 Turbo in which the 1.4-litre unit was positioned longitudinally where the rear seats would normally live, was turbocharged, and was rated at 160bhp. This was to be Renault's principal rallying 'homologation special' for the next few seasons, and it proved to be a very effective car.

At the same motor show there was also the fuel-injected 30TX and a more powerful TS version of the 14, with 69bhp instead of 59bhp.

Saab: The 99 Turbo finally went on sale in the UK, when the three-door model was priced at £7,850 and all the original supplies were painted black. But within weeks it was rendered obsolescent by the arrival of the new 900.

The 900 range was previewed in May and would go on sale in the UK in the spring of 1979, this effectively being no more than a long-nose version of the existing front-engine, front-wheel-drive, 99 family. At the time, and for many years afterwards, no-one could understand why Saab had done this – except as a facelift of the 99 – the difference being that the 'old' 99 would remain on sale for a number of years.

Technically and structurally, the 900 was like the 99, with a range of normally-aspirated and turbocharged 2-litre four-cylinder engines.

Skoda: Stung by the many criticisms published about the rear-engined Estelle, Skoda made a whole series of changes in April 1978. Modifications, subsequently tested by independents and found to be quite effective, included fitting different springs and anti-rollbars and changing damper settings, along with smaller wheels with wider rims.

Toyota: Imports of new-generation Carina and Celica models began early in the year. Carinas were available with a 1.6-litre engine, while for the sporty Celicas there was a choice of 1.6 and 2-litre types, the most powerful being a 118bhp twin-OHC version.

Because the new Starlet model was a conventional front-engine/rear-drive machine, there was undisguised relief from almost every one of Toyota's main rivals, who had feared that the Japanese giant would reveal a technically advanced front-drive car. For that reason the new Starlet made virtually no impact on the British market.

Triumph: From April 1, a new car called the TR7 V8 was homologated for international rallying. This, in effect, was a Rover V8-engined version of the TR7, a precursor of the TR8, but it began rallying nearly two years before the more sophisticated TR8 actually went on sale, solely in the USA.

TVR: A convertible style was introduced on the existing M-type/Taimar chassis, and instantly became a best-seller. Although convertibles would once again disappear from the TVR line-up in 1980, they soon returned, and by the 1990s almost every TVR being built was an open car.

Vauxhall: In October, two entirely 'new' ranges of Vauxhall were announced – both, in fact, being rebadged Opels, which were being built in Europe in Opel factories.

The car called a Vauxhall Carlton, therefore, was no more than an Opel Rekord with a modified Vauxhall-style nose, and fitted with the 2-litre version of the Opel cam-in-head engine.

The cars called Royale – saloon and coupe – were only lightly modified versions of the new Opel Senator/Monza types. Purely for product-planning reasons, the Vauxhall cars were only equipped with 2.8-litre engines at first – the 3-litre engines already available in the Opels were held back for another two years.

From April, the Cavalier was upgraded, the engine increased in size to 1,979cc, with power increasing to 100bhp. The latest (Opel) engine was also being fitted to current Opel models.

In the autumn, a new version of the Cavalier, the coupe hatchback, was added to the range: this was structurally identical to the latest Manta hatchback.

Some 18 months after it had been introduced – and homologated on the strength of one completed car – the Chevette HS finally went on sale, and there was an immediate storm in the world of rallying.

Although the HS was a fine road car, its own Vauxhall-designed cylinder head and the Getrag five-speed gearbox were not the same as the Lotus (Type 907) cylinder head and ZF gearbox used in works rally cars! The car's sporting homologation was rescinded until the cars' specification had been put right, and it would be a full year before they were once again competitive.

The road cars sold very slowly indeed – at £5,107 they were expensive – so only 400 were ever produced.

Volvo: In a major change of policy, a manual transmission was made available as an option on the 343 model, which was being built in the ex-Daf factory in Holland. Previous 343s and all Dafs had used a belt-drive auto-matic transmission, but this development had virtually been forced upon Volvo by customer demand. UK deliveries began in the autumn.

The old Volvo 66 (ex-Daf 66) was dropped during the year to make space for more 343s to be produced in Holland.

The weirdly-styled 262C coupe was shown off in the UK, with deliveries (in limited quantities) promised for 1979. The 262C was a two-door 'almost-four-seater' car with a style not nearly as successful as Mercedes-Benz, for example, would surely have achieved with the same car.

Industrial developments

Having made it clear to his workforce that he was the boss and would run British Leyland the way that he wanted to, Michael Edwardes started a massive restructuring of the business, first by splitting up the 'Leyland Cars' conglomerate which the Ryder Report had set up less than three years earlier. Austin-Morris was directed to go it alone, while Jaguar-Rover-Triumph came into being, Jaguar continuing to distance itself from as much of the BL Group as it could…

Weeks later, Edwardes announced the imminent closure of the TR7 plant at Speke, Liverpool – which had only a limited effect at the time as the workforce had been on strike for many weeks! There was a five-month hiatus before TR7 assembly began once again – this time at Triumph's older Canley factory, in Coventry.

GM-Europe revealed that it was planning a small front-wheel-drive Supermini, which clearly was a response to Ford's successful new Fiesta. No more details were available at this time except that the new small car would not be built in Britain or West Germany.

Chrysler's European ambitions came to an abrupt end in August as its entire European empire was sold to Peugeot-Citroen (who soon discovered a potentially calamitous commercial and financial situation). Peugeot paid $320 million, and gave Chrysler 1.8 million shares in the PSA business.

Chrysler's worldwide operations had been struggling since the first Energy Crisis, and it was only Government assistance which had persuaded the Americans to continue with their British subsidiary in recent years, whose market share had dipped to little more than 6 per cent. When the Government refused to give any more financial aid, either sale or closedown was inevitable.

Because the Government was owed a lot of aid money by Chrysler-UK, its approval was needed before the takeover could be formalized. This was eventually given in October, after which integration was swift – the Chrysler name, in fact, disappearing from all models (which would be renamed Talbot) in the summer of 1979.

Incidentally, it was altogether typical of the anarchy which existed among Britain's motor industry workforce at this time that a new Rolls-Royce Phantom VI, which had been commissioned by the SMMT as a Silver Jubilee present to The Queen, should have been ready in mid-1977, but was not actually handed over until 1978! A little of the overrun was due to Rolls-Royce's decision to update the specification somewhat, but most of the delay was due to strikes.

John DeLorean announced that he had secured massive Government aid to set up a factory close to Belfast, where his new gullwing sports coupe was to be built. The deal was said to be worth £65 million, and although the choice of engine – the PRV V6 unit – was revealed, very little else was known at this stage.

The new sporting car was supposed to be ready for volume sale before the end of 1980, with factory construction starting even before the end of 1978. Lotus took charge of all redesign and development work, though DeLorean missed their 'on sale' target by several months, sales actually beginning in 1981. But within a year of this, the project would descend into financial chaos and receivership.

Having failed to link up with Saab in 1977, Volvo now proposed a partial link with a national Government – that of Norway! Viewed from two decades later, this looks bizarre, and it made very little sense even in 1978, so was soon abandoned and forgotten.

In the USA, VW began building Golfs (rebadged as Rabbits) at a newly-completed assembly plant at Westmoreland, Pennsylvania, all for sale in North America. This project was very successful at first, but demand eventually fell away, and the plant would be closed down before the end of the 1980s.

From August 1, all production cars being sold in the UK had to pass a number of stringent tests to gain a National Type Approval certificate. Because this involved crashing a car into a concrete block at 30mph, the financial implications immediately made the sale of many low-production cars impractical.

The NEC – a new motor show site

In 1978, Britain's major motor show, the one sanctioned by the SMMT, was held for the first time at the new National Exhibition Centre on the outskirts of Birmingham.

Despite the inevitable pre-event moaning from those who wanted to combine business with London-based junketing, the move proved to be an enormous success. Compared with the problems of getting to London's Earls Court, and the impossibility of parking

close by, the NEC's facilities were ideal, for the site was close to the M6 and M42 motorways, built alongside a new railway station on the electrified London to Birmingham Intercity line, and had car parking facilities which were the envy of every other such facility in Europe.

More than 120,000 squeezed in on the busiest day and almost a million attended in all – both these being outright records for a British motor show. Earls Court had never attracted more than 660,000 – so those who had criticized the choice of Birmingham were silenced.

Ford, incidentally, had a stand completely devoid of cars as it was in the middle of an eight-week strike!

Technical developments

During the summer, Mercedes-Benz and Robert Bosch announced that a new anti-lock braking system had been developed and would be phased-in as an extra on production cars (and standard on the 450SEL 6.9) before the end of the year.

This system relied on the use of capable computers and electronic sensors which measured the rotation of each wheel: when the wheel suddenly slowed, tending to lock, the hydraulic pressure to that wheel could be released, then re-applied as soon as the skidding tendency had ended. Later in the year BMW also introduced Bosch ABS braking on the company's flagship 7-series models.

Nowadays Bosch treat this early installation as very old-fashioned, for ABS technology has marched inexorably forward in more recent years, but it was already an important development, far ahead of the crude system employed on Jensen cars in the late 1960s.

Men of Influence

Sir Michael Edwardes

It is not too much to suggest that Michael Edwardes – Sir Michael, as he soon became after taking up the challenge of running British Leyland – saved the rambling state-controlled business from liquidation.

Born and raised in South Africa, the diminutive Michael Edwardes originally studied law, then got involved in his father's electrical battery business. From there he joined the Chloride concern in Africa, moving to Britain (eventually to become Chloride's chairman) in the mid-1960s.

After joining the new state-controlled National Enterprise Board in 1975, while retaining the chair of Chloride, he rapidly became sucked into the economics, strategies and especially the politics of British Leyland. Immediately after Sir Richard Dobson was obliged to resign from the corporation, Michael Edwardes was offered the job of chairman and chief executive.

Accepting a three-year contract (which was later extended to five years), starting on November 1, 1977, he insisted on a free hand to run the business, not as a political toy but as – a business!

Under Sir Michael, British Leyland became BL, was

rationalized, downsized, split up into profit (or – mostly – loss) centres and made to look at least credible again. Decisions of which everyone approved were letting Jaguar loose to operate separately, approving the development of the Mini Metro, the expansion of Land Rover, the sacking of Longbridge's disruptive union convenor Derek Robinson, and the preparation of a viable Recovery Plan.

Less popular were the link-up with Honda and the closure of many factories – including the MG plant at Abingdon, the Triumph facility at Speke (LIverpool), Vanden Plas in North London and the Rover SD1/Triumph TR7 assembly plant at Solihull.

In many ways Sir Michael was a bristly little man who seemed to enjoy conflict and operating in a crisis, but he never seemed to compromise his beliefs for BL's survival. Five years on, when he returned to Chloride (and eventually to yet more industrial challenges), BL was in a much better shape than it had ever been, and much of the progress made until the mid-1980s was due to the policies he and his team had laid down.

1979

Following the deposition of the Shah of Iran in January, a second Energy Crisis erupted throughout the world and the price of crude oil doubled during the year – roughly from $12 to $26 a barrel. As a result, petrol prices continued to rise, and the much-forecast, much-feared £1 gallon finally made it to mainstream pumps in the UK in the spring.

There were some shortages in Europe, though none as severe as those locally found in the United States, and there was never any likelihood of rationing being imposed. On the other hand, by the end of the year a UK gallon cost about £1.20.

There was a shift in Britain's political climate in May when a Conservative administration was returned in the General Election after six years of Labour control. For the time being, though, there was no let-up in inflationary pressures. By the end of the year, prices were still rising at 17 per cent, though the rate of increase would rapidly decline over the next few years.

One result of the change of Government was a different taxation policy, direct taxation being reduced (income tax dropped from 33p to 30p in the pound in June), but VAT increased to compensate – from 8 per cent on cars, parts and labour, and 12.5 per cent on petrol, to 15 per cent all round. The duty on petrol was also raised by 7p.

This meant that all car prices rose sharply – a Mini 1000 by £155, a Vauxhall Carlton by £332, for instance – but the British consumer was so used to car prices being raised every 90 days or so by this time that this almost passed unnoticed!

It was a confusing year for car sales in Britain – sometimes they sagged, at other times they seemed buoyant – but by the end of the year two new records had been set: 1.7 million new cars had been registered in the UK during the year (breaking the previous record set in 1972) of which no fewer than 1.06 million were imports. This gave imports a market share of no less than 61 per cent – for the struggling British motor industry this was really depressing.

Compared with 1978, 260,000 more imported cars had been sold. Many of these were Fords, Vauxhalls and

Talbots, which had been produced in Europe, but it confirmed yet again that private owners preferred to buy technically advanced cars from Europe, or well-equipped machinery from Japan, rather than the often-humdrum products of British factories. Furthermore, exports were down – at 374,673 they were lower than they had been for the past two decades.

Fords were now Britain's best-selling cars, and would remain so, for British Leyland's market share was still on the decline, and would continue to slide as the 1980s progressed.

From March, new VW-Audi cars sold in the UK were covered by a six-year anti-corrosion bodyshell warranty, hailed at the time as the most extensive and comprehensive to be offered in Britain. It was the start of a trend which simply had to be matched by every volume-production car-maker in Europe, for such warranties were to become normal.

New models

Alfa Romeo: In April the new Six was revealed, perhaps best described as a very ordinary big Alfa Romeo with a magnificent V6 engine. British sales began in the autumn of 1980.

The car had an all-new steel monocoque shell, with four passenger doors and plenty of room, but even though it had de Dion rear suspension, like the smaller Giulietta/Alfetta models, it was a very stodgy machine with little character.

The 2.5-litre engine, however, was always well-liked, and even in the mid-1990s it was still being improved and made more powerful, having proved very successful in many different installations, both front and rear-wheel drive.

Midway through the year, the traditional reshuffle of engine sizes, power outputs and body styles continued on existing models. Alfa dealers could be excused for going cross-eyed with the problem of always having the right cars in stock...

This time around, the Alfasud Sprint coupe received a 95bhp twin-carburettor version of the 1.5-litre engine (suggesting that other Alfasuds would share this engine one day), while the medium-sized Giulietta was given the option of a 122bhp/1,779cc engine in place of the original 1.6-litre option.

Aro: Confusingly known as the Portaro in some quarters, because this was a Romanian 4x4 machine which was being assembled in Portugal, this Land-Rover competitor made a hesitant start in the British market in 1979. To add to the multi-national confusion, the engine was by Daihatsu of Japan.

More commercial vehicle than road machine at first, in exchange for a very low price, the Aro 240 offered a very basic specification, and only ever sold in tiny numbers in the UK, where the so-called 'road' version went on sale in 1982.

Audi: The new 200 arrived in September, for the 1980 model year, this effectively being a 100 model with a more impressive nose featuring rectangular headlamps, and with a choice of 2.2-litre five-cylinder engines, either normally-aspirated/136bhp, or turbocharged/170bhp, and a higher level of trim and equipment.

From January, the German company finally added a lower-powered carburettor version of the 2.1-litre five-cylinder 100 to the British range. Called the 100 L5S or GL5S, this version had a 115bhp engine, compared with the 136bhp rating of the fuel-injected models. Then, to crown a busy year, the company also introduced a 2-litre diesel version of the 100 for the 1980 season.

Austin: Even though the Maxi hatchback had never been wildly successful, it had now been on sale for a decade, but production was only pottering on because BL did not yet have a new model (one day it would be the Maestro) to replace it! The 1.5-litre versions were dropped towards the end of the year, leaving the 1.75-litre models to carry on alone.

Bitter: The small German manufacturer introduced the SC model, which was a smart 2+2 coupe based on the platform and running gear of the latest Opel Senator. Production was tiny, though a handful of these cars would eventually be sold in the UK.

BMW: Although the 6-series (coupe) and 7-series (saloon) ranges were relatively new – the 7-series had only been launched in 1977 – they were revised and rationalized in mid-1979 for sale in the UK from the autumn.

There were virtually no styling changes, but all the six-cylinder engines – 2.8, 3.2 and 3.5-litre versions – were fitted with Bosch fuel injection as standard, rated at 184, 197 and 218bhp respectively. (A turbocharged 745i was also revealed in Germany, though this was never marketed in the UK.) There were four-speed, five-speed and automatic transmissions, while ABS anti-lock braking was now optional on all models.

Chrysler-Europe: From the summer of 1979, all existing models, which had been variously sold as Chryslers, Simcas, or Matra-Simcas, were rebadged as Talbots. This was to emphasize the change of ownership of this business, which had taken place in 1978 when Peugeot bought the Chrysler business.

Before then, the old Hunters and 180/2-litre models were discontinued. *(For all details of 1979 model changes, see under Talbot.)*

Citroen: The front-drive CX range was still developing. From mid-year there were the new Reflex and Athena derivatives, these having the latest Peugeot-Citroen-Renault 2-litre overhead-camshaft four-cylinder engine, as also used in the Renault 20TS and Peugeot 505.

These were replacements for the original CX2000 models, the Reflex having a four-speed and the Athena a five-speed gearbox.

The mid-sized GS family progressed to GSA with a slightly larger (1,299cc) engine, a choice of four-door and five-door bodies and automatic transmission as an option.

Colt: The Mirage went on sale in the UK, complete with its unique two-range axle in conjunction with four forward gears, and a choice of 1.2 or 1.4-litre engines.

In Japan, a new range of four-door Lancer models was revealed, the first major restyle behind this badge since the early 1970s. These cars originally had 1.4 and 1.6-litre engines. British sales of what was still a very conventional car began at the end of the year.

Daihatsu: The front-wheel-drive Charade, launched in Japan in 1977, finally went on sale in the UK in September 1979. It was the first front-wheel-drive Daihatsu to be sold in the UK, and it was fitted with a *three*-cylinder

993cc overhead-camshaft engine.

Daimler: *(See under Jaguar for details of new models.)*

Datsun: The new-generation Skyline 240K, a conventionally-engined 2.4-litre fuel-injected six-cylinder coupe with a 2+2-seater style, went on sale in the UK early in the year.

In Japan, a new-generation 280C appeared, this having the same platform and running gear as before, but with a new and more angular style of body.

UK sales of the new-generation Z-car – the 280ZX – began in March.

Ferrari: The only front-engined four-seater in the range was updated in October to become the 400i. There were no styling changes, but the 4.8-litre engine was tuned to give 310bhp – and there was an automatic transmission option, which caused many Ferrari diehards to complain that the end of the world had come.

Fiat: The Ritmo/Strada cabriolet, to be built by Bertone, was previewed. Although not sensationally new in itself, it confirmed the trend back towards open-top motoring which had been signalled by the VW Golf cabriolet only a few months earlier. Two years earlier the convertible had seemed to be dead. Now there were two new models, and in due course many more would follow them.

Ford-UK: The British company was having a quiet year (the front-wheel-drive Escort Mk III was due on the scene in 1980), so there were only minor changes to most cars, and a reskin for the Cortina.

The latest Cortina, revealed in August, was actually marketed as Cortina 80 for a time, but most Ford fans called it a Cortina Mk V, even though it was never badged in that way.

Mechanically, the range was as before, except that the power of the V6 2.3-litre engine was increased from 108bhp to 116bhp. As before, there was a range of engines starting at 1.3 litres, but still no diesel.

Although many of the Cortina's external panels were new, the front and rear screens being deeper, the side windows larger, with different profiles, and a side-by-side comparison

with the Mk IV of 1976–79 showing up changes in most areas, the platform, running gear, cabin, overall dimensions and proportions were unchanged.

Also in August, the 2.3-litre Granada engine was improved, peak power going up to 114bhp, and there were trim/equipment improvements to match.

Ford-USA: Because the third-generation Mustang, which had been launched in 1978, was such a compact car, the company announced that it planned to deliver up to 500 of them in the UK as personal imports, with prices starting at £7,285. All these cars were processed through Ford's outlet in central London, for there was no dealer chain in Britain.

Honda: The second-generation Civic hatchback finally arrived in Japan, being a larger, smoother, roomier and bigger-engined statement of Honda's original transverse-engine/front-drive theme.

The new Civic was 8in longer than the older car, with different wheelbases for three-door and five-door types, and was fitted with a 1.33-litre version of the overhead-camshaft engine. Those in the know forecast that a conventional four-door saloon version (with a longer tail) would soon follow and that the joint-promotion 'Triumphonda' of 1981 would be based on that car. They were right.

Jaguar: The Series III XJ6/XJ12 models – all of them being long-wheelbase four-door saloons, badged either as Jaguars or Daimler Sovereigns – were introduced in March. Although looking basically as before, they had been treated to a newly reshaped cabin top, courtesy of Pininfarina, were much less 'fussy' at the front end, and were given a new and more logical instrument display.

As before there were 3.4 and 4.2-litre six-cylinder, and 5.3-litre V12-cylinder options. The 4.2-litre engine (which had been using Lucas fuel injection for US-market cars since 1978), now had fuel injection as standard for all markets. For Britain, therefore, the peak power output leapt from 172bhp to 205bhp (DIN), which was actually better than the numerically larger figures claimed for the original XJ6s of 1968, whose power was measured in a less stringent manner.

As previewed in 1978, the latest Rover-manufactured five-speed manual gearbox (without overdrive) was fitted on 3.4 and 4.2-litre cars. Automatic transmission, of course, was optional on all six-cylinder cars, and standard behind the V12 power unit.

Lancia: In September, the long-rumoured front-wheel-drive Delta finally went on sale. Although closely based on the transverse-engine/front-wheel-drive power train of the Fiat Strada, the Delta used an all-new platform, different suspension, and had a smart if rather angular five-door hatchback style by ItalDesign.

Original Deltas were available with Fiat 1.3 or 1.5-litre overhead-camshaft engines, though a good many more options (leading eventually to the turbo-charged 2-litre Delta Integrale) would follow during the 1980s.

The Delta was to have a long and very successful career, with UK sales beginning in mid-1980 and continuing until the 1990s, though the second-generation cars were not imported to the UK.

Early in the year the existing range of coupes and HPEs was revised and improved, though without major styling or engineering changes. Inside there was a revised facia/instrument panel, while under the bonnet there was a tiny increase in engine size (for speed limit reasons in Lancia's native Italy), while the power output of the 2-litre car was actually reduced to 115bhp.

From September the Beta hatchback range was given a new and controversial facia/instrument panel, with a 'Gruyere cheese' layout and instruments lurking in deep recesses. What *could* the designers have been thinking of?

Land-Rover: Starting in the spring, a V8 engine option was gradually filtered into the ever more complex Land-Rover range, this engine being coupled to the Range Rover's massive four-speed transmission.

Mazda: The latest model from this fast-expanding Japanese range was the 2000, announced in the UK in August, and only ever available as a capacious estate car. It would be renamed 929 in 1981, and would remain on the British market until 1987. This conventional front-engine/

rear-drive car had a 90bhp/1,970cc four-cylinder engine and a beam rear axle.

Although the excitingly-specified Wankel-engined RX-7 had been price-listed by the end of 1978, the first British deliveries in any numbers did not take place until the autumn of 1979.

Mercedes-Benz: Star of the Frankfurt motor show was a new-generation S-class, internally and later familiarly known as the W126 family.

Larger, sleeker and even more expensive than the previous S-class (which had been in production for nine years), the W126 was a beautifully-built, high-tech machine, with all-independent suspension and ABS braking – which gradually became available on all models – and would eventually be sold with a choice of normal or long wheel-bases and a huge variety of engines from a 2.8-litre six-cylinder to a 5.6-litre V8. This range would be colossally successful for Mercedes-Benz. Although UK sales did not begin until late 1980, the range would not be replaced until 1991.

The new 4x4 G-Wagen appeared in February, and although it was initially seen as a direct competitor to the Range Rover, it never came close to matching that car's character. Although its cross-country capability was high, the G-Wagen was powered at first by a series of rough and/or underpowered petrol and diesel engines, and it betrayed its military project ancestry in rather angular lines and a lack of interior trim and fittings.

Steyr-Daimler-Puch built them in Austria, but as these were always extremely expensive machines, sales in most countries (especially the UK) were very limited. Amazingly, Mercedes-Benz persevered with this original basic design until the mid-1990s, so at the end of a long career its overall sales were reasonably creditable.

The estate car derivative of the existing W123 saloons finally went on sale in the UK in May. Known colloquially as T-cars, these were equipped and detailed as every Mercedes-Benz buyer would expect and they immediately mounted a challenge for the market sector which big Volvo estates had held captive for so long.

MG: After a very long career, latterly with a Triumph Spitfire 1500 engine

and gearbox, the last MG Midget was built towards the end of the year. All that now remained at Abingdon was the ancient MGB, a car which had been starved of investment for years and would also be killed off in 1980.

Opel: In September, the new-generation Kadett was introduced, not only as GM-Europe's first transverse-engine/front-wheel-drive car, but with a new range of overhead-camshaft engines.

Except for one of its engines – the long-established 1.2-litre overhead-valve Opel unit – the Kadett was a totally new design based on a 98.9in front-drive platform. There was a choice of two and four-door saloons and three and five-door hatchbacks of similar overall styles. Technically this was a 'standard Eurobox' in almost every respect, for there was MacPherson-strut front suspension and a torsion-beam rear end.

The pundits forecast that a new-generation Vauxhall Astra would soon be launched in parallel with the Kadett, but although the new range was previewed late in 1979, it would not go on sale until early 1980.

The Ascona 400, a two-door saloon car fitted with a Cosworth-refined 2.4-litre 16-valve twin-cam engine, was unveiled in February and went on sale later in the year. This was strictly a 400-off 'homologation special' for approval into rallying's popular Group B category.

Later in the year, as a cheaper, halfway house towards Ascona 400 performance, Opel released the two-door 2000 model, in which the 2-litre cam-in-head engine was tuned to give 120bhp instead of 100bhp.

Peugeot: The most important new models of the year were the 505 family – a four-door saloon closely followed by a five-door estate car – destined to take over from the long-running and very successful 504 range. As with the 504, the 505 used a conventional front-engine/rear-drive layout, there was all-independent suspension and a range of engines starting with the 2-litre overhead-valve Peugeot unit, and eventually including corporate overhead-cam, diesel and even V6 power units.

Just before the end of the year the 104 range was rejigged, without style changes, but with a new model line-up. The 954cc and 1,124cc-engined saloons continued as before, but they were joined by a 57bhp/1,219cc version which was nearly identical to the Renault 14/Citroen Visa power unit, and there was also a new and more sporty 104S, which used a 72bhp/1,360cc version of the same engine.

In the three-door/short-wheelbase range, there was a 104ZR model with the 1,124cc engine, joined now by a 72bhp/1,360cc-engined 104ZS. On 104S and 104ZS models, the spare wheel was too large to be stowed when inflated, so was supplied 'flat', along with a 12-volt Porsche-type Englemann compressor to do the blow-up job! For once, it seems, French logic was missing…

It was clearly 'diesel' year for Peugeot, for the 604 flagship model was treated to an 80bhp/2.3-litre version of the well-proven engine, while the modern 305 got a new light-alloy 49bhp/1.55-litre overhead-camshaft diesel 'four'.

Porsche: For its 1980 model year, Porsche added to its big-car range by upgrading the original 928 to 928S and introduced a much more powerful 924, the 924 Turbo.

The 928S had a larger, 300bhp/4,664cc version of the V8 engine, and UK deliveries of right-hand-drive versions were promised for early 1980.

The 924 Turbo was a thoroughly redeveloped high-performance model with a 170bhp turbocharged version of the 2-litre engine: all 924s were given a totally new, Porsche-designed, five-speed transmission instead of the Audi-based design they had used for the first four years.

Finally, Sportomatic semi-automatic transmission was discontinued from the 911 range.

Renault: In a relatively quiet year for France's largest car-maker, a five-door version of the popular Renault 5 was introduced. Although this was mechanically the same as the original two-door, which was seven years old, it had a longer wheelbase and correspondingly more cabin space.

At the same time, an estate car version of the 18 appeared, and the latest example of the 14, called 14TS, received a 1.36-litre version of the transversely-mounted overhead-cam engine.

Meanwhile, development of the mid-engined 5 Turbo 'homologation special'

continued, and it was finally revealed that sales, initially only in France, would begin in the spring of 1980. Another new-model forecast concerned the Fuego coupe, but all details of this had to wait until 1980.

The last of 1.85 million hatchback 16 models was built at the end of the year, this car having been in production for nearly 15 years: it had finally been replaced by the still-evolving 20 range. At the same time, French production of the smaller 6 model also ended.

Rover: The V8S version of the 3500 was announced in July, being mechanically the same as before, but with a more upmarket interior and a specification which included gold-painted cast-alloy road wheels.

Saab: The long-nose 900 range, which had been introduced in Sweden during 1978, finally went on sale in the UK.

Subaru: Although the platform, flat-four engine and simple four-wheel-drive system were basically unchanged, a new and crisper range of body styles was announced in the summer, British sales beginning before the end of the year. For the first time these included four-door saloons.

Suzuki: The first of the little 4x4 models which grew up into the Kings Road-cruising Vitara was imported to the UK, its first incarnation being the LJ80, when it was fitted with a 41bhp/797cc engine.

Talbot: This old marque name was revived by Peugeot in the summer of 1979 by means of rebadging and an extensive marketing campaign, to take over from all existing Chrysler-UK, Chrysler-Europe, Simca and Matra-Simca types.

In the UK, all existing Avenger, Sunbeam, Horizon, Alpine and Matra-Simca Rancho models became Talbots – many cars being rebadged in dealers' showrooms.

The 16-valve twin-cam Lotus-engined Sunbeam-Lotus hatchback was previewed in March and nominally went on sale in mid-year as a Chrysler, though the vast majority of cars built in the 1979–81 period were badged as Talbots.

Developed to provide the company with a car to match the Escort RS in international rallies, the Sunbeam-Lotus was a completely re-engineered Sunbeam hatchback, with Lotus engine, ZF gearbox and heavy-duty rear axle. With 150bhp as standard, the capability of 240bhp in rally-tuned form, and a top speed of 125mph, this very promising car was duly homologated later in the year. More than 2,300 would be produced, and as a rally car it paid back its investment in 1981 when the Talbot works team won the Manufacturers' World Championship.

Triumph: The long-awaited and rumoured TR7 convertible was finally introduced in April, initially for sale in the UK only. Because of proposed, or impending, USA-market regulations regarding crash protection, the TR7 had originally been designed only as a closed car, but after those rules were abandoned an open-top derivative was speedily developed. In both America and the UK (where deliveries began at the end of 1979), the convertible version rapidly accounted for the majority of TR7 sales.

Triumph also started manufacturing Rover (not Triumph Stag) V8-engined TRs called TR8s, but these were only ever intended for sale in the USA, and were not to be officially launched there until the beginning of 1980.

Vauxhall: The Chevette HSR, a very limited-production (50-off) 'homologation special' with the unique Vauxhall 16-valve 2.3-litre engine, was announced in September. These cars were converted from unsold stocks of Chevette HS types, and were given special features including a twin-plate clutch, extra-wide front and rear wheel-arch flares, plastic body sills, different front and rear spoilers and wider cast-alloy wheels.

Volkswagen: In 1975, the Golf GTi had been a trendsetter, and now the trendsetter was a cabriolet version, which was to be assembled on behalf of VW by Karmann at Osnabruck.

Based on the platform and all the running gear of larger-engined Golfs, the cabriolet was a smart drop-top which featured a permanently fixed roll-over hoop behind the front seats. This model, in various guises and with different power outputs, was so successful that it would be built until the 1990s.

During the summer VW also launched the booted version of the Golf – the Jetta – which was effectively a conventional four-door saloon car with the same running gear as the familiar front-wheel-drive Golf hatchback and cabriolet models. In the beginning the Jetta was available with three different engines – 60bhp/1.3-litre, 70bhp/1.5-litre and 110bhp/1.6-litre.

After a great deal of delay, right-hand-drive versions of the fuel-injected Golf GTi and Scirocco models were finally put on to the British market, all previous UK deliveries having been of left-hand-drive examples.

To end an active year, the 1.5-litre diesel engine was also made optional for the Passat.

Industrial developments

Michael Edwardes' ruthless surgery at BL continued during the year, this time with the closure of the Vanden Plas business in Kingsbury, North London, also with a threatened close-down of the MG plant at Abingdon. The closure was postponed, even though the cars were said to be losing £900 apiece when sold in the USA, but this would finally take place in 1980.

Later in the year, the first news came of a technical link-up with Honda, a deal that was finally signed off over Christmas 1979, BL's immediate object being to gain access to a new small/medium-size car – the Ballade – which Honda was currently developing. There were still two years to go before the

British version of the Ballade would appear – badged as the Triumph Acclaim, though there was absolutely no connection with that once-proud Coventry marque.

Early in the year Chrysler UK (for which, really, read 'Peugeot', following the 1978 transaction) appointed George Turnbull as its new chairman. This must have given him a great deal of satisfaction, for he had started his working life as an apprentice in Coventry (at Standard) and had walked away from British Leyland in 1973 when he disagreed about plans which subsequently proved to be disastrously misguided.

Towards the end of the year the Byfleet-based Panther company – builders of extravagant pastiche models like the J72 and the De Ville as well as the more modest Lima two-seater sportscar, went into receivership. It would be some time before its future was settled.

Renault bought a 10 per cent stake in Volvo before the end of the year, this being placarded as a shrewd investment rather than a prelude to a full merger. In fact it made a good deal of sense for Renault to tie itself to Volvo in this way as the French company was a major supplier of engines for the Dutch Volvo business, and there were also links over the PRV V6 engine.

Saab and Lancia announced a new joint project for a new car, but would reveal little about the detail of the model to be developed. In fact this was the genesis of the Type 4 project, which eventually produced the Saab 9000 and the Lancia Thema in the mid-1980s. By then, however, Saab and Lancia would have grown apart again,

while Lancia would have drawn Alfa Romeo (the 164) and Fiat (the Croma) into the same co-operative venture.

The second proposed Motorfair, due to be staged at Earls Court in October, was cancelled four weeks before its intended opening date as a result of the failure to resolve a lengthy political battle involving the motor trade, the car manufacturers and the SMMT. The public were not best pleased.

Technical developments

When General Motors of Detroit introduced its new X-bodied Citation, Phoenix, Omega and Skylark models early in the year, it signalled a clear intention to follow Europe's lead in adopting transverse engines and front-wheel drive for most of its new-generation fast-selling models. This was a major change of thinking for American concerns, for up until then the only American-made FWD cars had been the massive and ultra-powerful Cadillac Eldorado/Oldsmobile Toronado models.

For the time being Ford and Chrysler said little, but they were also known to be working on new front-drive cars. Within a decade, not only would most American cars feature this layout, but they would also be smaller, lighter, and a good deal more fuel-efficient than before and in due course one or two of them would find their way onto the UK market.

Meanwhile, leaded petrol was already coming under attack, following a series of allegations about airborne lead's effect on health.

1980

For British motorists, the arrival of several new models was more important than the awkward economic news at home and overseas. This was the year in which BL's new Metro was launched (to a mainly friendly reception by the media), Ford revealed a brand-new front-wheel-drive Escort, and the Vauxhall Astra equivalent of the front-wheel-drive Opel Kadett went on sale. The Metro won most of the press headlines in the UK, but the prestigious European Car of The Year award went to the Escort!

Although Britain was sliding towards recession, the shift from direct to indirect taxation continued, so there were more income tax cuts in the March Budget, while taxes on petrol, alcohol and tobacco were raised. Interest rates were extremely high, which meant that the cost of borrowing, for car purchase, was also extremely burdensome.

Inflation in the UK finally peaked at 21.8 per cent (this being a side-effect of the shift to indirect taxation), but then rapidly began to fall, as it would continue to do for much of the 1980s.

Nevertheless it was a worrying time for Britain's motor industry, as sales eroded and the nation's unemployment rose steadily. Compared with 1979, total *and* import sales both fell by about 200,000, which proved that Britain's motorists were, for the moment, 'buying British' again.

The 'gentlemen's agreement' with the Japanese motor industry over sales in the UK was now well-established, with quotas being applied to the import of every Japanese marque. The overall limit was about 11 per cent of the total UK market, which did not please dealers or manufacturers, who could only expand their businesses if the overall sales level of cars expanded.

This led to the sometimes ludicrous situation of shiploads of Japanese cars having to remain on board on the high seas at the end of a calendar year so that the unofficial (but rigorously applied) quotas would not be exceeded.

New models

Alfa Romeo: The latest version of the front-engine/rear-transmission Giulietta, with 130bhp/2-litre twin-cam engine, went on sale in the UK in July.

At the end of the year the Alfetta-based GTV coupe range was thoroughly revised and given a visual and technical uplift for the 1980s. Not only was the facia/instrument styling improved considerably, but there was to be a new flagship, the GTV6, with a 160bhp version of the modern 2.5-litre V6 engine which had so recently gone into production to power the lumpy Alfa 6 saloon.

Already depressed by its poor anti-corrosion reputation in the UK, Alfa Romeo always struggled to make these cars into successes in this country. They deserved better.

Aston Martin: During the year the mid-engined Bulldog project car was shown, but there was no intention to put this interesting machine into production.

Audi: The revolutionary four-wheel-drive Quattro coupe appeared in March, with European sales starting during the summer. This was the first serious European attempt to build a four-wheel-drive car since the demise of the hand-built Jensen FF of the 1960s, and it was sufficiently successful to inspire many other car-makers to produce 4WD cars.

The basic layout followed that of the forthcoming Audi Coupe (this model not yet being ready for release), with an in-line five-cylinder engine mounted ahead of the line of the front wheels, though there were flared wheelarches to cover the fatter wheels/tyres of the Quattro.

Permanent four-wheel drive was provided via what was in effect a modified front-drive, five-speed transaxle, with a tiny grapefruit-sized centre differential (which was lockable) and a propeller shaft leading back to the rear of the car, which featured a chassis-mounted differential and semi-trailing rear suspension.

All this was made truly exciting by the use of a turbocharged 2.1-litre engine which produced no less than 200bhp – 30bhp more than the engine of the Audi 200 Turbo.

Audi made no secret of the fact that it intended to put developed versions of this car into World Championship rallying – the team starting its campaign (and its successes!) in 1981.

Although a number of left-hand-drive Quattros were sold in the UK in the next few years, the first right-hand-drive examples would not be delivered until the end of 1982.

The Audi Coupe was revealed at the Paris show in October. Visually it was similar to the Quattro, except that there were no flared arches. Technically it was a mixture of 80 and 100 engineering, originally with a 1.9-litre five-cylinder engine, plus front-wheel drive and a five-speed gearbox. Unlike the Quattro, the Coupe had a simple dead-axle rear suspension.

British sales would begin in March 1981, and in the next few years larger and more powerful 'fives' and an entry-level four-cylinder engine would also be added to the range.

Austin: The pre-launch build-up to the new Metro – BL's so-called make-or-break family car – began early in the year with the company's publicists taking every opportunity to fan the flames of speculation.

Looking back, it is difficult to see what a lot of the fuss was about, for although the Metro was a larger, smoother and more roomy restatement of the Mini theme, with a hatchback layout, it picked up the old Mini's transverse engine/transmission installation (noisy gearbox and all) and used the same basic Hydragas suspension as already fitted to the Allegro and Princess ranges.

Yet the Metro *was* an important new car for BL (there had been no new truly small car from this company since the Mini of 21 years earlier), and because it ushered in an age of new technology at Longbridge there was every chance of it becoming profitable for the struggling state-controlled business.

Early Metros were three-door hatchbacks and had a choice of 1-litre or 1.3-litre A-series engines with manual gearboxes, but all the expected derivatives – MGs, Vanden Plas types and automatic transmission options – would follow in the coming months.

Bentley: The new Mulsanne, introduced in October, was identical to the new Rolls-Royce Silver Spirit in all details except badging. *(See the Rolls-Royce entry for details.)*

BMW: In the UK it was a quiet year for the Bavarian car-maker. From September, however, the 316 was given a larger 90bhp/1,766cc engine instead of its original 1.6-litre unit – though it was not given the appropriate model title, which should have been 318!

Bristol: Anthony Crook, owner of the Bristol concern, continued to reshuffle his pack of hand-built, very limited-production cars. For 1980 the Beaufighter appeared as an evolution of the 412 type, complete with its rather curiously angular body style, built as a two-door 'convertible saloon'.

Although power was still by courtesy of Chrysler, for the Beaufighter there was a turbocharged version of the 5.9-litre V8. No power or torque figures were revealed.

Colt: Still yet to be named Mitsubishi on the UK market (though the first rumours of possible name changes were being heard), the range was increased late in the year by the addition of larger new-style Sigma and Sapporo models. There were new unit-construction platforms, with front-engine/rear-drive layouts, now with independent strut-type rear suspension and a new type of overhead-cam 2-litre engine. For some models, but not in the UK until 1983, there was a 2.6-litre engine, but a 2.3-litre diesel version, shown at the same time, was never sold in the UK.

Datsun: A new generation of front-engine/rear-drive Bluebirds were pre-viewed in Japan, but British deliveries were delayed until the summer. Running on an inch longer wheelbase than the previous Bluebird, the new car was 3 inches longer than before, a touch wider and with a more angular shape.

Although the engineering was still conventional – including a beam rear axle on coil springs and radius arms – this was the first Bluebird to use rack-and-pinion steering.

Just before the end of the year, a new-generation Laurel was also revealed, this being slightly larger and even more angular than the version which had been on UK sale for several years. Visually, it was easy to 'pick' the new car by its six-light style (which meant that there was an extra triangular-shaped window behind the rear door) and its backward-sloping front grille.

The new-generation Laurel used the same platform, front-engine/rear-drive

layout and chassis details as the older type, but in the UK (from 1981) it would only be available with the familiar 2.4-litre six-cylinder engine as used in cars like the 240Z and earlier Laurels for a decade or more.

Ferrari: At the Geneva motor show in March, the long-rumoured Mondial coupe, a Pininfarina-styled 2+2-seater, was finally announced. Although it was not as graceful as the shorter-wheel-base two-seaters from the same range, it seemed to be much more elegant than the Bertone-styled 308GT4 which it displaced.

With an eye to USA emissions regu-lations, the original Mondial used fuel injection, but the transversely-mounted 2.9-litre V8 engine had only 214bhp, which meant that it was not as fast as the ousted Bertone car. Changes and improvements would be needed dur-ing the 1980s, but this Mondial gener-ation sold well throughout the decade until eventually replaced.

Fiat: The most important new Fiat of the year was undoubtedly the small, angular, carry-all hatchback – the Panda. Built to dominate an entire sec-tor of its own market, it was also an obvious competitor for cars like the Renault 4 and the ageing Citroen 2CV.

This simple but space-efficient small car used the same basic transverse-engine/front-drive layout as the Fiat 127, which was matched by a dead axle sprung on crude half-elliptic leaf springs.

Clearly it was in for a long career – which, at the time, few would have guessed would stretch to more than 15 years.

Ford: Although the hype could not match the build-up to the launch of BL's Metro, the arrival of the new front-wheel-drive Escort Mk III, complete with a new range of overhead-camshaft (CVH) engines, was com-mercially as important to Ford. The company was astute – as ever, at this time – by launching the new Escort a couple of weeks before Metro-mania hit the British press.

Except that the 1.1-litre version used a modified Fiesta pushrod engine, this car was new from end to end. Not only was this the first front-drive Escort (with a transversely-mounted power unit), but the rather angular monocoque

was totally fresh, being immediately available in three-door and five-door hatchback styles, plus a three-door estate car (for the commercial vehicle market, a van version followed almost at once).

Most new Escorts were powered by a new type of single-overhead-cam four-cylinder engine, the CVH, and all of them used a four-speed transmission having much in common with that of the existing Fiesta and the new Mazda 323.

The big surprise was the launch of an Escort XR3. This was Ford's new approach to marketing special-interest machines, for the XR3 was effectively (and successfully, as it transpired – certainly in sales terms) a replacement for Escort RS models. Based on the 1.6-litre version, the XR3 had a 96bhp version of the engine, giving it a top speed of around 110mph.

Amazingly, when Escort deliveries began, there was a flood of criticism about the car's hard ride, and its rather peculiar wheel camber and ride-attitude angles. Ford made sev-eral hurried modifications before the new Mk III was truly satisfactory by mid-1981.

In advance of the launch of the Mk III Escorts, all the old-style rear-drive Mk IIs were dropped, including the well-loved RS2000.

Honda: Second-generation Civic sales began in the UK early in the year, introducing the latest 1,335cc engine and a five-speed gearbox to the British market. These cars were sold as hatch-backs in the UK, but not as saloons. The still-secret saloon was to be called Ballade, and as already mentioned, would also be cloned as the Triumph Acclaim late in 1981.

Lada: In Russia, the Lada saloon/ estate range was given a front-end facelift, but except for the substitution of cogged belt drive instead of chain drive to the engine's overhead camshaft, there were few mechanical changes. It continued to sell throughout the world on low prices rather than on any pre-tence to technical sophistication.

Lancia: Following the trend which was developing all over Europe, the Beta fastback was joined by a similar but longer and equally practical four-door saloon version of the design called the

Trevi. Mechanically as the Beta, and still with a wide choice of engines, it had the same awful facia style which had appeared on the Beta in 1979.

The mid-engined Monte Carlo sports coupe was re-introduced in March, this time with larger wheels/tyres, revised brakes, a different grille and improved equipment.

Lotus: The Esprit Turbo made its debut in February, the first cars being produced in the colours of Essex Petroleum, the Lotus F1 team's major sponsor.

Compared with normally aspirated Esprits, the Turbo had a 210bhp/2,174cc version of the familiar 16-valve twin-cam engine, and there were many chassis improvements, including an entirely new rear-end to the chassis-frame, with suspension changes to suit.

In May, Lotus added the 2.2-litre engine, in normally-aspirated/160bhp form, to the front-engined Elite and Eclat models, and from this point a Getrag five-speed gearbox took the place of Lotus' own-brand five-speeder, which had been used since the early 1970s.

Matra: In October, Matra introduced a replacement for its long-running and remarkably successful Bagheera, calling it the Murena. Although the new car kept to the same type of mid-engined sports coupe layout of the original, it was different in almost every detail.

Larger and with a smoother style, but still with the same three-abreast seating, the Murena used many facia/instrument components and chassis items from the latest Talbot Alpine/Solara range, there now being a choice between that car's 1.6-litre engine, or a 2.2-litre version of the old Chrysler 180/2-litre overhead-cam engine.

Mazda: The second-generation 323, announced in July, with UK sales due to begin early in 1981, was the first transverse-engine/front-wheel-drive car to come from the Japanese concern. It also hid a good deal of technical collaboration with Ford, which included a commonized front-drive transaxle (based on that of the Fiesta and also to be used on the new-generation Escort Mk III), though bodyshells and engines were totally different. The original cars were hatchbacks, but a conventional four-door booted saloon was destined

to follow them a few months later.

Available at first with a choice of new-type overhead-cam 1.3 or 1.5-litre overhead-camshaft engines, the 323 was a great advance on the previous type, and demonstrated that Japanese car-makers were making major changes to their cars for the 1980s

Mercedes-Benz: With the new-generation S-class cars now reaching production, it was time to give the SL/SLC models a mid-life freshener. In the spring, the latest, enlarged, light-alloy V8 engines were adopted, and the new-generation four-speed automatic transmissions were specified, so by mid-summer the 350SL/450SL/450SLC models had been dropped and the UK-market range had become:

280SL	185bhp/2.75-litre 'six'
380SL/380SLC	218bhp/3.8-litre V8
500SL	240bhp/5-litre V8

The rejuvenation and modernization of the engine range continued in mid-summer with the appearance of the new M102 family of four-cylinder overhead-camshaft engines, with cast-iron blocks and aluminium cylinder heads. Two sizes – 1,997 and 2,299cc – were immediately available, both engines sharing the same 80.25mm piston stroke.

These new engines immediately went into the current 200 and 230E saloons, along with the 230CE coupe and the 230TE estate types, though the first British deliveries were not made until the first weeks of 1981. Unknown at the time, these new 'building blocks' had been developed specifically to power a new, smaller and still-secret 190 model, which would not appear for a couple of years.

Morris: After a nine-year life, the Marina range was dropped and replaced by the Ital, which was really a major facelift of the old type.

With styling by ItalDesign (hence the name of the new model), the Ital had a new nose and tail. The Marina coupe style had been dropped, so Itals were only produced as four-door saloons or five-door estate cars. As before, there was a choice of familiar engines – 61bhp/1.3-litre A-series, or 78bhp/1.7-litre O-series – the old twin-carburettor engines having been dropped when the Marina series had been given a

final reshuffle in 1978.

A 2-litre version of the Ital was announced later in the year, though it was only ever available with automatic transmission.

Porsche: During the year the 924 Carrera was announced as a limited-edition, 210bhp version of the 924 Turbo model. This was the first car of this 924 family to use flared wheel-arches to cover wider wheels and tyres – the same theme being developed and refined a year later for the launch of the 944 model.

For 1981 there were to be further changes, with the 924 Turbo being uprated to 177bhp and the normally-aspirated 911SC to no less than 204bhp.

Reliant: Five years after the GTE had been relaunched in a wider and longer shape, it was reworked once again. From March, not only was it re-engined with the latest 135bhp/2.8-litre Ford-Germany V6, but a new derivative, the GTC convertible, was also introduced. Rather like the obsolete Triumph Stag, the GTC had a T-bar over the passenger compartment, with the soft-top folding up and over the bracing bars if required.

Renault: The Fuego coupe appeared in March, this effectively being a replacement for the long-running 15 and 17 coupe models. Like those cars, the Fuego had a range of Renault's well-known four-cylinder power units, longitudinally-mounted and with front-wheel drive.

Although Renault refuted suggestions that this was merely a rebodied 18, there were many common items in the platform, suspension and engine/transmission assemblies. The super-structure, however, was an all-new, almost-four-seater, three-door hatch-back, very smart and stylish, with a claimed drag coefficient (Cd) of only 0.347, which was exceptional for the time.

Later in the year the 20 range was further expanded with the addition of the overhead-camshaft 2.2-litre 20TX type.

The next development, which followed in the autumn, was the launch of two new derivatives of the 18. Commercially, the TD, which used an all-new 64bhp 2.1-litre diesel, was the more important, for this engine was quite unlike anything previously used by Renault, with aluminium block and head castings. If not yet in the UK, then certainly in Europe, diesel-engined cars were taking an ever larger share of the market.

The 18 Turbo was a more predictable car, for it used a turbocharged 110bhp version of the 1,565cc engine which had already been fitted to many Renault models throughout the 1970s. In the UK, when this car became available in 1981, Renault would advertise it as having 'Rush, with hush', but sales were always very limited.

Already nearing its 20th birthday, the Renault 4 'travelling suitcase' was given a new British lease of life in February when the 34bhp/1.1-litre engine became available in the 4GTL derivative. This unit was no more powerful, but much more torquey, making the cheap-and-cheerful 4 a more versatile load-carrier.

The 12 model, which had been introduced more than a decade earlier in 1969, was finally dropped, for the 18 of 1978 had always been meant as its replacement.

Rolls-Royce: The new Silver Spirit arrived in October to take over from the Silver Shadow, which had been on the market since 1965. The new car's career was set to be even longer than this, for after a series of postponements of various new model plans in the 1980s and 1990s, Rolls-Royce made it clear that there would be no all-new model until the end of the 1990s.

Although the Silver Spirit was slightly larger and more rounded and up-to-date than the obsolete Shadow, it used the same platform, chassis components, suspensions, engine and transmissions as the old car, which had in any case been persistently updated during the 1970s. Thus, it may have looked different (but not sensationally so), but it was no faster, no more refined and certainly did not handle any better than before.

From Rolls-Royce there was a normal-wheelbase Silver Spirit and a longer-wheelbase Silver Spur, while the near-identical new Bentleys were the Mulsanne and Mulsanne L.

The Corniche models carried on as before, picking up detail mechanical improvements made for the launch of the Silver Spirit.

Saab: The last 96 model with Ford-Germany V4 engine was built in January, which meant that all Saab production was now concentrated on the four-cylinder 99 and 900 models.

In October, the first lengthened, four-door saloon version of the 900 was shown, together with mechanical refinements for 1981 models.

Suzuki: The tiny rear-engined SC100 coupe went on sale in the UK early in the year, this being a very specialized Japanese minicar with a rear-mounted twin-cylinder engine and a very cramped four-seater cabin.

Talbot: The latest Alpines had a smoother nose than before (this having been phased-in during the winter of 1979/80), but in January a new derivative, the 88bhp/1.6-litre SX type, in which automatic transmission was standard, was added.

Then, in April, a four-door saloon version of the Alpine, the Solara, was added to the range. With the exception of the extended tail, the Solara was technically the same as the Alpine, the cabin of the car being almost exactly the same size. For the Solara there were 1.3-litre and 1.6-litre versions of the familiar front-wheel-drive, transverse-engine package, the 1.6SX only being available with automatic transmission. A manual transmission option was added in 1981.

The new, large, Tagora executive saloon was previewed at the Paris Salon in October, but did not go on sale in the UK until 1981. Effectively, though not in engineering terms, this car had started out as a replacement for the old Chrysler 180/2-litre, which had been in production since 1971. It was a car which had been conceived by Chrysler-Europe before the Peugeot takeover, then radically updated and improved before being launched as a Talbot.

Although almost the same size as the Peugeot 604, with which it had to compete both internally and on the French market, the Tagora was very different. Styled rather like a larger Solara, the C9 (as it had been coded for some time at Chrysler) was a big front-engined/rear-drive car which used modified 604-type rear suspension, but its own brand of MacPherson-strut front end, with a choice of the old-type Chrysler-France four-cylinder overhead-cam engine, enlarged to 2.2-litres, or the PRV 2.66-litre V6. There was also an 80bhp diesel option in France, but this was never marketed in the UK.

The Tagora was a good car, but unexciting, and there is evidence that Peugeot was glad to kill it off in the mid-1980s, which must have meant that it made a considerable financial loss for its sponsors.

Toyota: It was difficult to keep up with the new models so frequently announced by Japan's two giants – Toyota and Nissan-Datsun.

Early in 1980, a new-generation Corolla was put on UK sale – still a conventional front-engine/rear-drive car, but now with a coil-sprung back axle, and a choice of 1.3 or 1.6-litre engines in saloons, estates, coupes and liftbacks.

At the same time, the big Crown model was completely restyled, still with a six-cylinder overhead-cam engine, this time of 2,759cc, with fuel injection and 145bhp.

Triumph: The long-awaited 3.5-litre V8-engined TR8 sportscar was finally launched in the USA at the beginning of the year. This was never officially put on sale in the UK, though when production finally ended in 1981, a small number of right-hand-drive development, management and appraisal cars found their way into the enthusiasts' sector.

In the UK, the TR7 convertible went on sale in March, priced at £6,176, and even at this stage it was announced that the British Leyland O-series engine would be adopted when the existing Dolomite-type four-cylinder engine was withdrawn from production in 1981. If, that is, the TR7 was still being made by that time...

Rationalization with British Leyland led to all the old-type Triumph models – Dolomite saloons and the Spitfire sportscar – being killed off before the end of the year. Since TR7 assembly had already been transferred to the Rover factory at Solihull, this meant that car assembly in Coventry had come to an end.

The when-will-it-appear saga of the new BL 'Bounty' model continued for another year. By this time everyone seemed to know that the link-up with Honda would produce a similar model at BL, though not until the end of

1981. In October 1980, however, Honda's new Ballade four-door saloon was introduced – which gave people a year to ruminate on its possible future. Just before Christmas, BL revealed that it had decided to badge the new joint-project car as a Triumph Acclaim.

TVR: The all-new Tasmin appeared in January, a car which looked and was engineered completely differently from the old M-series/Taimar/Convertible types of the late 1970s which it replaced.

At first the new Tasmin was only available as a two-door hatchback coupe, but other derivatives, including a convertible, were already planned and appeared at the end of the year. The general layout was familiar to TVR-watchers, for there was a multi-tube backbone chassis-frame with all-independent suspension and four-wheel disc brakes (inboard at the rear).

Power was by Ford-Germany's fuel-injected 160bhp/2.8-litre Cologne V6, while the sharply-detailed body was in glassfibre. This was all such a culture shock for TVR customers that sales fell sharply during the year – they would not recover until the convertible version appeared.

Vauxhall: Nearly six months after the new-generation Opel Kadett had been announced, its near-identical relation, the front-wheel-drive Vauxhall Astra, went on sale.

This car had been previewed and displayed towards the end of 1979, though UK sales did not begin until March 1980. Original Astras had 1.3-litre overhead-camshaft 'Family 1' engines, and were sold as hatchbacks and estate cars. This range would then expand over the next few years, eventually including GTE models and several engine sizes.

The rationalization with Opel continued in October when a new Viceroy model was introduced, this being a badge-engineered version of the 2.5-litre/six-cylinder Opel Commodore, which was itself a close relative of the Opel Ascona/Vauxhall Carlton design, which had been brand new in 1978.

Volkswagen: At the end of the year a replacement for the seven-year-old Passat range, the medium-sized car from VW which had always been overshadowed by the Golf, was announced.

Mechanically there were few changes (much of the platform and suspensions were shared with the modern Audi 80), and the now-familiar longitudinal-engine/front-wheel-drive layout was retained, but this time there was also to be a 1.9-litre five-cylinder derivative. UK sales would begin in 1981.

Volvo: The fuel-injected 140bhp/2.3-litre 244GLT was introduced in March, this being the most sporting, so far, of the big Volvo range.

A five-door version of the 343, logically enough called the 345, was added to the Dutch-built range at the beginning of the year.

Industrial developments

Despite huge pressure from enthusiasts and from the public at large, BL closed down the MG factory at Abingdon before the end of the year. The fact was that, in spite of all the heat and light which had been generated, the old MGB was now virtually unsaleable in the USA, where thousands of unsold cars remained in stock. One reason was that the car was technically obsolete, the other that the rising value of the British currency made its price far too high.

BL also separated Jaguar from the main bulk of its business and installed a new managing director, John Egan, to run the operation. Egan arrived in April when the factory was at a standstill (paralysed by – guess what? – a strike), and immediately inspired a new approach to quality and labour relations. For the next few years sales increased persistently, as did profits, and the company was privatized in 1984.

In June, Rolls-Royce Motors was taken over by the Vickers Group. Although economists had long forecast that the privatized Rolls-Royce car company could not survive indefinitely without a larger partner, the move surprised everyone.

For Rolls-Royce, this move (which was not a rescue, as the company was very profitable at the time) came at the right moment because the new Silver Spirit/Bentley Mulsanne range was just about to be launched, and there would be inevitable disruption and interruptions in cash flow during the next year or so.

In September, Panther, which had accumulated debts of about £1 million, was just about to be closed down by the receiver when an offer was received from a Korean businessman, Young C Kim, who set about reviving the business. For the moment, only the Lima was reborn, but new models, or new developments, were reported to be on the way.

BL – Sir Michael versus industrial anarchy

For two years Sir Michael Edwardes and his team strove to keep British Leyland afloat, setting about a rationalization and downsizing of the business which should have been tackled years earlier.

Persistently, though, they were frustrated by a militant, anti-management workforce, not least at Longbridge, where the unions were led by convenor Derek Robinson, an avowed Communist.

Before the end of 1979 Robinson and his cronies were preaching disruption and industrial anarchy. To quote one document:

'The Leyland Combined Committee's policy of refusing to accept the transfer of work from one plant to another, unless the parent plant agrees, must be fully supported…in other industries like Upper Clyde Shipbuilders work-ins and occupations have been necessary to prevent closure. If necessary we shall have to do the same.'

Here was an attempt to take away management's right to run the business. When BL invited Robinson to withdraw his recommendations to the workforce, he refused. When it then instructed him to do so, on pain of being dismissed, he refused. He was sacked.

The crunch came early in 1980 when, as a result, BL faced a total and indefinite shut-down at Longbridge. Sir Michael made it clear that if the unions closed down Longbridge, he would begin to close down Austin-Morris for good, thus throwing thousands of workers on to the dole queues.

Fortunately, those workers showed more sense than their blinkered, self-seeking convenor and shop stewards. Longbridge returned to work and Austin-Morris' long struggle towards credibility could begin.

1981

Britain's motoring – and motorists – stayed in the doldrums this year, for the recession had deepened and unemployment was on its way up to the 3 million mark. No job meant no money, no money meant no car purchase – so it was a miracle that so many new cars were sold. Even so, retail sales drooped yet again, and the delivery of imports was still on the slide – down to 805,000.

In his Budget, the Chancellor added 20p to the price of a gallon of petrol, and yet another £10 to the price of annual licence fees for cars. Although inflation was now rapidly on the way down – to 12 per cent in 1981, and firmly into single figures the year afterwards – because of the Chancellor's latest imposts, the credit squeeze and the failure of Government to index income tax allowances in the Budget, motorists still did not feel well off.

As a consequence, motoring, and the British motor industry, seemed to mark time for another year. New cars sold at the same rate as in 1981, British Leyland (or BL, as we were now urged to call it) was still struggling to get back to a 20 per cent market share – half what it had been only a decade earlier – and imported cars still took more than half of the market.

Agreement was finally reached between the British car-makers and the Japanese industry over the level of Japanese imports to the UK. In July it was agreed formally that in future the JAMA would always limit its deliveries to 11 per cent of the British market. This deal has been honoured ever since, though of course the count has always excluded Japanese cars which have been built in the UK, as they have been from 1986, when Nissan opened its doors in County Durham.

Except for the arrival of the new front-wheel-drive Vauxhall Cavalier, 1981 was a year rather lacking in important new British cars, for BL's so-called 'new' Triumph Acclaim was only a slightly modified Honda Ballade. Even so, there was an air of anticipation, for Ford's Cortina replacement (to be called Sierra) was due in 1982, Vauxhall (for which, read GM-Europe) had a new Supermini almost ready to release, and even BL were talking

enthusiastically about a new LC10 medium-sized project which *might* be ready by the end of 1982.

Those looking forward to compulsory safety-belt usage also had to wait – patiently or not – for yet another attempt to push the legislation through Parliament was frustrated by procedural wrangling.

The last of Britain's major estuary road bridges – the Humber Bridge, linking the north and south banks of the big river – opened in June. Ever since, it has been considerably underused, thus confirming that it was only ever a 'political' bridge rather than one justified on transport and economic grounds.

New models

Alfa Romeo: After a decade of development, mainly of engines, transmissions and the fastback Sprint derivative, the Alfasud finally became available as a three-door hatchback, additional to the two-door and four-door saloons with separate boot: in fact the hatch replaced the two-door saloons in the UK line-up. The basic style and profile of the car was virtually unchanged, the principal difference being re-engineering around the tail to accommodate the lift-up hatch.

Audi: The first deliveries of 200bhp four-wheel-drive Quattros, all in left-hand-drive form, were made in March. Right-hand-drive cars would not be available until the end of 1982. Front-wheel-drive Audi Coupes also started their British career at the same time.

An additional version of the 200 'flagship' – the 200E, with normally-aspirated 136bhp/2.2-litre engine – was also added to the range.

Austin: From the summer, an automatic-transmission version of the Metro became available.

Early in the year the latest A-Plus engines began to be fitted to the front-drive Allegro, and at the same time a 1-litre engine took over from the original long-stroke 1.1-litre unit, while the power of the 1.3-litre version was boosted from 54 to 63bhp.

The Maxi, which had been introduced in 1969 to a distinctly lukewarm reception, was finally killed-off. It was typical of British Leyland's so-called

planning that this Austin-badged car had always been assembled at Cowley! One reason for the Maxi's death was that it made way for the Triumph Acclaim to be built at Cowley – that car, incidentally, being the only Triumph to be built there.

BMW: Nine years after the original series were launched, BMW introduced a new generation of 5-series cars. To the astonishment of observers, and many of BMW's rivals, the new cars looked very much like the old ones, which was reasonable as the latest car used the same platform, cabin, doors and major pressings as before, the main differences being to the front and rear styles, including an enlarged boot compartment with a higher lid line.

As previously, the latest 5-series used all-independent suspension, though there was new geometry at the front, and at the rear there was a new trailing-arm system in which the semi-trailing angle had been reduced from 20 to 13 degrees – this considerably reducing the range of camber changes.

As before, there was to be a complete range of overhead-camshaft engines, from a carburetted 80bhp/1.8-litre 'four' to a 184bhp/2.8-litre fuel-injected 'six'. British deliveries began in the autumn.

Citroen: Modern technology and the 2CV were finally married in the autumn, when front-wheel disc brakes (as already used in Dyane models) were standardized.

Colt: The Mitsubishi name had still to be officially adopted on UK-market versions of these cars.

In May, a new and very fast version of the Lancer was brought into the UK, the 2000 Turbo, which had a turbocharged version of the 2-litre 'balancer' engine more usually seen in Galants and Sapporos.

Because the power output of the standard car was a brawny 167bhp, and its top speed more than 130mph, this was a formidable performer, for which some rallying hopes were entertained.

The British sales problem was that at £8,299 the 2000 Turbo was expensive, and it was only available in limited numbers for about 12 months.

In March, a 1.2-litre version of the Mirage was added to the existing 1.4-

litre car, this time without the unique eight-speed (4 x 2) transmission of the larger-engined car.

Dacia: The Romanian company forecast in March that it would soon begin selling locally-assembled Renault 12s in the UK.

Daihatsu: The Cuore models had been introduced in Japan during 1980, and UK deliveries began in September behind the model name Domino.

The Domino was a very small (126in long) three-door minicar, whose bulk fell between the Mini and Metro packages. Although it had a transverse engine and front-wheel drive, the engine was a high-revving vertical-twin unit of only 547cc, which made the Domino something of a frantic little performer.

The medium-sized Charmant, a conventional front-engine/rear-drive model with a choice of 1.3 or 1.6-litre engines, was previewed during the year: UK deliveries were due to start in 1982.

Datsun: The parent company, Nissan, started the long process of changing the name on its export-market cars – from Datsun to Nissan – by putting a Nissan badge on the rear of every vehicle.

In addition, it was a very important time for new models from the Japanese giant, for there were totally new replacements for two mass-market ranges – the Sunny and the Violet – both with front-engine/front-drive installations.

The new-generation Sunny did not appear until December, which meant that British deliveries would not start until May 1982. This was the first front-wheel-drive Nissan to carry the Sunny badge, and the cars were powered by a family of new overhead-camshaft engines – 75bhp/1,270cc and 85bhp or 95bhp/1,488cc.

Slightly larger and more spacious than the previous model, with rather angular styling, like all current new Nissans, this was to be the start of an entire range of 1980s Sunnys and related cars. In the UK the range would comprise a four-door saloon, a coupe and an estate car.

The totally new generation of Violet models introduced in Japan in September also appeared on the UK market in 1982, but would carry the Stanza name.

Effectively, they were replacements for the old-style, rear-drive Violets, which were discontinued at this time.

The new Stanza was to be sold in the UK as a saloon or a hatchback with a choice of new-generation 1.6 or 1.8-litre overhead-camshaft engines. These cars were nearly 150lb lighter than the ousted Violets and were faster and more fuel-efficient.

Ferrari: During the year, the 308GTB and 308GTS models were upgraded to 308GTBi and 308GTSi, the letter 'i' indicating that fuel injection had been added to the specification of the V8 engine, which had been introduced in the Mondial of 1980. Such was the terrible toll being taken by ever-tightening exhaust emissions regulations that, even with injection, this engine was 36bhp *less* powerful than the original carburetted type of 1973.

Later in the year fuel injection was also added to the flat-12 engine in the Boxer. The result was a car called the 512BBi and a claimed power output of 340bhp at 6,000rpm.

Fiat: In mid-year, Fiat dropped the long-running 132 model and replaced it by the Argenta. This, however, was something of a smokescreen, for the Argenta was no more than a facelifted 132, which looked no better, handled no better and was certainly not a better sales package than the old 132.

For the 132-Argenta transformation, Fiat provided only four-door saloons, with new front and rear styling. There was a range of engines in its native Italy, but in the UK only the familiar 2-litre twin-cam was available.

British sales would not begin until 1982, but were always very limited as this was no longer a car which appealed to British drivers. The last in the UK would be sold in 1984, long before its front-wheel-drive replacement, the Croma, was ready.

Although the 127 was approaching the end of a long career, towards the end of the year Fiat gave it a new and smoother face, along with a five-speed gearbox and – for the 127 Sport – a 1.3-litre version of the Brazilian-built engine. British sales began in April 1982.

The well-established 131 Mirafiori range was partly revitalized with a new series of single-overhead-camshaft engines. There were no significant style

changes, and nothing was done to improve the handling. UK sales began in 1982.

The front-wheel-drive Strada/Ritmo range continued to expand. The latest arrival (in May) was the 105TC model, whose engine was a 105bhp version of the 1,585cc twin-cam unit more usually found in cars like the Fiat 131 and Lancia Beta/Trevi. British sales began early in 1982. At the Frankfurt motor show, there was also a prototype of the even fiercer, 125bhp/2-litre version of this car, to be called the Strada Abarth 125TC.

Ford: The Capri 2.8i appeared in March (but typically, first deliveries were not made until three months later...). This was the first project to be completed by the new Special Vehicle Engineering department at Dunton, and the car almost immediately took over from the lusty old 3-litre model.

There were no style changes, but the 2.8i combined a high-revving 160bhp fuel-injected version of the 2.8-litre Ford-Cologne V6 engine with stiffened suspension, wider (perforated alloy) wheels and tyres, and a transformed ride-and-handling characteristic. It could never revive overall Capri sales to the levels they had enjoyed a decade earlier, but it boosted the ageing model's image considerably.

Before the end of the year, the second SVE car – the Fiesta XR2 – began its career. Based on the earlier 1300S, the XR2 used the 84bhp version of the ageing 1.6-litre overhead-valve Kent engine, along with cast-alloy wheels looking like those of the Capri, but being totally different in detail. Style changes included the use of a circular-headlamp nose (like that of the Federal-specification cars), and this was the first 100mph Fiesta.

Shown as a prototype near the end of the year, but not yet ready for sale, was the Escort RS1600i, a special, limited-production version of the XR3, complete with 115bhp fuel-injected 1.6-litre CVH engine, modified and lowered suspension, and refined aerodynamic aids. This car was intended as the base model for a Group A motor-sport machine.

Before the end of the year the Granada range received a mid-life revision, which included major changes to suspension settings and improvements to the interior, but none at all to the engine or basic running gear.

Ford also revealed the Probe III research/concept vehicle. Unknown at the time, this car's five-door bodyshell was based closely on that of the Sierra to be announced in 1982, while the biplane rear spoiler was destined for the XR4i version of car in 1983.

Ginetta: The Suffolk-based company re-introduced the G4 two-seater open sportscar, some years after it had originally been dropped, but this time with a Ford Pinto 2-litre overhead-camshaft engine.

Honda: The front-wheel-drive five-door Quintet, a hatchback sharing its basic platform, running gear and suspension units with the Accord, went on sale in the UK.

Honda went to some lengths to make this a limited-supply car, advertising it with the tag line: 'You may have to pull a few strings to get one.'

Towards the end of the year, a larger, smoother and much more attractive range of Accords was put on sale in Japan, with UK deliveries due to begin in February 1982. The new car had a longer-wheelbase platform than the old, and by the time the UK range had matured would also have inherited a new 1.83-litre engine.

Isuzu: The Piazza sporting coupe was introduced during the year, though no British sales would take place until 1986.

The style, by ItalDesign, had already been seen in the 'Ace of Clubs' study, but the production car took shape around the platform of the old-style GM T-Car (Opel Kadett/Vauxhall Chevette of mid-1970s vintage), which meant that it was a front-engine/rear-drive machine with a beam rear axle. *(For details of the UK-market cars, five years on, see the 1986 section.)*

Jaguar: In July the V12 engine (if the Italian Supercar units could be discounted, this was still the only quantity-production V12 in the modern world) was revised, with new cylinder-head breathing details inspired by 'breathing wizard' Michael May, of Switzerland.

These changes were identified as the High Efficiency (HE) package, and although there were tiny changes to peak power and torque (power up to 299bhp, torque to 319lb.ft), a 20 per

cent improvement in fuel efficiency was claimed. To take advantage of this, all Jaguar's V12-engined cars were given higher overall gearing.

At the same time, the XJ-S was given a further package of improvements, including a tidying-up of the style in detail, new five-spoke alloy wheels and a return to burr-walnut for the facia panel.

Lancia: The Gamma saloon and coupe were shown in Italy with fuel-injected (instead of carburetted) flat-four engines, though this feature would not be added to UK-market cars until 1982.

UK sales of the Trevi four-door saloon began in mid-year, this car taking over almost at once from the older Beta fastback model. The Beta's reputation, in any case, had been badly hit by the scandal over premature rusting, a problem not helped by Lancia's decision to buy back the worst examples and put them through the crusher. Lancia's British sales had fallen from 11,500 in 1977 to 7,000 in 1980, and this sort of publicity was unwelcome.

Lotus: In mid-year the normally-aspirated mid-engined Esprit was upgraded to become S3 by adopting the latest chassis and suspension as already used in the more powerful Esprit Turbo model. At the same time, an optional set of 15in diameter road wheels became available – also from the Turbo model.

Earlier in the year the Turbo began to be sold in plain colours instead of the extrovert colour scheme of the Essex Petroleum company, which had been sponsoring the F1 team.

Marcos: Some years after the original company had been sold, then gone into receivership, designer/owner Jem Marsh bought back the rights and resumed making Marcos GTs in kit form. Reflecting what had gone before, these cars were available with a variety of Ford, Triumph and even Volvo engines. Kit prices for the car without the engine started at £3,000.

Mazda: The RX-7, at the time the world's only Wankel-engined car, was further improved, British sales beginning in the spring. Compared with the original, the 'Mk II' RX-7 had a more lusty 115bhp engine, and there were

minor style and equipment improvements.

Mercedes-Benz: For 1982, the company produced a new generation of V8 engines. Called the Energy Concept types, they included a slightly enlarged 3.8-litre (3,839 instead of 3,818cc), and there were detail changes to peak power and torque figures throughout the range. Weights were slightly down and fuel efficiency, it was claimed, was improved.

In September, the glossy, expensive and very carefully detailed and equipped two-door S-class coupes were revealed, using a shortened version of the platform of the latest S-Class saloons, but with a very smooth two-door, almost-four-seater super-structure. For the British market, where deliveries began almost at once, they would initially be sold in 201bhp/380SEC and 228bhp/500SEC forms, but additional versions would eventually be developed, these cars remaining in production throughout the decade.

The last of the very special (and very expensive!) 600 Grosser models was made during the year, this finally bringing to an end the life of a car which had been launched as long ago as 1963, but been little changed in the two decades which followed. There was no replacement model.

Morgan: This was the era in which Morgan made fewer than usual changes, and a production rate of about 10 cars per week was normal.

By the Malvern company's standards, therefore, there had been a positive tornado of change to the 4/4. At the end of the year, with first deliveries taking place at once, the design was updated by the fitment of two alternative new engine/transmission combinations – either the 96bhp/1.6-litre Ford Escort XR3 (CVH) engine plus four-speed gearbox, or a 98bhp/1.6-litre twin-cam Fiat engine plus five-speed gearbox.

The Rover V8-powered Plus 8 carried on with virtually no changes.

Opel: The Manta 400 'homologation special', first seen in March, was a coupe replacement for the Ascona 400, a lighter and rather more specialized car than before. There would be a considerable delay in building sufficient cars to satisfy sporting authorities that the car could be homologated, and only a handful of the road cars would ever come to the UK.

Although the new-generation front-drive Opel Ascona took over from the old rear-drive model later in the year, it was never imported to the UK, where the market was reserved for the new-generation Vauxhall Cavalier. Under orders from GM, indeed, Opel was beginning to run down its marketing efforts in Britain.

Panther: Under its new owner, Young C Kim, production of Limas (and a handful of J72s) resumed in January. From April, and to boost tiny sales, an extra version of the Lima was introduced, with a single-carburettor, 1.8-litre version of the Vauxhall engine (normally, Limas had a 2.3-litre engine).

For 1982, the J72 became the Brooklands, though the style was largely unchanged, and apart from the use of a fuel-injected Jaguar XK engine, technical changes were minimal.

Peugeot: Early in the year, the 305 range, which had been criticized for being technically dull, was livened up by the launch of the 305S type, which had an 89bhp version of the 1.5-litre engine. It was still not startling, and it would not be until 1983, and the arrival of the 205 range, that Peugeot's range would really begin to improve.

For 1982 there was a general reshuffle of cars, engines and transmissions, the most notable development being the arrival of a 2.5-litre version of the company's well-known and very rugged diesel unit.

Porsche: The launch of the 944 in July caused a real stir, for even though this car was no more than the 'definitive 924', with an own-brand 163bhp/2-litre overhead-cam engine at the front and a robust five-speed transmission at the rear, it was clearly just the start of a long stream of front-engined Porsches to be developed and sold during the 1980s. UK deliveries began in April 1982, the 944 becoming a Porsche best-seller for a number of years.

At the Frankfurt motor show the company also showed an early prototype of a 911 with four-wheel drive, though there was no question of it going on sale. This was the first indication of Porsche's determination to keep regenerating and improving the 911's

layout in order to prolong its life.

Range Rover: Some 11 years after the original model had been announced, a four-door version was finally put on sale in mid-year – and immediately took over as the best-selling version of the range. This Solihull-built car is not to be confused with the hand-built four-door versions which had been produced by Monteverdi of Switzerland, with tacit approval of British Leyland.

At the same time as the four-door style was introduced, the familiar alloy V8 engine was rejigged, with a lower-lift camshaft profile, but a higher compression ratio. The result was to reduce peak power by 5bhp, but to produce an engine with lower exhaust emissions. In general, performance and flexibility were unaffected.

Renault: Except for its transverse engines and front-wheel-drive transmissions, the rather angular Renault 9 four-door saloon, which arrived in the autumn, was new in every respect. A year later it would be joined by a shortened hatchback version, the 11.

Although similar in some marketing ways to the 14, there were no technical clashes as the 14 was based on Peugeot-based engines and transmissions, while the 9 was pure Renault. Originally there was a choice of 1,108cc (Renault 5 type), or a newly-developed 1,397cc version of the same five-bearing overhead-valve four-cylinder engine.

In October, the successful 5 Gordini (5 Alpine in France) was dropped in favour of a similar car, the 5 Gordini Turbo. Like its predecessor, this was a transverse-engine/front-wheel-drive car, but equipped with a 110bhp turbocharged version of the latest 1,397cc engine. With disc brakes at all four wheels and a top speed of a claimed 115mph, this little road rocket was to go on the British market early in 1982.

In February, the front-wheel-drive 20/30 range was further expanded with the launch of the 20TX. Still a four-cylinder car, the 20TX was really a grown-up 20TS, with a 115bhp/2.2-litre version of the overhead-cam Douvrin engine.

For 1982, the entire range received development changes, including a 45bhp/1.1-litre engine for the 5GTL, a 1.4-litre engine for the 5 Automatic, a 1.36-litre engine for the 14GTL, as well as a new 1.65-litre engine option

appearing in the Renault 18 range.

Saab: During the year, a limited-production, longer-wheelbase 900 saloon was introduced. Built in Saab's Finnish factory, this turbo-powered four-door CD model would be available in the UK from late 1982.

Skoda: The Czech manufacturer began to claw back some of its battered reputation for poor build quality and chancy handling by showing the Rapid coupe, which not only looked better than expected, but used rack-and-pinion steering and a semi-trailing-arm type of rear suspension. Handling was transformed, but not many British customers troubled to find out why, or how.

Subaru: From April, the size of this company's flat-four engine was increased, by a stroke change, from 1,595 to 1,781cc – this improvement being made to the entire range.

Suzuki: The three-cylinder Alto, which had been previewed in Japan at the end of 1980, finally came to the UK in mid-1981. Although it looked similar to many other superminis of the period, the Alto's three-cylinder overhead-camshaft engine inspired comment, and at £2,675 the price was certainly right.

Talbot: The Samba model appeared at the end of the year, too late for Europe's major autumn motor shows. Although this was an attractive little car – being available as a three-door hatchback or a very smart two-door cabriolet, the Samba was not mechanically new.

The platform was a shortened version (by 3.2 inches) of the Peugeot 104's, the general front-wheel-drive layout, suspension and steering all coming from the same car, and there was a wide choice of 104-style overhead-camshaft engines – 954, 1,124 and 1,360cc – and related transmissions. British sales would begin in February 1982.

Following the closure of the Linwood factory (see *Industrial developments*), the Sunbeam and Avenger ranges both dropped out of production, though stocks were to be found in dealers' showrooms for some months afterwards.

Later in the year the Alpine's 1.5-litre engine was dropped in favour of the

89bhp/1.6-litre unit already being used in the Solara.

Toyota: In April, a revised Cressida was announced, the new car using the same basic platform, but having a more angular body style and a choice of two new engines – a different (104bhp) 2-litre petrol engine, or a 2.2-litre diesel, the first to be offered by a Japanese car-maker. These cars always sold slowly, and would be dropped by Toyota-GB at the end of 1982, though the car remained in production in Japan for some years after that.

The Celica received a major facelift in mid-year with a more sloping nose and retractable headlamps, though without the main cabin, platform or running gear being affected.

At the same time a longer-wheelbase version called the Supra was revealed, this using a modified (twin-cam) version of the straight-six 2.75-litre engine already to be found in the Crown model. It would be some years before separately-engineered Supras were developed.

To match the revised Celica, Toyota also announced a much-changed four-door Carina in the autumn of 1981, this still being a front-engined/rear-drive car, though with crisper lines than before, and with all the technical improvements made to the latest Celica.

The massive 4x4 Land Cruiser, whose 1960s/1970s-generation models were so crude that they had to be withdrawn from the UK because so few people were prepared to buy them, was relaunched into the UK in mid-year. It was still a rugged vehicle, and none too refined by Range Rover standards, but this time it had a more acceptable estate car body style and a six-cylinder diesel engine.

Throughout its life in Britain, there were no alternative body styles (though other countries had them), nor any more refined alternative to the lusty diesel engine. Maybe that explains why it sold so slowly.

Triumph: After a long and not very heart-stopping wait, BL's 'Bounty' model, the Triumph Acclaim saloon, arrived in September. As expected, it was a mildly-redeveloped Honda Ballade saloon. Equipped with front-wheel drive and a choice of five-speed manual or three-speed automatic trans-

missions, the Acclaim had a 70bhp/1,335cc Honda engine.

The peripatetic TR7/TR8 range, which had been assembled on three different sites in seven years – Speke, Canley and Solihull – was finally dropped, production ending in October.

Scarred for too long by its controversial styling and questionable build quality, it was fatally harmed when the V8-engined TR8 sold only very slowly in the USA. With the dropping of the TR7/TR8, all domestic Triumph activity (disregarding the Acclaim) came to an end.

TVR: In the autumn, the Blackpool-based company announced the Tasmin 200 model, with a 2-litre single-overhead-camshaft Ford Pinto engine. Although cheaper than the V6-engined Tasmin at £9,885, it was a marketing flop – for only 16 would be sold.

Vauxhall: The new-generation front-wheel-drive Cavalier took over from the original front-engine/rear-drive type in the autumn of the year, and proved to be a car which was common in all respects (except badging and decoration) with the all-new Opel Ascona.

The latest Cavalier not only used transverse-mounted engines, but the larger 1.6-litre type was from an entirely new family of overhead-camshaft units, dubbed Family II by GM publicists. The range would expand considerably in the years to come, but initially there were just four-door notchback saloons and five-door hatchbacks, plus 1.3 or 1.6-litre engine options.

This Cavalier was to become a huge success (806,000 were sold in seven years), and its platform and running gear was also the foundation of the third-generation Cavalier which followed, and which was only finally abandoned in mid-1995.

No sooner had the Cavalier been introduced than its new type of 1.6-litre Family II engine/transmission was also made available in the Astra.

Volkswagen: The second-generation Polo arrived in the autumn of the year, this being a car with similar mechanical layout and range of front-wheel-drive engine options to the earlier Polo. The major item of controversy, however, was the choice of a very upright hatchback rear style, more

estate car than hatchback. According to VW, this had been done to maximize the interior space – but the fact that a conventional sloping-back coupe was already on the way was not stated at this point. As before, there was a booted saloon version called the Derby.

The other major new launch was of the new-style Scirocco, which retained the same Golf platform as before, but was now equipped with a new, larger, smoother and somehow less appealing 2+2 body style. As before, there was a choice of carburetted or fuel-injected 1.6-litre engines.

Zastava: First imports of Jugoslavian-built cars, closely based on Fiats, began in June and would continue until the early 1990s, when the outbreak of civil war and an embargo on trade cut Zastava off from the rest of the world.

The first cars to be imported were the ZL 3-series (Yugo, not BMW!), which were modified Fiat 128s, complete with a more sloping back and hatchback feature, these being available with 1.1 or 1.3-litre Fiat engines. The first 1,500 cars to be imported were brought into the UK with left-hand drive, then converted to right-hand drive at Zastava's new British HQ in Andover.

Build quality, fit and finish standards were all abysmal – equal, perhaps, to that of a Skoda or a Lada, but not up to Western European standards – but at least the prices were down in the bargain-basement level.

Later in the year, the new Yugo 45 model, which was Fiat 127-based, but also with modified styling, was added to the range, this having the familiar 903cc pushrod overhead-valve Fiat engine. As with the 3-series cars, the 45's principal attraction was its very low price.

Industrial developments

The break-up of the vast British Leyland Motor Corporation, so optimistically put together in the late 1960s, gathered force, both Alvis and Coventry Climax being hived-off and sold into private ownership.

At one stage there was even talk of closing down the huge new Solihull (Rover) assembly complex in 1982, but this was eventually changed. Instead of complete closure, all car assembly was to be moved to other sites and Land-Rover component assembly filling the vacated space.

In the meantime, the Triumph Acclaim was launched, and BL announced that it was planning a second joint project, the XX, which would not appear until the mid-1980s: this would be the Rover 800/Honda Legend.

Still struggling to make sense of its purchase from Chrysler, Peugeot decided to close down the Linwood factory, near Paisley in Scotland. The Linwood site had been opened in 1939 to build tanks and other military equipment, then had turned to making bodyshells in 1960, before Rootes started to build Hillman Imps in a new complex, alongside, in 1963.

But Rootes, then Chrysler and finally Peugeot had never made this plant profitable (principally because of an unco-operative workforce amongst which absenteeism was rife and strikes all too frequent). Peugeot's patience ran out early in 1981 and the lines emptied in mid-May; redundancy costs were £20 million, and there was also the matter of a £28 million Government loan to be settled.

Following the closure of Linwood, the only British Talbot cars were assembled at Ryton, which was producing Alpines and Solaras but was less than fully occupied. Early in the year, Talbot's UK market share was a mere 6 per cent – which was almost halved when the Avenger and Sunbeam models were dropped. Although Peugeot began assembling front-wheel-drive Horizons in the UK at the end of 1981, it would be a long time before Ryton could be brought back into profitability.

Lotus, which was strapped for cash (the more so after much of the DeLorean development cash had been diverted elsewhere...) set up a co-operative deal with Toyota during the summer. One immediate result was that Lotus incorporated many Toyota items into its latest developments of the Elite/Eclat generation – resulting in the appearance of the Excel derivative late in 1982.

Aided by many millions of pounds of Government finance, and by engineering from Lotus, DeLorean began building rear-engined DMC-12 cars in its new factory at Dunmurry, Northern Ireland, though the entire production was reserved for sale in the USA.

Pre-sale hype suggested that demand for the DMC-12 exceeded supply, but this was false, if not deliberately misstated. Not only were these cars much slower and more expensive than had been promised, but their handling was distinctly spooky. Early cars, it seemed, had poor build quality, and the stainless-steel body panels in reality stained very easily.

By the end of the year, only months after deliveries had begun, unsold cars began to pile up in the USA and in Northern Ireland. Could this project ever become profitable? We would find out in 1982...

Nissan had started to look for a new factory site in Europe, and there were strong rumours that it might choose one in the UK. But these were early days; Nissan would take ages to make up its mind, and the first cars to be assembled at its chosen British base in Sunderland would not be delivered until mid-1986.

In Italy, Alfa Romeo struck a deal with Nissan for a new joint project, but no details were issued at that stage. The result, to be seen in 1984, would be the Arna, whose bodyshell was Japanese and its engine Italian.

Motorfair – mending the rift

Following the 1979 debacle, when the Earls Court-based Motorfair was cancelled at a month's notice, the SMMT, the dealers and the motor industry reached a compromise that enabled the 1981 Motorfair to go ahead in October. Since then there have been alternating shows – in odd-number years they have been at Earls Court, and in even-number years at the NEC in Birmingham.

Technical developments

Whilst advances in turbocharger technology were to be seen most visibly in Formula 1 racing, the importance of turbos to the passenger car scene was increasingly being demonstrated as a useful way of meeting ever more stringent emissions limits without incurring an unacceptable loss of performance.

Meanwhile, the effectiveness of four-wheel drive was being demonstrated most emphatically by Audi in international rallying, but the growth in popularity of 4WD transmissions for passenger vehicles was being seen mainly through the growing interest in off-road vehicles and activities.

On the safety front, airbags were in the news once again – not because of their life-saving qualities, but because of the public's resistance to them. Not only did this cause GM to close down a lengthy development programme, but Mercedes-Benz, having said that it was to develop airbags, also discontinued its programme after only a few months.

1982

Economically this was an awkward year for the British motor trade, for as inflation dropped rapidly, unemployment continued to climb, the 3 million mark being breached in January. Later in the year there was widespread euphoria after Britain's triumph in the Falklands conflict, the nett result being a slight increase in sales.

At least the British Government abandoned hire purchase controls, which meant that the motor trade could now strike its own deals with customers without having to comply with Government regulations. At the time it was thought that about a quarter of all British new-car sales were furnished by hire purchase. Even so, there was a good deal of public gloom around, which may explain the significant fall in attendance at the motor show at the NEC – from 753,137 when last held in 1980, to 646,889. Even so, the vast halls of the Birmingham complex were still uncomfortably crowded at the weekends – proving, yet again, that the SMMT's move out of London had been well-judged.

Not only did the annual vehicle licencing fee go up by £10, but petrol prices were increased by 9p/gallon in the Budget of March 1982. This was also the year when the debate about lead-free fuels began to intensify. The oil companies insisted that lead-free fuel would cost more to refine, and therefore would be more expensive to buy, and they mounted a long-running campaign for tax reductions on lead-free fuel to encourage greater usage.

From August 1, the last of the current series of 'suffixed registration numbers' were introduced prior to the most significant change, in 1983, since the annual 'letter-numbering' of cars began in 1963. Whereas a 1982–83 car might have been registered – say – ABC 123Y, from August 1, 1983, onwards it would be registered A123 ABC...

At last, Britain's Parliament agreed to make the wearing of front seat belts compulsory. In May 1982 the compulsion date was set for Monday, January 3, 1983, but eventually was put back further, to Monday, January 31 – although many motorists had been wearing seat belts voluntarily for some time.

New models

AC: It was a measure of how slowly the 3000ME was selling that the company announced that it would supply cars direct from the factory at £2,000 below the recommended price of £13,301. Even so, there were very few takers.

Audi: The new-generation 100 appeared in September, not only with a superbly detailed four-door saloon shape, but one which was aerodynamically clean, having the very low drag coefficient (Cd) of 0.30, and styling which seemed to have made no compromises in achieving the right profile.

Under the shapely skin there were few technical surprises, as Audi was still committed to versions of its now-famous five-cylinder overhead-camshaft engines, while the suspension and steering layouts were all developments of those used in previous Audis.

By any standards, this was a trend-setting range of cars, which became available in the UK during the winter of 1982-83. Predictably, it was also crowned as European Car of the Year for 1983.

The first right-hand-drive 200bhp Quattros were sold in the UK before the end of the year, while a new and higher-performance version of the front-wheel-drive Coupe, the Coupe GT, was launched in April, this having a 130bhp/2.2-litre version of the five-cylinder engine.

At the same time, a 70bhp turbocharged version of the 1.6-litre diesel engine was added to the Audi 80 range.

Austin: The large front-wheel-drive Ambassador hatchback appeared in March, this effectively being a re-engined version of the Princess models of 1975-82, which were dropped. Even so, this expensively-redeveloped model was destined for a life of less than two years, for it would be dropped in the winter of 1983–84.

Although the Ambassador retained the same basic high-tail, low-nose wedge profile of the Princess, it was fitted with a lift-up hatchback door of the type which many pundits thought the Princess should always have had. The nose was more rounded than before and slightly longer – in fact BL

claimed that the only pressings not changed in some detail were the front door skins.

The smooth but expensive-to-build E6 six-cylinder engine had been dropped, engine choice being limited to 1.7-litre and 2-litre O-series 'fours', rated at 83bhp, 92bhp or 100bhp.

A more luxuriously trimmed version of the Metro, badged Vanden Plas, went on sale during the year, this having the same 72bhp version of the 1.3-litre A-series engine as the MG Metro.

The Allegro, which despite having been so widely derided by critics, managed to sell steadily for many years, was finally withdrawn in March 1982.

Bentley: There was a major surprise in March when the company announced an additional model, the massively powerful turbocharged Mulsanne Turbo saloon. Officially we were never meant to know how much power was produced by the boosted 6.75-litre engine, but figures later released in Germany put this at almost 300bhp.

Except for a painted (not stainless steel) radiator grille, the new version's style was unchanged, as was the softly-sprung chassis, but the performance was quite transformed, and the top speed was electronically restricted to 'only' 135mph.

When this car went on sale in September, it signalled the rebirth of Bentley as a distinctively different marque, and sales soon began to climb from a very low base.

Bertone: Early in the year, the Italian coachbuilder took over complete manufacture of the Fiat X1/9 sportscar. There were no mechanical changes, and only minor changes to the trim and decoration, but henceforth the cars were really Bertones rather than Fiats.

BMW: The most important new model of the year was held back until November, when a new 3-series range was introduced. Although these two-door saloons looked very similar to their predecessors (the 1975–82 variety), and indeed shared the modified platform and much of the old bodyshell's architecture, they had a new and smoother nose, while a four-door version was promised (though this would not be launched until early 1983).

Front and rear suspension changes

drew on 6-series and 7-series experience, which is to say that there was a reduced angle of trailing arm (and a new cross-beam/subframe to suit). The initial range – which would be expanded in the next few years – included 90bhp/1.6-litre and 105bhp/ 1.8-litre four-cylinder units, 125bhp/ 2-litre and 139bhp/2.3-litre 'sixes', all except the entry-level car having fuel injection. Four-cylinder cars had a four-speed gearbox, and six-cylinder cars a five-speed unit. This, though, was just the start, for BMW had much more to say about this range as the 1980s unfolded.

The 6-series coupe, which had been on sale since the mid-1970s, was revised once again in mid-year. From that time, British buyers had a choice of 184bhp/2.8-litre or 218bhp/3.4-litre versions of the famous overhead-cam six-cylinder engine, the larger engine actually having a new displacement of 3,430cc.

In addition, ABS braking had been standardized, there was a new type of independent rear suspension, with the semi-trail angle reduced to a mere 13 degrees, along with significant changes to the front-end geometry. All this, together with Michelin TRX tyres and a weight reduction approaching 150lb, made the 6-series cars more saleable than before.

The launch of the ETA-engined 528e was an interesting marketing move. As Renault once did with the much smaller and cheaper 5GTL, BMW introduced a version of its 5-series with an enlarged engine, in a lower and lower-revving state of tune. It was interesting...but a failure, as very few economy-first BMWs were sold to British drivers.

Bristol: In October, the new two-door fastback Brigand and Britannia models appeared, these using a lightly restyled version of the existing 603 model's bodyshell.

The chassis was a further development of that which Bristol had been refining continuously since the late 1940s, all cars using a 5.9-litre V8 Chrysler engine, Britannias in normally-aspirated form, while Brigands were turbocharged, with chassis changes to match. As ever, Bristol declined to reveal the peak power of these units, but the output was sufficient for Britannias to reach 140mph and Brigands 150mph.

Chevrolet: GM announced that it planned to bring selected models of these US-made cars back into the British market. Because of the imposition of National Type Approval on all new cars, UK sales had ended in the mid-1970s, but there seemed to be sufficient demand for NTP to be found for Caprice, Monte Carlo, Corvette and Celebrity models.

Later in the year, Camaros, Blazers, two Cadillacs and a Buick were added to that list. Even so, sales were always tiny, and the marketing effort was soon abandoned.

Citroen: The BX, announced in September, was a major new model by any standards, replacing the long-running GS range, though slightly larger and with more ambitious marketing intent. British sales did not begin until the autumn of 1983.

Unlike the new Audi 100 and Ford Sierra, this was not a smoothly styled car, though as expected it was technically advanced. Transversely-mounted engines, front-wheel drive and self-levelling hydropneumatic suspension, plus hatchback styling, were all as expected.

The 1.4-litre overhead-camshaft four-cylinder engine option was the Douvrin-built unit found in other Citroens and Peugeots, but the 1.6-litre aluminium-block type was brand-new and clearly designed with some built-in 'stretch' for a long and prolific life in these and other Peugeot-Citroen models. An iron-block 1.9-litre diesel derivative was also previewed, this being fitted to the Talbot Horizon (see Talbot) even before Citroen began to use it.

The LNA, a Peugeot 104-based three-door car which had been on sale in France for some time, finally went on sale in the UK, but it would serve as no more than a niche product in this market.

At the same time, Citroen also topped up the front-drive Visa range with the release of an 80bhp/1,360cc version, calling it the Visa GT.

Once again the CX range was reshuffled. Early in the year the 2-litre Reflex estate models were given 128bhp fuel-injected engines.

Colt: During the spring, turbocharged versions of the existing 2-litre Galant and Sapporo models went on sale in the UK, with Colt announcing its intention to make available turbo versions of all its models as soon as possible. This move was completed during the summer with the arrival of the 1400 (Mirage) Turbo.

Mitsubishi, the parent company, put two new models on sale in Japan – one the Cordia sports coupe, the other the Tredia four-door saloon version of the same design – British deliveries following in mid-summer.

Both these cars shared the same basic platform, complete with familiar Mitsubishi technology, which included transverse engines, four-by-two speed transmissions, and front-wheel drive. Both were in the current Japanese vogue with rather sharp-edged styles, and there were 1.4, 1.6 and 1.8-litre engines.

Dacia: This Romanian marque finally went on sale in the UK, the Denem being a slightly-modified version of the Renault 12, fitted with a 60bhp/ 1,289cc Renault engine.

This, though, was a spectacularly unsuccessful venture, for in July 1983 the British business appointed a receiver after only about 200 Denems had been sold from 50 dealerships. It would be 1984 before Dacia sales began again – this time of Duster 4x4 vehicles.

Datsun: Launched in the autumn was a new-generation Cherry, with a choice of rather angular three-door or five-door styles (there was no estate car) and of transversely-mounted front-wheel-drive engines and transmissions. Not technically exciting, but carefully priced, these cars would sell well in the UK for the next few years.

The new small front-drive Micra hatchback (which would later become so popular with driving schools all over the country), was previewed towards the end of the year, though British sales did not begin until June 1983. There was a choice of 50 or 55bhp/988cc aluminium engines and four or five-speed gearboxes.

DeLorean: Production of the rear-engined stainless-steel panelled coupe from Northern Ireland stuttered to a halt early in the year when the company collapsed, hopelessly insolvent. All work on future products, which reputedly had included turbocharged versions of the PRV V6 engine and a four-door saloon development, was immediately abandoned.

Although the DeLorean was never officially sold in the UK (National Type Approval was never achieved), the closure of the company resulted in a number of left-hand-drive cars eventually reaching private buyers.

Ferrari: This was the year in which *quattrovalvole* (four-valve) versions of the 2.9-litre V8 Dino engine were introduced to the entire Dino 308 and Mondial ranges. First to receive this mid-mounted unit was the Mondial 8 QV, of which British deliveries began in August. Compared with the last of the two-valve units, peak power had leapt from 214 to 240bhp and torque from 179 to 192lb.ft.

Another detail change, introduced at the end of the year, was the upgrading of the 4.8-litre V12 engine in the 400i four-seater saloon from 310 to 315bhp, with torque also rising from 289 to 304lb.ft.

Fiat: The Italian giant had a very quiet year, with no major releases. In November, however, the four-year-old Strada/Ritmo was given a major facelift with a smoother nose and four-headlamp style. The engine line-up was unchanged, though there were adjustments to the tune to encourage greater economy, along with transmission modifications to suit.

Ford: The arrival of the Sierra meant the end of an era for Ford as the last of the Cortinas was produced at Dagenham in July. Cortinas first went on sale in the autumn of 1962, rapidly becoming one of Britain's best-selling cars, and remaining a Ford mainstay for 20 years. No fewer than 4,279,079 Cortinas were produced.

The Sierra arrived amid great publicity in September, making many national newspaper headlines because of its 'aero' styling, which critics hastened to describe as 'jelly mould'. From the start, Sierras were offered as five-door hatchbacks or five-door estate cars. All had MacPherson-strut front suspension and semi-trailing arm/coil spring independent rear suspension.

There was some controversy because these were front-engine/rear-drive cars (one reason given was that this allowed a greater choice of engines to be fitted at home, in Europe and in far-flung countries). From the beginning there was a wide range on offer – 1.3, 1.6 and 2-litre overhead-cam Pinto, plus a German-built 2.3-litre V6. A 2.3-litre diesel engine alternative from Peugeot was also available. A new five-speed gearbox was provided for the more powerful versions. In October, prices began at £4,783, with the 2.3 Ghia costing no less than £8,567.

These and subsequent Sierras would be built for the next decade, only being replaced by the Mondeo at the beginning of 1993. A bespoilered V6-engined XR4i was previewed at this time, but full details had to wait until the spring of 1983.

Early in the year a five-speed gearbox was made available for various Escort models, including the XR3, this feature then gradually spreading throughout the range (either as a standard fitting or as an option).

The 115bhp Escort RS1600i, which had been previewed in 1981, was finally put on sale in the spring of 1982, though UK-market deliveries of right-hand-drive models were delayed until the end of the year.

In October, the XR3 gave way to the XR3i, which was a much improved car having a 105bhp fuel-injected engine, a five-speed transmission and a 115mph top speed, along with improved handling.

Then, to round off a complex year for Escort changes, an American-sourced CTX automatic transmission was made optional on 1.6-litre (non-XR3i) models.

Although it was not officially a factory car, there was considerable backing for the turbocharged Tickford Capri 2.8T, which was previewed in October. Deliveries began at the end of 1983, but ultimately the price of these cars, complete with an eye-catching body kit, would be too high, and only 100 examples would be produced.

For 1983 the ageing Granada was slightly updated, principally by the listing of a Peugeot 2.5-litre diesel engine instead of the original gutless 2.1-litre variety.

Honda: A new-generation Prelude was revealed – sleeker, more powerful and faster than before – with UK sales due to begin in 1983. Its chassis was based on that of the new-generation Accord, using that car's new platform, which gave it a longer wheelbase than before, and a 125bhp version of the three-valve 1.8-litre engine.

This particular Prelude was totally different from the original type, and much was made of the anti-lock braking system, the first on this size of car and the first from Japan.

Hyundai: The Pony range, a project which which had originally been inspired by George Turnbull in 1973–74, finally went on UK sale in February 1982.

In many ways this was a 'Korean Marina', for it was a very conventional front-engine/rear-drive car, to be sold with a choice of four-door saloon or two-door coupe styles, and a choice of Mitsubishi-supplied 1.2-litre or 1.4-litre engines. Technically it had no attraction to British drivers, but the build quality was excellent, and prices were always down in the bargain basement level.

Lancia: Although the Beta HPE model was showing its age (it had been launched in the mid-1970s), Lancia gave it one final makeover, adding a 122bhp fuel-injected version of the engine to the still-handsome sporting estate, with power-assisted steering.

A few weeks later the Beta Coupe was officially dropped and replaced by the Coupe 2000IE, which had the same fuel-injected 2-litre engine.

Later in the year, the four-door saloon Trevi was up-gunned with the launch of a *supercharged* (not turbocharged) version of the same 2-litre engine, this being rated at 135bhp and called the Volumex unit. For the next few years there would be a lively debate about the relative merits of turbocharged and supercharged engines – though the turbocharger won out in the end.

At Turin motor show time in November, the still-young Delta range was modified with an uprated 1.3-litre engine and changes to the front-end style. This car would be put on sale in the UK in 1983.

A four-door booted version of the Delta, badged Prisma, was also revealed. Apart from its increased length, this was technically the same as the Delta – the 1.3-litre version, however, would never be sold in the UK.

Lonsdale: Trying to find a way around the now-firm restrictions on Japanese car sales in the UK, British Mitsubishi distributors (still calling their cars Colt, of course) set up a deal with the company which built Mitsubishis in Australia. Late in 1982 it was announced that new cars called Lonsdale (the location of the ex-Chrysler factory) would be imported from 1983 – these, in fact, being rebadged versions of the Mitsubishi Galant. *(For further details of what, in the end, turned out to be a relatively short-lived project, see the 1983 section.)*

Lotus: Although the company had been heavily involved in the DeLorean design/development programme, there had still been time to rejig the design of the Eclat fastback coupe. By dipping into the Toyota corporate parts bin, and choosing to use gearboxes, rear axles and brakes from the Celica Supra, the latest car became the Excel in October and would be further improved in the years ahead.

Demand for the hatchback Elite had been falling steadily for some time, so none of these changes were made to that model, the last of which was built in the winter of 1982/83.

Maserati: The first fruits of Alejandro De Tomaso's Government-funded rescue of Maserati finally surfaced in February with the launch of the Biturbo model. This was a layout which would be developed, modified and disguised, but always retained for every new Maserati to be launched in the rest of the decade.

The original Biturbo was an angular-styled two-door four-seater coupe, with a front-engine/rear-drive layout, the brand-new engine being a 2-litre 60-degree V6, with three valves per cylinder, single-overhead-camshaft valve gear and twin Japanese-built turbochargers. The power output of the original model was 180bhp, though both engine size and power were set to soar on the models which followed later in the 1980s.

Mazda: The Japanese company previewed a new generation of 626 models in October (British sales would begin in the spring of 1983), these being totally different from the obsolete Montrose types. The new cars had transversely-mounted engines driving the front wheels, and were given a more angular style.

Although they would be commercially successful in Japan and other countries (by the mid-1980s they would be rebadged, remanufactured and sold as Ford Telstars in both Australia and New Zealand) they sold only slowly in the UK.

Mercedes-Benz: For the Stuttgart-based concern, the launch of the new 190 range was the most important product development for many years. For the first time, Mercedes-Benz was moving into a new size and price class, for the 190 saloon was smaller, lighter, more economical and cheaper than the existing 200 range, which continued in production.

Although 190 sales would not begin in the UK for a further year, there was already great interest in the new car's layout. Technically it was similar to the 200s, with all-independent suspension and a style that was a smaller restatement of what had gone before.

The overhead-camshaft four-cylinder engines – carburetted or injected – had been specially developed for the 190s, though they had already been fitted to some of the 200/230 types since 1980.

This range was more important for its marketing possibilities – clearly it represented head-on competition for the BMW 3-series, both in Germany and overseas – than for any technical innovation. The 190 series was set to have a decade-long life, with production running into millions.

MG: Although BL had killed off the marque when it dropped the MGB at the end of 1980, the MG badge was speedily revived, for in May 1982 a 72bhp/1.3-litre version of the Metro went on sale – the power pack being shared by the new Vanden Plas version of the same car. From October, a 93bhp turbocharged version, called Metro Turbo, was also announced, the engine work having been carried out for BL by Lotus' consultancy business.

Mini: After 22 years, the estate car version of this long-lived design was finally dropped. Henceforth, the only body type to remain in production (and which would do so well into the 1990s) was the two-door saloon.

Morris: BL revealed that it was planning to drop the Morris marque badge, but not until the Ital finally died away.

Nissan: The first of the Nissan (as opposed to Datsun) badged cars was the big and rugged 4x4 Patrol, which went on sale in February with a choice of 2.8-litre petrol or 3.3-litre diesel engine.

Opel: In October, the long-awaited GM supermini, badged Opel Corsa and to be built in Spain, was revealed. Although this was not for sale in the UK (GM admitted that an identical car, to be badged Vauxhall Nova, would go on sale in 1983), it caused a great deal of interest in the UK. Considerably smaller than the Kadett (Astra) range, which continued full-blast, the Corsa was a typical transverse-engine/front-drive design, to be sold in hatchback or saloon varieties. The style was simple, not to say angular and backward, and interestingly, the hatchbacks featured flared wheelarches, though no such flares appeared on the booted saloons.

When launched as an Opel, there was a choice of 1-litre overhead-valve or 1.2 and 1.3-litre Family I engines – the 1.3-litre engine having a five-speed gearbox.

The Manta range, which had already been in production for seven years, was revised and updated during the autumn with a slight restyle (including Manta 400-type sills under the doors) and a new 90bhp/1.8-litre version of the modern Family II engine, mated to a five-speed gearbox.

Panther: The Lima was killed off in the autumn and replaced by the similar-looking, but re-engined Kallista, a car whose chassis units, doors and most bodywork panels were produced in South Korea by the parent company before being shipped to Byfleet for final assembly.

With a longer wheelbase than before, Kallistas had more cockpit space and initially were supplied with a choice of Ford 1.6-litre CVH or 2.8-litre V6 power units. Sales did not begin until the spring of 1983.

Peugeot: The 505 estate car finally arrived in the spring to take over from the long-running 504 estate type, and later in the year an 80bhp 2.3-litre turbodiesel option was added to the 505 range.

Porsche: Early in the year, the first fully-convertible version of the rear-engined 911 went on sale. Previously, most cars had been fixed-head coupes, along with a proportion of removable-top Targas, but this was the first time a complete, and conventional, drop-top style had been offered. For the time being this body style was only available with the 204bhp/3-litre 911SC chassis.

At the end of the year the 928's original 4.5-litre engine was dropped in favour of the 300bhp/4.7-litre 928S version. The two cars had been running in parallel for some months.

Princess: In March, the front-wheel-drive models were replaced by modified, hatchback, versions badged as Austin Ambassadors. (For further details, see Austin.)

Range Rover: Many years after customers had started to ask for it, automatic transmission (by Chrysler) was finally made optional on the 4x4 – 12 years into the life of the big estate car.

Rover: More than five years after its original introduction, the SD1 fastback range was revised, facelifted and relaunched, final assembly being transferred from Solihull to the old BMC factory at Cowley (the last cars to be built at Solihull left in April). The facelift included a new facia style, an enlarged rear window and a new front airdam for high-specification models.

At the same time, a new derivative, the 2000, was introduced, using the British Leyland four-cylinder overhead-cam O-series engine, rated at 101bhp. Later in the spring came the 2400SD model, which was fitted with a 90bhp/2.4-litre four-cylinder turbocharged diesel engine by VM of Italy. It was originally available for export only, but UK sales began in June.

To round out the range, a 190bhp fuel-injected 3500 Vitesse derivative was announced in October, this having a tail spoiler, revised suspension settings and better brakes.

Saab: The 900 range continued to improve and expand, including the introduction of an updated turbocharged 2-litre engine, and the long-wheelbase 900CD (built in Finland and based on the four-door 900 Turbo) went on UK sale before the end of the year, but this car's high price – £14,995 – meant that sales were always very limited.

Subaru: A new type of 1.8-litre four-wheel-drive saloon appeared in mid-year, with an 81bhp version of the flat-four power unit and a new all-synchromesh gearbox. Later, automatic transmission became available on this model.

Suzuki: Quietly, and without fuss, the tiny (only 11ft 3in long) SJ410 4x4 estate car was introduced to the British market. This car, which later grew up into the Vitara, was much cheaper than almost any other four-wheel-drive machine on the UK market, and though it did not have the cross-country capability of machines like the Land-Rover, it appealed to a different clientele.

With a wheelbase of a mere 6ft 8in and barely room for four people, the SJ410 was a narrow and upright machine, with limited performance (its top speed was only 66mph), and a very hard leaf-spring suspension. Neither was its fuel economy – perhaps 26–30mpg in normal use – much of a bonus. But the British public forgave it all this because of the low price, which was originally £4,599.

Talbot: For 1983, the front-wheel-drive Horizon was given a new engine option – the brand-new Type XUD 1.9-litre overhead-cam diesel which Peugeot was developing for all its medium-sized cars. For the Horizon it was rated at 65bhp.

The autumn also saw the arrival of the 79bhp/1.36-litre Samba S hatchback and the Cabriolet.

In May, the old Humber Sceptre name was revived for a special-edition Solara model for which there were no mechanical differences.

Toyota: In what had been a quiet year for Toyota, the second-generation front-wheel-drive Tercel was the principal novelty. Unlike many contemporary FWD cars, this retained a 'north-south' engine position with a Triumph 1300-like location of the gearbox under and behind it, because this allowed the front-drive layout to be easily adapted for a 4x4 application in another Tercel derivative.

The original hatchback, though, had a 64bhp/1.3-litre overhead-cam engine and a choice of manual or automatic transmissions. At £4,562, this put it into the 1.4/1.5-litre price class, and

somehow it never integrated into Toyota's complex range.

TVR: The Blackpool company showed a turbocharged 2.8-litre engined prototype, the Tasmin Turbo, though this model never actually went into production.

Vauxhall: Although Vauxhall customers would have to wait until 1983 to take delivery of a new small car called the Nova, they could at least study the specification and layout of the car in 1982, as it was to be merely a rebadged Opel Corsa. (For all details, see under Opel.)

A 54bhp/1.6-litre diesel version of the Family II engine was launched on Astra and Cavalier models from mid-year, and later (for 1983) a five-speed transmission was progressively fitted to 2-litre models, with a promise that 1.6s would also inherit it in 1983.

Other changes for 1983 included the arrival of a 125bhp/1.8-litre fuel-injected engine for the front-wheel-drive Cavalier, and a front-end facelift for the four-year-old Carlton design.

Volkswagen: For the German company, this was the year in which engines were reshuffled and improved. The first 1.8-litre version of the overhead-cam four-cylinder unit appeared in the autumn, initially in 112bhp form for the Golf GTi, and there was a new turbodiesel, a 70bhp/1.6-litre version of VW's smooth-running engine, which was added to the Golf and Santana models.

Also launched was a 115bhp/1.9-litre five-cylinder version of the Santana, the GX5, the engine being yet another version of the Audi 'five' which had already been seen in several of that company's cars.

Only a year after it had introduced a new-generation Polo with estate car-like rear styling, protesting that a sloping back was no longer justified, in October 1982 the company introduced a new version of the Polo called the Coupe which – guess what? – had a sloping back just like the original type. VW hoped (in vain) that the motoring media would have short memories...

This was the year in which VW stopped building vehicles with air-cooled engines, because in the autumn the Transporter models (vans and what today might be called Multi

Purpose Vehicles) were given new 1.9-litre water-cooled engines to replace the old air-cooled boxer units.

Volvo: Early in the year, the Swedish concern launched a brand-new flagship, the very angular-style 760 range. Even more than the 264 type which it replaced (lower-powered, four-cylinder types would eventually be added to supplant the 244 models), the 760 had all the appeal of a rock-solid, square-edged tank, which emphasized safety over performance and mechanical ability in a marketing strategy which obviously appealed to many people.

Original cars used a choice of 156bhp V6 petrol and 82bhp six-cylinder diesel engines, and although they had four-wheel disc brakes, they were inflicted with a solid rear axle. Estate car versions were promised, along with a wider choice of engines.

A new variety of Dutch-built 300 series, the 360GLS/GLT types, appeared in September, these having either a 92bhp or a 115bhp version of Volvo's own 2-litre overhead-camshaft engine under the bonnet, and a five-speed all-synchromesh gearbox in the transaxle tail.

Zastava (Yugo): Importers of the Jugoslavian marque added the Yugo name to all cars, and for the next several years both the Yugo and Zastava names were freely to be used for all the Fiat-based cars brought in from that nation.

The rather angular three-door front-wheel-drive Yugo 45 was shown at the NEC at Birmingham, UK sales of this 903cc Fiat-engined car being due to begin in the early part of 1983.

At the end of the year, to add to the confusion, the old Fiat-based 1100 and 1300 models were renamed 311, 511 and 513 types.

Industrial developments

Well before it was ready to deliver its new Sierra models, Ford had to face legal action from Dutton, a small kit-car manufacturer, which already had a Sierra model of its own. Eventually, an uneasy compromise deal was struck which allowed Duttons still to be built – but the GRP-bodied Dutton estate car soon disappeared.

There was a change at BL, where the pugnacious Sir Michael Edwardes announced that he would step down after five years at the helm, to be replaced by the far less charismatic Sir Austin Bide. Technically, though, this was a quiet year, as the company was preparing to launch the new LM10 (Maestro) model, to be built at a radically modernized factory at Cowley.

The ludicrously over-optimistic DeLorean operation collapsed into receivership in February, with stocks of unsold cars piling up, huge financial losses continuing to mount, and John DeLorean already suspected of financial mismanagement. Renault sued for more than £10 million, which it said DeLorean owed it for the supply of engines and transmissions.

DeLorean had originally forecast that it could sell 20,000 cars a year, but well under half that figure had been built in 1981, many of them remaining unsold.

John DeLorean himself was later accused of massive financial fraud in connection with the project (these later being proved in court, though DeLorean has never returned to the British Isles to face the music), and towards the end of the year he was also accused of drug trafficking in the USA. It was all a very sordid end to a project which had once promised so much to the strife-torn people of Northern Ireland.

Technical developments

Two new mass-production cars – the Audi 100 and the Ford Sierra – confirmed that Europe's motor industry was about to move away from building craggily-detailed cars to producing smooth, shapely and wind-cheating alternatives.

This was an obvious reaction to the vast increase in fuel prices which had occurred in recent years, for the aim was to provide equal or even better performance at lower cost, by using less fuel.

There was still much to be learned about aerodynamic shaping, but with Audi claiming a drag coefficient (Cd) of only 0.30 for its new five-seater 100 and Ford claiming 0.32 for the Sierra, this was already a big step forward.

Some of the world's stylists and designers had obviously moved faster and reacted more logically than others, for many more new 'craggy' shapes would continue to appear. Nissan, in particular, was wrong-footed by this new styling trend – with a serious effect on its worldwide sales towards the end of the 1980s.

1983

Ahead of a General Election, the Chancellor announced sharply reduced taxation in his Budget. Since this was also a year in which the rate of inflation fell to 4.6 per cent, and the Conservative Government was returned with a landslide majority in June, there was a good deal of optimism in the British motor industry.

Of equal importance to business car users was that the Chancellor also introduced three benefit-in-kind car classes for taxation purposes – up to 1.3 litres, 1.3 to 1.8 litres and over 1.8 litres. At a stroke this invented the tax-break 1.8-litre car and encouraged big fleet-car suppliers like Ford to rush to produce 1.8-litre versions of their cars: Vauxhall already had 1.8-litre Cavaliers and Astras in its product range.

Even though unemployment rose alarmingly to yet another new post-war record (more than 12 per cent of the working population were out of work), the demand for cars remained buoyant. More than 1.87 million were sold, of which no fewer than 1.08 million (57.5 per cent of the market) were imports.

The law requiring front-seat safety belts, where fitted, to be worn in Britain was finally enacted on January 31, 1983. The House of Commons had first considered this measure in 1974 and had originally passed it in 1975, but legal wrangles held it up for a further *eight years*, during which time many hundreds of lives might otherwise have been saved.

The first steps were taken towards the introduction of lead-free petrol. In West Germany, which was more 'green' than other European countries, the first lead-free supplies were promised for 1986, and other countries were expected to follow shortly afterwards.

Yet another restriction on motorists came in May, when the first 'Denver Boots' were used to wheel-clamp illegally-parked cars in London's Chelsea, Kensington and Westminster districts.

Although the cross-channel hovercraft service was well-established and popular, there was not enough business for two British terminals to be used. In the winter of 1982/83, therefore, the original Ramsgate terminal was closed down, after which all hovercraft would arrive at and leave a modernized terminal at Dover.

The first of the new-style British registration numbers – with the 'year' letter at the start of the display, as in A123 ABC – appeared on August 1.

New models

Alfa Romeo: More than 10 years after the innovative front-wheel-drive Alfasud had gone on sale, the car's eventual successor, the 33 – a larger car with a five-door hatchback body – was introduced.

Using much of the platform, the flat-four engine and the front-wheel-drive transmission of the Sud, the 33, as usual with Alfa, was due to be built in a variety of guises over the next decade. The original 33 was sold with a choice of 79bhp/1.3-litre and 85 or 95bhp/1.5-litre engines. British deliveries began almost at once. Later in the year (though not yet for sale in the UK), a 4x4 version of the 33 was also shown.

During the summer, the manufacturing/marketing link with Datsun was spelt out with the launch of the Alfa Romeo Arna and its sister car, the Datsun Cherry Europe. Arna was an acronym for 'Alfa Romeo Nissan', and confirmed that the new car was actually a re-engineered Nissan/Datsun Cherry, fitted with a 1.2-litre flat-four overhead-cam Alfasud/33-type engine and its related transmission.

As it transpired, this car proved a marketing disaster, for potential Alfa customers hated the idea of an Italian-Japanese hybrid, and the Datsun/Nissan-badged alternative fared no better.

At the end of the year the Alfetta 2-litre model was treated to a fuel-injection engine, becoming the Gold Cloverleaf derivative.

Audi: Following the success of the new aerodynamically-shaped 100 range, an Avant version and more powerful 200 derivatives soon followed.

As expected, the new-generation Avant was mechanically identical to the conventional 100 saloons, but with a fastback/estate car type of bodyshell. The flagship 200 used exactly the same bodyshell as the 100 four-door saloon, with a choice of 2.1-litre five-cylinder engines – 136bhp (normally aspirated) or 182bhp (turbocharged).

During the year the latest 1.6-litre and 1.8-litre four-cylinder engines found their way into 80 models, as did the Quattro's four-wheel-drive installation for the new 136bhp/2.1-litre 80 Quattro saloon. Then, for 1984, there was yet another new version of the 'five' – a 115bhp/1,994cc unit for the 80 Quattro (and later for other models, too).

By this time, Audi had made it clear that four-wheel drive was to become optional on all present and future models. In September, with rallying in mind, the company showed the short-wheelbase 2+2-seater Quattro Sport. Only 200 examples of this car, which came with a 20-valve 300bhp engine and was much lighter than the conventional Quattro, were to be made, and officially none would be sold in the UK, though a few privately-imported cars (all with left-hand drive) eventually made it to these shores.

Austin: More than two years after the Metro had appeared, BL finally launched the next major new model in its Recovery Plan – the front-wheel-drive LM10, which had been badged an Austin Maestro. In every way, except that it looked smarter, this was a direct replacement for the Allegro.

In many ways this was much the most conventionally-engineered front-drive British Leyland car for many years. Although it was a neatly-styled and packaged five-door hatchback, there were no innovations hidden under the skin apart from the synthesized voice-warning package included in the specification of the upmarket models! Not only was this not very effective, it was also highly irritating, and was speedily discontinued following protests.

The transversely-mounted engines – A-series and R-series (much-modified E-series) – were straight out of the existing BL parts bin, and the influence of technical director Spen King was evident over the choice of simple steel springs rather than the use of Hydragas or similar complex systems.

There was no evidence of gearbox-in-sump layouts, for this was the first instance of end-on gearboxes being used, in this case a modified VW Golf design. Way back in the late 1970s, BL had been negotiating with Renault about gearbox supply for this car, which is where rumours of a BL-Renault merger had arisen in the first place.

Whereas the Metro had been widely placarded as BL's 'make or break' car, the Maestro (which would be built for more than a decade) was understood to be the car which would turn the state-owned corporation into a profitable business. High hopes...

BMW: Drawing on its motor racing experience to develop the M1 engine even further, BMW introduced the M635i coupe, which combined the familiar 6-series coupe body style with a 286bhp version of the M1's 3.5-litre 24-valve twin-cam engine.

Caterham: In a programme to build developments of a car based on the Lotus Seven S3, *any* change to the design had to be considered major. In March, therefore, the arrival of a long-cockpit version of the car (to allow more space for the passengers, but with no change to the wheelbase) was big news.

As before, there was a wide choice of engines, and from March 1983 prices started at £5,663, or £5,848 for the long-cockpit car.

Citroen: Still developing and evolving the large CX range, the company announced a CX25 TRD Turbo, which was powered by a 95bhp turbocharged version of the existing 2.5-litre diesel engine.

At the end of the year, the CX flagship was also revised, receiving the largest version of the four-cylinder engine, a 138bhp/2.5-litre unit.

Clan: There was a plucky, but short-lived, attempt to relaunch the rear-engined sports coupe that had originally been built at Washington, County Durham, in the early 1970s. Because the Rootes/Chrysler Imp engine was no longer available, the new company proposed to use Alfasud/33 engines, but this project soon folded.

Colt: In Japan, Mitsubishi revealed its first 'people mover', or MPV (Multi Purpose Vehicle), a seven-seater estate car called the Space Wagon, which was actually based on the underbody of the Tredia/Cordia front-wheel-drive models. Sales would begin in the UK in 1984.

The first of the 4x4 Shogun models (which were called Mitsubishi Pajero in most other markets) were delivered to British customers. The Shogun soon established itself as a major player in the leisure 4x4 sector. The original British-market variety had angular lines, three doors, a short (92.5in) wheelbase, and used a 102bhp/2.6-litre four-cylinder engine, like that of the Galant (Lonsdale) passenger cars. A five-door estate version soon followed.

A new-generation Galant was introduced in Japan – UK sales would begin in the summer of 1984 – being the first of this breed to have a transverse engine and front-wheel drive, and compared with the old-style Galant it had a longer wheelbase and more cabin space. As with other Colts (Mitsubishis) of the period, it had hard-edged styling, which would soon begin to date rather badly. The major surprise was that it had arrived only three years after the last major revision to the Galant line-up.

Dacia: Sales of the Denem (Renault R12-based, from Romania) stuttered to a halt in the spring, and Dacia temporarily disappeared from the British market.

This was the second attempt by British entrepreneurs to set up a Dacia business in the UK – another team had tried, but failed, to sell Dacia-built ARO 4x4s in 1981.

Daihatsu: The hard-working little twin-cylinder engine of the Domino was enlarged from 27bhp/547cc to 30bhp/617cc in February.

Daimler: A reshuffle of names in the autumn saw the Vanden Plas model disappear in favour of a Jaguar Sovereign.

Datsun: There was great excitement in Japan in mid-summer, when a new-generation Z-Car – the 300ZX – made its debut. Not only was this a larger, better equipped and more advanced car than the old 280ZX which it displaced, it was fitted with a completely new-generation 3-litre V6 engine, which had aluminium heads and single-overhead-camshaft valve gear. However, even though this was an aluminium engine, the new 300ZX was heavier than before.

UK deliveries would begin in 1984,

by which time this V6 engine had also been adopted for other new Nissan/Datsun cars.

A new model from Japan was previewed in Italy during the year – this being the Cherry Europe model, which went on sale in the UK in September. Unlike the other new-generation Cherry types, this was to be manufactured by Alfa Romeo in Italy, and was fitted with a choice of flat-four 1.2-litre or 1.5-litre Alfasud engines and transmission. (*For further details, see Alfa Romeo.*)

Fiat: The Uno range, effectively a replacement for the 127 models, was revealed in January 1983. It was a very important building block for Italy's largest car-maker, would be in production for more than a decade, and would sell in millions.

The style, by Fiat 'with contributions from Giugiaro/ItalDesign' (to quote Fiat spokesmen) was available in three-door or five-door hatchback forms. The platform was all new, but the rest of the chassis layout was conventional modern European supermini, with an initial engine choice of 903cc (OHV), 1,116cc and 1,301cc (OHC), all as found in the Strada and Panda models.

Five years after the Strada had originally gone on sale, a four-door booted saloon – the Regata – was launched. The Regata used the same basic platform, engine, transmissions and running gear as the Strada.

After a considerable delay following the launch, the Strada Abarth 105TC, complete with 105bhp/twin-cam 1.6-litre engine and the new long nose, finally went on sale in the UK, priced at £5,860.

Only a few weeks later, Fiat introduced an even more powerful Strada, the Abarth 130TC, which was like the 105TC, but fitted with a 130bhp/1,995cc version of the twin-cam engine.

Another new Strada derivative, also very much a niche model for the British market, was the cabriolet, which used the 1.5-litre single-cam engine and was manufactured by Bertone of Turin.

The arrival of a four-wheel-drive version of the Panda was a real surprise. It had been engineered by Steyr-Puch of Austria, and was using a new derivative of the small four-cylinder engine, this time with 965cc.

Apart from the badging, the four-wheel-drive Panda, which was not really an off-roader, but was meant to be useful in slippery/low-friction conditions, was obvious because of its higher stance, the sight of a differential in the beam rear axle, and fatter tyres. Even though it was underpowered, the Panda 4x4 would become successful in many markets, including the UK from 1984.

Ford: Commercially, the most important new Ford of 1983 was not a car, but an engine – a new 54bhp/1.6-litre four-cylinder diesel unit, which would eventually find a home in Fiestas, Escorts and the new Orion. The new engine, complete with an overhead-camshaft layout, but with cast-iron cylinder block and head castings, was previewed in May, though it was not actually fitted to cars for sale until the autumn.

Later enlarged to 1.8 litres and then turbocharged, this engine (which was built on redundant Kent engine manufacturing facilities at Dagenham) was to have a long career, for even in the mid-1990s Ford made it clear that a successor would not appear until the late 1990s.

The new Orion model, really a four-door booted saloon version of the front-wheel-drive Escort, was introduced in mid-summer, and went on sale a few weeks later. Although Ford always insisted that this was an extra line, not merely a modified Escort, customers never believed them, but it still took more than a decade before the Orion name was dropped in favour of Escort saloon. Mechanically, Orions were like the Escorts, though there would never be any XR or RS derivative, nor even any two-door versions.

A few weeks later came an extensively facelifted Fiesta, still recognisably based on the original 1976–83 variety, but with a new engine line-up which included a 1.3-litre version of the modern CVH overhead-cam unit and the aforementioned diesel.

There was also a new type of XR2 (though deliveries did not begin for some time), with a 96bhp/1.6-litre version of the CVH engine, allied to a five-speed transmission.

To round off a very busy year and top up on variants, the Escort cabriolet was introduced, this car to be assembled by Karmann in West Germany, and to be offered with a choice of 69bhp, 79bhp or 105bhp CVH engines.

The startlingly-styled Sierra XR4i went on sale in June. Unlike any other Sierra, it combined a unique cabin style (three windows each side) with a biplane rear spoiler. There was a Capri 2.8i-type 150bhp/fuel-injected 2.8-litre V6 engine, allied to the same type of five-speed transmission as the latest Capri 2.8i's.

Prices started at £9,170, and although this was always a controversial car (some complained about its handling, but few actually drove one to find out that they were wrong...), it sold well until replaced by a new four-wheel-drive XR4x4 in 1985.

In September, Ford also added a conventionally-styled three-door Sierra to its range, this car picking up many of the existing engine/transmission combinations (though a V6 type was never offered). This shell was also to be used as the basis of the Sierra RS Cosworth.

The 2.8-litre injected Capri was updated in January with the addition of a five-speed gearbox to replace the original four-speeder. Later in the year, the Capri range was considerably slimmed down – henceforth only 1.6LS, 2.0S and 2.8 Injection versions were in the range, all L, GL and Ghia types having been dropped.

Honda: Late in the year, the ambitious Japanese concern introduced the first of its CRX coupes, which had a very short (86.6in) wheelbase, only two seats and a fastback style.

Drawing on other Hondas for some of its hardware, the CRX had a transverse-engine/front-drive layout, these being 1,488cc three-valve overhead-cam units evolved from the latest aluminium Prelude type, which were expected to be used in the new-generation mass-production Civics due to be announced later in the year.

There were new suspension layouts, featuring longitudinal torsion bars at the front, along with a coil-spring/dead-axle system at the rear. All told, this was an appealing, though rather frantically revving little car, the first of several CRXs which have been made to this day.

The latest Civic duly appeared, complete with all the features seen on the CRX and described above. There was also a Shuttle derivative of the same theme, which was a high-roof estate car built on the Civic platform.

To rationalize the range further, the new 12-valve engines fitted to the new-generation Preludes were later standardized on the Accord models as well.

Hyundai: The Stellar four-door saloon, introduced in mid-year, was a real oddity. The platform, inner panels and all chassis components were pure Ford Cortina (final variety), though there was a new superstructure, while the engines and transmissions were from Mitsubishi.

This car, naturally, was damned by faint praise in the UK – and, in fairness, it sold in only limited numbers – but it helped to expand Hyundai's range while more new in-house designs were prepared.

Jaguar: The biggest news for some years was the arrival of a brand-new twin-cam engine, the AJ6 type, which was meant as an eventual successor to the old XK series, and would also feature in the new-generation saloons when they arrived in 1986.

The new engine had an alloy cylinder block and cylinder heads, and was rated at 225bhp from 3.6-litres. Its first application was in modified versions of the sporting XJ-S, for which a new cabriolet version was also revealed at the same time.

The existing SIII saloon range was re-arranged, for as the Daimler Vanden Plas model disappeared (see *Daimler, above*), it was replaced by the Jaguar Sovereign.

Jeep: In the USA, the world-famous 4x4 manufacturer introduced a new-generation Cherokee. This would eventually go on sale in the UK nearly a decade later, in 1993, by which time the engineering, if not the hard-edged styling, would have changed considerably. It was shown for the first time at Geneva in March 1984 (*for further details, see the 1993 section*).

Jensen: The remnants of the old Jensen business, Jensen Parts & Service Ltd, made a tentative effort to get the long-dead Interceptor back into production by showing a car at Motorfair in October. This, though, was in vain, for the Interceptor's time had passed, the company was no longer in a position to restart series production, and only a tiny handful of such machines would ever be sold before the enterprise was once again closed down at the start of the 1990s.

Lada: The Riva, released in the UK in May, was no more than a reskinned and improved version of the earlier Lada types, which were themselves direct developments (under licence) of the obsolete Fiat 124.

Compared with the earlier Ladas, Rivas had smoothed-out front and rear panels, along with different front and rear lighting arrangements. The 1200 and 1300 versions were available at first, 1500 versions following in 1985.

At the same time, the stubby little Niva 4x4 model became available in right-hand-drive form at the bargain price of £4,890.

Lancia: Still desperately reshuffling its pack to get the last few sales from its ageing Beta/Trevi and HPE/Coupe ranges, the Italian company added a supercharged (Volumex) option to the 2-litre Coupe and HPE types, dubbing them Coupe VX and HP Executive VX. In each case the engine was the same 133bhp unit already fitted to Trevi saloons.

Land Rover: For the first time in many years there was a new chassis design from Solihull. The latest solidly-engineered 4x4 from Land Rover (the hyphen was dropped from the name at this point), known as the One-Ten because its wheelbase was 110 inches, featured a new frame with coil-spring suspension of its live front and rear axles. All previous Land-Rovers had used leaf springs, but the One-Ten benefited from all the experience built up with the manufacture of Range Rovers since 1970 to provide a softer (a relative term!) ride.

Because the wheelbase was only marginally longer than that of the old Series III types, there were no major engineering changes to the aluminium-panelled bodies – which, as ever, were available in some profusion – though flexible wheelarch extensions allowed the wheels to take up even more extreme angles without damaging the coachwork.

As usual, petrol and diesel-powered four-cylinder engines were immediately available – 74bhp/2.3-litre petrol and 60bhp/2.3-litre diesel – along with a

114bhp version of the ubiquitous 3.5-litre light-alloy V8.

Lonsdale: This so-called new marque (see 1982) finally went on sale in the UK in May when two versions of the Australian-built Mitsubishi Galant were made available. Prices started at £5,699 for the 1.6-litre four-speed example, but these were conventional (not to say old-fashioned) machines – saloons or estate cars – which didn't seem to appeal to many British buyers. This short-lived experiment was brought to an end after only a year.

Marcos: The Wiltshire company, which had struggled back into life after a period of financial drama in the 1970s, introduced a revamped version of the 1960s design in October. Called the Mantula, it was powered by the latest Rover Vitesse 3.5-litre engine and its five-speed transmission.

Maserati: British fortunes of the Italian marque took a tumble early in the year when imports stopped. They would start up again, under new management, but sales would only ever be a tiny fraction of those of Ferrari, Maserati's major rival.

Matra: A few right-hand-drive Murenas found their way on to the British market, but these were privately converted machines (by Cartel, the British coachbuilders), not official imports from France.

Mazda: A four-door booted saloon version of the 323 model, previously only sold in the UK as a hatchback, was added in March.

Mercedes-Benz: Even as 190-range deliveries were beginning in the UK, the company was widening the range. The 2-litre diesel version (190D) was revealed at the Frankfurt motor show, while an exciting new 190E 2.3-16 version fitted with a Cosworth-designed 2.3-litre twin-cam 16-valve engine developing 185bhp was previewed.

MG: The marketing-led revival of the MG badge continued at BL. When the Maestro was launched, there was an MG version, complete with a Weber-carburetted 103bhp/1.6-litre engine and a five-speed gearbox. As usual, the traditionalists moaned...

Mini: After many years' absence from the British scene, the cheap-and-cheerful Moke, which was now to be built in Portugal, went back on sale in the UK at a price of £4,100. This time the specification included a 998cc version of the A-series engine, and 13-inch wheels, but its time had gone, and very few were delivered in the 1980s.

Opel: Having revamped the Manta coupes in 1982 by fitting a more modern, but smaller engine, in 1983 Opel re-introduced the old 2-litre cam-in-head engine as an option, this time in 110bhp fuel-injected form.

Panther: A fuel-injected version of the Ford 2.8-litre V6 engine (as used in the Capri 2.8i) was added to the Kallista range in October.

Peugeot: In January, the new 205 hatchback range was introduced. Except for the use of existing Peugeot-Citroen-Talbot engines and transmissions, this was a new concept, with a brand-new platform. The style – rounded and appealing – was quite unlike anything previously seen from Peugeot and was the first of a modern generation of such cars which changed the company's previously staid image.

This was set to be a very large range, with a life stretching into the mid-1990s, but at first there was only one body type – a five-door hatchback – and the engine choice was confined to 45bhp/954cc, 50bhp/1,124cc and 60bhp/1,360cc versions of the familiar (ex-Peugeot 104-type) alloy unit.

In the autumn, a 305GT model was announced, using a 93bhp version of the modern 1.6-litre Peugeot/Citroen engine. At the same time the 505GTi was also new, this version having a fuel-injected, 128bhp 2,165cc engine.

Porsche: For 1984, the long-lived 911 range was given a 3.2-litre version of the famous air-cooled flat-six engine, producing 231bhp, the highest output yet seen in a normally-aspirated 911.

Also new in the autumn was the 928 S2, with 310 instead of 300bhp and ABS braking as standard; at this time, anti-lock braking was still an expensive novelty.

Range Rover: Evolution of the big 4x4 estate car continued. From mid-year, a five-speed gearbox was standardized in place of the original four-speeder, the new box being a development of that used in cars like the Rover 3500 and Jaguar XJ6 SIII saloons.

Then, in August, the first of the In Vogue limited editions was launched, and before long the Vogue trim pack/specification was added as a regular flagship model.

Renault: Early in the year the hatchback Renault 11 arrived, this being a shortened version of the 9 saloon which was already on sale. Technically it was identical to the 9, in fact there were really no differences in layout and packaging ahead of the line of the rear seats. As with the newly-launched Austin Maestro, there was also an instrument voice synthesizer on certain models, a feature that was almost universally disliked.

Only months after the 11 had appeared, the range was augmented with a brand new 1,721cc overhead-camshaft engine, an 80bhp unit, widely expected to be fitted to many other cars in Renault's existing and planned future ranges.

At the same time Renault dropped the Peugeot-engined 14 after a seven-year career. The French company now hoped that the 9-11 duo would become very large sellers indeed – but in the UK they always had a boring image.

The 1984 model year Fuego range included a 132bhp turbocharged example.

Later in the year the entire range of Renaults was reshuffled and re-aligned for 1984. The principal mechanical change was that the 18 Automatic was given the 2-litre Douvrin engine in place of the old-style 1,647cc power unit.

The French company also introduced a new generation of 1.6-litre diesel engines, a 54bhp unit which originally found a home in 9s and 11s during the year and later would become optional on other models.

Too late for the public to see it at any of the autumn motor shows, the company also previewed the new front-wheel-drive 25 flagship model, which took over from the 30. Larger but lower, smoother and even better equipped than the 30, the original 25 had the ubiquitous PRV V6 engine as well as a choice of four-cylinder petrol and diesel engines, but like the 20/30

models that preceded it, the range would grow into an even larger family of cars in the years ahead.

In almost every way, the 25 was typical early-1980s Renault, complete with longitudinally-mounted engines/transmissions, all-independent suspension and soft seating.

Saab: In the spring, the first 16-valve version of the 900 Turbo engine was shown at the Geneva motor show. It would go on sale in the UK in mid-1984, rated at 175bhp from a normally-aspirated 2-litre power unit.

Suzuki: The original Swift hatchback was announced at the end of the year with a new three-door hatchback style and an enlarged version of the Alto's front-wheel-drive, three-cylinder engine, this time of 993cc.

Called Cultus in Japan, it was not ready to go on sale in the UK until 1984. Its 60bhp power output made it very brisk by supermini standards, and Swifts of this and later generations would continue to sell as well in the UK as restrictive Japanese quota limitations would allow.

Talbot: The remaining 150 examples of the Lotus 16-valve engined Sunbeam-Lotus were converted to a more plushy specification by Avon Coachworks of Warwick during the year. By the time some of these reached their first owners, their basic hardware was already more than two years old.

Less than three years after it had originally been revealed, the large and unloved Tagora was dropped. Even though many observers thought it looked equally as good as the Peugeot 604 with which it had to compete within the family, it had never sold well.

Toyota: This was the year in which a new-generation Corolla appeared, the first to carry this name with a transversely-mounted engine and front-wheel drive. Strangely, this was the last of the truly big-selling cars in the world (outside the USA) to adopt front-drive. For the time being coupes continued to be built in the classic front-engine/rear-drive form, though these would be phased out within two years.

More than 10 million Corollas had already been built, and Toyota was certainly looking to build millions of

this new type before it changed the style. Engine options included 1.3-litre and 1.5-litre 'fours', with manual or automatic transmission options.

The new-generation Camry (a Sierra/Cavalier-sized car), previewed in 1982, went on sale in the UK in April. Like most other new Toyotas of this period, the Camry had switched from rear-wheel to front-wheel drive, the transversely-mounted engine being hidden under a very sharp-edged style of a type which would soon fade from popularity.

The 89bhp/1.8-litre engine was a brand-new overhead-cam design, as was the platform and all other details. More popular in the USA and Japan than it ever was in the UK, this Camry generation would be replaced after only three years.

The four-wheel-drive version of the Tercel, promised when the front-wheel-drive car was introduced in 1982, finally appeared in January 1983 underneath a square-rigged five-door estate car body style.

Another new Toyota was the Space Cruiser 'people mover', a forward-control up-to-eight-seater with the 78bhp/1.8-litre engine mounted between the separate front seats, driving the rear wheels. Like its obvious new Japanese rival, the (Mitsubishi) Colt Space Wagon, it was only sold in the UK in small numbers.

During the year the heavy Land Cruiser was improved with the addition of a five-speed gearbox. Even so, this car was still no match for BL's Range Rover, even at a price of £12,440.

TVR: Without fuss, but with an enormous impact on its marketing potential, TVR added a 190bhp Rover Vitesse V8-engined 350i derivative of the Tasmin, which also included a five-speed Rover gearbox. In the next decade this layout would be extended and uprated until the last variant of all, a 320bhp 450SE, was put on sale.

Vauxhall: Several months after the near-identical Opel Corsa went on sale in Europe (and following a delay due to an industrial dispute), the new Nova was launched in May. Like the Corsa, this supermini-sized model was available as a four-door saloon or a three-door hatchback, with 1-litre overhead-valve, 1.2-litre and (soon) 1.3-litre overhead-camshaft engines.

A 1.3SR derivative soon followed.

The company also continued developing and refining its Cavalier range by adding a five-speed gearbox to diesel types and upgrading the specification of others.

In mid-year there was also a new version of the Carlton, the CD, which was fitted with the 110bhp fuel-injected version of the familiar 2-litre cam-in-head engine.

Volkswagen: Early in the year, the 112bhp/1.8-litre fuel-injected engine first seen in the Golf GTi late in 1982 was also added to the Scirocco range in January 1983. Less highly-tuned versions of the 1.8-litre engine also took over from the 1.6-litre type in the Passat and Santana.

Later in the year the first of a series of 16-valve twin-cam 1.8-litre engines was revealed. Rated at 139bhp, and being a clever conversion on the basis of the existing single-cam 1.8, this engine would eventually be fitted to Sciroccos and Golfs.

But all this was small beer compared with the launch of the second-generation front-wheel-drive Golf in August. After several millions of the original Golf had been sold in the preceding nine years, VW produced a new model which was effectively more of the same.

Larger, with a longer-wheelbase platform and a slightly more rounded body style (in-house this time, not by Giugiaro), the second-generation Golf was available in three-door or five-door hatchback forms at first (a four-door booted Jetta saloon was forecast, but was not yet available). As expected, there was a wide range of transversely-mounted engines – petrol from 55bhp/1.3 litres to 112bhp/1.8 litres, along with 54 and 70bhp versions of the 1.6-litre diesel.

Volvo: The 760 range, freshly introduced in 1982, continued to expand. First of all, a (VW-supplied) six-cylinder turbodiesel engine was added – this unit having 109bhp.

A few weeks later, the 760 Turbo also joined the range, this using a 173bhp turbocharged version of the existing Volvo 2.3-litre overhead-camshaft unit: British prices started at £13,249.

Industrial developments

In France, Matra ended its long-time partnership with Peugeot-Talbot (which meant a speedy end to building the front-drive Talbot Rancho estate car and the mid-engined Murena sports coupe), and at the same time it was announced that Renault was to take over as Matra's automotive partner. This was the start of the Espace project, which would become a huge success for both parties.

The most ambitious pan-European new-car project so far announced was revealed in May. This was the Type 4 programme, where the same basic platform and cabin was to be used by four of Europe's manufacturers – Saab, Fiat, Lancia and Alfa Romeo. In the next few years cars would be announced as the Saab 9000, Fiat Croma, Lancia Thema and Alfa Romeo 164.

Following the death of founder Colin Chapman in December 1982, Lotus went through a period of financial upheaval in 1983. American Express was paid off, and to replenish the available capital, both Toyota and British Car Auctions took substantial stakes, BCA's David Wickins becoming chairman.

Stability was assured for the time being, though Fraud Squad investigations of the Lotus/DeLorean imbroglio didn't help. In 1984, JCB, the construction machinery giant, would take an 11 per cent stake, while in 1985 Toyota also increased its stake. Then in 1986 (see that section of the book) the situation was finally resolved when General Motors took over the business.

In September there was great surprise when Dunlop announced that it was to sell its European tyre-making operations to the Japanese concern Sumitomo. Although there were many political protests about this – and the bad news was that the Japanese did not want the ancient Fort Dunlop facility in Birmingham – the shareholders agreed with the deal offered, which rapidly went ahead.

During the year BL set up a new historic organization, the British Motor Industry Heritage Trust, which was charged with preserving, enhancing and exhibiting everything which was important in the past of its own and other companies' heritage.

1984

It was no surprise that car sales in Britain should fall slightly this year. Not only was there the gloom of an increasingly bitter miners' strike, but unemployment was still very high. Of course, not all of those who were short of money would have been in the market for a new car, but the second-hand car trade which they probably favoured was also suffering something of a slump.

Had Britain still been a major car-exporting nation, this was a year in which the industry should have benefited, as the pound/dollar exchange rate moved decisively in favour of North America. However, British car exports slumped to 201,000 – they hadn't been so low since 1947!

Budget changes included an increase of £5 in Vehicle Excise Duty, bringing this to £90/year, and an extra 4.5p/gallon on petrol and 3.5p on diesel, which took petrol tax over £1/gallon for the first time.

This was the year in which the British Government guaranteed that lead-free petrol, rated at 95 octane, would be on sale in the UK by October 1989. Environmentalists wanted to know why it would take five years to bring this about, to which the oil companies responded that it was going to cost them millions of pounds to change their refineries to suit, while sceptics still insisted that the introduction of lead-free fuel would not reduce health hazards. Sometimes, it seemed, it was impossible to please *anybody*...

At the end of the year, the last contract was let for building the M25 motorway around London – this being the four-mile section between Brickett Wood and London Colney. When this was finished at the end of 1986 the entire ring would be opened.

Under the sea, there was slow progress towards building a Channel Tunnel. Although the British Government had abandoned an earlier project in 1975, the line and location of a rail tunnel (for cars to be transported by rail) had always been protected. Once again the British and French Governments resumed discussions about ways of restarting work – it having become clear that private finance would be needed.

New models

AC: The career of the mid-engined 3000ME staggered towards its close with the announcement that a new company, AC Scotland, was being set up to build and market the cars. The new entrepreneur, David McDonald, spoke confidently of building 400 cars a year, but in the end the project petered out with virtually no cars completed at all.

Moves to revive the design with a different engine – the Alfa Romeo 2.5-litre V6 – also failed.

Alfa Romeo: An estate car version of the new 33 model appeared, this being the first such body layout on the Alfasud/33 front-wheel-drive 'boxer engine' platform.

The new four-door 90 saloon was revealed in the autumn, with (very limited) British sales due to begin in 1985. This car was marketed as an eventual successor to the Alfetta (by now over 10 years old, and of which British deliveries would end in 1986), and it used the same basic chassis platform, complete with rear-mounted gearbox/final-drive unit. This meant, too, that a torsion bar front end and de Dion rear suspension were also continued.

Styling of this rather rounded car was by Bertone, and for the British market only the 2.5-litre V6 engine of the Alfa 6 would be fitted.

The slow-selling Alfa 6 was modified as a Gold Cloverleaf derivative, Bosch fuel injection becoming standard, along with automatic transmission. At the same time Bertone gave the car a new nose and tail, but none of this made much difference to demand in the UK, which remained tiny.

Audi: Although the German company made much of its 'new' 80 range for 1985, in truth this was a mildly facelifted 1978–84 model, with the five-cylinder engine options deleted because they were reserved for the new 90 (*see below*) which arrived a few weeks later.

Among the novelties was the combination of a 90bhp/four-cylinder engine with the quattro four-wheel drive system, while the line-up of four-cylinder models was slightly reshuffled.

The 90, when it appeared in October, proved to be mostly a spin-off of five cylinder-engined cars from the existing 80 range, though the engines were either slightly smaller (1,994cc) or larger (2,226cc) than those in the previous 80. Front-wheel-drive and four-wheel-drive types were available.

The most exciting new model of Audi's year was the 200 Quattro Turbo, which combined all the equipment and four-door style of the 200 flagship with four-wheel drive and a 182bhp turbocharged version of the 2.1-litre five-cylinder engine.

At this time the German company seemed to enjoy playing 'mechanical Meccano' with its bodies, engines and transmissions, and by the end of the year it had made four-wheel drive available under all its body styles and behind most of its engines. The last new cars to arrive, to complete an increasingly complex model jigsaw, were the Coupe GT, 100 saloon, 200 saloon and Avant types.

Austin: The Montego range of four-door saloons was introduced in April, using the same basic platform, suspensions and running gear as the Maestro which had been launched a year earlier. The Montego, however, had a longer wheelbase and was therefore more roomy, with a sizeable boot compartment and was a more upmarket car with a 2-litre engine at the top of an eight-car range. A capacious estate car version was added in October. Prices of Montego models started at £5,281.

Bentley: In August, Rolls-Royce produced a 'bargain basement' version of the familiar Mulsanne, calling it the Eight. Mechanically it was identical to the Mulsanne, but it had a lower level of trim and furnishings. Even so, the price was no less than £76,108.

Bitter: During August, it was announced that the first imports of this Opel-based German car would be sold in the UK, starting in 1985, though only a handful of them seem to have been delivered here.

BMW: Late in the year the 5-series range was padded out with a 105bhp (fuel-injected) 518i, which replaced the earlier 90bhp 518, and the M535i, which was given the 218bhp/3.5-litre six-cylinder engine already used in 6-series and 7-series models.

Bristol: Still developing new versions of their car on the ancient but effective Chrysler-engined chassis, Bristol introduced the Beaufort convertible as a companion to the Beaufighter, although said it was for export only.

Caterham: In a major innovation by its own traditional standards, the company introduced de Dion rear suspension under its stark Lotus Seven-type machines in place of the original beam rear axle.

Citroen: It was the year of the GTi for the French company. The still-new BX range was expanded further, first with the arrival of the 1.9-litre diesel engine, and from October with the addition of the BX GTi, which used a 105bhp/1.9-litre version of the new-generation overhead-cam engine. In many ways this was similar to the 1.6-litre fuel-injected engine already fitted to the Peugeot 205GTi.

Also new at the same time was the Visa GTi, which used the 105bhp/1.6-litre engine of the Peugeot 205GTi, along with the big CX GTi Turbo, which had a 168bhp version of the 2.5-litre four-cylinder engine.

Clan: The history of this interesting little two-seater sports coupe became yet more complicated. The original type had been built in the early 1970s, but the company closed down. A revised Clan had been previewed from a Northern Ireland-based company in 1983, but nothing more was heard of it.

Now, the original company's owner, Paul Haussauer, proposed to import newly-manufactured cars from Cyprus, where the rights to the old company apparently existed. Nothing more, as far as is known, was ever again heard of that project, either...

Colt: Following a management upheaval inside the British concession-aires, the Colt name finally took a back seat, to be replaced by that of the parent company, Mitsubishi. (For details of subsequent new models, see under Mitsubishi.)

Daihatsu: The first Fourtrak 4x4 models arrived in the UK, these having a choice of 87bhp/2-litre petrol or 72bhp/2.76-litre diesel engines. Because prices started at £6,899 (for the soft-top version), they fell into the middle of the increasingly competitive 4x4 sector.

Dacia: Following a hiatus while one British concessionaire collapsed and another was appointed, the Romanian marque went on sale again in the UK.

This time there was no sign of the Renault 12-based Denem, which was unsaleable, all efforts instead going into the import of Duster 4x4s. After a rather muddled, low-key summer, the official relaunch of Dacia was at the British motor show in October.

With prices starting at £5,995 these were much cheaper than Land Rovers or Colt Shoguns, but more costly than Lada Nivas or the tiny Suzukis. Accordingly, there was a small niche, which Dacia hoped to exploit.

Datsun: At long last, after three years of dual-badging on some models, it was decided to call all British-market cars Nissan, just as they had been in the rest of the world for years! (For further details, see under Nissan.)

Ferrari: The sporting world was electrified by the launch of the new 288GTO, which looked similar to the existing 308GTV QV, but was very different under the Pininfarina-styled skin. Although still mid-engined, this time it had an in-line instead of transversely-mounted V8 engine. This was a 400bhp twin-turbocharged 2.85-litre development of the familiar 90-degree V8. The car was claimed to have a top speed of nearly 190mph, and was billed as the fastest Ferrari road car of all time. But not for long – only a few years hence it would be eclipsed by the F40!

Only a car like the 288GTO could possibly overshadow the arrival of another phenomenal Ferrari – the Testarossa, which was shown for the first time in October. The easiest way to describe this mid-mounted (5-litre flat-12) supercar is as a re-engineered and rebodied Boxer 512BBi, for the chassis and general layout were the same as on that model, which had been dropped to make way for it.

Compared with the Boxer, however, the new Testarossa had a 48-valve engine producing 390bhp, and startling styling which featured long rows of cooling strakes/louvres on the flanks.

Fiat: The long-running 131 Mirafiori range of saloons was dropped and replaced by the front-wheel-drive Regata, which had been previewed in 1983. The Regata went on sale in the UK at the beginning of the year, and a 1.93-litre diesel-engined version was announced in Italy during the spring.

Ford: In October, the Escort RS Turbo – a limited-production 'homologation special' intended to replace the now-dropped RS1600i – was unveiled. Based on the XR3i, this had a 132bhp turbocharged version of the 1.6-litre CVH engine, was fitted with a viscous coupling limited-slip differential as standard (this was a world first for this component) and larger wheels with bigger wheelarch extensions to cover them.

In March, a strange new E-Max version of the 1.6-litre Sierra was introduced, this having a revised Pinto engine with a different bore and stroke (81.3 x 77mm instead of 87.67 x 66mm). There were minor power and torque changes, but a claimed significant improvement in fuel efficiency.

Then, late in the year, a more conventional 1.8-litre version of the CVH engine arrived, this being a 'taxation special' intended to help fleets wanting to buy cars with engines under the 1.8-litre limit imposed by modern benefit-in-kind legislation.

Rounding off the Sierra reshuffle, the three-door cars were dropped, along with the 2.3-litre V6-engined cars – both due to low demand.

For 1985, the Capri 2.8i became the 2.8 Injection Special, complete with a limited-slip differential and several other features and fittings improvements, but with unchanged engine and transmission.

The 200-off RS200 Group B rally car was previewed in November, though deliveries would not begin until 1986. This all-new two-seater monocoque coupe had a mid-mounted 1.8-litre BD engine, turbocharged to produce 250bhp in basic form, along with permanent four-wheel drive and a glassfibre body on a mainly steel tub.

Honda: As something of an experiment, the high-and-narrow Jazz hatchback was imported into the UK from the spring. This front-wheel-drive machine was Metro-sized with a Civic 1200 engine, but its rather angular looks did not appeal to British drivers.

The Jazz would be withdrawn before the end of 1985 – less than two years after the UK launch.

Jeep: A new company was set up in the UK to import the latest CJ-7 models, but sales were very restricted. Jeep would not become a major player in the UK until Chrysler took control of distribution in the early 1990s.

Lancia: The 2-litre, transverse-engined, four-door Thema model – Lancia's version of the pan-European Type 4 design – was introduced in November. Although it looked rather different from the Saab 9000 and used totally different running gear, there were many obvious similarities and common areas.

Lancia (a Fiat-owned company) admitted that the Thema had much in common with the forthcoming Fiat Type 4, to be introduced in 1985, and that much development and design work had been shared.

For the Thema there would be fuel-injected and turbocharged four-cylinder petrol engines plus – a real surprise, this – a V6 version, which used the 2.85-litre Peugeot-Renault-Volvo engine. A diesel engine, sold in Italy, was never marketed in the UK.

Surprisingly, the Thema was placarded as a successor to the Gamma range, which was dropped, whereas it was much more similar to the old Trevi. Before the arrival of the Thema, the front-wheel-drive Trevi range had finally been dropped from the British market, more than a decade since the original Beta version of this car went on sale: it was Lancia's unshakeable 'rust-bucket' reputation which had hurt the range's sales so badly.

The front-drive Delta hatchback range was further developed. The HF Turbo arrived in mid-summer, this having a 130bhp/1.6-litre turbocharged version of the existing twin-cam engine. It seemed that Lancia's flirtation with supercharging (on Trevis and other Beta-family models) had been brief...

Land Rover: From February, the four-cylinder diesel option in One-Tens was enlarged from 2,286cc to 2.5 litres.

In June, the new Ninety model arrived to take over from the old Series III, this effectively being a short-wheelbase (near to 90 inches) version of the One-Ten range, which meant that all 4x4s now being built at Solihull had coil-spring/live-axle front and rear suspensions.

Lonsdale: This invented marque – the cars were really old-type rear-drive Australian-built Mitsubishis – was killed off during the summer, just ahead of the launch of new-generation front-wheel-drive Mitsubishi Galants (see Mitsubishi). In fact the last 300 unregistered cars were left in dealer showrooms, registered and sold as second-hand cars, until the spring of 1985.

Mercedes-Benz: At the end of 1984, with deliveries beginning early in 1985, a new medium-sized model, the W124 family (which would later be dubbed the E-class) was introduced. Except for its new style, this was a totally predictable Mercedes-Benz, produced only in four-door saloon form at first, though estate cars and coupes would eventually follow. With all-independent suspension, a high-level of crash-protection and safety performance, not to mention what would become a colossal range of engines, starting from a 109bhp/2-litre 'four' to (eventually) a 326bhp/5-litre V8, this was to be one of Mercedes' best-selling cars of the next decade.

Earlier in the year, the company was still concentrating on the 190 model, launching a completely new 2-litre, four-cylinder diesel engine version in October, with British deliveries beginning almost at once.

MG: As with the Maestro, so with the Montego, Austin-Rover announced an MG-badged version, this particular model being a four-door saloon with a fuel-injected 117bhp/2-litre engine. Priced at £8,165, it was at once faster, more roomy and more expensive than the MG Maestro 1600, currently priced at £6,775.

After a very short life of little more than a year, the Maestro 1600 was dropped, to be replaced by the Maestro 2.0EFI, which used the same 2-litre engine/transmission package as the Montego EFI.

Mitsubishi: The original British marque title of Colt was downgraded from April, the proper name of Mitsubishi taking prominence. Within months, Colt had virtually disappeared, except as a model name.

There was a new-generation front-drive Mirage at the beginning of the year. Not only did this have a wider range of four-cylinder engines, but there was no longer any sign of the unique 4x4 transmission.

Mitsubishi also introduced a new generation of Lancers, these also being front-wheel-drive cars. With sharp-edged styling, they were available with 1.2, 1.5 or 1.8-litre engines.

Finally, the new-generation front-wheel-drive Galants (first shown in Japan in 1983) went on sale in the UK. At a stroke this marketing move killed off the short-lived Lonsdale marque.

An 83bhp/2.35-litre diesel option was added to the 4x4 Shogun range, which originally had only been available with a petrol engine. Towards the end of the year the range was enlarged with the arrival of the longer-wheelbase five-door model, which soon came to take the majority of Shogun sales. First UK deliveries were of the 2.3-litre diesel-engined example, the 2.6-litre petrol unit being phased in during 1985.

Morris: With the arrival of two new BL cars – Austin Montego and Rover 200 – the Morris marque was finally abandoned. The last private cars to be so badged were the Itals.

Triumph disappeared at the same time. From this moment on, BL only built Austin, MG and Rover-badged private cars.

Naylor: The TF1700 was a praise-worthy attempt to produce a visual incarnation of the old MG TF, the body being precisely the same style that Naylor brothers was already supplying for TF restorations.

Under the skin, though, was a new style of ladder chassis, with a 1.7-litre O-series Austin-Rover engine and related transmission/suspension components. Even though Naylor worked hard to gain National Type Approval, its problem was that prices started at £12,950 – for which one could buy an extremely good example of a real and properly restored MG TF from the mid-1950s.

Nissan: The Japanese parent company's name was officially adopted for all models sold in Britain from the beginning of the year. But the changeover was not instant or tidy, so there was confusion for a short time with cars variously being seen with Datsun, Nissan, or even both badges on their tail!

Early in the year, a new-generation Bluebird was announced, and although this looked very much like the previous variety, it actually had a transversely-mounted front-wheel-drive engine/gearbox layout and all-independent suspension. This was the model which in due course would be produced at the new British factory – a project which went public in the spring of 1984.

Another model new to Britain in 1984 was the smart, though rather angular Silvia coupe, a classic front-engine/rear-drive car falling approximately into the Capri/Manta price and size bracket, and equipped with a turbocharged 130bhp/1,809cc engine.

The 300C, with the new V6 3-litre engine, replaced the old straight six-engined 280C. It developed 155bhp in the saloon, but only 150bhp in the estate. As before, sales would be very restricted.

Panther: The first mid-engined Solo was introduced, but this proved to be a one-off prototype as it was fitted with a Ford XR3i 1.6-litre engine and rear-wheel drive. A complete redesign, to four-wheel drive and a more powerful engine, would soon follow.

Peugeot: Early in the year, the amazing new 205GTI was introduced, an agile, 105bhp/1.6-litre version of the existing 205 design, but with three instead of five doors and with firmed-up handling and very responsive steering.

The 205GTI immediately took over from the Golf GTi as a media darling, and even though it had definite lift-off/on-the-limit handling flaws, for years it was touted as the standard other manufacturers had to beat.

The 305 range was updated in the autumn by the fitment of the 1.76-litre diesel as already found in the Peugeot 205, and at the end of the year the 305GTX arrived, using the same 105bhp/1.9-litre overhead-cam engine as the latest Citroen BX GTi (and closely related to the 205GTI's 1.6-litre unit).

The 604 model had never been a great success in the UK, so to boost its fortunes the diesel version was given a more powerful engine – it was now rated at 94bhp – and alloy wheels and a rev-counter became standard.

Reliant: The arrival of the small Scimitar SS1 in October marked the launch of the first new-shape Reliant sportscar since 1968.

The SS1, which was much smaller than old-type GTEs and GTCs, eventually replaced these cars at Tamworth, though production was always to be very limited. As before, there was a ladder-style chassis, front-engine/rear-drive layout, and a rather lumpy body styled by Michelotti and produced in glassfibre.

On the original cars there was a choice of Ford Escort CVH engines of 1.3 or 1.6 litres, though a more powerful Nissan engine would follow in the next few years.

Renault: After the 25, the most significant new Renault arrivals of the year were the new-generation 5 and the Espace MPV, or 'people mover', which had been developed in conjunction with Matra, who were to manufacture them.

The Espace was a large up-to-seven-seater estate car, with a longitudinally-mounted engine and front-wheel drive. Although the monocoque was conventionally made from pressed steel panels, all skin panels were made from rustproof GRP/polyester mouldings.

The first cars were fitted with a 110bhp/2-litre engine, though a whole family of diesels, V6s with manual and automatic transmissions, were being developed to follow up. British sales began in the summer of 1985.

This car had an interesting style, with a long sloping front and a vast screen. Although it *looked* like a forward-control layout, it was actually nothing of the sort, for the windscreen was situated about 5 feet ahead of the driver's eyes.

Apart from getting the new 25 range into the showrooms, Renault also enlarged the 11 range by adding a 1.4 litre-engined Turbo (with 105bhp), and a 55bhp diesel, as already found in the related 9 model.

In the late autumn, Renault also previewed a new-generation 5 model, though this was clearly premature, having been forced on the company by leaks. Effectively this was a 1985 car, which actually went on sale in the UK in February 1985.

Compared with the original type of 5, the new car looked virtually the same, if a little smoother and better

equipped inside, but it had a transverse engine installation instead of the inline engines/transmissions used from 1972–84.

As expected, there was to be a wide choice of four-cylinder engines, petrol and diesel. This range would eventually be supplanted by the Clio, but versions of the so-called *Supercinque* were still being built in the mid-1990s, more than a decade after the shape had been launched.

Rolls-Royce: A long-wheelbase six-door limousine version of the Silver Spur was announced, the conversion having been engineered by Robert Jankel Design. It added no less than 36 inches to the length of the already massive car.

Rover: BL signalled its decision to promote and boost the Rover marque name by replacing the Honda-based Triumph Acclaim by a new-generation Honda-based Rover 200.

Except that this was based on a new platform, with different hard-edged styling (almost identical to the latest Honda Civic saloon), and had Civic/CRX-type 1.3-litre engines, this was really an update of the Triumph Acclaim. BL stylists had worked hard to give it a patina of 'Rover' features in the cabin, and it began to appeal to an older generation of drivers, even though they had wanted a Rover but in fact had been given a slightly Anglicized Honda. BL's marketing chiefs, however, had hit the bull's-eye, for this car was a great commercial success.

Saab: After a long gestation, the new 9000 Turbo model (the first of the pan-European Type 4 machines to be unveiled) was finally introduced. Although the 175bhp 16-valve engine had already been seen in top-of-the-range 900s, the rest of the car was completely new. Built around a bigger platform/monocoque (as a five-door hatchback at first, though four-door saloon versions would follow), it was the first four-stroke Saab to have the engine transversely-mounted; a top speed of 136mph was claimed.

Seat: The Spanish manufacturer, which had been freed of previous links with Fiat, started producing own-brand models, notably the ItalDesign-styled Ibiza in the summer of 1984. As expected, this was a front-wheel-drive car with a transversely-positioned engine of 1.1 or 1.5 litres, both units having been developed with advice from Porsche. Although not yet on sale in the UK, the first imports were forecast for 1985.

Skoda: Still struggling to improve the Estelle's image, the Czech company introduced the Series 2 early in the year, having wider tracks. modified suspension settings and some detail style changes.

Subaru: Although still light-years away from the fire-breathing, rally-winning image which it would develop in the 1990s, Subaru continued to introduce new models.

For 1985, there was a new L-series range, which was strongly based on the existing flat-four-engined chassis, though at first only with front-wheel drive. Four-wheel-drive versions, and body derivatives other than the original four-door saloon, would soon follow.

Talbot: Traditionalists sobbed into their warm beer in October when they saw that special editions of the Talbot Solara and Alpine models were launched carrying the names Minx and Rapier. Mechanically there were no changes, and the revival of ancient Hillman and Sunbeam model names seemed to do nothing for the cars' prospects.

Toyota: Early in 1984 the Carina II was launched, a transverse-engined front-wheel-drive replacement for the original Carina. This was always a rare car in the UK because Toyota concentrated on selling its smaller models.

The first of the mid-engined MR2 sports coupes was shown at the NEC motor show in October, with British deliveries promised for early 1985. Like the old Fiat X1/9, which had clearly inspired it, the MR2 used a transverse engine/transmission package from a front-wheel-drive Toyota (in this case a 'hot' Corolla), but mounted behind the two-seater cabin.

Triumph: To the great relief of all true Triumph enthusiasts, the marque name was killed-off in mid-year when the Japanese-inspired Acclaim was dropped, to be replaced by a second-generation Honda, though this car

would be badged as a Rover 200.

TVR: The Tasmin range continued to expand, and from the autumn yet another flagship, the 390i, went on sale. Like the 350i, this used mainly Rover SD1 engine/transmission technology, though the 390i had a fuel-injected 3.9-litre engine which was supplied to TVR by Andy Rouse.

Vauxhall: After a life of less than five years, the original Astra (or Opel Kadett) was dropped, to be replaced by the second-generation car in September. This used the same basic platform, suspension and chassis layout, and there was the same wide choice of engines and transmissions. The original range included 1.2, 1.3, 1.6 and 1.8-litre petrol engines, plus the 1.6-litre diesel.

In what was purely a rebadging move – for the cars were technically little changed and were still built in West Germany – the Opel Senator became the Vauxhall Senator. There was a choice of 2.5-litre or 3-litre six-cylinder engines, both with fuel injection.

Volkswagen: The Golf II range went on sale in the UK in February, with the eagerly-awaited 112bhp/1.8-litre Golf GTi II following in April.

After the launch of the Golf II, the company announced the Jetta II four-door saloon. Although they went to great lengths to emphasize that the Jetta was not simply a booted Golf, that is almost precisely what it was.

Volvo: The old 240/260 range was drastically slimmed (more estate cars than saloons remained), but at the same time the 740 (four-cylinder) branch of the new 7-series range continued to expand.

For 1985 there would be carburettor-engined and fuel-injection types and eventually a turbocharged model.

Yugo: The Jugoslavian marque added to its range with the 55GLS, a bespoilered and larger-engined version of the 45.

Industrial developments

As part of its privatization programme, the British Government decided to hive

off Jaguar from BL – and as soon as rumours about this began to spread, a number of corporate buyers expressed interest. The Government, however, was determined to release this company to 'popular capitalism', made sure that no company could hold more than 15 per cent of the equity, and retained a 'Golden Share' – meaning effective control – for the foreseeable future.

Flotation was announced in the spring, but shares went on the market in July. By that time Jaguar was turning a pre-tax profit of £50 million (in 1983), a figure which would rise to £91.5 in 1984. Shares which were sold at 165p each soon soared to a large premium.

This was also the period when the volume cars section of BL became generally known as Austin-Rover, with company spokesmen agreeing that these were the only two marque names they wanted to promote in the future.

After dithering for more than three years over whether or not to build, and if so where, Nissan finally opted to build a brand-new car assembly plant at Washington, near Sunderland, in the north-east of England.

Technical developments

Perhaps not directly linked to automotive technology – but cars were important to it – was the development of portable (cellular) telephone networks. Using hundreds of radio masts dotted around the country (initially close to motorways and main roads), and computer-sensed transfer of signals from one mast to another as the subscriber drove along, the cellular system would soon revolutionize telephone usage in Britain.

Vodaphone was one of the pioneers, stating that it would be open for business during 1985, but a rival organization, Cellnet, followed shortly afterwards.

Sinclair C5 – a colossal flop

The rumours of Sir Clive Sinclair's forthcoming 'people's car' had been circulating for months, and the established motor industry had been somewhat concerned. Sir Clive was a people's champion, pollution-free electric power was fashionable, and Lotus Engineering had been consulted – what could go wrong?

When the motoring press was introduced to the C5 in December they were staggered. They were even more appalled when test drives began early in 1985. The C5 runabout, in a nutshell, was awful. As one wag commented: 'If this is the answer, it must have been a damned silly question!'.

The C5 was a travesty of a machine, not even a car but a tiny open single-seater three-wheeler, powered by a rear-mounted electric motor produced by a washing machine company, with pedal power to assist, all built up in an ex-Hoover factory in South Wales. It was very slow – with a top speed of 15mph – and with a range in ideal conditions of only 24 miles it was almost totally impractical.

Priced at £399, it was a complete non-starter. Sir Clive had hoped to sell 500,000 C5s a year, but only 9,000 had been made and only half of these sold (many as curiosities) when the project was abandoned in the middle of 1985 and the receiver called in by October. By that time Sinclair Vehicles had debts of £6.4 million. This meant that the loss on each £399 C5 was actually £711!).

It took ages for the balance of production to be sold, and 10 years later, in the mid-1990s, it was still possible to buy brand-new C5s, packaged and ready to be powered up. So much for the so-called caring generation.

Men of Influence

Sir John Egan

Although he was little known when he arrived at Jaguar in 1980, John Egan soon became the darling of Fleet Street, who dubbed him 'the man who saved Jaguar'. Throughout the 1980s, in fact, Egan was as powerful a Jaguar figurehead as Sir William Lyons had ever been (the two kept in close contact), and masterminded the privatization of the company in 1984.

Before joining Jaguar, John Egan (born in 1939) had completed impressive spells with BL's Unipart division, and later with Massey Ferguson. Then, to quote Sir Michael Edwardes' book *Back from the Brink*:

'Early in 1980 I suggested to Ray Horrocks and Berry Wilson that John Egan...whom we had failed to recruit the previous year, might be worth approaching again. Between them they very quickly had John Egan in the top job at Jaguar reporting to Ray...he rejoined the company in April during a strike at Jaguar over a grading issue, and immediately became deeply involved in the negotiations. Bridges were built with the workforce from that first day...'

Although Egan had an uphill struggle, not least in convincing unions and suppliers that he *would* close down the business if quality and labour relations did not improve, he turned the business round. Helped along by a particularly vigorous public image campaign, he convinced the world (particularly the North American one) that Jaguar was on the way back.

He was Jaguar's chief executive until 1984, when the company was hived-off from the rest of BL and privatized, then for a short time he was managing director under Hamish Orr-Ewing's chairmanship. After Orr-Ewing stood down in March 1985, though, Egan was back as the undisputed boss of Jaguar, a position he would hold until 1990.

During his time in charge, he masterminded the launch of the new-generation XJ6 range (the XJ40 cars), the purchase of Whitley as a technical centre, the setting-up of a pressings venture in Telford, the support of Tom Walkinshaw's ambitious TWR racing enterprise – and the evolution of the XJ220 supercar.

Until 1988 he seemed to keep every possible ball in the air, but as sales and profits collapsed thereafter he was happy to receive approaches from General Motors and later Ford. After the Ford takeover of 1989 it was clear that he would not stay for long as a member of the Ford empire.

Amicably, it seems, he left Jaguar in mid-1990, soon becoming chief executive of the British Airports Authority, where once again he presided over a period of great expansion.

1985

Once again the Chancellor's Budget hit hard at the motorist. Annual Vehicle Excise Duty rose again, this time to £100, while petrol taxation was raised so that the average price of a gallon of four-star became 203.6p from late March (or 44.8p/litre in mid-1990s parlance). Major increases were also made to the benefit-in-kind taxation on drivers with company-owned cars, though the capacity limits – 1.3 and 1.8 litres – were unchanged.

Even so, in Britain new car sales jumped to a new all-time record, with more than 1.9 million leaving the showrooms during the year. UK production was still flat (but everyone was holding their breath to see what effect the new Nissan factory would have in the future), while no fewer than 1.07 million imported cars were sold – a market share of 56 per cent.

There was, however, one very significant increase. Diesel-engined cars were becoming much more popular, for more than 66,000 had been sold, compared with a 1984 figure of 45,000.

The most important marketing trend was that a positive flood of new models had appeared from the Far East (Japan in particular, but also from Malaysia and South Korea). The motor manufacturers in what became known as the Pacific Rim countries sensed that there was a good deal of market expansion to come, which they were gearing up to meet, cutting model cycles to no more than four years.

This was an aggressive and (in the short term) successful strategy, but as the market turned down in the early 1990s, these companies would also have to trim back their activities.

New models

AC: Although production of the 3000ME had moved to Scotland a year earlier, with a new Alfa Romeo-engined derivative promised, this project soon collapsed. Virtually no Ford-engined 3000MEs were built in Scotland, while the Alfa-engined car was abandoned before a single car was delivered. During October a receiver was called in, and the marque went into suspended animation.

Nothing more would be heard from AC for some years, then Ford bought up the rights, subsequently sold them to Brian Angliss, who put a new front-engined Ace into production in the early 1990s.

Alfa Romeo: Named to celebrate the Italian company's 75th Anniversary, the new 75 saloon range, introduced in May, was a direct replacement for the long-running Giulietta models.

Like the ousted Giulietta, the new 75 used a modified version of the car's platform, and therefore had a front-mounted engine, a rear-mounted gearbox/final-drive unit and de Dion rear suspension. There was a big choice of four-cylinder twin-cam engines and the big V6, though the entry-level 1.6-litre cars were never sold in the UK. The new car's style was an in-house design and included the same curious broken-back waistline feature as on the 33.

The four-wheel-drive estate car version of the 1.5-litre boxer-engined 33 also went on sale in the spring.

Aston Martin: Early in the year the company made a deal with Zagato, of Italy, for a limited run of 50 very fast coupes based on the Vantage platform and running gear.

All 50 were sold – after hefty deposits had been demanded and paid – before a single car was delivered or even the final price settled. The final Zagato was neat enough except for the bonnet-line being so low that a sizeable bonnet bulge was needed to clear the engine air cleaner.

Bentley: Continuing its move up-market, the company announced the Turbo R in May, being a development of the Mulsanne Turbo with stiffened-up suspension and more responsive handling, but with no more performance than before.

BMW: Several new derivatives of the 3-series range were added in the autumn, though only two of them were scheduled for sale in the UK.

The 325i was like the 323i, but with a 171bhp 2.5-litre version of the straight-six engine. Once available in the UK, from October, it was a direct replacement for the 323i model.

The 325iX (originally called 325-4) was a four-wheel-drive version of the 325i, using the same 2.5-litre engine, but having a very similar four-wheel-drive conversion as that engineered for the Ford Sierra XR4x4. This was logical, for FF Developments had been consulted by both firms when the system was evolving.

A new-generation M5 model made its debut in February, having the same type of 286bhp/3.5-litre six-cylinder engine as the M635CSi coupe, along with firmed-up suspension and better equipment.

Citroen: In the Visa, the new 1.77-litre diesel replaced the earlier 1.36-litre type, the new engine now being specified for a whole variety of cars in the Citroen and Peugeot ranges.

During the autumn, a five-door estate version of the BX range was added to the line-up.

The CX range, which was already 11 years old, was further modified with a new nose and the addition of a 115bhp/2.2-litre engine to fill in the gap between the 2-litre and 2.5-litre power units.

Daihatsu: A replacement for the original Domino appeared in Japan in August (sales would begin in the UK in the autumn of 1986), this being a rather upright, tall and narrow front-wheel-drive hatchback. The engine, though still tiny at 846cc, was considerably larger than that of the original Domino.

The Charade range was expanded with the arrival of a 46bhp turbodiesel engine.

Ferrari: The best-selling 308GTB/GTS models were dropped in the autumn, to be replaced by the near-identical looking 328 types. These had larger (3,185cc) V8 engines with 270bhp, and would take this long-running model forward for a further four seasons before it was replaced by the 348GTB.

The only front-engined four-seater saloon in the range, which had looked virtually the same since its launch in 1972, was updated yet again in March, become the 412i, with yet more power and an enlarged engine – 340bhp and 4,942cc.

Fiat: A year after the Lancia Thema was previewed, Fiat finally launched the very similar-under-the-skin Croma hatchback, this being the third version of the pan-European Type 4 model to reach the showrooms.

The Croma shared the same basic platform as the Thema and had a similar choice of engines – twin-cam and diesel (though the diesels were never to be sold in the UK). The major structural difference, of course, was that the Croma was a five-door hatch, whereas the Lancia was a four-door saloon.

Although the Croma started its career amid great corporate enthusiasm, it was to be no more successful than many other larger-engined Fiats had been in previous decades. British sales would begin in 1986, but would die away to a trickle within four years.

The Uno Turbo appeared in April, this being a re-engineered and much more powerful version of the three-door Uno hatchback. Power was boosted to 105bhp.

Later in the year the mainstream Uno range was also updated by the fitment of the new 999cc FIRE engine in place of the old 907cc unit.

Ford: The new-style Granada range – smooth five-door hatchbacks with suspension and other chassis components based on those of the Sierra, were revealed in March. With structures totally different from the previous Granadas, the new cars offered a big choice of engines, from 90bhp/1.8-litre to 150bhp/2.8-litre. New-type, enlarged, V6 engines were already known to be on the way, though these would not be ready until 1987.

A 4x4 version (see details of the Sierra XR4x4, below) was also revealed in the autumn, and was only available with the most powerful 2.8-litre V6 engine. At the end of the year this new range was voted European Car of the Year by a large jury of European journalists.

Although it would be more than a year before deliveries actually began, Ford stunned the world with the preview of its sensational Sierra RS Cosworth model in March 1985, which had the largest free-standing rear spoiler/aerofoil ever seen on a road car. Intended to be the basis of a Group A racecar for Touring Car events, it combined the normal Sierra three-door structure with a newly-developed 204bhp/2-litre Cosworth engine, which might have had a Pinto engine cylinder block, but was other-

wise entirely special, complete with a 16-valve twin-cam head and turbo-charging.

With a top speed of 150mph in standard form, and with the possibility of more than 300bhp in racecar tune, this was clearly a very promising tool. It would not begin its works competition career, however, until homologated in 1987.

In the spring, the Sierra gained two new models – a 115bhp fuel-injected version of the 2-litre rear-drive car, and a new five-door XR4x4, which combined the engine of the XR4i (which had been dropped) with a four-wheel-drive installation, which was based on the FF Developments system and had two viscous-coupling limited-slip differentials. The same four-wheel-drive system, or developments of it, would be used on several Fords built in the next decade, including the Sierra and Escort RS Cosworths.

Honda: The most important new Honda of the year was a new-generation Accord family comprising saloons and a very smart sporting estate model known as the Aerodeck. This third-generation Accord would eventually spawn off a new type of Prelude.

The entirely new platform accommodated new-type coil-spring/wishbone suspension at front and rear, and a 2-litre version of the three-valve engine which had hitherto only been seen in 1.8-litre form.

This engine, too, found its way into the 1976-model Preludes, which were facelifted, but retained the same basic cabin as before.

Although it would not be sold in the same quantities, the new Legend (previewed in October) was commercially important. Not only was it the first Honda to use a new family of four-cam V6 engines (allied to front-wheel drive), it was also the sister car of the Rover 800s, which would not actually be seen until the summer of 1986. For political reasons, the Legend would not go on sale in the UK until October 1986, after the Rover 800 appeared.

Dipping its toe into the four-wheel-drive market, the company introduced an all-wheel-driven version of the Shuttle five-door estate car early in the year. Like normal front-drive Shuttles, this had a 12-valve 1.3-litre engine.

The Quintet Integra was introduced

in March 1985 (UK sales would begin the following year), this being a front-drive five-door hatchback, with smooth lines and a choice of 1.5 or 1.6-litre engines, which fitted neatly between the smaller Civic and larger Accord models.

Hyundai: The South Korean manufacturer finally joined the front-wheel-drive brigade with the launch of the second-generation Pony, which still used Mitsubishi engines, this time transversely-mounted.

Isuzu: This Japanese manufacturer announced that it intended to start selling cars in the UK in 1986, and that the first model would be the Piazza coupe.

The Piazza Turbo, with its 150bhp/2-litre engine, was then launched in the UK in October, with deliveries beginning during the winter. However, although the front-engine/rear-drive 2+2-seater coupe by ItalDesign was smart enough, it hid the use of a modified 1970s-type Opel Kadett chassis platform, the style itself being a development of the Ace of Spades show car which ItalDesign had revealed as long ago as 1979. Not surprisingly, the Piazza was a marketing failure in the UK, and at one time it was branded 'the worst car in Japan'.

Jaguar: It was mix-and-match time at Jaguar, for in July the company combined the modern XJ-S cabriolet body style with the latest version of the 5.3-litre V12 engine, this being rated at 295bhp. Even with a slightly less aerodynamic body style than the normal coupe, the V12 cabriolet had a top speed of around 150mph.

Lada: The first official pictures of a car later known as the Samara were revealed in January, though the first examples would not reach the UK until the end of 1987.

The new Samara went into production later in 1986, proving to be almost standard 'Euro-box', with a transversely-mounted engine, front-wheel drive and a three-door hatchback body style. The Russians had produced their own body style – a neat and unadorned shape – but Porsche had advised on the development of the new family of overhead-cam engines.

Lamborghini: The amazing mid-mounted V12-engined Countach was made even more exciting from March with the launch of the 5000 *quattrovalvole* version, with four-valves-per-cylinder heads and an engine enlarged to 5.2 litres, peak power output becoming 455bhp at a spine-tingling 7,000rpm.

With a claimed top speed of more than 180mph, maybe this was an impractical car for ordinary usage, but to the hundreds of rich men who queued up to buy such status, that was not an issue. It was the sheer presence of the Countach which counted for so much.

Lancia: The Italian company announced a chunky three-door hatchback model called the Y10 (inevitably, this was soon nicknamed 'White Hen'...), the smallest-ever car to carry a Lancia badge.

Although the platform and the upright style were unique, the transverse engine, transmission and basic front suspension were all shared with Fiat models like the Panda and Uno, while there was a unique type of dead beam axle rear suspension.

The Y10, in fact, was the first Fiat Group car to use a new generation of high-economy four-cylinder overhead-camshaft engines in the FIRE family (Fully Integrated Robotised Engine), a 45bhp/1-litre unit.

Land Rover: To match the increased-size diesel engine introduced in 1984, the four-cylinder petrol engine was now increased to the same 2.5-litre capacity, power and torque figures being increased by 8 per cent.

Lotus: The Excel, whose roots were in the Elite of 1974, carried on for 1986 with an update to SE specification, with a higher-powered (180bhp) version of the 2.2-litre 16-valve engine.

Marcos: A convertible version of the Rover V8-engined Mantula was introduced in October. This was the first drop-head Marcos to have been put on sale.

Mazda: The third-generation 323 model appeared in mid-summer, a front-wheel-drive car based on an all-new and rather angular hatchback body style. Both 1.3 and 1.5-litre engines were available, while a 1.6-litre – normally-aspirated or turbocharged – was also promised.

Later in the year a turbocharged twin-cam 1.6-litre engine (with 132bhp DIN) was mated to four-wheel-drive transmission and introduced as the top-of-the-range derivative of the new 323 family. This type would become a competent, if not outstanding, Group A rally car.

An all-new second-generation RX-7 coupe was introduced in September, having a new platform and two-door sports hatchback style and a 175bhp/2,354cc version of the famous twin-rotor Wankel engine. The new RX-7 was faster and considerably heavier than the original variety. Although it sold very well in the USA (its principal market), it was not a success in the UK, mainly because of its cost.

Mercedes-Benz: Entry-level 190s had been launched with only 90bhp in 1982, but the power of the 2-litre carburetted engine was increased to 105bhp in the winter of 1984/85.

A 2.6-litre six-cylinder engine (with 160bhp) was added to the 190 range from the end of the year, though British customers had to wait until 1987 to get their hands on this car.

The 185bhp Cosworth-designed twin-cam 2.3 litre-engined 190E 2.3-16 went on sale in the UK in mid-year at £21,045. For this price there was the combination of a 140mph top speed, flashing acceleration and traditional Mercedes-Benz quality.

The 560SEL arrived in the autumn (with a 300bhp/5.6-litre version of the V8 engine) as a long-wheelbase flagship example of the S-class saloon family.

At the Frankfurt motor show the company also showed its first four-wheel-drive installation – 4-Matic – which it proposed to use in some of the medium-sized models.

MG: In April, the Montego Turbo saloon was announced, fitted with a 150bhp 2-litre O-series engine. It was a very fast car, but it was also unruly, for there was a ferocious amount of torque steer from the front-wheel-drive installation.

This, and the difficulty of establishing the MG badge as credible on what was otherwise a very mundane car, meant that sales were disappointing.

Mitsubishi: The Cordia coupe was dropped briefly from the British range during the summer, then came back in the autumn with a new engine, a 135bhp 1.8-litre turbocharged unit almost identical to that being fitted to the 200ZX sports coupe.

The fast-and-furious Starion coupe, originally introduced to the UK in 1982, was improved with a more powerful (177bhp) intercooled turbocharged engine. At the same time, anti-lock braking was standardized.

Morgan: By its own modest standards, the relaunch of a model called the Plus 4 was a big move. Basically, though, the new car was merely a 4/4 to which a 122bhp/2-litre twin-cam Fiat engine (and its related five-speed gearbox) had been grafted, for the styling of the car was not changed.

Nissan: A new-generation Sunny appeared in Japan in October, with UK deliveries beginning in 1986. Like its predecessor, this was a car with hard-edged styling, front-wheel drive and a variety of engines. Cars didn't come much more boring than this one...

A new Auster model was shown at the Tokyo motor show in November, and it was made clear that this would be the car to be produced at the new British Nissan factory in County Durham from 1986. *(For further details, see the Nissan entry in the 1986 section.)*

A new-generation Laurel, with 2.4-litre straight-six engine and rather angular four-door saloon styling, went on sale in the UK in the autumn. At a time when other makers were turning to more rounded 'aero' styles, Nissan's liking of sharp-edged cars was making them look rather old-fashioned.

Opel: A specially converted cabriolet version of the Ascona model went on sale in the UK with a choice of 90bhp/1.6-litre or 115bhp/1.8-litre engines. A Vauxhall version, technically identical, was more popular.

Peugeot: The most important new Peugeot of the year was the 309 saloon, which was designed to replace the old Talbot Horizon (which was dropped).

Although it had a very ordinary style, not nearly as curvaceous or as attractive as the 205, it shared a lengthened version of that car's platform, the same type of suspension (including transverse torsion bar rear springs) and was immediately available with a wide choice of the 205's engines – 1.1, 1.3 and 1.6-litre four-cylinder petrol units. It was also known that a GTI version and the ubiquitous Peugeot-Citroen diesel unit would be added at a later date.

The 309s would be built in France and at the Ryton-on-Dunsmore factory in the UK (where they took over from the old Horizon/Alpine/Solara types).

The 505 range was given a mid-life facelift in the summer, and for the first time this car was available with an entry-level 1.8-litre engine, while the 2-litre engine was power-boosted to 108bhp.

Porsche: The 944 Turbo was introduced during the spring, this being a comprehensively re-engineered and developed turbocharged version of the 944 2+2-seater coupe. The new car's engine produced 220bhp from 2.5 litres, and the top speed was claimed to be over 150mph.

Later in the year there was a big package of changes for the 924/944 models, which included the arrival of the 924S to replace the 924 (the change being based around the use of a detuned – 150bhp – 2.5-litre 944 engine), and the showing of prototype 16-valve twin-cam heads for the 944 (which would eventually turn it into the 944S) and a convertible version of the 944.

The 911 Turbo was further improved with a 330bhp engine, while an optional front-end style, which included hidden headlamps, also became available.

The four-wheel-drive 959 supercar, which had a 450bhp twin-turbo version of the 2.85-litre Porsche flat-six engine which had been seen several times since 1983, was still undergoing extensive testing and was still not ready for sale.

Proton: This Malaysian-built car was first revealed to the British public, although UK sales were not yet organized. There was a great deal of hype about new cars from a new car-making nation, but it was easy to see that the new Proton was in fact little more than a slightly-modified Mitsubishi Lancer.

Range Rover: Even though it was now 15 years old, development of this car continued. In October, a 165bhp fuel-injected version of the engine became available, and there was even more to come, a diesel version being slated for 1986.

Reliant: The old-style Scimitar GTE/GTC models were dropped during the year as Reliant concentrated on the newer and much smaller SS range of sportscars.

Renault: The second-generation front-wheel-drive 5 hatchback (dubbed the *Supercinque* in France) went on sale in the UK in February with transversely-positioned front-drive engines ranging from 42bhp/956cc to 72bhp/1,397cc. Five-door versions followed later in the year.

In November a new range, the front-wheel-drive 21 model, was introduced to take over from the old 18. By dipping into its corporate parts bin for various major components, Renault had developed this car in double-quick time – it was the first (and, even 10 years later, the only) car to be sold with transverse *and* in-line four-cylinder engines!

This was achieved by using the transverse 1.7-litre engine from the 9 and 11 types, then the in-line 2-litre and 2.1-litre diesels previously found in 18s. Although the overall silhouette was always the same, there were differences in wheelbase (transverse-engined cars had a longer-wheelbase), yet the overall lengths were the same.

In March, a much under-estimated car, the Alpine V6 GT, was introduced. This Renault-badged model was a direct replacement for the old Alpine-Renault A310-V6, which had never been marketed in the UK.

Like the Porsche 911 for which it was an obvious competitor, the Alpine had a steel backbone chassis, a 160bhp/2.85-litre version of the familiar PRV V6 engine mounted in the extreme tail, and a curvaceous 2+2-seater coupe body in glassfibre. For no very good reason, this car never sold in the numbers that it deserved, for many independent observers felt that it could out-do the Porsche in many ways.

Two more versions of the 25 joined the range, one being a stretched version, the V6-engined Limousine, the other the 25 Turbo, which featured a

182bhp/2,458cc development of the familiar V6 engine.

Rover: A 1.6-litre engine was added to the new 200 range, this being rated at 85bhp or 103bhp.

For the last limited-production run of the SD1 Vitesse model, there was originally to be a newly-developed twin-plenum engine with 230bhp, but before the end of the year the sporting camshaft which was necessary was abandoned, and peak power reverted to near the 190bhp level. Very few of these cars appear to have been made, for this engine was developed as an homologation exercise to help the TWR racing Rovers hold out against their latest competition in the European Touring Car Championship.

The company also previewed the new XX joint project with Honda – now to be badged Rover 800 – by talking about, rather than showing it, though the Honda equivalent – the Legend – was introduced in October *(see Honda, above)*. At the same time Rover revealed a new 16-valve twin-cam four-cylinder 2-litre engine, the M16, which was destined for this car and other new Austin-Rover projects.

Seat: The first UK imports of these Spanish-built cars, some still with a lot of Fiat heritage and some with all-new and independent engineering, began in October.

The Malaga was a new model in mid-summer, this being recognizably developed from the bodyshell of the Fiat Regata (Seat had been controlled by Fiat for many years until the 1980s). Larger and more expensive than the all-Spanish Ibiza, the Malaga used a Fiat platform and suspensions allied to the Porsche System four-cylinder engines announced for use in the Ibiza.

The second model in the UK range, the Ibiza, had been introduced in 1984 and featured all-new styling by ItalDesign.

Subaru: The latest L-type range was further improved, not only with the launch of an estate car, but with the as-expected appearance of four-wheel drive. Top of this range was a 130bhp turbocharged version of the 1.8-litre flat-four power unit.

The two-door XT Coupe, a new style from this once-mundane company, was revealed in March. Although this was based on the platform of the latest L-type saloons, and had the same turbocharged 1.8-litre flat-four engine, it had air suspension and a totally original two-door coupe body style. British deliveries began later in the year.

Suzuki: The original Swift had used a sub-1-litre three-cylinder engine, but from March it was joined by the 1.3GS model, with a 1.3-litre four-cylinder derivative of the same basic engine.

Talbot: The French marque, invented by Peugeot in 1979 to wean the market away from the Chrysler models which it had bought, was under sentence of death, for this had not been a successful exercise.

As old models like the Horizon died away, they were replaced by new Peugeots (such as the 309), or simply allowed to wither on the vine. In the UK, the Horizon, the Alpine and the Solara all breathed their last in 1985, while the Samba would die in 1986.

Toyota: A new-generation Starlet appeared during the year, this being a front-wheel-drive car (previous Starlets had front-engine/rear-drive layouts) with a new 999cc overhead-cam engine. Because of quota problems with Japanese cars, this model was only ever available in very limited quantities.

The new-generation Corolla range was fleshed out further with two new hatchbacks – a mundane 74bhp 1.3-litre car and an excitingly-specified 120bhp 1.6-litre twin cam-engined GT.

In the autumn, an entirely new type of Celica GT was introduced in Japan (British sales would begin in a few months' time). This was the first front-wheel-drive/transverse-engined Celica, based on the platform and suspension of the Camry saloon, but with a new 16-valve 2-litre 136bhp engine and a very sleek three-door coupe/hatchback body style.

This Celica would soon form the basis of the Celica GT-Four (four-wheel-drive) machine, which would eventually become an extremely successful rally car; this installation was shown at motor shows during the autumn.

Trans Cat: An attempt was made to market the Portuguese-made and Peugeot diesel-engined 4x4, but the effort soon evaporated, and only a

very few such machines were ever sold in the UK.

Vauxhall: The Carlton range was expanded in the autumn with the addition of a 115bhp 2.2-litre cam-in-head engine to the range.

The Cavalier convertible, technically identical to the Opel Ascona equivalent (see above) was introduced in the autumn, available only with the 1.8 fuel-injected engine.

Volkswagen: This was a year in which VW introduced many derivatives of its current models, but no startlingly new styling. There were new engine and transmission types.

The first of the supercharged Polos was shown in the autumn, this G40 model having a 115bhp 1.3-litre power unit.

The Golf Synchro appeared in September, this being a four-wheel-drive version of the existing front-engined Golf II.

The first of a very widely-used 16-valve 1.8-litre engine was introduced for the Scirocco and Golf GTi 16V models in May. This unit featured a twin-cam cylinder head, one camshaft being driven off the other by gear wheels, and it produced a 'green' 139bhp.

The Santana was dropped after only four years – but this was not a confession of failure as the car was immediately renamed Passat saloon, which in fact was what (technically) it had always been!

Volvo: In October, the staid Swedish company astonished everyone by releasing the 480ES coupe, a new sporting-estate machine of the type made famous by Lancia with the Beta HPE – and by Volvo with the 1800ES.

This three-door sporting hatchback, in fact, was to be built in Holland, and was the first of the 400-series, which used a brand-new platform with front-wheel drive, and was powered by Renault's modern 1.7-litre overhead-cam engine. The 440 and 460 family car types, however, would not be revealed for two more years, and UK deliveries of 480ES models would not begin until 1987.

The original 480ES used a 109bhp engine, but it was already known that a more powerful, turbocharged, version was being developed.

The massive, square-rigged, but impressively practical five-door estate car version of the 740/760 range was unveiled in February, with UK deliveries beginning in October.

Industrial developments

Ford of Europe and Fiat spent much time during the year trying to work out how to merge without losing their individual identities, but eventually gave this up as impossible. The two giant companies then reverted to being bitter rivals, their next encounter being to fight for ownership of Alfa Romeo...

After a great deal of more fruitful negotiation, on the other hand, VW looked set to take a majority share in Seat of Spain, and would soon set about integrating it into the worldwide VW empire. The first move was to start Polo assembly in Spain, but dedicated new cars, based on VW model platforms, could not be readied until the early 1990s.

During the spring, Honda gained planning permission to build a new factory at Swindon on a disused airfield to the north of the town. At first there was only to be a pre-delivery inspection plant, then an engine plant, but bodyshell production and assembly facilities were also planned. This was just the first stage of a massive development, which eventually led to the manufacture of complete cars.

In Italy, the Arna project (the joint Nissan-Alfa Romeo production deal combining the Nissan Cherry with Alfa Romeo boxer engines) rapidly fell apart. Few people, it seems, liked the idea of a good (Alfa Romeo) engine in a very boring (Nissan) car, so the experiment was halted in the winter of 1985/86, production ending in November.

Technical developments

Traction control made its first tentative appearance on BMW and Mercedes-Benz models. ASR (Antrieb schlupf regelung) was almost a mirror image of ABS anti-lock braking in that it used the same type of wheel-speed sensors to detect when wheels began to spin. At this point the electronic brain instructed the engine to reduce power.

As ever, there was still much to do with the refinement of such an intricate system, but by the early 1990s it had gone into mass production and was becoming available, usually as an option, on many middle-class cars.

Meanwhile, four-wheel drive was suddenly appearing as a transmission option on a number of ranges of cars, including the Ford Sierra XR4x4, the BMW 325iX and the Mercedes-Benz 4-Matic. Although the percentage take-up of such systems was always very limited (no more than 5 per cent of a range usually had four-wheel drive), it was to become a very 'hot' marketing feature for the next few years.

Men of Influence

Sir Clive Sinclair

If ever a prototype of the 'Batty Inventor' was needed, Sir Clive Sinclair certainly provided the pattern. Even before the ludicrous C5 car burst on the scene, he was already a well-known inventor.

Born in 1940, he came to specialize in electrical and electronic engineering, setting up his own small firm when he was only 18 years old. He published a survey of transistor receivers in 1959, wrote a British Semiconductor Survey in 1963, then invented the first practical small, hand-held, electronic calculator in the early 1970s.

The calculator was followed by the notorious 'black watch' – an electronic wristwatch which needed to have a button pressed to show off the time – small personal computers more useful for playing games than any more serious purpose and the world's first miniature flat-body TV.

Some of these products made him rich (the calculators and the computers, particularly), but the C5 was a disaster which cost him dear. He did not seem to learn from this mistake – namely that the public did not care for electrically-driven *anything* if it was slow and with a short range – for in the next few years he went on to invent an electrically-powered pedal cycle, and produced an electric-powered add-on pack for normal bikes.

Generously backed by the British Government at critical stages in his career, he seemed to make more money than he lost, and he approached the 1990s with as many ideas (few of them commercially successful) as he had dredged up in the 1980s.

1986

Britain was still developing an economic boom, this being helped along in March by another expansionary Budget in which the main blow on motorists came in increased taxation on cars provided to employees for business use.

At the same time there were proposals that the tax-break limits should be changed from 1.3 and 1.8 litres to 1.4 and 2 litres. This change was actually enacted in 1987, which encouraged fleet-car users to trade up to slightly larger cars.

By this time, what was wrongly called the investment boom in classic cars was under way. Foolish people with more spare money than sense were beginning to bid heavily against each other for desirable classic cars, the result being that notional values rose rapidly. Even so, it would be three years before the bubble burst, precipitating a sudden fall in values.

The M25 motorway, the 117-mile ring around London, was finally completed on October 29. As forecast, almost immediately it was filled with more traffic than it had ever been intended to accept, rush-hour traffic jams became normal (and got worse) – and there were immediate forecasts of widening schemes and the need for a further, outer ring.

New models

Alfa Romeo: The Arna joint project with Nissan having crawled to a dismal end during 1985, all plans for a replacement model were abandoned.

Alpine-Renault: (See Renault, below.)

Aston Martin: After a 13-year break, a fuel-injected version of the famous V8 was reintroduced. The original V8 of 1969 had used a Bosch injection system, but this had been dropped in 1972, to be replaced by Weber carburettors. The latest installation used a Weber-Marelli system, distantly related to that specified for the Ford Sierra RS Cosworth.

Had this system been available a year earlier, the bonnet bulge in the limited-edition Zagato coupe could have been made a lot smaller. The first

of these cars was delivered during the year, priced at £87,000. There was no shortage of demand, especially as the engine was rated at 432bhp and the claimed top speed was way above 180mph.

Audi: In September, a new-generation 80 range was introduced, taking over from the cars which had been on sale for eight years (with more than 3 million examples).

The style and bodyshell were entirely new, more rounded, but with a smaller boot (which instantly drew much criticism and would need to be enlarged), but under the skin the choice of in-line engines, transmissions, front or four-wheel drive and various trim packs was much as before.

Audi made it clear that new-generation 80s would be four-cylinder cars, and that a forthcoming new-generation 90 would embrace the five-cylinder types. Petrol engines varied, therefore, between 75bhp/1.6 litres and 112bhp/1.8 litres, with a 1.6-litre diesel as before.

There were changes to the four-wheel-drive Quattros, a Torsen differential having been fitted to the centre instead of the original simple bevel-gear system. The most interesting technical innovation (as an on-cost option) was Procon Ten – a complex safety installation of wires in tension, which pulled the steering column forward when the car was involved in an accident.

Continuing to juggle their assets, Audi also produced a 1.8-litre, 112bhp, four-cylinder-engined Coupe GT for 1987.

Austin: A new direct-injection four-cylinder diesel engine, which had been developed jointly with Perkins, was unveiled during the year, with a promise that it would be fitted to Maestros and Montegos during 1987 – a promise that had to be broken as more development work was needed. Normally-aspirated and turbocharged versions of this 2-litre unit were already being prepared.

Bentley: (For changes to 1987 models, see Rolls-Royce, below.)

Bitter: The Opel-based coupes and convertibles disappeared during the year as the company hit financial

trouble. In spite of several promises in the years which followed, Bitter never returned.

BMW: The arrival of a second-generation 7-series was a major event for BMW, for the original type had been on the market for eight years and was thoroughly out-of-date by 1976.

Larger and sleeker than the first 7-series, the latest type stuck to the familiar formula of using overhead-cam straight-six cylinder engines and an all-independently suspended chassis, but this time there were only two engines at first – 184bhp/3 litres and 211bhp/3.5 litres.

A brand new V12 engine was briefly previewed at the same time and promised for future use in the new 7-series.

Just as Ford's Sierra RS Cosworth finally arrived in the showrooms, BMW's obvious rival – the M3 – also appeared. Destined to sell better than the Cosworth, and to be equally as successful in saloon car racing, the M3 was always a thoroughly civilized road car.

Based on the normal two-door 3-series shell, the M3 had a revised-slope rear window to aid the aerodynamics, and was powered by a high-revving normally-aspirated 200bhp/2.3-litre four-cylinder twin-cam engine. This was an obvious relative of the famous F1 engines which Brabham had been using for some time, and was therefore expected to be completely 'bomb-proof'.

Although it was only ever available in left-hand-drive form, the M3 soon became a firm favourite among BMW followers in the UK, and there would be even better Evolution versions in the next few years.

During the year an early prototype of the structurally unique Z1 two-seater sportscar was revealed, though UK deliveries were not yet ready to begin. Except for the new and complex rear suspension (which would eventually be seen on BMW family cars), most of this car's running gear was lifted from the 325i. Its main innovation, however, was that the two passenger doors did not swing out or up to open, but slid down into recesses in the monocoque structure.

Citroen: The much-rumoured AX, a small transverse-engined front-wheel-drive car in the hotly contested super-mini hatchback category, arrived in September. Although it was smaller, it would eventually take over from the Visa, but the two cars were produced simultaneously for the next three years, the Visa in diminishing numbers.

Technically, the AX was familiar, though this time with Peugeot-inspired coil-spring suspension at front and rear. However, although the engines carried familiar Peugeot-type bore and stroke dimensions – giving 954, 1,124 and 1,360cc – they were all from the brand new TU family. The obvious difference was that whereas the old Peugeot engines had been installed with the cylinder block lying back 72 degrees, the TUs were installed vertically.

The BX range continued to expand, for in mid-year the 125bhp/1.9-litre GTi model was added, with a claimed top speed of 123mph.

Clan: The much-delayed Clover model – effectively a re-engineered 1970s-style Crusader with an Alfa Romeo boxer flat-four engine behind the seats, and with bodywork changes to accommodate wider wheel tracks – was finally unveiled in March. At £9,200, however, it was an expensive and none-too-well developed proposition, and it died within the year.

Dacia: The company was still struggling to establish its Duster 4x4 models and added a Renault 55bhp/1.6-litre diesel engine to the range from October.

Daihatsu: A new-generation Domino model, replacing the original type withdrawn in 1985, reappeared in 1986, this time with a longer wheelbase, a five-door body style and an 846cc engine.

Daimler: In October, a new-generation car appeared, the 3.6 being a badge-engineered replica of the XJ40-type Jaguar Sovereign.

Evante: This Lincolnshire-conceived two-seater sportscar, at first glance merely a restyled 1960s-type Lotus Elan, but much different under the skin, including a new type of twin-cam engine, was previewed at the end of the year, though it was not yet ready for production, and then only as a kit-car.

Fiat: There was a major update for the Panda model with the fitment of new-generation overhead-camshaft FIRE engines (of 768cc or 999cc), and the use of the modern Lancia Y10 rear suspension, which featured a coil-sprung axle beam with a pivot in the centre of the car. This was almost as 'independent' as the torsion-beam/coil-spring installation currently being chosen by many of the world's manufacturers.

At the same time, the Panda 4x4 was updated, also with the 999cc engine, though its simple leaf-spring rear end was not altered.

Later in the year the company launched a new 60bhp/1.7-litre diesel engine, fitting it to Uno models, and eventually specifying it for later Tipo and Punto ranges.

Ford: The front-wheel-drive Escorts and Orions were given a front-end facelift, a new facia layout and a comprehensive reshuffle of engines, which would carry them on until 1990.

These cars (the Escort was unofficially known as the Mk IV), retained virtually the same chassis, though a new mechanical (rather than electronic) SCS (Stop Control System) by Lucas was standardized on the revised Escort RS Turbo and became optional on all other types.

The 1.3-litre models now used overhead-valve (Valencia-type) engines instead of CVH units, and there was a new 1.4-litre CVH engine, rated at 75bhp.

The Escort RS Turbo, once a limited-production 'homologation special', was reintroduced as a mainstream car, with softer suspension, high gearing and different glassfibre panel cladding, including sills under the doors.

Dipping its toe even further into the limited four-wheel-drive market, the company launched the Sierra 4x4 estate, matching the same running gear and transmission of the XR4x4 to upmarket Ghia trim.

Towards the end of the year, a pair of much-modified 60-degree overhead-valve V6 engines (which had been forecast two years earlier) were revealed. In 130bhp/2.4-litre and 150bhp/2.9-litre forms, these would be standardized in Granada/Scorpio models during the winter of 1986/87.

The long-lived Capri finally dropped out of production at the end of the year. The last car was assembled immediately before Christmas. Since 1969, nearly 1.9 million Capris had been produced.

Honda: The Japanese company signed an agreement with Austin-Rover for Ballades (very similar to Rover 200s) to be built at Longbridge. The first cars were delivered towards the end of 1986, and were mechanically identical to the Rover 200, but with new front-end styles.

Before mid-summer, the CRX coupe was relaunched in the UK, this time with a new 125bhp 16-valve twin-cam engine, which was much more suited to this agile little car.

At the same time the Integra, which had first been seen in Japan in 1985, also went on UK sale with a choice of engines – an 85bhp/1.5-litre and a much more powerful 16-valve 125bhp/1.6-litre.

Isuzu: The Piazza Turbo was selling very slowly, but the importers cheered themselves up by announcing that the Trooper 4x4 model would be imported from 1987.

All this, however, was in vain, as the importing company collapsed into receivership in November, only a year after the sale of Piazzas in the UK had begun. Later it transpired that the original importer *could* have opted to sell Troopers first and Piazzas next, but made the wrong decision... Almost immediately, International Motors of West Bromwich (Robert Edmiston's enterprise, which already imported Subarus and Hyundais) opened talks with the Japanese and in consequence would become official Isuzu importers early in 1987.

Jaguar: When the new-generation XJ6 (coded XJ40) appeared in October it brought few surprises, for the car had been long-rumoured, much-photographed in disguised form and regularly discussed in the motoring press.

In layout it was very similar to the old-type XJ6, which was dropped after an 18-year career, though every detail was different. New-type AJ6 six-cylinder engines – a single-cam 165bhp/2.9-litre and a twin-cam 221bhp/4-litre – were standard, with a choice of Getrag manual or ZF automatic transmissions. From the start, there was a

Daimler equivalent of the 3.6-litre model.

Jeep: In the USA, the Wrangler replaced the old CJ-7, which was historically significant. Although the Wrangler was still recognizably derived from the previous cars, it was the first not to carry a CJ (Civilian Jeep) title.

With a ladder-style chassis, hard leaf-spring front and rear suspension, and functional rather than comfortable accommodation, this was a Jeep in the old style, though now with a choice of GM four-cylinder or own-brand six-cylinder engines and the option of automatic transmission.

There would be no official UK deliveries until the early 1990s, and then only in very limited numbers.

Lamborghini: The massive four-wheel-drive LM model was shown, to the amazement of everyone, who did not expect to see such a cross-country car powered by a 420bhp/7.25-litre four-cam V12 engine.

It was never Type Approved for sale in the UK, though one or two privately-imported examples were seen on (and off!) our roads in the next few years...

Lancia: The much-rumoured Thema 8.32 was finally launched in April, still a front-wheel-drive car, but powered by a charismatic 210bhp 2.9-litre Ferrari V8 engine, as latterly seen in the 308GTB QV sportscars! Naturally, ABS braking was standard, but because no form of traction control had yet been developed, this was sure to be a car with demanding handling in certain conditions!

The four-wheel-drive version of the Prisma, with a 108bhp/1.6-litre twin-cam engine, was shown in April, but this was only a prelude to the much more ferocious Deltas to follow.

These, called Delta HF 4WD, and fitted with a 165bhp version of the same four-wheel-drive system, were launched in May, and immediately became Italian cult cars (in the same way that the Ford Sierra RS Cosworth briefly became *the* car to own in the UK). Fortunately for Lancia, no sooner was the car announced than FISA announced a Group A requirement for World Championship rallying in 1987 and the new Delta 4WD proved to be an ideal basis for Lancia's next rally car! The Delta HF 4WD was the first of a series of amazingly talented and surefooted Deltas, which became Integrales for 1988, and were given 16-valve engines for 1990.

Land Rover: Turbocharged versions of the 2.5-litre diesel engine, producing 85bhp, were introduced for Ninety/One-Ten models towards the end of the year.

Lotus: From October, the Esprit Turbo was improved by the fitment of a more powerful (215bhp) engine, which had 10 per cent more torque than before and could be run on 95 octane unleaded fuel.

Maserati: Development of the V6-engined Biturbo continued, with the launch of a *six*-valve cylinder head (incorporating three inlets and three exhausts) for the 420S. For British enthusiasts, though, there was even better news – imports of this Italian marque were to begin again at the beginning of 1987, four years after previous sales had stopped. The concession would then change hands *again* – and would shortly afterwards fail.

Mercedes-Benz: In March, British deliveries of the latest S-class cars began. Although there were virtually no style changes, the use of 3-litre 'six' and 4.2-litre V8 engines was a novelty.

At the same time, new 300SL and 420SL varieties of the long-running SL two-seater roadster models were also phased in.

Mitsubishi: Just before the end of 1986, the Shogun 4x4 range was updated, notably with a more torquey and larger-capacity diesel engine and an automatic transmission option.

Morgan: In a major innovation by its own conservative standards, the company started treating its wooden body skeletons with Cuprinol, to delay the rotting which tended to occur after the wood was repeatedly wetted.

Nissan: The 'British Bluebird' finally appeared in the spring, less than two years after construction of the factory in County Durham had been started; the first cars were completed in April.

In spite of a great deal of pre-launch speculation and some hype from Nissan, with the Auster name mentioned in 1985 proving something of a red herring, the cars being built at Washington were no more than slightly updated versions of 1984-generation Japanese Bluebirds.

There was a choice of 1.6, 1.8, 1.8 Turbo and 2-litre petrol and 2-litre diesel four-cylinder engines, packaged inside four-door saloon or five-door hatchback styles.

Even while capped by the UK-Japanese gentlemen's agreement, which had limited sales since the late 1970s, Nissan was currently selling over 100,000 cars a year in Britain because British-built cars did not count towards the quota, and the company was looking for an increase in sales in the coming years.

A new-generation Sunny (badged Pulsar in Japan and some other countries) appeared in mid-year, British sales beginning in the autumn. Like its predecessors, this was a very mundane front-wheel-drive car, sold with several engines (1.3, 1.6 and 1.7-litre diesel) and a choice of body styles – saloon, coupe and estate.

As already indicated, the Arna joint project with Alfa Romeo had finally come to an end, and all thoughts of producing a second-generation model were abandoned.

Opel: Although a brand-new Omega range (also sold as a Vauxhall Carlton) was announced in August, it was never to be sold in the UK. The Opel badge, in fact, was set to disappear from Britain in 1988, two decades after postwar imports had begun.

Peugeot: The very chic little 205 cabriolet was unveiled early in the year. At almost the same time, the exciting little 205GTI's engine was uprated from 105 to 115bhp, making a good car even better. But that was only an interim measure, for the 130bhp/1.9-litre GTI engine was shown in October and was added to the 205GTI and (eventually) to the 309GTI models.

Further downmarket, though, a 1.9-litre diesel engine was also phased in to the 309 range, and would soon find use in other models.

During the year the 604 model was finally dropped, so to partially replace it, a 2.8-litre V6-engined version of the 505 was launched, having 170bhp and a top speed of more than 125mph.

Porsche: Still there were no new-shape cars from Porsche (whose last innovation had been the 928 of 1977, nearly a decade earlier), but the company continued to upgrade its running gear, mainly with more powerful engines.

The 944S arrived in July, this being the first 944 to use a twin-overhead-camshaft version of the 2.5-litre four-cylinder engine. With 190bhp and a very impressive torque curve, this was an engine with a lot of potential locked inside.

The 928 series moved up to 928 Series 4 (there never was an S3 in the UK, this name having been reserved, internally, for the more recent USA-market cars), with a 320bhp/5-litre version of the V8 engine, which had twin overhead camshafts and 32 valves.

In the autumn, the 911 Club Sport was announced, a limited-edition, lightweight version of the normal 911, coming complete with a 231bhp/3.2-litre flat-six engine. The weight was down and so was the price – to £34,390.

Because the four-wheel-drive 959 had originally been conceived as a 400-off Group B car for competition use, it virtually found itself out of a job after Group B rallying was banned from the end of 1986. Even so, the first deliveries of 959s were made at the end of the year.

Range Rover: The long-awaited diesel engine option appeared in April, not with a version of the V8 on which so much abortive time and money had been spent, but with a four-cylinder 2.4-litre VM unit from Italy, which was turbocharged and produced 112bhp. This engine was much criticized for a lack of low-end torque (the BBC's *Wheelbase* team being the loudest complainers).

Reliant: Sales of the Scimitar SS had got off to a slow start, mainly because the chosen Ford engines were not powerful enough. To rectify this, Reliant launched the 1800Ti version in mid-year, using a 135bhp Nissan 1.8-litre turbocharged engine, which was the same as that used in the contemporary Nissan Silvia ZX coupe. The new car's top speed was claimed to be over 125mph – but it still did little for the Scimitar's image.

Although the Scimitar GTE sporting estate had been dropped, there was interest in its revival, so Reliant spent months negotiating the sale of the tooling and the manufacturing rights to other concerns. A deal proposed by Peter Boam and John McCauley, who planned to put the car back into production in Nottingham, failed during the winter of 1986/87.

Renault: Turbocharged versions of the 1.4-litre overhead-valve engine were introduced for the 5 and the 9, adding to those already available in the 11. Soon afterwards, the 5 range was given the 1.6-litre diesel which was already being used in the 9 and 11 models.

What most enthusiasts still knew as the Alpine-Renault GTA was launched in Britain as the Renault GTA (the Alpine trademark being reserved for use by Peugeot-Talbot in the UK), with a choice of rear-mounted normally-aspirated or turbocharged V6 engines.

With very high performance and remarkably civilized handling characteristics, the GTAs deserved to sell better than they ever did, especially as only 25 specialist Renault dealers were appointed to look after them. But unhappily for Renault, they were no match for the Porsche 911s in the marketplace, even though those cars were considerably more expensive.

After only a short and presumably unsuccessful run, the long-wheelbase 25 Limousine was quietly abandoned – only 800 having been sold, of which 10 had been sold in the UK.

After a 25-year career, the 4 estate car was finally dropped from the British market, though it was still in production in France.

Rolls-Royce: In October, the existing range (along with the equivalent Bentleys) were upgraded with the standardization of fuel-injected engines and ABS brakes. The engines were more powerful than before – variously from 10 to 22 per cent, depending on the model – but following tradition, the company declined to release figures.

Rover: Nearly a year after the Honda Legend on which it was based had gone on sale, the Rover 800 range was finally ready. Even so, some derivatives announced in July were not actually in the showrooms before the end of the year, a problem which did nothing for the company's credibility at the time.

Like the Legend, with which it shared a platform, front-wheel-drive layout and much of the inner structure, the 800 was a big four-door saloon. Engines were transversely mounted, there being a choice of 120 or 140bhp twin-cam H16 'fours', or the smooth and high-revving 173bhp 2.5-litre Honda V6, which also had twin overhead camshafts per bank.

Whereas Honda was already planning to displace the Legend by another model before the end of the 1980s, Rover was to stick with this layout (heavily facelifted, and with several extra engine choices) for a full decade.

Seat: The Ibiza range was expanded – downwards – by the offer of the ancient Fiat-based 903cc engine instead of the modern Porsche-influenced overhead-cam types which had been introduced at first.

Sterling: For record purposes, I note here that Rover's 800 was to be marketed in the USA as a Sterling, through a new series of dealerships.

Suzuki: The front-wheel-drive Alto was added to the list of superminis on the European market.

The latest version of the Swift hatchback was the GTi, which was fitted with a 101bhp/1.3-litre 16-valve twin-cam engine. This quite transformed what had been an unexceptional hatchback into a real little fire-breather. British sales began in November.

The company also started to sell the small SJ400 Santana 4x4 models in the UK, using cars manufactured in a Spanish factory. Deliveries would begin in 1987 (*for more details see that section*).

Talbot: When the front-wheel-drive Samba was dropped during the year, this was the end of a marque name which had only been re-introduced to the British market in 1979. Thereafter, all cars in this section of the Peugeot-owned sector were covered by Peugeots.

Toyota: The Celica GT-Four, the 175bhp/2-litre four-wheel-drive version of the front-wheel-drive coupe, went on sale towards the end of the year, but first UK deliveries were delayed until early 1988 because there were not enough lead-free fuel pumps in the UK to cater for this catalyst-only car before then!

There was an all-new Supra sports GT hatchback coupe in March, this time with no link to the smaller Celica GT. The new-generation Supra was still a front-engine/rear-drive car, and was powered by a special new twin-overhead-cam 3-litre straight-six engine.

Big, and considered graceful when new, the Supra would remain in production for seven years and nearly a million examples proved its commercial success.

Later in the year a graceful, if technically conventional, new-generation Camry was launched with a choice of petrol and diesel engines. Toyota GB was far too busy selling fleets of Corollas and Supra flagships to give too much attention to this new Camry, so its career in the UK was rather blighted by neglect.

A supercharged version of the mid-engined MR2, with a 40 per cent power increase over normal models, was revealed in Japan, though there were doubts that this car would ever be sold in the UK.

TVR: At the motor show, the new, but retro-look S model was shown in prototype form. With a new chassis and suspension, a Ford V6 engine and an open two-seater style derived from the old Convertible of the late 1970s, the S was meant to be much cheaper than existing Tasmin-based cars. Sales of S models did not begin until the summer of 1987.

The 420SEAC appeared during the year, having evolved from a 4.2-litre lightweight version of the 390SE, but going into limited production with a civilized interior, various high-tech body panel materials and a free-standing aerofoil on the rear deck behind the seats.

Vauxhall: The new Belmont four-door saloon was introduced at the beginning of the year, this being a notchback version of the Astra hatchback, with the same wide range of front-wheel-drive engines and trim packs.

Somehow or other, in the years which followed, the Belmont developed a very dull and mundane image, though it sold well enough for Vauxhall to keep it in the range until the style was changed in 1991.

A brand-new Carlton series was launched in August, being a badge-engineered derivative of the new Opel Omega (see Opel, above) and replacing the original Carltons which had been on sale for eight years.

Big, rounded and with a choice of four-door saloon or five-door estate car body styles, the new Carltons had all-independent suspension and a choice of 1.8 and 2-litre petrol engines, a 2.3-litre diesel and – at the top of the range from its introduction in March 1987 – a Carlton GSi 3000 with a 170bhp/3-litre overhead-cam six-cylinder engine.

Other changes for 1987 included the arrival of sporty 2-litre-engined versions of the Astra GTE and the Cavalier SRi (both of which were not ready for delivery until March 1987), along with the launch of a Bertone-bodied Astra cabriolet.

Industrial developments

Having failed in its bid to join with Fiat, Ford of Europe next tried to buy the Austin-Rover business from BL, but this was also foiled when the Government turned down the offer. Ford, which had gone a long way with negotiations, was not best pleased by this turn of events.

In what was a very complex industrial year, Austin-Rover was separated from the old Leyland truck and bus divisions, which were both sold. The rump of Rover was now confined to cars and the profitable Land Rover business.

Someone at Ford, however, must have been enthusiastic about takeovers and empire building, for the company then spent some high-profile time trying to buy Alfa Romeo. This strategy also got a long way down the road to completion before Fiat stepped in, used its Italian influence to stave off the Ford approach and became Alfa's new owners instead!

Looking back, there is evidence that the Ford-Alfa deal had been completed apart from the formalities before zenophobic Italian nationalism set in. Fiat was encouraged to bid for Alfa, finally doing the deal in November, and as a result ended up with control of more than 90 per cent of the entire Italian motor industry.

Consequent on the failure of its talks with Ford, Austin-Rover's chairman, Ray Horrocks, resigned and left the company. The BL company changed its name to the Rover Group. In the meantime, Rover's corporate chairman, Sir Austin Bide, had retired, his place being taken by the smooth-talking and very effective Canadian, Graham Day.

After a whirlwind two-year build period, the new Nissan factory opened at Washington, County Durham, beginning by building Nissan Bluebirds, mainly from kits imported from Japan, but soon progressing to entirely local manufacture. This was the first Japanese 'invasion' of Britain's motor industry – though both Toyota and Honda would soon follow – and 29,000 Bluebirds were produced in the first 12-month period.

After a lengthy, but seemingly amicable series of negotiations, Seat of Spain finally became a subsidiary of VW in the spring. Before the end of the year the Spanish company was assembling VW Polos, Polo Classics and Passats, while work on 'VW-Seats' got under way.

In January, Lotus, which had led a tortured and financially perilous existence in recent years, was finally taken over by the world's largest car-making group, General Motors, for no less than £22.75 million.

For the record, immediately before that takeover, Lotus' largest individual shareholders had been British Car Auctions (29 per cent), Toyota (20 per cent) and JCB (18 per cent), with the Chapman family interests still controlling about a fifth of the total shareholding.

For the time being, Alan Curtis became Lotus' chairman, Mike Kimberley continuing as chief executive.

The ambitious Naylor TF1700 sports-car project failed in the spring when the receiver was called in. The Naylor was a line-by-line copy of the 1950s-style MG TF, except that there was a different chassis and Austin-Rover mechanicals underneath.

The project really failed because it was more costly to buy a Naylor TF1700 than a fully-restored, genuine MG TF of 1953–55. The entire project was eventually bought and relaunched as the Hutson, but only a handful of those cars were destined to be produced.

Channel Tunnel – a start at last

Britain and France had been talking about constructing a fixed cross-channel link since the 18th century, and there had been a short-lived project in the 1970s (see the 1975 section).

Now, in 1986, a new privately-financed project was approved, and this time it was serious. The Channel Tunnel Group was awarded the contract to build a railway tunnel, which would feature shuttle trains and massive ferry-style terminals on both sides of the Channel. Access on the British side would be from the extended M20 motorway, close to Folkestone.

The finalized tunnel was to be 31 miles long, the shuttle crossing being expected to take no more than 35 to 40 minutes. Completion was originally set for 1992/93, but in the event the complete infrastructure would not be in operation until 1995.

Although the French immediately built a TGV (*Train a Grand Vitesse* – high-speed train) link to the mouth of the tunnel, there were innumerable delays to a tunnel link on the British side, this not being expected to be built until 2002 or even later. Although the Government came in for much criticism over this delay, most was due to protests made by Kent residents – who wanted a rail link, but not near to them.

Lead-free petrol – a slow start in the UK

In the first half of the year, BP and Esso became the first British oil companies to make lead-free petrol available in Britain, though the demand was extremely low for the first few years. In 1986, lead-free petrol cost between 4p and 5p a gallon *extra* compared with normal leaded supplies. Then, as later, lead-free was rated at 95 octane, compared with 97 or 98 octane for four-star.

Five million Minis

The 5-millionth Mini was built in February 1986, nearly 27 years after the first of these tiny front-wheel-drive cars were produced at Cowley and Longbridge. It still used the traditional layout of a transversely-mounted A-series engine, with the four-speed gearbox 'in the sump'.

Although the Mini's heyday was well past (production had peaked in the early 1970s, but dropped off dramatically once the more modern Metro had appeared in the 1980s), BL still found it profitable to build the car. In fact it would still be in production – in significantly changed form – 10 years later when the first edition of this book was being written.

Men of Influence

Rod Mansfield

Although Rod Mansfield was never a top boss at Ford, through the work of his Special Vehicle Engineering team he became the best-known of all that company's design engineers, and was regularly profiled and interviewed in the specialist press.

It was typical of him, therefore, that after retiring from Ford in 1995, he was almost immediately attracted back into the motor industry to take charge of Lotus.

Bristol-born, with no motor industry heritage but always with a passion for cars, he first worked for AC Cars, then joined Ford in 1960 as a development engineer. After tackling a variety of design, development and product planning tasks in the next decade, he became the fifth employee of the newly-formed Advanced Vehicle Operation in 1970, going on to engineer and develop successful Escorts and Capris in the RS line-up.

At the same time he managed to indulge himself racing various Escorts – Twin-Cams and Mexicos, principally – before moving back into Ford's mainstream engineering division. Then, in 1980, came the chance to set up and manage a new division called Special Vehicle Engineering, which would make him famous and Ford sporty once again.

Under Mansfield, SVE developed sporting cars such as the Capri 2.8i, the Fiesta XR2, the Escort XR3i, the Sierra XR4x4 and the original Escort cabriolet, but in the mid-1980s its two most famous products were the original Escort RS Turbo (1984) and the Sierra RS Cosworth (1985).

There was more to come in the late 1980s, including the Sierra Cosworth 4x4 (with four-wheel drive) and the Escort RS Cosworth. Then, in 1990, Ford sent Mansfield to rejuvenate Aston Martin (which it had controlled since 1987) as technical director (where the DB7 project was finally set in train), but after less than two years he was once again diverted, this time to Ford-USA, where he established the equivalent of the Ford-UK Special Vehicle Engineering department.

Finally retiring – or so he thought – at the end of 1994, he spent only months at home before being attracted to Lotus in the aftermath of the Bugatti financial traumas, becoming managing director just ahead of the launch of the new Elise model, only to leave abruptly after falling out of favour with Bugatti's volatile Romano Artioli. It was not difficult to do that!

1987

If there was ever a time which was good for British drivers, this was it. New cars were appearing from all angles, new roads seemed to be opening up to improve horrid old journeys, and there seemed to be plenty of money around to finance new cars, and motoring in general. Looking back, some of this might have been an illusion, but it felt good at the time.

Once again British motorists were relieved to find few changes in the annual Budget. The annual Vehicle Excise Duty stayed at £100 and there was actually a *reduction* of 5p/gallon on lead-free petrol. The tax-break changes proposed in 1986 were formalized – which meant that it now made much sense for fleet-car users to have sub-1.4-litre or sub-2-litre cars.

UK car sales were still increasing as the economic boom progressed, 2.08 million being delivered during the year – an all-time record, and the first time that the British market had absorbed more than 2 million new cars in a year. But there was still two more years of expansion to go – the peak not coming until 1989.

Of those 2.08 million, Ford sold 29 per cent, including 178,000 Escorts, 153,000 Fiestas and 140,000 Sierras, which were the country's top three best-sellers.

New models

By this time, most new models were announced with a multiple choice of engines, or at least the promise of a wide choice as time went buy. Back in the 1950s, of course, North American companies had been the masters of this craft, but by the 1960s it was Mercedes-Benz who seemed to offer the widest choice of all.

By the mid-1980s, though, almost every new car – British, European or Japanese – arrived as a multi-choice offering. For that reason, and to keep each section down to a readable length, we now have to summarize more than for earlier years.

Alfa Romeo: The first official pictures of the new 164 saloon (Alfa's version of the Saab-Lancia-Fiat Type 4 plat-

form) were released in April. They showed a more graceful car than its closely related rivals, almost entirely due to sympathetic treatment by Pininfarina, who had shaped the shell.

Two new versions of the 75 saloon appeared in February. The Twin Spark 2.0 featured a much-revised four-cylinder twin-cam, whose cylinder head was a brand-new casting with a narrower opposed-valve layout, two spark plugs per cylinder and different breathing arrangements.

The 75 3.0 V6 used a new version of the celebrated single-cam V6 unit, now enlarged to 2,959cc and producing 188bhp.

The flat-four engine family used in the smaller front-drive Alfas was still developing. The final stretch, to 1,712cc, was unveiled early in the year, originally in 118bhp/single-cam form, and was slotted into a newly badged 33 Green Cloverleaf model, which went on UK sale at £8,599. Later in the year the same engine also became available in the 33 Sportwagen which, unlike the discarded Sportshatch, only had front-wheel drive.

Aston Martin: Having sold 50 of the limited-edition Vantage-based Zagato models, the company announced that it was to produce 25 convertible versions of the same basic style. This time the cars were priced at £149,500, but once again there was no problem in selling them all ahead of production taking place.

This time the cars were to be fitted with 305bhp fuel-injected engines, which meant that there was no longer any need for a power bulge in the bonnet. First deliveries were made in 1988.

The long, low and flat four-door Lagonda model was given a facelift/reskin, with most of the sharp edges replaced by radiused corners. It was a low-investment change which seemed to work well and kept the car in production for a few more years.

Audi: In May, more than six months after the last of the earlier-style 90s had been produced, a new-generation 90 was introduced. This, as expected, was no more than a five-cylinder, top-of-the-range development of the new-type 80.

There were no styling differences between the new 90 and 80, the basic

bodyshells being the same, while both cars shared the same in-line front-engine/front-wheel-drive (or quattro) layouts.

There were three versions of the new car – a 115bhp/2-litre, a 136bhp/2.2-litre and a 136bhp/2.2-litre with the quattro four-wheel-drive installation. Like the latest 80 quattro, the 90 quattro now had a Torsen-type centre differential.

The Procon Ten safety system introduced for the 80 in 1986 was forecast to be ready for the 90 by 1988.

After a seven-year life, the famous four-wheel-drive Quattro (later to be known as the *Ur*, or original, model) was upgraded for 1988 with a larger engine of 2,226cc, along with the Torsen centre differential which featured in the latest 80/90 models.

In the USA, the company was obliged to take massive recall action to modify automatic transmission cars after a TV show accused them of running away when left unattended with the engine idling. These accusations were later shown to be groundless, but Audi's reputation in that continent was irreparably harmed; fortunately for the Germans, there was no backwash in the UK.

Austin: In a half-hearted attempt to emphasize Rover and sideline Austin, BL took the Austin badge off the back of the Montego, but this did not work, as everyone continued to call it an Austin Montego.

BMW: The much-rumoured 3-series Touring (an estate car to everyone but BMW...) was finally launched in mid-summer. Compared with the 3-series saloons, the chassis was virtually unchanged, though in the UK it would only be offered with the 325i six-cylinder engine.

At the time the Touring was launched, a new type of overhead-camshaft four-cylinder engine, the 1.8-litre M40, a 115bhp fuel-injected unit, took over from from the old-style 105bhp engine, whose roots were in the 1960s with the original BMW 1800 model. In many ways the combustion and valve layout of the new 'four' was like that of the new V12.

The radically-different Z1 roadster, announced during the year, was probably a commercial failure, since only 8,000 of them would be sold before the project was closed down.

As previewed in 1986, the front-engine/rear-drive Z1 used mainly familiar 3-series running gear (including the 2.5-litre six-cylinder engine), but featured a new and complex type of rear suspension and those ingenious doors which opened by being slid down into the capacious sills. With the doors retracted and the soft-top folded back, most of the passengers' bodies were exposed to view – and to the weather. This made the Z1 only suitable for warm-weather territories, but you would never find a BMW enthusiast who would admit that.

As forecast in 1986, V12-engined versions of the new 7-series model, the 750i and 750iL, were announced in mid-year. Although there were no major styling changes, there was a great boost in performance, for the 5-litre overhead-cam V12 produced 300bhp and gave a claimed top speed of 155mph, which was electronically limited.

The 750iL, in fact, had a 4.5in longer wheelbase than the existing six-cylinder cars, but this stretch had been carried out very subtly and was barely noticeable, which was just what BMW had intended.

Bugatti: The first rumours appeared of a rebirth of the once-famous French marque, this time to be built in Italy. These stories were soon confirmed, but it would be another five years before a new car, as opposed to a mere project, appeared, and the entire venture would go financially wrong in 1995.

Citroen: A new and more sporty version of the AX model, the 85bhp/1.36-litre GT, went on UK sale in October, and at the same time the AX Sport also appeared. This was a highly-tuned 95bhp/1,294cc car, the slightly shorter piston stroke of its engine allowing it to compete in domestic 1.3-litre race and rally categories.

The BX range was *still* expanding, and in 1987 it was topped out by the launch of the GTi, with a 160bhp/1.9-litre 16-valve engine derived from that used in Peugeot 205 T16 turbocharged cars of a year earlier.

Although Visas were still listed in the UK, by the end of the year only diesel-engined versions were still available, and these would disappear in 1988.

Still working on the big CX theme,

Citroen produced an astonishingly powerful turbocharged/intercooled diesel version producing no less than 120bhp from 2.5 litres, with a claimed top speed of more than 120mph.

Daihatsu: A new-generation Charade appeared to replace the original model which had been in production for six years. As before, Diahatsu stuck to using three-cylinder in-line engines (which, the company claimed, were shorter, lighter and cheaper-to-build than 'fours') to drive the front wheels.

There were seven models in the new generation, including 51, 67 and 99bhp petrol-powered versions, along with a 47bhp diesel. The most sporting was the GTti, with a high-revving 12-valve turbocharged twin-cam unit.

The Fourtrak 4x4 was revised at the end of the year, with more powerful engines and softened suspension settings.

Ferrari: The most sensational new model of the year was Ferrari's F40, a celebration model to commemorate 40 years of Ferrari road-car production. In some ways it was more of a racing than a road car, for its cabin was sparsely trimmed and furnished, its manners harsh – and its performance well ahead of that of any previous Ferrari.

Although the F40 used elements of the obsolete 288GTO's running gear, the multi-tube chassis was special and the turbocharged 2.9-litre V8 engine produced a staggering 450bhp. The claimed top speed (never authenticated by testers in the UK) was 201mph, and even before there was any indication of prices, the waiting list exceeded Ferrari's promised production run. At first, Ferrari stated that it would produce 500 cars, but well over 1,000 would eventually leave the lines at Maranello. Until the F50 arrived in 1995, it was the fastest Ferrari that money could buy.

Fiat: In September, the new 126 Bis (Bis = second-generation) took over from the original type, which had been on sale for 15 years. Structurally and in its style, the 126 Bis was much as before, though there was a new facia and better interior. The important innovation, however, was that the old-type air-cooled engine had been discarded and replaced by a parallel-twin water-cooled unit of 704cc with the cylinders laid down horizontally.

It didn't sound much, but peak power was up from 24 to 26bhp, and there was a 12 per cent torque improvement. The other development of major importance was that the 126 Bis was to be built at the FSO factory in Poland.

Like Ford, Fiat matched the new-style CVT continuously-variable automatic transmission to a 1.1-litre engine, launching the Uno Selecta in May.

Ford: Continuously variable automatic transmission (CVT) became optional on 1.1-litre Fiesta models. At first this sounded very attractive and a surefire best-seller, but sales of this car (and its related Fiat Uno) were surprisingly restricted.

In January, the new four-door notchback version of the Sierra, badged Sapphire, went on sale. Along with the existing five-door hatchbacks, these cars had a smoother nose than the original types, but there were no significant mechanical changes.

Although it was only a 500-off limited-production car, the Sierra RS500 Cosworth was enormously important to Ford. As a 224bhp version of the 1986-model Sierra RS Cosworth, it was really no faster than before (and considerably more expensive at £19,950!), but its engine could be tuned to produce more than 500 reliable horsepower for Group A racing, which made it almost unbeatable in touring car racing – until regulations were rewritten to nullify its advantages.

Honda: The fourth-generation Civic range, only the hatchback version of which was destined for sale in the UK, was announced in September, along with a new but closely-related CRX coupe. The new cars were longer, wider and lower than before, with double-wishbone suspension all round and new 16-valve twin-cam engines.

The front-wheel-drive CRX looked similar to its mid-1980s predecessor, but had a totally new style and was powered by a 130bhp 1.6-litre twin-cam engine.

In addition, a new-generation Prelude coupe was introduced in September, this being a lower, wider and smoother restatement of the well-known two-door four-seater coupe theme. The new car's running gear had much in common with that of the Accord which had been launched two years earlier.

The most powerful version had a newly-developed 150bhp 2-litre twin-cam engine, and this was the first four-wheel-steering car to go on sale in the UK.

The very smart Legend coupe – a two-door four-seater model – was announced early in the year. Rover, which had only recently begun deliveries of 2.5-litre Honda-engined 800s, were dismayed to see Honda listing a new and more torquey 2.7-litre engine for the coupe! This meant that customers would soon be expecting to see the 2.7 in Rovers – but they had to wait until early 1988 for it.

Isuzu: International Motors finalized a deal to take over the UK import concession, but abandoned the Piazza to its fate (the 534 unsold cars were snapped up by the Alan Day dealership and repriced at a bargain price of £8,995) in favour of the Trooper 4x4 model.

A redeveloped Piazza, with suspension work carried out by Lotus, was reintroduced at the end of 1987, this time at a retail price of £10,998, but the first UK deliveries were delayed until March 1988.

Troopers went on sale in April with a choice of short or long wheelbase, petrol or diesel power, all vehicles having torsion-bar independent front suspension, with prices starting from £9,999.

Lada: The front-wheel-drive Samara, which had been previewed as long ago as 1985, finally went on sale in the UK.

Lancia: Only 18 months after the original four-wheel-drive Delta HF 4WD had gone on sale, Lancia introduced an altogether better version, the 185bhp (eight-valve) Delta Integrale, which was not only more powerful, but had wider wheel tracks and larger wheels (with flared arches to suit) and better brakes.

Lotus: In October, the mid-engined range of normally-aspirated and turbocharged Esprits was relaunched, this time with a more rounded X180-style GRP body over the same basic chassis and running gear. Power outputs remained at 172bhp (for the normally-aspirated engine) and 215bhp (for the turbocharged).

Mazda: A new-generation 626 family appeared in the autumn, this being the same (Sierra) size as before, but with a new, more rounded and altogether more attractive shape. As before, the 626 was a transverse-engined/front-wheel-drive car with a choice of 1.8 or 2-litre engine.

Mercedes-Benz: A pair of new two-door E-class coupes first appeared in March, badged as the 230CE and 300CE, with four-cylinder and six-cylinder engines respectively. Based on the layout of the W124 saloons, though with a shortened wheelbase/platform, they were set for a 10-year life.

Middlebridge: (See under Reliant, below.)

Mitsubishi: The long-running front-engine/rear-drive Starion coupe was improved with what became known as the wide-body style. The original bodyshell and mechanical layout were modified with flared front and rear wheelarches and wider wheels and tyres. The Starion, nevertheless, was close to the end of its run, for the last of these cars would be produced in 1989.

The Galant Sapporo, revealed in October, was a flagship version of the latest Galant with a new and longer nose which included four headlamps. It was always very rare in the UK, and should not be confused with the completely different 1970s-vintage Sapporo coupe.

Nissan: Even though the Laurel was only a slow-selling car in the UK, Nissan treated the existing square-edged style to a technical makeover, which included giving it independent rear suspension.

Later in the year the rather gawky Sunny SLX coupe was made a lot faster by equipping it with a larger (1.6-litre) and higher-revving engine of 122bhp.

The new British operation, which was already producing 100,000 Bluebirds a year, announced that it was to double its size and would start building a new-generation Micra in the early 1990s.

Opel: The Monza model was discontinued, leaving Mantas as the only Opel-badged GM cars still on sale in the UK.

Panther: Three years after showing a car called Solo (see the 1984 section), Panther previewed a very different Solo, this model having an in-line, mid-mounted, 204bhp Sierra RS Cosworth engine and four-wheel drive. But it was a long way from being ready for sale and there was an embarrassingly long delay before deliveries began at the end of 1989.

A 1.6-litre version of the Kallista was reintroduced, this time with an in-line version of the Ford Fiesta XR2 power unit.

Peugeot: The introduction of the 405 range was the most commercially important launch the French company had tackled for some years. With a wide range of engines either available at once or promised for the near future, this front-wheel-drive car was aimed squarely at the fast Sierra/Cavalier market.

With styling by Pininfarina, the 405 was immediately available as a four-door saloon, and a five-door estate car was promised. There were four different tunes of petrol engine, spanning 92bhp to a 16-valve 160bhp, and diesels were also being developed. British-market deliveries would begin in January 1988 from cars produced at the British Ryton plant.

The 309 GTI, with 130bhp/1.9-litre engine, arrived in February. Those who tried both cars later decided that the 309GTI handled and behaved even better than the highly rated 205GTI on which its chassis and running gear was based.

Porsche: More than 10 years after the turbocharged version of the 911 had first gone on sale, in March Porsche finally made it available on the Targa and cabriolet versions.

Before the end of the year, rumours began to circulate of a new-generation 911 with a much simpler four-wheel drive system than that installed in the 959.

As the world's stock markets crashed (temporarily, as it happened), so did the market for Porsches, and after selling about 50,000 cars a year the company suddenly had to face up to a much lower demand. Part of the problem was that the so-called 'yuppie' types could no longer afford Porsches, but another factor was that all Porsches were now beginning to look old.

Reliant: Rights to the obsolete, out-of-production Scimitar GTE/GTC models were sold to the Middlebridge Group during the year. This car would eventually re-appear in 1988 with the Ford 2.9-litre V6 engine, badged as a Middlebridge.

In an attempt to give the smallest Scimitar model more performance, the 1.3-litre Ford engine was dropped in favour of a 75bhp 1.4-litre Ford type. The difference was minor and the effect on sales negligible.

Renault: The 5 range was rejigged in the spring, without changing the style. The 956cc-engined entry-level car was dropped, the 1,237cc engine of the 9 and 11 types was phased in, the 1.4-litre engine was given more power (from 60 to 68bhp) and a 1.7-litre version was added to what was already a crowded line-up of three-door and five-door hatchbacks.

During the year the flagship of the 21 range, the 21 Turbo, was revealed. This featured a turbocharged and intercooled version of the 2-litre engine producing no less than 175bhp.

Saab: The 99 (renamed 90 in its final year or so) finally died out during the year after a 20-year production life during which more than 600,000 had been built in Sweden and Finland.

Skoda: After a decade of suffering ridicule for the weird habits of its rear-engined Estelle, the company launched the new Favorit, a transverse-engined, front-wheel-drive hatchback (with an estate car to follow). Still down at bargain-basement price levels, the Favorit was a much more roadworthy example, which sold well in the UK for some years until replaced by the similar Felicia in the mid-1990s.

Suzuki: The small 1-litre Spanish-built Santana 4x4s went on sale in the UK during the year. These cars, in developed form, would be renamed Vitara, and even though they were not very capable off-road machines, they were much cheaper than most of their rivals and found a ready sale among trendy types and those irreverently known as 'Sloane Rangers'. Later in the year this car became available with a 63bhp/1.3-litre engine, though with a top speed of only 74mph it was still not a quick 4x4.

Toyota: It was a surprisingly quiet year for the Japanese giant, in Britain at least. The Corolla range was fleshed out later in the year with a 123bhp/1.6-litre twin-cam engine.

Vauxhall: In Germany, Opel introduced a new large car called the Senator, and it was announced that a near-identical Vauxhall model would go on UK sale during the summer.

Looking similar to the latest Carlton, and using the same 107.5in-wheelbase platform and main cabin, the Senator had different front and rear styles, while as before there was to be a choice of 140bhp/2.5-litre and 177bhp/3-litre cam-in-head six-cylinder engines.

Senators were instantly recognizable by their 'egg-crate' front grille and would soon find distinctive use in the UK as high-performance police cars.

When the Opel Corsa GTE, with 1.6-litre injected engine, was introduced in Germany, GM admitted that there would eventually be a Vauxhall Nova equivalent – but this did not appear until 1988.

Volkswagen: The German company was having another of those mix-and-match years, mating engines to bodies in new combinations. One of these, first seen in April, was the 139bhp Jetta GTi 16V.

This was also the year in which the company suffered in a craze inspired by a pop group, The Beastie Boys. Because *they* wore VW badges as medallions, many thousands of their fans did likewise...by stealing roundels from the front grille of current VW models.

Volvo: In the autumn there was a mid-life facelift for the 760 series, including a slightly more rounded nose (for the time being, the original nose was retained on the 740 types) and with coil-spring independent suspension now standardized on all 760 saloon types.

Industrial developments

Although several other firms had tried to buy Rover from the British Government in recent years, this must surely have been for potential rather than for business logic. During the year the company, although shorn of the truck and bus divisions, admitted that in 1986 it had made losses of £862 million and that to finance this its net borrowings had risen to a staggering £1 billion. Ever helpful, though, the Government agreed to fund these losses, to inject up to £680 million, and to make Rover ripe for privatization.

By spending what was jocularly called petty cash, Ford-UK took control of Aston Martin in September, instantly endorsed the development of the new Virage (which would be introduced in 1988), and underpinned the struggling Newport Pagnell firm, really for the first time in half a century.

Later in the year Ford also took majority control of the AC marque, which was struggling to finalize the design of a new Ace car, the other major shareholder being Brian Angliss. However, the alliance would end in tears after a few years as the two sides always disagreed over the layout of the new car.

After one high-profile attempt had failed, Reliant finally sold the rights to Scimitar GTE and GTC manufacture, this time to the Middlebridge Group, who proposed to relaunch the cars in 1988. It was a brave effort which would ultimately fail, for the GTE's time was past and demand was almost non-existent.

Chrysler bought control of Lamborghini in April, thus giving the Italian maker of supercars the financial stability which it had lacked for several years. One result of the buyout, though delayed by a couple of years, would be the launch of the mid-engined V12 Diablo.

Fiat took control of FSO in Poland, promising to spend up to £400 million to modernize the plant and concentrate assembly of the 126 (and later successors) in that country.

The UK concession for Maserati changed hands yet again, this time to a Leeds-based consortium, but the new company was no more successful than the old, which had suffered major cashflow difficulties. Maserati sales soon tailed off in the UK, seemingly permanently.

Porsche of Germany took control of its UK import business, buying out the AFN operation which had been founded in the mid-1950s.

Panther, the small British-based sportscar maker which was already owned by a Korean business, was taken over by Ssangyong. Even so, it would be another eight years (to 1995) before a Ssanyong-badged car, actually a 4x4 estate car, went on sale in the UK.

Technical developments

Ford and Fiat collaborated in the use of a continuously variable transmission (CVT) in its front-wheel-drive cars. This was a much more advanced derivative of the Daf belt-drive system of the 1960s and 1970s, this time using steel-element belts and self-adjusting pulleys.

Catalytic converters, already well-known in the USA, were first mentioned in the UK when Toyota decided to import Celica GT-4s with this item as standard equipment. First imports were delayed until the winter, by which time sufficient unleaded petrol outlets existed to make this worthwhile!

'Cats', which relied on exotic metals like platinum to help convert noxious to harmless gases as they passed from the engine to the outside world, were still not required by law in the UK, but would become so in the early 1990s.

Such converters were always controversial, not only because they were extremely expensive (they added hundreds of pounds to the cost of a car) but because they were not at all effective until thoroughly warmed-up, which meant that millions of town use-only cars have never employed them properly.

The Japanese had spent much time researching the possibilities of four-wheel steering. Of course, there was nothing new about the principle (military and commercial vehicles had been using such layouts for decades), but to make four-wheel steering suitable for use in fast passenger cars was an extremely delicate business.

Mazda was first to unveil a production-standard layout in which the front steering was conventional, but the rear-wheel steering was much less pronounced and controlled electronically. In this system the rear wheels were arranged to steer away from the front pair at low speeds (thus reducing the turning circle), but to steer *with* the front wheels at high speeds to encourage transient stability.

Toyota and Mitsubishi soon joined the race to put 4WS onto the market (Mitsubishi made it available on a 4WD Galant at the same time). However, such a feature was always an expensive and (in some people's view) wholly unnecessary innovation, which would make only limited progress in the next decade.

Men of Influence

Henry Ford II

It is often said that death dignifies a man's reputation, and certainly this was very true of Henry Ford II, who died in 1987, aged 70. Much criticized during his lifetime, not only for his business methods but for his unconventional marital lifestyle, he was reverently saluted after his death. He had retired from active management several years earlier.

HF2, as he was sometimes known, was the grandson of the *original* Henry Ford and the personality who saved the ailing American giant car company from extinction in the mid-1940s. HF2 was Edsel Ford's son, and after his father died he was released from the US Navy in 1943 so that he could return to the 'family business'. At the time he was only 26 years old, so his grandfather's old cronies, like Harry Bennett, thought they could run him, rather than the other way around.

Although Ford was still the world's second-largest carmaker in the mid-1940s, it was at one time losing $10 million a week, but Henry Ford hired the right management team, turned it round, sacked diehards like Bennett and saw Ford recover. By the 1950s it was once again highly profitable, with even more manufacturing plants all round the world.

Henry Ford II was on the main board of Ford for 37 years, ruling his company with an iron and (apparently) idiosyncratic hand. When personalities like Lee Iacocca were rising through the ranks he was happy to indulge them and the publicity they generated, but once they neared management peaks he became nervous, even vicious.

Iacocca, his heir apparent, was brutally passed over, then sacked in 1978, after which Ford passed over the reins to more predictable lieutenants, who would run the business as he would have wished.

For the last decade of his life he had more time for pleasure, and mainly lived in Britain, near Henley-on-Thames.

1988

Following 1987's boom year, the British motoring market was even busier in 1988. UK car sales rose to yet another new record (2,277,306) as Britain's motorists decided that the 1980s boom would continue indefinitely.

Sales and production figures make intriguing reading a few years down the road. Although UK car production was still well down on the record figures of the early 1970s, and exports of complete cars (although not of major components like engines) were still weak, imports rose to yet another record of 1,356,902, which was higher than total domestic production.

Meanwhile, 'Big Brother' came a stage closer in Britain when spy camera evidence was used for the first time in court to trap drivers who had crossed traffic lights at red. The first convictions came in Nottingham, where the local authority had generated something of a reputation for its anti-motorist stance.

New models

Alfa Romeo: The 1.7-litre flat-four engine, first seen in 1987, was applied to the smart little Sprint coupes during the year.

Aston Martin: The new Virage, launched at the motor show in October, but not ready to go on sale until the summer of 1989, was the first British-inspired new-shape Aston Martin to be revealed since 1969.

With a new box-section chassis developed in conjunction with the Cranfield Institute of Technology, and an aluminium body shaped by the newly-fashionable Heffernan/Greenley partnership, the Virage used a 32-valve version of the famous 5.3-litre V8 engine, the top end of which had been developed by Callaway Engineering of the USA.

Excitingly-specified though it was, this new Aston Martin was almost universally seen as the 'last of the dinosaurs', and pundits were already looking forward to a smaller, cheaper, new-generation car which they were quite sure would follow. It did – but not until 1992.

Audi: More than eight years after the first of the Quattro coupes had been shown, Audi introduced an entirely new coupe shape. This car, in a whole variety of front-drive and four-wheel-drive, four, five and (eventually) six-cylinder forms, was to become an important part of Audi's line-up for the next few years.

More rounded than before and somehow less aggressive looking, the new car used many chassis components and the modified platform of the 80/90 range. At launch time, there was the choice of 136bhp/2.2-litre and 170bhp/20-valve/2.3-litre five-cylinder engines.

The old-style Quattro, however, was not quite dead, for Audi agreed to keep it going for a short time, updated with the latest 220bhp/20-valve twin-cam version of the ageing five-cylinder engine. At the time, indeed, Audi said it would keep the Quattro going as long as there were buyers – these eventually disappearing in 1991.

For the first time since the mid-1970s the German company produced a new engine. A 90-degree V8 was a new configuration for Audi, and it was an all-Audi unit not destined to be shared with any other marque.

The new engine, a 3.6-litre unit, was a technical *tour de force* with twin-camshaft cylinder heads and four valves per cylinder, and in many ways it was a doubling-up of the VW Golf GTi 16-valve engine for the top ends of the two units were nearly identical.

The engine was to power the Audi V8 model which followed later in the year. Based closely on the 100/200 Quattro bodyshell, this was a 250bhp super-saloon whose principal marketing problem was that apart from a slightly altered nose it looked almost identical to the smaller-engined cars.

Four-wheel drive was standard, for Audi believed that there was too much power to commit to front wheels only: although the familiar quattro-type lay-out was used, this time there was automatic transmission – a 'first' from Audi. The latest Procon Ten safety system of hauling the steering column forward in case of accidents was also standardized.

Early in the year the 100/200 range of Audis was freshened-up with an interior revamp and with the Torsen centre differential used on quattro types.

Austin: After an embarrassing series of delays, the diesel version of the Montego was finally put on sale in October. This used a Perkins-developed direct-injection 2-litre engine which had evolved from the old O-series petrol engine. In turbocharged form it produced 80bhp, while Rover claimed 102mph for the Montego which it powered.

BMW: The arrival of a new-generation 5-series was eagerly awaited as the first officially leaked pictures had been shown late in 1987. Although the new car used the same choice of overhead-camshaft engines and transmissions as the old, it was a larger and smoother-styled series of cars, with different front and rear suspensions, owing more in engineering to the modern 7-series than the previous 5-series layout.

This new generation would have an eight-year career (the next series would be announced in 1995, for UK sale in 1996) during which there were to be no significant style changes, though eventually there was an extremely large choice of inline and V-formation petrol and diesel engines.

Initially, four of the new-type 5-series went on sale, the 520i, 525i, 530i and 535i derivatives, all with the same smooth new four-headlamp style.

Later in the year, an exciting new 5-series flagship, the M5, was also revealed. Except for its distinctive 17in alloy wheels, visually this looked like other 5-series models, but there was a 315bhp/3.5-litre six-cylinder engine under the bonnet, using the latest version of the 24-valve twin-cam cylinder head.

With a claimed top speed of 155mph (electronically restricted), this automatically became the fastest and the most desirable of the 5-series.

Only two years after the original type had gone on sale, BMW replaced the M3 with a car it called the M3 Evolution. Developed purely with Touring Car racing in mind (where the turbocharged Sierra RS500 Cosworths usually beat the M3), the Evolution had 16in wheels, modified aerodynamic aids, and a 220bhp version of the 2.3-litre engine.

As with the original M3, it was only available in left-hand-drive form, even in the British market. Later in the year, a convertible version of the original-specification M3 was also put on sale.

At the other end of the 3-series scale, for 1989 there was a revised 316i with the new 102bhp fuel-injected M40-type engine instead of the old carburetted 1.8-litre engine.

Citroen: The BX range received yet another engine in May, this time a turbocharged 90bhp/1,769cc diesel of the type which had just been adopted for the Peugeot 405. Four-wheel drive was also added to the very wide range of fittings at the end of the year.

In the autumn, a new small (1.36-litre) diesel, producing 51bhp, was announced and promised for use in the AX by 1989, and in similar small Peugeot models.

Daihatsu: The Sportrak had a name confusingly close to that of the existing Fourtrak model, but it was a different, smaller and – above all – cheaper restatement of Diahatsu's four-wheel-drive ambitions.

Launched in October 1988, but available in the UK from March 1989, the Sportrak started life with an 84bhp 16-valve 1.6-litre engine and a five-speed primary gearbox. There was independent front suspension (which Land Rover still declined to fit to its own machines), a choice of soft-top and hardtop bodies and a well-trimmed interior.

Significantly, Daihatsu saw the Sportrak as a second car for use as a leisure vehicle, not necessarily a working machine.

Fiat: The Tipo was introduced in January with a platform and front-wheel-drive engineering which were also to be the basis of forthcoming Lancia and Alfa Romeo models.

By 1980s standards, the Tipo was a conventional transverse-engined, front-drive car, with a rather stumpy five-door style. One reason for this (not made clear at the time) was that the door pressings and outlines were to be the same on conventional notchback Fiat and Lancia saloons, which rather compromised the short-tail hatchback shape.

Engines were being offered in the new 1,372cc and 1,580cc sizes of the long-established 128/Strada overhead-cam type, whose heritage dated back to 1969. Strangely, the fastest car in the original Tipo range was the 1.9-litre turbodiesel!

Ford: At the end of 1988, Ford released official pictures of a new-generation Fiesta which was to go on sale in 1989. The car's release, however, was held back until the new year (see the 1989 section for all technical details).

In January, the second-generation Sierra RS Cosworth appeared, using the same 204bhp turbocharged 2-litre engine and rear-wheel-drive transmission as the original three-door 'whale-tail' car, but within a four-door notchback Sapphire-shaped shell. More expensive, the new model was conceived as a businessman's express rather than as a detuned racing car, being both slower and less exciting than the extrovert three-door machine.

In May, the 1.8-litre version of the Sierra was considerably changed in detail. Out went the British-built 1.8-litre Pinto-type engine, which was reaching the end of its life, and in its place came a 1.8-litre CVH engine built in the USA with a different bore, stroke, capacity and cylinder head layout, but with the same power output.

Later in the year came the launch of the MT75 five-speed gearbox, a new-generation manual transmission intended for use in the company's higher-powered Sierra and Granada/Scorpio models. This was notably larger and more robust than the five-speeders it replaced, and featured a synchronized reverse gear.

The company's small diesel engine – which powered Escort, Orion and Fiesta models – was enlarged from 1,608 to 1,753cc in the autumn, giving 60 instead of 54bhp and 81 instead of 70lb.ft of torque, but in this form it was not to be fitted to existing Fiestas, which were about to be dropped.

Ginetta: The Essex-based specialist maker, still tenuously in business despite years of difficulty for this sector of the motor industry, introduced the limited-production G32 coupe, which used a two-seater layout similar to that of the Fiat X1/9 of the 1970s, or the Toyota MR-2 of the 1980s. Power was by the 105bhp/1.6-litre Ford Escort XR3i version of the CVH engine.

Honda: The new Concerto, which was announced in mid-year, was more important to British drivers than it first appeared. The front-wheel-drive Concerto eventually went on sale in the UK at the end of 1989, but it was also the basis of the next-generation Rover 200 model, though with a different nose style. Concertos had a choice of 1.5 or 1.6-litre engines, were worthy and carefully built models, but were almost completely devoid of character.

A brace of rather different high-roof estate-type Shuttles went on sale in April – both with transverse-engine layouts, one with 90bhp and front-wheel drive, the other with 116bhp and full-time four-wheel drive, the latter also incorporating a six-speed gearbox with an SL (for Super Low), or crawler gear.

Hyundai: The first of the Sonata models was shown in October, this being an altogether larger and more upmarket car than existing Pony models, in a completely different league from the old-style Cortina-based Stellars.

The Sonata was a front-wheel-drive car with a choice of 1.8, 2.0 and 2.4-litre engines, and would go on UK sale in mid-1989.

Isuzu: Only a year after it had been launched in the UK, the Trooper 4x4 model was improved with a choice of 111bhp/2.6-litre petrol and 95bhp/2.8-litre turbodiesel engines.

Jaguar: Still being developed, even though it was already nearly 13 years old, the XJ-S gained ABS braking as standard equipment early in the year. Prices roses sharply to suit.

Then, in March, the XJ-S convertible appeared, directly replacing the cabriolet model, which had only been available since the end of 1983.

The company announced stronger links with TWR's JaguarSport enterprise (TWR was currently racing Jaguar-powered sportscars) by supporting the launch of the XJR-S, which was an updated, body-kitted version of the XJ-S model. Only months later a similar cosmetic job was done on the XJ6, to produce the XJR 3.6.

Lancia: Only three years after its birth, the Type 4 Thema was substantially revised, with a choice of normally-aspirated or turbocharged 'balancer' 2-litre 16-valve twin-cam engines. Lancia was acting as a pace-setter for other corporate cars here, for this engine would eventually find a use in several other important Alfa Romeo, Fiat and Lancia cars, including the rally-winning Delta Integrale.

Lexus: A very important new marque name appeared towards the end of the year with the introduction of the brand-new Lexus LS400 four-door saloon. Aimed squarely at the big Mercedes-Benz/BMW/Jaguar market, the Lexus was a Toyota product, but marketed entirely separately.

The LS400, which had smooth but almost totally anonymous styling, was new from end to end. Like its rivals, it had front-engine/rear-drive mechanicals, and was powered by a 250bhp 4-litre V8 engine, which had twin overhead camshafts per bank and four valves per cylinder.

Toyota had gone to infinite pains to make the Lexus as refined and as capable as possible. In quality, fit and finish it was certainly as good as any car which it had to beat in the show-rooms, and during the next few years it would sell in increasing numbers.

Lotus: Rumours began to spread that the next-generation Elan (which would appear, in fact, in 1989) would use an engine imported from Isuzu and would have front-wheel drive. Neither rumour was denied (for both were quite true), the supply of the Isuzu engine being logical because the Japanese concern, like Lotus, was controlled by General Motors.

Maserati: The Italian company's range of cars, all based around the same front-mounted twin-turbocharged V6 engine, continued to expand, but as UK imports had once again ended this was of little significance to British car buyers.

Mazda: The company finally entered the 'mini' market in the UK (it had been strong in that sector in Japan for many years) with the launch of the rather narrow and upright front-drive 121 models – sold with either a 56bhp/1.1-litre or a 65bhp/1.3-litre four-cylinder overhead-cam engine.

Mercedes-Benz: Although the first official pictures were shown of a new-generation SL roadster range – the first since 1971 – this car would not be launched until 1989 *(for all technical details, see the 1989 section).*

The range-heading 190E 2.3-16 was upgraded in mid-summer with a larger engine, becoming the 190E 2.5-16. From this point the Cosworth-developed 16-valve twin-cam engine became a 204bhp/2,498cc unit. As before, this was backed by a Getrag five-speed transmission. There were no style or major equipment changes.

Like BMW, Mercedes-Benz had an eye to future exhaust emission rules, replacing the original carburetted 200 (E-class) model with a new-type fuel-injected 200E, which sold for £17,150 and had a 122bhp/2-litre four-cylinder engine.

MG: Still playing the heritage card for all it was worth, Rover introduced the MG Maestro Turbo towards the end of the year, putting it on sale during the winter of 1988/89.

The specification was predictable enough, for this was an MG Maestro into which the engine/transmission package of the unsuccessful MG Montego Turbo had been inserted.

The cars were actually completed by Tickford in Coventry (who had only recently built the Ford Sierra RS500 Cosworth) and featured very prominent transverse rear spoilers and had a claimed top speed of at least 125mph.

Mitsubishi: Like other Japanese car-makers, Mitsubishi was developing a positive blizzard of new models in the late 1980s. In 1988 it was time for new Colt and Lancer ranges (interrelated, with the same basic front-drive layout) to take over from cars which had only been on sale for four years – and in turn these new types would be super-seded only four years later.

Two more derivatives of the modern Galant family – with 143bhp/2-litre injected or 74bhp/1.8-litre turbodiesel engines – were added in mid-year.

Taking the successful Shogun model further upmarket, a new 150bhp/V6 3-litre engine was announced in Japan in the autumn, which would also be used in other future Mitsubishis and would become the favoured choice in later-generation Shoguns. It was not until world markets turned down and the Japanese received a severe financial fright that model cycles began to be stretched.

Morgan: That very British maker of sportscars reverted towards an all-British Plus 4 during the year by replacing the 2-litre Fiat twin-cam engine

with the 16-valve twin-cam M16 2-litre from Rover.

In many ways this was the nicest and best-balanced of all the four-cylinder types offered so far, for the high-revving engine, backed by Rover's own five-speed gearbox, gave a power/weight ratio of 160bhp/tonne.

Nissan: The new front-wheel-drive Maxima (a model name not seen before on a Nissan) was revealed during the year as a replacement for the old rear-drive Laurel, with UK sales promised for 1989. This was the first of a new breed of Nissans, having a 3-litre V6 engine driving the front wheels and rounded rather than angular lines – a sure sign that the Japanese company's stylists had finally decided to fall into line with the rest of the motoring world.

But the prettiest new Nissan of 1988 was the 200SX coupe which appeared in October. Replacing the old-style Silvia coupe, the 200SZ retained a front-engine/rear-drive layout, this time with a much more powerful, 2-litre, twin-cam engine. UK deliveries would begin in 1989.

The second-generation Prairie – larger, faster, more powerful and more pleasingly-shaped than before – took over from the first-generation types (which had been made for six years) in the autumn, though British sales did not begin until 1989. The new-type Prairie had all-independent suspension, its base engine being a 2-litre model.

Opel: The last of the Manta coupes was delivered to a British customer in May, and with it, all sales of Opels in the UK ended. This brought to an end a 21-year period in which two GM-owned concerns – Opel and Vauxhall – had come progressively closer together. Opel had taken over design leadership for all new cars, and by the 1980s new Vauxhalls were nothing more than Opels with a different badge. Thereafter, Vauxhalls were only sold in the UK, and Opels were sold in the rest of Europe.

Peugeot: The increasingly popular 405 range, which was already proving to be *exactly* what many fleet managers had been looking for, expanded further with the arrival of two different diesel engine options – a normally-aspirated 70bhp/1.9-litre and a turbocharged 92bhp/1.77-litre.

Porsche: Enthusiasts for Stuttgart's flat-six air-cooled cars found something new to drool over during the year when the Type 964 – it was still officially badged as a 911 Carrera – appeared. Subtly smoother in shape than the earlier 911 from which it had evolved, it had a 250bhp/3.6-litre version of the famous engine as well as permanent four-wheel drive.

Apart from the existing 959, a supercar in every way, including its performance and price, the new Carrera 4 was the first Porsche road car to offer all-wheel drive. Its chassis was radically different from before – it had coil spring instead of torsion bar front suspension, plus coil spring/semi-trailing arm rear suspension (so all historic links with the VW Beetle had gone at last) – the platform was clearly quite new, and indeed Porsche later claimed that 85 per cent of the parts were new, though that figure included many modified versions of old components. Furthermore – although it was not mentioned at the time – a simpler, rear-drive version of the new Carrera 4 was also on the way and would appear in 1989.

Towards the end of the year, the front-engine/rear-drive 944 went one stage further with the release of a 165bhp version of the 2.7-litre single-cam engine, and a 211bhp twin-cam 16-valve version of the same engine, opened out to 2,990cc, was also launched, making this the largest four-cylinder engine in current production. Without the twin Lanchester balancer shafts, which were a part of the specification, this unit would surely not have been smooth enough to go on sale.

Renault: An ambitious new range – the 19 family of hatchbacks – appeared in June, though other versions would follow, including notchback saloons in 1989.

The 19 was a replacement for the gawky 9/11 models, and used several different combinations of the transverse-engine/front-wheel-drive theme. As by now expected from Renault, the new car was no beauty, although the five-door style was longer, wider *and* taller than the ousted 11.

There was a new engine family, which Renault called the Energy type, of which an 80bhp/1.4-litre overhead-cam version was expected to be the most popular, while higher up the range there was a new 140bhp/1,764cc power unit for the sporty models. Renault was nothing if not keen (and clever) on engine design.

A four-wheel-drive version of the Espace, called the Quadra, was announced, using the same 118bhp/2-litre engine as was being forecast for future use in the 21.

Rover: As expected, Rover followed Honda's lead by offering the enlarged 2.7-litre V6 in its top-of-the-range 800 models. The 827 model – a direct replacement for the 825 types which had been on sale for less than two years – had 177bhp and significantly increased torque.

Later in the year, the company also announced five-door fastback/hatchback versions of the 800 platform, the style being a distinct throwback to the old SD1 type of the previous decade.

Saab: More than three years after it launched the 9000 as a hatchback, Saab added a notchback design to the range early in the year, using a slightly-modified version of the front-wheel-drive platform, and retaining the same wide choice of engines and power outputs.

Later in the year, to further liven up the 9000's rather staid image, Saab also introduced the 9000T16 Carlsson (named after Erik Carlsson, the company's legendary rally driver *cum* PR man).

Seat: A new model from Spain looked just like a Fiat Panda at first glance, but it was badged as a Seat Marbella. Although it was almost pure Fiat, with the same shell, old-fashioned pushrod engines (which dated from the 1950s), plus a high-and-narrow style, it was made and marketed independently, and at £4,199 for the 903cc-engined version it was around £300 cheaper than the equivalent Panda. Fiat was not best pleased, but at the time of the divorce from Seat in the early 1980s this sort of situation had been envisaged, and accepted.

Subaru: A new-generation Justy arrived near the end of the year, with a choice of single-cam three-cylinder or four-cylinder engines and an improved version of its simple four-wheel drive.

Suzuki: The Vitara 4x4 arrived in October to take over from the earlier SJ410/SJ413 types on which it was based. Although the Vitara shared many of the older car's components, it was significantly larger in many ways – with a 6in longer wheelbase, wider tracks, independent front suspension and an altogether more upmarket interior and (Suzuki hoped) image.

Vitaras could not approach the on-the-limit off-road capabilities like various Land Rover models, but as they were much cheaper and definitely of the Kings Road-cruise tendency, they soon became very popular.

A new-generation Swift was revealed in September, this car having more rounded lines than before, with a lowered nose. As before, there was front-drive, and a choice between related three and four-cylinder engines.

Toyota: By now confirmed as the largest car-maker in Japan (having passed Nissan, whose fortunes were in decline), Toyota introduced a new family of Sierra/Cavalier-sized Carinas to the UK in the spring. Available as a four or five-door saloon or an estate car, with a choice of engines, the Carina would have sold much better if Toyota GB had not deliberately restricted sales because of the quota limitations.

Two years after the smart front-engine/rear-drive Supra had been launched, Toyota finally produced a turbocharged version of that car's 3-litre twin-cam engine, which produced no less than 232bhp.

TVR: With the retro-look S model now firmly and successfully in production, the company developed a V8 S, which was powered by the Rover-derived light-alloy V8 engine as already found in other TVRs, and this soon became a more popular option than the original Ford V6 engine, which in turn grew from 2.8 to 2.9 litres displacement.

Later in the year, it was engine-upgrade time for the Tasmin-derived cars – the 390SE getting a full 4-litre and the SEAC a 4.5-litre version of the ubiquitous Rover-based V8.

Vauxhall: The arrival of the third-generation Cavalier in August was commercially the most important new-model launch of the year. Taking over from the 1981–88 Cavalier, the new type was aimed directly at what was generally referred to as the Sierra market sector (for middle-sized cars) from which many thousands of fleet cars were chosen every year.

In spite of the pre-launch hype about the new Cavalier's novelties, this was really no more than a restatement of existing technical themes inside and underneath an all-new and rather smoother body style. As before there were to be four-door saloon and five-door hatchback types – though, surprisingly, there would never be an estate car version.

The basic layout was transverse-engine/front-wheel drive, with petrol and diesel engines from 75bhp/1.4 litres to 156bhp/2 litres, but there was also a four-wheel-drive car mated to the 130bhp eight-valve version of the 2-litre engine.

Although previewed in 1987, the 1.6-litre Nova GTE did not actually go on sale until June 1988. With 100bhp and a five-speed gearbox, but without the same immediate sporty image, it was an obvious competitor for cars like the Ford Fiesta XR2 – but it was more expensive, and in any case the XR2 was soon due to be retired, so Vauxhall was really several years behind the game.

Volkswagen: The third-generation Passat appeared in February, this being the first of the type to use a transverse instead of an in-line engine, which also meant that an entirely new type of front-wheel drive (similar in many ways to that of the latest Golf) was adopted.

Bigger, more rounded and more versatile than before, the Passat was immediately available with 1.6 and 1.8-litre eight-valve, 1.8-litre 16-valve and 1.6-litre diesel engines. In October, a 2-litre version of the 1.8-litre engine was phased in – the Passat being the first of many VW-Audi models to pick up that engine size.

Later in the year, the long-rumoured sporting Corrado hatchback coupe appeared, a car which would always be built for VW by Karmann. Although the Corrado was really a next-generation Scirocco, it did not replace that car, the two models continuing to be built at Karmann for another four years.

Like the Scirocco, though, the Corrado was based on a Golf platform – in this case the second-series Golf GTi – though with a new type of three-door almost-four-seater style. At first, there was to be a choice of 139bhp/16-valve or 160bhp/supercharged G-Lader/eight-valve 1.8-litre engines. A narrow-angle 2.8-litre V6 engine (the VR6 unit) was rumoured to be following up.

Four-wheel-drive Synchro versions of the Golf and Jetta models finally went on sale in the UK at the end of year, in both cases mated to the rather humble 90bhp/eight-valve/1.8-litre engine – a combination which hardly necessitated 4WD in the first place! For that reason, therefore, UK demand was very low.

In March, the company celebrated the completion of the 10 millionth Golf.

Volvo: Years later than expected and forecast, the 440 hatchback finally went public in May. Using the same basic platform, front-wheel-drive engineering and Renault engine as the 480 hatchback coupe (which was the first of this breed), the 440 had a typically-Volvo (hard-edged) style, which looked obsolete from the day it was announced. Amazingly, Volvo suggested that the new 440 would help them dissolve the company's staid image.

Put on the market and greeted by waves of indifference from motoring writers, it would nevertheless sell reasonably well for six years, before being dropped in 1995, at which point few realized that it had died because they had been ignoring it for years.

A third member of this 400-series range was still to come – the 460, a four-door notchback saloon, which would eventually reach the British market in 1990.

This most conservative of car-makers caused great astonishment in March, when it announced a twin-cam 16-valve 2.3-litre engine which also included twin Lanchester balance shafts. Originally offered in the 740GLT, it would soon find use in other Volvo models.

The 480 Turbo (a hatchback coupe) was announced in January, but as its engine only produced 120bhp (compared with 109bhp for the normally-aspirated model) one wondered what all the fuss was about.

Westfield: Following its bruising court battle with Caterham, after which it was told to stop making Lotus Seven lookalike models, Westfield regrouped and launched the new SEi, which still looked somewhat similar to the Caterham Seven, but had an altogether different, brand-new, tubular chassis-frame and all-round independent suspension.

Like the Caterham (formerly Lotus) Seven, the Westfield would continue to look the same for the next decade, but would use a whole variety of engines. At first, though, the SEi was powered by a much-modified old-style Ford Kent unit of 110bhp/1.6 litres. A more modern CVH-powered Westfield followed during 1989.

Industrial developments

This was the year in which the British Government finally rid itself of the perenially loss-making Rover/Land Rover car/4x4 combine, accepting what looked then (and still looks today) the ludicrously low bid from British Aerospace of £150 million, while at the same time agreeing to write off up to £550 million of accumulated debt. It also transpired during the next two years or so that the Government had additionally offered certain sweeteners to reduce the purchase price even further. In return, BAe had to guarantee not to sell the company for at least five years – a commitment that was only *just* honoured before BAe sold out at a profit to BMW of Germany.

Nissan announced that it was to set up a new R&D facility in the UK to service the needs of the modern British plant.

When the last French-assembled Citroen 2CV was built at the ancient Levallois factory in Paris, in February, it was the end of a very long era for a much-loved car. Although 2CVs would still be built in Portugal and Spain for a time, it ruled a line under an amazing 40-year career in France.

Technical developments

Jaguar's XJ220, revealed with great pomp and circumstance at the motor show in October, looked sensational, but turned out to be a false start. Conceived in their spare time by an informal group of engineers known as the Saturday Club, the XJ220 was a gorgeous mid-engined two-seater with a claimed top speed of 220mph.

Powered by a 500bhp racing version of the famous V12 engine, with twin-overhead-camshaft cylinder heads and four-valve combustion chambers, this car also had four-wheel drive. Many months later (after, indeed, the much changed XJ220 production car had been shown) it was learned that the first car had never even turned a wheel before it was shown in public, and that no-one knew if the car really would reach its claimed speed! This project then went to ground – and it would be another year before anything else was heard. (See 1989...)

During the year Honda unveiled a very clever system of variable valve timing intended for use in its twin-cam engines. A steel spring-loaded pin moved under oil pressure inside a casing attached to the intermediary rocker arms to effect a change in valve lift, and even in timing, by moving the rockers from one cam profile to another, which could provide power improvements without ruining flexibility. This patented system would be phased-in on some high-revving Hondas before the end of 1989.

Men of Influence

Enzo Ferrari

The legendary master of the world's most famous motor company had been frail for years, had not appeared in public since October 1987, nor actively in charge of the company for some time, but his death at 90, in August 1988, inspired mountainous eulogies.

In real life, as opposed to fiction and the PR broadsheets, Enzo Ferrari had been a despot who ruled his empire by whim and fear, but there is no doubt that under his thumb the Ferrari business produced some of the most charismatic race and road cars in the world for more than 40 years.

Born in 1898, his first job was testing Lancia vans, but he eventually drove racecars, joined Alfa Romeo in 1929, setting up Scuderia Ferrari to run the works racing team. Then, after setting up his own company in Maranello to make and repair machine tools, he began to build Ferrari-badged cars immediately after the Second World War.

The first Ferraris had single-cam V12 engines and were racing cars which could also be used on the road, but the split between racing and road cars was complete by the end of the 1940s. Thereafter Ferrari's passion was for racing – single-seater and two-seater sportscars – with a small but gradually increasing number of road cars being sold at exorbitant prices to help finance the sport.

Ferrari F1 racecars were supreme in the early 1950s, the early 1960s and the mid-1970s, but were by no means as dominant, nor for so long, as some of the hagiographers would have one believe. Ferrari, however, never wavered in its support of F1, and except for periodic 'withdrawals' for political or industrial reasons, the team was ever-present on the grids.

Ferrari road cars like the 250GT of the 1950s, the 275GTB and Daytona of the 1960s, the mid-engined Dinos and Boxers of the 1970s and the Testarossas of the 1980s, were all ferociously fast, always with better-built chassis than (Pininfarina-styled) bodies and invariably desirable.

Ferrari himself was no engineer, so he hired and ruthlessly discarded those he thought could do the design job for him. His personal life was shattered in 1956 when his only 'official' son, Dino, died – after which he became increasingly embittered and cynical. He was a latter-day ruler of all he surveyed, and expected everyone to come to him, rather than the other way round. Although he occasionally left Italy, throughout his life he never flew and always resisted setting foot into a train if he could.

Having sold 50 per cent of his business to Fiat in 1969 in exchange for their control over his road car enterprises, he retained the other half interest and insisted that his beloved racing cars should always be under his personal control. Although he did not attend F1 races after Dino had died, he kept in close touch with his team directors and was ever-present, if only at the end of a telephone.

Towards the end of his life, the existence of a second (illegitimate) son – Piero Lardi – was acknowledged, and 10 per cent of the business was bequeathed to him, the rest going to Fiat.

Ferrari the company was expected to change after 'the old man' died – and so it did, becoming more commercial and less exciting to watch and to be a part of. Ferrari, in any case, died at the height of the 'investment' boom, so after his death the value of old-type Ferraris plummeted and demand for new models also fell away. Even so, with the backing of cash-rich Fiat, Ferrari's future was assured, well into the 21st century.

1989

In March, just before the British economic boom, which had been developing steadily in the mid-1980s, finally overheated, the Chancellor's Budget brought pleasant surprises to British motorists, who were beginning to think they deserved them after a difficult decade.

To encourage the use of unleaded fuel, the tax on a gallon was reduced by 4p, which made unleaded between 8p and 10p cheaper than four-star. Predictably, the demand for unleaded petrol soared – from 6 per cent of the market to 14 per cent in a single month.

However, the Bank of England raised interest rates drastically during the year (which caused mortgage and hire purchase rates to go through the roof) and quite suddenly the so-called value of collectors' or classic cars suddenly eroded.

This was the start of a serious British recession which would see unemployment rise towards the 3 million mark and UK car sales slump badly, from 2.4 to 1.6 million in only two years. Paradoxically, though, UK car sales *and* imports both reached an all-time high during 1989. Not only were 2,373,391 cars sold during the year, but a massive 1,370,589 of them – nearly 58 per cent – were imports (many of them, of course, being Fords and Vauxhalls brought in from factories in Spain, Germany and Belgium).

New models

Alfa Romeo: 'It's so ugly, it's beautiful!', is how one nonplussed British journalist greeted the SZ coupe which was launched in March. Based on the platform of the existing front-engine/rear-drive 75 saloon, the SZ's startlingly brutal Zagato two-door fixed-head coupe body hid a 210bhp/3-litre version of the famous V6 engine.

Audi: Although a four-valves-per-cylinder twin-cam head had appeared on the 200-off short-wheelbase Quattro Sport in 1983, nothing further had come of this – until 1989. Starting in May, a developed variety of four-valve head began to appear on the company's five-cylinder engines – thus the

'20-valve' phenomenon arose.

The original 20-valve-equipped road car was the 200 Quattro 20V, whose 2,226cc engine produced a brawny 220bhp. This, and four-wheel drive, ensured a top speed of 150mph in great security. This engine would soon be fitted to other sporting Audis.

In the autumn, every car in the Audi range to be sold in the UK was fitted with a three-way catalyst as standard, which meant that prices had to rise (by at least £300), and that all new Audis had to run on unleaded petrol.

The entry-level 90 model inherited a 2.3-litre instead of a 2-litre five-cylinder engine, and for the first time there was a 20-valve 90 Quattro (price £19,460).

Because the 200 models were dropped (they had always been far too costly to sell well in the UK), the 100 range was expanded to fill the gap, so for the first time a turbocharged 100 went on sale.

Bentley: *(For technical changes, see the Rolls-Royce entry.)*

BMW: The new 8-series coupe was introduced in the autumn, being a replacement for the 6-series which had originally been launched in the mid-1970s. Bigger, heavier and altogether more powerful than the 6-series, the new model was based on some new-generation 5-series/7-series chassis components, but had a new type of complex five-link independent rear suspension, and was powered by the 300bhp/5-litre V12 engine, linked to a six-speed gearbox. BMW made much of the fact that the top speed was 155mph – but that this was electronically limited, and could have been more if necessary.

Z1 roadster deliveries, in left-hand-drive form, began in the UK before the end of the year. Priced at £36,925, it was no surprise that there were few takers in Britain for this over-hyped product.

Citroen: The arrival of the large new XM model was a major investment for Citroen, this being the car which replaced the CX models which had been running since 1974.

Styled by Bertone as a five-door hatchback, the new front-wheel-drive XM featured an advanced type of self-levelling hydropneumatic suspension, making this Citroen even more com-

plex than any previous model.

From the start there was a choice of five different engines, all developments of existing Peugeot-Citroen units. These included full 2-litre versions of the XU family, which already powered many Peugeot 405s and Citroen BXs, the PRV V6 was enlarged to 170bhp/3 litres, while the diesel was not only larger than before but had three valves per cylinder.

In yet another example of 'mechanical Meccano' which Citroen had applied to the BX, well over six years after it had originally been put on sale as a front-drive 1.4-litre car, the company announced the BX 4x4, which linked the corporate 1.9-litre engine with a full-time four-wheel-drive installation.

Daihatsu: Another Japanese car with a peculiar name, the Daihatsu Applause was a front-drive family saloon with a 1.6-litre engine. Devoid of charisma, it would always be a slow-seller in the British market.

Dodge: At the Detroit motor show, Chrysler stunned everyone by showing the Dodge Viper concept car, and the V10-engined monster caused such a reaction that the company decided to turn it into a production proposition.

Ferrari: The long-running Mondial was replaced by the Mondial T in the spring, the latest car not only featuring a 300bhp/32-valve/3.4-litre version of the famous V8 engine, but also relocating it in the 'north-south' position and driving it through a brand-new five-speed transmission. Top speed was expected to be at least 155mph. A cabriolet version of this 2+2-seater chassis was soon made available.

Later in the year, at the Frankfurt motor show, the new mid-engined 348tb (coupe) and 348ts (spider) twins arrived, taking over from the long-running 328GTB/GTS, whose roots were in the early 1970s. The new-generation 348 used the same in-line 300bhp/3.4-litre 32-valve V8 engine and layout as in the latest Mondial, but the new cars had a very different and somehow subdued style by Pininfarina, featuring side strakes/cooling guides to the engine bay, which harked back to the larger Testarossa model.

Fiat: Towards the end of the year, the new Tempra saloon arrived as a direct replacement for the old-fashioned Regata. This was effectively a four-door notchback saloon version of the Tipo hatchback, with the same basic platform, engine range, inner panels and doors – and was also closely related to the latest Lancia Dedra saloon.

In the autumn, for the start-up of the 1990 model year, the Uno was given a front-end facelift and several changes to the engine line-up. The new Uno fleet included a turbocharged 118bhp/1.37-litre unit and a 1.1-litre version of the modern FIRE engine.

Following the changes made to the related Lancia Thema in 1988, the Croma was also revised during 1989. Although there were no style changes, there was a new type of turbodiesel (not sold in the UK) and a four-speed automatic option instead of the original three-speeder.

The venerable mid-engined X1/9 (theoretically badged as a Bertone since 1982, but always known as a Fiat) was finally dropped during 1989, more than 16 years after a smaller-engined version had first been put on sale.

In all that time there had been just one engine change and only minor alterations of style, but around 180,000 cars had been sold.

Ford: The big news of the year was the launch of a new-generation Fiesta, with a completely new platform, finally replacing the original Fiesta of 1976–88 vintage.

The new car was somewhat larger, with a longer wheelbase and a more roomy cabin. As expected, there was all-independent suspension, a choice of three-door or five-door coachwork, and the usual broad line-up of petrol and diesel engines, starting from a 55bhp/1.1-litre unit and topping out (for the time being) with a 110bhp 1.6-litre XR2i model.

Later in the year, the company also launched a new eight-valve 2-litre twin-cam engine, the I4, which immediately took over from old-style single-cam 2-litre Pintos. Developing either 109bhp (carburetted) or 125bhp (fuel-injected), this engine was fitted to Sierras and Granada/Scorpios from mid-year. A 16-valve version was known to be under development, but this would not be launched until 1991.

A well-known model name – 1600E

– was reintroduced in mid-year, but this time it was a great disappointment, being merely a cosmetic makeover of the existing Orion 1.6i Ghia saloon.

Honda: The amazingly complex, effective, but somehow unexciting mid-engined NSX supercar was previewed in the spring, but would not go into production until 1990. In almost every way – in engineering, detail construction and build quality – the NSX was a better car than the Ferrari 328GTBs with which it had to compete, yet few of them found buyers in the UK.

The basic mid-engined rear-drive layout was familiar to most motoring enthusiasts. In Honda's case, however, the NSX's monocoque was mainly built from aluminium (to reduce weight and minimize the risk of corrosion), while power was by a 270bhp 24-valve 90-degree V6 engine, a derivative of the Legend's power unit.

A new-generation Honda Accord range made its world debut in the autumn, this having a wider, flatter and more graceful style than its predecessor. British sales would begin at the end of the year, but would only persist until 1993, when yet another new Accord would take over, that car actually cloning the Rover 600 and being built in the UK, in Swindon.

The 1989-variety Accord used an all-new platform and body style on a longer wheelbase than before, had a transverse-engine/front-wheel-drive layout, as expected, and there was a choice of new-design 'balancer' 16-valve 2-litre or 2.2-litre engines, plus a saloon or an Aerodeck (hatchback/estate) style. Prelude-type four-wheel steering was available on the top-of-the-range model, which had a 150bhp/2,156cc engine.

Further changes to the appealing little CRX coupe for 1990 model year included the arrival of a 160bhp/1.6-litre VTEC twin-cam engine option. This would also be fitted to other Hondas in the coming months.

Jaguar: The amazing XJ220 supercar was introduced in December, well over *two years* before sales could possibly begin (the first deliveries, in fact, took place in mid-1992).

Although the styling studies shown at the time – no real car existed – showed a car very similar to the XJ220 seen at

the NEC in 1988, the car to be sold was very different under the skin. Shorter, lighter and with rear instead of four-wheel drive, it was to be powered by a slightly detuned version of the twin-turbocharged 3.5-litre V6 engine which the racing TWR Jaguar XJR-11s had been using all season.

This engine, incidentally, was a lineal development of the four-cam 90-degree V6 which had been designed in 1984 for use in Austin-Rover's short-lived MG Metro 6R4 rally car.

The production car was set to be built in a new factory at Bloxham, near Banbury, by a company half owned by Jaguar and half by TWR. Demand was colossal, for although the company stated that only 350 were to be built, more than 1,200 orders were received in a matter of days – all of them with a deposit of £75,000 + VAT!

This was boom time, though, and the bubble would eventually burst. Priced at £361,000 in 1989, that price was to be indexed to British inflation, and chosen customers would be asked to make a further interim payment of £100,000 while construction was going ahead.

By 1993, when production was in full swing, many customers tried to back out of the deal, but found the contracts they had signed were watertight. All sorts of legal action was threatened and actioned, but in the end many customers refused to take their cars, walked away from moneys paid and total production eventually halted at 271 cars. The last cars were apparently *still* unsold in 1996.

Only three years after it had introduced the XJ40 shape of XJ6 saloon, Jaguar gave it a brace of new AJ6-type 24-valve twin-cam engines – one of them a new 200bhp 3.2-litre, the other a 223bhp 4-litre, both being versions of the original 3.6-litre, which had been in production for six years.

By this time, around 100,000 of this body style had been produced – but there was still no sign of the V12-engined version which had been rumoured for so long.

Following the launch of the TWR-modified XJ-S in 1988, the company supported a further modification, namely the development of a 6-litre V12-powered version. At the time this was thought to be a totally TWR initiative, but in the early 1990s the same basic 6-litre engine would be applied to mainstream Jaguars as well.

Lamborghini: With the Countach coming towards the end of its life, and the Diablo nearly ready for launch, there was just time to introduce the Countach Anniversary model, of which 430 cars were due to be made. Mechanically these were virtually the same as the previous Countach model.

The Diablo was previewed at the end of the year, a massively powerful supercar by any standards, which used the same basic layout as the Countach, complete with a 492bhp/7.7-litre V12 engine. Development of this car would never have been possible without Chrysler finance.

At first glance, the Diablo was faster, more capable and more attractive than the Countach had ever been, but testers later damned it with faint praise, pointing to its cockpit and handling deficiencies. Even at this stage, there were rumours of a pending 4x4 version, which excited all the technical buffs.

Lancia: The new Dedra range of four-door saloons were revealed in April. Totally different from any previous Lancia (and fitting in above the Delta range, which was still in production), the Dedras were closely based on the platform, cabin, doors and running gear of the Fiat Tipo.

More upmarket and faster than the Tipo, the Dedra arrived with a choice of 1.6, 1.8 or 2-litre/eight-valve petrol engines or a 92bhp/1.9-litre turbo-diesel, but the diesel was never put on sale in the UK, where deliveries would begin in 1990.

The four-wheel-drive Integrale took a further step in May with the launch of the 16-valve model. Previous Integrales had used the ageing eight-valve Fiat-based twin-cam, but this engine was the latest turbocharged 16-valver, as already being used in the Thema and being prepared for other Fiats and Lancias. Except for a bonnet bulge, needed to clear the bulkier engine, there were no style changes. Peak power was up from 185 to 200bhp. As before, the Integrale was readily available in the UK, but only ever with left-hand drive.

Still trying to establish some sort of UK market for the tiny square-backed Y10, Lancia revised it during the year, adding both a 1.1-litre FIRE engine

and a 1.3-litre GT model as well.

Land Rover: The Discovery arrived in September, fleshing out a Land Rover range which had previously had a yawning gap between the old-style Land Rover 90/100 models (now to be called Defenders), and the glossy, up-market Range Rover series.

The Discovery used a mildly modified Range Rover chassis, still with the traditional 100in wheelbase, and came with a choice of 145bhp/3.5-litre carburetted V8 or 111bhp/2.5-litre turbo-diesel units.

For the first year at least, the Discovery was only to be available with manual transmission and a new-style three-door estate car bodyshell (with interior style by Conran Associates) – but there were many more derivatives already in the pipeline.

Lotus: British pundits were adamant that the brand-new front-wheel-drive Elan which appeared in October was not only the star of the London Motorfair, but was also the most important new car of the year. Technically that might have been so, but this Elan would be a commercial failure, being far too expensive to build, and it never made any money for the firm.

Built around a traditional steel backbone chassis, and with a VARI-style GRP-based bodyshell, the Elan had a transverse (Isuzu) 16-valve/1.6-litre twin-cam engine driving the front wheels. Normally-aspirated types had 130bhp, but most Elans would be built with the 165bhp turbocharged unit.

Wide, sinuously-styled, but short, the Elan had excellent steering and road-holding – better than any Lotus previously put on sale. Deliveries began in the spring of 1990.

Less than two years after the new-shape (X180) Lotus Esprit had been introduced, the company offered a much more powerful (264bhp) version of the Turbo model, claiming a top speed of 165mph.

Marcos: The long-running Mantula (ex-Marcos GT) coupe was revised for 1990, with independent rear suspension becoming optional.

Maserati: Still developing the Biturbo theme – but still, it seemed, unable to establish any lasting base in the UK, Maserati announced a twin-cam

24-valve version of its 90-degree V6 engine, the result being a 245bhp output from 2 litres.

Mazda: The MX-5 sportscar, rumoured for some time, finally went on sale in the USA, badged as the Miata, and immediately became a big hit. Strangely from a company which normally produced transverse-engined, front-wheel-drive cars, this was a front-engined, rear-drive two-seater. Mazda admitted openly that they had engineered the MX-5 to have some of the character and ethos of an MG Midget, and this new car, with its urgent high-revving 1.6-litre twin-cam engine, rounded lines and small proportions, seemed to get it all exactly right. UK deliveries would begin in the spring of 1990.

In March, a new-generation 323 range was introduced in Japan, this being a restatement of the familiar transverse-engine/front-wheel-drive theme, but with an enlarged platform and more rounded body styling. The five-door hatchback version, in particular, had a much lower and more curvaceous nose than before. Called the Astina in Japan, this soon became a fast-selling type in the UK, along with the three-door hatchback and four-door saloons which accompanied it.

Although the Wankel-powered RX-7 was not a big seller in the UK, it was very successful in its principal export market, the USA. This justified a mid-life facelift in June, when the Wankel engine's peak power was pushed up to 205bhp.

Mercedes-Benz: The new-generation SL roadster (for which a detachable hardtop was also available) went on sale in the spring, this being the first all-new SL platform since 1971. (The old-style SL remained in production for a few months, but the last of all was produced before the summer shutdown in Sindelfingen.)

Larger, heavier, smoother and more powerful than the old-fashioned variety, the new SL picked up much of its chassis engineering from the S-class and medium-sized (later to be known as E-class) family car ranges. Naturally, there was all-independent suspension, four-wheel disc brakes, anti-lock braking, loads of electronics and a mass of other advanced equipment.

One of the features was a safety

rollover bar, which could either be erected by the driver, or could be retracted, but set to operate automatically if the car turned over in an accident. Three engines were available at first – a 190bhp/3-litre single-cam 'six', a 231bhp/3-litre 24-valve twin-cam and a 326bhp/5-litre 32-valve twin-cam V8. An even more extravagant version, with a 6-litre V12 – was also under development!

In the autumn, the W124 (later to be called E-class) was given a makeover, with detail style changes and the addition to the line-up of a 24-valve twin-cam 3-litre engine developing 220bhp and – for the first time in Europe – a *five*-speed automatic transmission option.

The G-Wagen, which had gone into production 10 years earlier, was also much revised, though without major styling changes. Inside there was a much more car-like facia panel and a new engine option – a 3-litre/175bhp six-cylinder.

Mitsubishi: The Shogun range was revised during the year, though without styling changes. From the spring of 1989, all Shoguns were built on the longer of the two original wheelbases, and the rear live axle was now located by coil springs and radius arms.

Engines, too, were reshuffled, for there was a new 139bhp/overhead-cam/3-litre V6, while the 2.5-litre turbo-diesel was boosted to give 94bhp. Thus equipped, the Shogun became an even more viable rival to the Range Rover, and sold extremely well in the UK.

Lancer changes introduced late in the year included catalyst-equipped engines (these were still novelties, but would become universal in Europe in the next two years or so), a hatchback body option and a four-wheel-drive installation on some models.

The modern Galant range was widened even further. At long last the four-wheel-drive/four-wheel-steer version (this chassis was already being used by the works team in World Championship rallying), was made available in the UK without turbocharging and offering 142bhp, for £16,969 – which made a few potential Sierra RS Cosworth customers think again.

Towards the end of its life, the old-type Starion was given a different, lean-burn, 2.6-litre four-cylinder engine,

which produced 153bhp. There were no changes to the appearance or the chassis specification because this car was soon to be replaced by the USA-built 3000GT.

Nissan: The new-generation 300ZX coupe was launched early in the year, this being a faster, smoother and altogether more capable car than its predecessors. There were two versions of the 3-litre V6 engine, which even in normally-aspirated form produced 222bhp, giving a claimed top speed of more than 140mph, while the 280bhp turbocharged version's top speed rose to 155mph.

Styled in the USA, but engineered and developed in Japan, this was a telling example of the way that Japanese technology was now the equal of any in the world.

It was reshuffle time with the Sunny range, for the Ls gained a new 16-valve 1.4-litre engine, the 1.6-litre engine received a 16-valve head, while the quirky ZX coupe was given a 1.8-litre/16-valve engine. At the same time the ageing Micra was also given a new engine option, a 60bhp/1.2-litre unit.

Panther: The mid-engined four-wheel-drive Sierra RS Cosworth-engined Solo coupe finally staggered into production at the very end of the year, more than five years after the first rear-drive prototype was shown – and was almost immediately seen to be a sales disaster. Far too expensive (at £39,850) for what it offered, it was capable, but virtually unsaleable. Apparently Panther was losing money even at that high price, so it was no wonder that the project was abruptly terminated in the summer of 1990.

The long-running Kallista (son of 1976-vintage Lima) was given a final tweak in mid-year with the introduction of a 150bhp Ford 2.9-litre V6 engine to replace the obsolete 2.8-litre type. Prices started at £11,950. Kallista demand, however, was falling, and the lines would be halted completely in 1990.

Peugeot: In September, the company unwrapped the new large 605 saloon range, thus starting the career of a fine car which never sold anything like as well as it should have done. The 605 was a direct replacement for the old 604 (which had been in production

since the mid-1970s). Although it looked very similar to the 405 – Pininfarina had shaped both bodyshells – it was totally different in every detail, being a larger car with a longer wheelbase.

As expected, this was a transverse-engine/front-wheel-drive machine (the 604 had a front engine and rear drive) and there was a choice of engines from day one, including a 115bhp or 130bhp/2-litre 'four', and two versions of the ageing PRV 90-degree V6 in 3-litre form, one being a 12-valve version with 170bhp, the other a 24-valver with 200bhp.

Two new versions of the 405 saloon arrived during the spring, these being four-wheel-drive conversions of the original front-wheel-drive layout. Both used a 1.9-litre Type XU engine, the GL x 4 having an eight-valve/110bhp unit and the more sporty Mi16 x 4 a 16-valve/twin-cam/160bhp version, giving a claimed top speed of 134mph.

The latest version of the 309 saloon was a ferociously fast derivative, complete with the 160bhp/1.9-litre 16-valve twin-cam engine normally found in the 405 Mi16.

Porsche: As forecast, a rear-drive version of the new-generation Carrera 4 – logically enough, called Carrera 2 – was revealed during the year, British-market deliveries beginning in the autumn.

Porsche, who had dropped the previous type of semi-automatic transmission (Sportomatic) from the 911 nearly a decade earlier, came back into this sector with a new type of transmission called Tiptronic. The new system was based around a ZF torque converter, a lock-up clutch and a four-speed epicyclic gearbox, with sophisticated electronic control systems which suited the sporting character of the 911 much better than before. In one particular mode, it could be used as a clutchless manual transmission, which made many otherwise reluctant 911 customers a lot happier.

The 330bhp/5-litre 32-valve V8-engined Porsche 928GT was the fastest version yet of this long-running front-engine/rear-drive sports coupe, which eventually went on UK sale in March, priced at a staggering £55,441.

The 928s had never sold as well as the rear-engined air-cooled 911s, which mystified many unbiased observers who found it a much better car. There was no doubt, though, that the 928 never had the charisma or sheer character of the 911.

Proton: After a long delay following the start of production in Malaysia, the first Proton cars went on sale in the UK in March, but the Saga models were really no more than lightly facelifted Mitsubishis.

Range Rover: In October, two 1990-model cars were announced, both being more powerful than before. The V8 engine was enlarged, now being a 185bhp/3.9-litre version of the famous light-alloy design, while the VM turbodiesel was enlarged to 119bhp/2,500cc, giving much better low-speed torque.

Reliant: A revised version of the slow-selling SS1 sportscar was launched in October, with a neater front-end style and better detailing. There were two engines to choose from – the 75bhp/1.4-litre Ford CVH and the 135bhp/1.8-litre Nissan unit.

Renault: Having filled out the range of engines for the 21, which included a new 65bhp normally-aspirated diesel of 1,870cc (which wasn't really powerful enough for this car) and a 12-valve/140bhp version of the 1,995cc unit, Renault concentrated on body style options, adding a five-door hatchback version to the existing saloons and estates for 1990.

Later, a four-wheel-drive version of the 21, the Quadra, was introduced, this having the 175bhp turbocharged engine at first, though a lower-powered (140bhp) version would also be offered.

The Renault 19 Chamade, previewed at the end of the year, was a four-door saloon version of the 19 hatchback with the same basic range of engines.

Although the 25 was a slow seller in the UK, the company revealed yet another variant in July – this being a 160bhp/3-litre version of the car, priced at £17,520. Later, the 12-valve 2-litre arrived, to produce the TXi.

Rolls-Royce: From October, for the 1990 models, the Silver Spirit (and equivalent Bentley) saloon models (but not the Corniche convertibles) were equipped with electronically-sensed adaptive damping, and at the same time there were wider-rim wheels.

Rover: In August, the company previewed an all-new K-series four-cylinder engine, this originally having eight-valve/single-cam or 16-valve/twin-cam layouts, to be made in sizes between 1.1 and 1.4 litres. Intended for use in cars like the revised Minis and in the Honda-based Rover 200, it was to become a very important building block for Rover during the 1990s and would eventually be stretched to 1.8 litres.

Then, in October, the company revealed the new 200 hatchback range, this being closely based on the Honda Concerto. Taking over from the first-series Rover 200 (which had been on the market for five years), the new-generation model had a choice of two 16-valve engines at first – the 94bhp/1.4-litre K-series and the 115bhp/1.6-litre single-overhead-cam Honda unit.

Even at this stage, Rover admitted that there was an additional body style to come, this being a four-door saloon to be called a Rover 400, and that this would appear in 1990.

Saab: In the autumn, a heavily-redesigned version of the existing twin-cam engine was unveiled, this being a long-stroke 2,290cc unit with twin Lanchester balancer-shafts to make it feel smoother than before. The first version was a normally-aspirated 150bhp unit, used in the 9000 structure, but – as usual with Saab – several other derivatives were already being developed.

Subaru: The Japanese company surprised everyone with the launch of a smooth new Sierra/Cavalier-sized car, the Legacy, which had a choice of 1.8 or 2-litre flat-four engines, two or four-wheel drive, and – as a flagship model – a 220bhp turbocharged 4x4 version which clearly was destined for use in World Championship rallying. The Legacy was a step ahead of the more mundane flat-four-engined Subarus of the past, and the engine was totally new.

Toyota: Towards the end of the year the second-generation mid-engined MR2 took over from the original type, which had been on sale for five years.

The new-generation MR2 was larger and smoother-styled and was offered with a choice of 2-litre engines (still transversely mounted), which made it a more flexible sports coupe than before. The 119 and 158bhp twin-cam engines were closely related to those already being used in the larger Camry saloon and Celica GT models. The new MR2 was to be a lasting success in the UK.

A new-generation Celica – as previously, produced in 2-litre form with front-wheel drive, or (as the GT-Four) with four-wheel drive – was introduced during the year.

Based on a modified version of the earlier car's platform, its much more rounded body style proved controversial in that it offered much less glass area and seemed less elegant than the previous style. As before, front-drive cars used a normally-aspirated engine and the four-wheel-drive model a 200bhp turbocharged derivative.

A new-generation 4x4 off-roader, a big three or five-door estate car called the 4-Runner, was revealed in March. Different in many ways from the even bigger, old-fashioned, Land Cruiser, it would not go on UK sale until 1993 – *for all further details see that section.*

Although it was only a minor player in the UK concessionaire's line-up, the Camry was still considered valuable. A new twin-cam 156bhp flagship version of the V6 engine was offered from January.

For 1990 there was a substantially redesigned Land Cruiser with a longer wheelbase and more curvaceous lines. The VX, as it was known, would go on UK sale in 1990 with an enlarged six-cylinder diesel engine.

Although exactly right for rugged world markets, the Land Cruiser was not the most suitable player for the UK, where 4x4s were rarely put to practical use and smooth power units and upmarket interiors were thought more important.

Vauxhall: The most sensational new Vauxhall of the year (perhaps of *any* year) was the Lotus-Carlton, which used a 360bhp/3.6-litre twin-overhead-camshaft version of the existing six-cylinder engine equipped with twin turbochargers, one feeding each group of three cylinders.

In the manner of the Ford Sierra RS Cosworth, the rest of the Carlton was thoroughly revised, with new suspension settings, fat wheels and tyres and a *six*-speed all-synchromesh ZF transmission.

In every way, including its 180mph top speed and its near-£50,000 price, this was a monster for which there seemed to be no obvious market. Its engine made it too large for saloon car racing (there was now a very high minimum-weight clause for such large units), it was far too costly to compete in the BMW/Mercedes-Benz market, and its gearing was almost ludicrously high. The cars were all built at Lotus, in Norfolk (there was also an Opel-badged derivative), and when deliveries began in 1990 they would sell steadily, but at a disappointingly low rate, for the next two years.

Soon after the Lotus-Carlton was previewed, a normally-aspirated 3-litre version of the same engine, rated at 204bhp, was introduced for use in the Senator and the Carlton GSi. UK sales began towards the end of the year, when almost at once this new Senator became a very popular pursuit car choice by British police forces.

The smart new Calibra hatchback coupe was previewed in the autumn (though it would not be ready for sale until the summer of 1990), this car being developed on the platform of the latest-generation Cavalier and featuring the same transverse-engine/front-wheel-drive layout.

In the first phase there would be a choice of 115bhp (single-cam) and 150bhp (16-valve/twin-cam) 2-litre engines, though more powerful versions would follow. Testers commented that the Calibra's principal drawback was that it still felt like a Cavalier rather than a purpose-built high-performance sports coupe.

As expected, the 4x4 version of the Cavalier was given the 150bhp 16-valve version of the 2-litre engine from October, sales of the original eight-valve model having been extremely disappointing.

The Astra/Belmont range was given a new-style nose for 1989, but with few other changes, while 1990-model Novas were to be little changed except for the addition of a new Isuzu 1.5-litre diesel engine option.

Perhaps this was premature, but as Isuzu put a new four-wheel-drive Amigo sports utility on sale in the USA, rumours began to spread that it might eventually be built in Europe. This eventually came true, for the Amigo was the forerunner of the Vauxhall Frontera.

Volkswagen: A limited number of Rallye Golf G60 models went on the UK market during the year, these combining the 160bhp supercharged engine with the latest Synchro four-wheel-drive mechanism. The price for this limited-interest model was £16,940.

New Passat derivatives included a 160bhp/G-Lader supercharged four-wheel-drive type and a normally-aspirated 68bhp/1.9-litre diesel.

Volvo: At the end of the year, with sales due to begin early in 1990, the 460 saloon (a four-door notchback version of the 440 hatchback) was revealed, sharing the same basic platform and Renault-manufactured engines.

Yugo: The Sana, a Fiat-engined five-door hatchback with Italian (Giugiaro) styling, which had first been seen in Yugoslavia three years previously, finally went on sale in Britain. Smoother and more upmarket than existing Yugos, it was still a crudely-detailed design by Western European standards and very few were ever sold in the UK.

Industrial developments

Towards the end of the year, after a brisk takeover battle, Ford beat GM to ownership of Jaguar, paying an astonishing £1.6 *billion* to gain control in November 1989.

For Jaguar, the takeover came only just in time, for as the US market went into recession, sales were slipping, profits had almost disappeared again, and there was simply not enough cashflow to finance the development of new models.

In Europe, with Alfa Romeo now settled in Fiat's hands, it was Saab's turn to become an obvious takeover target, for though it was protected by the wealth of its Scania parent, it was a loss-making company, small by world standards, and would benefit from having a larger partner.

During the autumn both Fiat and Ford were rumoured to be in pursuit, but in December it was General Motors, frustrated in its bid to buy Jaguar, which took a 50 per cent stake in the Saab business and immediately started planning a new-generation 900 around the platform of GM-Europe's Cavalier/Calibra range.

During April, Toyota announced that it was to begin making cars in the UK. Settling on a site south-west of Derby, it began construction of a factory which would start producing a new-generation Carina E in 1992. The Derby factory was also to be fed by a new castings facility in Clwyd, North Wales.

Having earlier admitted that its new Swindon facility would build engines, Honda now agreed that it was also planning to produce complete cars – and that a new-generation model (it would be a new Accord, from which the Rover 600 was also to be cloned) would be assembled there in its entirety.

At the same time, Honda bought a 20 per cent share of Rover, while Rover in turn bought a 20 per cent stake in Honda. This was as close, corporately, as the two organizations would ever get.

In Britain, Fiat was anxious to revive the fortunes of its Lancia offshoot, whose annual sales had been eroding. Anticipating that it could do a better marketing job than Lancar (the business controlled by the Heron Group), Fiat bought back the franchise during the year.

However, it was all to no avail. New Lancia models, based on the Fiat Tipo, were already on the way, but these would do little to stop the inexorable slide in Lancia sales in Britain. By the mid-1990s Fiat had pulled the plug on the whole operation, the Lancia franchise being dropped after 40 years.

Technical developments

Slowly but surely, unleaded petrol was making headway in the UK. By Budget time, unleaded petrol was claiming about 6 per cent of the market, a figure which rocketed to 14 per cent in the following month and was expected to continue rising, not only because of the favourable reduction in tax on unleaded fuel, but also because ever more new cars were capable of running on unleaded without changes being made to the engine settings. During the year, a higher-rated (98 octane) super unleaded grade also became available, though this was only really needed for very high-output engines.

1990

This was the year in which the recession in the British motor industry bit hard and was due to get worse. Total car sales dropped by no less than 300,000 compared with the all-time record of 1989, for people not only had less money to spend, but were feeling gloomy about their future, and were not willing to take out hire (or lease) purchase contracts at the very high interest rates which were then being imposed. Naturally, this led to short-time working in some factories, and the postponement of investment in several businesses.

It was also the year in which the British Government misguidedly tried to apply means testing to drivers who committed motoring offences, and for a time a series of ludicrously high fines were levied on affluent drivers. This was soon seen to be scandalously wrong, and the legislation was abandoned a few months later. There were red faces all round – but no apologies.

As construction of the Channel Tunnel forged ahead, a new type of cross-channel ferry, the giant catamaran Seacat model, came into service. Notwithstanding the potential threat imposed by the new tunnel, during the next few years several more new and larger ships would be added to fleets.

The Department of Trade and Industry signalled a further move towards metrication by declaring that all fuel must be sold in litres rather than gallons by the end of 1994 – though in fact almost all garages began to do so straight away. Cynics suggested that this was a good way of allowing the Chancellor to impose more price rises, as a small increase on a litre would not look as obvious as a large increase on a (4.546-litre) gallon!

New models

Alfa Romeo: The 33 range of hatchbacks was given a new and slightly longer nose early in the year. This change was accompanied by revised, even more powerful, versions of the flat-four engine, the most powerful of which was now a 137bhp/16-valve 1.7-litre unit.

After many years when the Spider had not officially been available on the British market (though hundreds of them had been imported on a personal basis through Bell & Colvill, of Surrey), official imports began again of the final facelifted model. The latest car had revised nose and tail contours, but under the skin the main monocoque, the famous twin-cam 2-litre engine and the front-engine/rear-drive layout were just as they had always been since the late 1960s.

Before the end of the year, there was a new 2.5-litre V6-engined version of the 75, while the 3-litre V6 version was standardized around the 192bhp engine.

At the same time, the 164 was also slightly uprated, the latest Cloverleaf model having a 200bhp version of the 3-litre V6 engine.

Aston Martin: Still showing few signs of a long-term development strategy (though more aggressive interest from new-owners Ford would soon attend to that), in October the company showed a prototype soft-top version of the Virage. Called Volante, and therefore carrying on an Aston Martin tradition, the prototype was a two-seater, which meant that it appealed to even fewer people than such a high price ensured. It did not go into production in that form, but would be relaunched as a 2+2 at the Geneva show in March 1991.

As ever, there was much talk about a 'new DB4', or the DP1999 project, but for a time this never seemed to progress beyond paper studies or 'good idea' status. But in November Ford installed ex-SVE manager Rod Mansfield at Aston Martin as engineering director, and guided by Walter Hayes (who had become chairman), this new project was soon firmly under way, and the DB7 of 1992 was the result.

Audi: At the end of the year the first of a new family of V6 engines was introduced. This was a 174bhp/2.8-litre single-cam unit with a 90deg angle (it used some of the same tooling as the existing Audi V8), and Audi was at pains to insist that it had nothing in common with the new VR6 engine being developed by VW.

Eight years after the aerodynamically-styled 100 range had gone on sale, Audi announced an all-new style and platform. First previewed in October, it would go on UK sale in mid-1991. Described by pundits as a conservative new car, the new-generation 100 used a similar mechanical layout to earlier types, though there was one important innovation – the use of the 2.8-litre V6 engine.

Just as the well-loved Quattro (the *Ur* model) was ready to breathe its last, it was supplanted by a new-shape Coupe S2 (it did not carry the Quattro name), which combined the latest coupe shape with the new Torsen centre differential-equipped four-wheel-drive system and power by the same 220bhp/2.2-litre five-cylinder engine.

With a top speed of nearly 150mph, this new car was as rapid as the original type of Quattro, though testers did not find it quite as exciting to drive.

From September, all 1991 model year cars were fitted with the Procon Ten safety system as standard (for details, see the 1986 section).

BMW: At the end of the year, a new-generation 3-series family was introduced, all these cars having a new platform, more sophisticated multi-link rear suspension and a smooth body style (four-door saloons only, at first, though a rather different two-door coupe was planned) which looked rather like that of the current 5-series.

All these new BMWs had the same basic front-engine/rear-drive layout, there immediately being a choice of 316i, 318i, 320i and 325i models, varying from 1.6-litre/eight-valve to 2.5-litre/24-valve types.

The second-evolution (old-style) M3 model went on sale early in 1990 (less than a year before the entire 3-series range was to be replaced), just in time to be homologated for use in Group A Touring Car racing. Compared with earlier M3s, the Evo-2 version had a larger, 2,467cc version of the famous four-cylinder 16-valve engine, which produced 238bhp in road-car form and something like 350bhp when fully tuned for racing.

To match the more powerful engine, there were further flared wheelarches, new adjustable front and rear spoilers and racing-type front seats.

Early in the year, too, there was a new (but old-style) 318iS model, with 136bhp/1.8-litre 16-valve engine, and a new entry-level 5-series car, the 518, which had a 115bhp/1.8-litre eight-valve engine. There always seemed to be something new coming out of Munich!

Starting in March, the company began making a new family of six-cylinder engines with 24-valve twin-cam cylinder heads. Intended to upgrade the 5-series range, these engines borrowed much from the latest M40-type four-cylinder units (and therefore also had some relation to the new V12 units). With the same bore, stroke and swept volumes as before, they had much in common with the old 12-valve engines, but the new 2-litre produced 150bhp, the new 2.5-litre unit no less than 192bhp.

Caterham: The ever-young Lotus Seven-based sportscar seemed to go on improving – and becoming more desirable. During the year yet another new derivative – the HPC, complete with a 175bhp version of the Vauxhall 16-valve 2-litre engine – was added to the range. HPC stood for High Performance Course, which was offered free to buyers of the new car.

Daihatsu: The Sportrak 4x4 model, widely criticized as being too slow when put on sale in 1989, was improved with a more torquey and powerful fuel-injected version of its engine in mid-year.

Dodge: The amazing Viper, with its 400bhp V10 engine, finally reached production status in the USA, but UK deliveries were still years away, and even then the car would only be available in left-hand-drive form. Not that enthusiasts with fat wallets minded this, for they were already seeing it as the natural successor to the 1960s AC (Shelby) Cobra.

Ford: The most important introduction of the year was the arrival of new-generation Escorts and Orions, another front-wheel-drive range which took over from the original types which had been running throughout the 1980s.

Because of its uninspiring specification, the new car was received with howls of abuse by many motoring writers. Although it was more rounded and slightly sleeker than before, its character was dull indeed. The same range of engines – pushrod and single-cam – were used, the suspension systems were like those of the 1989-generation Fiesta, and although there

was a complete range of hatchbacks, estate cars and convertibles, there was barely any character in sight.

Although it was already known that new 16-valve twin-cam engines were being developed, these would not go on sale until 1992, and because there were no sporting types in the range at first, no-one had a good word to say about the latest car.

It was a great credit to Ford's formidable marketing organization that, dull or not, the new-generation car immediately rose to the top of the best-seller lists, where it would stay in future years…

To balance this false start, at the end of the year there was the very proud introduction of the Scorpio 24V model, which used a newly-developed 195bhp Cosworth 2.9-litre V6 engine, with twin overhead camshafts per bank, which was not only powerful and torquey, but also environmentally 'green'.

At more than £27,000, this Scorpio was not only the fastest in the range, but also comfortably the most expensive. Compared with the old-style pushrod overhead-valve-engined models, though, it was such an advance that it would sell well for several years.

Early in the year the Sierra (which had been on sale since 1982) was given one last package of changes. Slight styling alterations identified it in the showrooms, but the two principal improvements to 'bread-and-butter' cars were the arrival of a 1.8-litre turbodiesel to replace the old Peugeot design of the 1980s, and the launch of a 2-litre I4 (twin-cam)-engined version of the XR4x4, complete with four-wheel drive.

The car which earned most of the headlines, however, was the Sierra Cosworth 4x4, which combined the latest XR4x4-type four-wheel drive (complete with MT75 gearbox) with a 220bhp version of the four-door saloon Sierra Cosworth chassis. This was a remarkably accomplished car (though too expensive at £24,995), for which Ford had major plans in the World Rally Championship. It was also the car which eventually gave rise to the Escort RS Cosworth – a smaller and more extrovert car which did not go on sale until 1992.

The fastest-ever Fiesta, the RS Turbo, was introduced in the spring, this being based on the XR2i layout, but having a 133bhp turbocharged 1.6-

litre CVH engine similar to that of the Escort RS Turbo. This car, in fact, would only have a short life, for it would be replaced by the 16-valve RS1800 in 1992.

Five years after the original Granada/Scorpio hatchback had gone on sale, Ford added a four-door saloon version of the same platform to the range.

Ginetta: Now under new ownership, Ginetta announced the starkly trimmed but potentially very fast G33 two-seater sportscar, which was previewed with a Rover V8 engine.

Honda: Only five years after the original model had appeared, the second-generation Legend went on sale in Japan towards the end of the year in saloon and coupe models. Larger, and with smoother styling than the first type, Legend 'Mk 2' used a larger, 3.2-litre, version of the V6 engine, which was already seen in earlier Legends (and in Rover 800s).

No sooner had the new Legend appeared than it was rumoured that Rover would follow suit with a Mk 2 800, but this did not happen. There *would* be a much revised Rover 800 in the next year or so, but this was purely a styling facelift on the existing platform.

The much-discussed VTEC 16-valve twin-cam engines finally went on sale in the UK in mid-year, featuring in the Civic and CRX models. As already described in 1988, these featured variable camshaft arrangements, carefully (and electronically!) controlled according to engine revs.

Hyundai: The new Sonata saloons, which had been introduced in Korea during 1989, went on sale in the UK early in 1990. By almost any standards – transverse-engine, front-wheel drive, all-independent suspension and a high level of equipment – these were conventional cars of the period, and with their Mitsubishi-derived four-cylinder engines they took over from the ancient Ford Cortina-derived Stellar models.

The rather gawky-looked S coupe – or Scoupe, as it soon came to be known – went on UK sale in mid-summer. The platform of this car was based on the new-generation Pony family cars (which would not appear in the UK until September), having the usual type of transverse-engine/front-drive layout. All the initial cars used an

82bhp/1.5-litre engine, but a series of more powerful engines would follow in 1992.

The revised Pony X2 range of family cars went on sale in the autumn, these using the same basic mechanical layout as the superseded 1985–89 models.

Not content with all this activity, Hyundai then introduced the Lantra (originally badged as an Elantra in Korea), which would go on UK sale in 1991. The Lantra slotted into the range above the new Pony, but below the Sonata, and was an obvious competitor in the very popular British 1.6 to 2-litre category, which was actually beginning to look just a little bit overcrowded.

Lamborghini: The Diablo, already officially previewed at the end of 1989, finally went on sale during the summer of 1990, rapidly gaining the reputation of a super-fast mid-engined two-seater with every facet in excess of the Countach, which had finally been dropped.

Land Rover: As expected, a five-door version of the Discovery 4x4 vehicle appeared in the autumn, just one year after the original three-door type had gone on sale. At the same time a more powerful, fuel-injected, version of the V8 engine was standardized.

Mahindra: This Indian-built derivative of the old-style American Jeep CJ four-wheel-drive machine (which, itself, had links with the legendary Jeep of the Second World War) finally went on sale in the UK. There were two versions – the Indian Brave and the longer-wheelbase Indian Chief – both with the same bone-shattering ride and lack of creature comforts which the Jeep had always exhibited.

Unhappily, within months, the interconnected British companies which were importing the cars ran into serious financial problems and fell into the hands of the receiver. Within weeks, importation was started up again by a new concern – though this made virtually no difference to Mahindra's British sales, which were always tiny.

Marcos: Still building the 1960s-shape Mantula, the company introduced an entry-level 2-litre model in September with power by Ford's latest twin-cam engine.

Mercedes-Benz: At the end of the year, a new-generation S-class model was previewed. First impressions were that it was larger, heavier and technically even more complex than the decade-old range which it was to replace. All details would be held back until 1991 (see that section for analysis).

The gloriously powerful and extrovert 500E arrived at the end of the year, mixing amazing 155mph performance with the conventional looks of the well-known mid-size saloon (E-class, as it would eventually be known).

Except for the use of the big front spoiler and the slightly flared wheel-arches, the 500E looked similar to other cars in this family, but under the bonnet there was a 322bhp 32-valve 5-litre V8 engine to give it quite startling performance. At £57,200 when it finally came onto the British market, it could only ever expect to be a slow seller, but Mercedes-Benz didn't mind that as all assembly was to be carried out by Porsche in Stuttgart: this was the performance flagship intended to match, and beat, anything which BMW could provide.

Although this car was virtually unknown in the UK, the 190E 2.5-16 Evolution II made quite a stir in its native Germany. Like the evolution BMW M3, this car had been produced to make the model more competitive in Touring Car racing (particularly the high-profile German series), and featured extrovert front and rear spoilers and a modified 2.5-litre engine which produced 235bhp.

The rear spoiler of the Evolution II was so high that the driver could look under it through his rear-view mirror – in some ways this being reminiscent of the Dodge/Plymouth NASCAR-winning machines of 20 years earlier.

Quite overshadowed by this launch, but commercially much more important, was the appearance of a 109bhp 1.8-litre version of the 190E model, this becoming the smallest-engined and cheapest Mercedes-Benz saloon of the day.

Middlebridge: Less than two years after the career of the Scimitar GTE had been relaunched under the Middlebridge banner, a receiver was appointed, as the Japanese-owned company was in serious financial problems, from which it would not recover.

Mitsubishi: In the USA, an ambitious joint project between Mitsubishi and Chrysler came to fruition with the launch of two near-identical high-performance sports coupes – the Dodge Stealth and the Mitsubishi 3000GT.

The new 3000GT effectively took over from the old Starion, but was utterly different in detail and technically quite new. Under the skin of this front-engined coupe there was a twin-turbocharged V6 engine, four-wheel drive and four-wheel steering, so with a claimed top speed of around 165mph this was a much more costly car than the old Starion, and was effectively shooting for sales against the ageing Porsche 928 family and cars like the Honda NSX and Nissan 300ZX and Skyline GT-R models (the latter was not sold in the UK).

This car had been conceived at the height of the boom in car sales, customer confidence and economic boom, but in the light of the recession it made much less marketing sense. British sales, very few in number, would begin in 1992.

Early in the year the company also announced the Diamante saloon, styled very much like the latest Galant, but a full size larger. Complete with front-wheel drive, but using the same basic 3-litre V6 engine as other top-of-the-range Mitsubishis, this was clearly aimed to fight in the BMW/small Mercedes-Benz market sector, where it struggled to establish itself.

Even though the downmarket Diamante name was ditched in the UK in favour of an old favourite, Sigma, very few were sold in Britain.

Nissan: The new Sierra/Cavalier-sized Primera family, a transverse-engined/rear-drive type, which was to take over from the Bluebird in Europe, and be assembled at the Nissan factory near Sunderland, was unveiled early in the year and went on sale in the summer.

Rounded where the Bluebird had been hard-edged, technically interesting where the Bluebird had been run-of-the-mill, and with a sporty character contrasting sharply with that of the old Bluebird, the Primera used a family of new-generation engines, with 16 valves and twin overhead camshafts. Rival engineers soon found that it had a very capable chassis, and used Primeras as comparator cars for their next-generation models.

At the time there were suggestions that the new Primera might hit sales of Sierras, Cavaliers and Peugeot 405s very badly – but in the event the British public showed little interest, and the vast majority of sales were achieved overseas.

In five years – 1990 to 1995 – the Primera would almost become a forgotten car in the UK, and few could understand this, least of all Nissan's product planners.

In the summer, Nissan introduced a new-generation Sunny range, a family of front-wheel-drive cars which included hatchbacks and saloons and a choice of engines from 1.4 to 2 litres, including a diesel option. UK sales would begin early in 1991.

At the end of the year the Sunny GTi-R (R for Rally) was previewed, this being another 'homologation special' intended to become a World Rally Championship contender. Although based on the new-generation Sunny hatchback shell, its engine was a 230bhp/2-litre 16-valve turbocharged unit, and there was a sophisticated permanent four-wheel-drive installation.

Although the specification was promising, and the price also promised to be very competitive (lower, by several thousands, than the Escort RS Cosworth, it was said), the GTi-R was only ever to be available in left-hand-drive form. Never strongly marketed in the UK, where only 50 cars were delivered, the GTi-R would have a short and ignominious works rallying career, not least because the turbo intercooler was placed atop the engine – where it got too hot and failed to do its job...

Panther: In October, the company announced the death of the four-wheel-drive Solo sports coupe, of which a miserable 12 cars had been sold.

Peugeot: In what was a very quiet year for the French company, the only significant new arrival was a 1.77-litre turbodiesel engine added to the 205 range for 1991.

Porsche: Fleshing out the latest type of 911 chassis, there was a new-generation 911 Turbo in 1990. Like the newest Carrera 2 and Carrera 4, this had the latest platform and coil-spring rear suspension, while the famous flat-six engine was now a 320bhp/3.3-litre single-cam unit.

Proton: In Malaysia, the Mitsubishi-based Saga was updated with 12-valve versions of the 1.3 and 1.5-litre engines. It took some time for the delivery pipeline to fill, so UK deliveries did not begin until January 1991. Proton's naming sense went a bit over the top when they first described these new versions as Megavalve types...

Range Rover: To celebrate the 20th anniversary of the model's birth, the company built 200 CSK models. CSK stood for Charles Spencer King – better known as 'Spen' King, who designed the original Range Rover. All 200 were built in two-door form, in black, with stiffened suspension settings, but with the standard 3.9-litre fuel-injected engine.

Renault: The French company's major announcement of the year was the new front-drive Clio model, which was meant to be a replacement for the second-generation 5 (though at least one version of the 5 would continue alongside it into the mid-1990s).

Rounded where the 5 had been craggy, and more roomy inside, the Clio was really a half-class further upmarket. By transverse-engine standards, this was a conventional chassis layout, and there was a full range of engines covering 49bhp/1.1-litre all the way to 140bhp/1.8-litre – and even more powerful versions were already being planned.

Rover: As predicted, the new 400 series – a booted saloon version of the new 200 which had appeared in 1989 – finally went on sale in the spring. The platform, all the styling ahead of the rear window, the front-wheel-drive layout and some of the engines, were common, but in general power outputs were higher, for this was meant to be a faster and more upmarket car.

Almost a year after the new 200 Series had gone on sale, Rover added three-door coupe versions to the range, including in this a new 216GTi twin-cam derivative. By the end of the year the range was fully fleshed out, with diesel versions yet to come.

Later in the spring, there was a substantially re-engineered Metro, now officially badged as Rover. At last, the ancient A-series engine and gearbox-in-sump layout (which dated from 1959) had been ditched.

The second-generation car kept the same basic style and proportions as before, but had a longer and more rounded nose, which hid a choice of the brand-new eight-valve K-series engine in 1.1 or 1.4-litre form, these being mated to end-on four-speed or five-speed transmissions.

At the top of the range, too, there was a Metro GTi, which used a 95bhp/1.4-litre version of the 16-valve K-series engine. Sales of revised Metros would be brisk, but not sensationally so, as it was all too obvious that this was still a 10-year-old car which had been given a makeover.

To the great delight of Mini enthusiasts, a totally updated Mini-Cooper was put on sale in mid-summer, this being a 1990 restatement of the car which had made so many BMC headlines (as an Austin or a Morris) in the 1960s.

As before, the 1990 Mini-Cooper was an A-series-engined front-wheel-drive two-door saloon, but there were many different details. This time the engine was a 61bhp 1.3-litre unit with only a single carburettor, and there was a strident but appealing body striping package to make it stand out from its neighbours. More and higher-performance derivatives of this model were already being developed.

In mid-summer a diesel-engined version of the 800 range was announced, this car having a turbocharged 118bhp/2.5-litre four-cylinder VM unit.

The (ex-Austin) Maestro was given a diesel engine option from March, this being a normally aspirated 60bhp version of the 2-litre type which had already been fitted to the Montego (but in turbocharged form).

Saab: The latest cocktail from Saab's choice of bodies, engines and tuning levels was the CD 2.3 Turbo model which appeared in September. This had a 200bhp engine, and a claimed top speed of 143mph.

Suzuki: A new-generation Swift went on UK sale in the spring, this slightly larger and more high-tech machine now having a 92bhp/1.6-litre engine and four-wheel drive.

Toyota: The new Previa MPV (or people-mover) was one of the first seriously thought-out new approaches to packaging this kind of car since the

Range Rover came along in 1970.

A large car by any standards (it was nearly 6ft tall and was a full six-seater), the Previa had a long sloping nose and five doors, the rear side doors being the van-like sliding variety. The packaging was unique in that there was a specially-designed 2.4-litre four-cylinder unit, mounted almost on its side, under and behind the front seats, with the gearbox tacked on behind and driving the rear wheels.

It was a brave idea, but in the UK at least it was only a partial success, for this was always an expensive proposition, while the lofty stance made it less handy than its obvious MPV rivals such as the Renault Espace.

Also in mid-summer came the launch of the third-generation Camry, the largest, most high-tech and best equipped Toyota of the early 1990s, which slotted neatly into a complex range immediately under the Lexus models, which were even larger, faster and more expensive.

The latest Camry was a large but smooth and carefully-detailed four-door saloon, with transverse-engine/front-drive, courtesy of 2.2-litre four-cylinder or 3-litre V6 engines. Very well-specified, with transmission choices, ABS and electric-everything, these would be costly cars when they went on sale in the UK in 1991.

A new-generation Starlet (the Metro-sized hatchback) appeared early in the year, looking more rounded than the previous-generation types. There would be a choice of 1-litre and 1.3-litre engines.

A 2-litre diesel-engined option was added to the Carina before the end of the year – diesel demand in Europe, incidentally, was always much higher than in Japan.

TVR: Continuing the development of existing styles, the company turned the S2 into the S3 and S3C (C = Catalyst) in mid-year, these cars retaining the same chassis, but having longer doors to give easier access to the cockpit, and a new-style facia layout.

A sensationally-smooth new Rover-powered two-seater Griffith model was previewed at the Birmingham motor show, but was little more than a mock-up, and would be completely redeveloped (being based on a new-style Tuscan racecar chassis) before sales began in 1991. (For details of the

production car, see the 1991 section.)

Vauxhall: Deliveries of the Calibra coupe, which had been previewed at the 1989 show, began in the summer. Then, from the end of the year, a four-wheel-drive version of the 16-valve car (using the same engine/transmission package as the Cavalier 4x4) was added to the range.

The Nova had already been on the market for seven years, so a facelift was long overdue. This was made in September, to keep the model going for another two years or so before the new-generation Corsa could take over.

Volkswagen: For 1991, the Polo, which had been on sale almost throughout the 1980s, was given a late-life makeover, with a new nose and interior, but with few mechanical innovations.

One further version of the Polo was previewed in the UK, this being the supercharged (G40) 113bhp version of the 1.3-litre car.

In Germany, the company announced a supercharged (160bhp) single-cam version of the Golf GTi, but stated that it would never be made in right-hand-drive form.

The first right-hand-drive Corrado coupe/hatchback models went on sale at the end of the year.

Volvo: After eight years, the 760 Series gave way to the 960 series, though this represented little more than a major facelift to the existing monocoque (with a more rounded, but still angular, tail) and with a brand new 2.9-litre inline 24-valve six-cylinder engine replacing the ageing PRV V6 to which Volvo had been faithful since 1974.

Industrial developments

As forecast in 1989 when Ford took over the business, 'Mr Jaguar' – John Egan – left the company in the spring, to be replaced by Ford nominee Bill Hayden, a ruggedly successful production expert with 40 years' service for Uncle Henry.

In a surprise move (surprising because it had not been leaked, or forecast, in advance) the Vickers Group bought the world-famous Cosworth business

from Carlton Communications. Vickers, who already controlled Rolls-Royce, stated that there was no question of merging the two businesses together – a pledge which was to be honoured through the next several years.

Reliant, which had always been trading with difficulty after the old-style Scimitar programme closed down, eventually called in the receiver in October. A revival would follow in January 1991, when a consortium headed by Cyril Burton rescued the sportscar side of the company. Meanwhile, the Metrocab business was sold to another concern.

AC was in the news once again – for all the wrong reasons. Ford, who had a controlling shareholding, decided that it could no longer do business with the other major shareholder, Brian Angliss, and applied for the company to be put into liquidation.

But that was only the beginning of the wrangle, which eventually reached the courts and ended up with Ford walking away, with Angliss determined to carry on, on his own.

Renault and Volvo started the process of merging their operations – at least, that was the plan – by deciding to put their truck businesses close together. Since Renault already supplied Volvo with engines for several of its car models – including all the 300 and 400-series Volvo cars produced in Holland, this made a lot of commercial sense.

The merger moves, however, would take a long time to work out, and in the end would collapse because the philosophies of the two companies were so very different.

Following the collapse of Communist Eastern Europe, West European car-makers made haste to set up links with car concerns in those nations. GM and Fiat laid plans to build cars there, Volkswagen set up investment programmes with Wartburg (Polo and Golf models were to be built where Trabants were once produced), and before long it would complete an agreed takeover of Skoda: just before the end of the year, VW announced that it was to take a minority stake in the Czech car-maker and that it hoped to complete the takeover in 1991.

Those who had wondered how erstwhile Eastern European cars could be so cheap (and nasty!) eventually found out when they managed to inspect the factories. Without exception, these were technologically backward and run down, often with facilities which had barely improved in 40 years, and they were paying demeaningly low wages to a supine workforce.

All this would change in the early 1990s as the once-hated capitalist concerns arrived, to clean up, tear up, then modernize the businesses which had been starved of proper investment for decades.

Technical developments

Airbags, probably the most over-hyped and expensive safety fitment to be applied to modern cars, were beginning to make their presence felt, and in the next three years or so would find themselves fitted ever more more widely.

Originally proposed, tested – and rejected – in the early 1970s as a substitute (not an addition) to safety belts, this North American invention featured the fitting of a tighty-packaged airbag, either in the hub of the steering wheel, or behind panels ahead of the front-seat passenger.

With a retail cost of around £300 per bag, these fittings were totally dormant until the car was involved in an accident, during which an explosive inflation turned them into pillows ready to cushion the passengers' faces before they could hit the wheel or the facia – if the safety belts allowed them to stretch that far. Once inflated, the bags speedily deflated again, and because it was a one-time-only system, the whole system then had to be replaced.

Originally intended to be used *without* safety belts, airbags made a contribution for the 1990s as an additional injury-reduction aid. The fact (heavily disputed by some safety researchers) was that efficient, properly designed and correctly worn safety belts could provide all the protection required, and there is still much discussion as to the cost effectiveness of airbags.

What other car fitting, of similar value, may never have its use in the life of the vehicle?

The new Trafficmaster system was previewed in the UK, and if it could be brought to market without incurring horrendous financial losses appeared to be a promising way to avoid traffic jams.

Subscribers would get a multi-image video display screen for fitment to their cars, which would show maps of motorway and main road systems. This would receive radio-type signals from central transmitters, whose information would be receiving intelligence from sensors mounted on over-bridges.

If traffic began to move slowly, or even stop, the sensors would trigger off warning signals through the transmitters, which would then flash up the jam on the VDU screens inside the cars. It was a great idea – and it worked very well. The only problem, at first, was that the system was expensive, but costs came down – and utility went up – as the network expanded in the early 1990s.

Men of Influence

Bob Lutz

Although Bob Lutz was widely supposed to have been unhappy at missing the top job at Chrysler in the early 1990s when Lee Iacocca finally retired, he could nevertheless be proud of the impact he had already made on the world's motor car industry. The arrival of the sensational Dodge Viper of 1990 was just the latest of a series of fast and sporty cars developed under his control since the 1970s.

Born in Zurich, Switzerland, in 1932, but domiciled in the USA by the 1950s, the dynamic young Lutz served in the US Marine Corps as a fighter pilot for five years before gaining science and business degrees at Berkeley University, California. After that he joined General Motors in its New York planning department, and his whirlwind progress through the American and European motor industries was under way.

Enthusiastic, energetic and keenly interested in anything which offered fun as well as profit, he worked up through Opel and GM-France before joining BMW as its sales vice-president. This was the period in which BMW not only developed the first 5-series cars and the 3.0CSL 'Batmobiles', but also provided engines for F2 racing.

Then it was time for him to move to Ford, where for the next decade and more he ran increasingly large divisions. Starting as Ford-Germany's general manager, he became its president in 1977 and its chairman in 1979. This was the period when the Fiesta was put on sale, RS models were developed and sold widely, and Ford of Europe seemed to be winning everywhere in motorsport. It was at this time, too, that he came to know Lee Iacocca at Ford.

Vice-president of Ford's international automotive operations from 1982-84, he then returned as chairman, Ford of Europe, until 1986, when he surprised everyone by moving back to the USA, to Chrysler.

Having seen the way he worked at Ford when *he* was at Ford, Chrysler's boss, Lee Iacocca hired him to inject some life, excitement and pizzazz back into another firm. Having become president under Iacocca, he urged the development of new cars – not only the high-profile Dodge Viper, but the much-praised LH family which would appear in 1992 to rival the very successful Ford Taurus.

It was under Lutz that Chrysler once again started serious exports of its cars back to Europe (this would include the successful relaunch of Jeep in Britain), and when Chrysler started making cars which looked, felt and drove as well as any of their rivals in Detroit. It had been decades since they had done that...

1991

Perhaps it was because the country was slipping into a deep recession, but the Budget, revealed in March, was broadly neutral as far as motorists were concerned. Although annual road tax stayed at £100/year (for the sixth year running), petrol duty went up by 15.3p/gallon on unleaded fuel, 17.7p/gallon on leaded and 14.9p/gallon on diesel fuel. This meant that for the first time a gallon of unleaded fuel cost more than £2. And there was worse to come because the standard rate of VAT was to be increased from 15 to 17.5 per cent on April 1, which added another 4p to the price of a gallon. The VAT rise also affected the price of cars – a £10,000 car going up by more than £200.

The completion of the M40 motorway, now running all the way from London to the motorway ring south of Birmingham, signalled the completion of the basic British motorway network. Though it was not generally realized at the time, this would be the last major motorway opening, for in the 1990s most work would be confined to making improvements to the existing network. The M40 offered a very viable alternative to the increasingly overcrowded M1/M6 route to Birmingham, though it took well over a year for this message to sink in.

It is interesting to observe that some new laws are respected, whereas others are not. When the wearing of front seat belts became compulsory in the early 1980s, more than 90 per cent of passengers immediately complied, but when the law was extended to the wearing of rear seat belts, on July 1, 1991, it was ignored (and often still is) by the majority of passengers.

New models

Alfa Romeo: The new 155 was previewed before the end of the year, this being a direct replacement for the 75 range and based on the existing Fiat Tipo/Tempra platform. It would go on sale in 1992 – for further details see that section.

Still juggling their engines, transmissions and bodyshell combinations (an art at which the company had been adept for three decades), Alfa introduced the four-wheel-drive 33 Permanent 4 to Britain in the spring, along with a revitalized Sportwagen, both with a 137bhp/16-valve/1.7-litre flat-four engine. It was a brave effort, but it had little effect, for this was the period when British Alfa Romeo sales gradually slid away.

Aston Martin: The Virage Volante finally made it to customers in 2+2 form, six months after it had been previewed as a two-seater. Deliveries were intended to start before the end of the year, but at a suggested price of around £150,000 it was not expected to be a big seller!

Incidentally, it was 1961 all over again for a short time as the company authorized one of its specialists, Richard Williams, to build up four new DB4GT Zagatos, using previously allocated but unissued chassis numbers from the original batch of cars. This brought the total production, over the years, to 23.

Audi: Although there were important changes to the 80 range for 1992 (these cars being announced in August/September 1991), there were few visual clues. Even so, with a 2.6in increase in wheelbase, more than 3in added to the overall length, a new rear suspension layout and a much increased boot size (helped by the relocation of the spare wheel in a carry-flat position), this was certainly more than a mere facelift.

As expected, and especially since the 90 range was being dropped (see below), the engine range was wider than ever, starting with an 80bhp/2-litre/eight-valve 'four' and extending all the way to the 174bhp/2.8-litre V6, which was a new flagship unit. Thus re-equipped, the 80 range was ready to carry on for a further three years, when it would be replaced by the A4 model.

Just before the improved 80 range was announced, the larger-engined derivatives, always badged as 90s, were dropped as their mechanical package had been included in the latest 80 models.

After a great deal of development, several showings at motor shows and several delays, the 90-based cabriolet finally went on sale in 1981. This four-seater soft-top, which would eventually become famous because the Princess of Wales chose to drive one at the time she was going through the traumas of her separation from the Prince, was originally powered by a 133bhp/2.3-litre five-cylinder engine, though a 2-litre model would later be added to this range.

The fastest new Audi of the year was the new 100-based S4 saloon, which combined the structure of the modern four-door 100 with the well-proven four-wheel drive system and a 230bhp/20-valve/turbocharged/2,226cc five-cylinder engine.

In effect this was a saloon car relative of the modern Coupe S2 (which used the same basic engine/transmission package), though it was 10bhp more powerful, and for the first time the manual gearbox had six forward speeds.

To make the car more distinctive there was a new front bumper/lower spoiler, more flaring to the wheelarches, and special five-spoke alloy road wheels. An estate car version appeared soon afterwards – this certainly being the fastest load-carrier Audi had yet put on sale.

It was a very busy new-car year for the company, for in the autumn a new turbocharged diesel version of the 100 – the 100TDi – also went on sale, this combining a 2.5-litre five-cylinder turbocharged engine with a six-speed transmission (as used in the latest high-performance Audis).

The V8 also received a boost for 1992 with a 280bhp/4.2-litre version of the V8 engine, which replaced the original 250bhp/3.6-litre type: UK deliveries began in January 1992.

In Britain, the importers signalled the death of the original turbocharged (Ur) Quattro with the launch of the Coupe S2 which was intended to replace it. More rounded that the original type, but with the same 220bhp/20-valve five-cylinder engine as the last of the original types, the S2 had a difficult job to build its own reputation, especially at a price of £29,394.

Bentley: The Continental R coupe, launched in March, was the first unique Bentley – totally different, that is, from a Rolls-Royce body style – for many years, in fact since the original Continental coupe of 1952, nearly 40 years earlier. Based around the existing platform of the Bentley Turbo R, but with an impressive two-door four-seater fixed-head coupe style, it used an (estimated) 360/380bhp version of the 6¾-litre V8 engine and had a potential top speed of around 150mph. When deliveries began early in 1992, the Continental R was priced at £175,000 – yet there was a healthy demand by Bentley standards.

BMW: The most important arrival of BMW's year was the estate car version of the modern 5-series. BMW, however, were not anxious to compete against Volvo and Mercedes-Benz at this end of the market, so called its new car a Touring instead. Late in the year, too, the company also previewed the latest two-door 3-series cars, which would officially go on sale in 1992 as coupe models. Although based on the same platform as the 3-series saloons, most of their superstructure and cabin was subtly different in shape.

From October, BMW began delivering 325td and 525tds models in Britain – these being the first diesel-engined BMWs to be sold in the UK. The engine was a 115bhp (325) or 143bhp (525) 2.5-litre six-cylinder unit based on, but much modified from, the company's existing petrol-powered 'six' – and was well insulated from the cabin to remove most traces of diesel engine noise, smell and behaviour. Even so, it soon became clear that Britain was not a good market for diesel BMWs, and sales were very limited.

Bugatti: Here was the classic case of an over-ambitious supercar, conceived at exactly the wrong time (just as the market was turning decisively downwards) by a company with very shaky finances.

The V12 engine, complete with four small turbochargers, had already been previewed, and first pictures of the wedge-styled car itself were shown early in 1991. The new EB110, as it would eventually be known, had a difficult act to follow, for although it was to be built in the area of Italy (near Modena) which had inspired so many other magnificent machines, it would have to build a reputation from scratch.

At a very glossy, expensive and high-profile launch in France, the EB110 was finally unveiled in September, priced at more than £250,000, which guaranteed that demand would be very limited indeed. The first deliveries,

in penny numbers, would not be made until 1992.

Caterham: Still developing the Seven concept, there was yet another engine variant from mid-summer, this being the latest fuel-injected 103bhp/1.4-litre Rover K-series 16-valve unit.

Citroen: The arrival of the new ZX range was probably the most important European event of the motoring year, as it was soon being assessed against its rivals as the best hatchback in small/medium category.

Falling into the middle of the hotly contested Ford Escort/Vauxhall Astra/VW Golf/Rover 200 class, the new ZX had a neat but not outrageous style, and was based around a new platform, with conventional steel springs, which was certain to be shared by Peugeot (eventually, the 306 range) in the next few years.

As expected, much of the engineering, particularly of the suspension and the engine/transmission packages, was shared with Peugeot, for there was a wide choice of corporate TU and XU engines ranging from the 75bhp/1.36-litre to the 130bhp/1.9-litre types. More engine choice, including diesels and turbodiesels, would follow.

Evante: For some time this tiny Lincolnshire-based company had been trying to put a 1960s Lotus Elan-style sportscar (with a different engine and chassis) back into production, but the effort failed in December when the receiver was called in. There were attempts to revive the marque in 1992, but these failed.

Ferrari: Maybe the 512TR, which was introduced almost at the end of 1991, was no more than a modified Testarossa (with virtually the same wide, flat, two-seater supercar style (including those air-intake strakes along the flanks), but it was still an astonishingly fast car by any standards. Now with 422bhp (DIN) instead of 390bhp from its 4.9-litre flat-12 four-cam normally-aspirated engine, it came with a typically exaggerated top speed claim of nearly 195mph, though British testers could only reach 175mph.

Fiat: A completely new-generation 500 – actually to be badged Cinquecento – was introduced in April, this

being a short, relatively high, but smoothly detailed miniature four-seater. Unlike the previous-generation 500 and 126 types, this was a front-engine/front-wheel-drive car in the true BMC Mini tradition, and Fiat took the brave step of having it assembled exclusively by its associate company FSM, in Poland. Frustratingly for British motorists, UK deliveries would not begin until mid-1993.

The Tipo 16V, with 148bhp 2-litre engine, finally appeared in March, three years after the Tipo had first been seen in public, this embarrassing delay having been caused because prototypes had not been able to match the best that VW, GM and Ford were already offering. The 16V model was powered by the latest 2-litre 'balancer' engine already found in other (larger) Fiat and Lancia models.

Ford: The new-generation Escort RS2000, which had been previewed a year earlier, finally went on sale in the autumn of 1991. Advertised behind the punchline *The Champ is Back*, the latest front-wheel-drive Ford had a 150bhp/16-valve/2-litre version of the company's modern I4 twin-cam, along with four-wheel disc brakes and (compared with other Escorts) much improved handling.

In October, the company officially previewed its new-generation 16-valve Zeta engine family, stating that this would be fitted to an increasing number of front-wheel-drive Fords from 1992. Unknown at the time was that this engine was central to the layout of the successor to the ancient Sierra – to be called Mondeo – which would be introduced early in 1993. The new engine would soon have to be renamed Zetec to get round trademark difficulties with Lancia of Italy!

FSO: Because of the political and industrial upheaval which followed the collapse of Communism in Eastern Europe, deliveries of these cars stopped during the year, leaving the dealer chain in the lurch. FSOs would not return to the UK until the end of 1993, by which time the Polonez had been restyled and renamed Caro.

Ginetta: Having previewed the car in 1990, Ginetta finally put the productionized G33 on sale in mid-1991, still with a tightly-profiled two-seater GRP body which incorporated two humps behind the seats, and with a wrap-round windscreen. Production cars were to be equipped with a 200bhp/3.9-litre fuel-injected Rover V8 engine, the result being searing performance, with a claimed top speed of 150mph, all at a price of £18,187.

Hindustan: Suddenly it was 1956 all over again! When the last of the Nuffield Morris Oxfords, as restyled in 1956, had gone out of production, the tooling had been shipped to India, where the cars had been in production ever since. Now, in the 1990s, the latest version, badged as a Hindustan Ambassador, was said to be almost ready to be re-imported in limited numbers to the UK. In fact there would be several bureaucractic and legislative obstacles before this 'blast from the past' was ready for sale – to those with spare money and (hopefully) a sense of humour – in mid-1992.

By that time the British promoters – Fullbore Motors – had decided that the ancient BMC B-series engine was not powerful enough, and had opted for the already optional-in-India 74bhp 1.8-litre Isuzu engine, and its matching five-speed gearbox. This was a small mercy for what, by common media consent, was probably the worst 'new' car to hit British roads for a long time.

Honda: A new-generation Civic was introduced in Japan in the summer, with UK deliveries starting in November. Like previous Civics, this was a wide-ranging line of cars, all with front-wheel drive, and four-cylinder engines from 1.3 to 1.6 litres, mostly available in saloon, hatchback and coupe derivatives.

Power outputs ranged from 75bhp to 160bhp, for some derivatives used the latest high-tech VTEC, 16-valve variable valvegear units, so within the usual annoying quota limitations Honda were able to sell a large number of all types.

A new-generation Prelude was introduced in September, with UK deliveries due to begin in 1992. The new Prelude was lower, wider and sleeker than before, with distinctive triangular-pattern tail-lamps, while Honda claimed the NSX styling had influenced the way that it looked at the front.

For the UK market there would eventually be a choice of 133bhp/2-litre, 2.2-litre or even 160bhp/2.3-litre engines, all being high-revving 16-valve types.

Isuzu: Having ditched the Piazza Turbo sports coupe, Isuzu next launched a new-generation Trooper 4x4 range, which would arrive on the UK market in 1992. Bigger, heavier and with larger/more powerful engines than before, it would sell steadily in the UK until the British importers were obliged to give it up in favour of a Vauxhall Monterey from the same Isuzu source.

Jaguar: The revised XJ-S (now designated XJS) launched in April was really the first new Jaguar to have been authorized by the new owners, Ford, though of course the engineering had been completed before the takeover.

Structurally and mechanically the XJS was much as before, except that the side-window glass profile had been changed, there being a larger rear quarter-window. Jaguar claimed that 40 per cent of the body panels were new – for which read 'modified', and to re-align the car with the latest XJ6s, the six-cylinder engine had been enlarged to 4 litres, giving 223bhp.

At the rear, the style had been changed to incorporate new horizontal tail-lamps, though there were no changes to the nose, where the big rectangular headlamps dominated as before. This was expected to be the last major change made to the XJS, though it would carry on in full production until 1996.

For 1992, the JaguarSport-built XJR-S was given a more powerful, 333bhp, version of its 6-litre engine.

Jeep: Chrysler, inspired by Bob Lutz, who had spent many of his working years in Europe, announced that it was to start selling right-hand-drive Jeep Cherokee 4x4s in the UK from the end of 1992.

The modern Cherokee, powered by either a four-cylinder 2.5-litre or a six-cylinder 4-litre engine, had been on sale in the USA since 1984, which meant that it would have been in production for eight years before British sales began.

Smaller than the Land Rover Discovery, but considerably larger than the Wrangler (an evolution of the classic small Jeep which was still not available in the UK in RHD form), the Cherokee was already a well-proven off-road 4x4 and was almost bound to sell well by trading on its famous name. A British dealer chain was set up in the next 18 months, and once deliveries began the Cherokee did, indeed, become very popular.

Kia: When launched in the UK by the Korean manufacturers, this was a new marque for British drivers to consider, but the car itself – the Pride – was familiar enough as it was a lightly-modified version of the old-type Mazda 121, which had just been superseded.

As with the old Mazda, there was a choice of 1.1 or 1.3-litre engines. Imported by the group which also dealt with Mazdas, the Kia gave them a second bite at the sub-mini market at a low entry-level price.

Lancia: The final evolution of the famous Delta Integrale, which was intended to keep the car supreme in rallying for yet another season, was introduced in August, and a few left-hand-drive versions would eventually be sold in the UK.

Developed from the previous Integrale 16-valve car, the latest version had wider wheel tracks, further flared wheelarches and a 2-litre engine which had been boosted to no less than 210bhp at 5,750rpm.

Lotus: Now that the front-wheel-drive Elan was safely in production, it was the turn of the Esprit for a further (but by no means final) facelift. Starting in October, the bodyshell was rerigged internally, giving more cabin space, while a large free-standing aerofoil was placed high above the tail. The normally-aspirated Esprits had been dropped in 1990, which allowed Lotus to concentrate on the latest 264bhp version of the Turbo.

In October, too, the company showed a hardtop version of the front-drive Elan, but this proved to have been premature, as none seem to have been sold before the Elan project closed down in mid-1992.

Mahindra: No sooner had the British concession been established for these Indian-produced derivatives of the Jeep 4x4 than the vehicle was updated. Late in 1991, the latest CJ-5 based car was badged as a Marksman. In many ways this was a difficult car to sell, for although it looked like one, it wasn't a Jeep – and with prices starting at £10,400 it was not even the cheapest of the more basic 4x4 breed.

Mazda: The MX-3 coupe appeared in March 1991 with what was claimed to be the world's smallest production six-cylinder engine, a light-alloy 60-degree 24-valve V6 with twin-cam heads and 134bhp.

The MX-3 itself was a likeable but unsensational 2+2-seater sports hatch-back with transverse engine and front-wheel drive, but its significance was that it carried a version of the platform of the next-generation 323 (not due for two or three years) and was the first Mazda to use this sweet and high-revving engine. Developments would soon find their way into the new-generation 626 and MX-6 models, would be handed down to the Ford Probe 24V of the future, and in race-tuned form would also power Ford's successful Mondeo Touring Car racers to be campaigned from 1993.

The MX-6 was introduced in September. Bigger in every way than the MX-3, and with a choice of 2.2-litre four-cylinder or 2.5-litre V6 engines driving the front wheels, the MX-6 was shaped around the platform of a new-generation 626 (which would appear a few weeks later). Only the V6-engined type would be sold in the UK.

Most significantly, the MX-6 was to be manufactured in the USA, along with the new 626, and the second-generation Ford Probe (to be launched in 1992) was also to share the same platform and be built in the same Michigan factory.

The new-generation 626, which appeared just before the end of 1991, was larger and heavier than the 1987–91 generation. As already previewed, it ran on a new platform layout, shared with the MX-6, though there would be a choice of 1.8 and 2-litre 'fours' and the high-revving 2.5-litre V6.

Towards the end of the year the company unveiled the third-generation RX-7 sports coupe, a slightly smaller, more sinuously styled and lighter car than the model it replaced, but with a massively more powerful twin-rotor Wankel engine, which developed 255bhp and guaranteed a top speed of nearly 150mph.

Once again this was a fine car which simply did not sell in the UK after it

was launched in the second half of 1992 – its high initial price didn't help – because it could offer no real competition to the Porsche 911.

The new-generation 121 arrived early in the year, a strange, rounded little four-seater powered by a high-revving 73bhp/1.3-litre engine. Except for its controversial looks, this was a bland little front-wheel-drive car which the buying public seemed to decide offered nothing over the many competing European machines.

Mercedes-Benz: The new S-class saloons – standard and long-wheelbase – were proudly launched at the start of the year, when the company admitted that they had been developed over a very long period, virtually without regard to cost.

Design and development had started in the early 1980s, and if only the cars had appeared in the affluent and confident late 1980s they would have sold better than they did in 1991. Instead, the S-class was seen to be much too heavy and thirsty – in general, just 'too much'…

There was more cabin space than before, double glazing in the windows and a wide choice of engines, but these cars were definitely only for the rich, and those who cared little for what the rest of the world thought of their wasteful tastes. Power started with a 231bhp/3.2-litre 'six' and went all the way up to a 408bhp/6-litre V12.

In the meantime, the long-promised E-class cabriolet finally appeared, this being a carefully developed and equipped drop-top version of the 300E-24. Called the 300CE-24, it had a power-operated top which incorporated a glass rear screen, while automatic transmission was standard.

Mini-Moke: In the UK this famous name was thought to be long dead – surviving saloons were being badged as Rovers – until Portuguese-built Mini-Mokes began to be imported, reviving a model which had once been in production in the UK, but had dropped off the market in 1968 – 23 years earlier. The 1990s style Mini-Mokes looked almost the same as in the 1960s except that they were now supplied with a full rollcage and a 'bull bar' at the front. In the early 1990s no-one was complaining about these unfriendly accessories…

Mitsubishi: Eight years after the original versatile 4x4 went on sale, a new-generation model was launched. Called the Pajero in most other markets, the latest Shogun had a new chassis, on which was mounted new and more rounded bodywork and a revised range of engines.

UK-market sales began in May of a range featuring 2.5-litre diesel and 3-litre V6 petrol engines and two wheel-bases, all the cars being better finished and more luxuriously equipped than before.

The company reinforced the MPV (Multi Purpose Vehicle) cult in May with the introduction in Japan of a new-generation seven-seater Space Wagon, a 1.8-litre front-wheel-drive car. The Space Runner, a shorter-wheelbase derivative of the same design, followed later. Since these launches came at the same time as Ford was announcing its get-together with VW to produce its own MPV, it was clear that this was suddenly a fashionable market sector.

During the year the long-running Colt range was renewed yet again, now with a more rounded body style and the usual choice of transversely-mounted four-cylinder engines.

Nissan: The Pulsar name, which in other markets had been applied for years to what we knew as Sunny models, made a tentative appearance in the UK on saloon versions of the new Sunny range.

The 200SX was revised during the year with a more powerful version of the turbocharged engine – up from 164bhp to 171bhp.

Peugeot: The new, delicately-styled and commercially very important little 106 range was introduced in August and immediately set new standards for what might be called the Fiesta/Nova/Metro class.

Looking similar to, but even tidier than the 205, and with a totally different and somewhat smaller platform/superstructure, in some ways the 106 was a further evolution of what had already been achieved in-house with the Citroen AX.

Like that car, it used a range of already-developed four-cylinder engines and front-wheel-drive transmissions, the smallest being a 45bhp/954cc unit. The 106s all had three-door hatch-back shells at first, and were lighter and more fuel-efficient, yet almost as roomy as the 205 had ever been.

The 106, and the larger 306 which would follow in the relatively near future, would bracket the long-established 205, but not kill it off completely, for all three cars, in various forms, would still be made alongside each other in the mid-1990s. A 78bhp/1.77-litre turbo-diesel engine option was added to the already-massive 205 range in the spring.

Porsche: Ten years after it had been introduced, the 944 was finally dropped in mid-summer – but effectively lived on in the shape of the newly-launched 968. Much hyped beforehand as a new type of front-engine/rear-drive Porsche, the 968 was eventually revealed as a much-modified 944 instead.

The basic 944 bodyshell and front-engine/rear-transmission layout were retained, but there was a new 928-like nose style with smoothly-detailed 'lie-back' headlamps, and power was by a 240bhp/16-valve/3-litre version of the famous twin-balancer shaft four-cylinder engine. Both coupe/hatch-back and convertible versions were available.

Although the 968 was an extremely fast and capable 2+2-seater, it sold nothing like as well as Porsche had hoped because it was so obviously developed from another old Porsche design. After the initial surge of interest, it became something of a forgotten model, and would be dropped altogether during 1995.

Quite dwarfed by the arrival of the 968 was the final evolution of the 928 theme, this time by enlarging the V8 engine to 330bhp/5.4 litres and giving the car the title 928GTS. But this did little to improve the 928's sales, which for several years past had been very slow. In fact it was barely worth keeping the car in production at the established rate of just two cars a day, but so much pride seemed to be at stake that Porsche was reluctant to drop it altogether.

Renault: At the Geneva motor show in March, two of the company's more limited-production machines – the Espace and the rear-engined Alpine GTA coupe – were both given thorough makeovers.

The Espace had detail changes to the front-end style, though the sloping nose and boxy shape, all in glassfibre, were retained. There was a new engine line-up, including the 2.8-litre PRV V6 for the first time, along with a choice of 2.2-litre petrol and 2.1-litre diesel four-cylinder options, while the interior was redesigned, this time to include a middle row of seats, which could be swivelled to make the interior even more versatile.

The GTA, which for no good reason had always sold extremely slowly in the UK, was given a revised body with pop-up headlamps, while the rear-mounted V6 engine was enlarged to the full 3 litres, and with turbocharging gave a most exhilarating 250bhp – 25 per cent more than the earlier GTA.

The 16-valve version of the 19 hatchback, which had first been seen in France in 1988, finally went on UK sale early in the year, adding much-needed spice to a range of cars which had failed to establish an exciting marketing image.

Powered by a 16-valve 137bhp/1.76-litre engine, it was a 128mph machine which seemed to offer great value for money. In future years Renault would even try to make it into a British Touring Car Championship winner, but without lasting success.

Rocket: This innovative two-seater sportscar – which looked more like a single-seater racing car of the 1950s than a normal road car – was introduced in June. At first, many observers treated it as a joke – and a very expensive one at £28,000 – but with top F1 designer Gordon Murray behind the layout, this was a serious concept, and when a steady trickle of orders was received from wealthy people wanting a 'toy', the car went into production.

Powered by a mid-mounted six-cylinder Yamaha Genesis motorcycle-type engine, mounted across the frame, with exposed wheels barely covered by cycle-type mudguards, the Rocket normally had only the driver on board, with a panel behind him which covered a second seat. The rear seat passenger was obliged to sit with legs on either side of the driver ahead.

There was no windscreen or any other form of weather protection, so it was necessary to wear a full-face helmet at all times.

Rover: During the spring, the 800 range was widened yet further with the launch of the new 820 Turbo. This used a 180bhp turbocharged version of the M16 2-litre 16-valve engine, which made this model more or less a match for the existing 827 types (which had 177bhp Honda engines).

Then in November, just a few weeks *after* the British Motorfair, a new-generation 800 range was introduced, this being a much-facelifted derivative of the original. Rounded where the first 800s had been sharp-edged, and this time with a traditional style of Rover radiator grille, the new model retained the same platform and transverse-engine/front-drive layout.

The engine choice was somewhat simplified, there now being T-series (improved M16) 16-valve 2-litre, VM 2.5-litre diesel and Honda 2.7-litre V6 types, backed by the usual bewildering array of trim and equipment specifications.

Later in the spring came the 220GTi, which matched a normally-aspirated 135bhp version of the 2-litre M16 engine to the three-door 200 shell. This was a prelude to the launch (in October 1992) of a new range of rebodied 200 coupes, while in November, the 400 range of saloons picked up the same M16 2-litre engine.

Diesel-engined versions of the 200 and 400 series – 66bhp/1.9-litre normally-aspirated and 87bhp/1.77-litre turbocharged – became available during the spring, these engines being provided by Peugeot rather than made by Rover. These XU-derived engines were virtually the same as used in various Citroen BX, ZX and Peugeot 205 models.

The Metro GTi 16V, with 95bhp, replaced the older eight-valve model in mid-year, though the Metro had such a staid image that it was difficult for it to develop any type of sporting image, even with the advanced K-series engine.

Building on the instantly revived reputation of the Mini-Cooper, a new Mini-Cooper S was put on sale during the spring, this being a factory-approved aftermarket conversion of the Mini-Cooper, with a twin-SU carburettor/78bhp version of the 1990/91 Mini-Cooper's 1.3-litre engine.

Greeted with glee by the many Mini enthusiasts who had never gone away, this was really no more than a restatement of a 1960s design, with few modern improvements, which caused

Autocar & Motor to label it 'obsolete but irresistible'.

Then, only months later, Rover turned its factory-built Mini-Cooper into a fuel-injected model so that it could meet future exhaust emission requirements. From November 1991, therefore, the Mini-Cooper cost £720 more than before, but it had a 63bhp instead of a 61bhp engine.

Some 32 years after the original Mini had gone into production, Rover finally got round to showing a convertible version of the car and promised to put a limited number of 75 on sale during the summer. This machine featured a full-blown body kit, flared wheelarches and a Mini-Cooper type of 1,275cc engine, and it cost £12,250.

Saab: There seemed to be no end to the permutations which could come from one basic four-cylinder engine design, and two body platforms. In March, there was the new 9000CD Carlsson, a top-of-the-range model which combined the four-door saloon shell, the turbocharged 2.3-litre engine, a 220bhp setting and a special body kit. All this, combined with the name of Saab's most famous rally driver – Erik Carlsson – added up to a 141mph car at a £27,000 price.

Sao: Here was a new marque which the British had never encountered before. Launched in June, the Penza was a South African-built car based on updated old-style (pre-1989) Mazda 323 hatchbacks and saloons.

Accordingly, its only attraction was as a low-priced machine with a 1.3-litre overhead-cam engine and front-wheel drive, which sold only slowly without major changes in the ensuing years.

Seat: First clear evidence of the Spanish company being controlled by Volkswagen came in the spring with the introduction of a new range of Toledo saloons. Although the style was neat, anonymous and new, industry watchers soon realized that the new shell had been developed around the platform, suspension and full line-up of VW-sourced running gear from the current Jetta model.

The new Toledos, to be built in Spain, had been styled by Giugiaro/ItalDesign, who had clearly been hampered by the use of the Jetta platform,

for this was a car which always looked curiously narrow for its class, though its cabin had similar basic dimensions to those of the Jetta.

All Toledos had front-wheel drive, and when it was mature the engine range spanned 75bhp/1.6 litres to 150bhp/2 litres, with (as expected) a VW diesel option.

Subaru: The fast but strange-looking SVX coupe, which had been previewed in Japan in 1990, went on sale in the USA during 1991, with UK deliveries promised for 1992. Powered by a brand-new, flat-six, 230bhp/3.3-litre boxer engine, which drove all four wheels through an automatic transmission, this was obvious competition for cars like the Nissan 300ZX and especially the latest Mitsubishi 3000GT.

The 2+2-seater coupe body was round and sleek in most ways, but had weird side-detailing of glass and shut lines, this being an amalgam of original Giugiaro/ItalDesign styling and Japanese productionizing ideas.

Although this was a fast (140mph-plus) sports coupe, it was also expensive (£27,999 when it went on sale in the UK in April 1992) and was therefore always likely to be a rarity.

The Legacy range of flat-four-engined cars was still being expanded, and at the Earls Court Motorfair, in October, the company showed two new 2-litre models – one with a 123bhp normally aspirated engine and the other a four-cam/197bhp turbocharged version of the saloon, which was destined to be used in World Championship rallying.

(The engine and many other mechanical parts from the 197bhp Legacy would eventually be used in the smaller and more nimble Impreza, the car which helped Colin McRae to become World Rally Champion in 1995.)

Toyota: The seventh-generation Corolla range appeared in Japan in mid-year, but as usual with such an important Japanese car, UK deliveries would not begin until a year later, in mid-1992. Compared with the previous generation, the latest Corollas were an important bit larger, more powerful and faster, but were still middle-of-the-road cars in the Escort/Astra category.

To make sure that its Celica GT-Four would remain a rally-winning car, the company introduced a 5,000-off 'homologation special' version in the

autumn, the engine of which had been tuned to 205bhp. It would go on limited-sale (440 examples) in the UK badged as the Carlos Sainz model – to salute the fact that the Spanish driver had used Celicas to become World Rally Champion.

TVR: For the Blackpool company this was certainly the year of the V8, for it launched the V8S development of the S sportscar and the Griffith finally went on sale at the end of the year.

The V8S was a lineal derivative of the S3, which was still being built with a 2.9-litre Ford V6 engine, but had a 240bhp fuel-injected, TVR-modified, 3.95-litre version of Rover V8 engine. With a top speed of 146mph, it rapidly took over as the best-selling version of the 1970s-style S range.

The Griffith which had been previewed in 1990 was never put on sale, but a 4-litre or 4.3-litre V8-engined car with the same basic style was! This car had a version of the racing Tuscan chassis, the style was almost unchanged, and demand for the new Griffith was immediately beyond the factory's capability to produce.

Vauxhall: A new-generation Astra was previewed in July, deliveries beginning a few weeks later. This replaced a car which had been running for seven years with relatively minor changes.

The newly-launched Astra (developed from a new-type Opel released at the same time) was based on the same platform as before, but was a slightly larger car, with a smoothly-detailed style available in hatchback, saloon or estate forms. The old Belmont saloon name had disappeared.

All cars had transverse-engine/front-drive layouts (there was no 4x4 alternative), and were to be offered with a choice of seven four-cylinder engines, ranging from a 60bhp/1.4-litre all the way to a 150bhp/2-litre, and there were to be two diesel alternatives. In many ways this was perceived to be a better car than the still-new Escort, and Vauxhall's sales leapt as a consequence.

The Calibra Turbo was previewed in Germany in the autumn, but was not ready for UK launch until 1992. (For details, see the 1992 section.)

Following a great deal of rumour, Vauxhall confirmed that it was to sell a sporty 4x4 model, closely based on the Japanese Isuzu Amigo. This, in fact, was a real mix-and-match project, for although the chassis and the style were almost pure Isuzu Amigo, two of the engines – petrol and diesel – were supplied by Opel while one came from Vauxhall, and there was also an Opel-badged version for sale in Europe.

The Frontera officially went on UK sale close to the end of the year with a choice of short or long-wheelbase styles and three different engines – the 115bhp/2-litre Cavalier-style 'four', a 125bhp/2.4-litre 'four' from Opel and a 100bhp/2.3-litre turbodiesel, also from Opel.

But 4x4 fanatics never took to Fronteras – which were described as recreational four-wheel-drives, but since these vehicles found a ready sale with buyers jocularly described as 'Knightsbridge farmers', Vauxhall was able to sell many thousands of them.

Volkswagen: The long-rumoured narrow-angle V6 engine, the VR6, finally broke cover at the Geneva motor show in March, when it became optional on the Passat model, though it would soon be added to the Golf and Corrado ranges as well.

Developed rather agonizingly and haltingly over several years, the VR6 was totally different from the Audi V6 engine which had surfaced in 1990, for it was very short, and only had a 15-degree angle between cylinder banks. In some ways this was more of a narrow-angle straight-six than a vee engine, and was specifically engineered for transverse installation (the Audi engine was an in-line unit, and could therefore be a lot wider – there were, in fact, no common parts).

In some ways the VR6 was advanced – narrow vee-angle, careful balancing, one cylinder head for two banks – but in another it was rather backward-looking – single-overhead-camshaft valvegear, long stroke, no 'stretch' capability. Even so, this was an extremely sweet engine, which revved smoothly, was very 'clean', and had a great deal of character, particularly when matched to the smaller platform of Golf/Corrado cars.

Following a massive investment in new facilities, VW introduced the third-generation Golf in August, showing a range of new cars intended to take them through the 1990s. The general transverse-engine/front-drive layout was as before – all the engines and transmissions were developments of those previously seen in earlier Golfs, Corrados and Passats – but the new platform/structure was slightly larger, stiffer and (according to VW) safer than ever before.

It took a little time for the entire range to enter the British market (starting in February 1992), but the wide choice of engines eventually spanned 60bhp/1.4-litre all the way to 174bhp/2.8-litre VR6, with a turbodiesel and many other variants. For the time being there was no 16-valve GTi version, this model being delayed until the engineers were satisfied with the power and refinement of their latest 2-litre engine.

Interestingly enough, there was no sign of a four-wheel-drive version, for although this had been tried and offered on various earlier-generation cars, it had not been a sales success, and was therefore dropped. Similarly, the G-Lader supercharged engines had also been dropped, and would not reappear in future years.

Naturally there would also be a successor to the Golf-based Jetta, but the new-generation car (to be called Vento) would not appear until the end of the year, nor go on volume sale until 1992. VW went to some lengths to stress that the Vento was not merely a booted version of the new Golf – yet it was almost precisely that.

From the autumn the Corrado coupe was upgraded, not only to include the new VR6 engine as an option, but also to have a 2-litre version of the well-known 16-valve four-cylinder unit instead of the original 1.8-litre. Surprisingly, although these cars always received rave road tests in the UK, they never seemed to sell very well.

Volvo: The most important new model to have been launched by Volvo for many years arrived in July. This was the 850 family, which not only had front-wheel drive with transverse engines, but looked more rounded than before, promised to be real driver's cars instead of safety-first 'tanks', and were clearly the first of an entirely new wave of Volvos.

Although looking rather similar to the latest 940/960 cars, the 850 saloons and estate cars were rather smaller and considerably lighter. The original version, badged 850GLT, featured an in-line five-cylinder 2.5-litre twin-cam/20-valve engine producing 170bhp, though both smaller and larger engines were to be launched in the months ahead.

The new engine was a close relative of the in-line 'six' which had been introduced for the 960 type of 1990, for this new family of power units was designed on the modular principle. UK deliveries would begin in May 1992, by which time there would also be 2-litre and 2.5-litre engines.

Still aiming (successfully) to confuse its public, and sometimes even its dealers, Volvo produced yet another derivative of the 740/760/960 range in the spring. Called the 940 SE Turbo, this was effectively the new-style 940/960 body, but with a 155bhp/2-litre version of the turbocharged four-cylinder engine. Yes, there already was a 940 Turbo, but that car had a 165bhp/2.3-litre version of the same engine…

Much derided in its day, both for its stodgy image and for its looks, the old 360-series family was finally killed off at the end of 1991. If British demand had not been inexplicably so strong in the latter years, it would probably have gone much earlier.

Westfield: Now fully recovered from its bruising design and 'copycat' battle with Caterham (see the 1988 section), the Midlands-based company launched an exciting new version of the SE two-seater.

Titled the SeiGHT, it was powered by a much-modified Rover V8 3.5-litre engine and produced the most phenomenal performance, with 0–60mph claimed in a mere 4 seconds!

Industrial developments

After 11 years at the helm of Aston Martin, Victor Gauntlett finally stepped down from the chairmanship, to be replaced by ex-Ford VP Walter Hayes. It was the end of one era, and the start of a higher-profile Ford-backed one.

There was a major upheaval in the British distribution networks when Nissan of Japan announced that it was to take back all the rights to sell its cars from Nissan UK, whose reclusive boss Octav Botnar had finally proved impossible to do business with on a sensible basis.

Botnar (who would later flee the country, accused of multi-million pound tax fraud) had fought this decision to the bitter end, but lost – and the only major result was that Nissan's market share had gradually slipped away from more than 10 per cent to less than half of that.

Along the way there were court cases, the Fraud Squad invaded the Nissan UK HQ in Worthing, senior executives were arrested, and Botnar himself fled to Switzerland. A warrant for his arrest was later issued, but in 1996 there was talk of a 'financial accommodation' with the Inland Revenue as a possible basis of a return to the UK. A new Nissan-owned company, Nissan Motor (GB), was set up to handle British sales from January 1, 1992.

Rover admitted defeat in the USA by pulling its Sterling (Rover 800) range out of the market there – this being the third humiliating withdrawal from the United States since the 1960s. Rover Sterling sales had started well in 1987, but had fallen away dramatically in the 1990s. Even though the still-to-be-announced 800 Coupe had been developed specifically with the US market in mind, Rover's owners (British Aerospace) decided that they could not wait for it, and closed all the showrooms.

Rolls-Royce, badly hit by the deepening British recession, decided to close down its last London coachbuilding base in Willesden. The Hythe Road factory had been producing Phantom VI and Corniche/Bentley Continental models for some years – but Phantom VI assembly (which had been at a snail's pace) was to close down, while final assembly of the other models was relocated at the main factory at Crewe.

It had taken nine months of operating in receivership, but in the end the automotive side of Reliant (but not that making Metrocab taxis) was rescued by the component manufacturer Beans Industries.

Beans, once independent in the 1950s, then swept into the Leyland (eventually British Leyland) maw in the 1960s and 1970s, but had been back in private hands for some years. Robin three-wheeler assembly restarted in the autumn, but there would be a long hold-up before the Scimitar SST went back into production.

Once again the British Maserati concession was in trouble. The umpteenth company which had been bringing in Maseratis from Italy since the 1960s went into receivership in April, admitting that only nine cars had actually been delivered in the first four months of 1991.

Unlike Ferrari, Maserati had never truly managed to establish itself in the British market – only 151 cars had been sold in the peak year of 1989, and the figure fell to 75 for the whole of 1990. It did not help, of course, that the Biturbo family was neither as fast, nor as attractively-styled, as the Ferraris with which it had always had to compete.

Once again the concession was revived – this time by Meridien of Lyndhurst, which was an established Maserati dealer, though even that enterprising concern could not raise the level of sales above a trickle.

Men of Influence

Victor Gauntlett

When Victor Gauntlett stepped down from the chairmanship of Aston Martin at the end of 1991, it brought to an end the era of wealthy individuals propping up a famous name which, by all logical criteria, should have been dead and closed down decades earlier.

Victor Gauntlett always seemed to be wrapped in the aura of the ex-public school boy who had stumbled on a job which he enjoyed, an all-round Good Chap and a man with money who would use it to keep other people happy. In some ways it was a good act, for the real Gauntlett was a man who had already made his money by succeeding with other businesses, and within limits was always determined to turn round Aston Martin.

Having started his working life in the oil industry, he first worked for BP then, in the 1970s, left to set up his own oil company, Pace Petroleum, which was soon a sizeable, if still a niche-market player in the UK oil distribution and garage business. By the late 1970s he was well-known for supporting Nigel Mansell when he ran out of money on the way to being a racing driver, for owning a mouth-watering collection of old-style cars, then for injecting money into Aston Martin and becoming a director.

The glamour of Aston Martin eventually proved too much, so when Alan Curtis moved on to take interests at Lotus, Gauntlett's Pace Petroleum company got together with CH Industrials to buy the company. Within a few years this enterprise had developed one branch of the business – Aston Martin Tickford – into a sizeable technical consulting concern, which Gauntlett soon released to do its own thing.

Against insuperable odds, and seemingly without any help from Government sources, Gauntlett and his associates kept Aston Martin firmly afloat until Ford came along with an attractive offer in 1987. Ford thought so much of Gauntlett that he was persuaded to stay on as chairman for another four years, and it is widely considered that he only agreed to step down because he was happy with the calibre of his successor – Walter Hayes of Ford.

This was one of those very rare years when taxation on cars and motoring actually came down (it was, after all, an election year). After a great deal of lobbying from the British motor industry, with the SMMT doing most of the talking, the Government finally agreed to reduce Special Car Tax, which was a unique type of impost not applied to any other consumer item.

Introduced in 1973, when VAT arrived to take over from purchase tax, SCT had been set at 10 per cent of the ex-factory price of the car (see the 1973 section for details) and had never been changed since that time.

The first reduction, from 10 to 5 per cent, was made in the Budget of March 1992, while the last 5 per cent was abandoned in November 1992, so all the hated SCT disappeared during this calendar year. This chopped about £400 off the price of a mid-range Ford Escort, £600–800 off a mid-sized BMW, and well over £1,110 off the price of a 4-litre Jaguar.

That was the good news. The bad news was that the annual licence fee rose to £110 (the first increase for eight years), while unleaded petrol and diesel rose in price by 5p/gallon and leaded fuel by 10p/gallon. Once again there were changes to the way company car taxes were levied on their users – taxation now to be applied according to value rather than with regard to engine size.

In fact these fiscal measures had a negligible effect on sales of cars in Britain, where the retail dealer chain was still in deep gloom. Not only had the private-sale market wilted badly, but the even more important fleet car market (where cars were usually bought regularly and in bulk) was also in the doldrums. It was not until that immeasurable (but vital) element – the 'feel-good factor' – returned that car sales would once again be on the rise.

New models

Alfa Romeo: The new 155 family, previewed at the end of 1991, went on sale in January 1992. Using a modified version of the Fiat Tipo platform and front-wheel-drive layout, the 155 was an altogether faster and more upmarket car, with a wide choice of twin-cam four-cylinder and 2.5-litre V6 engines. There was a four-wheel-drive version – the 190bhp/2-litre turbocharged 155 Q4 – which would only briefly be offered for sale in the UK, and then only in left-hand-drive form.

In its original state the 155 was criticized for looking rather anonymous and lacking image, which was one reason for Alfa using much-modified (and very successful!) versions of the car in Touring Car racing in future years.

Incidentally, it was not at all obvious from Alfa's original publicity literature that the 155's four-cylinder engines were Fiat-derived, not descendants of the old Alfa Romeo twin-cams – but by this time Alfa Romeo was already being rapidly reshaped as a Fiat 'corporate' concern.

The 164 family of four-door saloons was upgraded yet again during the autumn, this time with improved, twin-cam/four-valves-per-cylinder versions of the 3-litre V6 engine. The Super model had 210bhp, whereas the Cloverleaf had 230bhp. These were remarkably poised front-wheel-drive cars which, had they carried any other badge but Alfa Romeo, would have sold much better in the UK, where Alfa's image had come under considerable strain.

Aston Martin: Still making headlines, if not many cars, the company launched a rather gawky estate car derivative of the Virage in March, though only a handful were ever expected to be sold.

At the same time, a 465bhp/6.3-litre engine conversion was offered for all normal Virages, a makeover which cost a mere £50,000 extra...

Then, at the end of the year, the ferociously powerful 550bhp Vantage version of the Virage was introduced, this using a twin supercharged (not turbocharged) version of the 32-valve V8 5.3-litre engine. Expected to sell at more than £150,000, it had a claimed top speed of 186mph, and was clearly aimed at only a few very rich clients.

With different-style 18in wheels, the ZF six-speed gearbox, flared wheelarches and other subtly different styling details, this was clearly a complete step ahead of the 330bhp Virage – yet it still had the aura of a 'dinosaur' almost from the day it was launched.

Audi: A new and smaller version of the modern 90-degree V6 engine, with 150bhp and a 2,598cc capacity, joined the 174bhp/2.8-litre version during the summer and would eventually be fitted to a variety of 80s, Coupes and 100s. Intended eventually to take over from the old 2.3-litre five-cylinder units which Audi had been fitting since the late 1970s, it actually ran on in parallel with this entirely different unit for some years.

An estate car version of the new-generation 80 model was introduced during the summer, and like the saloons it would eventually be available in front-wheel or four-wheel drive and with a whole variety of engines.

UK deliveries of the cabriolet model began in July, originally in 133bhp/ 2.3-litre/five-cylinder form.

There was no end, it seemed, to the way engines, body styles and badges could be mixed. From the end of the year the latest new model was the S2 estate, based on the 80 estate, but fitted with the 230bhp/turbocharged/ 20-valve/five-cylinder engine already found in the S2 Coupe. This was also the occasion for Audi to announce a revised S2 Coupe, with the same engine and a six-speed gearbox.

Bentley: In 1991 Bentley had introduced its most expensive ever coupe, but in 1992 it produced a new entry-level model, the Brooklands four-door saloon which, at £91,000, took over from the Eight and the Mulsanne models. There were no styling and few major mechanical changes, though the Brooklands now had automatic ride control and was more firmly suspended than the Eight/Mulsanne models had been.

BMW: The arrival of a new breed of 32-valve V8 engine, with twin overhead camshafts per bank, set new standards at this price level when BMW launched the original developments in 218bhp/3-litre and 286bhp/4-litre guise.

The new V8s were eventually intended to take over from the long-running straight 'six' family which had already been running for nearly 25 years, but this would be a gradual business. The first two V8-equipped BMWs were badged as 730i and 740i versions of the well-known 7-series four-door saloons. It was already known that these V8s were destined for use in 5-series models and in the big 8-series coupe, the V8-engined 5-series cars actually being introduced in December.

The 850CSi coupe went one stage further in the autumn, getting a newly-developed 380bhp/5.6-litre version of the V12 engine. The top speed was still limited to 155mph by electronic means, but it accelerated even faster and more fiercely than before, and was only immediately available with a six-speed manual transmission.

Yet another variation of the modern-generation M5 appeared in mid-year, a 340bhp/3.8-litre 24-valve derivative of the latest straight-six 5-series four-door saloon. Like the previous M5, which it replaced, this called up all manner of superlatives from testers, especially as it was still a totally practical and refined touring model.

The first four-wheel-drive 5-series cars – 525i saloon and Touring types – went on UK sale in mid-year, using a developed version of the system previously seen only in the 325iX model. This layout, more familiar to the British in cars like Ford's Sierras and the Escort RS Cosworth, was matched to a straight-six engine. Prices started at £25,500.

Announced towards the end of the year (but tantalizingly not available in the UK until 1993), the new-generation M3 was a magnificently developed two-door 3-series coupe powered by a 286bhp/3-litre straight-six engine with 24 valves and twin overhead camshafts.

Unlike the original M3, this was not meant to be the basis for a competition car, but was at the time the ultimate statement of what BMW's engineers could do with the modern 3-series platform and chassis components.

The engine was a stretched version of the 325i's 24-valver, a five-speed gearbox was retained, and the chassis was aided by 235/40-section tyres on 17in cast-alloy wheel rims. Much quieter and more comfortable than the original M3, this new-generation car had its top speed limited to 155mph/250kph.

Showing that it meant the M3 to be a fast road car, not just a competition-based model, BMW also revealed the M3 convertible at the end of the year.

Citroen: Previewed in November, but not ready to go on sale until early 1993, was a new middle-sized saloon called Xantia. This was a direct replacement for the long-running BX range (which had been on sale for 10 years), and it shared many components with the Peugeot 405 model.

However, because this was a Citroen, it had XM-style hydropneumatic self-levelling suspension, though the wide choice of four-cylinder engines – petrol and diesel types – were all mirrored by those just introduced for the revised Peugeot 405 range. These spanned a 71bhp diesel to a 155bhp/2-litre 16-valve petrol engine. The four-wheel-drive feature seen on top-of-the-range BX models was dropped as sales had been slow.

For much of the year, Peugeot-Citroen concentrated on updating its mid-size four-cylinder engines, so the most important new Citroen model to go into production during the year was the expanded ZX range, which now included a three-door style, a new 155bhp/16-valve/2-litre engine and a 92bhp turbodiesel (see under Peugeot for how this dovetailed with their latest cars).

Daihatsu: Yet another tiny Japanese town car, badged as the Mira, was unveiled and British sales would begin in 1993. Powered by a three-cylinder 847cc engine, the little Mira had a neat front-wheel-drive installation.

Daimler: The last of the old-style V12-engined Double-Six saloons was produced in December (see under Jaguar, below).

Ferrari: Towards the end of the year the Italian company sent many a pulse racing with the introduction of the big 456GT, its first new front-engine/rear-drive V12-engined car for two decades. The 456 was a direct replacement for the venerable 412i, which had dropped out of production three years earlier.

By many supercar standards this was an old-fashioned (or unfashionable?) design, for the bulky engine was up front, the transmission was at the rear in unit with the axle, and it was a long-nosed, short-tailed 2+2-seater coupe. No matter, because it had a 442bhp/5.5-litre V12 engine and the performance was colossal. In any case, the looks (by Pininfarina) were rounded and sensuous, so there were absolutely no complaints from anyone who might have been in this market. UK deliveries would begin, slowly, in 1993, when the price was a hefty £145,999.

Ford: The sensational Escort RS Cosworth, which had been previewed in 1990 and rallied several times since then, finally went on sale in the spring. Basically, this used a shortened version of the Sierra Cosworth 4x4 floorpan and all its running gear, but was topped by an Escort-like cabin, with a massive high-mounted rear aerofoil to provide downforce.

In road-car tune, there was 227bhp from its Cosworth YB-type 16-valve 2-litre turbocharged engine, but until FISA started to apply turbocharger restrictions, works rally cars often developed around 400bhp.

Smaller, more nimble, but more expensive than the Sierra Cosworth 4x4 (which carried on until the end of the year), the Escort RS Cosworth was an extremely capable car which did everything in motorsport which Ford had hoped for. Unhappily, Britain's insurance companies seemed determined to kill it off with high premiums, and sales were always disappointing.

The new-generation 16-valve Zetec engine, in 1.8-litre form, was fitted to a whole series of revised Fiestas, Escorts and Orions in the spring of the year. New high-performance versions of the Fiesta were introduced in January (with sales beginning in March). The XR2i-16V had 105bhp, while a version to be known as the Fiesta RS1800 had 130bhp – these cars replacing the old CVH-engined XR2i/RS Turbo types respectively.

Then, in February, the same engines were fitted to Orions (saloons) and Escorts (hatchbacks, estates and cabriolets). The most high-profile of these were the XR3i models, making a reappearance with a choice of 105 or 130bhp engines.

Later in the year, the Escort/Orion range was given a comprehensive makeover, only two years after it had been launched (to a disappointing reception). There was a new 'smiley face' nose with a separate grille, a new rear aspect including larger tail-lights and more glass, and the bodyshells were stiffened internally. The XR3s and RS2000s were given more flamboyant rear spoilers, but these were still nowhere near as large as the Escort RS Cosworth's.

Mechanical changes included the standardization of fuel injection on all engines, the addition of CTX automatic transmission on 1.6-litre and 1.8-litre models, a new 1.6-litre version of the Zetec engine, and power-assisted steering as standard on all Zetec-fitted Escorts.

This was a much better specification than the earlier type, as the sales figures and road test reports would soon confirm, although cabriolets would not become available until May 1993.

In March the Granada/Scorpio range was given a front-end facelift, with smoother detailing. At the same time there was a new facia style, and at long last a big, handsome and very useful estate car version was added to the range.

After a long and glamorous career, the Sierra RS Cosworth dropped out of production towards the end of the year. Not only had it been overtaken in the eyes of Ford fans by the new Escort RS Cosworth, but it also had to make way (in Belgium) for the Sierra's replacement, which would make its debut early in 1993.

Ford-USA: The second-generation Probe sports hatchback/coupe was introduced at the Detroit Auto Show in January with the news that UK deliveries would follow in mid-1993. The new Probe used the same platform and basic front-wheel-drive layout as the newly-launched Mazda 626/MX-6 models seen in 1991.

The Probe was a smoothly-detailed 2+2-seater and would go on sale in Britain with a choice of 2-litre 'four' and 2.5-litre V6 engines, both being USA-built Mazda units.

Ginetta: The sportscar maker plunged into receivership in September, but bravely showed the new cars it *wanted* to sell if the administrators would allow it — both being developed G33s, one with a 1.8-litre Ford Zetec engine, the other with a 3.9-litre V8.

Honda: Early in the year, a new-generation CRX sports coupe was launched. Not only did this front-wheel-drive car have a choice of four-cylinder engines, the most powerful of which was the 160bhp 1.6-litre VTi type, but there was a unique body feature. The new CRX featured an aluminium roof panel which could be folded and stored in the boot. In manual form there was nothing new about this feature (the Fiat X1/9, for instance, had had such a roof 20 years earlier), but there was an optional electrically powered version which required seven motors to do its job.

Having freed the side and centre roof locks, a button was pressed, after which the car's bootlid rose, roof carriers folded out from the boot area, clamped on to the roof panel, then folded it all back into the boot, after which the bootlid closed once again. As with the manual lift-off hood, there was nothing new here (Ford-USA cars had used similar mechanisms in the 1950s), and as expected this added 55lb to the car's weight and decimated the carrying capacity of the boot.

Apart from this, the platform, chassis components and all running gear were closely derived from the latest-generation Civic family, which had been launched in 1991.

Only three years after the previous-generation Accord had been introduced in Japan, yet another range was shown. This car was doubly significant, not just because it had been introduced so soon after its ancestor, but because it was known to be the basis of a new Rover model to be launched in 1993 and badged Rover 600.

Nor was this only a facelift, for the car was built on a new and slightly shorter-wheelbase platform, with rather more rounded body lines than before, which (like the latest Toyota Carina E) included three side windows. All the time, too, the Accord was edging slowly upmarket, for there would be a wider choice of more powerful engines, all of them with four valves per cylinder, including a 2.3-litre 16-valve 'four'.

The first British-built Accords were assembled at Swindon in October, though the official British launch would be delayed until the spring of 1993.

Hyundai: In October, the modest little Scoupe gained a new engine option, a 114bhp/1.5-litre turbocharged unit, which gave it a claimed top speed of 121mph.

Almost immediately afterwards, the Lantra range was topped out with a new 124bhp/1.8-litre engine option, a 16-valve twin-cam with a twin balancer-shaft layout to make it as smooth as possible.

Jaguar: Deliveries of the 212mph XJ220 finally began in mid-year, nearly four years after the first concept car had been revealed (at the NEC Motor Show in October 1988). The selling price had risen with inflation and was now set at a staggering £415,544.

Although there had been huge demand for the car in 1988 and 1989, Jaguar said it would only ever build 350 cars. In the meantime, and because the recession had struck hard, with the value of all so-called collector's cars plummeting, many tried to walk away from their orders, and the XJ220 never achieved the fame that it deserved. In the end, assembly would end in 1994 after only 271 cars had been produced.

The last of the long-established V12-engined XJ12 cars was built (the same basic car had originally gone on sale in 1972, with one major facelift taking place in 1979). It would be replaced in 1993 by a new 6-litre version of the XJ40-style car.

For 1993, the latest XJ6 models were slightly different from 1992 types, notably by trim changes, some engine refinements and a new-type front spoiler. The XJS was also improved by changes to the driving position (steering wheel moved forward, seats back...) and with a manual gearbox option now available on the 4-litre/six-cylinder derivatives.

Jeep: After many years of not being regularly on sale in the UK, and never in right-hand-drive form, the rugged and world-famous four-wheel-drive Jeep range was finally made available to British drivers at the end of the year.

Two of the three current models — the Wrangler (a lineal descendant of the legendary Second World War Jeep) and the Cherokee (a Range Rover-sized estate car) — would make up the majority of sales, for the Grand Cherokee (a much larger estate than the Cherokee) could not really compete on price or refinement in the Range Rover class.

For 1993, Wranglers and Cherokees were both available with the same choice of engines — a 122bhp/2.5-litre four-cylinder or a 184bhp/4-litre straight-six petrol engine. This became the established choice for the smaller Wranglers, but the larger Cherokee would also have turbodiesel and V8 engine options in future years.

Lancia: Sales of these cars in the UK were still slipping ominously away. The endearing little Y10 was dropped from the British market in 1992, and flagship cars like the 8.32 (complete with Ferrari V8 engine) had been negligible sellers.

In an attempt to revive their image, the Thema saloons were revamped in the autumn. The normally-aspirated 2-litre version was given new Bosch Motronic fuel injection/engine management control, making it more tractable although slightly less powerful than before.

Land Rover: The Discovery, which had now been on sale for three years, progressed a stage further in the autumn when a ZF automatic gearbox was made an option on V8-engined types.

Lotus: In a major shock announcement, Lotus killed off the front-wheel-drive Elan in June. Although this car had received rave notices from the motoring press, it had always been perceived as expensive, particularly in North America, where it was a marketing failure. Lotus later admitted that the car had never been profitable.

After the announcement, the production lines were closed and cleared almost immediately, and there was a brief surge of demand for still-to-be-sold cars. However, the FWD Elan was not quite dead after all, for several hundred more cars would eventually be produced in 1994–95 around a batch of already-delivered engine/transmissions units from Isuzu.

The long-running Excel, which had been in production for nearly a decade, and was itself developed from the 1976 Eclat, was also allowed to die, the last car, apparently, being delivered to Hazel Chapman, Colin Chapman's widow.

Marcos: The latest version of the by now very old Marcos design was the Mantara, introduced in October, which was a 4.5-litre version of the recent Rover-engined car: it was available as both a coupe and a convertible.

Maserati: Somehow the Maserati concession in the UK kept struggling on, selling very few cars, whose styling was generally considered to be gawky by comparison with Ferraris. In mid-

1992 the latest derivative of the long-running Biturbo range, the Shamal coupe, went on UK sale at £63,450. The 3,217cc twin-turbo V6 engine produced no less than 326bhp, a top speed of nearly 170mph being claimed.

Mazda: The first of the new top-of-the-range models, the Xedos 6, was introduced in the spring, UK sales beginning in mid-year. Larger, smoother and altogether more upmarket than any previous Mazda, this was an obvious move into BMW/Audi territory.

The Xedos had an extremely rounded and smoothly detailed body style, with a small radiator grille and a short tail, all hiding a conventional front-wheel-drive layout. Different engines were to be fitted for Japanese-market cars, but for the UK there was to be a 2-litre version of the new twin-cam/24-valve V6 at first, though a smaller-capacity 'four' would follow in 1993.

McLaren: The world's fastest road car, the McLaren F1, was revealed in mid-year, well before it was ready to go into production. Not that there were too many impatient customers, for it was expected to retail for around £540,000.

As expected, this mid-engined supercar coupe was powered by a specially-developed 6-litre V12 BMW power unit, an engine of superlatives, which not only had 48 valves and four camshafts, but produced 627bhp in production form, thus guaranteeing a top speed of at least 230mph.

The F1's cabin was a uniquely laid-out three-seater, with the driving seat in the centre and slightly ahead of the two passenger seats, one on each side. No expense had been spared in specifying the chassis, with space-age materials, carbonfibre and gold leaf figuring in profusion.

This was not a 'sensible' car by any standards, but it was a superb statement of what automotive technology, enterprise and ambition could produce. However, it had arrived several years behind the boom, so by the time deliveries began in 1993 many of the potential buyers had fled, and deliveries were not expected to creep up to a total of 100 until 1997, when the design was due to be abandoned.

Mercedes-Benz: From September the mid-size 200E, 220E, 280E and

320E (popularly referred to as the E-class) were substantially changed for 1993, though without any style changes. All the petrol engines were given four-valve/twin-cam cylinder heads, which meant increases in power and torque – the 200E gained 18bhp and the new 320E no less than 40bhp, for instance. Even so, this E-class range only had three more years to run before being replaced by completely restyled models in 1995.

The new-generation two-door, four-seater S-class coupes, closely based on the latest S-class saloons, but with a shorter wheelbase, were introduced in January. Like the saloons, these were sumptuously-equipped machines, the most powerful of which had a 402bhp/6-litre V12 engine.

The 400E saloon – an E-class four-door saloon fitted with a 268bhp/4.2-litre V8 engine – was introduced in Germany in February, but although it was promised for the UK in 1993, it was never officially put on sale.

From mid-year there was also a new flagship derivative of the SL roadster range, this being the 600SL, which was powered by a 395bhp/6-litre V12 engine. Heavier, even faster and considerably more expensive than the 5-litre V8 type, which continued, the 600SL was a no-expense-spared indulgence for all who bought it – yet according to testers it was really no better than the 5-litre model.

MG: The new MG RV8 was previewed in June, and finally went on sale in October. Broadly based on the layout of the MGB V8, which had been killed off in 1976, the RV8 was an open roadster, not a GT, and had been updated in several ways. Body monocoques were manufactured by the small Heritage concern in Faringdon, Oxon, which was already producing classic-type MGB bodyshells for use in restorations. Unlike old-style MGBs, these featured flared wheelarches, and there was an upmarket wooden facia and door cappings, along with very plush trim and fittings.

The engine was a 187bhp/3.9-litre Rover V8, and a top speed of 135mph was claimed. Sales were due to begin in the spring of 1993, after which customers would soon find that this car was expensive, and had an irritating mixture of 1990s performance, retro-look styling and a positively archaic combination of ride and handling.

In Britain, in spite of what MG enthusiasts would have you believe, the £26,500 RV8 was not a success, and most cars from the 2,000 production run (which ended in 1995) were exported to Japan.

Mini: *(See under Rover, below.)*

Mitsubishi: A new-generation Galant, larger, smoother and more upmarket than the last, was put on sale in Japan in May, though British deliveries would not begin until 1993, following its first European appearance at the Amsterdam show in February.

Compared with the earlier type, the latest Galant had newly-developed multi-link suspension and updated engines, including 2-litre and 2.5-litre V6s, which in some models were mated to four-wheel drive and four-wheel steering.

During the summer, the Space Wagon MPV people carrier was upgraded with a 131bhp 2-litre engine in place of the original 1.8-litre type from which it was developed.

Revised Lancer liftback models, which shared much of the running gear of the latest Colt hatchbacks, were introduced in October.

Nissan: A totally new Micra was introduced in the spring. Called the March in some markets, not only was this car important in its own right, but it was also the second model which Nissan had promised would be built in its British factory.

Rounded where the earlier Micra had been sharp-edged, the new Micra was also smaller than before. There was a choice of two new 16-valve twin-cam engines – a 1-litre and a 1.3-litre – front-wheel drive and an appealing character.

The Serena model jumped on the fast-developing MPV bandwagon when introduced towards the end of the year. Like in the Toyota Previa, which was an obvious competitor, its engine was under the front seats, though it drove the rear wheels as expected.

The Serena, therefore, was even higher than expected, and had rather ungainly handling characteristics. It was by no means the best-packaged nor (as it transpired) the best-selling of the modern generation of MPVs.

The 3-litre V6-engined Maxima, which had first been seen in 1988, then dropped from the British line-up at the end of 1991, reappeared during the summer, having been mildly facelifted and reworked. At £20,500, it was in the Ford Scorpio/Vauxhall Senator class, and sales would always be very limited.

Peugeot: There was a thorough mid-life makeover for the best-selling 405 range, which took effect in Britain in November. The basic style was not changed, but at the rear the bootlid was now arranged to open all the way down to bumper level, and there was a redesigned interior with a 605-like facia/instrument panel.

This was accompanied by a reshuffle of engines. The established 1.9-litre units were dropped, and in their place came newly-developed 101bhp/1.8-litre and 118bhp/2-litre derivatives, along with a 150bhp/2-litre 16-valve engine which was considerably more torquey than the obsolete 160bhp/1.9-litre type. There was also a new 92bhp/1.9-litre turbocharged diesel engine.

At the same time as the 405 was facelifted, a limited-production (2,000-off) 200bhp/2-litre version of the Mi16 was put on sale in France, but only a handful ever seem to have been sold in the UK, for it was only built in left-hand-drive form, at an approximate price of £22,500.

The little 106 model range was expanded considerably in the autumn with the arrival of five-door types (to add to the original three-door models) as well as small diesel engines, similar to those currently being used in the Rover Metro.

Porsche: Because the 968 model, which had been launched in 1991, had proved to be a relative failure (its sales were a mere fraction of those forecast), Porsche was in serious financial trouble, so some of its new model programme had to be delayed.

In October, though, the already formidable Porsche 911 Turbo was given a 360bhp/3.6-litre version of the flat-six engine, which boosted its already formidable performance to give a claimed top speed of 174mph – a pace which could only really be proved on the speed limit-free autobahns of Germany.

Range Rover: Years after it had first been rumoured, the top Range Rover models finally became available with air suspension, along with a 4.2-litre engine and an 8in longer wheelbase. The air suspension of the Vogue LSE type's beam axles (so long in development) had many advanced features, including five different ride height settings and the ability to 'kneel' to allow access. The engine was a longer-stroke version of the famous light-alloy V8 (TVR had already made similar changes of its own on this engine), which produced 200bhp.

Just before the end of the year came a new type of diesel engine, a 111bhp/2.5-litre unit designed and built by Rover (as opposed to the earlier VM-type) which was already being used in the Land Rover Discovery.

Reliant: The Scimitar SST, which had always sold slowly, and had suffered badly from the company's financial problems in 1990 and 1991, was being revived by Beans Industries, and a revised version, called the Scimitar Sabre, was shown during the year.

Still based closely on the old SST, and using the same turbocharged 1.8-litre Nissan engine, the Sabre had a restyled and rather smoother nose, with hidden headlamps. Even so, at £14,900 it was still not an entrancing prospect, so the sales rate did not increase.

Renault: The 25 range was finally dropped at the beginning of the year, to be replaced by a new Renault flagship – the Safrane. As expected, this big front-wheel-drive machine, which was smoother and had a larger cabin than the 25, was to be built with a wide choice of engines.

It was an entirely different car from the 25, which had used in-line engines, whereas the Safrane had transverse units which, in the UK, ranged from a 105bhp/2-litre 'four' to a 170bhp/3-litre V6, this last being a final development of the old PRV engine which was also still being used by Peugeot and Volvo.

The 19 range was reshuffled during the year, notably with the addition of a 95bhp/1.8-litre model to the range, which was actually a slightly enlarged version of the familiar 1,721cc unit which had been used in various Renault (and Volvo) cars for some years.

The last of the cheap, cheerful, but amazingly useful and long-running Renault 4 range was produced at the end of the year, total production having amounted to a staggering 8,135,424 cars.

Rover: After a big delay and a great deal of rumour, the smart and dignified 800 coupe, a two-door four-seater 800-series flagship, was finally introduced in March. This was the car that had originally been intended for sale mainly in the USA, but as Rover (Sterling) had withdrawn from that market by this time, it was wasted.

The platform and all the running gear came from the latest 827/Sterling models, as did the front end and the general proportions, but the two-door shell was otherwise very different and bore a striking resemblance to the current Ford-USA Thunderbird.

Too expensive and specialized to appeal to British motorists, the coupe disappeared almost as soon as it had been launched, and very few were sold. It must have been a financial and marketing disaster.

The latest in the ever-widening 800 line-up was the Vitesse (which had been previewed at the end of 1991), which was fitted with a 180bhp turbocharged version of the T16 twin-cam 2-litre four-cylinder engine and went on sale in February, when the VM-engined turbodiesel versions also hit the showrooms.

In October, a trio of smart three-door 200 coupes were launched, these being built on developed versions of the existing front-drive 200 platform and running gear. The 111bhp/1.6-litre and 136bhp/2-litre engines were familiar enough, but the 197bhp/2-litre turbocharged engine was new for this chassis, and at a launch price of £18,313, this model was considered to be a bargain.

The use of a Torsen-style limited-slip differential was a novelty, but although it was supposed to act like traction control, in practice it was very rough and ready compared with more sophisticated layouts, and the 200 coupes would always be criticized for this trait.

The 200 convertible, closely based on the latest-generation hatchback type, was previewed in March and went on sale in the summer. Available in 1.4-litre or 1.6-litre form, it had an optional power-operated soft-top.

Tidying up all this activity for 1993, the 200/400 range was revised in October. The 400 four-door saloon cars received a traditional type of radiator grille (though without sheet-metal changes), this being the sum total of the style modifications.

Mechanically, there was a 103bhp instead of the 95bhp version of the 1.4-litre engine, a new (Honda) 111bhp/1.6-litre unit, while the M16 engines gave way to the latest 800-style T-series, which meant a minor drop in power to 136bhp.

Both styles – 200 hatchback and 400 saloon – were now to be available with the 197bhp turbocharged 2-litre engine of the new 200 coupes, but they were only intended to be manufactured in very limited quantities.

In the spring, a diesel option was announced for the latest Metro range, this being a 53bhp/1.36-litre Peugeot, which was mated to Rover's own Peugeot-derived gearbox.

A new type of automatic transmission became optional on the Metro during the year. A Volvo-developed CVT system was offered, this matching what Fiat, Ford and Nissan were already doing with their small/medium-sized cars. Earlier-generation Minis and Metros had used the conventional AP automatic transmission.

Finally, at the NEC Motor Show, the company unveiled the Longbridge-built (as opposed to imported) version of the Mini cabriolet, and a Metro cabriolet. Neither was yet ready for sale, nor likely to sell in large numbers, but it all added up to variety on an amazing scale at Rover. Mini cabriolet assembly, however, was much delayed (surely it could never have been justified on economic grounds?) and first deliveries did not take place until 1994.

Seat: The old-style Fiat Panda-based Marbella hatchback was perked up in the spring with the launch of a 903cc-engined entry-level version, which had a five-speed gearbox and sold for a mere £4,133.

There was also time for the modern VW-based Toledo range to be reshuffled. From March, a new 75bhp/1.6-litre entry-level model became available to add to the 1.8, 2-litre and diesel-engined models already on sale.

Subaru: In a very low-key introduction, the tiny (Metro-sized) Vivio hatch-back was put on sale in the UK in May. Because it was powered by a 658cc twin-cylinder engine, driving the front wheels, it was only ever seen as distinctly marginal motoring by the British public, and very few were sold.

In Japan, a new range of saloons and estates badged as Imprezas were previewed. These took over from the old Leone range, and like them had flat-four engines with either front-wheel or four-wheel-drive transmission. Smaller and lighter than the Legacy, which remained in production, the Imprezas would become Subaru's front-line rally cars from the end of 1993.

Toyota: Although it appeared in Japan, badged as a Corona, this particular new model was due to be produced at the new Derby factory in the UK from the end of the year, badged as the Carina E.

To be aimed squarely at the large Sierra/Cavalier market, this medium-sized front-wheel-drive car was launched in four-door saloon or five-door hatchback styles. The two were very similar, except that hatchback cars had an extra rear quarter-window aft of the rear doors.

As expected, there would be a choice of engines, ranging from a 1.6-litre twin-cam to a 16-valve 2-litre twin-cam, with a diesel option. UK production would begin later in the year.

TVR: In October, there were two major innovations at the NEC Motor Show. One was the launch of yet another Rover-engined two-seater roadster, this one called the Chimaera, and the other the display of a mock-up of a brand-new in-house V8 engine, the AJP8.

The Chimaera used the same chassis and running gear as the charismatic Griffith, but it had rather less rounded lines and was that important bit more 'touring' than 'sports'. In 1993, when it finally went on sale, it rapidly took over from the Griffith as the most dominant model on the assembly lines at Blackpool.

The AJP8 engine, on the other hand, suffered one delay after another. Originally intended to be ready within the year, even at the end of 1995, more than three years after it had first been shown, it was only just beginning to appear in the first cars (Cerberas) to be delivered to customers.

Vauxhall: The fastest and most capable Calibra coupe of all was introduced in April, this being the turbocharged 4x4 version, which not only had 201bhp and a 150mph-plus top speed, but also a *six*-speed manual gearbox.

Although it was cannily priced at £20,950 – several thousands less than Ford's Sierra Cosworth 4x4, for instance – the Calibra Turbo 4x4 for some reason turned out to be a resounding flop. It was great to look at, and technically fascinating, but apparently it was never felt to have an inspiring chassis. More importantly, too, there was no competition heritage to help build an image.

A totally new 170bhp/2.5-litre V6 engine with twin cams per head was previewed during the year, this being destined for use in several models in the current and planned Cavalier, Senator and (soon) new Saab models. For space, rather than technical, reasons, it had a 54-degree angle between its cylinder banks.

The Cavalier range was revamped for 1993, notably with the launch of two very high-performance models – the 201bhp Turbo 4x4 (with a turbocharged 2-litre engine and a six-speed gearbox) for £19,539, and the promise of a V6-engined version in the spring of 1993. Side-impact beams were fitted inside the doors, airbags became standard in the steering wheel of top-of-the-range models, and there was a new V-styled grille, complete with the Vauxhall griffon symbol.

Still expanding its Astra range, Vauxhall introduced an 82bhp/1.7-litre turbodiesel version during the year.

Volkswagen: After a long delay, caused because the original examples were not good enough, the Golf GTi 16V 2-litre model finally went on sale. At last it had a 150bhp version of the long-established twin-cam engine, and would go on UK sale early in 1993.

Even so, this was not the sparkling and cheeky Golf GTi of old, for many years of development, safety regulations and the addition of a lot of extra equipment had made it a much heavier car than before.

Production of the long-running Scirocco sports coupe ended during the summer, though its sales in the UK had been in heavy decline for some time. The Scirocco was not to be replaced – the Corrado being a larger and rather more ambitious restatement of the VW/Karmann front-wheel-drive sporting-VW theme.

Industrial developments

When Rover announced that it was finalizing a new high-tech assembly facility at its Cowley factory complex near Oxford, it obscured the sad fact that the historic Morris Motors Cowley factories were to be abandoned. From 1993, it seemed, assembly was to be concentrated in what many older hands still called the Pressed Steel buildings.

Within two years, not only would the Cowley North and Cowley South be emptied of cars, they would also be razed to the ground, then redeveloped into light industrial parks. It was one of a series of radical changes planned for Rover by its owner, British Aerospace, who seemed to be more interested in asset-stripping than in developing car sales.

Assembly of new Toyota Carina E models began at the new Burnaston (near Derby) factory towards the end of the year.

Ginetta went into receivership in September, but the company was hoping for a rescue – which would follow in 1993.

Once again an importer of Italian supercars was in trouble. This time, it was the turn of the Lamborghini importer, Portman Lamborghini, who ceased trading for a time before returning to the market after a financial restructure in mid-summer. Sales of Countachs and the new Diablos had been hard-hit by the onset of the recession.

In a move generally agreed to have staved off major financial trouble for TWR, Benetton of Italy bought 50 per cent of TWR's business. As so often before, this was a master-stroke by the canny Tom Walkinshaw, who not only saw his business shored up, but soon found himself in a position of real authority in the Benetton F1 team.

Technical developments

Was the arrival of Ford's twin-cam 16-valve Zetec engine a major technical, or industrial development? Certainly it was a very important new venture for Britain's market leader – its first mass-production four-valves-per-cylinder twin-overhead-camshaft unit. (The RS2000's 16-valve engine, an entirely different type, didn't really count as it was being built in limited quantities for just one sporting model.)

Ford, rarely considered to be the leader in producing major building blocks like engines, had clearly concluded that this sort of engine layout was essential to its future and the image it needed to project. Engineers and managers who pointed out that similar power characteristics could be coaxed from simpler and cheaper-to-build engines had lost their battle, being told that 16 valves, belt-driven camshafts and obvious dashes of high-tech fittings, were now 'sexy' and essential marketing tools in the modern showroom. The days of Ford-is-cheapest, Ford-is-simplest, were over, seemingly for good.

Vauxhall's Lotus-Carlton had been the first European car to fit a six-speed gearbox as standard, but that was a very limited-production machine which used an off-the-shelf American box. The Calibra Turbo 4x4 of April 1992, though, was certainly the first European-developed car to have a six-speeder as standard – and it was also a world 'first' for a transverse installation. Some thought this was gilding the lily – and in fact very few other six-speed models would be launched in the next few years.

Jaguar's XJS became the first UK-built car to fit a driver's airbag as standard, this feature being added to the standard specification from May. It was the first of many such updates.

1993

Because the Government was changing the way that it went about and advertised its financial planning, there were two Budgets in 1993. However, in spite of the depth of the recession in the UK, both Budgets looked like a wholesale attack on cars and motoring.

In the first, unveiled in March, not only was four-star petrol increased in price by 15p/gallon (with unleaded and diesel going up by 12p/gallon), but the price of an annual licence disc jumped by £15 to £125.

At the same time, a wholesale rejig of the taxation of benefit-in-kind company cars was proposed, this time by taxing cars according to their retail price when new.

Then, in November, there was a further impost of an extra 14p/gallon on fuel and another £5 on the cost of an annual vehicle licence (Excise Duty).

Nevertheless, the combined effect of Honda and Toyota starting up car manufacture in the UK, the build-up of Micra production at the Nissan factory near Sunderland, and a general reaction to the end of the UK recession, saw UK car sales leap by nearly 200,000 compared with 1992. UK car production, in fact, was at its highest level for nearly two decades, though the purely *British* element of that output was still very low.

Although the Government announced that it was to begin experiments into ways of imposing road pricing – which meant logging automatic tolls on cars using certain stretches of road – three years later there was no sign that the technology was yet up to the job.

Road pricing had originally been proposed as early as the 1960s. Apart from it being universally unpopular with the motorist, it was always going to be difficult to administer.

British drivers, though, had no cause to be complacent, for it began to look as if some form of road pricing would be introduced early in the 21st Century.

New models

AC: The story of the new-generation Ace seemed to have been dribbling on for years, but at the London Motor Show in October the company showed yet another variation, this one having a front-mounted Ford-USA 5-litre V8 engine.

Although it was still not ready for production (the factory kept itself busy building a few old-type Cobras), this was almost the finalized design, which ultimately would go on sale during 1994.

Alfa Romeo: Production of the near-legendary Spider finally ended in April 1993 after an unbroken run which began in 1966, 27 years earlier, and rumours began to spread about the arrival of a new-generation car (see 1994 for further details).

Asia: The Rocsta 4x4, which resembled a very small edition of the Jeep Wrangler, was mechanically different, this Korean range relying on Mazda power units. There was a choice of 1.8-litre petrol and 2.2-litre diesel four-cylinder engines. British sales were due to begin in 1994.

Aston Martin: Many years after previous Aston Martin management had started talking about the need for a new-generation car which was a lot smaller than the V8 (later Virage) range, a prototype – the DB7 – was finally unveiled. This was still a year away from production, but it caused great interest.

The new car had been inspired by the company's new chairman, Walter Hayes, who had acted instead of merely talking about the project. Based on the pressed-steel platform, suspension and running gear of the updated Jaguar XJS (whose replacement would not, in fact, appear until 1996), the DB7 had a sleek new 2+2-seater coupe style which Hayes assured everyone had a flavour of earlier DB4GT-style cars of the 1960s.

Aston Martin was at pains to suggest that there was a lot of unique engineering in the DB7, but the more one was allowed to delve into it, the more Jaguar – XJS in particular – was revealed. The engine was a modified version of the Jaguar 3.2-litre AJ6, with an Eaton supercharger (not turbocharger) which helped to liberate well over 300bhp, and was backed by a choice of Jaguar-related manual or automatic transmissions.

The DB7 was scheduled to be built on the same assembly lines as the Jaguar XJ220 – at Bloxham, near Banbury – which meant that manufacture could not begin until XJ220 production had ended. This was forecast to be in mid-1994, and because there was a slight overrun in XJ220 deliveries this date slipped back to the autumn of 1994. (For further details, see the 1994 section.)

Audi: The latest complex combination of engines and body styles came in January, when Audi launched the S4 estate, which not only used the 280bhp/4.2-litre V8 engine from the larger Audi V8 model, along with four-wheel drive, but was also scheduled to be manufactured by Porsche. It was only ever to be built with left-hand drive and consequently was sold in the UK to special order only.

Except for its new multi-spoke alloy wheels, the S4 saloons and estates looked much like existing Audi 100 models, and although Audi's marketing staff did not confirm this, it meant that there was now direct in-house competition for the Audi V8 saloon, which was larger, heavier and really no faster or more desirable.

Bentley: (See Rolls-Royce, below.)

Bristol: When the new Blenheim was introduced in September, journalists had to scratch their heads before remembering when the previous newly-named Bristol had been unveiled. After a great deal of research, they discovered that it had been 11 years earlier, when the Britannia and Brigand types had appeared.

The Blenheim of 1993, however, was not truly new, for it was a closely-based development of the Britannia/Brigand types, which in turn had been an evolution of the 603 style which first surfaced in 1976.

There was more in the Blenheim, in fact, which was not new than was fresh, but because these hand-built cars were always so carefully built and nicely detailed, everyone forgave them for that.

The chassis was yet another minor improvement of the frame which had been evolving since the 1950s, the bodyshell was almost (if not entirely) indistinguishable from the old 603/Britannia/Brigand, while as ever, the engine/transmission package came from Chrysler-USA. As usual, neither power nor torque outputs were quoted, though Bristol claimed a top speed of around 140mph and felt sure there were sufficient customers willing to pay £109,980 to keep the small factory and workforce happy and occupied.

Citroen: From mid-year, two diesel-engined versions of the Xantia – a 71bhp normally-aspirated and a 92bhp/1.9-litre turbodiesel – were added to the range, and at the same time an entry-level 89bhp/1.6-litre was added.

Daewoo: The Korean car-maker (which would eventually advertise itself as 'The largest company you've never heard of...' – which was certainly correct in UK terms) announced that it would began selling cars in Britain in 1995. *(For further details, see the 1995 section.)*

Daihatsu: A new-generation Charade was introduced in Japan early in the year, British deliveries beginning later in the season. More rounded than before, this latest front-wheel-drive Japanese hatchback would eventually be available in 1.3, 1.5 and 1.6-litre guises.

From mid-summer there was a much-modified Fourtrak 4x4 leisure vehicle, fitted with a completely new chassis-frame and having an independent front suspension by coil springs and double wishbones, allied to a rigid rear axle sprung on coils and located by five links.

Visually the Fourtrak was much as before, but the latest car (which was available in 2.8-litre diesel and turbo-diesel forms) was a much more saleable proposition in a market sector which was still dominated by the Land Rover Discovery.

Daimler: *(See under Jaguar, below.)*

Ferrari: The much-rumoured 348 spider finally went on sale during the year. Mechanically it was identical to the existing 348tb coupe.

Later in the year both types were given even more performance with their V8 engine tuned to produce 320 instead of 300bhp.

Fiat: The new Punto range of three and five-door hatchbacks, which were intended to take over from the Uno,

were previewed in mid-summer, went on sale a few weeks later, and would come to the UK in 1994.

As expected, the new Punto was to be fitted with a wide range of well-proven four-cylinder engines, rated from 55bhp/1.1-litres to – eventually – a 2-litre/16-valve unit, some versions had new six-speed manual transmissions, and it was slightly larger than the replaced Uno. Styling was by Giorgetto Giugiaro at ItalDesign, and with a 10mm longer wheelbase the Punto had a larger cabin than the Uno.

This represented a major investment, even by Fiat standards, and it was clear that this was a new platform on which many other Fiat, Lancia and Alfa Romeo models would be based during the 1990s. Even at first there were no fewer than 22 Punto derivatives on the Italian market, though not all of these would make it to the UK in 1994.

During the summer, the smart new coupe, which was a two-door car based on the floorpan and running gear of the modern Tipo hatchback, went on sale, though British deliveries would not begin until mid-1995.

Like the Tipo, the coupe had a front-engine/front-wheel-drive layout, and for sale in the UK there would eventually be a choice of two 2-litre/16-valve engines, one normally-aspirated (142bhp) and one with turbocharging (195bhp).

These controversially-styled cars (by Pininfarina, who would assemble them) came with definite and distinctive angled creases/styling lines on the flanks, had rounded headlamp covers in the steeply-sloping front end, and incorporated many technological advances, including ABS and traction control.

The coupe was aimed squarely at the rather limited mid-size market, which was already covered by the GM Calibra and the VW Corrado, with the Ford-USA Probe also due in 1994.

Tidying up its big range of Tipo models early in the year, Fiat-UK dropped the 1.8ie SX model, replacing it with a 115bhp/2.0ie GT instead.

Ford: Long-rumoured and certainly long-awaited, the new Mondeo was launched at the beginning of the year and went on general sale a few weeks later. As a direct replacement for the Sierra (which had been in production for just over 10 years), the Mondeo was different – and better – in every respect.

Front-wheel drive where the Sierra had been rear-drive, with 16-valve engines where the Sierra had been lumbered with a choice of old-fashioned power, the Mondeo was not only modern, but also felt startlingly so. Publications which had been prepared to rubbish the new Ford were astonished by the car's steering, handling and general capability, the general consensus being that it went immediately to the top of the medium-sized class. Straight away, too, what had been known as the Sierra/Cavalier class now became the Mondeo class.

In the first stage, Mondeos were available with four-door saloon or five-door hatchback styles, with a choice of 1.6, 1.8 or 2-litre 16-valve twin-cam Zetec engines, along with a 1.8-litre overhead-cam turbodiesel. An estate car option would follow within a few months, while an all-new 60-degree four-cam V6 (to be built in the USA) was promised for the future. The Mondeo, in fact, got off to an extremely good start, and did not falter in the next few years.

In the autumn, a prototype Escort RS2000 4x4 was shown by Ford, but this was premature as the company was not yet ready to deliver cars. First deliveries, in fact, would not be made until the autumn of 1994. Like other 4x4 conversions of transverse-engine/front-wheel-drive layouts, this car featured three differentials, and in this case the torque split was approximately 40 per cent front/60 per cent rear.

In a marketing move which suggested that the company had failed to establish the Orion as a separate model line, the name was dropped from the autumn. Henceforth all four-door saloon versions of the Escort (for that was precisely what the Orion had always been) would also be badged as Escorts. It was just 10 years since the first of the cars carrying the Orion name had been unveiled.

The Granada/Scorpio range, which had been extensively facelifted in 1992, was improved still further for 1994 with the launch of a new flagship version of the estate car with a 195bhp four-cam V6 Cosworth-developed engine. Saloon car versions of this type had been on sale since early 1992.

Almost unnoticed, too, went the addition of a turbocharged VM 2.5-litre diesel engine option, replacing the Peugeot-supplied 2.5-litre diesel which had been available for some years. With 115bhp instead of 92bhp, this improved the car's performance considerably, though it was always a very rare car in the British market.

Details of the Maverick 4x4 will be found in the Nissan section, for the Ford was a rebadged clone of the Japanese vehicle, both types being built in a Nissan factory in Spain.

FSO: Following the political tumult which had swept across Eastern Europe in the early 1990s, FSO of Poland had temporarily stopped exporting cars to the UK, but the marque reappeared at the end of 1993 with the Caro range of hatchbacks. These extremely cheap (by British standards) machines were little more than modified Polonez models with a new and rather smoother face – and it is worth recalling that the Polonez itself was based on the Fiat 1300/1500 platform of the early 1960s. There was a choice of engines, the petrol-powered unit being by Fiat, the diesel engine by Citroen.

Hyundai: The new-generation Sonata range of four-door saloons were introduced at the Frankfurt show in September, with UK deliveries due to begin around the turn of the year. Compared with the first-generation Sonata, the latest car was slightly larger, more rounded and at first would be sold with a 136bhp/four-cylinder engine, though a 3-litre V6 was already slated for introduction at the end of 1994.

Jaguar: Many years after it was known that design work had commenced, Jaguar finally put a V12-engined version of the latest-shape XJ6 on sale. The new type featured a 318bhp/6-litre engine, had new-style alloy wheels to identify it and was easily capable of 150mph.

As before, the engine was matched only to an automatic transmission (a four-speed GM unit with sport and economy settings). The Jaguar version, logically enough, was called XJ12 and cost £46,600, and there was a Daimler-badged Double-Six which cost an extra £5,100.

Kia: Hitherto, the only Korean Kia on sale in the UK had been the small Pride model, but from mid-summer it was joined by a larger Escort-sized front-wheel-drive family saloon called the Mentor, which had an 81bhp/1.6-litre Mazda-derived power unit and transmission. Sales began at the end of the year.

The Sportage, a leisure-market 4x4 off-roader, made its first tentative appearance in the UK towards the end of the year, with a body styled in Britain by IAD. Charitably, this 126bhp/2-litre machine could be described as cheap and cheerful, and it made little impact on the burgeoning 4x4 market.

Lamborghini: Although very few people could afford to buy one, there was great technical interest in the Diablo VT, which appeared in February. Visually, it looked exactly the same as the original mid-engined/rear-drive Diablo, but there was permanent four-wheel drive, along with power-assisted steering (which was not fitted to the RWD type) and adaptive damping. The Viscous Traction feature (hence the VT part of the title), diverted up to 29 per cent of the engine torque to the front wheels.

A supercar by any standards, this 492bhp/200mph monster was expected to cost at least £160,000 when British sales began later in the year. Then the company astonished everyone by previewing the 525bhp Diablo SE30, an anniversary version of the normal model (the first Lamborghini had been introduced in 1963). The SE30, with a claimed top speed of 220mph, would go on sale in 1994.

Lancia: Although a new-generation Delta was previewed, then introduced, in Italy, it was of only passing interest to British drivers because Lancia was soon to withdraw from the UK market, where the latest Delta would never officially appear.

Land Rover: The Discovery 4x4 range was enlarged still further in April with the introduction of an entry-level machine, the Mpi, which used the Rover 800-style 2-litre 16-valve engine.

Later in the year it was revealed that Honda, Rover's partner, was to market the Discovery in Japan, rebadging it as the Honda Crossroads.

Towards the end of the year the Discovery took a further step upmarket with the arrival of the 180bhp/3.9-litre fuel-injected version of the alloy V8 engine. This model range was now

firmly into Range Rover territory, but since a new-generation Range Rover (larger, faster, glossier and with yet more powerful engines) was due for launch in 1994, Land Rover was not troubled.

Lexus: The second model in this top-of-the-line Toyota marque appeared at the end of 1992 and was first seen in the UK in 1993. Known as the GS300 and based on the Toyota Aristo, it was smaller than the LS400, with a different body monocoque and platform.

With styling by Giugiaro and a front-wheel-drive package based around a 220bhp/3-litre 24-valve V6 engine, the GS300 was a fast and capable car which was intended to compete at the top end of the BMW 5-series and Mercedes-Benz E-class category. Although it was Jaguar XJ-size, it was really too small and too limited in its quality fittings to compete there.

Lister: With no relation to the famous 1950s racing sportscars (except that the new owner gained permission to use the name), this Leatherhead-based marque, controlled by Laurence Pearce, grew out of a business which had begun by manufacturing stunningly fast conversions for the Jaguar XJS.

The new Storm, however, which was introduced in October, prior to deliveries beginning in 1994, was a front-engine/rear-wheel-drive car built around a honeycomb sandwich monocoque and used much-modified Jaguar XJS running gear except for a Getrag six-speed gearbox of the type found in cars like the BMW 8-series. The engines were bored and stroked to a full 7 litres and given two belt-driven superchargers.

The style was in the 'brutal' school, for this was definitely a car whose looks were an acquired taste. Pearce stated that he would be happy to build 10 Storms a year, and with a claimed top speed of 200mph and a selling price of nearly £220,000, he was probably wise.

Lotus: The mid-engined Esprit Turbo progressed to S4 from March with a package of modifications which included yet another facelift – including new front-end and rear spoiler details, plus power-assisted steering and revised suspension settings. There were no important changes to the 2.2-

litre turbocharged four-cylinder engine.

Maserati: The Italian concern continued to squeeze every possible variation out of its decade-old Biturbo theme. The latest two-door/four-seater model to appear was a 280bhp/2.8-litre twin turbocharged V6, which was given the famous name of Ghibli, though the latest car was neither as fast nor as beautiful as the original Ghibli of the 1960s.

Mazda: The second of two top-of-the-range flagships, the oddly-named Xedos 9, was shown in August and would eventually go on sale in the UK in 1994. Rather like the Toyota-based Lexus (but not abandoning the original badge), the new car was bigger, faster, better-equipped, glitzier and altogether more upmarket than any other Mazdas. With a transverse engine and front-wheel drive, the Xedos 9 was powered by an aluminium 168bhp/2.5-litre V6 of the type which was already being used in 626s, MX-3s, MX-6s and, of course, the Ford Probe.

The popular MX-5 roadster was improved in Japan in mid-summer with the fitment of a larger and more powerful 1.8-litre version of the twin-cam engine. The new engine produced 128bhp and made the MX-5 much easier to drive fast and was much more flexible in heavy traffic. UK deliveries would begin in May 1994.

Mercedes-Benz: A new-generation 'small' saloon range – to be called the C-class – was introduced in February, the launch coming just over 10 years after the first 190E had gone on sale.

Compared with the earlier (W201) variety, the new C-class was a few inches larger, not least in the amount of rear-seat space it offered. Although it had an all-new platform and style, it retained the same basic type of all-independent suspension, and there was a wide range of four, five and six-cylinder engines, ranging from a 75bhp diesel to a 197bhp 2.8-litre 'six', but not all the engines would go on sale in the UK when deliveries began in October 1993. All the engines, including the diesels, had four valves per cylinder, and there were to be no fewer than four different trim packages available on all types – Classic, Esprit, Elegance and Sport.

Production of the much-admired

190E 2.5-16, complete with Cosworth-developed 16-valve cylinder head, finally came to an end in mid-summer. This was a signal not only that assembly of the old-style compact cars had ended, but that Mercedes-Benz had now evolved its own range of high-performance twin-cam engines with four valves per cylinder.

During the summer, and without fuss, a pair of different SL roadsters appeared, these being the SL280 (with 2.8-litre 24-valve 'six') and the SL320 (with 3.2-litre 24-valve 'six'). In all respects, not least in styling and build quality, the SL range carried on as before.

An entry-level model, the S280, with 197bhp/2.8-litre six-cylinder engine, was added to the S-class saloon family during the summer with British prices starting at £37,500.

Morgan: Development work was still going steadily ahead at Malvern, and in the autumn a new derivative appeared of the 4/4, known as the 4/4 1800, using the modern Ford Zetec 16-valve engine in 128bhp/XR3i tune.

Nissan: The Terrano II, launched early in the year, was a new type of 4x4 estate car sold in short-wheelbase three-door or longer-wheelbase five-door varieties, with a choice of 122bhp/2.4-litre petrol or 99bhp/2.7-litre turbodiesel four-cylinder engines.

Aimed squarely at the Vauxhall Frontera category rather than the more expensive Land Rover Discovery sector, the Terrano II was a smoothly styled, but rather narrow and upright machine, with independent front suspension and a choice of trim packs.

There was also an identical (apart from badging and cosmetics) version of this model called the Ford Maverick. Nissans were sold through Nissan dealerships in the UK, Mavericks through Ford dealerships, there being no agreement for either marque to have an unchallenged run in the market. The result was that neither car sold as well as it might...but neither company was likely to admit to that.

Later in the spring there was a revised Patrol 4x4, this time with a 124bhp/six-cylinder diesel engine, which was available in short-wheelbase three-door or longer-wheelbase five-door estate car form.

Towards the end of the year a new-

generation 200SX was introduced in Japan, as before a front-engine/rear-drive car (such layouts were becoming increasingly rare...) with a 200bhp version of the 2-litre engine previously found in the four-wheel-drive Sunny GTi-R. Compared with the earlier-type 200SZ, the new car had a 50mm/2in longer wheelbase and a more rounded cabin.

Peugeot: The smart new 306, which had a new-looking monocoque based on the platform of the Citroen ZX and was a size larger than the long-running 205, appeared in January. It was a direct replacement for the 309, and although some 205 models were immediately dropped, this meant that Peugeot's smaller-car range was now looking crowded with 106, 205 and 306 models in the line-up.

Although very smoothly styled, and clearly with a new and very modern cabin, the 306's underpinnings – chassis and engine/transmission units – were all very familiar, especially as they were also being used in the Citroen ZX. Transverse engine/transmission packs, too, were modified versions of those already found in 205s, 405s and Citroen ZXs, ranging from 1.4 to a full 2 litres. Diesel-engined versions were added later in the year.

Here was a new car which everyone seemed to like from the start – it certainly sold extremely well in the years which followed.

The 106 range, which had been launched in the UK at the end of 1991, was spiced up even further from October with the arrival of the high-revving 100bhp/1.3-litre Rallye model.

Porsche: Only four years after thoroughly re-engineering the rear-engined 911 range, Porsche produced yet another new technical package under the familiar skin, making what was effectively a third-generation 911 with much-modified styling.

Starting in mid-1993, the 911's facelifted style included laid-back ellipsoid headlamps, more subtly flared wheelarches and integrated front and rear bumper/spoilers, but that was only the visual part of the package.

Although the rear-mounted flat-six air-cooled engine layout was retained, the floorpan/platform was rejigged yet again, this time matching the existing MacPherson-strut front end to a new multi-link double-wishbone/coil-spring rear end. At the same time the engine was reworked to a 270bhp/3.6-litre installation and linked to either a close-ratio six-speed manual or a Tiptronic four-speed automatic gearbox.

The new 911 (which, confusingly, did not get any new model labelling) immediately took over from the old, British deliveries starting before the end of the year.

Although it was clear that the front-engined 968 model was already in deep trouble, with demand slumping towards zero, Porsche produced a harsh new offshoot, the Club Sport, which traded refinement and comfort for even better roadholding and offered potential for use in motorsport.

Proton: For the first time since it put cars on sale in the UK, the Malaysian manufacturer introduced a new shape – one which was not a revamped Mitsubishi, although much of the mechanical equipment still came from that concern. This was the front-wheel-drive Persona, which would have a choice of 1.5 or 1.6-litre engines at launch, which would eventually be joined by a 1.3-litre version.

These were larger and better-equipped cars than the original bargain-basement types, and would gradually be built into a range of three-door or five-door (hatchback) or four-door (saloon) models.

Reliant: The Scimitar Sabre sportscar was changed yet again in October, this time by replacing the old Ford CVH engine option by a 103bhp/1.4-litre Rover K-series unit. Reliant claimed that this increased the top speed of the small-engined car to 120mph.

Renault: The limited-edition Clio Williams was introduced early in the year to celebrate Williams-Renault's 1992 F1 Constructor's World Championship. Based on the existing Clio 16V, the Williams had a 150bhp/1,998cc version of that car's engine and was clearly going to be the basis of a useful competition car. Only 2,500 were slated to be produced, which made this an instant collector's car, which it remained until the Williams 2 appeared...

At the same time, the Clio RSi was introduced, this also being based on the 16V, but having a 1.8-litre eight-valve engine, though for marketing purposes it retained the same body kit as used for the 16V model. This was a less powerful car and consequently a lot easier to insure in the UK.

Rolls-Royce: From August, the existing and very long-running Silver Spirit range was upgraded for the 1993 season, it being tacitly agreed that this would be the last major change before a new-generation car appeared towards the end of the 1990s.

For 1994, therefore, the latest Silver Spirits (and their Bentley equivalents) had 20 per cent more peak horsepower (but as ever, the figure was not spelt out), together with new-type GM three-speed automatic transmission, twin airbags, new electronic controls and a heap of other development changes. Prices started at £96,401 for the Bentley Brooklands, though most Rolls-Royces, with options, cost well over £100,000.

Rover: The new 600 range of four-door saloons was launched in April, these being based very closely on the latest Honda Accords. The platform, suspension and engine choices were all pure Accord, but although there were a number of obvious body 'hard-points' which had been shared, much of the detail of the body style was unique to Rover.

The new-generation 600 was destined to be manufactured in the completely revamped Cowley facility, whereas the Accord was being produced at Honda's Swindon factory. Later, when it became clear that neither car was selling as well as hoped (or forecast), the question was asked why these cars could not have been constructed on the same assembly line?

Naturally they had transverse engines and front-wheel drive, and at first there would be a choice of 129bhp/2-litre or 156bhp/2.3-litre Honda four-cylinder engines. Turbodiesel and turbocharged petrol engines would be added in the next year or so.

The much-promised and much-delayed British-built Mini cabriolet finally went on sale in mid-summer, but would never sell in significant numbers, perhaps not surprisingly since it had appeared no less than 34 *years* after the original Mini saloon had gone on sale. Some magazine testers described it as the worst British new car

of the year – and in view of the very limited sales achieved for this expensive Mini derivative, one wonders why Rover bothered with it.

The 200 hatchback range was finally updated, just as the 400 had been in 1992, with a facelifted car complete with traditional Rover grille being put on sale from November. Side-impact beams were standardized in the doors of 200s *and* 400s, and there was a minor reshuffle to the wide range of engines (including normally-aspirated and turbodiesels in both 200 and 400 types), principally to commonize with the 400 saloon, but nothing radical was now expected until a new generation of these cars appeared in 1995.

Saab: Three years after GM had taken a 50 per cent financial stake in the Swedish car-maker, it produced a new range of 900 models, UK deliveries of which began in the autumn. As expected, the new-type 900 (which replaced the car which had been on the market for 15 years) was based on the platform, suspension and some of the engine/transmission options of the latest GM Opel Ascona/Vauxhall Cavalier.

Clothed in styles which had a definite family resemblance to previous Saabs – and with no obvious connection to the Cavalier – the new-type 900 was sold as a five-door hatchback at first, but three-door coupe derivatives and a smart two-door convertible would be added to the range in 1994.

There were to be three engines – the 2-litre and 2.3-litre 16-valve Saab 'fours', along with the new corporate GM 170bhp/2.5-litre V6 unit which was already being used in medium-sized GM-Europe cars.

Although there were serried ranks of cynics ready to criticize this very GM-influenced Saab, the public took to it at once, and Saab's financial fortunes (which had been hard-hit in the late 1980s and early 1990s) immediately began to improve.

Seat: Building on its new relationship with VW, the Spanish car-maker replaced the long-running Ibiza range with a new-generation transverse-engine/front-wheel-drive family which was based very closely on the platform of the still-to-be-revealed new-type VW Polo.

Larger, smoother in style and better

built than the earlier Ibiza, the new car would be sold at first in three-door and five-door hatchback styles, with a wide choice of VW-derived engines from a 55bhp/1.3-litre to a 115bhp/2-litre and including diesels. A super-economy 1-litre engine would soon follow.

The new Cordoba saloon was revealed in September, this effectively being a four-door notchback version of the Ibiza (which had only been put on sale early in the year). Those who knew their way round the labyrinthine technicalities of Seat-owners VW realized that the Cordoba was really a VW Vento with a makeover, as was proved when the wide choice of VW engines and transmissions was listed – although of course the Cordoba was to be built entirely in Spain.

Ssangyong: From the end of the year it was necessary to learn how to spell – and pronounce – a new marque name from Korea when the company unveiled a big and brawny Land Rover Discovery-sized 4x4 estate, which carried British styling and used Mercedes-Benz engines.

As far as the British were concerned, this was all a bit premature, for the first UK showing would be at the NEC in October 1994, and deliveries would begin in 1995. *(For all further details, see the 1995 section.)*

Subaru: In Japan, a new-generation range of Legacy saloons and estates was announced at the Tokyo motor show. Based on the previous car's platform and flat-four boxer engine layout, the new-type Legacy would go on sale in the UK in 1994, as before with the option of either front-wheel or four-wheel drive and a choice of engines and power outputs.

Suzuki: The tiny Cappuccino sports-car, with its three-cylinder 657cc engine, made its first appearance in the UK during the year. Although it was filled with many modern technological gizmos, all packed into a length of just 10ft 10in, those who expected it to be a latter-day replacement for MG Midgets and the like were to be sorely disappointed, as it was too small, too cramped and too frantic to make much of an impression. *Autocar & Motor* described the Cappuccino as 'an underpowered and expensive fashion accessory…'

Toyota: A new-generation Supra coupe appeared at the beginning of the year, this car (like the rival Mazda RX-7) being a larger, more rounded and considerably faster machine than the model it replaced.

The new-type Supra featured a much-changed version of the old-type Supra's straight-six 3-litre engine, this time having twin turbochargers (one each feeding the forward and rear-ward trio of cylinders) and producing 320bhp. To keep the performance in check at very high speeds (but totally pointless in the speed-limited USA…) was a large, high-mounted, transverse rear spoiler. When it went on UK sale in August 1993, the new Supra was both too extrovert and too expensive for British drivers, and sales were limited.

Toyota also announced a new-generation Celica sports coupe in the autumn, with a sleeker and altogether more attractive body style that its precedessor's. This type would eventually go on sale in the UK in early 1994, with a choice of normally-aspirated or turbocharged engine with front-drive and four-wheel-drive transmission, respectively.

In the autumn, the latest-generation Toyota 4x4 leisure vehicle, to be known as the 4-Runner, came to the UK. Smaller than the Land Cruiser, more rounded and much more modern in its concept, this was now squarely in Land Rover Discovery territory and would be available in 3-litre V6 (petrol) and 3-litre four-cylinder (diesel) form. With independent front suspension, a five-speed main gearbox and a very high level of equipment and features, it looked likely to widen the Toyota 4x4 market still further.

In fact Toyota's 4x4 ambitions stretched further than this, for the company also showed a much smaller concept car – the RAV-4 – at the Tokyo show in October. This was an advanced and fast little car meant to compete in the Suzuki Vitara sector – but little more would be heard of it until its arrival on the British market in 1995. *(For further details see the 1995 section.)*

TVR: Although frantically busy making and selling Griffith and Chimaera two-seater sportscars, the company also found time in October to show the first prototype of a longer-wheelbase 2+2 coupe to be called the Cerbera.

This launch, however, was very premature, for the design would be radically updated before being shown again towards the end of 1994 – and deliveries would not begin before the end of 1995. *(For further details, see the 1995 section.)*

In the meantime, the Griffith was given a 340bhp/5-litre TVR-developed version of the ubiquitous Rover V8 engine, the performance of this machine being quite colossal. With a top speed of 161mph and 0–100mph in around 10 seconds, who needed a Porsche?

Vauxhall: Early in the year, GM finally introduced a replacement for the Opel Corsa/Vauxhall Nova which had been running for a full decade. The new-generation cars were all to be badged as Corsas, with either the Opel (in most territories) or the Vauxhall name appended. (In Australia, incidentally, these cars were sold and badged as Holden Barinas.)

Built on the basis of an entirely new platform, with rounded styling in three-door or five-door hatchback form, the Corsa was a larger car than the Nova it displaced, with a 4in longer wheelbase and 3in wider tracks. As expected from GM, it was a conventionally-engineered front-wheel-drive car to be sold in a myriad of versions, the first six ranging from a 44bhp/1.2-litre to a 108bhp/1.4-litre and including two 1.5-litre diesels, with various extra types to be added later. As before, this car was totally manufactured in Spain and would immediately become an important part of Vauxhall's UK line-up.

Just before the end of the year, with deliveries due to begin in the spring of 1994, a new range of medium/large Omega saloons and estates was announced as a direct replacement for the long-running Carlton models. Like the little Corsa, in fact, the Vauxhall Omega was no more than a badge-engineered Opel Omega, sharing its style, structure and engineering.

With a smoother and more rounded style, which Vauxhall claimed was more rigid and roomy than the old Carlton, this new front-engine/rear-drive car was to be built with a choice of 2-litre four-cylinder, 2.5 or 3-litre V6 petrol engines, plus a 2.5-litre turbo-diesel manufactured by BMW. Outputs spanned 113bhp to 207bhp.

The V6-engined Cavalier went on sale in the UK in March, priced at

£16,085. Surprisingly, in view of the power and torque provided, it was still only a front-wheel-drive model. Prices started at £16,085.

The Lotus-Carlton supercar was dropped early in the year, well before its original planned demise – simply because it was not selling. Although it was an amazingly fast high-performance machine, it had always been marketed at an unrealistically high price (£45,271 at the end), and total assembly of Vauxhall and Opel-badged cars was a mere 950, of which 323 were Vauxhalls.

Like several other manufacturers, sales of Vauxhall's hot hatches had been hit very badly by a combination of the recession and rapacious insurance premiums, so to counter this a new 'warm hatch' version of the Astra, the 123bhp/1.8-litre 16-valve Astra GSi, went on sale in September. This was at once a faster car than the 115bhp SRi which it replaced, and slower than the 148bhp/2-litre Astra GSi which continued.

Volkswagen: For 1994, starting in September, the Passat which had first been revealed in 1988 was updated. The existing platform, basic running gear and inner panels were retained, but almost every exterior panel was new, the 1994 model looking smoother than before. As usual there was the same wide range of VW engines – four-cylinder petrols and diesels, plus the very successful VR6.

A new-generation Golf convertible (to be manufactured by Karmann) was announced in mid-year, finally bringing to an end the 14-year career of the earlier first-generation open-top Golf. The latest model was based on the Golf III platform, thus confirming that no Golf II-based open car would ever go on sale.

There were more signs of VW's retreat from advanced technology when the much-vaunted supercharged G60 1.8-litre-engined Corrado and Passat models was dropped at the end of the 1993 model year.

Hugely controversial when they were launched in the 1980s – when VW insisted that supercharging was superior to turbocharging, even though their customers seemed to disagree – the G60-engined VWs (which had also included 'blown' Golfs, although these had never formed part of the latest Golf III range) had never sold well.

Having earlier abandoned four-wheel drive, too, VW had now dropped all the advanced engine and transmission fittings of the 1980s and was reverting almost to a Volvo-type safety-first philosophy.

Volvo: After a considerable delay while sales of saloons built up, an estate car version of the front-wheel-drive 850 family finally went on sale during the spring.

Later in the year it became clear that Volvo was to use the 850 to help change its desperately stodgy image. Although a sedate 10-valve/five-cylinder version of the 2.5-litre engine was added at one end of the range, the 225bhp 850 T-5 Turbo saloons and estates (with a claimed top speed of 150mph) appeared at the other to remind us that Volvo's engineers knew a lot, even if they were not always allowed to practice it... Then, to cap it all, the company announced that it was to enter cars in the 1994 British Touring Car Championship, with Tom Walkinshaw's TWR concern building and running the cars.

To keep them going for another two years or so, Volvo gave the Dutch-built 440/460 front-wheel-drive cars a new nose with a distinct family likeness to the latest 850, though there were no significant mechanical improvements.

Industrial developments

During the summer Renault and Volvo agreed to move steadily towards a full merger, which seemed to make a lot of technical sense, particularly as Volvo had been using Renault engines for some time. A study of proposed shareholding arrangements showed that Renault would be in control.

The theory, which was very persuasive, was that the companies could begin to get together on commonized medium-sized car designs for the late 1990s and that – equally important – the massive truck arms of the two companies could be brought together.

Volvo's president Pehr Gyllenhammar had been the inspiration behind this massive deal, but like others which he had previously proposed for Volvo (he had tried to sell out to the Norwegian state in the 1970s!), it all went wrong

and the astonishing news broke in December that the long-planned merger had been abandoned.

There had been a revolt within Volvo, it seems (it was the Swedes, not the French, who had pulled out), one result being that Gyllenhammar abruptly left the company of which he had been president for two decades. The two companies drew back from closer links, preparations were made for cross-shareholding arrangements to be unscrambled, and there was a great loss of face all round.

One result was that Volvo had to start again with thoughts of new large cars, though the already-signed medium-size car deal with Mitsubishi (which would mature in 1995) was not affected.

After a great deal of rumour and counter-rumour in the European automotive and financial press, Fiat finally confirmed that it was taking control of Maserati, which was ailing financially and had been unable to produce a new car, other than one based on the Biturbo of the early 1980s, for more than 10 years.

'We plan to sustain Maserati as a low-volume specialist car-maker', said Fiat managing director Paolo Cantarella. He was right: Fiat had no choice...

Also in Italy, Chrysler decided to part with its troublesome investment in Lamborghini, disposing of it to an Indonesian consortium of which Tommy Suharto (son of the country's premier) and ex-Lotus managing director Mike Kimberley were important members. This transaction, in fact, would not be finalized until the early spring of 1994, when Kimberley would move to Italy as Lamborghini's managing director.

General Motors sold Lotus to Bugatti of Italy in September, a move which apparently made money for GM and landed Bugatti with an expensive asset which it hoped could become a 'cash cow' to help support the build-up of production of its own supercar in Italy.

For the time being there were no immediate changes at Lotus except that Bugatti promised to put the recently killed-off front-drive Elan back into production, using stocks of Isuzu engine/transmission units which were already at Hethel. But this arrangement would only persist until early 1995, when Bugatti's finances finally began to collapse. (*For further details of what subsequently happened at*

Lotus, see the 1995 section.)

Ginetta, which had failed in September 1992, was rescued again in 1993, coming back to life in a deal led by Martin Pfaff, who had been at the head of the company when it had foundered. The reborn Ginetta company was once again to build cars, this time in a factory in Rotherham.

Yugo Cars, the British importers of the Yugo marque, went into receivership early in the year and never recovered. The cause was not a lack of demand for the cars (which had been ultra-cheap and had a guaranteed market), but was a result of the civil war which had broken out in the Balkans, splitting Yugoslavia asunder. Deliveries of Yugo cars were badly hit at once (the last were sent to the UK in mid-1992), then totally disrupted when all trade with the breakaway nation of Serbia was banned by order of the United Nations.

Evante, the small Lincolnshire-based maker of sportscars, had originally gone into liquidation in 1991. There had been repeated attempts to revive the concern, but these were finally abandoned in mid-1993.

Technical developments

A newly-enacted EC law made it compulsory for all new cars to be fitted with catalytic converters from January 1, though cars without 'cats' could still be sold in Britain provided they had been manufactured after July 1, 1992.

Once again the disbelievers made the point that catalytic converters – which were extremely expensive because of the exotic rare metals used in their construction – were totally ineffective in cars used only for commuting, but the 'green' fringe chose to ignore this unpalatable fact...

The fitment of airbags was unstoppable, and from 1993/94 they would progressively become standard or optional on almost every make of car. In the UK, at mass-market level, Ford stated that it would make steering-wheel airbags standard on all its new cars from the late autumn of 1993, which was a clear indication that within months all its major rivals would have to follow suit.

Passenger-side airbags became optional on most cars (but standard on very few) at the same time, but it is a measure of public indifference to driving safety that the take-up was very limited.

Men of Influence

Peter Wheeler

To quote the famous Remington shaver adverts on TV, in 1981 Peter Wheeler: '...liked the product so much that I bought the company...' – in this case TVR, at the ripe young age of 38.

Trained as a chemical engineer, Wheeler started his first business in 1972 with a capital of £200. He then made his fortune selling specialized equipment to the booming North Sea industry. Along the way he bought his first TVR sportscar – a Taimar Turbo – soon becoming known to, and friendly with, TVR's then owner, Martin Lilley.

Tall and gangling, with a lugubrious moustache, Peter Wheeler was a self-made man, determined to plough his hard-earned money into a business he could enjoy more than chemical engineering:

'I gradually came to know people and be drawn into the company's activities. It was Stewart Halstead [sales director] who actually got me involved, and I became a shareholder when I saw that there were certain problems which I could help to solve.'

One of those problems was a lack of capital, for although the Lilleys, father and son, had kept TVR afloat since rescuing it from bankruptcy in 1965, the development of the new-generation Tasmin of 1980 had drained most of the reserves away.

Peter Wheeler therefore took control at the end of 1981, completely buying out Martin Lilley. At first he was the company's chairman, with Stewart Halstead as his managing director, but after parting company with Halstead a few years later he became chairman, managing director, sole shareholder – in fact the absolute master of the thriving sportscar business in Blackpool.

Wheeler's first move was to initiate a 'large-engine' policy at TVR, the 350i being the first obvious fruits of that strategy. Next, he gradually moved the company upmarket, with bigger, faster and ever more expensive cars, making sure that he underpinned the old business by inspiring the S models of 1986 and beyond, which were really a throwback to the 1970s.

By the 1990s Wheeler would have seen TVR expand so far that it was making record numbers of cars, ever more of which were built in-house. Never frightened to take a chance, Wheeler's team produced a series of stillborn prototypes, but none of these were more ambitious than the all-new AJP8 engine project which occupied him for much of the early 1990s.

Some 15 years after buying TVR, the company was bigger, more profitable and more famous than ever before – and Wheeler was still the boss of all he surveyed.

1994

In a motoring year which was largely optimistic (UK production and sales were rising steadily), the Government did its best to dampen any enthusiasm. Indeed, it was now stated policy to carry on increasing the price of fuel in real terms – by raising the duty by at least inflation plus 5 per cent in the years ahead. There was also talk of introducing comprehensive road-pricing measures and the introduction of more tolls.

Compared with 1993, UK car sales rose again – but were still only back to the levels of a decade earlier – with more cars than ever being both exported *and* imported.

Expenditure on roads was cut once again, new road schemes being either downgraded, postponed or cancelled altogether, and politicians made any number of soothing noises intended to placate the 'green' lobby, which was strident in the media, even though little supported on the ground.

By this time it had become fashionable to protest about road schemes, even when construction had begun, with all manner of illegal activities being tolerated by the liberal media. Roads suffering from the attention of malcontents included the connection of the M65 from Blackburn to the M6 at Preston, and the extension of the M77 in Glasgow, towards Kilmarnock.

New models

AC: After a multi-year design and development saga, the first of the new-generation 5-litre V8-engined Ace roadsters was delivered in June, marking the beginning of limited series production.

Alfa Romeo: One of Italy's most important new cars of the year was the stylish new Alfa Romeo spider, described as the first *new* Alfa spider for 28 years, for it finally took over from the graceful old Pininfarina-styled Giulia-based car which had first been seen in 1966.

Except for the title, and the fact that Pininfarina had once again been responsible for the style, there was no connection between new and old

models, for the 1994 example had a transversely-mounted engine and front-wheel drive, the latest type of four-cylinder/2-litre 16-valve Twin Spark engine (a Fiat-based unit, not a descendant of the famous old Alfa twin-cam), and there was also the promise of a 3-litre/V6-engined version later.

The open-top two-seater and its closed relative, the GTV coupe, were both previewed at the Paris motor show in October 1994, but would not go on sale in Europe until 1995, and in Britain until mid-1996.

The 33 came to the end of its long British-market career in the autumn, when the first of the 145/146 range appeared. The 145 was first to be introduced, this car having a three-door hatchback style.

Based on the platform and suspensions of the Fiat Tipo, but with an entirely fresh cabin, the 145 was totally different from any previous Alfa Romeo and was even more closely based on the engineering and platform of another make of car than the 164 had been.

At first there was great resistance to buying an Alfa-badged hatchback, but the reason for its launch became clearer towards the end of the year when it was joined by the larger and more roomy five-door Type 146, with which it shared almost all its running gear.

British sales of 145s began in 1994, but the 146 would not join in until 1995. In their original format, both cars were powered by further developments of the famous flat-four engine used for two decades in the previous Alfasud and Type 33 ranges. For the 145 and 146 there were to be 103bhp/1.6-litre single-cam and 129bhp/1.7-litre twin-cam versions. Even then, it was widely suggested that more conventional Fiat-type four-cylinder engines would be fitted later in the 1990s.

In order that it could compete more effectively in the British Touring Car Championship, there was a special 2,500-off version of the 155 called the 155 Silverstone, which at £13,575 was no more than a dressed-up version of the existing 2-litre model.

The all-important aerodynamic additions comprised a low, flat and wide front spoiler (or 'splitter') under the front bumper, and a transverse rear spoiler on the bootlid. Alfa Romeo also provided instructions to allow the splitter to be moved further forward

and the rear spoiler pushed up on sturdy pylons to increase downforce.

These add-ons, while effective, did little for the appeal of the road car – and were speedily protested in the BTCC, but in 1994 (though not in 1995) they helped the 155s to reign supreme and win the Championship.

Asia: The arrival of the Rocsta (built by a subsidiary of Kia) put another Jeep-like 4x4 on to British roads. This was a South Korean machine which had been on sale in its home market since 1986. With a choice of 1.8-litre petrol or 2.2-litre diesel engines, a very short (84in) wheelbase and hard beam-axle/leaf-spring front and rear suspension, this was a rough-and-ready machine which harked right back to the 1940s original-style Land-Rovers and early Jeep CJ types. Because of its hard ride and limited fittings and performance, it was always destined to be a slow seller in the UK.

Aston Martin: Deliveries of the new DB7 *(see 1993 for original details)* began in the autumn of that year at a price of £78,500 and a top speed of 157mph. Since the new car was not only smaller, lighter, very much cheaper and more modern-looking than the old-type Virage (which remained in production), it immediately began to sell faster than any previous Aston Martin.

Audi: During the year the German company decided to simplify the way it described its cars. Like Mercedes-Benz with their designations, Audi found it ever more difficult to differentiate the new 100 from the old, and the 80 from the 90, all of which required specialist knowledge from its customers.

Instead, it was decided to use A prefixes in future, the lowest number representing the smallest car and the largest number the largest. Thus, a replacement for the 80, to be launched later in the year, would be the A4, the existing middle-size 100 would become the A6, and the new-generation big (aluminium) Audi would become the A8. Although it would take a few years for the naming system to become complete, it was logical, if not romantic.

The all-new A4 range (a direct replacement for the 80 which had been on sale for eight years) appeared in October and was seen to be shorter but slightly wider than the cars it replaced. As expected, the range included four-cylinder and V6 engines (the old-style five-cylinder had gone, at last), petrol and diesel-powered, from 90 to 150bhp and a choice of front-wheel and four-wheel drive, all in a new structure more rounded than before running on a new 103in-wheelbase platform.

The major novelty was that the 1.8-litre four-cylinder engine had a brand-new twin-cam cylinder head featuring *five* valves per cylinder – three inlet and two exhaust – while the old-type two-valve 1.6-litre unit had a new crossflow cylinder head. Many engine experts raised their eyebrows at this venture because so far all attempts to make five-valve heads work in competition engines had failed – Audi, though, claimed that its new layout offered very effective cooling and excellent combustion. British sales of A4 models would begin in spring 1995.

During the summer the company performed yet another of its platform/engine/transmission juggling tricks, launching the A6 2.5TDi, which combined the existing A6/100 front-wheel-drive structure and layout with a newly-developed 140bhp/2.5-litre five-cylinder direct-injection turbodiesel engine. The result was a car which could reach 129mph, yet was good for about 40mpg. The only snag was its British price, which reached a discouraging £23,451 when it went on sale later in the year.

Having trailed the market with a concept car in 1993, the company then astonished the world's technicians by introducing the big new A8 four-door executive saloon to replace the V8 model. Not only was the A8 available in two or four-wheel-drive forms with a choice of 2.8-litre V6 and 4.2-litre V8 engines (the 4x4 2.8-litre version was not available in the UK at first), but much of the hull was made from aluminium.

This had been a major philosophical and development effort by Audi, who wanted to get away from the use of steel in the search for lightness and protection from corrosion. In the A8 there was a massive cage-like structure in box-section aluminium pressings, the car being mainly encased in aluminium skin panels and even had some aluminium suspension members.

According to the figures, though, the lightness campaign seemed to have failed, for a V8-engined A8 was actually heavier than the Audi V8 which it replaced. More surprisingly and creditably, although this was a large car, its carefully rounded styling made it look much smaller than, in fact, it was.

From August, the 1995-model 100s were given a makeover, with a barely noticeable exterior facelift, which included different headlamps and grille and some smoothing of the front-end contours. One of the novelties was the use of a 115bhp/2.5-litre five-cylinder turbodiesel engine, for which a six-speed manual gearbox was an option.

Helped by Porsche, who were contracted to build the production cars, Audi introduced the very fast but extremely practical RS2 estate, an 80-based car fitted with a 315bhp/2.2-litre five-cylinder, 20-valve engine and four-wheel drive. Although the running gear was based on that of the other Audis, this was the most powerful Audi road car yet to go on sale.

The RS2 was colossally fast (with a top speed of around 160mph), very expensive (more than £45,000 when it went on sale in the UK), but an extremely capable load-carrier.

Bentley: The long-running Continental (ex-Corniche) range finally died away, 28 years after the first two-door car of this type had been built. (*For further details, see Rolls-Royce, below.*)

BMW: A new-generation 7-series range of four-door saloons appeared in May, these replacing the cars which had been on sale since 1986. Although the styling and platform of the new car was different from that of the old in almost every way (the wheelbase was 3.8 inches longer, which meant that the cabin was more spacious), the style was only an evolutionary improvement, which led many observers to wonder what the fuss was about.

The new 7-series, though, was a car designed to take on the Mercedes-Benz S-class and anything which Jaguar could throw at it, it was extremely carefully developed and it was to be available with 3-litre and 4-litre V8s, or even a 326bhp/5.4-litre V12. In fact these celebrated engines, and the transmissions to match them, were the only carry-over parts from the old 7-series.

At the end of the year a long-wheelbase 750iL was added to the new line-up, this effectively being a direct replacement for the old-type 750iL, this time fitted with a 326bhp/5.4-litre V12 engine. UK deliveries of the new 7-series began in August 1994, priced from £39,800.

The new 3-series Compact appeared in the spring, though UK deliveries would not begin until October. Much hyped beforehand, the Compact proved to have a shorter-wheelbase version of the modern 3-series platform matched to a three-door hatchback cabin, and for the first two years at least it would only be powered by 1.6 or 1.8-litre four-cylinder petrol or diesel engines.

Compared with the 3-series saloons and coupes, the Compact was a cheaper, simpler, entry-level product, with an old-style semi-trailing link rear suspension which had been adopted for packaging reasons. It was neither a light nor a cheap car, but it allowed customers to get a step on the BMW 'ladder-of-opportunity' at a lower price level than before.

Confirming that the new-generation M3 model was not, nor had ever been intended to be, a motorsport contender, there was a convertible version from January 1994.

There was no end, it seemed, to the different models which could be wrung from the basic 3-series design, but in 1994 the new 318TDS, a 90bhp/1.7-litre turbodiesel version, seemed (and proved) to be the least desirable of all. By a considerable margin, this was the slowest of all 1990s BMWs. Diesel-engined BMWs sold steadily in Europe, it seemed, but were always failures in the UK.

Caterham: At the October motor show, the Kent-based company showed an early prototype (in fact it was the *only* prototype) of a new type of two-seater sportscar, based on the long-running Seven, but with an all-enveloping body style.

Given the title '21' (to celebrate the fact that Caterham had now been car manufacturers for 21 years), this was a premature launch, for a finalized prototype would not be shown until the autumn of 1995, with first deliveries following in mid-1996.

Citroen: Advanced suspension systems had always been a feature of

Citroen cars, hence the October 1994 launch of a top-of-the-range Xantia Activa, complete with computer-sensed no-roll suspension. This car, with a 2-litre 16-valve engine, looked otherwise standard, yet it changed the entire cornering behaviour of the Xantia and represented a breakthrough which was sure to be copied by other manufacturers in coming years.

Along with three other makers – Fiat, Lancia and Peugeot – the company previewed a new MPV estate car or people carrier, which was an obvious competitor to the successful Renault Espace and the latest cars from Japan. All four companies planned to build cars at the same factory in Northern France, and would share the same structure, basic style and transverse-engine/front-drive layouts. The launch, however, was premature, for there would be no UK deliveries until the autumn of 1995. (For details, see the 1995 section.)

During the summer, a brand new type of 16-valve cylinder head was released for the well-known 1,998cc engine. The first car to benefit was the XM, the 1995 range including a new 135bhp/2-litre engine. Clearly, this particular engine tune would be adopted by other models in the Citroen and Peugeot ranges.

Daewoo: The Korean conglomerate finally decided that it would begin selling cars in the UK, announcing that sales would commence in 1995. Two cars would be involved – the Nexia and the Espero – both of them being based on old-style GM-Europe models which had been facelifted. (For details, see the 1995 section.)

Daimler: New six-cylinder and V12 models, near-identical to the latest X300 Jaguars, were introduced in the autumn. (For further details, see Jaguar, below.)

Ferrari: To the applause of almost everyone who saw it, the company announced the new 3.5-litre V8 F355 model to take over from the 348tb, which had sold well, but had somehow never stirred the senses.

The consensus was that the F355, with no less than 380bhp and a top speed of 173mph, was the best all-round Ferrari road car yet produced, and there were many willing to state

that it was better than the much larger, but ageing, flat-12 512TR model.

Like its predecessor, the two-seater F355 had its 90-degree V8 engine mounted longitudinally, behind the seats, and driving the rear wheels. It was beautifully balanced and styled (by Pininfarina), and almost immediately became a best-seller by any supercar standards.

Backing up the arrival of the F355, the F512M arrived in October as a facelifted derivative of the mid-mounted, flat-12-engined 512TR, both cars being derivatives of the Testarossa, which meant that the basic design of this car stretched back to the original mid-engined Boxer of the early 1970s. At 440bhp, its peak output was only 12bhp ahead of that of the 512TR, but there was a small weight saving, and Ferrari fanatics seemed to be content with the looks of the new car.

During the year rumours began to spread about the so-called F130 (it would actually be badged F50), a sensational new successor to the F40, which had finally dropped out of production. The first official pictures, released in November 1994, showed it to be a mid-engined two-seater with a removable roof section, so that it could be used as a coupe or a spider (with twin humps behind the passengers' heads), but all technical information would have to wait until 1995.

Fiat: One of the most surprisingly successful new cars of the year was the Cinquecento Sporting, sometimes succinctly described as Fiat's new Mini-Cooper. Using the basic design of the new and rather upright front-wheel-drive Polish-made Cinquecento, Fiat provided it with a 54bhp/1.1-litre FIRE-type engine instead of the archaic Fiat 127-type previously used, allied that to revised suspension and cast alloy wheels, and endowed the new Sporting with a truly cheeky character.

For young buyers who were itching to buy the nearest thing to a hot hatch their insurance company would allow, this would be a very attractive proposition.

(For details of the newly-previewed Ulysse MPV, see the Citroen entry.)

Ford: The first of a gradual but definite retreat from a sporting image began in the spring, when the company ditched the XR labels from its

Fiesta and Escort models (there were no Mondeo XRs, in any case...) in favour of less-powerful and less-specialized Si models.

Ford said that this was because hot hatches were being strangled by rapacious insurance premiums, but the opposing view was that these cars had latterly not been special enough, or marketed at all.

As partial replacements, therefore, the new Fiesta and Escort Si models used a 90bhp/1.6-litre 16-valve Zetec engine, along with power-assisted steering, these cars going on sale during the spring. They were identified by large and bulbous new front and rear bumpers which, up to a point, mirrored what was already being planned for a new-generation Fiesta in late 1995. At the same time, the 128bhp/1.8-litre RS1800, which continued, was given power-assisted steering, a big improvement for a car which hitherto had been very hard work to drive in towns.

In a similar move, the Escort RS Cosworth was visually detuned in May and given a slightly different turbocharged engine. With the homologation run complete (and with the Escort RS Cosworth winning World Championship rallies), Ford henceforth reverted to using a smaller turbocharger with quicker response and less turbo lag, though the peak power and torque figures were largely unchanged. At the same time the vast rear spoiler (and the associated front splitter) became 'delete options'. By this time, though, insurance company demands had made the Escort RS Cosworth difficult to sell.

Early in the year, the US-manufactured Probe sports coupes went on sale in the UK. These cars, which had been introduced in the USA in 1992, had a complex heritage, for they were built in a factory owned jointly with Mazda, were engineered by Mazda, and were based on the latest Mazda 626/MX-6 platform and running gear.

There were to be two engines for the UK, both Mazda-derived – a 114bhp/2-litre 16-valve 'four' and a 164bhp/2.5-litre 24-valve V6. The V6 had already made its mark in the UK in the successful British Touring Car Championship works Mondeos.

The Mondeo 24V (with V6 engine) promised in 1993, but not available until the autumn of 1994, was immediately hailed as the best of all the Mondeos, despite the fact that the 168bhp engine almost totally filled the bonnet. With a top speed of 139mph and 0–100mph acceleration in 21.8sec, it was a startlingly effective machine compared with any comparable Sierra that it replaced.

After a series of false starts, the Escort RS2000 4x4 finally went on limited sale in the summer, though it was typical of Ford at the time that the launch was low-key, the marketing support nil, and the 4x4 feature disappeared almost without trace. The same basic transmission was fitted to the Mondeo 2-litre a few months later, matched to the 2-litre 16-valve Zetec engine.

In the autumn a startling facelift (if that is the right word) for the long-established Scorpio range was launched. There was no five-door version of the latest type, the choice being limited to a four-door saloon and a five-door estate. Although previewed well in advance, deliveries did not begin until January 1995.

The rear end was rounded off with a full-width strip of lights, while at the front there was a rounded, doleful nose, with what many people called 'Marty Feldman' headlamps of a most unattractive shape.

Almost everyone condemned the style, which rather detracted from the suspension revisions which had improved the ride and handling balance, the smart new interior, and the revised engine line-up, which featured eight and 16-valve (RS2000-based) 2-litre units, a 150bhp 12-valve OHV 2.9-litre V6, which Cosworth was to manufacture, and the Cosworth-type four-cam V6 which had been tuned to produce 204bhp.

The new-generation Galaxy MPV (whose design was shared with the VW Sharan) was previewed in October, though deliveries would not begin until 1995. (See the 1995 section for details.)

Honda: A new-generation Civic, which was due to go on UK sale in the spring of 1995, was previewed in October. It was a car with a lot in common with the next-generation Rover 400, also due for launch in 1995, and was also a direct replacement for the Concerto.

The new-type Civic was a rounded car with the usual wide choice of transverse-engine/front-drive power units ranging from an 89bhp/1.4-litre to a full-house, high-revving 124bhp/1.6-litre V-Tec 16-valve twin-cam. As ever, though, Honda was to have difficulty in enhancing its image in the UK, for in spite of its remarkable racing record (both in F1 and with motorcycles), the age-profile of its customers was still perceived as too high. Honda disliked being stuck with the description of building an 'old-man's car', but that was what they had…

Hyundai: Yet another new family of Korean-built cars, the Accent, went on UK sale towards the end of the year. This was a direct descendent of the mundane Pony models, and was advertised as Korea's first completely home-grown car, as the engines had been designed in-house, there no longer being any links with Mitsubishi.

The Accent was an Escort/Astra-sized car, with the world-standard transverse engine/front-wheel-drive layout, and would be available in 1.3 and 1.5-litre forms with hatchback or saloon bodywork.

Jaguar: In September, the eight-year-old XJ6/XJ12 range of models (and their associated Daimlers) were dropped, to be replaced by a new range of X300 cars, which retained the same basic structure, but looked very different in detail.

Front and rear detailing was much more curvaceous than before, the front end having four circular headlamps and the rear a pair of large, Series III-style stop/tail/turn indicator clusters. The interiors had been retouched, with a new facia design and a very high level of equipment.

As before, these big, graceful and now exceptionally well-built cars were produced with a choice of 24-valve/twin-cam six-cylinder or single-over-head-cam V12 engines. The 'sixes' were AJ16s, much-modified versions of the previous AJ6, and now came in 216bhp/3.2-litre, 246bhp/4-litre and supercharged 321bhp/4-litre guises – the latter being available in a car called the XJR. The V12 was what would probably be the last development of the famous single-cam unit, which dated from 1971, this time in 318bhp/6-litre form. With prices starting at £28,950, costs were significantly increased compared with the outgoing models, but then so was the quality and what industry observers now called the perceived value. Considering that the old car's platform and basic running gear had all been retained, the new models felt much more modern than they had any right to do, and demand was high.

A few months before the much-changed XJ6/XJ12 types appeared, the long-running XJS sportscar was also given the updated/uprated 4-litre six-cylinder engine, along with a package of minor trim and equipment improvements, for which the latest car was priced at £50,500.

Land Rover: In March, the Discovery was rejigged and upgraded, mainly by the introduction of a brand-new five-speed manual gearbox and improvements to the 300Tdi (111bhp/2.5-litre) turbodiesel engine, though without affecting peak power and torque outputs.

Lexus: Only three years after the original LS400 had gone on sale, Lexus (for which, read Toyota) put a new-generation LS400 on the market in Japan, UK deliveries being due to start in 1995.

Using the same basic platform as before, the new-type LS400 was at once slightly more roomy in the cabin but lighter, with a more powerful 4-litre V8 engine, and a considerably higher price of £42,863 when it reached the UK. More rounded than the original type, this was a bland style, but the car was built to the highest possible quality standards and was aiming directly at sales in the BMW 7-series and Jaguar XJ market.

Lotus: As forecast, a final run of 800 front-drive Elans were manufactured during the year, starting in mid-summer and using left-over Isuzu engine/transmission packs which had been in stock when the lines had closed down in 1992. There were no visual and few technical differences between the earlier and latest front-drive cars: the latest car had lower-section tyres on wider rims, and the compulsory catalytic converter had trimmed 10bhp off the peak power output. In 1994 the price had risen to £24,500, making it even more difficult to sell than before.

Later in the year, the long-running Esprit Turbo range (turbocharged mid-engined Lotuses had been on sale since 1980) was modified yet again. A new derivative, the S4S, went on sale, complete with a 285bhp engine, revised suspension and 17in/18in diameter road wheels. The price was now £53,995.

Marcos: The latest development of the 1960s-type sportscar was the Mantara-based LM500, an open-top or coupe two-seater with a 5-litre/300bhp version of the Rover engine. The LM stood for Le Mans, into which race two of the cars were entered later in the year without success. Jem Marsh realized that this was probably the last, the fastest and the least refined of all the cars in this family, but he did not need to sell many to make the investment worthwhile for his small Wiltshire-based concern.

Maserati: Now under Fiat control, Maserati was able to complete development of the new Quattroporte (four doors) and launch it in the spring.

Although still based on the platform of the 1980s-type Biturbo model – which is to say that it had a twin-turbo V6 engine driving the rear wheels – this time, for the UK, the 2.8-litre engine produced 284bhp and the car had a claimed top speed of more than 160mph. With styling by Gandini, the new Maserati did not look sufficiently modern to sell for long, and with a price of around £57,000, its prospects were always very limited in the UK.

Mazda: During the summer and autumn, the new-generation 323 range of hatchbacks and saloons took over from the previous generation. The new car was a transverse-engine/front-drive design, with an even more rounded body profile from all angles, and the range of five engines included a diesel and a 167bhp/2-litre V6.

With the bloom now off the early-life reputation of the MX-5 sportscar, Mazda freshened up its UK prospects by introducing a stripped-out version in May. Mechanically the same as the existing 1.8-litre type, by dropping the anti-lock brakes, airbag, power-assisted steering and alloy road wheels it was possible for the price to come down to £14,495 – almost £3,000 cheaper than the regular version. But as so often happens with such promotions, the majority of MX-5 sales contin-ued to be of the more expensive type!

Mercedes-Benz: With very little fuss, the company fleshed out the SL road-ster range during the year, dropping the original SL300 type and replacing it with two new cars – the 193bhp/2.8-litre SL280 (£53,200) and the 231bhp/3.2-litre SL320 (£58,000). There were no styling and few other specification changes.

During the year, the company established a precedent by listing the AMG-modified C36 (C-class) and E36 (E-class) models as fully fledged production cars, both with a long-stroke version of the existing 3.2-litre 24-valve twin-cam six-cylinder engine, giving 280bhp/3,606cc. At the same time AMG also provided an integrated body kit, different springs and dampers and bigger wheels and tyres. The orig-inals had been approved conversions, but Mercedes-Benz had been so impressed with AMG's work that it swept them into the corporate listings with a full warranty.

By a large margin these were much the most expensive of the ranges for which they became the flagships – the C36 costing £38,250 in July 1994, compared with £25,100 for the C280 model.

Before the end of the year a third AMG-engineered car had been added to the official Mercedes-Benz range, this being the SL60 sportscar. Based on the existing SL500, this car used an enlarged 5,956cc twin-cam 32-valve V8 engine which produced a lusty 375bhp and guaranteed colossal (though electronically speed-limited) performance.

Mitsubishi: A new range-topping Shogun model appeared in February, this having a brawny 204bhp/3.5-litre 24-valve V6 engine, while at the same time there was a respecified version of the 2.8-litre turbodiesel engine with 123bhp, but only in the long-wheelbase five-door body.

Nissan: A new-generation Maxima was announced in May, though by the time it went on UK sale in the spring of 1995 it would have been renamed QX. Bigger, more roomy and distinctly more upmarket than the car it replaced, the new Maxima/QX was more rounded than before, with a 2in longer wheelbase and a choice of new-generation alloy V6 engines, one of 2 litres, the other 3 litres.

The British importers revealed that it would have to stop selling the 300ZX in the UK because the Japanese engineers were unable to justify the re-engineering work in modifying right-hand-drive cars to take account of future exhaust emissions and catalytic converter regulations.

Peugeot: During the summer the still-modern 106 range was revised yet again, this time by enlarging the diesel unit from 1.36 to 1.5 litres. The new unit was more powerful (58bhp) and torquey than before.

(For details of the newly-previewed Type 806 MPV, see the Citroen section.)

Porsche: Following the revamped chassis given to the rear-wheel-drive 911 model towards the end of 1993, Porsche tidied up its range from sum-mer 1994 by putting a similar new four-wheel-drive 911 on sale.

Like the 1993 rear-drive car, the latest 911 Carrera 4 featured coil-spring front and rear suspension and had all the same styling touches, including the carefully integrated front and rear bumpers and the lay-back oval head-lamps. As before, power was by a 272bhp/3.6-litre version of the leg-endary flat-six engine. All that was needed now was for the 911 Turbo to be updated, but that would not hap-pen until 1995.

To follow the limited-production 968 Club Sport of 1993, Porsche now announced the 968 Sport model, which was mechanically standard except for the Club Sport's suspension and 17in wheels, though most of the trim and fittings ditched from the CS had been reintroduced for the Sport type. Confused? Not many Porsche customers seemed to be – but, then, not many of these cars were sold either.

Range Rover: It had taken 24 years for Rover to produce a new-generation Range Rover, which was introduced in September, and even then it did not bury the old type, which continued as the Range Rover Classic.

The new car took the philosophy of the existing Range Rover one complete stage further, and yet more upmarket. There was a smooth, subtly rounded and very spacious new five-door estate car-type bodyshell and a choice of petrol and diesel power units.

All the new Pegasus types (this was the car's project code when it was being developed) ran on a 108in wheelbase (like the old-style Vogue LSE) with variable ground-clearance air suspension of their beam axles. The venerable alloy V8 engine had been reworked yet again, there now being a choice of 190bhp/3.95-litre and 225bhp/4.5-litre types, while the diesel option was to be a turbocharged straight-six-cylinder BMW unit producing 134bhp.

The choice of the BMW engine, in fact, had been made years before BMW had decided to buy the Rover Group, and it was the sight of this new Range Rover which had been one of the strong influences which persuaded management to make the bid in the first place!

Renault: The new Mondeo/Cavalier-sized Laguna appeared in January, a five-door hatchback which was a direct replacement for the long-running Renault 21. Rounded and delicately smooth where the 21 had been rather more angular and gawky, the Laguna was a typical pan-European transverse-engined front-wheel-drive car, which was to be built in many different forms, with petrol and diesel four-cylinder and V6 engines. UK deliveries began in the spring, and – helped along by a very successful debut season in the British Touring Car Championship – the Laguna soon built a fine reputation, which the 21 had somehow lacked.

There would be no Laguna estate car until October 1995, which meant that the old Renault 21 Savanna estate stayed on the market until then.

Even though the Espace MPV had now been on the market for eight years, Renault was still developing the concept. During the year the latest model to reach UK showrooms was a 110bhp/2.2-litre version, which was only marketed with automatic transmission.

Rolls-Royce: In an interesting product-planning move, the company launched a new cocktail, which comprised the longer-wheelbase Silver Spur bodyshell, the turbocharged 6.75-litre V8 engine, as normally used in the Bentley Turbo R, with a slightly different grille and fittings.

The new car was to be called Flying Spur, would have a top speed of more than 130mph, yet only 50 were to be produced. It was priced at a breathtaking £148,545.

Late in the year, the last of the Corniche convertibles was produced (along with the equivalent Bentley), this bringing to an end an unbroken 28-year life. Introduced in 1966 merely as a two-door Mulliner-Park Ward special-bodied version of the Silver Shadow, the Corniche name was officially adopted in 1971. Because the Silver Spirit platform was basically the same as that of the Silver Shadow, Corniche assembly continued after the saloon car was replaced in 1980.

Rover: At the end of the year, the long-running Metro (which was already past its 14th birthday) was given a further major facelift. With a new nose and even more prominent Rover badge, it ceased to be called a Metro, and was renamed the Rover 100 series.

As before, there were 1.1 and 1.4-litre K-series petrol engines and a 1.5-litre Peugeot diesel, with power outputs spanning 56 to 74bhp.

There was still activity to fill out every corner of the 800 range. From May, the latest was called the 800 Vitesse Sport, and came complete with a 197bhp turbocharged 2-litre T-series twin-OHC 16-valve engine and a claimed top speed of 143mph.

A 400 Touring estate car was previewed in March, with sales due to begin in June. Although the 400 was a Honda-based car, there was no Honda equivalent to this five-door load-carrier, which was produced with a choice of 416SLi, 420GSi and 418SLD (diesel) engines.

Saab: After a decade of producing a wide variety of four cylinder-engined 9000s, Saab announced its first V6-engined derivative in September 1994, this using a 210bhp/3-litre version of the modern GM unit (which had become available to Saab following GM's purchase of a shareholding in 1990, and was already being used in the new-generation Saab 900 and latest GM ranges).

The style of the new 3-litre 9000 was virtually unchanged, but this was by far the smoothest version of the car yet put on sale – if not the fastest, for there was a high-output four-cylinder turbo version which took that title. The claimed top speed was more than 140mph, and UK deliveries began towards the end of the year.

Seat: Less than three years after it had gone on sale in the UK, the VW-based Cordoba range was revised. The original 1.3-litre engine was dropped in favour of a 60bhp/1.4-litre VW unit, while the 148bhp/16-valve 2-litre VW engine took over from the original 128bhp/1.8-litre type. At the same time, the wider-track VW Golf GTi suspension was adapted to the Seat's VW-based platform.

Skoda: Having been taken over by VW in 1991, the Czech car-maker had been busy. VW investment allowed the company to rework the front-drive Favorit, turning it into the facelifted, better-built, but essentially similar machine called the Felicia.

Compared with the Favorit, the platform, engines, transmissions and running gear had all been retained, although the overhead-valve 1.3-litre engine was now more powerful and benefited from VW's fuel injection expertise.

When the Felicia was introduced at the end of 1994, there were promises that VW-style petrol and diesel engines would be made available in the future, though these had not been released by the end of 1995.

The body style, though based on the Favorit's structure, featured a complete set of smoother and more nicely detailed outer panels, though the heritage was still obvious. UK deliveries would begin in the spring of 1995, with a choice of 54 or 68bhp engines.

Suzuki: At the end of the year, the Vitara was given the new top-of-the-range option of a 134bhp/2-litre 24-valve V6 engine, which was clearly much more powerful and much more sophisticated than any of the four-cylinder engines previously used in one of the world's smallest off-road 4x4 vehicles.

Toyota: Having shown a concept car at the Tokyo motor show in 1993, the company launched the small, high-performance, RAV-4 4x4 model at the Geneva show in March, with British sales set to start in mid-summer.

The RAV-4 was different from other 4x4s by being smaller, more rounded, faster, with a theme that was considerably less 'off-road' than 'leisure market'. Not only did it have independent suspension all round, but its 133bhp/2-litre fuel-injected engine could push the short-wheelbase three-door four-seater up to a 105mph top speed. Although to some older eyes the RAV-4 looked like an overgrown Tonka toy, it was a very effective machine, and immediately began to sell well in the UK.

From March, the mid-engined two-seater MR-2 model, which had been on sale in the UK since 1990, was given the latest 173bhp Celica GT engine instead of the 158bhp unit used previously. Surprisingly, Toyota claimed no performance improvements.

TVR: Still embarrassed by the over-running development of its new AJP8 engine, the company juggled with its resources, this time adding a pair of 5-litre Rover-based V8 engines to the Chimaera catalogue, rated at 290 or 340bhp.

In the 'hope springs eternal' department, prices of Cerberas were being quoted with a variety of engines, but there was absolutely no chance of these cars being delivered for a long time, for development of them had barely begun.

Vauxhall: The much-rumoured Tigra coupe was finally introduced in September. Based on the platform and all the running gear of the latest front-wheel-drive Corsa, the Tigra was a curvy, 2+2 sports coupe model with a rather cramped cabin and styling which certainly did not appeal to everyone.

At launch there was a choice of two different 16-valve four-cylinder engines – an 89bhp/1.4-litre and a 105bhp/1.6-litre. In its looks and character this was definitely a car for the young, and early signs were that Vauxhall would find it difficult to sell enough to make the Tigra project worthwhile.

During the spring the new Monterey 4x4 off-roader estate car went on sale, this being a rebadged version of the largest Isuzu Trooper Citation, with a choice of 3.1-litre petrol or diesel engines.

Then, as later, there was great confusion as to the respective roles of this so-called Vauxhall and the Trooper, which continued to be sold in the UK through a different distribution network. Vauxhall, for its part, marketed

the Monterey as a much larger and more capable machine than the smaller Isuzu-based Frontera, charging premium prices, which automatically meant that it was fighting for the top of the Land Rover Discovery market.

Like other major British car-makers, Vauxhall reacted to the insurance industry's rapacious demands by trimming back the power of its sporty cars. The 16-valve 2-litre engine was detuned from 150 to 133bhp for use in the Calibra and Cavalier models, but for the time being the higher-powered engine remained in the Astra GSi.

Later in the year, the Astra was given a thorough engine range makeover, with a whole series of 16-valve twin-cams taking over from the long-established eight-valve single-cam units which had been around since the late 1970s. These included a 100bhp/1.6-litre, the promise of a 134bhp/2-litre to be phased in during the coming winter, and the addition of a 67bhp/1.7-litre 'light-pressure' turbodiesel. Visually, the Astra received the new-style corporate V-grille to carry it into the later 1990s.

A few weeks later, a similar engine range 'clean-up' was applied to the Cavalier (though that car only had one more season to run before being replaced by the new-generation Vectra of 1995). In this case there were new-style Ecotech engines, including a 134bhp/2-litre 16-valve (to replace the old-style 113bhp eight-valve unit). Meanwhile, the Cavalier 4x4 (an ultra-sporting saloon) was dropped due to an inexplicable lack of sales.

To round off the new-for-1995 reshuffle, there was a new 89bhp/1.4-litre 16-valve engine for the more sporty versions of the Corsa.

Volkswagen: The major event of the year for the German concern was the launch of a new-generation Polo in October, with a brand-new platform to replace that of the old-type Polo, which had been on sale since 1981. Because of the lengthy time gap between the launch of the previous platform and this one, plus the fact that it was also to be the foundation for future Seats and (probably) Skodas, it represented a colossal new investment.

The fact that this, the third-generation Polo, was as large as the original Golf had been in the 1970s (and very much heavier!) proved the inexorable growth

of all family cars during this period and the influence that safety engineering had had on vehicle layouts.

Like all current VWs, the new Polos were transverse-engine/front-drive machines, built as three-door or five-door hatchbacks with a choice of single-overhead-cam engines (which were beginning to look old-fashioned) ranging from 45bhp/1.05-litre to 75bhp/1.6-litre models, together with a 64bhp/1.9-litre diesel.

VW emphasized that these were safe, secure and solid little cars, claims borne out by their rather limited performance, but there was no doubt that there was a new high level of comfort and build quality. Most observers immediately put the Polo at the top of the class.

Amazingly, the Corrado sports coupe was still selling too slowly all round the world – no-one, least of all VW, could really understand why – so in mid-1994 the range was shaken up, the existing 136bhp 16-valve unit being replaced by a 115bhp/2-litre eight-valve entry-level model and a 148bhp/2-litre 16-valve engine.

The new-generation Sharan MPV, whose design and construction was to be shared with the Ford Galaxy, was previewed in October, but deliveries were not due to begin until mid-1995. (For details see the 1995 section.)

Volvo: Late in the life of the Dutch-built 440/460 range (they were due to be replaced by a Mitsubishi-inspired car at the end of 1995), there was the option of the 90bhp/1.9-litre Renault turbodiesel, as already found in Renault 19s and other mid-size Renaults.

The Swedish company continued to reshuffle and make the most of its resources, and for 1995 offered a 170bhp/2.5-litre version of the modern six-cylinder 24-valve twin-cam engine in the 960. So much of this was going on at Volvo that at times even the dealers were confused by the sheer variety of what was on offer.

In the autumn, a limited-edition T-5R model (2,500 cars were to be built) took over from the already outrageously fast T-5 range. For 1995, therefore, the T-5R saloons and estates had turbocharged 240bhp/2.5-litre five-cylinder 20-valve engines driving the front wheels through grippy 205/45-17 wheels and tyres.

With a top speed of around 145mph,

a sporting character previously quite alien to Volvo, and the fact that all the British examples were to be produced in bright yellow or a glossy black, the T-5R (R for Racing? Volvo wasn't saying anything...), this was a remarkably different sort of Volvo. Clearly, the Swedish company was determined to change its image for the late 1990s.

Industrial developments

The biggest news of the year – of the decade, probably – came in February when BMW was suddenly revealed as the new owner of the Rover Group. Previous owner British Aerospace was delighted, and minor-shareholder Honda was appalled.

British Aerospace had taken control in 1988, paying a mere £150 million for a loss-making group. Five years later it sold out all its interests to BMW for £1.3 billion – a remarkable capital gain, which naturally caused many politicians to state that this was scandalous.

Later it was learned that British Aerospace had also been negotiating with Honda, but the Japanese company had not apparently been willing to make a full purchase bid. When BMW came in with a straightforward bid, BAe was delighted to do a deal.

Within days BMW was talking airily of reviving famous but long-dormant British names like Austin-Healey and Riley, Honda was crying 'foul', and all co-operative programmes were hastily being wound-up. However, except that BMW finance was now to underpin Rover's activities, there would be no obvious synergy between the two concerns for some time, and even two years later there seemed to have been little actual amalgamation.

BMW was in the news in another direction, too, at the end of the year, when Rolls-Royce announced that it had decided to use BMW engines – modified V8s and V12s – in its next generation of models, which were expected to be revealed near the end of the 1990s.

Until the last moment, Mercedes-Benz had been rumoured to be in line for this contract, but a last-minute switch was made. One consequence was that the existing chief executive, Peter Ward, immediately left the company (his views had been overridden) and Chris Woodwark took his place.

(Both Rolls-Royce and Cosworth were Vickers subsidiaries. Woodwark, who was already running Cosworth, later revealed that Cosworth would carry out the technical development work on at least one of the engines intended for use in the new Rolls-Royce.)

There was dispute, amicably settled in the end, between Vauxhall and the IM Group, the importers of Usuzu cars. Vauxhall gained agreement from GM, who held a major, but not controlling, stake in Isuzu, to begin importing 'Vauxhall Montereys', which were modified Isuzu 4x4s, while IM continued to sell Isuzu Troopers of a substantially older design. From 1997, however, Vauxhall was to become the sole UK importer of Isuzu models.

Times were still difficult for Reliant. In receivership in 1990/91, it had been rescued by Beans Industries. Now, at the end of 1994, it was Beans which found itself in financial trouble, so once again Reliant was threatened with closure. This time it seemed to be final, for although the company was bought by an aviation-based company, Avonex, the marque did not reappear in the price lists in 1995.

Lancia withdrew from the British market during the year, quite simply because they were selling very few cars. From a peak of around 12,000 cars/year sold in 1978, deliveries had dropped inexorably throughout the 1980s and early 1990s, such that only 701 cars had been sold in 1992 and fewer still in 1993.

This was a classic case of a poor quality and reliability image overtaking the technical merits of the front-wheel-drive cars, for not even a staggeringly successful rally programme (which should have done wonders for the image of the Delta and its replacement, the Dedra) could counter that.

The British design consultancy, IAD of Worthing, was taken over by Daewoo to be converted into its European base. This was a godsend to IAD, which had been suffering financially for some time.

Channel Tunnel opened

The Channel Tunnel was supposed to be ready for business in May 1994, but cynics all across the country were sure that the date would slip – and they were right. Connecting Folkestone with Calais, it would begin operations haltingly during the summer, but would not truly get into its stride until mid-1995, when four shuttle trains an hour were moving in each direction. At first the cost of taking a car through the tunnel started at £220 return (for a car plus any number of passengers), but this price then see-sawed, going down at off-peak periods and for special promotions, and soaring at peak times.

This had been one of the world's most ambitious civil engineering projects and it was plugged into the British and French railway systems. Not only was it meant to take conventional rail traffic, but there was to be a 24-hour vehicle-carrying shuttle service between massive terminals close to motorway/autoroute systems on each side of the Channel.

Completion of the tunnel (or tunnels – for in fact there were three bores, two of them for rail traffic and a centre one for services) had been a major achievement, but costs had soared to around £10 billion, and even in 1995 the high-clearance ferry vans needed to carry lofty 4x4 estate cars and MPVs had not been delivered, while early complaints centred on the way that low-slung or heavily-laden cars could be damaged by scraping their bodywork while being driven onto and off the Shuttle.

Technical developments

Citroën's new 'active roll control' suspension system, as premiered in the Xantia Activa model, was the first major breakthrough in overall suspension design for some years. It was fitting that it came from the marque which had pioneered hydropneumatic springs and self-levelling in the 1950s.

Normally, when a car goes round a corner, forces cause the bodyshell to lean towards the outside of the curve – to roll. Citroën's Activa principle eliminated roll because of the superfast reaction of electronic sensors. When the springs on the outside of the car tended to compress due to cornering forces, modified hydropneumatic jacks were pumped up to counter the tendency.

Although this sounds simple enough, the development of control systems to make a no-roll system practical had occupied many years – British firms had been dabbling with such a system in the early 1970s, but could not master the detail, nor contain the costs.

McLaren F1 – the fastest ever road car

This was the year in which the astonishing 627bhp/6.1-litre/V12 three-seater McLaren F1 road car was finally road-tested, to prove conclusively that it was the world's fastest road car. With a sale price of £540,000, and such colossal performance that no car was ever to be entrusted to mere mortals, McLaren chose *Autocar & Motor's* test team to produce the figures, but even this experienced bunch could find nowhere in the British Isles to prove the claimed top speed of 230mph-plus which McLaren's Jonathan Palmer had already verified at the Nardo high-speed circle in Southern Italy.

Even so, there was enough space on Bruntingthorpe's long runway for more than 210mph to be achieved with the car still accelerating…

With the blessing of *Autocar & Motor*, I merely quote this sample from a comprehensive set of figures published on May 11, 1994:

Maximum speeds:

6th:	230mph+ (claimed)
5th:	180mph
4th:	150mph
3rd:	125mph
2nd:	95mph
1st:	65mph

Acceleration:

0–60mph:	3.2sec
0–100mph:	6.3sec
0–150mph:	12.8sec
0–200mph:	28.0sec
Standing-start ¼-mile:	11.1sec

– all this from a car that was able to return an overall fuel consumption of 15.2mpg. Astonishing!

Men of Influence

Bernd Pischetsrieder

It was only after BMW took over Rover in 1994 that the British motoring media had to buckle down and learn to spell, and pronounce, the name of the BMW chief executive. However, he had become famous in the European motor industry well before that.

Born in Munich in 1948, he studied mechanical engineering at Munich University before joining BMW in 1973 as a production planning engineer, and steadily worked his way up through the BMW hierarchy in the next two decades. By 1982, when still only 36 years old, he had become production director of BMW South Africa, then in 1985 he returned to Germany as BMW's head of quality assurance.

In 1987 he became the head of BMW's technical planning department, joined the board of directors in 1991 (with responsibility for production), then became chairman of the board in May 1993.

Almost from the day that BMW took control of Rover in February 1994, it became clear that Pischetsrieder was not only a formidable businessman, but also a real motoring enthusiast. His technical, financial and business qualifications were not in doubt – what had been done at BMW in the previous decade spelt that out – but it was his fond remarks about Rover's heritage, and the dormant marques still owned by the Group, which made it seem that he might also want to inject a bit of fun and excitement into the 'new' Rover Group.

One of his first moves was to approve final development and production of the new MGF sportscar, which would be launched in 1995 – he had already approved the building of the BMW Z3 roadster, which would also make its debut that year.

1995

Without doubt, this was one of the most important years ever for new-model launches, Britain's motoring enthusiasts being given a regular feast of descriptions of cars of all types, British and imported.

Although UK car sales rose slightly once again, press comment made much of the fact that the 'feel-good' factor was still absent. The reality was that no more cars were being sold in the UK than there had been in 1986, and it began to look as if the motor trade was in a 'mature' state. Short of another massive economic boom, therefore, it looked as if there would never again be the amount of activity as had been seen in 1988 and 1989.

The fragile optimism in the motor industry was badly hit by a November Budget which offered no favours, for there was yet another increase in petrol duty – equal to about 3.5p/litre or 15p/gallon – along with increased benefit-in-kind taxation on company cars. The Vehicle Excise Duty became £140/year (except for old classic cars – see the panel), and a small reduction in income tax rates did little to balance this.

Modern technology let the British Government down at one stage when experiments with traffic volume-sensed variable speed limits on the M25 motorway had to be postponed for months in order to 'de-bug' the computer software.

The theory – which took ages to bring into practice – was that sensors on gantries over the eight-lane M25 in the Heathrow area would sense the amount of traffic flowing, then alter the speed limit signs to suit – the more traffic, the lower the speed limit.

The Government moved to make the driving test more difficult by proposing that a written test about driving should also be included in the examination of skills, but this was not enacted until 1996.

New models

AC: Because the old-style pushrod V8 engine was being abandoned in the USA, AC had to pick up an alternative for its Ace, this being the latest 4.6-litre

32-valve twin-cam unit as fitted to a variety of 1996-model Fords. The specification for 1996 was otherwise little changed.

Alfa Romeo: The 155, still a modern car by European model-cycle standards, received a thorough technical makeover in the spring, which included a wider front track necessitating flared wheelarches, and the adoption of the latest corporate twin-spark 2-litre 16-valve engine, which had Fiat-Lancia origins, although Alfa did its best to hide this.

Expansion of the modern front-drive 145/146 range continued with the addition of a 150bhp/2-litre four-cylinder engine (155 type) to the Cloverleaf derivatives. These cars were previewed at the London Motor Show and were to be added to the range in 1996. They involved major changes to the front end of the platform, but the cars' exterior style was unchanged.

Audi: In the UK, much of the year's effort was spent in building up the sales and reputation of the latest A4 model which had taken over from the long-running 80 range.

A third version of the A8 flagship appeared in Germany, using a 230bhp/3.7-litre shorter-stroke version of the big V8 engine and featuring front-wheel rather than four-wheel drive. Like the other A8s, it was only available with automatic transmission. First UK deliveries were promised for later in the year, but in fact were delayed until 1996.

The long-running Coupe range (including quattro-transmission derivatives) was finally killed off towards the end of 1995, almost 15 years after the first of an earlier-generation Coupe had entered the market.

Bentley: The new Azure drop-head coupe, revealed in March, was a beautifully-finished flagship derived from the Continental R coupe. With a 385bhp turbocharged version of the old-fashioned 6.75-litre V8 engine, and with a complex power-operated soft-top which added £27,000 to the selling price, the Azure had a Pininfarina connection, for the plan was that every Azure would be shipped to Italy for roof fitting before being returned to Crewe for completion.

(For details of changes to four-door

saloons, see under Rolls-Royce, below.)

BMW: Helped along by a great deal of Hollywood-style hype, the Z3 roadster, a two-seater sportscar to be built in BMW's new North American factory, was previewed during the year and was set to feature in the latest James Bond movie, *Golden Eye*.

The Z3 used a traditional front-engine/rear-drive layout, with rounded styling rather similar to that of the Mazda MX-5, and one could quite see why BMW was at pains to make this a more expensive car than the new MG MGF *(see MG, below)*, a model and marque which was now in the BMW fold.

The Z3 used the platform of the latest 3-series Compact, which meant that the old-style semi-trailing arm rear suspension was used, and at first there was to be a choice of 1.8-litre engines, though only the 140bhp 16-valve unit was scheduled to travel to the UK when British deliveries began in 1996.

The prolific series of new model launches had continued in February with the release of first examples of a new family of in-line six-cylinder alloy-block engines intended to take over from the iron-block units which had been in production since the late 1970s.

The 323i was a conventional 3-series model with a 170bhp/2.5-litre 24-valve version of this new engine, whereas the excitingly-specified 328i used a torquey 193bhp/2.8-litre 24-valve version of the same type. Although the latest 2.8-litre engine had similar power to the iron-block 2.5-litre it replaced, it had 15 per cent more peak torque and was no less than 70lb lighter.

The top-of-the-range M3, the second generation of which which had only been launched in 1992, was further improved during the year, becoming more powerful, lighter – and in consequence faster and more expensive.

Using the technology already blooded in building a road-car engine for McLaren, BMW enlarged the 24-valve 3-litre twin-cam engine to 3.2 litres with a longer stroke, incorporated variable valve time, and thus offered 321 instead of 286bhp. At the same time the six-speed gearbox of the modern M5 was specified.

The latest car had doors pressed

from aluminium, there were changes to the suspension settings, larger-section rear tyres took over and the level of equipment was even higher than before, all of which made the latest M3 a formidable machine.

Then, in September, a new-generation 5-series four-door saloon was introduced, with British sales due to begin in 1996. It was no insult to BMW to say that this car was almost exactly as expected, for it was a slightly larger car than the previous 5-series, having a new and longer-wheelbase platform and a more spacious cabin.

The style was reminiscent of the latest 7-series, the independent suspensions were derived from that car, while the initial engine line-up was of six-cylinder units ranging from a 143bhp/2.5-litre diesel to a 193bhp/2.8-litre petrol version, though more engines, including V8s, were confidently expected to be added during 1996.

Almost lost in this blizzard of brand-new BMWs was the introduction of the entry-level 728i which, logically enough, was a new-type 7-series fitted with the latest 193bhp/2.8-litre six-cylinder engine, which still gave it a claimed top speed of 140mph.

Caterham: The 21 project, shown as a single prototype in 1994, progressed further towards production, being exhibited in October 1995 with a choice of Rover K-series 1.6-litre engines – but production cars were still not promised until 1996.

Citroen: From mid-summer the very successful Xantia range was reshaped, in particular by bringing the engine line-up into the same sequence as for the new Peugeot 406, 16-valve engines taking over in the 1.8-litre and 2-litre sizes, which meant more power and (according to Citroen) better fuel economy.

Daewoo: This new-to-Britain marque finally went on sale in April. For the previous few months Daewoo had run their series of corporate adverts claiming Daewoo to be 'the world's largest company you have never heard of...' and introducing what it claimed was a new way of selling cars.

Daewoos were to be marketed through agencies quoting non-negotiable new car and trade-in used car values, the initial deal to include

three years or 60,000 miles of cost-free servicing, a year's free road tax and no delivery charges. Also, customers buying M-plate cars in the spring were to be offered brand-new N-plate cars in August as an early trade-in, for no extra charge. The financial deal looked unusually good – until people compared the actual costs with the specification of the cars being offered.

Two models were introduced – the Nexia and the Espero. Although both were fresh faces to the UK, neither was newly-engineered. The Nexia was a descendant of the Daewoo Le Mans, a car that had been launched in 1986 as a lightly-modified version of the Opel Kadett/Vauxhall Astra of 1984–89 vintage. The Espero was a reskinned derivative of the old-style Opel Ascona/Vauxhall Cavalier, which had been engineered in the 1970s and had gone out of production in 1988.

But although the motoring press treated these cars with a certain amount of scorn, the public seemed to like what it saw, considered the high-priced cars to be bargains, and as a result sales built up steadily during the year.

Daihatsu: The small Hijet revealed in the spring of 1995 was more of a converted van with windows than a purpose-built MPV, for this shape had already been seen on British roads as a small load-carrier. It was small by any standards, could carry only six passengers (who had to huddle close together), and it had to struggle along with a three-cylinder 45bhp/993cc engine. High and narrow, it had a hard van-like ride, its only real attraction being a low price of £7,995.

Daimler: (For details of longer-wheelbase models, see Jaguar, below.)

Ferrari: The sensational F50 sports-car, the successor to the F40, was officially unveiled in March, with sales beginning later in the year. This was to be such an exclusive car that Ferrari stated it would only produce 349 of them (a number deliberately chosen to be memorable and, according to Ferrari: 'one less than 350!'), of which only 25 were scheduled to be delivered to British buyers.

The heart of this magnificent mid-engined/rear-drive machine was that it had an enlarged and detuned version

of Ferrari's early-1990s V12 F1 engine, in this case producing 520bhp from 4.7 litres. Allied to it was a six-speed gearbox, race-type suspension and a sufficiently slippery body shape to let Ferrari claim a top speed of 202mph.

This was a hi-tech missile for rich people, though even at a UK price of £329,000 there was still a queue to buy. With a chassis and body structure in carbonfibre, this was not a car which could be maintained, especially repaired, by the owner – indeed, it was one of the biggest motoring indulgences of the 1990s.

Fiat: In mid-summer, the new twins – Bravo and Brava – appeared, caught most technical writers' imaginations and soon went on to win the European Car of the Year competition.

Bravo (shorter-wheelbase/three-door) and Brava (longer-wheelbase/five-door) hatchbacks effectively took over from the Tipo platform for they immediately offered a big choice of specifications ranging from an 80bhp/1.4-litre to a 147bhp/2-litre, with a normally-aspirated 65bhp/1.9-litre diesel alternative. The 1.4s had 12-valve heads, the other four-cylinder petrol engines having 16 valves. Top of the range was a new 'modular' 2-litre five-cylinder unit, with 147bhp.

The new Barchetta two-seater sports-car was announced during the spring, this being a 1.75 litre-engined front-wheel-drive machine falling into direct competition with cars like the Mazda MX-5.

The platform of the Barchetta was derived from that of the latest Punto family car, but with a torquey 130bhp engine and a claimed top speed of more than 120mph, this was clearly going to be a fast machine. With a rounded style by Fiat's own team, and some mechanical links to the recently launched coupe, as far as British buyers were concerned the car's only drawback was that it was only to be built with left-hand steering.

Ford: The long-expected new-generation Fiesta arrived in September, a car based on the outgoing model (and retaining the same basic platform, cabin and suspensions), but with new nose and tail styles, a much-modified interior and a new engine line-up.

Although the old-type 1.3-litre OHV

and 1.8-litre diesel engines carried on, a brand-new Zetec SE twin-cam 16-valve engine was introduced. In its initial form, this engine was a 74bhp/1.25-litre unit, but Ford freely admitted that a 1.4-litre version would soon follow and that there was enough space within the design for 1.7 litres to be possible. Like its predecessor, the new Fiesta was expected to be one of Britain's best-sellers in the next few years. On early examples, testers reported impressive improvements in quality and passenger comfort.

In February, full details were released of the ambitious new Galaxy MPV, which was to be produced in a brand-new factory. Set up as a joint project with Volkswagen, the Galaxy was joined by a near-identical VW model called the Sharan, and before the end of 1995 it was revealed that there would eventually be a Seat version of the same design (Seat, of course, being controlled by Volkswagen).

All models shared the same big five-door high-roof estate car style and were pitching for what industry-watchers called the 'Renault Espace' market. All had transversely-mounted engines and front-wheel drive, with all-independent suspension and a deceptive style which looked as if it featured forward control, but did not.

There was a choice of three engines – a 115bhp/2-litre eight-valve twin-cam of the type used in early-1990s Sierras, Scorpios and Transit vans, a 90bhp/1.9-litre VW turbodiesel (as found in Passats, Golfs and Ventos) and VW's 174bhp/2.8-litre VR6 (V6).

The cabin featured three rows of seats, most of which were instantly removable, or could be swivelled, which made this an extremely versatile load-carrier. British deliveries did not begin until mid-summer, and for political reasons Fords and VWs were priced at very similar levels.

Little more than four years after the current range of front-wheel-drive Escorts had gone on sale, Ford revamped the design yet again. From early in the year the cars received a restyled nose, with a smaller oval grille, there was a totally different facia, a lot of work on refinement and build quality, but almost no changes to the existing line-up of engines and transmissions.

The retreat from a performance image continued apace. The XR models had disappeared in 1994, and

towards the end of 1995 Ford announced that it was to stop producing Escort RS Cosworths during the winter and to phase out the RS2000 models during 1996. It was a sad retreat from what had once been a dominant marketing stance.

Honda: At the end of the year, the Accord range (to which Rover's 600 family was so closely related) was given a facelift and a new engine line-up. The first UK deliveries were promised for March 1996.

The car received a new nose, complete with a definite grille aperture, which the earlier types had lacked. At the same time the engine line-up was changed to include an entry-level 113bhp/1.8-litre, the earlier 2.3-litre engine being dropped, while Rover's 104bhp/2-litre L-series turbodiesel was a new option.

Hyundai: A new-generation Lantra appeared during the summer, UK deliveries starting later in the year, taking over from the original-generation Lantra, which had been in production since 1990.

Here was yet another transverse front-engine/front-drive car selling in the 1.6 to 2-litre Ford Mondeo/Vauxhall Cavalier-Vectra bracket. Because it was Korean rather than Japanese, this meant that there would be no quota restrictions on sales, which made British manufacturers wary of its qualities.

Jaguar: During the summer, a longer-wheelbase version of the four-door saloon shell was introduced as an option to the conventional cars (and, of course, to the Daimlers). This took over from the Majestic conversions and offered more than 4 inches of additional rear seat legroom in a body nearly 5 inches longer overall and weighing an extra 50lb. The longer shell was available on all six-cylinder and V12 models, the entry-level XJ6 costing an extra £2,750.

The last of the V12-engined XJS models was built at the end of the year, though production of six-cylinder types was due to continue until the mid-1996 launch of the new-generation XK8.

Jeep: The popular Cherokee, which had already been a part of the worldwide scene for more than 10 years, became more European in 1995 when

it gained the option of an Italian VM turbodiesel engine. This 116bhp/2.5-litre engine was also a lot lighter than the petrol-engined alternatives of this design.

Lamborghini: Not to be outdone by Ferrari and the launch of the F50, the company put the very limited-production rear-wheel-drive Diablo SE30 Jota on sale during the year. Although it was much bigger and heavier than the F1-technology Ferrari, it was still a colossally fast machine, for it had a 590bhp/5.7-litre V12 engine and a claimed top speed of more than 210mph. At £192,200, surely a car like this was at the outer limits of practical road use?

At the end of the year, an open-top Diablo roadster also went on sale – not that anyone would want to drive an open-top car at the colossal speeds of which the Diablo was capable!

Lotus: The company rocked under the financial storm which broke during 1995 around its Italian parent, Bugatti, but it managed to carry on, a new managing director, Rod Mansfield (an ex-Ford SVE manager) was appointed and an exciting all-new lightweight two-seater sportscar, the Elise, was previewed.

The basic mechanical layout was familiar enough – like the MG MGF, it used a mid-position 1.8-litre Rover K-series engine/transmission pack, but the novelty was in the chassis, which was an aluminium monocoque, bonded rather than welded together. The smooth and rounded body was in glassfibre composite, as expected, the entire car was very light (the prototype was claimed to weigh no more than 1,485lb) and sales were due to begin in mid-1996. Technically, of course, the new Elise was fascinating, but in view of previous marketing (and pricing) problems at Lotus, observers were cautious about the car's prospects.

Mazda: Although the MX-5 sportscar was already six years old, there was as yet no sign of a new model. In the spring, in fact, Mazda reintroduced a 1.6-litre version, which effectively sent it back to its roots. This, though, was a 1.6 with a difference, much less powerful than the original (it had 88bhp instead of 115bhp), and with latter-day equipment such as airbags, anti-lock brakes and alloy wheels all stripped out of the specification. The result was a 109mph car, which made it significantly slower than almost every hot (or even 'warm') hatchback on British roads, but which was to sell at £12,995 – £1,500 cheaper than any other MX-5 on the UK market.

McLaren: Although the F1 road-car had always been a technical *tour de force*, its incredibly high price – £634,500 at the end of 1995 – meant that only a very few, very rich, people could ever afford to buy one. To no-one's surprise, therefore, at the end of the year the company announced that it would wind up the production lines at the end of 1997, the (unspoken) likelihood being that only 100 F1s would have been built instead of the 350 mentioned when the car was introduced in the early 1990s.

Mercedes-Benz: The new E-class, revealed in the spring, took over from the previous W124 E-class cars which had been in production for more than a decade, and made a real sensation among all Mercedes-watchers by being the first of this make to have a sloping nose style with elliptical headlamps.

Mechanically, though, the new E-class was conventional Mercedes-Benz, complete with all-round multi-link independent suspension and a wide choice of four, five and six-cylinder petrol and diesel engines.

Larger, stronger and faster than before, this was clearly a range which Mercedes-Benz would be building for up to 10 years, and it was already rumoured that new V6 and V8 engines would be added to the range within two or three years.

The C-class grew even larger in the autumn when the company announced the C230 Kompressor model, this using a slightly enlarged, supercharged (not turbocharged) derivative of the familiar four-cylinder 16-valve twin-cam C-class engine, which produced an easy 193bhp.

This was the first supercharged petrol-engined Mercedes-Benz car to have been put on sale since the 1930s, though the engine itself was originally developed for the short-wheelbase R-class roadster, which was not in fact due to appear until 1996.

At the end of the year the company previewed its own version of what an MPV should look like, but this was a provisional announcement as production was not due to begin until the autumn of 1996.

MG: The mid-engined MGF sportscar, officially previewed in March, but not actually on sale until the autumn, was the most talked-about new British car for some years and it encouraged many people to believe that BMW (through Rover) was serious about reviving and encouraging the old marques which it had acquired in the takeover.

Based on a new platform, the MGF actually used many existing components from the Rover 'parts bin'. The mid-engine/transmission layout used developed versions of the 1.8-litre K-series power packs which would also be seen in the new-generation Rover 400 (announced a few weeks later, but put on sale first), while the all-independent suspension used Hydragas units of the type used in the Rover 100 (ex-Metro).

Body structures were to be produced in Coventry by the Mayflower Group (who had also taken a financial stake in the tooling of the car) at a factory better known as Motor Panels (which already supplied pressings to Rover for the Land Rover Discovery), and first sales were to be concentrated in the UK. Rover had no plans to try to sell this car in the USA, to the disappointment of MG enthusiasts there.

Mitsubishi: Early in the year, the Japanese company unveiled a new front-drive car, the Carisma, which it had developed in concert with Volvo, and was to be built alongside a new Volvo version of the model *(see Volvo, below)* at Volvo's Dutch factory.

The Carisma was initially criticized for having no charisma, but Mitsubishi did not rise to that joke at all. As forecast and expected, it was a conventional transverse-engine/front-drive car of Ford Mondeo/Vauxhall Cavalier size, which Mitsubishi also saw as competing head-on with cars like the Nissan Primera and Toyota Carina. Slightly larger than the Lancer, but smaller than the Galant, it was effectively an additional model range for this maker.

Initially, the Carisma had a choice of 90bhp/1.6-litre and 115bhp/1.8-litre single-cam engines, which were sup-

plied complete from Japan. The only major item to be sourced from Europe was the five-speed manual transmission, which came from Volvo's erstwhile European partner, Renault.

Nissan: A completely new range of Sunny models was announced in Japan in January, the latest cars being smoothly rounded restatements of a familiar (and, to many) technically boring front-wheel-drive scene. The latest cars ran on a longer wheelbase with different-style rear suspension. Although hatchbacks and saloons were both shown at that stage, only hatchbacks figured in the UK line-up before the end of the year. The major surprise came in October when, after a series of puzzling TV adverts, it became clear that these cars would not be called Sunny, but Almera.

Although a new-generation Primera was shown in Japan towards the end of the year, the British Nissan organization showed no signs at this stage of replacing the original-type Primera they were already building at the Sunderland factory.

Peugeot: The long-awaited 406, the replacement for the very successful 405, was launched during the summer. Because it came from such a successful company, it was awaited with great interest in the UK by all the major rivals in this medium-sized category, including Ford and Vauxhall.

The 406 was really a modernized restatement of the 405 theme, with very similar styling and package within a slightly larger envelope. This meant that all models had transversely-mounted engines and front-wheel drive. UK sales of this new four-door saloon began towards the end of the year, the original range including 1.8-litre and 2-litre petrol engines and 1.9 and 2.1-litre turbodiesels.

Porsche: Rounding off the 911's chassis transformation, a new-type Turbo was launched early in the year. Not only was this a more powerful car than ever before – it had a 408bhp 3.6-litre flat-six engine with twin turbocharging, but it was equipped with permanent four-wheel drive of the type which Porsche had been producing since the mid-1980s. There was also a six-speed gearbox (the original 911 Turbos of the mid-1970s had only four speeds), the largest 18in diameter wheel/tyre combination yet seen on a 911 road car, and a large rear aerofoil to provide permanent downforce, so this was immediately seen as a very desirable car indeed. British sales began in the spring, when road tests proved that the 408bhp Turbo had a top speed of 180mph, so the £91,950 price tag looked to be justified.

Whenever Porsche engineers had a spare moment, they seemed to develop a new derivative of the rear-drive 911, and during 1995 there were several of these. In the spring the 911GT2 arrived in the UK at a staggeringly high price of £131,000. This price, though, was explained by the use of a 430bhp/twin-turbo version of the new Turbo's 3.6-litre engine, but in a rear-drive chassis, this being matched by yet more suspension modifications, including the use of 18in diameter wheels, those at the rear having 11in wide rims and 285/35-section tyres! The GT2, in fact, was a limited-production (50-off), more civilized version of the latest works Porsche race-cars, even though it had been subject to a drastic weight-limitation programme and weighed only 2,679lb.

Later in the summer, the 911RS model appeared, this car having a 300bhp/3.75-litre version of the flat-six engine, a twin-level rear spoiler, racing-style front seats, with the rear seats removed completely. In a way this car harked back to the famous early 1970s 911 Carrera RS, which had only had a 210bhp/2.7-litre engine, but this time it was to be available with two-wheel or four-wheel drive.

Yet another body derivative of the evergreen 911 appeared in October, this being the new-type Targa, which had a rollback glass roof allied to permanent body sides and fixed rear quarter-windows.

Both of the front-engined/rear-drive Porsches, the 928 and the 968, were killed-off during the summer. The 928 was merely ancient, while the 968 (only launched in 1992) had been a marketing failure since its introduction, its sales in the previous two years having been down to a trickle.

Range Rover: One year after stating that the original-style model was to continue alongside the new, the company found that sales had dried up, so

production of the earlier model was discontinued before the end of 1995.

Renault: The most important new model this year was the Megane, a much more versatile car than the 19 range it was intended to replace. Right from the start, Renault revealed that there would be hatchback, saloon, coupe, convertible *and* small MPV derivatives. In many ways the Megane was a direct descendant of the 19, using the same type of transverse engine/transmission, front-wheel-drive and suspension layouts, but the platform and style were completely fresh.

Earlier in the year, the company had surprised everyone with the launch of the mid-engined Spider, an open-top two-seater sportscar which was quite out of character with anything the Regie had produced for many years.

Based on an all-new platform and layout, the Spider was stark, and it was made clear that the first batch of cars, to be built at the ex-Alpine factory in Dieppe, would not even have a windscreen or fold-down hood – though these would be added later in the run.

This, then, was a car for the goggles and crash helmet brigade, even when used on the road, and would have a 150bhp/2-litre Clio Williams type of engine/transmission pack. The chassis was an aluminium spaceframe, while the bodyshell (from Alpine) was in glassfibre.

Still expanding the fast-selling Safrane range, Renault introduced a 115bhp/2.5-litre turbodiesel engine option during the summer.

The Clio Williams saga continued. The first series had arrived in 1993, with numbered dashboard plaques and the (unstated) inference that there would be no more. But in 1994 the Williams 2 had arrived – and in 1995 the Williams 3 was introduced, mechanically as before except for the use of anti-lock brakes, an electric sunroof and other extra fittings and a UK price of £15,025. A run of 700 original models and 450 Williams 2s had been sold – but this time the run was to be limited to 300 cars.

Rolls-Royce: During the summer, the long-running Silver Spirit (and its near-identical relatives, the Bentley Brooklands and Turbo R models), were given a styling and equipment makeover. There were no changes to the basic

style, but many detail improvements were incorporated.

Visually, the most noticeable external changes were the use of 16in diameter road wheels on the Rolls-Royce (and 17in on the Bentley Turbo), the fitment of body-colour bumpers, a reduction of radiator size, and the deletion of front quarter-windows.

Inside there were facia/instrument panel changes, including the integration of the console into the panel, while the ancient pushrod engine was given many revisions which resulted in a slight (unspecified) increase in peak power and torque.

Rover: A new-generation 200 range appeared in October, unrelated to the new 400 which had preceded it (*see below*), but with a few links with the past. It fell squarely into the Escort/Astra class.

Using a modified bulkhead and inner front end from the old-style Honda-based 200, the new car had its own new platform, and a choice of rounded three-door or five-door body styles with a positively bewildering choice of engines and trim packs.

The suspension layout was similar to the old-style car's, as was the basic front-engine/front-drive layout. There were six different engines in the line-up, four of them being from the Rover K-series and two L-series 2-litre diesels, making almost a clean break from Honda.

A new-generation 400 range, replacing the original 400s which had been on sale for the previous five years, appeared in March. Based on the latest Honda Civic, though with mostly Rover-based four-cylinder engines and unique skin panels, they received a surprisingly muted reception. Five-door cars went on sale in the spring, with four-door saloon versions following in the autumn.

The rounded style was seen as bland, the cars' character was definitely 'family' rather than sporting, and the prices were quite a lot higher than expected. More than one motoring observer suggested that these were Escort-sized cars trying to sell at Mondeo prices, which might not have been totally fair, but summed up the impression which grew in the market place. At the time, Rover made it clear that this was to be the last of the Honda-based cars.

Ssangyong: The big and capable Musso off-road 4x4 estate car from Korea, which had been previewed as long ago as 1993, finally went on UK sale during 1995, falling into the middle of the hotly contested Land-Rover Discovery/Mitsubishi Shogun/ Isuzu Trooper class.

This was a truly cosmopolitan design, for although it was assembled in South Korea, its styling was by Britain's Ken Greenley, and the engine was a 94bhp five-cylinder Mercedes-Benz diesel.

Suzuki: The Baleno, previewed early in the year and on UK sale from the spring, was yet another new name for British buyers to learn, this being an Escort-sized car from Japan and rather similar to the competing Hyundai Accent, which had recently gone on sale. Bland but efficient, it was originally sold for £8,795 in 97bhp/1.6-litre form, the engine being shared with the latest Vitara (4x4) and Swift models.

Tata: A strangely old-fashioned two-door estate car called the Gurkha arrived late in the year, masquerading as an off-roader, but only being fitted with a front-mounted (Peugeot) engine driving the rear wheels.

Actually a conversion of a Loadbeta van, with generous ground clearance and dated mechanicals, it had a well-equipped cockpit, but otherwise had little going for it.

Toyota: The Carina E pushed further into Mondeo and fleet-sales territory with a 103bhp/1.8-litre version of the twin-cam engine, and at the same time there were price cuts across the range.

Only a year after the original short-wheelbase RAV-4 4x4 model had been introduced, the longer-wheelbase five-door version was added to the range.

The long-running Land Cruiser 4x4 was facelifted in the spring with a new and more rounded nose, an updated interior package and a more powerful 202bhp/4.2-litre six-cylinder petrol engine.

TVR: The Cerbera 2+2 sports coupe, much modified and redeveloped since it had originally been previewed in 1993, was finally ready to go on limited UK sale at the end of 1995. The production-standard car was no longer a stretched Chimaera (which the prototype had been), but a new TVR in its own right. Much of the delay had been caused by lengthy development and production problems with the new TVR-designed AJP8 engine.

Although based on the same basic multi-tubular backbone chassis design as used for other TVRs, the Cerbera had a 101in wheelbase, allowing a more spacious cabin than any previous model. The AJP engine was a 350bhp/ 4.2-litre unit with single-overhead-cam cylinder heads, and TVR claimed a top speed of around 170mph.

At first this looked rather unlikely, but too many pundits had underestimated Peter Wheeler and his sportscar-making company before, so more humble pie had to be eaten at the end of the year when the first cars reached their customers at the considerable price of £37,000.

Vauxhall: Previewed during the summer, but not on sale until late autumn, the Vectra, engineered by Opel, was effectively a fourth-generation Cavalier. GM, however, was continuing its policy of rationalizing model names with Opel.

Compared with the last of the Cavaliers, the Vectra was really more of the same – slightly more rounded, slightly more roomy, but still available as a typically wide-ranging Mondeo-competitor in five-door hatchback form.

No fewer than six different engines were listed (though not all were immediately available), ranging from a 74bhp/1.6-litre to a 168bhp/2.5-litre V6, with an 81bhp turbodiesel included. All but the diesel and the base 1.6-litre used four-valve/twin-cam cylinder heads, though there was no sign of turbocharging or four-wheel-drive transmissions, as seen on the departing Cavalier, neither of which had sold well.

The Isuzu-based Frontera 4x4 was given a mid-life mechanical facelift during the spring. There was a new type of chassis, complete with multi-link rear suspension, and a fresh range of engines, including an Opel-derived 136bhp/2.2-litre petrol and an Isuzu 111bhp/2.8-litre diesel.

Volkswagen: The new Sharan MPV was almost identical to the Ford Galaxy MPV except for using its own 115bhp/2-litre petrol engine instead of the Ford unit (*see the Ford entry*). UK deliveries began during the summer.

The company lost patience with the slow-selling Corrado coupe and decided to drop it in mid-summer, a full two years before any replacement VW sports coupe could possibly be ready. The last run of UK-market Corrados, dubbed Corrado Storm, had the VR6 engine and a very high specification. In seven years, a total of about 10,000 Corrados had been sold on the UK market.

Volvo: Months after the introduction of the Dutch-built Mitsubishi Carisma, the closely-related Volvo, originally called S4 (saloon) and F4 (estate car), but later renamed S40 and V40 after trademark disputes with Audi, also made its appearance. With 1.8 and 2-litre engines, and an overall length of 176in, it fell squarely into the hotly contested European medium-size family/business category.

The two cars shared the same platform, basic front-wheel-drive layout and suspensions, though Volvo were at pains to point out that their version had different skin styling and a different line-up of engines.

The S40/V40 types, in fact, used four-cylinder twin-cam petrol engines developed from the same basic design as five and six-cylinder units already to be found in larger Volvos, while the diesel engine was from Volvo's long-time partner Renault.

Prior to the launch of the new Mitsubishi-linked medium-sized Volvos, the company began phasing out the existing 440/460/480 cars. First to go was the three-door sporting hatchback 480 models, a move marked by the launch of a limited-production Celebration version.

The limited-production 850 T-5R was dropped in the autumn, only to be replaced by the 250bhp 850-R, which was intended to become a mainstream model. Another new 850 derivative, also due for sale in the UK in 1996, was the 850 TDi, which used a transversely-mounted five-cylinder 140bhp/2.5-litre diesel engine.

Industrial developments

After much internal debate – a good deal of it leaked to the press – Jaguar (which is to say Ford) finalized its forthcoming X200 project. This new-generation series, which was expected to appear in 1998, was to be built in a newly-developed factory in the grounds of the company's existing body/paint plant at Castle Bromwich.

To historians, of course, this was the ex-Spitfire aircraft plant, ex-Fisher & Ludlow and ex-BMC bodyshell production factory, which was currently producing shells for the XJ6 and XJS models. By the time Ford/Jaguar had finished the redevelopment, a brand new assembly plant would take shape over the ground once occupied by the old buildings.

In the UK, Lamborghini's fortunes took another turn in what had always been a complex history. In January, the UK concession was awarded to Porsche Cars Great Britain. Previously, Lamborghini had always been represented by small concerns, with no dealer network, but there was real industrial muscle behind this latest move.

Proving that the Rocket project was more than a rich man's toy, the Light Car Company was taken over in April by a new group of investors. Over 30 Rockets had been sold in the first three years, and the new group had plans to increase that modest rate of sales.

The reborn Bugatti concern of Italy finally collapsed during the year, colossally in debt, and for a time this also threatened to drag down Lotus.

Bugatti, it seemed, had always been living on borrowed money (and unpaid bills), and it had only been a matter of time before the laws of economics caught up with the image. With sales of the EB110 supercar falling way behind expectations, there had been no chance of putting the EB112 into production.

The future of Lotus, however, seemed to be secure, for although the parent company was wound up, a related company, Bugatti Luxembourg, carried on – and Lotus was a subsidiary of that offshoot. For the time being, at least, Lotus would carry on and remain profitable because of the large list of clients tapping into its engineering expertise, although there were destined to be more storm clouds ahead...

Technical developments

The most intriguing new development of the year was Lotus' new approach to chassis design with the new Elise sportscar. To keep the weight down, the company elected to use an aluminium monocoque, not welded or riveted, but bonded together. This process used Ciba-Giegy technology, the bonding being developed by Hydro Aluminium Automotive in Denmark (a country which had no indigenous motor industry of its own).

On the Elise, the tub looked slightly reminiscent of that of a 1970s racing sportscar, stretched the technique of aluminium extrusions to its limit and was claimed to provide a very stiff and very light assembly. Lotus conceded that this type of chassis could only be used when production rates were limited.

Licence fees abolished for 25-year-old cars

To end on a happy note, although the British Government had spent several years threatening to impose a 'tax on possession' in the form of Vehicle Excise Duties on all cars, whether they were on the road or laid up for restoration, in November 1995 there was a complete and welcome reversal.

Instead, in his November Budget statement, the Chancellor announced that henceforth all cars more than 25 years old (which, in that particular case, meant built before the end of 1969) could be used on the roads without paying any Excise Duty at all. Such cars were to display a nil-value tax disc.

The new quarter-century ruling was to roll forward with every year which passed, so from January 1, 1996 all pre-1971 cars would qualify. This was thought to benefit about 150,000 owners of classic cars.

APPENDIX A

Price comparisons – now and then

No-one needs to be told that prices have been rising continuously since 1945. However, when comparing car prices 'then' with 'now' it helps to know how much prices in general have changed over the last 50 years.

Thanks to the Central Statistical Office, I have been able to assemble the following table *which has been reformulated, and is specific to this book.* Taking January 1946 as my base point (no accurate figure is available for 1945), it shows how the Retail Price Index has changed over the years:

Calendar year (1946 = 100)	Retail Price Index	Calendar year (1946 = 100)	Retail Price Index
1946	100	1971	276
1947	107	1972	295
1948	115	1973	322
1949	119	1974	374
1950	121	1975	465
1951	133	1976	542
1952	140	1977	627
1953	143	1978	680
1954	146	1979	771
1955	151	1980	909
1956	158	1981	1,017
1957	163	1982	1,105
1958	168	1983	1,156
1959	170	1984	1,213
1960	172	1985	1,287
1961	176	1986	1,331
1962	183	1987	1,386
1963	186	1988	1,454
1964	192	1989	1,567
1965	201	1990	1,716
1966	209	1991	1,816
1967	215	1992	1,884
1968	225	1993	1,914
1969	237	1994	1,960
1970	252	1995	2,008

Thus, in 1994/95, the Retail Price Index was at approximately 20 times its 1946 level and eight times the level it had been in 1970. Accordingly, if one can make any valid comparisons, a 1970 Ford Escort 1100 (£807 at the end of the year) cost the equivalent of about £6,500 in the mid-1990s. Similarly, the £3,123 Jaguar E-type V12 of 1971 would cost about £23,000 in 1995 after applying the Retail Price Index. One has to ask the question: Have relative values – prices compared with incomes – changed out of all proportion?

APPENDIX B

CARS in the UK: 1971 to 1995
Specifications and performance data

NOTES:

i) Cars listed are those which were officially sold in the UK, either by their manufacturers, or by official importers. Private imports, test cars, and (in a few cases) British models only sold overseas are not listed.

ii) With some limited-production models, many items of optional equipment were available. In those cases I have produced what was a 'typical specification'.

iii) Production figures are totals, not UK deliveries. In some cases, where models were introduced pre-World War Two, these figures include prewar production too. Except where stated, these figures come from factory sources.

In some cases accurate figures are not available and are quoted as 'Est' (for estimated). N/A = not available. Where a car is in production, with figures still building up, 'In prod' is quoted.

iv) 'Years built' refers to the production life of these cars, not necessarily the years in which they were sold in the UK. For example, a foreign car built from 1975–1984 may have been sold in the UK for only two of those years. For cars still in production when this book is published, dates are quoted like this: 1992–Date.

v) Body styles are those officially marketed by the factory. Some types were not available in the UK.

vi) Accepted engine positions are: F – ahead of the driving seat; M – behind the driving seat, but ahead of the rear wheels; R – behind the line of the rear wheels. In some cases engine tunes changed during the production run. Where possible, these are summarized in the tables.

vii) Quoted engine sizes and tunes are for such cars sold in the UK. Other sizes, types and power outputs which may have been available in other markets are not quoted.

viii) Prices quoted are total retail figures for the cheapest original version, including all purchase or VAT/Special Car Taxes, and are

those listed when the car first went on sale in the UK. They do not include engine or transmission options, or other optional extras.

ix) Performance figures, where available, were those recorded by independent testers. In the tables these are quoted on the same line as the appropriate engine specification. Where such tests have not been found, factory-recorded figures are sometimes shown instead.

Abbreviations:

Body styles

Conv	Drophead/Convertible/Cabriolet
Cpe	Coupe
Est	Estate car
Htch	Hatchback
Limo	Limousine and Landaulette
Sal	Saloon
Spl	Special coachwork
Spts	Sportscar
Targa	Removable roof panels
Ute	Utility (especially 4x4s, etc)

Engine and transmission

F/F	Front-engine/front-wheel drive
F/R	Front-engine/rear-wheel drive
F/4	Front-engine/four-wheel drive
R/R	Rear-engine/rear-wheel drive
M/R	Mid-engine/rear-wheel drive
M/4	Mid-engine/four-wheel drive
R/4	Rear-engine/four-wheel drive
IL	In-line engine
(Tr)	Transversely mounted
V	Vee-engine
HO	Horizontally-opposed engine
Rot	Rotary (Wankel) engine
AirC	Air-cooled
SV	Side-valve
IOEV	Overhead inlet/side exhaust valve
OHC	Single overhead camshaft per head
2OHC	Twin overhead camshaft per head
OHV	Overhead valves, pushrod-operated
2-Str	Two-stroke engine
Diesel	Diesel
Auto	Automatic transmission
SemiAuto	Semi-automatic
O/D	Overdrive
PreS	Preselector

Chassis

I	Independent
DD	De Dion
Beam	Beam axle
C	Coil springs
TrL	Transverse leaf spring
1/4E	Quarter-elliptic leaf spring
1/2E	Half (semi)-elliptic leaf spring
Tor	Torsion bar
Air	High-pressure air suspension
HP	Hydro-pneumatic (and Oleopneumatic) suspension
Rubber	Rubber springs
HydroL	Hydrolastic suspension
HydraG	Hydragas suspension
Disc	Disc brakes
Drum	Drum brakes
R & P	Rack-and-pinion steering
Worm	All other steering types
N/A	Not available/not known
N/Q	Not quoted by manufacturer

Cars from North America:

Except in isolated cases, it has not been practical to give details of North American cars price-listed in the UK since 1945. In many cases cars were listed but not stocked, the choice of engine, transmission and body options was enormous, and deliveries were only made against special orders. Cars seen at British Motor Shows, and subsequently listed, were often sold only in ones and twos – and then not always in the specification listed in British magazines at the time!

Many North American cars seen on British roads were originally imported for use by North American government departments, businesses, individuals and military service personnel. Although such cars were often registered in the UK, then sold on to British buyers in due course, in many cases these models and derivatives were not even price-listed as being for sale in the UK.

Individual specifications and performance details of North American cars tested by *Autocar*, *Autocar & Motor*, and *Motor* since the import ban was lifted in 1953 have been included and marked with stars: **

Make and model	Production Figures	Years Built	Body Styles	Mechanical Layout	Engine Make (if not own)	Capacity/ (cc)/Layout/ Valves	BHP/ rpm	Torque (lb.ft)/rpm	Transmission gearbox/automatic transmission
AC									
428	81	1965–1973	Cpe Conv	F/R	Ford-USA	7014/V8/ OHV	345/4600	462/2800	-/Auto
3000ME	82	1979–1984	Cpe	M(Tr)/R	Ford-UK	2994/V6/ OHV	138/5000	174/3000	5-spd/-
Cobra Mk IV	In prod	1983–1996	Spts	F/R	Ford-USA	4948/V8/ OHV	225/4200	300/3200	5-spd/-
Ace	In prod	1994–1996	Spts	F/R	Ford-USA	4942/V8/ OHV	260/5250	320/3250	5-spd/Auto
Alfa Romeo									
Giulia saloons	836,323 (All Giulias)	1962–1974	Sal	F/R	—	1290/4IL/ 2OHC	82/6000 89/6000	77/4900 101/3200	5-spd/-
						1570/4IL/ 2OHC	92/6200 95/5500 98/5500 102/5500 112/6500	108/3700 100/4400 96/2900 105/4400 112/4200	5-spd/- 5-spd/-
Sprint GT/ GTV family	210,495	1963–1975	Cpe	F/R	—	1290/4IL/ 2OHC	89/6000 96/6000	101/3200 101/3200	5-spd/- 5-spd/-
						1570/4IL/ 2OHC	106/1000 109/6000 115/6000	103/3000 103/2800 119/5500	5-spd/- 5-spd/- 5-spd/-
						1779/4IL/ 2OHC	122/5500	137/2900	5-spd/-
						1962/4IL/ 2OHC	132/5500	134/3000	5-spd/-
Duetto/1750/ 2000 Spider	N/A	1966–1993	Spts	F/R	—	1290/4IL/ 2OHC	89/6000	101/3200	5-spd/-
						1570/4IL/ 2OHC	109/6000	103/2800	5-spd/-
						1779/4IL/ 2OHC	122/5500	137/2900	5-spd/-
						1962/4IL/ 2OHC	115/5500 133/5500 120/5800	119/3000 134/3000 118/4200	5-spd/Auto 5-spd/- 5-spd/-
1750 saloon	101,883	1967–1972	Sal	F/R	—	1779/4IL/ 2OHC	122/5500	139/3000	5-spd/-
2000 saloon	89,840	1970–1977	Sal	F/R	—	1962/4IL/ 2OHC/	131/5500	134/3000	5-spd/-
Montreal	3,925	1970–1977	Cpe	F/R	—	2593/V8/ 2OHC	200/6500	173/4750	5-spd/-
Alfetta	424,739	1972–1984	Sal	F/R	—	1570/4IL/ 2OHC	108/5600	105/4300	5-spd/-
						1779/4IL/ 2OHC	122/5500	123/4400	5-spd/-
						1962/4IL/ 2OHC	122/5300 130/5400	129/4000 131/4000	5-spd/- 5-spd/-
Alfetta GT/ GTV/GTV6	279,821	1976–1987	Cpe			1570/4IL/ 2OHC	108/5600	105/4300	5-spd/-
						1779/4IL/ 2OHC	122/5500	123/4400	5-spd/-
						1962/4IL/ 2OHC	130/5300 122/5300	131/4000 129/4000	5-spd/- 5-spd/-
						2492/V6/ OHC	160/6000	157/4000	5-spd/-
Giulietta	255,762	1977-1985	Sal	F/R	—	1570/4IL/ 2OHC	109/5600	105/4300	5-spd/-
						1779/4IL/ 2OHC	122/5300	123/4000	5-spd/-
						1962/4IL/ 2OHC	130/5400	131/4000	5-spd/-
Alfasud	906,734	1972–1984	Sal Htch Est	F/F	—	1186/4HO/ OHV	63/6000 68/6000	71/3500 67/3200	4-spd/5-spd/- 5-spd/-
						1286/4HO/ OHC	68/6000 76/6000	67/3200 76/3500	5-spd/- 5-spd/-
						1350/4HO/ OHC	79/6000	81/3500	5-spd/-
						1490/4HO/ OHC	84/6000 95/6000 105/6000	98/3500 96/4000 98/4000	5-spd/- 5-spd/-
Alfasud Sprint	96,450	1977–1990	Spts Cpe	F/F	—	1286/4HO/ OHC	76/6000	76/3500	5-spd/-
						1490/4HO/ OHC	85/6000 95/6000	98/3500 96/4000	5-spd/- 5-spd/-

Suspension Front	Rear	Steering	Brakes (Front/rear)	Wheels/Tyres	Length (in)	Weight (lb,unladen)	Top speed (mph)	0–60mph (sec)	Standing 1/4-mile (sec)	UK Total Price (£: at Launch)
IC	IC	R & P	Disc/Disc	205-15	176	3115	139	5.9	14.4	£4250
IC	IC	R & P	Disc/disc	195/60-14	157	2483	120	8.5	16.3	£12,432
IC	IC	R & P	Disc/disc	225/50-16/ 255/50-16	162	2620	135	5.3	N/A	£25,000
IC	IC	R & P	Disc/disc	225/50-16 235/50-16/	174	3175	144 (Claimed)	5.9	N/A	£56,250
IC	BeamC	Worm	Disc/disc	155-15	163	2152	97	15.3	19.8	£1225
IC	BeamC	Worm	Disc/disc	155-15	163	2240	106	13.1	18.9	£1659
IC	BeamC	Worm	Disc/disc	155-15	163	2307	108	11.3	18.3	£1599
IC	BeamC	Worm	Disc/disc	155-15	161	2046	102	13.2	19.1	£1749
IC	BeamC	Worm	Disc/disc	155-15	161	2117	102	13.8	19.6	£1649
IC	BeamC	Worm	Disc/disc	155-15	161	2090	112	10.6	N/A	£1650
IC	BeamC	Worm	Disc/disc	155-15	161	2286	113	11.1	17.7	£1950
IC	BeamC	Worm	Disc/disc	165-14	161	2180	115 (Est)	N/A	N/A	£2128
IC	BeamC	Worm	Disc/disc	165-14	161	2292	116	11.2	18.0	£2248
IC	BeamC	Worm	Disc/disc	165-14	161	2288	120	9.2	16.4	£2439
IC	BeamC	Worm	Disc/disc	155-15 or 165-14	167, later 162 from 1970	2181	106 (Claimed)	N/A	N/A	£1749
IC	BeamC	Worm	Disc/disc	155-15	167	2195	111	11.2	17.7	£1895
IC	BeamC	Worm	Disc/disc	165-14	167, later 162 from 1970	2292	116	9.2	17.1	£2199
IC	BeamC	Worm	Disc/disc	165-14 to 195/60-15	162	2291/ 2445	116	8.8	17.1	£2439
IC	BeamC	Worm	Disc/disc	165-14	162	2245	116	9.8	17.1	
IC	BeamC	Worm	Disc/disc	195/60-15	167	2444	118 (Est)	9.4	N/A	£15,950
IC	BeamC	Worm	Disc/disc	165-14	173	2447	116	10.8	17.5	£1898
IC	BeamC	Worm	Disc/disc	165-14	173	2447	113	9.1	17.1	£2026
IC	BeamC	Worm	Disc/disc	195-14	156	2794	137	7.6	15.4	£5077
ITor	DDC	R & P	Disc/disc	165-14	168	2293	103	11.5	18.0	£2649
ITor	DDC	R & P	Disc/disc	165-14	168	2436	110	10.8	17.7	£2449
ITor	DDC	R & P	Disc/disc	165-14	173	2512	108	10.1	17.6	£4800
ITor	DDC	R & P	Disc/disc	185/70-14	173	2513	113	9.6	17.2	£6865
ITor	DDC	R & P	Disc/disc	185/70-14	165	2310	112 (Claimed)	N/A	N/A	£3799
ITor	DDC	R & P	Disc/disc	185/70-14	165	2393	117	9.4	17.0	£3498
ITor	DDC	R & P	Disc/disc	185/70-14	165	2423	120	8.7	16.5	£4799
ITor	DDC	R & P	Disc/disc	185/70-14	165	2408	118	9.5	17.0	£5020
ITor	DDC	R & P	Disc/disc	195/60-15	165	2668	130	8.8	16.7	£9495
ITor	DDC	R & P	Disc/disc	185/70-13	166	2359	105	10.5	17.6	£4499
ITor	DDC	R & P	Disc/disc	185/70-13	166	2520	107	10.6	17.5	£5165
ITor	DDC	R & P	Disc/disc	185/65-14	166	2486	112	9.5	16.8	£5800
IC	BeamC	R & P	Disc/disc	145-13	153	1830	92	14.1	19.5	£1399
IC	BeamC	R & P	Disc/disc	145-13	153	1870	99	12.9	19.1	£1718
IC	BeamC	R & P	Disc/disc	145-13	153	1842	98	12.8	N/A	£2999
IC	BeamC	R & P	Disc/drum	165/70-13	153	1888	101	11.8	18.4	£3000
IC	BeamC	R & P	Disc/disc	165/70-13	157	2025	98	12.2	18.2	£4100
IC	BeamC	R & P	Disc/disc	165/70-13	154	1915	102	11.6	18.5	£3499
IC	BeamC	R & P	Disc/disc	165/70-13	157	1967	107	9.9	17.4	£5550
IC	BeamC	R & P	Disc/disc	165/70-13	155	1907	99	13.1	19.2	£3999
IC	BeamC	R & P	Disc/drum	165/70-13	158	2040	103	11.2	18.6	£4299
IC	BeamC	R & P	Disc/drum	165/70-13	158	2040	107	10.0	16.9	£5165

Make and model	Production Figures	Years Built	Body Styles	Mechanical Layout	Engine Make (if not own)	Capacity/(cc)/Layout/Valves	BHP/rpm	Torque (lb.ft)/rpm	Transmission gearbox/automatic transmission
							105/6000	98/4000	5-spd/-
						1712/4HO/OHC	118/5800	108/3500	5-spd/-
33	196,300	1983–1994	Htch	F/F	—	1350/4HO/OHC	79/6000	82/3500	5-spd/-
							86/5800	87/4000	5-spd/-
						1490/4HO/OHC	85/6000	98/3500	5-spd/-
							95/5750	96/4000	5-spd/-
							105/6000	100/4500	5-spd/-
						1712/4HO/OHC	118/5800	109/3500	5-spd/-
				F/F (and F4)		1712/4HO/2OHC	137/6500	119/4600	5-spd/-
33 Sport-wagon	64,120	1985–1994	Est	F/4	—	1490/4HO/OHC	95/5750	96/4000	5-spd/-
							105/6000	100/4500	5-spd/-
				F/F	—	1712/4HO/OHC	118/5800	108/3500	5-spd/-
							137/6500	118/4600	5-spd/-
Arna	61,750	1983–1986	Htch	F/F	—	1186/4HO/OHC	68/6000	66/3200	5-spd/-
						1350/4HO/OHC	71/5800	77/3000	5-spd/-
						1490/4HO/OHC	95/5800	96/4000	5-spd/-
90	N/A	1984–1987	Sal	F/R	—	2492/V6/OHC	156/5600	155/4000	5-spd/Auto
75	187,300	1985–1992	Sal	F/R	—	1779/4IL/2OHC	120/5300	123/4000	5-spd/-
						1962/4IL/2OHC	148/5800	137/4700	5-spd/-
						2492/V6/OHC	156/5600	155/4000	5-spd/Auto
						2959/V6/OHC	188/5800	184/4000	5-spd/-
							192/5600	181/3000	5-spd/-
Alfa 6	81,750	1980–1985	Sal	F/R	—	2492/V6/OHC	160/5800	162/4000	5-spd/Auto
164	In prod	1987–Date	Sal	F/F	—	1962/4IL/2OHC	148/5800	137/4000	5-spd/-
						1995/4IL/2OHC	146/5800	140/5000	5-spd/-
						2959/V6/OHC	192/5600	181/3000	5-spd/Auto
							200/5800	198/4400	5-spd/Auto
						2959/V6/2OHC	210/6300	202/5000	5-spd/Auto
							230/6300	210/5000	5-spd/-
SZ/RZ	1000/800	1989–1993	Spts Cpe Spts	F/R	—	2959/V6/OHC	210/6200	181/4500	5-spd/-
155	In prod	1992–Date	Sal	F/F	—	1773/4IL/2OHC	126/6000	121/5000	5-spd/-
						1779/4IL/2OHC	129/6000	122/5000	5-spd/-
						1962/4IL/2OHC	143/6000	138/5000	5-spd/-
						1970/4IL/2OHC	150/6200	138/4000	5-spd/-
						2492/V6/OHC	166/5800	161/4500	5-spd/Auto
							163/5800	159/4500	5-spd/Auto
				F/4	—	1995/4IL/2OHC	190/6000	219/2500	5-spd/-
145	In prod	1994–Date	Htch	F/F	—	1596/4HO OHC	103/6000	99/4500	5-spd/-
						1712/4HO/2OHC	129/6500	109/4300	5-spd/-
						1970/4IL/2OHC	150/6200	138/4000	5-spd/-
146	In prod	1995–Date	Htch	F/F	—	1596/4HO/OHC	103/6000	99/4500	5-spd/-
						1712/4HO/2OHC	129/6500	109/4300	5-spd/-
						1970/4IL/2OHC	150/6200	137/4000	5-spd/-
Spider/GTV	In prod	1995–Date	Spts Cpe Spts	F(Tr)/F	—	1970/4IL/2OHC	150/6200	137/4000	5-spd/-

Alpine-Renault

Make and model	Production Figures	Years Built	Body Styles	Mechanical Layout	Engine Make (if not own)	Capacity/(cc)/Layout/Valves	BHP/rpm	Torque (lb.ft)/rpm	Transmission gearbox/automatic transmission
A310	2,334	1971–1976	Spts Cpe	R/R	Renault	1605/4IL/OHV	140/6250	109/5000	5-spd/-

For later models, see **Renault**

Suspension Front	Rear	Steering	Brakes (Front/rear)	Wheels/ Tyres	Length (in)	Weight (lb, unladen)	Top speed (mph)	0–60mph (sec)	Standing ¼-mile (sec)	UK Total Price (£: at Launch)
IC	BeamC	R & P	Disc/disc	190/55-340	158	2148	107	10.8	18.0	£7145
IC	BeamC	R & P	Disc/drum	185/60-14	158	2148	114	9.5	17.6	£8999
IC	BeamC	R & P	Disc/drum	165/70-13	158	1962	100 (Est)	N/A	N/A	£5690
IC	BeamC	R & P	Disc/drum	165/70-13	158	2005	105	11.7	18.0	£5995
IC	BeamC	R & P	Disc/drum	165/70-13	158	2008	105	10.8	18.1	£6000
IC	BeamC	R & P	Disc/drum	165/70-13	158	2008	105	10.8	18.0	£6590
IC	BeamC	R & P	Disc/drum	195/55-340	158	2038	118	9.8	17.2	£6995
IC	BeamC	R & P	Disc/drum	185/60-14	158	2060	117	9.1	16.5	£8999
IC	BeamC	R & P	Disc/disc	185/60-14	160	2138/2359	128	8.9	16.7	£11,790
IC	BeamC	R & P	Disc/disc	175/70-13	163	2135	110	10.9	18.0	£7999
IC	BeamC	R & P	Disc/disc	175/70-13	163	2135	112 (Est)	N/A	N/A	
IC	BeamC	R & P	Disc/drum	185/60-14	165	2155	115	9.5	17.5	£9969
IC	BeamC	R & P	Disc/drum	185/60-14	165	2237	126 (Est)	N/A	N/A	£13,448
IC	IC	R & P	Disc/drum	175/70-13	157	1865	95 (Est)	N/A	N/A	£4350
IC	IC	R & P	Disc/drum	165/70-13	157	1874	98	13.1	19.3	£4620
IC	IC	R & P	Disc/drum	175/70-13	157	1863	108	10.2	17.5	£5590
ITor	DDC	R & P	Disc/disc	195/60-15	173	2745	126	9.0	16.8	£10,850
ITor	DDC	R & P	Disc/disc	185/65-14	170	2519	116	10.3	17.5	£8949
ITor	DDC	R & P	Disc/disc	195/60-14	170	2519	124	9.3	16.3	£11,899
ITor	DDC	R & P	Disc/disc	195/60-14	170	2697	130	8.9	16.7	£11,649
ITor	DDC	R & P	Disc/disc	195/60-14	170	2668	137	7.5	16.1	£15,299
ITor	DDC	R & P	Disc/disc	195/60-14	170	2668	137 (Est)	N/A	N/A	£17,315
ITor	DDC	R & P	Disc/disc	195/70-14	184	3241	115 (Auto)	11.4	18.2	£11,900
IC	IC	R & P	Disc/disc	195/60-15	179	2940	126	9.5	17.7	£17,560
IC	IC	R & P	Disc/disc	195/65-15	179	3087	130 (Claimed)	9.9	N/A	£16,850
IC	IC	R & P	Disc/disc	205/55-15	179	3005	138	7.9	16.2	£20,250
IC	IC	R & P	Disc/disc	195/65-15	179	3150	143	7.8	16.4	£25,965
IC	IC	R & P	Disc/disc	195/65-15	179	3483	147	7.4	15.8	£25,100
IC	IC	R & P	Disc/disc	205/55-16	179	3374	153 (Claimed)	7.7	N/A	£28,100
IC	DDC	R & P	Disc/disc	205/55-16/ 225/55-16	160	2778	153	6.9	N/A	£40,000
IC	IC	R & P	Disc/disc	205/50-15	175	2844	123	10.3	17.9	£14,140
IC	IC	R & P	Disc/disc	185/60-14	175	2651	123	10.3	17.9	£13,580
IC	IC	R & P	Disc/disc	195/60-14	175	2673	124	9.3	17.1	£15,100
IC	IC	R & P	Disc/disc	205/50-15	175	2863	125	8.2	N/A	£15,990
IC	IC	R & P	Disc/disc	195/55-15	175	2838	131	8.4	16.6	£19,050
IC	IC	R & P	Disc/disc	205/50-15	175	3021	133 (Claimed)	8.4	N/A	£17,765
IC	IC	R & P	Disc/disc	205/50-15	175	3215	139	6.7	15.2	£21,024
IC	IC	R & P	Disc/drum	175/65-14	161	2508	110	11.5	18.3	£10,995
IC	IC	R & P	Disc/disc	185/60-14	161	2624	124 (Claimed)	9.8	N/A	£12,950
IC	IC	R & P	Disc/disc	195/55-15	161	2734	129 (Claimed)	8.0	N/A	£14,884
IC	IC	R & P	Disc/drum	175/65-14	168	2681	114	11.4	18.2	£11,195
IC	IC	R & P	Disc/disc	185/60-14	168	2701	126	10.2	N/A	£13,655
IC	IC	R & P	Disc/disc	195/55-15	168	2811	130 (Claimed)	8.5	N/A	£15,392
IC	IC	R & P	Disc/disc	195/60-15	169	2982	122	9.4	17.3	£19,950
IC	IC	R & P	Disc/disc	165-13/ 185-13	165	2075	130	8.6	17.3	£4300

Make and model	Production Figures	Years Built	Body Styles	Mechanical Layout	Engine Make (if not own)	Capacity/(cc)/Layout/Valves	BHP/rpm	Torque (lb.ft)/rpm	Transmission gearbox/automatic transmission
American Motors									
Pacer **		1976 model	Cpe	F/R	—	4229/6IL/ OHV	110/3500	195/2000	Auto
ARO									
240/Ranger	N/A	1978–Date	Ute	F/4	Mitsubishi	2530/4IL/ OHV Diesel	30/3600	39/2200	4-spd/-
					Peugeot	2112/4IL/ OHV Diesel	59/4500	86/2500	4-spd/-
Asia									
Rocsta	In prod	1986–Date	Ute	F/4	Kia	1789/4IL/ OHC	77/5500	98/3000	5-spd/-
						2184/4IL/ OHV Diesel	61/4050	93/2500	5-spd/-
Aston Martin									
DBS-6	899	1967–1973	Sal Est	F/R	—	3995/6IL/ 2OHC	282/5500 325/5500	288/3850 290/4500	5-spd/Auto 5-spd/Auto
DBS-V8/ AM V-8/ Vantage	2,666	1969–1989	Sal Conv	F/R	—	5340/V8/ 2OHC	N/Q N/Q (Vtge)	N/Q N/Q	5-spd/Auto 5-spd/-
Volante/ Vantage Volante	562	1977–1989	Conv	F/R	—	5340/V8/ 2OHC	N/Q 406/6200	N/Q 390/5000	5-spd/Auto 5-spd/Auto
Lagonda	7	1974–1976	Sal	F/R	—	5340/V8/ 2OHC	N/Q	N/Q	5-spd/Auto
Lagonda	645	1977–1990	Sal	F/R	—	5340/V8/ 2OHC	280/5000 300/5000	N/Q N/Q	Auto/- Auto/-
Zagato Cpe/Conv	90	1986–1989	Cpe Conv	F/R	—	5340/V8/ 2OHC	432/6000 305/5000	395/5100 320/4000	5-spd/- 5-spd/-
Virage/ Volante	In prod	1988–Date	Cpe Est Conv	F/R	—	5340/V8/ 2OHC 6347/V8/ 2OHC	330/6000 456/6000	340/3700 460/4000	5-spd/Auto 5-spd/Auto
Vantage	In prod	1992–Date	Cpe	F/R	—	5340/V8/ 2OHC	550/6500	550/4000	6-spd/-
DB7	In prod	1994–Date	Cpe	F/R	Jaguar	3239/6IL/ 2OHC	335/5750	361/3000	5-spd/Auto
Audi									
60/70/80/90	416,852	1965–1972	Sal Est	F/F	—	1496/4IL/ OHV	55/4750	83/2500	4-spd/-
						1696/4IL/ OHV	72/5000 80/5000	94/2800 98/3000	4-spd/- 4-spd/-
						1760/4IL/ OHV	90/5200	108/3000	4-spd/-
100	796,787	1968–1976	Sal Est	F/F	—	1760/4IL/ OHV	100/5500	111/3200	4-spd/Auto
						1871/4IL/ OHV	115/5500	117/4000	4-spd/Auto
100 Coupe S	30,687	1969–1976	Cpe	F/F	—	1871/4IL/ OHV	115/5500	117/4000	4-spd/Auto
100	1,609,929	1976–1982	Sal	F/F	—	1984/4IL/ OHC	115/5500	116/3500	4-spd/Auto
						2144/5IL/ OHC	115/5500 136/5700	122/4000 134/4200	4-spd/Auto 4-spd/Auto
						1986/5IL/ OHC Diesel	70/4800	90/2800	5-spd/-
100 Avant	132,333	1977–1982	Est	F/F	—	1588/4IL/ OHC	85/5600	92/3200	4-spd/Auto
						2144/5IL/ OHC	115/5500	122/4000	4-spd/Auto
						1986/5IL/ OHC Diesel	70/4800	91/3000	4-spd/-
80	939,931	1972–1978	Sal Est	F/F	—	1296/4IL/ OHC	60/5500	68/2500	4-spd/-
						1470/4IL/ OHC	75/5800 85/5800	83/3500 89/2500	4-spd/- 4-spd/-
						1588/4IL/ OHC	100/6000 110/6100	97/4000 103/5000	4-spd/- 4-spd/-
80	3,100,000 (Est)	1978–1986	Sal	F/F	—	1588/4IL/ OHC	85/5600 110/6100	88/3200 103/5000	4-spd/- 5-spd/-
						1595/4IL/ OHC	75/5000	92/2500	5-spd/Auto
						1781/4IL/	90/5200	107/3300	5-spd/-

Suspension Front	Rear	Steering	Brakes (Front/rear)	Wheels/ Tyres	Length (in)	Weight (lb, unladen)	Top speed (mph)	0–60mph (sec)	Standing 1/4-mile (sec)	UK Total Price (£: at Launch)
IC	Beam1/2E	Worm	Disc/drum	185-14	172	3455	96	14.8	19.8	£5041
IC	Beam1/2E	Worm	Drum/drum	6.50-16	159	3693	68 (Claimed)	N/A	N/A	£5582
IC	Beam1/2E	Worm	Drum/drum	6.50-16	159	3693	68 (Claimed)	N/A	N/A	£5582
Beam1/2E	Beam1/2E	Worm	Disc/drum	215/75-15	141	3748	70 (Claimed)	N/A	N/A	£10,300
Beam1/2E	Beam1/2E	Worm	Disc/drum	217/75-15	141	3748	70 (Claimed)	36.5	N/A	£9500
IC	DDC	R & P	Disc/disc	GR70-15	181	3760	140 (Est)	N/A	N/A	£5500
IC	DDC	R & P	Disc/disc	GR70-15	181	3760	148	8.6	16.3	£6897
IC	DDC	R & P	Disc/disc	GR70-15	181	3800 183	162	6.0	14.1	£6897
IC	DDC	R & P	Disc/disc	GR70-15	184	4001	170 (Est)	5.4	13.7	£20,000
IC	DDC	R & P	Disc/disc	GR70-15	181	3954	140 (Est)	7.7	15.6	£33,864
IC	DDC	R & P	Disc/disc	275/55-15	181	3637	165 (Est)	N/A	N/A	£87,000
IC	DDC	R & P	Disc/disc	GR70-15	194	4410	149 (Claimed)	N/A	N/A	£14,040
IC	DDC	R & P	Disc/disc	GR70-15	208	4459	143	8.8	16.4	£24,570
IC	DDC	R & P	Disc/disc	225/60-16	208	4662	145	8.4	N/A	£79,500
IC	DDC	R & P	Disc/disc	255/50-16	173	3638	186 (Est)	N/A	N/A	£87,000
IC	DDC	R & P	Disc/disc	255-50-16	176	3638	160 (Est)	N/A	N/A	£125,000
IC	DDC	R & P	Disc/disc	255/60-16	185	4295	157	6.8	14.7	£120,000
				255/55-17	185	4410	157 (Est)	N/A	N/A	£145,500
IC	DDC	R & P	Disc/disc	285/45-18	185	4267	174	6.1	14.4	£184,000
IC	DDC	R & P	Disc/disc	285/45-18	187	4368	186 (Claimed)	4.6	12.9	£177,600
IC	IC	R & P	Disc/disc	245/40-18	182	3859	157	5.8	14.3	£78,500
ITor	BeamTor	R & P	Disc/drum	6.15-13	173	2080	86 (Claimed)	N/A	N/A	£1068
ITor	BeamTor	R & P	Disc/drum	165-13	173	2251	89	13.4	20.0	£1147
ITor	BeamTor	R & P	Disc/drum	165-13	173	2459	97 (Est)	N/A	N/A	£1096
ITor	BeamTor	R & P	Disc/drum	165-13	173	2184	100	12.8	18.7	£1194
IC	BeamTor	R & P	Disc/drum	165-14	182	2310	106	11.9	18.7	£1475
IC	BeamTor	R & P	Disc/drum	165-14	182	2340	109	9.9	17.6	£1876
IC	BeamTor	R & P	Disc/drum	185-14	173	2397	112	10.6	17.7	£2418
IC	BeamC	R & P	Disc/drum	165-14	184	2535	107	10.9	17.7	£4890
IC	BeamC	R & P	Disc/drum	165-14	184	2630	108	10.7	18.0	£5790
IC	BeamC	R & P	Disc/drum	185/70-14	184	2632	109	11.8	18.7	£5599
IC	BeamC	R & P	Disc/drum	185/70-14	184	2668	93 (Claimed)	N/A	N/A	£7089
IC	BeamC	R & P	Disc/drum	165-14	181	2436	100	12.6	18.8	£4955
IC	BeamC	R & P	Disc/drum	165-14	181	2579	108 (Est)	N/A	N/A	£6020
IC	BeamC	R & P	Disc/drum	185/70-14	181	2666	91	16.6	20.3	£7089
IC	IC	R & P	Disc/drum	155-13	165	1840	92 (Claimed)	N/A	N/A	£1275
IC	IC	R & P	Disc/drum	155-13	165	1885	96	13.2	19.0	£1544
IC	IC	R & P	Disc/drum	155-13	165	1885	101	11.5	18.7	£1653
IC	IC	R & P	Disc/drum	175/70-13	165	1885	106	9.5	17.2	£2237
IC	IC	R & P	Disc/drum	175/70-13	165	1903	106	9.6	17.4	£2910
IC	IC	R & P	Disc/drum	175/70-13	173	2050	101	12.0	18.4	£4650
IC	IC	R & P	Disc/drum	185/60-14	173	2139	109	10.2	17.4	£6171
IC	IC	R & P	Disc/drum	175/70-13	173	2051	99 (Claimed)	N/A	N/A	£6551
IC	IC	R & P	Disc/drum	175/70-13	173	2238	106	10.1	17.5	£8093

Make and model	Production Figures	Years Built	Body Styles	Mechanical Layout	Engine Make (if not own)	Capacity/(cc)/Layout/Valves	BHP/rpm	Torque (lb.ft)/rpm	Transmission gearbox/automatic transmission
						OHC	112/5800	118/3500	5-spd/-
						1921/5IL/ OHC	115/5900	113/3700	5-spd/Auto
						1994/5IL/ OHC	115/5400	121/3200	5-spd/Auto
						1588/4IL/ OHC Diesel	70/4500	98/2600	5-spd/-
				F/4	—	2144/5IL/ OHC	136/5900	130/4500	5-spd/-
90	97,302	1984–1986	Sal	F/F	—	1994/5IL/ OHC	115/5400	122/3200	5-spd/Auto
				F/4	—	2226/5IL/ OHC	136/5700	139/3500	5-spd/-
200	73,571	1980–1983	Sal	F/F	—	2144/5IL/ OHC	136/5700	136/4200	5-spd/Auto
							170/5300	195/3300	5-spd/Auto
80	N/A	1986–1994	Sal	F/F	—	1595/4IL/ OHC	75/5200	92/2700	5-spd/-
							100/6000	96/3200	5-spd/-
				F/F	—	1781/4IL/ OHC	90/5200	111/3300	5-spd/Auto
							112/5800	118/3400	5-spd/-
				F/4 and F/4	—	1781/4IL/ OHC	112/5800	118/3400	5-spd/-
					—	1984/4IL/ OHC	115/5400	124/3200	5-spd/Auto
							90/5400	109/3000	5-spd/Auto
					—	1984/4IL/ 2OHC	137/5800	133/4500	5-spd/-
					—	2309/5IL/ OHC	133/5500	137/4000	5-spd/Auto
					—	2598/V6/ OHC	150/5750	165/3500	5-spd/Auto
					—	2771/V6/ OHC	174/5500	180/3000	5-spd/Auto
					—	1588/4IL/ OHC Diesel	80/4500	114/2800	5-spd/-
					—	1896/4IL/ OHC Diesel	90/4000	134/2300	5-spd/-
90	153,937	1986–1991	Sal	F/F	—	1994/5IL/ OHC	115/5400	127/4000	5-spd/-
						2226/5IL/ OHC	136/5700	137/3500	
						2309/5IL/ OHC	136/5500	140/4000	5-spd/Auto
							170/6000	162/4500	5-spd/Auto
				F/4	—	2226/5IL/ OHC	136/5700	137/3500	5-spd/-
					—	2309/5IL/ OHC	170/6000	162/4500	5-spd/-
100	1,071,729 + 308,385 Avant	1982–1990	Sal Est	F/F	—	1781/4IL/ OHC	75/4600	102/2500	4-spd/5-spd/Auto
						1921/5IL/ OHC	100/5600	110/3200	5-spd/Auto
						1994/5IL/ OHC	115/5200	125/3000	5-spd/Auto
						2144/5IL/ OHC	136/5700	133/4800	5-spd/Auto
						2226/5IL/ OHC	138/5700	138/3500	5-spd/Auto
							165/5500	177/3000	5-spd/Auto
						1986/5IL/ OHC Diesel	87/4500	126/2750	5-spd/-
				F/4	—	2226/5IL/ OHC	138/5700	139/3500	5-spd/-
200	77,571	1983–1989	Sal Est (Avant)	F/F	—	2144/5IL/ OHC	136/5700	133/4800	5-spd/Auto
							182/5700	186/3600	5-spd/Auto
				F/4	—	2144/5IL/ OHC	182/5700	186/3600	5-spd/-
						2226/5IL/ 2OHC	200/5800	199/3000	5-spd/-
Quattro	10,629	1980–1989	Cpe	F/4	—	2144/5IL/ OHC	200/5500	210/3500	5-spd/-
						2226/5IL/ OHC	200/5500	210/3500	5-spd/-
Quattro Sport	200	1983–1985	Cpe	F/4	—	2135/5IL/ 2OHC	306/6700	258/3700	5-spd/-
Quattro 20V	931	1989–1991	Cpe	F/4	—	2226/5IL/ 2OHC	220/5900	228/1950	5-spd/-
Coupe GT	173,747	1980–1988	Cpe	F/F	—	1781/4IL/ OHC	90/5200	107/3300	4-spd/Auto
						1921/5IL/ OHC	115/5900	114/3700	5-spd/Auto
						1994/5IL/ OHC	115/5400	121/3200	5-spd/Auto
						2144/5IL/	130/5900	126/4800	5-spd/-

Suspension Front	Rear	Steering	Brakes (Front/rear)	Wheels/ Tyres	Length (in)	Weight (lb,unladen)	Top speed (mph)	0–60mph (sec)	Standing 1/4-mile (sec)	UK Total Price (£: at Launch)
IC	IC	R & P	Disc/drum	185/60-14	173	2164	117	9.3	17.0	£8995
IC	IC	R & P	Disc/drum	175/70-13	173	2249	116 (Claimed)	N/A	N/A	£7596
IC	IC	R & P	Disc/drum	175/70-13	173	2271	114	N/A	N/A	£9032
IC	IC	R & P	Disc/drum	165-13	173	2170	96	12.8	19.5	£7616
IC	IC	R & P	Disc/disc	175/70-14	173	2607	120	8.8	16.6	£11,474
IC	IC	R & P	Disc/drum	185/60-14	174	2429	111	9.6	17.2	£9995
IC	IC	R & P	Disc/disc	195/60-14	174	2646	118	9.0	16.7	£13,492
IC	IC	R & P	Disc/disc	205-60-15	184	2774	110	10.5	17.9	£10,334
IC	IC	R & P	Disc/disc	205/60-15	184	2910	125	7.5	16.3	£12,950
IC	IC	R & P	Disc/drum	175/70-14	173	2249	106 (Est)	N/A	N/A	£9558
IC	IC	R & P	Disc/drum	195/65-15	173	2624	109 (Est)	12.0	N/A	£13,456
IC	IC	R & P	Disc/drum	175/70-14	173	2338	112	11.1	18.2	£9224
IC	IC	R & P	Disc/disc	175/70-14	173	2434	119	9.8	17.7	£11394
IC	IC	R & P	Disc/disc	175/70-14	173	2618	115	10.9	18.2	£14,100
IC	IC	R & P	Disc/disc	195/65-15	177	2286	120	10.6	18.4	£12,475
IC	IC	R & P	Disc/drum	195/65-15	177	2624	110 (Est)	N/A	N/A	£13,459
IC	IC	R & P	Disc/disc	205/50-15	173	2665	130	8.7	16.7	£16,697
IC	IC	R & P	Disc/disc	195/65-15	177	2800	137	N/A	N/A	£16,605
IC	IC	R & P	Disc/disc	195/65-15	177	2933	132 (Claimed)	N/A	N/A	£19,195
IC	IC	R & P	Disc/disc	195/65-15	173	2926	133	8.3	16.5	£19249
IC	IC	R & P	Disc/drum	175/70-14	173	2403	107 (Claimed)	N/A	N/A	£10972
IC	IC	R & P	Disc/drum	195/65-15	177	2800	108 (Claimed)	N/A	N/A	£14,700
IC	IC	R & P	Disc/disc	195/60-14	173	2446	122 (Claimed)	N/A	N/A	£13,994
IC	IC	R & P	Disc/disc	195/60-14	173	2446	126	9.5	17.2	£15,391
IC	IC	R & P	Disc/disc	195/60-14	173	2580	128 (Est)	N/A	N/A	£14,999
IC	IC	R & P	Disc/disc	205/50-15	173	3014	137	8.5	16.9	£19,460
IC	IC	R & P	Disc/disc	195/60-14	173	2689	125	9.5	16.7	£18,999
IC	IC	R & P	Disc/disc	205/50-15	173	2911	137 (Claimed)	N/A	N/A	£22,285
IC	IC	R & P	Disc/drum	165-14	189	2381	102 (Claimed)	N/A	N/A	£8772
IC	IC	R & P	Disc/drum	165-14	189	2521	109 (Claimed)	N/A	N/A	£8894
IC	IC	R & P	Disc/drum	185/70-14	189	2756	118 (Claimed)	N/A	N/A	£11,039
IC	IC	R & P	Disc/disc	185/70-14	189	2664	128	9.5	17.4	£9618
IC	IC	R & P	Disc/disc	185/70-14	189	2858	120	10.0	17.5	£15,332
IC	IC	R & P	Disc/disc	205/60-15	189	2866	134 (Est)	N/A	N/A	£19,440
IC	IC	R & P	Disc/drum	185/70-14	189	2764	111	12.6	18.6	£12,670
IC	IC	R & P	Disc/disc	205/60-15	189	2954	117	9.3	17.0	£16,156
IC	IC	R & P	Disc/disc	205/60-15	189	2778	124 (Est)	N/A	N/A	£13,411
IC	IC	R & P	Disc/disc	205/60-15	189	2844	142	8.4	16.2	£17,013
IC	IC	R & P	Disc/disc	205/60-15	189	3387	139	7.3	15.3	£23,043
IC	IC	R & P	Disc/disc	205/60-15	193	3348	144 (Est)	N/A	N/A	£29,992
IC	IC	R & P	Disc/disc	205/60-15	173	2786	138 (Est)	6.5	14.6	£14,500
IC	IC	R & P	Disc/disc	215/50-15	173	2934	135	6.3	14.7	£29,445
IC	IC	R & P	Disc/disc	235/45-15	164	2807	154	4.8	13.5	Special Order
IC	IC	R & P	Disc/disc	215/50-15	173	3069	141	6.3	14.5	£32,995
IC	IC	R & P	Disc/drum	175/70-13	171	2095	107 (Claimed)	N/A	N/A	£11,677
IC	IC	R & P	Disc/drum	185/60-14	171	2352	113	9.9	17.0	£7475
IC	IC	R & P	Disc/drum	185/60-14	171	2464	118	8.9	17.2	£9219
IC	IC	R & P	Disc/disc	185/60-14	171	2366	120	8.8	16.9	£9173

Make and model	Production Figures	Years Built	Body Styles	Mechanical Layout	Engine Make (if not own)	Capacity/(cc)/Layout/Valves	BHP/rpm	Torque (lb.ft)/rpm	Transmission gearbox/automatic transmission
					—	2226/5IL/ OHC	136/5700	137/3500	5-spd/Auto
				F/4	—	2226/5IL/ OHC	136/5700	139/3500	5-spd/-
Coupe S2	In prod	1988–Date	Cpe	F/F	—	1984/4IL/ OHC	112/5300	124/3250	5-spd/Auto
						2226/5IL/ OHC	136/5700	137/3500	5-spd/-
						2309/5IL/ OHC	133/5500	138/4000	5-spd/Auto
						2309/5IL/ 2OHC	167/6000	159/4500	5-spd/Auto
						2598/V6/ OHC	150/5750	166/3500	5-spd/Auto
						2771/V8/ OHC	174/5500	181/3000	5-spd/Auto
				F/4	—	2226/5IL/ OHC	136/5700	137/3500	5-spd/-
						2309/5IL/ OHC	133/5500	138/4000	5-spd/-
						2309/5IL/ 2OHC	170/6000	162/4500	5-spd/-
						2771/V6/ OHC	174/5500	181/3000	5-spd/-
Cabriolet	In prod	1991–Date	Conv	F/F	—	1984/4IL/ OHC	115/5400	121/3200	5-spd/Auto
						2309/5IL/ OHC	123/5500	137/4000	5-spd/Auto
						2598/V6/ OHC	150/5750	166/3500	5-spd/-
S2 (Quattro)	In prod	1990–Date	Cpe	F/4	—	2226/5IL/ OHC	220/5900	228/1950	5-spd/-
			Est			2OHC	230/5900	275/1950	5-spd/6-spd/-
RS2	In prod	1994–Date	Est	F/4	—	2226/5IL/ 2OHC	315/6500	302/3000	6-spd/-
100/A6	In prod	1990–Date	Sal Est	F/F (or F/4)	—	1984/4IL/ OHC	101/5500	116/2750	5-spd/Auto
						2226/5IL/ 2OHC	230/5900	258/1950	6-spd/Auto
						2309/5IL/ OHC	133/5500	132/4000	5-spd/Auto
						2598/V6/ OHC	150/5750	166/3500	5-spd/Auto
						2771/V6/ OHC	174/5500	180/3000	5-spd/Auto
						1896/4IL/ OHC Diesel	90/4000	149/1900	5-spd/Auto
						2460/5IL/	115/4000	196/2250	6-spd/-
						OHC Diesel	140/4000	214/1900	6-spd/-
V8	19,341	1988–1994	Sal	F/4	—	3562/V8/ 2OHC	250/5800	251/4000	Auto/-
						4172/V8/ 2OHC	280/5800	295/4000	Auto/-
100 S4	In prod	1991–Date	Sal Est	F/4	—	2226/5IL/ 2OHC	230/5900	258/3200	6-spd/Auto
A8	In prod	1994–Date	Sal	F/F	—	2771/V6/ OHC	174/5500	184/3000	Auto/-
						3697/V8/ 2OHC	230/5500	233/2700	Auto/-
				F/4	—	4172/V8/ 2OHC	300/6000	295/3300	Auto/-
A4	In prod	1994–Date	Sal Est	F/F or F/4	—	1595/4IL/ OHC	101/5300	103/3800	5-spd/Auto
						1781/4IL/ OHC	125/5800	127/3950	5-spd/Auto
						OHC	150/5700	155/1750	5-spd/Auto
						2598/V6/ OHC	150/5750	166/3500	5-spd/Auto
						1896/IL/ OHC Diesel	90/4000	149/1900	5-spd/Auto

Austin

Mini – see **Mini** marque, below

Make and model	Production Figures	Years Built	Body Styles	Mechanical Layout	Engine Make (if not own)	Capacity/(cc)/Layout/Valves	BHP/rpm	Torque (lb.ft)/rpm	Transmission gearbox/automatic transmission
1100/1300	1,119,800 (Approx)	1963–1974	Sal Est	F(Tr)/F	—	1098/4IL/ OHV	48/5100	60/2500	4-spd/Auto
						1275/4IL/ OHV	58/5250	69/3000	4-spd/Auto
						OHV	70/6000	74/3250	4-spd/Auto
1800	210,000 (Approx)	1964–1975	Sal	F(Tr)/F	—	1798/4IL/ OHV	80/5000	100/2100	4-spd/-
						OHV	86/5300	101/3000	4-spd/Auto

Suspension Front	Rear	Steering	Brakes (Front/rear)	Wheels/ Tyres	Length (in)	Weight (lb,unladen)	Performance Top speed (mph)	0–60mph (sec)	Standing 1/4-mile (sec)	UK Total Price (£: at Launch)
IC	IC	R & P	Disc/disc	185/60-14	174	2288	122	8.8	16.5	£12,384
IC	IC	R & P	Disc/disc	195/60-14	171	2674	119	8.6	16.9	£14,569
IC	IC	R & P	Disc/disc	205/60-15	172	2492	122 (Claimed)	10.9	N/A	£15,250
IC	IC	R & P	Disc/disc	205/60-15	172	2672	129	9.7	17.3	£17,995
IC	IC	R & P	Disc/disc	205/60-15	172	2580	128 (Claimed)	N/A	N/A	£16,960
IC	IC	R & P	Disc/disc	205/60-15	172	2646	137 (Claimed)	N/A	N/A	£19,994
IC	IC	R & P	Disc/disc	205/60-15	172	2878	133 (Claimed)	9.3	N/A	£18,427
IC	IC	R & P	Disc/disc	205/60-15	172	2878	138 (Claimed)	8.0	N/A	£22,999
IC	IC	R & P	Disc/disc	205/60-15	172	2819	124	9.5	17.0	£22,486
IC	IC	R & P	Disc/disc	205/60-15	172	2933	128 (Claimed)	N/A	N/A	£19,994
IC	IC	R & P	Disc/disc	205/60-15	172	2907	137 (Claimed)	N/A	N/A	£22,200
IC	IC	R & P	Disc/disc	205/60-15	172	3087	138 (Claimed)	8.0	N/A	£25,499
IC	IC	R & P	Disc/disc	195/65-15	172	2977	116 (Claimed)	N/A	N/A	£19,245
IC	IC	R & P	Disc/disc	195/65-15	172	2976	123 (Claimed)	10.8	N/A	£21,995
IC	IC	R & P	Disc/disc	195/65-15	172	2976	129	9.1	17.1	£23,386
IC	IC	R & P	Disc/disc	205/55-16	172	3249	148	5.9	14.5	£29,394
IC	IC	R & P	Disc/disc	205/55-16	172	3248	147	5.7	14.5	£29,083
IC	IC	R & P	Disc/disc	245/40-17	178	3517	158	4.8	13.5	£45,705
IC	IC	R & P	Disc/drum	195/65-15	189	2889	113 (Claimed)	11.9	N/A	£17,650
IC	IC	R & P	Disc/disc	225/50-16	189	3625	147	6.4	14.9	£34,211
IC	IC	R & P	Disc/disc	195/65-15	189	3014	125 (Claimed)	10.2	N/A	£19,248
IC	IC	R & P	Disc/disc	195/65-15	189	3087	133	9.1	17.0	£20,635
IC	IC	R & P	Disc/disc	195/65-14	189	3080	135	9.0	16.9	£24,636
IC	IC	R & P	Disc/disc	195/65-15	189	3087	110	13.9	N/A	£19,940
IC	IC	R & P	Disc/disc	195/65-15	189	3363	121	12.3	18.9	£22,315
IC	IC	R & P	Disc/disc	205/60-15	189	3241	129	9.5	17.3	£23,451
IC	IC	R & P	Disc/disc	215/60-15	192	3770	144	9.0	16.8	£40,334
IC	IC	R & P	Disc/disc	215/60-15	192	3762	153	7.7	15.9	£43,548
IC	IC	R & P	Disc/disc	225/50-16	189	3625	144	6.4	14.9	£31,083
IC	IC	R & P	Disc/disc	225/60-16	198	3484	135	11.2	18.3	£34,499
IC	IC	R & P	Disc/disc	225/60-15	198	3709	135	9.2	17.0	£42,499
IC	IC	R & P	Disc/disc	225/60-16	198	3859	155	8.3	16.2	£46,699
IC	IC	R & P	Disc/disc	195/65-15	176	2635	119 (Claimed)	11.9	N/A	£14,920
IC	IC	R & P	Disc/disc	195/65-15	176	2695	126	10.3	17.7	£16,745
IC	IC	R & P	Disc/disc	205/55-16	176	2860	137	8.2	16.5	£20,925
IC	IC	R & P	Disc/disc	205/55-16	176	2833	137	9.1	N/A	£20,387
IC	IC	R & P	Disc/disc	195/65-15	176	2734	114 (Claimed)	13.3	N/A	£17,347
IHydroL	IHydroL	R & P	Disc/drum	5.50-12	147	1780	78	22.2	22.7	£593
IHydroL	IHydroL	R & P	Disc/drum	5.50-12	147	1780	88	17.3	20.7	£672
IHydroL	IHydroL	R & P	Disc/drum	145-12	147	1900	93	15.6	20.0	£910
IHydroL	IHydroL	R & P	Disc/drum	175-13	164	2645	90	17.1	20.5	£769
IHydroL	IHydroL	R & P	Disc/drum	165-14	164	2645	93	16.3	19.9	£999

Make and model	Production Figures	Years Built	Body Styles	Mechanical Layout	Engine Make (if not own)	Capacity/(cc)/Layout/Valves	BHP/rpm	Torque (lb.ft)/rpm	Transmission gearbox/automatic transmission
							96/5700	106/3000	4-spd/-
3-litre	9,992	1967–1971	Sal	F/R	—	2912/6IL/ OHC	124/4500	161/3000	4-spd (+O/D)/Auto
Maxi	472,098	1969–1981	Htch	F(Tr)F	—	1485/4IL/ OHC	74/5500	84/3500	5-spd/-
						1748/4IL/ OHC	84/5500	105/3000	5-spd/Auto
							91/5250	104/3400	5-spd/-
Sprite	1,022	1971	Spts	F/R	—	1275/4IL/ OHV	65/6000	72/3000	4-spd/-
2200	20,865 (Incl. Morris 2200)	1972–1975	Sal	F(Tr)/F	—	2227/6IL/ OHC	110/5250	126/3500	4-spd/Auto
Allegro	642,350	1973–1982	Sal Est	F(Tr)/F	—	998/4IL/ OHV	44/5250	52/3000	4-spd/Auto
						1098/4IL/ OHV	48/5250	60/2700	4-spd/-
							45/5250	55/2900	4-spd/-
						1275/4IL/ OHV	59/5300	69/3000	4-spd/Auto
							62/5600	73/3200	4-spd/Auto
						1485/4IL/ OHC	68/5500	80/3250	5-spd/Auto
							77/5750	83/3250	5-spd/-
						1748/4IL/ OHC	75/5000	100/2600	5-spd/Auto
							90/5500	103/3100	5-spd/Auto
1800/ 2200	19,000 (This includes Morris and Wolseley figures)	1975 only	Sal	F(Tr)/F	—	1798/4IL/ OHV	82/5200	102/2750	4-spd/Auto
						2227/6IL/ OHC	110/5250	125/3250	4-spd/Auto
Ambassador	43,427	1982–1984	Htch	F(Tr)/F	—	1695/4IL/ OHC	83/5200	97/3500	4-spd/Auto
						1993/4IL/ OHC	92/4900	114/2750	4-spd/Auto
							100/5200	120/3250	4-spd/Auto
Metro	1,518,932	1980–1991	Htch	F(Tr)/F	—	998/4IL/ OHV	41/5400	51/2700	4-spd/-
						1275/4IL/ OHV	63/5600	72/3100	4-spd/-
							73/6000	73/4000	4-spd/-
Maestro	605,410	1982–1994	Htch	F(Tr)/F	—	1275/4IL/ OHV	68/5800	75/3500	4-spd/5-spd/-
							64/5400	73/3500	4-spd/5-spd/-
						1598/4IL/ OHC	81/5500	91/3500	4-spd/5-spd/Auto
						1994/4IL/ OHC Diesel	62/4500	88/2500	5-spd/-
							81/4500	116/2500	5-spd/-
Montego	571,457	1984–1994	Sal Est	F(Tr)/F	—	1275/4IL/ OHV	68/5600	75/3500	4-spd/Auto
						1598/4IL/ OHC	85/5600	97/3500	5-spd/Auto
						1994/4IL/ OHC	102/5500	121/3000	5-spd/-
							115/5500	134/2800	5-spd/-
						1994/4IL/ OHC Diesel	81/4500	116/2500	5-spd/-

Bedford

Make and model	Production Figures	Years Built	Body Styles	Mechanical Layout	Engine Make (if not own)	Capacity/(cc)/Layout/Valves	BHP/rpm	Torque (lb.ft)/rpm	Transmission gearbox/automatic transmission
Beagle	N/A	1964–1973	Est	F/R	—	1057/4IL/ OHV	40/5200	55/2600	4-spd/-

Bentley

Make and model	Production Figures	Years Built	Body Styles	Mechanical Layout	Engine Make (if not own)	Capacity/(cc)/Layout/Valves	BHP/rpm	Torque (lb.ft)/rpm	Transmission gearbox/automatic transmission
T1/T2	2,280	1965–1980	Sal	F/R	—	6230/V8/ OHV	N/Q	N/Q	Auto/-
						6750/V8/ OHV	N/Q	N/Q	Auto/-
Corniche/ Continental	1,280	1966–1994	Cpe Conv Spl	F/R	—	6230/V8/ OHV	N/Q	N/Q	Auto/-
						6750/V8/ OHV	N/Q	N/Q	Auto/-
Mulsanne	2,039	1980–1992	Sal	F/R	—	6750/V8/ OHV	N/Q	N/Q	Auto/-
Eight	1,734	1984–1992	Sal	F/R	—	6750/V8/ OHV	N/Q	N/Q	Auto/-
Turbo/R	In prod	1982–Date	Sal	F/R	—	6750/V8/ OHV	N/Q	N/Q	Auto/-
Brooklands	In prod	1992–Date	Sal	F/R	—	6750/V8/ OHV	N/Q	N/Q	Auto/-
Continental R	In prod	1991–Date	Cpe	F/R	—	6750/V8/ OHV	385/4000	553/2000	Auto/-
Azure	In prod	1995–Date	Conv	F/R	—	6750/V8/ OHV	385/4000	553/2000	Auto/-

Suspension Front	Rear	Steering	Brakes (Front/rear)	Wheels/ Tyres	Length (in)	Weight (lb,unladen)	Top speed (mph)	0–60mph (sec)	Standing $1/4$-mile (sec)	UK Total Price (£: at Launch)
IHydroL	IHydroL	R & P	Disc/drum	165-14	164	2645	99	13.7	19.4	£1105
IHydroL	IHydroL	R & P	Disc/drum	185-14	186	3290	100	15.7	20.1	£1418
IHydroL	IHydroL	R & P	Disc/drum	155-13	158	2160	86	16.6	20.6	£979
IHydroL	IHydroL	R & P	Disc/drum	155-13	158	2160	89	15.8	20.2	£1103
IHydroL	IHydroL	R & P	Disc/drum	165-13	158	2216	97	13.2	19.4	£1375
IC	Beam1/2E	R & P	Disc/drum	5.20-13	138	1575	94	14.6	19.7	£924
IHydroL	IHydroL	R & P	Disc/drum	165-14	167	2620	104	13.1	18.7	£1340
IHydraG	IHydraG	R & P	Disc/drum	145-13	152	1794	79 (Est)	N/A	N/A	£3519
IHydraG	IHydraG	R & P	Disc/drum	145-13	152	1822	81	19.9	21.2	£974
IHydraG	IHydraG	R & P	Disc/drum	145-13	152	1850	83	19.4	20.9	£1541
IHydraG	IHydraG	R & P	Disc/drum	145-13	152	1822	82	18.4	20.9	£1009
IHydraG	IHydraG	R & P	Disc/drum	145-13	152	1857	92	14.9	19.5	£3979
IHydraG	IHydraG	R & P	Disc/drum	145-13	152	1920	94	14.0	19.6	£1164
IHydraG	IHydraG	R & P	Disc/drum	155-13	152	1980	95 (Est)	N/A	N/A	£4246
IHydraG	IHydraG	R & P	Disc/drum	155-13	152	2011	96	12.4	18.6	£1254
IHydraG	IHydraG	R & P	Disc/drum	155-13	152	1904	100	11.0	17.9	£1577
IHydraG	IHydraG	R & P	Disc/drum	185/70-14	175	2557	96	14.9	20.1	£2117
IHydraG	IHydraG	R & P	Disc/drum	185/70-14	175	2600	104	13.5	19.2	£2424
IHydraG	IHydraG	R & P	Disc/drum	185/70-14	179	2659	95	15.7	20.1	£5105
IHydraG	IHydraG	R & P	Disc/drum	185/70-14	179	2675	100	14.3	19.6	£6108
IHydraG	IHydraG	R & P	Disc/drum	185/70-14	179	2732	103	11.8	18.6	£6917
IHydraG	IHydraG	R & P	Disc/drum	135-12	134	1675	84	18.9	21.6	£3095
IHydraG	IHydraG	R & P	Disc/drum	155/70-12	134	1737	94	13.5	19.2	£3995
IHydraG	IHydraG	R & P	Disc/drum	185/55-13	134	1828	103	11.8	18.6	£7325
IC	IC	R & P	Disc/drum	155-13	158	1929	96	12.3	18.5	£4955
IC	IC	R & P	Disc/drum	155-13	158	2017	95	13.0	19.1	£5682
IC	IC	R & P	Disc/drum	165-13	158	2083	102	12.0	18.4	£5225
IC	IC	R & P	Disc/drum	175/70-14	158	2414	90 (Est)	N/A	N/A	£7584
IC	IC	R & P	Disc/drum	175/70-14	158	2414	101 (Est)	N/A	N/A	£8183
IC	IC	R & P	Disc/drum	165-13	176	2094	95 (Est)	N/A	N/A	£5281
IC	IC	R & P	Disc/drum	165-13	176	2225	99	11.9	18.4	£5660
IC	IC	R & P	Disc/drum	180/65-365	176	2249	107	10.3	17.8	£7195
IC	IC	R & P	Disc/drum	180/65-365	176	2367	115	9.5	17.8	£9577
IC	IC	R & P	Disc/drum	185/65-14	176	2423	101	13.2	19.1	£10,908
ITrL	Beam1/2E	R & P	Drum/drum	4.00-12	150	1680	73	29.1	22.6	£620
IC	IC	Worm	Disc/disc	8.45-15	204	4659	115	10.9	17.6	£6496
IC	IC	Worm	Disc/disc	8.45-15	204	4659	117	10.2	17.5	£9148
		R & P (T2)		205-15 235/70-15	204	4930	119	9.4	17.7	£22809
IC	IC	Worm	Disc/disc	8.45-15	204	4978	115 (Est)	N/A	N/A	£9789
IC	IC	Worm	Disc/disc	8.45-15	204	4978	120	9.6	17.1	£11,491
		R & P		205-15 235/70-15						
IC	IC	R & P	Disc/disc	235/70-15	207	4907	119	10.0	17.1	£49,629
IC	IC	R & P	Disc/disc	235/70-15	207	4950	120	N/A	N/A	£49,497
IC	IC	R & P	Disc/disc	235/70-15	207	4926	135	6.7	14.6	£58,613
				255/65-15 255/65/17	207	4939	143	7.0	15.4	£79,397
IC	IC	R & P	Disc/disc	235/70-15 235/65-16	207	5182	127 (Claimed)	N/A	N/A	£100,686
IC	IC	R & P	Disc/disc	255/60-16 255/55-17	210	5402	151	6.1	14.7	£175,000
IC	IC	R & P	Disc/disc	225/55-17	210	5755	150 (Claimed)	6.3	N/A	£215,000

Make and model	Production Figures	Years Built	Body Styles	Mechanical Layout	Engine Make (if not own)	Capacity/(cc)/Layout/Valves	BHP/rpm	Torque (lb.ft)/rpm	Transmission gearbox/automatic transmission
Bitter									
SC	450	1982–1986	Sal Cpe	F/R	Opel	2969/6IL/ OHC	180/5800	179/4800	5-spd/Auto
BMW									
1500/1800/ 2000	334,165	1962–1972	Sal	F/R	—	1499/4IL/ OHC	80/5700	87/3000	4-spd/-
						1773/4IL/ OHC	90/5250 110/5800	106/3000 109/4000	4-spd/Auto 4-spd/-
						1766/4IL/ OHC	90/5250	106/3000	4-spd/Auto
						1990/4IL/ OHC	100/5500 120/5500	116/3000 123/3600	4-spd/Auto 4-spd/-
1502/1600/ 1602	349,955	1966–1977	Sal Conv Est	F/R	—	1573/4IL/ OHC	75/5800 85/5700	87/3700 91/3000	4-spd/- 4-spd/-
2002/Tii	409,922	1968–1976	Sal Conv Est	F/R	—	1990/4IL/ OHC	100/5500 130/5800	116/3500 131/4500	4-spd/5-spd/Auto 4-spd/5-spd/-
2002 Turbo	1,672	1973–1974	Sal	F/R	—	1990/4IL/ OHC	170/5800	177/4500	4-spd/5-spd/-
2500/2800	137,455	1968–1977	Sal	F/R	—	2494/6IL/ OHC	150/6000	155/3700	4-spd/Auto
						2788/6IL/ OHC	170/6000	174/3700	4-spd/Auto
2800CS/ 3.0CS/3.0CSI	28,661	1968–1975	Cpe	F/R	—	2788/6IL/ OHC	170/6000	173/3700	4-spd/Auto
						2985/6IL/ OHC	180/6000 200/5500	188/3700 200/4300	4-spd/Auto 4-spd/-
3.0CSL	1,039	1972–1975	Cpe	F/R	—	3003/6IL/ OHC	200/5500	199/4300	4-spd/-
						3153/6IL/ OHC	206/5600	211/4200	4-spd/-
3.0S 3.0Si/3.3L	61,420	1971–1977	Sal	F/R	—	2985/6IL/ OHC	180/6000 200/5500	188/3700 200/4300	4-spd/Auto 4-spd/Auto
						2985/6IL/ OHC	180/6000 200/5500	188/3700 200/4300	Auto/- Auto/-
						3295/6IL/ OHC	190/5500	213/4000	Auto/-
						3210/6IL/ OHC	2000/5000	210/4250	Auto/-
5-Series	699,094	1972–1981	Sal	F/R	—	1766/4IL/ OHC	90/5500	105/3500	4-spd/Auto
						1990/4IL/ OHC	115/5800 130/5800	119/3700 131/4500	4-spd/Auto 4-spd/Auto
						1990/6IL/ OHC	122/6000	118/4000	4-spd/Auto
						2494/6IL/ OHC	145/6000	153/4000	4-spd/Auto
						2788/6IL/ OHC	170/5800 177/5800	173/4000 173/4300	4-spd/Auto 4-spd/Auto
3-Series	1,364,039	1975–1982	Sal	F/R	—	1573/4IL/ OHC	90/6000	90/4000	4-spd/-
						1766/4IL/ OHC	90/5500	103/4000	4-spd/5-spd/Auto
						1990/4IL/ OHC	109/5800 125/5700	116/3700 127/4350	4-spd/Auto 4-spd/Auto
						1990/6IL/ OHC	122/6000	118/4000	4-spd/Auto
						2315/6IL/ OHC	143/6000	140/4500	4-spd/Auto
6-Series	80,361	1976–1989	Spts Cpe	F/R	—	2788/6IL/ OHC	184/5800	177/4200	4-spd/5-spd/Auto
						3210/6IL/ OHC	200/5500 197/5500	210/4250 210/4300	4-spd/Auto 4-spd/5-spd/Auto
						3430/6IL/ OHC	218/5200	224/4000	5-spd/Auto
						3453/6IL/ OHC	218/5200 218/5200	224/4000 228/4000	5-spd/Auto
						3453/6IL/ 2OHC	286/6500	251/4500	5-spd/-
7-Series	292,280	1977–1986	Sal	F/R	—	2788/6IL/ OHC	170/5800 184/5800	172/4000 177/4200	4-spd/Auto 4-spd/5-spd/Auto
						2985/6IL/ OHC	184/5800	188/4000	4-spd/Auto
						3210/6IL/ OHC	197/5500 197/5500	206/4250 210/4300	4-spd/5-spd/Auto 5-spd/Auto
						3430/6IL/	218/5200	228/4000	5-spd/Auto

Suspension Front	Rear	Steering	Brakes (Front/rear)	Wheels/ Tyres	Length (in)	Weight (lb, unladen)	Top speed (mph)	0–60mph (sec)	Standing 1/4-mile (sec)	UK Total Price (£: at Launch)
IC	IC	Worm	Disc/disc	215/60-15/ 235/55-15	191	3341	133 (Claimed)	N/A	N/A	£26,950
IC	IC	Worm	Disc/drum	6.00-14	177	2337	92 (Claimed)	N/A	N/A	£1567
IC	IC	Worm	Disc/drum	6.00-14	177	2403	100	13.7	19.0	£1440
IC	IC	Worm	Disc/drum	5.90-14	177	2470	107	11.3	18.4	£1540
IC	IC	Worm	Disc/drum	165-14	177	2492	102	11.8	18.4	£1699
IC	IC	Worm	Disc/drum	165-14	177	2446	104	11.7	17.7	£1777
IC	IC	Worm	Disc/drum	175-14	177	2536	114	9.7	17.3	£1798
IC	IC	Worm	Disc/drum	165-13	167	2161	97 (Est)	N/A	N/A	£2299
IC	IC	Worm	Disc/drum	165-13	167	2161	99	11.8	18.4	£1298
IC	IC	Worm	Disc/drum	165-13	170	2183	107	10.6	17.4	£1597
IC	IC	Worm	Disc/drum	165-13	170	2227	116	8.3	16.4	£2299
IC	IC	Worm	Disc/drum	185/70-13	166	2381	130	7.3	16.0	£4221
IC	IC	Worm	Disc/disc	175-14	185	2938	121	9.3	17.2	£2958
IC	IC	Worm	Disc/disc	175-14	186	2955	124	8.9	16.7	£3245
IC	IC	Worm	Disc/drum	DR70HR14	183	2845	128	8.5	16.3	£4997
IC	IC	Worm	Disc/disc	195/70-14	183	3030	131	8.0	16.2	£5345
IC	IC	Worm	Disc/disc	195/70-14	183	3030	139	7.5	15.4	£6199
IC	IC	Worm	Disc/disc	195/70-14	183	2845	133	7.2	15.2	£6399
IC	IC	Worm	Disc/disc	195/70-14	183	2775	137 (Claimed)	N/A	N/A	£6899
IC	IC	Worm	Disc/disc	195/70-14	185	3114	127	8.0	15.9	£3555
IC	IC	Worm	Disc/disc	195/70-14	185	3114	131	7.4	15.7	£3999
IC	IC	Worm	Disc/disc	195/70-14	189	3291	120 (Est)	N/A	N/A	£6499
IC	IC	Worm	Disc/disc	195/70-14	189	3548	124	9.9	17.3	£7859
IC	IC	Worm	Disc/disc	195/70-14	189	3548	124 (Claimed)	N/A	N/A	Special order
IC	IC	Worm	Disc/drum	175-14	182	2711	101	12.9	18.8	£3299
IC	IC	Worm	Disc/drum	175-14	182	2712	106	11.3	18.0	£2999
IC	IC	Worm	Disc/drum	175-14	182	2759	114	10.5	17.5	£3499
IC	IC	Worm	Disc/drum	175-14	182	2889	107	11.1	18.1	£6099
IC	IC	Worm	Disc/disc	175-14	182	2976	117	10.6	17.8	£4099
IC	IC	Worm	Disc/disc	195/70-14	182	3035	124	9.0	16.7	£4699
IC	IC	Worm	Disc/disc	195-14	182	3260	129	8.7	16.8	£8599
IC	IC	R & P	Disc/drum	165-13	171	2285	100	12.9	19.0	£2799
IC	IC	R & P	Disc/drum	165-13	171	2436	102	11.3	18.0	£5355
IC	IC	R & P	Disc/drum	165-13	171	2285	108	10.2	17.3	£3349
IC	IC	R & P	Disc/drum	185/70-13	171	2315	113	9.6	17.3	£4749
IC	IC	R & P	Disc/drum	185/70-13	171	2390	111	9.8	17.4	£4999
IC	IC	R & P	Disc/disc	185/70-13	171	2625	126	8.3	16.7	£6499
IC	IC	Worm	Disc/disc	205/70-14	187	3170	130	8.5	16.7	£16,635
IC	IC	Worm	Disc/disc	195/70-14	187	3240	131	8.1	14.9	£13,980
IC	IC	Worm	Disc/disc	195/70-14	187	3240	130 (Est)	N/A	N/A	£17,462
IC	IC	Worm	Disc/disc	195/70-14	187	3175	139	7.3	15.6	£22,950
IC	IC	Worm	Disc/disc	195/70-14	187	3447	140	8.5	16.2	£16,499
IC	IC	Worm	Disc/disc	240/45-15	190	3458	156	6.1	14.7	£32,195
IC	IC	Worm	Disc/disc	195/70-14	191	3374	120	9.0	16.5	£8950
IC	IC	Worm	Disc/disc	195/70-14	191	3286	120 (Est)	N/A	N/A	£10,115
IC	IC	Worm	Disc/disc	205/70-14	191	3484	116	10.0	N/A	£10,540
IC	IC	Worm	Disc/disc	205/70-14	191	3585	122	8.9	16.7	£11,550
IC	IC	Worm	Disc/disc	205/70-14	191	3374	127	8.0	16.4	£13,643
IC	IC	Worm	Disc/disc	205/70-14	191	3506	130	7.8	15.9	£18,860

Make and model	Production Figures	Years Built	Body Styles	Mechanical Layout	Engine Make (if not own)	Capacity/(cc)/Layout/Valves	BHP/rpm	Torque (lb.ft)/rpm	Transmission gearbox/automatic transmission
						OHC			
						3453/6IL/ OHC	218/5200	228/4000	5-spd/Auto
M1	454	1979–1980	Spts Cpe	M/R	—	3453/6IL/ 2OHC	277/6500	239/5000	5-spd/-
3-Series	1,167,130 (Incl. all types)	1982–1990	Sal Est Conv	F/R	—	1596/4IL/ OHC	102/5500	105/4250	5-spd/Auto
						1766/4IL/ OHC	90/5500	103/4000	4-spd/Auto
							105/5800	105/4500	4-spd/Auto
						1796/4IL/ OHC	115/5500	122/4250	5-spd/Auto
						1796/4IL/ 2OHC	136/6000	127/4600	5-spd/-
						1990/6IL/ OHC	125/5800	125/4000	5-spd/Auto
						2315/6IL/ OHC	139/5300	151/4000	5-spd/Auto
							150/5300	148/4000	
						2494/6IL/ OHC	171/5800	164/4000	5-spd/Auto
325iX	15,815	1985–1990	Sal Est	F/4	—	2494/6IL/ OHC	171/5800	164/4000	5-spd/-
M3	17,184	1986–1990	Sal	F/R	—	2302/4IL/ 2OHC	200/6750	177/4750	5-spd/-
							220/6750	181/4750	5-spd/-
						2467/4IL/ 2OHC	238/7000	177/4750	5-spd/-
5-Series	722,327	1981–1987	Sal	F/R	—	1766/4IL/ OHC	90/5500	103/4000	4-spd/Auto
							105/5800	107/4500	4-spd/5-spd/-
						1990/6IL/ OHC	125/5800	121/4500	4-spd/Auto
							129/5800	128/4500	5-spd/Auto
						2494/6IL/ OHC	150/5500	158/4000	4-spd/Auto
						2693/6IL/ OHC	125/4250	177/3250	Auto/-
						2788/6IL/ OHC	184/5800	177/4200	5-spd/Auto
M535i	1,650	1980–1981	Sal	F/R	—	3453/6IL/ 2OHC	218/5200	228/4000	5-spd/-
M535i	9,483	1984–1987	Sal	F/R	—	3430/6IL/ OHC	218/6500	229/4000	5-spd/-
M5	2,205	1984–1987	Sal	F/R	—	3453/6IL/ 2OHC	286/6500	250/4500	5-spd/-
5-Series	N/A	1987–1995	Sal Est	F/R	—	1796/4IL/ 2OHC	115/5500	122/4250	5-spd/Auto
						1990/6IL/ OHC	129/6000	121/4300	5-spd/Auto
						1990/6IL/ 2OHC	150/5900	140/4700	5-spd/Auto
						2494/6IL/ OHC	170/5800	164/4300	5-spd/Auto
						2494/6IL/ 2OHC	192/5900	181/4700	5-spd/Auto
						2986/6IL/ OHC	188/5800	192/4000	5-spd/Auto
						3430/6IL/ OHC	211/5700	225/4000	5-spd/Auto
						2997/V8/ 2OHC	218/5800	214/4500	5-spd/Auto
						3982/V8/ 2OHC	286/5800	295/4500	6-spd/Auto
						2498/6IL/ OHC Diesel	143/4800	192/2200	5-spd/Auto
							115/4800	163/1900	5-spd/Auto
				F/4	—	2494/6IL/ 2OHC	192/5900	181/4700	5-spd/Auto
M635CSi	5,803	1984–1990	Spts Cpe	F/R	—	3453/6IL/ 2OHC	286/6500	251/4500	5-spd/-
M5	In prod	1988–Date	Sal	F/R	—	3453/6IL/ 2OHC	315/6900	265/4750	5-spd/-
						3795/6IL/ 2OHC	340/6900	295/4750	6-spd/-
7-Series	522,894	1986–1994	Sal	F/R	—	2986/6IL/ OHC	197/5800	203/4000	5-spd/Auto
						3430/6IL/ OHC	217/5700	232/4000	Auto/-
						2997/V8/ 2OHC	218/5800	210/4500	5-spd/Auto
						3982/V8/ 2OHC	286/5800	290/4500	Auto/-
						4988/V12/ OHC	300/5200	332/4100	Auto/-
							300/5200	332/4100	Auto/-
Z1	8,000	1986–1990	Spts	F/R	—	2494/6IL/	170/5800	164/4300	5-spd/-

Suspension Front	Rear	Steering	Brakes (Front/rear)	Wheels/Tyres	Length (in)	Weight (lb, unladen)	Top speed (mph)	0–60mph (sec)	Standing ¼-mile (sec)	UK Total Price (£: at Launch)
IC	IC	Worm	Disc/disc	205/70-14	191	3374	129	7.5	15.9	£15,395
IC	IC	R & P	Disc/disc	205/55-16/ 225/50-16	172	3120	162	5.5	13.8	£37,570
IC	IC	R & P	Disc/drum	175/70-14	170	2439	112	10.1	17.4	£11,125
IC	IC	R & P	Disc/disc	175/70-14	170	2183	109 (Est)	N/A	N/A	£5950
IC	IC	R & P	Disc/disc	175/70-14	170	2205	111	10.7	17.8	£8650
IC	IC	R & P	Disc/drum	195/65-14	170	2391	115	9.3	16.9	£11,590
IC	IC	R & P	Disc/disc	195/65-14	170	2552	125	9.3	16.8	£14,750
IC	IC	R & P	Disc/disc	195/60-14	170	2315	119	8.0	16.4	£8595
IC	IC	R & P	Disc/disc	195/60-14	170	2381	124	8.1	16.0	£11,750
IC	IC	R & P	Disc/disc	195/65-14	170	2316	131	7.4	15.4	£11,495
IC	IC	R & P	Disc/disc	195/65-14	170	2679	132	6.8	15.7	£17,250
IC	IC	R & P	Disc/disc	205/55-15	171	2762	139	7.1	15.7	£22,750
IC	IC	R & P	Disc/disc	225/45-16	171	2809	146	6.6	15.2	£26,960
IC	IC	R & P	Disc/disc	225/45-16	171	2762	151 (Est)	6.3	N/A	£34,500
IC	IC	Worm	Disc/disc	175-14	182	2554	102 (Est)	N/A	N/A	£7595
IC	IC	Worm	Disc/disc	175-14	182	2554	108	10.3	17.7	£8970
IC	IC	Worm	Disc/disc	175-14	182	2686	115 (Est)	N/A	N/A	£9235
IC	IC	Worm	Disc/drum	195/70-14	182	2906	117	10.5	17.6	£11,450
IC	IC	Worm	Disc/disc	175-14	182	2841	125 (Claimed)	N/A	N/A	£10,995
IC	IC	Worm	Disc/disc	175-14	182	2919	111	10.2	17.8	£11,495
IC	IC	Worm	Disc/disc	195/70-14	182	2907	133	8.7	16.8	£11,745
IC	IC	R & P	Disc/disc	195/70-14	182	3305	139	7.1	15.7	£13,745
IC	IC	R & P	Disc/disc	220/55-390	181	3116	143	7.4	15.6	£17,950
IC	IC	R & P	Disc/disc	220/55-390	182	3153	147	6.0	15.4	£31,295
IC	IC	R & P	Disc/disc	205/65-15	186	2932	119	11.5	18.3	£16,450
IC	IC	Worm	Disc/disc	195/65-15	186	3084	128	11.6	N/A	£15985
IC	IC	Worm	Disc/disc	225/60-15	186	3281	128	9.6	17.1	£18,915
IC	IC	Worm	Disc/disc	205/60-15	186	3286	133	8.7	16.6	£19240
IC	IC	Worm	Disc/disc	225/60-15	186	3381	138	8.7	16.5	£24,200
IC	IC	Worm	Disc/disc	205/65-15	186	3326	134	8.1	16.4	£23,875
IC	IC	Worm	Disc/disc	225/60-15	186	3507	141	7.4	15.9	£24,995
IC	IC	Worm	Disc/disc	225/60-15	186	3447	144 (Claimed)	7.8	15.9	£30,650
IC	IC	Worm	Disc/disc	225/60-15	186	3630	149	7.0	15.3	£33,950
IC	IC	Worm	Disc/disc	195/65-15	186	3263	129	10.7	N/A	£20,100
IC	IC	Worm	Disc/disc	195/65-15	186	3230	121 (Est)	N/A	N/A	£22,430
IC	IC	Worm	Disc/disc	225/55-16	186	3462	136 (Claimed)	N/A	N/A	£25,500
IC	IC	Worm	Disc/disc	240/45-415	187	3458	150	6.0	14.6	£32195
IC	IC	Worm	Disc/disc	235/45-17	186	3682	157	6.4	15.0	£43,500
IC	IC	Worm	Disc/disc	245/40-18	186	3801	170	5.4	14.0	£52,480
IC	IC	Worm	Disc/disc	205/65-15	193	3470	131	10.5	17.7	£19,850
IC	IC	Worm	Disc/disc	225/60-15	193	3883	145	9.0	16.7	£24,850
IC	IC	Worm	Disc/disc	225/60-15	193	3828	139	9.8	17.5	£36,950
IC	IC	Worm	Disc/disc	225/60-15	193	3947	146	7.9	16.1	£43,950
IC	IC	Worm	Disc/disc	240/50-15	193	4070	152	7.3	15.2	£48,250
IC	IC	Worm	Disc/disc	225/60-15	198	4101	155	7.7	15.9	£53,750
IC	IC	R & P	Disc/disc	225/45-16	155	2948	136	7.9	15.9	£36,925

Make and model	Production Figures	Years Built	Body Styles	Mechanical Layout	Engine Make (if not own)	Capacity/(cc)/Layout/Valves	BHP/rpm	Torque (lb.ft)/rpm	Transmission gearbox/automatic transmission
3-Series	In prod	1990–Date	Sal Conv Est	F/R	—	1596/4IL/ OHC	100/5500	104/4250	5-spd/Auto
						1796/4IL/ OHC	113/5900	119/3000	5-spd/Auto
						1990/6IL/ 2OHC	150/5900	140/3000	5-spd/Auto
						2494/6IL/ 2OHC	189/5900	177/4700	5-spd/Auto
						2OHC	192/5900	180/3500	5-spd/Auto
						2793/6IL/ 2OHC	193/5300	206/3950	5-spd/Auto
						1665/4IL/ OHC Diesel	90/4400	140/2000	5-spd/-
						2498/6IL/ OHC Diesel	115/4800	164/1900	5-spd/Auto
							143/4800	192/2200	5-spd/Auto
8-Series	In prod	1989–Date	Cpe	F/R	—	3982/V8/ 2OHC	286/5800	295/4500	5-spd/Auto
						4988/V12/ OHC	300/5200	332/4100	6-spd/Auto
						5576/V12/ OHC	380/5300	406/4000	6-spd/Auto
3-Series Coupe	In prod	1992–Date	Cpe	F/R	—	1596/4IL/ OHC	102/5500	111/3900	5-spd/Auto
						1796/4IL/ 2OHC	140/6000	129/4500	5-spd/Auto
						1991/6IL/ 2OHC	150/5900	140/4200	5-spd/Auto
						2494/6IL/ 2OHC	192/5900	180/3500	5-spd/Auto
						2494/6IL/ 2OHC	170/5500	180/3950	5-spd/Auto
						2793/6IL/ 2OHC	193/5300	206/3950	5-spd/Auto
M3	In prod	1992–Date	Cpe Conv Sal	F/R	—	2990/6IL/ 2OHC	286/7000	236/3600	5-spd/-
						3201/6IL/ 2OHC	321/7400	258/3250	6-spd/-
3-Series Compact	In prod	1993–Date	Htch	F/R	—	1596/4IL/ OHC	102/5500	110/3900	5-spd/Auto
						1796/4IL/ 2OHC	140/6200	129/4500	5-spd/Auto
						1665/4IL/ OHC Diesel	90/4400	140/2000	5-spd/-
7-Series	In prod	1994–Date	Sal	F/R	—	2793/6IL/ 2OHC	193/5300	206/3950	Auto/-
						2997/V8/ 2OHC	218/5800	214/4500	Auto/-
						3982/V8/ 2OHC	286/5800	295/4500	Auto/-
						5379/V12/ OHC	326/5000	362/3900	Auto/-
Z3	In prod	1995–Date	Spts	F/R	—	1895/4IL/ 2OHC	140/6000	132/4300	5-spd/-
5-Series	In prod	1995–Date	Sal	F/R	—	1991/6IL/ 2OHC	150/5900	140/4200	5-spd/Auto
						2495/6IL/ 2OHC	170/5500	180/3950	5-spd/Auto
						2793/6IL/ 2OHC	193/5300	206/3950	5-spd/Auto
						2498/6IL/ OHC Diesel	143/4600	206/2200	5-spd/Auto
Bristol									
411	600	1969–1976	Sal	F/R	Chrysler	6277/V8/ OHV	335/5200	425/3400	Auto/-
						6556/V8/ OHV	264/4800	335/3600	Auto/-
412	N/A	1975–1980	Sal Conv	F/R	Chrysler	6556/V8/ OHV	N/Q	N/Q	Auto/-
						5898/V8/ OHV	172/4000	270/2000	Auto/-
603	N/A	1976–1982	Sal	F/R	Chrysler	5898/V8/ OHV	N/Q	N/Q	Auto/-
						5211/V8/ OHV	N/Q	N/Q	Auto/-
Beaufighter	N/A	1980–1992	Sal	F/R	Chrysler	5898/V8/ OHV	N/Q	N/Q	Auto/-

Suspension Front	Rear	Steering	Brakes (Front/rear)	Wheels/ Tyres	Length (in)	Weight (lb,unladen)	Top speed (mph)	0–60mph (sec)	Standing ¼-mile (sec)	UK Total Price (£: at Launch)
IC	IC	R & P	Disc/drum	185/65-15	175	2767	120	11.2	18.2	£14,250
IC	IC	R & P	Disc/drum	185/65-15	175	2524	122	10.2	17.5	£15,285
IC	IC	R & P	Disc/disc	205/60-15	175	2800	132	9.1	16.9	£17,950
IC	IC	R & P	Disc/disc	205/60-15	175	2855	141	7.3	15.8	£18,650
IC	IC	R & P	Disc/disc	205/60-15	175	3043	143 (Claimed)	6.8	15.3	£23,750
IC	IC	R & P	Disc/disc	205/60-15	175	3073	143	6.4	15.4	£23,050
IC	IC	R & P	Disc/drum	205/60-15	175	2851	114	13.5	19.3	£17,990
IC	IC	R & P	Disc/disc	195/65-14	175	2944	123 (Est)	12.0	N/A	£18,950
IC	IC	R & P	Disc/disc	205/60-15	175	2902	134	8.8	16.8	£22,250
IC	IC	Worm	Disc/disc	235/50-16	188	3925	153	8.1	16.2	£54,490
IC	IC	Worm	Disc/disc	235/50-16	188	4152	159	7.1	15.5	£61,950
IC	IC	Worm	Disc/disc	235/45-17/ 265/40-17	188	4112	155 (Claimed)	6.0	N/A	£77,500
IC	IC	R & P	Disc/disc	185/65-15	174	2624	121 (Claimed)	N/A	N/A	£15,995
IC	IC	R & P	Disc/disc	205/60-15	174	2703	132	9.3	17.0	£17,250
IC	IC	R & P	Disc/disc	205/60-15	174	2900	133 (Claimed)	10.0	N/A	£18,950
IC	IC	R & P	Disc/disc	205/60-15	174	3043	144	7.2	15.6	£21,750
IC	IC	R & P	Disc/disc	205/60-15	174	2889	141 (Claimed)	7.8	N/A	£22,035
IC	IC	R & P	Disc/disc	205/60-15	174	3076	139	6.6	15.3	£23,600
IC	IC	R & P	Disc/disc	235/40-17	175	3352	162	5.4	13.9	£32,450
IC	IC	R & P	Disc/disc	225/45-17/ 245/40-17	175	3175	155 (Claimed)	N/A	N/A	£36,550
IC	IC	R & P	Disc/drum	185/65-15	166	2513	117	9.9	17.5	£13,350
IC	IC	R & P	Disc/disc	205/60-15	166	2767	128	9.8	17.4	£15,290
IC	IC	R & P	Disc/drum	185/65-15	166	2635	109 (Claimed)	N/A	N/A	£15,150
IC	IC	Worm	Disc/disc	215/65-16	196	3682	140 (Claimed)	9.4	N/A	£38,850
IC	IC	Worm	Disc/disc	215/65-16	196	3795	140	10.3	17.8	£39,800
IC	IC	Worm	Disc/disc	235/60-16	196	3947	155	8.8	16.7	£47,750
IC	IC	Worm	Disc/disc	235/60-16	202	4516	155	6.5	15.0	£69,450
IC	IC	R & P	Disc/disc	205/60-15	158	2585	123	8.4	16.3	£N/A
IC	IC	R & P	Disc/disc	205/65-15	188	3109	137 (Claimed)	10.0	N/A	£22,950
IC	IC	R & P	Disc/disc	205/65-15	188	3303	137	8.0	16.3	£24,870
IC	IC	R & P	Disc/disc	225/60-15	188	3168	142	8.9	15.3	£29,320
IC	IC	R & P	Disc/disc	205/65-15	188	3263	131 (Claimed)	10.2	N/A	£24,700
IC	BeamTor	R & P	Disc/disc	185-15 205-15	193	3726	138	7.0	15.0	£6997
IC	BeamTor	R & P	Disc/disc	205-15	195	3775	140 (Claimed)	N/A	N/A	£8973
IC	BeamTor	R & P	Disc/disc	205-15	195	3780	140	7.4	15.9	£14,584
IC	BeamTor	R & P	Disc/disc	205-15	195	3780	135 (Est)	N/A	N/A	£14,584
IC	BeamTor	R & P	Disc/disc	205-15	193	3931	140 (Est)	8.6	16.5	£19,661
IC	BeamTor	R & P	Disc/disc	205-15	193	3931	120 (Est)	N/A	N/A	£19,360
IC	BeamTor	R & P	Disc/disc	225/70-15	195	3850	140	6.7	15.0	£37,999

Make and model	Production Figures	Years Built	Body Styles	Mechanical Layout	Engine Make (if not own)	Capacity/(cc)/Layout/Valves	BHP/rpm	Torque (lb.ft)/rpm	Transmission gearbox/automatic transmission
Brigand/Britannia/Beaufort	N/A	1982–1993	Sal Conv	F/R	Chrysler	5898/V8/OHV	N/Q	N/Q	Auto/-
Blenheim	In prod	1993–Date	Cpe	F/R	Chrysler	5898/V8/OHV	N/Q	N/Q	Auto/-

Bugatti

EB110GT	N/A	1992–1995	Cpe	M/4	—	3500/V12/2OHC	553/8000	451/3750	6-spd/-

Buick

Century **	—	1978 model	Sal	F/R	—	4995/V8/OHV	145/3800	245/2400	Auto

Cadillac

Eldorado **	—	1972 model	Cpe	F/R	—	8194/V8/OHV	235/3800	385/2400	Auto
Seville **	—	1988 model	Sal	F(Tr)/F	—	4467/V8/OHV	155/4000	240/8000	Auto

Caterham

Super Seven S4	40	1973–1974	Spts	F/R	This model was a rebadged Lotus Seven S4. For all details – see **Lotus**				
Super Seven S3	In prod	1974–Date	Spts	F/R	Ford	1298/4IL/OHV	72/6000	68/4000	4-spd/-
					Rover	1396/4IL/2OHC	110/6000	96/5000	5-spd/-
							130/7400	99/5000	6-spd/-
						1589/4IL/2OHC	138/7000	115/5000	5-spd/-
					Ford	1598/4IL/OHV	84/6500	96/3600	4-spd/-
							110/6500	100/4600	4-spd/5-spd/-
					Ford	1698/4IL/OHV	135/6500	122/4500	4-spd/5-spd/-
							150/6500	N/Q	5-spd/-
					Lotus	1558/4IL/2OHC	126/6500	113/5500	4-spd/-
					Vegantune	1598/4IL/2OHC	130/6500	113/5500	5-spd/-
					Cosworth	1598/4IL/2OHC	155/6700	N/A	5-spd/-
							170/6700	N/A	5-spd/-
					Vauxhall	1998/4IL/2OHC	175/6000	155/4800	5-spd/-

[Note: Other very limited-edition types, with different engines, have also been made. Many optional extra/engine tunes were also available]

21	In prod	1995–Date	Spts	F/R	Rover	1589/4IL 2OHC	115/6000	107/3000	5-spd/6-spd/-
							138/7000	115/5000	5-spd/6-spd/-
						1796/4IL/ MG VVC To do 2OHC			

Chevrolet

Vega 2300 **	—	1971 model	Cpe	F/R	—	2286/4IL/OHC	80/4400	121/2600	4-spd/-
Blazer **	—	1978 model	Ute	F/4	—	5737/V8/OHV	165/3800	255/2800	Auto
Caprice **	—	1979 model	Sal	F/R	—	5002/V8/OHV	130/5000	245/2000	Auto
Corvette **	—	1984 model	Cpe	F/R	—	5737/V8/OHV	201/4200	289/2700	Auto
Corvette **	—	1986 model	Cpe	F/R	—	5737/V8/OHV	235/4100	330/2700	5-spd/-

Chrysler (USA/Canada/Australia)

Charger 770 **	—	1972 model	Cpe	F/R	—	5210/V8/OHV	230/4400	340/1600	Auto

Chrysler (Europe)

180/2-litre	N/A	1970–1980	Sal	F/R	—	1812/4IL/OHC	97/5600	106/3000	4-spd/Auto
						1981/4IL/OHC	110/5600	118/3600	Auto/-
Alpine	108,405 (UK assembly)	1975–1979	Htch	F(Tr)/F	—	1294/4IL/OHV	68/5600	79/2800	4-spd/-
						1442/4IL/OHV	85/5600	93/3000	4-spd/-

Suspension Front	Rear	Steering	Brakes (Front/rear)	Wheels/Tyres	Length (in)	Weight (lb, unladen)	Top speed (mph)	0–60mph (sec)	Standing ¼-mile (sec)	UK Total Price (£: at Launch)
IC	BeamTor	R & P	Disc/disc	215/70-15	193	3850	140 (Est)	N/A	N/A	£46,843
IC	BeamTor	R & P	Disc/disc	215/70-15	191	3850	140 (Est)	6.9	N/A	£109,980
IC	IC	R & P	Disc/disc	245/40-18/ 325/30-18	173	3453	212 (Claimed)	4.5	12.8	£285,500
IC	BeamC	Worm	Disc/drum	195/75-14	196	3315	104	11.9	18.2	£7467
IC	BeamC	Worm	Disc/drum	L78-15	223	4928	110	10.7	17.4	£6599
IC	IC	R & P	Disc/disc	215/65-15	189	3416	117	9.8	17.3	£28,995
IC	BeamC	R & P	Disc/drum	165-13	131	1162	90 (Est)	N/A	N/A	Special Order
IC	DDC	R & P	Disc/disc	185/60-14	133	1191	105 (Est)	6.8	15.6	£13,376
IC	DDC	R & P	Disc/disc	205/45-16	133	1269	109	6.0	14.6	£16,995
IC	DDC	R & P	Disc/disc	195/55-15	133	1221	115	6.0	14.7	£17,039
IC	BeamC	R & P	Disc/drum	185/70-13	131	1142	99	7.7	15.7	£2887
IC	BeamC DDC (1985 on)	R & P	Disc/drum	185/70-13	131	1162	105 (Est)	N/A	N/A	£5416
IC	BeamC	R & P	Disc/drum	195/60-14	131	1162	111	5.6	14.6	£7624
IC	DDC (1985 on)		Disc/drum	195/60-14	131	1162	114	5.3	14.6	£8441
IC	BeamC	R & P	Disc/drum	165-13	131	1162	114	6.2	14.9	£2196
IC	DDC	R & P	Disc/drum	195/70-13	131	1162	114 (Est)	N/A	N/A	£8512
IC	DDC	R & P	Disc/drum	195/70-13	131	1162	120 (Est)	N/A	N/A	£9363
IC	DDC	R & P	Disc/drum	195/70-13	131	1162	125 (Est)	N/A	N/A	Special Order
IC	DDC	R & P	Disc/disc	205/45-16	134	1383	126	5.2	13.6	£18,493
IC	DDC	R & P	Disc/disc	205/45-16	150	1429	118 (Est)	6.4	N/A	£18,750
IC	DDC	R & P	Disc/disc	205/45-16	150	1429	131 (Est)	5.8	N/A	£19,749 Special order
IC	BeamC	Worm	Disc/drum	A70-13	169	2246	95	16.4	20.5	£2058
Beam1/2E	Beam1/2E	Worm	Disc/drum	H78-15	184	5152	90	14.5	20.0	£9009
IC	BeamC	Worm	Disc/drum	235/70-15	212	4066	100	13.9	19.6	£11,996
ITrL	ITrL	R & P	Disc/disc	225/50-16	177	3127	142	6.6	15.0	£28,757
ITrL	ITrL	R & P	Disc/disc	255/60-16	177	3173	151	6.0	14.8	Special Order
ITor	Beam1/2E	Worm	Disc/drum	185-14	183	3276	114	9.3	16.7	£2999
IC	BeamC	R & P	Disc/disc	175-14	176	2334	99	13.6	19.0	£1498
IC	BeamC	R & P	Disc/disc	175-14	176	2450	101	12.8	19.2	£1822
ITor	IC	R & P	Disc/drum	155-13	167	2314	90	16.9	20.5	£2164
ITor	IC	R & P	Disc/drum	155-13	167	2314	100	12.9	19.0	£2375

Make and model	Production Figures	Years Built	Body Styles	Mechanical Layout	Engine Make (if not own)	Capacity/ (cc)/Layout/ Valves	BHP/ rpm	Torque (lb.ft)/rpm	Transmission gearbox/automatic transmission
Avenger	150,413	1976–1979	Sal Est	F/R	—	1295/4IL/ OHV	59/5000	69/2600	4-spd/-
						1599/4IL/ OHV	69/4800	91/2900	4-spd/Auto
							80/5400	86/4400	4-spd/Auto
Sunbeam	104,547	1977–1979	Htch	F/R	—	928/4IL/ OHC	42/5000	51/2600	4-spd/-
						1295/4IL/ OHV	59/5000	69/2600	4-spd/Auto
						1599/4IL/ OHV	69/4800	91/2900	4-spd/Auto
							80/5400	86/4400	4-spd/Auto
							100/6000	96/4600	4-spd/-
Sunbeam- Lotus	N/A (Incl. in Talbot figures)	1979	Htch	F/R	Lotus	2174/4IL/ 2OHC	150/5750	150/4500	5-spd/-
Horizon	N/A (See Talbot figures)	1977–1979	Htch	F(Tr)/F	—	1118/4IL/ OHV	59/5600	67/3000	4-spd/-
						1294/4IL/ OHV	68/5600	76/3000	4-spd/-

Note: All Chrysler-Europe cars remaining in production in mid-1979 were rebadged as **Talbot** models. For all further details, see the **Talbot** entry.

Citroen

Make and model	Production Figures	Years Built	Body Styles	Mechanical Layout	Engine Make (if not own)	Capacity/ (cc)/Layout/ Valves	BHP/ rpm	Torque (lb.ft)/rpm	Transmission gearbox/automatic transmission
2CV	3,872,583	1948–1990	Sal	F/F	—	375/2HO/ OHV AirC	9/3500	N/Q	4-spd/-
						425/2HO/ OHV AirC	12/3500	17/2900	4-spd/-
						602/2HO/ OHV AirC	29/6750	29/3500	4-spd/-
DS19/DS21/ DS23	1,456,115 (All DS and ID models) (Incl. 1,375 Cabriolets)	1955–1975	Sal Est Conv	F/F	—	1911/4IL/ OHV	75/4500	101/3000	4-spd/-
							83/4500	105/3500	4-spd/-
						1985/4IL/ OHV	84/5250	106/3500	4-spd/-
							91/5900	104/3500	4-spd/-
							99/5500	104/3500	4-spd/-
						2175/4IL/ OHV	100/5500	121/3000	4-spd/-
							106/5500	123/3500	4-spd/5-spd/Auto
							125/5500	145/4000	4-spd/5-spd/-
						2347/4IL/ OHV	115/5500	135/3500	5-spd/Auto
							130/5250	144/2500	5-spd/Auto
ID19 family	—	1956–1975	Sal	F/F	—	1911/4IL/ OHV	62/4000	92/3000	4-spd/-
							66/4500	98/2500	4-spd/-
							74/4750	98/3500	4-spd/-
						1985/4IL/ OHV	78/5250	106/3000	4-spd/-
							81/5500	100/3000	4-spd/-
							89/5500	106/2500	4-spd/-
							91/5900	104/3500	4-spd/-
							99/5500	104/3500	4-spd/-
Ami 6	1,039,384	1961–1971	Sal Est	F/F	—	602/2HO/ OHV AirC	22/4500	30/2800	4-spd/-
Ami 8/Super	800,775	1969–1979	Sal Est	F/F	—	602/2HO/ OHV AirC	32/5750	30/4000	4-spd/-
						1015/4HO/ OHC AirC	54/6500	50/3500	4-spd/-
Dyane 4/6	1,443,583	1967–1984	Sal	F/F	—	435/2HO/ OHV AirC	24/6750	21/4000	4-spd/-
						602/2HO/ OHV AirC	29/6750	29/3500	4-spd/-
							32/5750	31/3500	
SM	12,920	1970–1975	Cpe	F/F	—	2670/V6/ 2OHC	170/5500	172/4000	5-spd/-
							178/5500	178/4000	5-spd/-
GS/GSA family	2,473,499	1970–1987	Sal Htch Est	F/F	—	1015/4HO/ OHC AirC	56/6500	52/3500	4-spd/-
						1129/4HO/ OHC AirC	57/5750	59/3500	4-spd/-
						1220/4HO/ OHC AirC	60/6500	64/3250	4-spd/SemiAuto
							65/5750	67/3250	4-spd/-
						1299/4HO/ OHC AirC	65/5500	72/3500	5-spd/Auto
CX range	1,042,460	1974–1989	Sal Est	F(Tr)/F	—	1985/4IL/ OHV	102/5500	112/3000	4-spd/-
						1995/4IL/ OHC	106/5500	122/3250	4-spd/5-spd/-
						2165/4IL/ OHC	115/5600	130/3250	5-spd/-
						2175/4IL/ OHV	112/5500	123/3500	4-spd/Auto
						2347/4IL/ OHV	115/5500	131/3000	4-spd/Auto
							128/4800	145/3600	5-spd/-
						2473/4IL/ OHC	168/5000	217/3250	5-spd/-

Suspension Front	Rear	Steering	Brakes (Front/rear)	Wheels/Tyres	Length (in)	Weight (lb,unladen)	Top speed (mph)	0–60mph (sec)	Standing 1/4-mile (sec)	UK Total Price (£: at Launch)
IC	BeamC	R & P	Disc/drum	155-13	163	1889	90	17.5	20.6	£1755
IC	BeamC	R & P	Disc/drum	155-13	163	1929	94	13.7	19.1	£1931
IC	BeamC	R & P	Disc/drum	155-13	163	2013	95	13.6	19.2	£2516
IC	BeamC	R & P	Disc/drum	145-13	151	1757	77	24.3	22.7	£2324
IC	BeamC	R & P	Disc/drum	155-13	151	2002	92	14.8	21.0	£2400
IC	BeamC	R & P	Disc/drum	155-13	151	1953	95	12.9	19.2	£2692
IC	BeamC	R & P	Disc/drum	155-13	151	2004	100 (Est)	N/A	N/A	£3213
IC	BeamC	R & P	Disc/drum	175/70-13	151	2037	107	10.7	18.5	£3779
IC	BeamC	R & P	Disc/drum	185/70-13	151	2166	121	7.4	15.6	£6995
ITor	IC	R & P	Disc/drum	145-13	156	2081	95	15.3	20.3	£2740
ITor	IC	R & P	Disc/drum	145-13	156	2131	95	15.4	20.0	£2869
IC	IC	R & P	Drum/drum	125-400	149	1120	41	N/A	34.4	£565
IC	IC	R & P	Drum/drum	125-400	149	1176	47	N/A	31.1	£598
IC	IC	R & P	Drum/drum	125-15	151	1322	67	32.8	24.3	£899
IHP	IHP	R & P	Disc/drum	165-400	189	2464	87	23.3	22.6	£1486
IHP	IHP	R & P	Disc/drum	165-400	189	2780	92	18.4	21.7	£1745
IHP	IHP	R & P	Disc/drum	180-380	189	2811	92 (Est)	N/A	N/A	£1796
IHP	IHP	R & P	Disc/drum	180-380	189	2878	97 (Est)	N/A	N/A	£1799
IHP	IHP	R & P	Disc/drum	180-380	189	2878	105 (Est)	N/A	N/A	£1852
IHP	IHP	R & P	Disc/drum	180-380	189	2878	107	14.4	19.5	£1977
IHP	IHP	R & P	Disc/drum	185-15	189	2844	110 (Est)	N/A	N/A	£1879
IHP	IHP	R & P	Disc/drum	185-15	189	2960	118	12.3	18.9	£2107
IHP	IHP	R & P	Disc/drum	185-15	189	2904	111 (Est)	N/A	N/A	£2282
IHP	IHP	R & P	Disc/drum	185-15	189	2955	120	10.4	17.6	£2811
IHP	IHP	R & P	Disc/drum	165-400	189	2464	85 (Est)	N/A	N/A	£1498
IHP	IHP	R & P	Disc/drum	165-400	189	2720	87	21.1	22.3	£1498
IHP	IHP	R & P	Disc/drum	165-400	189	2744	97	15.6	21.0	£1499
IHP	IHP	R & P	Disc/drum	180-380	191	2668	99 (Est)	N/A	N/A	£1563
IHP	IHP	R & P	Disc/drum	180-15	191	2668	100	14.2	19.6	£1699
IHP	IHP	R & P	Disc/drum	180-15	191	2777	104 (Est)	N/A	N/A	£1459
IHP	IHP	R & P	Disc/drum	180-15	191	2668	105	14.5	19.6	£1734
IHP	IHP	R & P	Disc/drum	180-15	191	2788	105 (Est)	N/A	N/A	£1607
IC	IC	R & P	Drum/drum	125-15	155	1400	68	44.0	25.2	£824
IC	IC	R & P	Disc/drum	135-15	157	1545	72	31.7	24.5	£649
IC	IC	R & P	Disc/drum	135-15	157	1775	88	17.1	20.5	£1025
IC	IC	R & P	Drum/drum	125-380	154	1224	67	63.2	26.0	£549
IC	IC	R & P	Drum/drum	125-15	154	1312	69	30.8	24.3	£610
IHP	IHP	R & P	Disc/disc	195/70-15	193	3197	139	9.3	17.1	£5480
IHP	IHP	R & P	Disc/disc	205/70-15	193	3197	142	8.3	16.5	£6154
IHP	IHP	R & P	Disc/disc	145-15	152	1867	90	18.0	21.5	£1001
IHP	IHP	R & P	Disc/disc	145-15	152	2039	93	16.0	20.2	£2490
IHP	IHP	R & P	Disc/disc	145-15	152	1886	94	14.9	20.1	£1315
IHP	IHP	R & P	Disc/disc	145-15	152	2072	94	15.4	20.0	£1729
IHP	IHP	R & P	Disc/disc	145-15	152	2184	98	14.1	19.5	£4060
IHP	IHP	R & P	Disc/disc	185-14/175-14	181	2788	110	12.2	18.8	£3195
IHP	IHP	R & P	Disc/disc	185-14/175-14	181	2713	109	12.5	18.2	£5697
IHP	IHP	R & P	Disc/disc	195/70-14/185/70-14	181	2836	111	10.8	17.6	£9290
IHP	IHP	R & P	Disc/disc	185-14/175-14	181	2822	112	11.6	18.2	£3495
IHP	IHP	R & P	Disc/disc	185-14/175-14	181	2990	113	11.8	18.1	£4991
IHP	IHP	R & P	Disc/disc	175-14	181	3000	118	10.1	17.4	£6530
IHP	IHP	R & P	Disc/disc	210/55-390	181	3107	130	7.6	15.7	£12,990

Make and model	Production Figures	Years Built	Body Styles	Mechanical Layout	Engine Make (if not own)	Capacity/ (cc)/Layout/ Valves	BHP/ rpm	Torque (lb.ft)/rpm	Transmission gearbox/automatic transmission
						2175/4IL/ OHV Diesel	66/4500	93/2750	4-spd/-
						2473/4IL/ OHV Diesel	75/4250	111/2000	5-spd/-
							95/3700	159/2000	5-spd/-
							120/3900	188/2000	5-spd/-
CX Prestige	(Incl. above)	As above	Sal	F(Tr)/F	—	2347/4IL/ OHV	128/4800	145/3600	5-spd/Auto
Visa	1,254,390	1978–1988	Htch Conv	F/F	—	652/2HO/ OHV AirC	36/5500	38/3500	4-spd/-
				F(Tr)/F	—	954/4IL/ OHC	45/6000	51/2750	4-spd/-
						1124/4IL/ OHC	57/6250	59/3000	4-spd/-
							50/5400	61/2500	4-spd/-
						1219/4IL/ OHC	64/6000	67/3000	4-spd/-
						1360/4IL/ OHC	80/5800	79/2800	5-spd/-
							60/5000	77/2500	5-spd/-
						1580/4IL/ OHC	105/6250	99/4000	5-spd/-
							115/6250	97/4000	5-spd/-
						1769/4IL/ OHC Diesel	60/4600	82/2000	4-spd/-
LNA	223,772	1978–1986	Htch	F(Tr)/F	Peugeot	1124/4IL/ OHC	50/5500	62/2500	4-spd/-
AX	In prod	1986–Date	Htch	F(Tr)F	—	954/4IL/ OHC	45/5200	54/2400	4-spd/-
						1124/4IL/ OHC	55/5800	66/3200	4-spd/5-spd/-
						1294/4IL/ OHC	95/6800	83/5000	5-spd/-
						1360/4IL/ OHC	65/5400	83/3000	5-spd/-
							75/6200	82/4000	5-spd/-
							85/6400	85/4000	5-spd/-
							100/6800	90/4200	5-spd/-
						1360/4IL/ OHC Diesel	54/5000	62/2500	5-spd/-
						1527/4IL/ OHC Diesel	58/5000	70/2250	5-spd/-
BX	2,333,240	1982–1994	Htch Est	F/F	—	1360/4IL/ OHC	62/5500	79/2500	4-spd/-
							73/5600	82/3000	5-spd/-
						1580/4IL/ OHC	93/6000	97/3500	5-spd/Auto
						1905/4IL/ OHC	105/5600	119/3000	5-spd/Auto
							125/5500	128/4500	5-spd/Auto
						1905/4IL/ 2OHC	155/6500	133/5000	5-spd/-
						1769/4IL/ OHC Diesel	90/4300	134/2100	5-spd/-
						1905/4IL/ OHC Diesel	65/4600	88/2000	5-spd/Auto
				F(Tr)/4	—	1905/4IL/ OHC	107/6000	121/3000	5-spd/-
BX GTi 4x4	Incl. above	1990–1994	Htch	F(Tr)/4	—	1905/4IL/ OHC	125/5500	128/4500	5-spd/-
ZX	In prod	1991–Date	Htch Est	F(Tr)/F	—	1360/4IL/ OHC	75/5800	85/3800	5-spd/-
						1580/4IL/ OHC	89/6400	98/3000	5-spd/-
						1761/4IL/ OHC	103/6000	113/3000	5-spd/-
						1905/4IL/ OHC	130/6000	118/3250	5-spd/-
						1998/4IL/ OHC	123/6000	130/2700	5-spd/Auto
						1998/4IL/ 2OHC	155/6500	135/3500	5-spd/-
						1905/4IL/ OHC Diesel	71/4600	90/2000	5-spd/Auto
							92/4000	148/2250	5-spd/-
XM	In prod	1989–Date	Sal Est	F(Tr)/F	—	1998/4IL/ OHC	115/5800	126/2250	5-spd/-
							130/5600	132/4800	5-spd/-
							145/5400	166/2200	5-spd/-
						1998/4IL/ 2OHC	135/5500	135/4200	5-spd/Auto
							150/5300	177/2500	5-spd/Auto
						2963/V6/ OHC	170/5600	177/4600	Auto/-
						2975/V6/ OHC	170/5600	173/4600	5-spd/Auto
							200/6000	191/3600	5-spd/-
						2088/4IL/ OHC Diesel	110/4300	183/2000	5-spd/Auto
						2445/4IL/ OHC Diesel	130/4300	217/2000	5-spd/-

Suspension Front	Rear	Steering	Brakes (Front/rear)	Wheels/Tyres	Length (in)	Weight (lb,unladen)	Performance Top speed (mph)	0–60mph (sec)	Standing ¼-mile (sec)	UK Total Price (£: at Launch)
IHP	IHP	R & P	Disc/disc	185-14/ 175-14	181	3140	89	20.8	21.9	£4514
IHP	IHP	R & P	Disc/disc	185-14/	181	2960	97	17.0	20.7	£5697
IHP	IHP	R & P	Disc/disc	175-14	181	3052	106	12.5	19.0	£10,862
IHP	IHP	R & P	Disc/disc	195/70-14	181	2978	112	10.1	17.8	£15,096
IHP	IHP	R & P	Disc/disc	185-14	194	3252	115	11.7	18.5	Special order
IC	IC	R & P	Disc/drum	135-13	147	1621	76	26.1	23.8	£2950
IC	IC	R & P	Disc/drum	145-13	147	1786	83 (Claimed)	N/A	N/A	£3895
IC	IC	R & P	Disc/drum	145-13	147	1764	89	15.4	19.4	£3250
IC	IC	R & P	Disc/drum	145-13	147	1748	78	20.1	20.6	£3278
IC	IC	R & P	Disc/drum	160/65-340	147	1780	96	12.8	19.1	£3721
IC	IC	R & P	Disc/drum	160/65-340	147	1851	103	11.2	18.1	£4596
IC	IC	R & P	Disc/drum	155/70-13	147	1731	93	14.9	19.5	£5162
IC	IC	R & P	Disc/drum	185/60-13	147	2013	109	9.7	17.4	£5899
IC	IC	R & P	Disc/drum	185/60-13	147	1937	113	9.1	17.1	£6496
IC	IC	R & P	Disc/drum	145-13	145	1984	89	19.1	21.1	£4550
IC	IC	R & P	Disc/drum	135-13	135	1651	83	16.0	20.3	£2990
IC	ITor	R & P	Disc/drum	135/70-13	138	1411	83	18.1	20.7	£4399
IC	ITor	R & P	Disc/drum	135/70-13	138	1393	100	12.6	17.9	£5049
IC	ITor	R & P	Disc/drum	185/60-13	138	1742	110	9.3	17.0	£6899
IC	ITor	R & P	Disc/drum	155/70-13	138	1508	99	11.0	18.1	£5900
IC	ITor	R & P	Disc/drum	165/65-13	138	1632	107 (Est)	N/A	N/A	£6450
IC	ITor	R & P	Disc/drum	155/65-14	138	1795	107	9.0	16.8	£7914
IC	ITor	R & P	Disc/drum	185/60-13	138	1806	114	9.3	17.1	£9995
IC	ITor	R & P	Disc/drum	145/70-14	138	1632	91	16.2	20.3	£7211
IC	ITor	R & P	Disc/drum	155/70-13	138	1742	98 (Claimed)	12.7	N/A	£6800
IHP	IHP	R & P	Disc/disc	145-14	167	1951	96 (Est)	N/A	N/A	£4790
IHP	IHP	R & P	Disc/disc	165/70-14	167	2095	99	14.3	19.3	£7758
IHP	IHP	R & P	Disc/disc	170/65-365	167	2114	106	10.7	17.9	£5600
IHP	IHP	R & P	Disc/disc	165/70-14	167	2280	112	10.0	17.3	£7289
IHP	IHP	R & P	Disc/disc	185/60-14	167	2259	121	9.0	16.6	£9184
IHP	IHP	R & P	Disc/disc	195/60-14	167	2365	130	7.9	16.2	£12,300
IHP	IHP	R & P	Disc/disc	165/70-14	167	2346	104	11.9	18.3	£10,885
IHP	IHP	R & P	Disc/disc	165/70-14	167	2261	98	14.4	19.7	£6100
IHP	IHP	R & P	Disc/disc	165/70-14	167	2437	114 (Claimed)	N/A	N/A	£12,945
IHP	IHP	R & P	Disc/disc	185/60-14	166	2500	115	10.6	17.8	£13,900
IC	ITor	R & P	Disc/drum	165/70-13	160	2083	105	11.9	18.7	£8680
IC	ITor	R & P	Disc/drum	175/65-14	160	2302	108	11.5	18.6	£11,140
IC	ITor	R & P	Disc/drum	175/65-14	160	2370	112	10.7	18.0	£10,425
IC	ITor	R & P	Disc/disc	185/60-14	160	2326	124	9.1	17.1	£11,140
IC	ITor	R & P	Disc/disc	185/60-14	160	2326	125 (Claimed)	8.4	N/A	£12,575
IC	ITor	R & P	Disc/disc	195/55-15	160	2536	137 (Claimed)	8.0	N/A	£14,500
IC	ITor	R & P	Disc/drum	165/70-13	160	2335	97	14.7	20.7	£9490
IC	ITor	R & P	Disc/drum	175/65-14	160	2514	110	11.0	18.3	£11,370
IHP	IHP	R & P	Disc/disc	185/70-15	185	2822	120 (Est)	10.2	N/A	£14,499
IHP	IHP	R & P	Disc/disc	195/60-15	185	3150	120	11.2	19.0	£15,949
IHP	IHP	R & P	Disc/disc	205/60-15	185	3086	131 (Est)	8.2	N/A	£17,745
IHP	IHP	R & P	Disc/disc	195/65-15	185	3076	127 (Est)	9.1	N/A	£15,995
IHP	IHP	R & P	Disc/disc	205/60-15	185	3120	134 (Est)	N/A	N/A	£17,090
IHP	IHP	R & P	Disc/disc	205/60-15	185	3296	138 (Claimed)	N/A	N/A	£26,310
IHP	IHP	R & P	Disc/disc	205/60-15	185	3310	134 (Auto)	9.5	17.3	£20,099
IHP	IHP	R & P	Disc/disc	205/60-15	185	3252	143	7.5	15.5	£26,910
IHP	IHP	R & P	Disc/disc	195/65-15	185	3205	116	12.4	18.8	£18,450
IHP	IHP	R & P	Disc/disc	205/65-15	185	3495	125 (Claimed)	10.4	N/A	£20,525

Make and model	Production Figures	Years Built	Body Styles	Mechanical Layout	Engine Make (if not own)	Capacity/ (cc)/Layout/ Valves	BHP/ rpm	Torque (lb.ft)/rpm	Transmission gearbox/automatic transmission
Xantia	In prod	1992–Date	Htch Est	F(Tr)/F	—	1580/4IL/ OHC	90/6000	98/2600	5-spd/Auto
						1761/4IL/ OHC	103/6000	112/3000	5-spd/Auto
						1761/4IL/ 2OHC	112/5500	114/4250	5-spd/-
						1998/4IL/ OHC	123/5750	132/2750	5-spd/Auto
						1998/4IL/ 2OHC	135/5500 150/5300	133/4200 173/2500	5-spd/- 5-spd/-
						1905/4IL/ OHC Diesel	71/4600 92/4000	90/2000 148/2250	5-spd/- 5-spd/-
Synergie	In prod	1994–Date	Est	F(Tr)/F	—	1998/4IL/ OHC	123/5750	127/2650	5-spd/-
						1905/4IL/ OHC Diesel	92/4000	148/2250	5-spd/-

Clan

Crusader	315	1971–1974	Spts Cpe	R/R	Chrysler-UK	875/4IL/ OHC	51/6100	52/4300	4-spd/-
Clover	40	1984–1986	Spts Cpe	R/R	Alfa Romeo	1490/HO/ OHC	105/6000	98/4000	5-spd/-

Colt (later badged Mitsubishi, from 1984)

Lancer	N/A	1973–1979	Sal Est	F/R	—	1238/4IL/ OHC	55/5200	62/3000	4-spd/-
						1439/4IL/ OHC	68/5000	77/3000	4-spd/Auto
						1597/4IL/ OHC	82/5500	85/3000	4-spd/Auto
Galant	N/A	1973–1980	Sal Est Cpe	F/R	—	1597/4IL/ OHC	82/5500	85/3000	4-spd/Auto
						1995/4IL/ OHC	90/5250 125/6200	102/3000 126/4000	5-spd/Auto 5-spd/-
Celeste	N/A	1975–1981	Htch Cpe	F/R	—	1597/4IL/ OHC	73/5000 82/5000	85/3000 101/3500	4-spd/- 4-spd/-
						1995/4IL/ OHC	90/5250	102/3000	5-spd/Auto
Sigma	N/A	1976–1980	Sal Est	F/R	—	1597/4IL/ OHC	75/5000	86/3000	4-spd/Auto
						1995/4IL/ OHC	85/5000	101/3500	5-spd/Auto
Lancer	N/A	1979–1983	Sal	F/R	—	1410/4IL/ OHC	68/5000	77/3500	4-spd/-
						1597/4IL/ OHC	82/5500	96/3500	5-spd/-
						1997/4IL/ OHC	168/5500	181/3500	5-spd/-
Galant/ Galant Sigma	N/A	1980–1983	Sal Est	F/R	—	1597/4IL/ OHC	75/5000	85/3000	4-spd/5-spd/Auto
						1997/4IL/ OHC	102/5500 170/5500	105/3500 180/3500	5-spd/Auto 5-spd/-

Note: The **Mitsubishi** marque name was officially adopted in 1984.

Dacia

Denem	N/A	1969–Date	Sal Est	F/F	Renault	1289/4IL/ OHV	60/5250	70/3000	4-spd/-
Duster	N/A	1981–1990	Ute	F/4	Renault	1397/4IL/ OHV	65/5250	72/3200	4-spd/-
					Renault	1595/4IL/ OHC Diesel	54/4800	75/2250	4-spd/-

Daewoo

Nexia	In prod	1994–Date	Sal Htch	F(Tr)/F	GM	1498/4IL/ OHC	75/5400	91/3200	5-spd/-
						1498/4IL/ 2OHC	90/4800	101/3600	5-spd/Auto
Espero	In prod	1991–Date	Sal	F(Tr)/F	GM	1498/4IL/ 2OHC	90/4800	101/3600	5-spd/Auto
						1796/4IL/ OHC	95/5400	107/2800	5-spd/Auto
						1998/4IL/ OHC	103/5000	121/3000	5-spd/Auto

DAF

| Suspension | | Steering | Brakes | Wheels/ | Length (in) | Weight | Performance | | Standing | UK Total |
Front	Rear		(Front/rear)	Tyres		(lb,unladen)	Top speed (mph)	0–60mph (sec)	¼-mile (sec)	Price (£: at Launch)
IHP	IHP	R & P	Disc/disc	175/70-14	175	2580	109 (Claimed)	12.4	N/A	£10,895
IHP	IHP	R & P	Disc/disc	175/70-14	175	2714	115	11.9	18.4	£12,095
IHP	IHP	R & P	Disc/disc	175/70-14	175	2721	120 (Claimed)	10.0	N/A	£12,195
IHP	IHP	R & P	Disc/disc	185/65-14	175	2729	123 (Claimed)	10.6	N/A	£12,795
IHP	IHP	R & P	Disc/disc	185/65-14	175	2864	126 (Est)	9.3	N/A	£13,605
IHP	IHp	R & P	Disc/disc	205/60-15	175	3102	132 (Est)	8.9	N/A	£18,480
IHP	IHP	R & P	Disc/disc	195/55-14	175	2668	99 (Est)	N/A	N/A	£10,895
IHP	IHP	R & P	Disc/disc	195/55-14	175	2692	111	13.4	19.3	£15,995
IC	IC	R & P	Disc/drum	195/65-15	175	3329	110 (Claimed)	14.6	N/A	£16,200
IC	IC	R & P	Disc/drum	205/65-15	175	3451	100 (Claimed)	17.2	N/A	£17,200
IC	IC	R & P	Drum/drum	155-12	152	1278	100	12.5	18.8	£1410
IC	IC	R & P	Disc/disc	185/60-13	148	1345	110	8.6	16.7	£9200
IC	Beam1/2E	Worm	Disc/drum	155-13	156	1730	92	14.3	19.1	£1625
IC	Beam1/2E	Worm	Disc/drum	155-13	156	1797	96	11.6	18.7	£1760
IC	Beam1/2E	Worm	Disc/drum	155-13	156	1885	102	12.3	18.6	£2089
IC	Beam1/2E	Worm	Disc/drum	165-13	165	2072	92	13.9	19.5	£1698
IC	Beam1/2E	Worm	Disc/drum	165-13	165	2205	100	11.9	18.5	£2186
IC	Beam1/2E	Worm	Disc/drum	185/70-13	162	2218	107	11.7	18.2	£2995
IC	Beam1/2E	Worm	Disc/drum	165-13	162	2050	90 (Est)	N/A	N/A	£2299
IC	Beam1/2E	Worm	Disc/drum	165-13	162	2162	95	13.0	18.9	£2299
IC	Beam1/2E	Worm	Disc/drum	175/70-13	162	2160	104	11.2	19.1	£2599
IC	BeamC	Worm	Disc/drum	165-13	170	2216	93 (Claimed)	N/A	N/A	£2995
IC	BeamC	Worm	Disc/drum	165-13	171	2316	97	13.4	19.2	£3499
IC	BeamC	Worm	Disc/drum	155-13	166	2061	90 (Est)	N/A	N/A	£4399
IC	BeamC	Worm	Disc/disc	165-13	166	2187	95	13.5	18.9	£4799
IC	BeamC	Worm	Disc/disc	175/70-14	166	2336	127	8.6	16.1	£8499
IC	IC	Worm	Disc/drum	165-13	176	2216	98 (Claimed)	N/A	N/A	£5225
IC	IC	Worm	Disc/drum	165-14	176	2702	103	11.9	18.3	£5999
IC	IC	Worm	Disc/disc	185/70-14	176	2712	124 (Claimed)	N/A	N/A	£9379
IC	BeamC	R & P	Disc/drum	145-13	171	2116	94	12.9	19.3	£3190
IC	Beam1/2E	Worm	Disc/drum	175-14	149	2685	72	22.7	22.6	£5995
IC	Beam1/2E	Worm	Disc/drum	175-14	149	2536	68 (Est)	N/A	N/A	Special order
IC	IC	R & P	Disc/drum	175/70-13	168	2156	100	11.4	18.3	£8295
IC	IC	R & P	Disc/drum	175/70-13	168	2156	105 (Claimed)	12.0	N/A	£9495
IC	IC	R & P	Disc/drum	185/65-14	182	2392	105 (Claimed)	12.6	N/A	£10,695
IC	IC	R & P	Disc/drum	185/65-14	182	2448	104 (Claimed)	12.0	N/A	£11,295
IC	IC	R & P	Disc/drum	185/65-14	182	2602	109	10.8	17.9	£12,195

Make and model	Production Figures	Years Built	Body Styles	Mechanical Layout	Engine Make (if not own)	Capacity/(cc)/Layout/Valves	BHP/rpm	Torque (lb.ft)/rpm	Transmission gearbox/automatic transmission
Daffodil/ 750/33	312,367	1962–1975	Sal	F/R	—	590/2HO/ OHV AirC	22/4000	33/2500	Auto/-
						746/2HO/ OHV AirC	26/4000	42/2800	Auto/-
44/46	200,258	1966–1976	Sal Est	F/R	—	844/2HO/ OHV AirC	34/4500	51/2400	Auto/-
55/66	310,528	1968–1975	Sal Cpe Est	F/R	Renault	1108/4IL/ OHV	46/4600 55/5600	62/2800 61/3800	Auto/- Auto/-
						1289/4IL/ OHV	57/5200	69/2800	Auto/-

Note: In the UK the Daf 66 officially became the Volvo 66 in 1975.

Daihatsu

Make and model	Production Figures	Years Built	Body Styles	Mechanical Layout	Engine Make (if not own)	Capacity/(cc)/Layout/Valves	BHP/rpm	Torque (lb.ft)/rpm	Transmission gearbox/automatic transmission
F20LK	N/A	1976–1984	Ute	F/4	—	1587/4IL/ OHV	66/4800	81/3400	4-spd/-
Charade	N/A	1977–1983	Htch	F(Tr)/F	—	993/3IL/ OHC	50/5500 52/5600	54/3000 55/3200	5-spd/- 5-spd/SemiAuto
Domino	N/A	1980–1986	Htch	F(Tr)/F	—	547/2IL/ OHC	27/6000	28/3500	4-spd/-
						617/2IL/ OHC	30/5700	33/3500	4-spd/-
Domino	N/A	1985–1990	Htch	F(Tr)/F	—	846/3IL/ OHC	44/5500	50/3200	5-spd/-
Charade	N/A	1981–1987	Htch	F(Tr)/F	—	993/4IL/ OHC	51/5600 68/5500	56/3200 78/3200	5-spd/- 5-spd/-
						993/4IL/ OHC Diesel	37/4600 46/4800	45/3500 63/2900	5-spd/- 5-spd/-
Charade	579,700 (Incl. GTti)	1987–1993	Htch	F(Tr)/F	—	993/3IL/ OHC	51/5600 67/5500	56/3200 78/3500	5-spd/- 5-spd/-
						993/3IL/ 2OHC	99/6500	96/3500	5-spd/-
						1295/4IL/ OHC	89/6500 75/6500	77/5000 75/3900	5-spd/Auto 5-spd/-
						993/3IL/ OHC Diesel	47/4800	63/2300	5-spd/-
Charmant	N/A	1981–1987	Sal	F/R	Toyota	1290/4IL/ OHC	64/5400	72/3600	5-spd/Auto
						1588/4IL/ OHC	74/5400 82/5600	87/3600 96/3600	5-spd/Auto 5-spd/Auto
Fourtrak	N/A	1984–1993	Ute	F/4	—	1998/4IL/ OHC	87/4600	116/3000	5-spd/-
						2237/4IL/ OHC	91/4200	132/2500	5-spd/-
						2765/4IL/ OHV Diesel	72/3600 87/3500 90/3400	125/2200 155/2200 165/2200	5-spd/- 5-spd/- 5-spd/-
Fourtrack Independent	In prod	1993–Date	Ute	F/4	—	2765/4IL/ OHV Diesel	101/3400	181/1900	5-spd/-
Sportrak	In prod	1988–Date	Ute	F/4	—	1580/4IL/ OHC	85/6000 94/5700	93/3500 95/4800	5-spd/- 5-spd/-
Applause	In prod	1989–Date	Htch	F(Tr)/F	—	1589/4IL/ OHC	91/6000 105/6000	96/3500 99/4800	5-spd/- 5-spd/Auto
Mira	In prod	1990–Date	Htch	F(Tr)/F	—	659/3IL/ OHC	63/7500	68/4000	4-spd/-
						847/3IL/ OHC	40/5500	48/3200	5-spd/-
Charade	In prod	1993–date	Sal	F(Tr)/F	—	1296/4IL/ OHC	84/6500	77/5000	5-spd/Auto
						1499/4IL/ OHC	90/6200	87/3600	5-spd/-
						1590/4IL/ OHC	105/6000 88/6200	99/4000 88/3600	5-spd/- 5-spd/-
Hijet	In prod	1994–Date	Est	F/R	—	993/3IL/ OHC	47/5300	56/4000	5-spd/-

Daimler

Make and model	Production Figures	Years Built	Body Styles	Mechanical Layout	Engine Make (if not own)	Capacity/(cc)/Layout/Valves	BHP/rpm	Torque (lb.ft)/rpm	Transmission gearbox/automatic transmission
DS420 Limo	4,206	1968–1992	Limo	F/R	—	4235/6IL/ 2OHC	245/5500	282/3750	Auto/-
Sovereign SI/SII	45,413	1969–1979	Sal Cpe	F/R	—	2792/6IL/ 2OHC	140/5150	150/4250	4-spd (+O/D)/Auto
						3442/6IL/ 2OHC	160/5000	189/3500	4-spd (+O/D)/Auto
						4235/6IL/ 2OHC	173/4750	227/3000	4-spd (+O/D)/Auto
Sovereign Coupe SII	1,598/399	1975–1977	Cpe	F/R	—	4235/6IL/ 2OHC	173/4750	227/3000	4-spd (+O/D)/Auto
						5343/V12/	285/5750	294/3500	Auto/-

Suspension Front	Rear	Steering	Brakes (Front/rear)	Wheels/ Tyres	Length (in)	Weight (lb,unladen)	Top speed (mph)	0–60mph (sec)	Standing 1/4-mile (sec)	UK Total Price (£: at Launch)
ITrL	IC	R & P	Drum/drum	5.20-12	142	1268	50	N/A	29.6	£681
ITrL	IC	R & P	Drum/drum	5.20-12	142	1460	63	50.7	25.4	£778
ITrL	IC DD1/2E (46 only)	R & P	Drum/drum	135-14	130	1646	74	31.2	24.1	£747
ITor	IC	R & P	Disc/drum	135-14	153	1730	80	22.5	22.8	£852
ITor	IC/DD1/2E	R & P	Disc/drum	155-13	153	1725	84	23.0	22.3	£1050
ITor	DD1/2E	R & P	Disc/drum	155-13	153	1875	84	19.4	21.3	£1399
Beam1/2E	Beam1/2E	Worm	Drum/drum	6.00-16	137	2337	65 (Est)	N/A	N/A	£3799
IC	BeamC	R & P	Disc/drum	155-12	137	1517	83	16.1	20.6	£2989
IC	BeamC	R & P	Disc/drum	155-12	137	1499	85	15.6	19.7	£3099
IC	IC	R & P	Drum/drum	145-10	126	1260	72	26.6	22.8	£2799
IC	IC	R & P	Drum/drum	145-10	126	1260	68 (Claimed)	N/A	N/A	£2950
IC	IC	R & P	Disc/drum	145/70-12	126	1362	85	14.7	19.7	£3995
IC	BeamC	R & P	Disc/drum	155-13	140	1635	85	16.7	20.4	£3399
IC	BeamC	R & P	Disc/drum	165/70-13	140	1622	100	11.8	18.4	£4999
IC	BeamC	R & P	Disc/drum	165/70-13	140	1722	77	20.8	21.9	£4699
IC	BeamC	R & P	Disc/drum	165/70-13	140	1588	84 (Est)	N/A	N/A	£5199
IC	IC	R & P	Disc/drum	155-13	142	1499	90 (Est)	13.3	N/A	£5299
IC	IC	R & P	Disc/drum	165/70-13	142	1757	93	11.3	18.2	£6599
IC	IC	R & P	Disc/disc	175/60-14	142	1808	114	7.9	16.4	£7699
IC	IC	R & P	Disc/drum	165/70-13	142	1784	106 (Est)	10.5	N/A	£8680
IC	IC	R & P	Disc/drum	165/70-13	142	1850	97	11.2	18.3	£6949
IC	IC	R & P	Disc/drum	165/70-13	142	1812	80	20.9	22.0	£6299
IC	BeamC	R & P	Disc/drum	155/70-13	163	1923	91	14.2	19.5	£4299
IC	BeamC	Worm	Disc/drum	175/70-13	163	2090	94	13.2	19.2	£4999
IC	BeamC	R & P	Disc/drum	185/60-14	165	2064	95	12.2	18.6	£6050
Beam1/2E	Beam1/2E	Worm	Disc/drum	215-15	162	2933	81 (Claimed)	N/A	N/A	£7,234
Beam1/2E	Beam1/2E	Worm	Disc/drum	215-15	162	3043	81 (Claimed)	N/A	N/A	£14,325
Beam1/2E	Beam1/2E	Worm	Disc/drum	215-15	162	3362	84 (Est)	N/A	N/A	£7,906
Beam1/2E	Beam1/2E	Worm	Disc/drum	215-15	162	3656	83	17.9	20.7	£12,699
Beam1/2E	Beam1/2E	Worm	Disc/drum	215-15	162	3656	84 (Est)	N/A	N/A	£12,849
IC	BeamC	Worm	Disc/drum	255/70-15	164	3844	84 (Claimed)	N/A	N/A	£15,650
ITor	Beam1/2E	Worm	Disc/drum	195R-15	145	2788	89	16.1	20.3	£8995
ITor	Beam1/2E	Worm	Disc/drum	195R-15	145	2591	93 (Est)	13.9	N/A	£10,995
IC	IC	R & P	Disc/drum	185/60-14	168	2191	109 (Est)	N/A	N/A	£9,250
IC	IC	R & P	Disc/drum	185/60-14	168	2191	110	10.1	17.6	£10,250
IC	IC	R & P	Disc/drum	155/60-13	130	1389	84 (Claimed)	N/A	N/A	£N/A
IC	IC	R & P	Disc/drum	145/70-12	130	1506	80	21.1	21.9	£6395
IC	IC	R & P	Disc/drum	165/70-13	148	1854	94	10.8	18.0	£7995
IC	IC	R & P	Disc/drum	165/70-13	148	1852	97 (Claimed)	12.1	N/A	£9695
IC	IC	R & P	Disc/disc	175/60-14	148	1929	111	9.5	17.2	£10,850
IC	IC	R & P	Disc/drum	165/70-13	148	1918	106	11.0	18.1	£9695
IC	Beam1/2E	R & P	Disc/drum	155-12	130	2062	N/A	N/A	N/A	£7995
IC	IC	Worm	Disc/disc	H70HR-15	226	4706	105 (Est)	N/A	N/A	£4424
IC	IC	R & P	Disc/disc	205-15	190	3388	117 (Claimed)	11.0	18.1	£2356
IC	IC	R & P	Disc/disc	205-15	195	3708	117	10.9	18.0	£4965
IC	IC	R & P	Disc/disc	205-15	190	3703	124	8.8	16.5	£2714
IC	IC	R & P	Disc/disc	205-15	190	3724	124	8.8	16.5	£5590
IC	IC	R & P	Disc/disc	205-15	190	3885	148	7.6	15.7	£6959

Make and model	Production Figures	Years Built	Body Styles	Mechanical Layout	Engine Make (if not own)	Capacity/ (cc)/Layout/ Valves	BHP/ rpm	Torque (lb.ft)/rpm	Transmission gearbox/automatic transmission
						OHC			
Double Six SI/SII	5,040	1972–1979	Sal	F/R	—	5343/V12/	265/5850	304/3500	Auto/-
						OHC	285/5750	294/3500	Auto/-
Sovereign SIII	29,354	1979–1987	Sal	F/R	—	4235/6IL/ 2OHC	205/5000	236/3700	5-spd/Auto
Double Six SIII	11,568	1979–1993	Sal	F/R	—	5343/V12/ OHC	299/5500	318/3000	Auto/-
3.6/4.0	10,313/ 8,876	1986–1994	Sal	F/R	—	3590/6IL/ 2OHC	221/5000	248/4000	5-spd/Auto
						3980/6IL/ 2OHC	223/4750	278/3650	5-spd/Auto
Double Six	In prod	1993–Date	Sal	F/R	—	5994/V12/ OHC	318/5350	353/2850	Auto/-
Six 4.0	In prod	1994–Date	Sal	F/R	—	3980/6IL/ 2OHC	245/4800	289/4000	5-spd/Auto

Datsun (renamed Nissan in the British market from 1984)

Make and model	Production Figures	Years Built	Body Styles	Mechanical Layout	Engine Make (if not own)	Capacity/ (cc)/Layout/ Valves	BHP/ rpm	Torque (lb.ft)/rpm	Transmission gearbox/automatic transmission
Bluebird (Type 510)	1,696,974	1968–1971	Sal Est	F/R	—	1295/4IL/ OHC	72/6000	76/3600	4-spd/-
						1428/4IL/ OHC	85/6000	86/3600	4-spd/Auto
						1595/4IL/ OHC	96/5600	100/3600	4-spd/Auto
1800 Laurel/	164,985 (Incl. Laurel)	1968–1973	Sal Est	F/R	—	1815/4IL/ OHC	105/5600	115/3600	3-spd/4-spd/Auto
C30 2000	-	1968–1974	Sal Est	F/R	—	1990/4IL/ OHC	114/5600	124/3200	4-spd/Auto
240Z/ 260Z/2+2	622,649	1969–1978	Spts Cpe	F/R	—	2393/6IL/ OHC	151/5600	146/4400	5-spd/-
						2565/6IL/ OHC	162/5600	152/4400	5-spd/-
						2565/6IL/ OHC	162/5600	152/4400	5-spd/-
Sunny B110	1,226,843	1970–1973	Sal Est	F/R	—	1171/4IL/ OHV	68/6000	70/3600	4-spd/-
						1428/4IL/ OHC	85/6000	86/3600	4-spd/Auto
280ZX	414,358	1978–1983	Cpe Targa	F/R	—	2753/6IL/ OHC	140/5200	149/4000	5-spd/Auto
						2753/6IL/ OHC	140/5200	149/4000	5-spd/Auto
Cherry 100A	389,807	1970–1974	Sal Cpe Est	F(Tr)/F	—	988/4IL/ OHV	59/6000	60/4000	4-spd/-
						1171/4IL/ OHV	69/6000	70/4000	4-spd/-
Cherry FII	668,038	1974–1978	Sal Cpe Est	F(Tr)/F	—	988/4IL/ OHV	45/5600	56/4000	4-spd/-
						1171/4IL/ OHV	52/5600	68/3600	4-spd/Auto
Cherry N10	1,001,508	1978–1982	Sal Htch Est Cpe	F(Tr)/F	—	988/4IL/ OHV	45/6000	47/4000	4-spd/-
						988/4IL/ OHC	50/6000	55/4000	4-spd/Auto
						1171/4IL/ OHV	52/5600	58/3600	4-spd/Auto
						1270/4IL/ OHC	60/5600	71/3600	4-spd/Auto
Sunny 120Y	2,360,670	1973–1977	Sal Cpe	F/R	—	1171/4IL/ OHV	53/6000	70/4000	4-spd/-
Sunny 120Y (B310)	1,770,814	1977–1981	Sal Cpe Est	F/R	—	1171/4IL/ OHV	65/6000	68/3600	4-spd/Auto
							52/5600	59/4000	4-spd/-
						1397/4IL/ OHV	63/5600	73/3600	5-spd/-
Violet 140J/160J	765,910	1973–1977	Sal Cpe	F/R	—	1428/4IL/ OHC	65/5800	85/3600	4-spd/-
						1595/4IL/ OHC	72/6000	98/4000	4-spd/5-spd/-
Violet 140J/160J (Type A10)	610,614	1977–1981	Sal Cpe Est	F/R	—	1397/4IL/ OHV	63/5600	72/3600	4-spd/-
						1595/4IL/ OHC	81/5600	89/3600	4-spd/-
							87/5800	91/3800	5-spd/-
Bluebird 160B/180B (Type 610)	1,050,263	1971–1976	Sal Est	F/R	—	1595/4IL/ OHC	90/6000	97/4000	4-spd/Auto

Suspension Front	Rear	Steering	Brakes (Front/rear)	Wheels/Tyres	Length (in)	Weight (lb, unladen)	Top speed (mph)	0–60mph (sec)	Standing 1/4-mile (sec)	UK Total Price (£: at Launch)
IC	IC	R & P	Disc/disc	205-15	190/195	3881/4116	146	7.4	15.7	£3849
IC	IC	R & P	Disc/disc	205-15	195	4116	147	7.8	15.7	£4812
IC	IC	R & P	Disc/disc	205-15	195	3875	127	10.0	17.4	£12,983
IC	IC	R & P	Disc/disc	205-15	195	4234	150	8.1	16.2	£15,689
IC	IC	R & P	Disc/disc	220/65-390	196	3903	137	7.4	15.8	£28,495
IC	IC	R & P	Disc/disc	225/55-16	196	3991	141	8.2	16.3	£36,500
IC	IC	R & P	Disc/disc	225/60-16	196/203	4354/4404	155 (Est)	6.8	N/A	£51,700
IC	IC	R & P	Disc/disc	225/60-16	198/203	4023/4073	143	6.9	15.3	£49,950
IC	Beam1/2E	Worm	Drum/drum	5.60-13	162	2184	87	18.1	21.4	£889
IC	Beam1/2E	Worm	Disc/drum	5.60-13	162	2075	92	14.6	19.2	£970
IC	Beam1/2E	Worm	Disc/drum	5.60-13	162	2184	91	15.4	20.1	£948
IC	IC	R & P	Disc/drum	6.50-13	171	2172	96	13.1	19.2	£1386
IC	Beam1/2E	Worm	Disc/drum	165-14	177	2262	100	12.6	18.6	£1799
IC	IC	R & P	Disc/drum	175-14	163	2284	125	8.0	15.8	£2288
IC	IC	R & P	Disc/drum	195/70-14	163	2565	115	10.1	16.8	£2896
IC	IC	R & P	Disc/drum	195/70-14	175	2630	120	9.9	17.3	£3499
IC	Beam1/2E	Worm	Disc/drum	6.00-12	151	1590	89	15.3	19.9	£865
IC	Beam1/2E	Worm	Disc/drum	155-13	151	1590	91	15.6	20.1	£970
IC	IC	Worm	Disc/disc	195/70-14	171	2650	112	9.8	17.1	£8103
IC	IC	Worm	Disc/disc	195/70-14	179	2850	111 (Auto)	11.3	18.3	£8999
IC	IC	R & P	Drum/drum	155-12	142	1445	86	16.8	20.5	£766
IC	IC	R & P	Drum/drum	155-12	142	1445	93 (Claimed)	N/A	N/A	£1242
IC	IC	R & P	Disc/drum	155-12	151	1638	80	20.3	21.7	£1989
IC	IC	R & P	Disc/drum	155-12	151	1664	86	16.5	20.2	£2259
IC	IC	R & P	Disc/drum	155-13	153	1831	78	21.3	21.7	£2597
IC	IC	R & P	Disc/drum	155-13	153	1720	87 (Claimed)	N/A	N/A	£2597
IC	IC	R & P	Disc/drum	155-13	153	1764	90 (Claimed)	N/A	N/A	£3371
IC	IC	R & P	Disc/drum	155-13	153	1764	93 (Claimed)	N/A	N/A	£3594
IC	Beam1/2E	Worm	Disc/drum	155-12	156	1757	90 Est	16.0	21.0	£1049
IC	Beam1/2E	Worm	Disc/drum	155-13	156	1749	94 (Est)	N/a	N/A	£3256
IC	BeamC	Worm	Disc/drum	155-13	156	1880	83	19.1	21.5	£2659
IC	BeamC	Worm	Disc/drum	155-13	157	1797	93 (Claimed)	N/A	N/A	£2982
IC	Beam1/2E	Worm	Disc/drum	165-13	162	2183	94	15.3	20.0	£1295
IC	Beam1/2E	Worm	Disc/drum	165-13	162	2249	99 (Claimed)	N/A	N/A	£1585
IC	BeamC	Worm	Disc/drum	165-13	161	1984	90 (Claimed)	N/A	N/A	£2756
IC	BeamC	Worm	Disc/drum	165-13	161	2083	96 (Est)	N/A	N/A	£2826
IC	BeamC	Worm	Disc/drum	165-13	161	2149	104	11.8	18.5	£3147
IC	IC	Worm	Disc/drum	165-13	166	2172	100	12.4	18.5	£1240

Make and model	Production Figures	Years Built	Body Styles	Mechanical Layout	Engine Make (if not own)	Capacity/(cc)/Layout/Valves	BHP/rpm	Torque (lb.ft)/rpm	Transmission gearbox/automatic transmission
			Cpe			1770/4IL/ OHC	105/6000 115/6000	108/3600 112/4000	4-spd/Auto 4-spd/Auto
Bluebird 160B/180B (Type 810)	722,923	1976–1979	Sal Est	F/R	—	1595/4IL/ OHC	81/5600	89/3600	4-spd/-
						1770/4IL/ OHC	88/5600 90/5800	98/3600 100/3800	4-spd/Auto 4-spd/-
Laurel 200 (C130)	387,492	1972–1977	Sal Cpe	F/R	—	1990/4IL/ OHC	114/5600	124/3200	4-spd/Auto
						1998/6IL/ OHC	115/5600	120/3500	4-spd/Auto
Laurel 200 Six (C230)	423,209	1975–1981	Sal Cpe	F/R	—	1998/6IL/ OHC	108/5600	113/3600	4-spd/Auto
						2393/6IL/ OHC	113/5200	129/3200	5-spd/Auto
Skyline 240K (C110)	700,155	1972–1977	Sal Cpe Est	F/R	—	2393/6IL/ OHC	130/5600	145/3600	4-spd/Auto
Skyline 240K (C210)	576,797	1977–1981	Sal Cpe Est	F/R	—	2393/6IL/ OHC	127/5600	132/3600	5-spd/Auto
Cedric 240C/ 260C/ 280C (Type 230)	923,892	1971–1979	Sal Cpe Est	F/R	—	2393/6IL/ OHC	130/5600	141/3600	4-spd/Auto
						2565/6IL/ OHC	140/5200	159/4000	4-spd/Auto
						2753/6IL/ OHC	125/4800	145/3200	4-spd/Auto

[In the UK the 'Datsun' badge was dropped, in favour of 'Nissan' in 1984. For all models ultimately sold in the UK under the Nissan label, see 'Nissan' below]

De Tomaso

Make and model	Production Figures	Years Built	Body Styles	Mechanical Layout	Engine Make (if not own)	Capacity/(cc)/Layout/Valves	BHP/rpm	Torque (lb.ft)/rpm	Transmission gearbox/automatic transmission
Mangusta	400	1967–1972	Spts Cpe	M/R	Ford-USA	4727/V8/ OHV	305/6200	392/3500	5-spd/-
Pantera	N/A	1971–1994	Spts Cpe	M/R	Ford-USA	5763/V8/ OHV	330/5400	325/3600	5-spd/-
							350/6000	333/3800	5-spd/-
Deauville	355 (Est)	1970–1989	Sal	F/R	Ford-USA	5763/V8/ OHV	330/6000	325/3500	5-spd/Auto
Longchamp	N/A	1972–1989	Cpe Conv	F/R	Ford-USA	5763/V8/ OHV	330/6000	325/3500	5-spd/Auto

Dino

Make and model	Production Figures	Years Built	Body Styles	Mechanical Layout	Engine Make (if not own)	Capacity/(cc)/Layout/Valves	BHP/rpm	Torque (lb.ft)/rpm	Transmission gearbox/automatic transmission
246	3,761	1969–1973	Spts Cpe	M(Tr)/R	—	2418/V6/ 2OHC	195/7600	166/5500	5-spd/-

308GT4 – Originally badged **Dino**, this was renamed **Ferrari** in 1975. For all details, see entry under **Ferrari**.

Dodge

Make and model	Production Figures	Years Built	Body Styles	Mechanical Layout	Engine Make (if not own)	Capacity/(cc)/Layout/Valves	BHP/rpm	Torque (lb.ft)/rpm	Transmission gearbox/automatic transmission
Viper	In prod	1992–Date	Spts	F/R	—	7997/V10/ OHV	400/4600	450/3600	6-spd/-

Enfield

Make and model	Production Figures	Years Built	Body Styles	Mechanical Layout	Engine Make (if not own)	Capacity/(cc)/Layout/Valves	BHP/rpm	Torque (lb.ft)/rpm	Transmission gearbox/automatic transmission
8000 Electric car	108	1969–1976	Sal	F/R	—	Electric	8hp rating	N/Q	Auto

Evante

Make and model	Production Figures	Years Built	Body Styles	Mechanical Layout	Engine Make (if not own)	Capacity/(cc)/Layout/Valves	BHP/rpm	Torque (lb.ft)/rpm	Transmission gearbox/automatic transmission
Sports Car	N/A	1986–1991	Spts	F/R	—	1699/4IL/ 2OHC	140/6500	129/5250	5-spd/-

Fairthorpe

Make and model	Production Figures	Years Built	Body Styles	Mechanical Layout	Engine Make (if not own)	Capacity/(cc)/Layout/Valves	BHP/rpm	Torque (lb.ft)/rpm	Transmission gearbox/automatic transmission
Electron/ Minor	Approx 500	1956–1973	Spts	F/R	Standard/ Triumph	948/4IL/ OHV	38/5000	49/2800	4-spd (+O/D)/-
						1147/4IL/ OHV	63/5750	67/3500	4-spd/-
						1296/4IL/ OHV	75/6000	75/4000	4-spd/-
					Coventry-Climax	1098/4IL/ OHC	71/6500 83/6800	67/4750 72/4750	4-spd/-
TX-GT/S/SS	Approx 50	1967–1976	Spts Cpe	F/R	Triumph	1998/6IL/	104/5300	117/3000	4-spd/-

| Suspension | | Steering | Brakes | Wheels/ | Length (in) | Weight | Performance | | | UK Total |
Front	Rear		(Front/rear)	Tyres		(lb,unladen)	Top speed (mph)	0–60mph (sec)	Standing 1/4-mile (sec)	Price (£: at Launch)
IC	IC	Worm	Disc/drum	165-13	166	2248	103	12.5	18.5	£1359
IC	IC	Worm	Disc/drum	165-13	166	2251	105	10.3	17.9	£1499
IC	IC	Worm	Disc/drum	165-14	168	2304	99 (Claimed)	N/A	N/A	£3148
IC	IC	Worm	Disc/drum	165-14	168	2390	101	13.6	19.1	£2950
IC	IC	Worm	Disc/drum	185/70-14	168	2348				
IC	Beam1/2E	Worm	Disc/drum	165-14	175	2262	100	12.6	18.6	£1749
IC	Beam1/2E	Worm	Disc/drum	165-14	175	2342	101	14.8	20.3	£2225
IC	BeamC	Worm	Disc/drum	185/70-14	178	2584	101	14.8	20.3	£2890
IC	BeamC	Worm	Disc/drum	185/70-14	182	2737	99	11.8	18.2	£5957
IC	IC	Worm	Disc/drum	175-14	176	2580	111	11.3	17.9	£1997
IC	IC	Worm	Disc/disc	185/70-14	181	2768	109	11.0	17.8	£6001
IC	Beam1/2E	Worm	Disc/drum	175-14	185	2503	103	12.3	18.4	£2026
IC	Beam1/2E	Worm	Disc/drum	175-14	185	2550	112 (Claimed)	N/A	N/A	£2099
IC	Beam1/2E	Worm	Disc/drum	195/70-14	185	3080	106	12.8	18.7	£5135
IC	IC	R & P	Disc/disc	185-15/ 205-15	168	2915	155 (Claimed)	N/A	N/A	Special order
IC	IC	R & P	Disc/disc	185/70-15/ 215/70-15	168	3110	159	6.2	14.4	£6696
IC	IC	R & P	Disc/disc	285/40-15/ 345/35-15	168	3219	160	5.4	13.6	£41,410
IC	IC	R & P	Disc/disc	215/70-15	191	4000	143 (Claimed)	N/A	N/A	£8992
IC	IC	R & P	Disc/disc	215/70-15	178	4000	149 (Claimed)	N/A	N/A	£9945
IC	IC	R & P	Disc/disc	205/70-14	167	2609	148	7.1	15.4	£5486
IC	IC	R & P	Disc/disc	275/40-17/ 335/35-17	175	3356	146	4.6	13.1	£55,000
IC	Beam1/2E	R & P	Drum/drum	145-10	112	2150	37	N/A	N/A	£550
IC	IC	R & P	Disc/disc	195/60-14	N/A	N/A	132 (Claimed)	6.4	N/A	£N/A
IC	BeamC	R & P	Drum/drum	5.60-13	132	1288	75	17.9	20.8	£720
IC	IC	R & P								
IC	IC	R & P	Disc/drum	155-13	137	1000	85 (Est)	N/A	N/A	£700
IC	ITrL	R & P	Disc/drum	155-13	143	1035	90 (Est)	N/A	N/A	£826
IC	BeamC	R & P	Drum/drum	5.20-15	132	1204	90 (Est)	N/A	N/A	£1050
IC	IC	R & P	Disc/drum	155-13	144	1792	110 (Est)	N/A	N/A	£1310

Make and model	Production Figures	Years Built	Body Styles	Mechanical Layout	Engine Make (if not own)	Capacity/(cc)/Layout/Valves	BHP/rpm	Torque (lb.ft)/rpm	Transmission gearbox/automatic transmission
						OHV	112/5300	117/3000	4-spd/-
					Triumph	2498/6IL/ OHV	140/6000	152/3000	4-spd/-
						OHV	132/5450	153/2000	4-spd/-
TX Tripper	N/A	1970–1976	Spts	F/R	Triumph	1296/4IL/ OHV	75/6000	75/4000	4-spd/-
						2498/6IL/ OHV	132/5450	153/2000	4-spd/-

Ferrari

Make and model	Production Figures	Years Built	Body Styles	Mechanical Layout	Engine Make (if not own)	Capacity/(cc)/Layout/Valves	BHP/rpm	Torque (lb.ft)/rpm	Transmission gearbox/automatic transmission
365 GT 2+2	800	1967–1971	Spts Sal	F/R	—	4390/V12/ OHC	320/6600	268/5000	5-spd/-
365GTB4 Daytona	1,406	1968–1974	Spts Cpe Spts	F/R	—	4390/V12/ 2OHC	352/7700	318/5400	5-spd/-
365GTC/4	500	1971–1972	Spts Sal	F/R	—	4390/V12/ 2OHC	340/6600	268/5000	5-spd/-
365GT4 2+2/ 400GT	525/502	1972–1979	Spts Sal	F/R	—	4390/V12/ 2OHC	320/6200	318/4000	5-spd/-
						4823/ 2OHC	340/6500	347/3600	5-spd/Auto
Dino 308GT4	2826	1973–1980	Spts Cpe	M(Tr)/R	—	2926/V8/ 2OHC	250/7700	210/5000	5-spd/-
Dino 308 GTB/GTS	2,897/ 3219	1975–1981	Spts Cpe Spts	M(Tr)/R	—	2926/V8/ 2OHC	250/7700	210/5000	5-spd/-
365GT4BB/ 512BB/ 512BBi	387/ 929/ 1,007	1973–1984	Spts Cpe	M/R	—	4390/12HO/ 2OHC	344/7200	302/3900	5-spd/-
						4942/12HO/ 2OHC	360/6200	332/4600	5-spd/-
400i/412i	1,308/ 576	1979–1989	Sal	F/R	—	4823/V12/ 2OHC	310/6400	289/4200	5-spd/Auto
							315/6400	304/4200	5-spd/Auto
						4942/V12/ 2OHC	340/6000	333/4200	5-spd/Auto
308GTBi/ 328GTB	2,237/ 7,412	1981–1988	Spts Cpe Targa	M(Tr)/R	—	2926/V8/ 2OHC	214/6600	179/4600	5-spd/-
						3185/V8/ 2OHC/	240/7000	192/5000	5-spd/-
							270/7000	224/5500	5-spd/-
Testarossa	N/Q	1984–1992	Spts Cpe	M/R	—	4942/12HO/ 2OHC	390/6300	362/4500	5-spd/-
Mondial 8/ QV	4,274	1980–1989	Spts Cpe Conv	M(Tr)/R	—	2926/V8/ 2OHC	214/6600	179/4600	5-spd/-
						3185/V8/ 2OHC	240/7000	192/5000	5-spd/-
							270/7000	224/5500	5-spd/-
Mondial t	N/Q	1989–1993	Conv Spts Cpe	M/R	—	3405/V8/ 2OHC	300/7200	283/4200	5-spd/-
288GTO	271	1984–1987	Spts Cpe	M/R	—	2855/V8/ 2OHC	400/7000	366/3800	5-spd/-
F40	1,200	1987–1992	Spts Cpe	M/R	—	2936/V8/ 2OHC	478/7000	425/4000	5-spd/-
348tb/ts	N/A	1989–1994	Spts Cpe Targa Spts	M/R	—	3405/V8/ 2OHC	300/7000	239/4200	5-spd/-
							320/7200	237/5000	5-spd/-
F355	In prod	1994–Date	Spts Cpe Spts Conv	M/R	—	3496/V8/ 2OHC	380/8250	268/6000	6-spd/-
512TR	N/A	1992–1994	Spts Cpe	M/R	—	4943/12HO/ 2OHC	428/6750	362/5500	5-spd/-
456GT	In prod	1992–Date	Cpe	F/R	—	5474/V12/ 2OHC	442/6250	405/4500	6-spd/-
F50	In prod	1995–Date	Spts	M/R	—	4698/V12/ 2OHC	520/8500	347/6500	6-spd/-
F512M	In prod	1994–Date	Spts Cpe	M/R	—	4943/12HO/ 2OHC	440/6750	368/5500	5-spd/-

Fiat

Make and model	Production Figures	Years Built	Body Styles	Mechanical Layout	Engine Make (if not own)	Capacity/(cc)/Layout/Valves	BHP/rpm	Torque (lb.ft)/rpm	Transmission gearbox/automatic transmission
500/500D/ 500F	Est 3,408,000	1957–1977	Sal Est	R/R	—	479/2IL/ OHV AirC	13/4000	18/2500	4-spd/-
							17/4000	20/2500	4-spd/-
						499/2IL/ OHV AirC	18/4600	22/3000	4-spd/-
500 Giardiniera	327,000	1960–1977	Est	R/R	—	499/2IL/ OHV AirC	17/4600	22/3200	4-spd/-
1800/ 2100/2300	Est 185,000	1959–1968	Sal Est	F/R	—	1795/6IL/ OHV	85/5000	93/3000	4-spd/-
							97/5300	101/3000	4-spd/-
						2054/6IL/ OHV	95/5200	106/3000	4-spd/-
						2279/6IL/ OHV	105/5300	123/2800	4-spd (+O/D)/Auto
850	1,780,000 (Approx)	1964–1974	Sal	R/R	—	843/4IL/ OHV	37/5100	41/3400	4-spd/SemiAuto
							47/6200	44/3600	4-spd/-

[Later 850s were supplied from Seat in Spain, as re-badged Seat 850s, which were mechanically identical]

| Suspension | | Steering | Brakes | Wheels/ | Length (in) | Weight | Performance | | Standing | UK Total |
Front	Rear		(Front/rear)	Tyres		(lb, unladen)	Top speed (mph)	0–60mph (sec)	¼-mile (sec)	Price (£: at Launch)
IC	IC	R & P	Disc/drum	155-13	144	1736	115 (Est)	N/A	N/A	£1546
IC	IC	R & P	Disc/drum	155-13	144	1736	127 (Est)	N/A	N/A	£1658
IC	IC	R & P	Disc/drum	165-13	147	1736	125 (Est)	N/A	N/A	£1693
IC	IC	R & P	Disc/drum	165-13	146	1120	85 (Est)	N/A	N/A	£1151
IC	IC	R & P	Disc/drum	165-13	146	1568	112	8.0	16.0	£1412
IC	IC	Worm	Disc/disc	205-15	196	3490	152	7.1	15.2	£7500
IC	IC	Worm	Disc/disc	215/70-15	174	2825	174	5.4	13.7	£8750
IC	IC	Worm	Disc/disc	205-14	180	3200	152	7.3	15.7	£10,251
IC	IC	Worm	Disc/disc	215/70-15	189	3963	150	7.1	15.2	£12,783
IC	IC	Worm	Disc/disc	215/70-15	189	4180	156 (Auto)	8.0	16.0	£22,464
IC	IC	R & P	Disc/disc	205/70-14	169	2866	154	6.9	14.9	£7699
IC	IC	R & P	Disc/disc	205/70-14	174	2784	154	6.5	14.8	£11,992
IC	IC	R & P	Disc/disc	215/70-15	172	3197	171	6.5	14.0	£15,492
IC	IC	R & P	Disc/disc	215/70-15/ 225/70-15	172	3340	163	6.2	13.6	£26,000
IC	IC	Worm	Disc/disc	215/70-15	189	4035	156 (Auto)	8.0	16.0	£31,809
IC	IC	Worm	Disc/disc	215/70-15	189	4035	N/A	N/A	N/A	£38,496
IC	IC	Worm	Disc/disc	240/55-16	189	4035	158 (Claimed)	N/A	N/A	£55,599
IC	IC	R & P	Disc/disc	205/70-14	174	2784	149 (Est)	N/A	N/A	£21,810
IC	IC	R & P	Disc/disc	220/55-390	174	2784	155	5.7	14.2	£23,173
IC	IC	R & P	Disc/disc	220/55-390	174	2972	159	5.5	14.1	£32,220
IC	IC	R & P	Disc/disc	225/50-16/ 255/50-16	177	3675	171	5.2	13.5	£62,666
IC	IC	R & P	Disc/disc	240/55-390	180	3108	138	9.3	N/A	£24,488
IC	IC	R & P	Disc/disc	220/55-390	180	3152	146	6.4	14.5	£25,851
IC	IC	R & P	Disc/disc	220/55-390	180	3152	149	6.3	14.8	£37,500
IC	IC	R & P	Disc/disc	205/65-16/ 225/55-16	179	3414	154	5.6	14.2	£62,500
IC	IC	R & P	Disc/disc	225/55-16/ 265/50-16	169	2558	190 (Claimed)	N/A	N/A	Special Order
IC	IC	R & P	Disc/disc	245/40-17/ 335/35-17	172	2425	201	4.5	N/A	Special order
IC	IC	R & P	Disc/disc	215/50-17/	166	3226	163	5.6	13.8	£67,499
IC	IC	R & P	Disc/disc	255/45-17	166	3226	163	5.9	14.4	£78,999
IC	IC	R & P	Disc/disc	225/40-18/ 265/40-18	167	3136	173	4.6	13.0	£83,031
IC	IC	R & P	Disc/disc	235/40-18/ 295/35-18	176	3535	175	5.0	13.2	£129,954
IC	IC	R & P	Disc/disc	255/45-17/ 285/40-17	186	4020	193	5.1	13.5	£145,999
IC	IC	R & P	Disc/disc	245/30-18/ 355/30-18	176	2706	201 (Claimed)	3.7	N/A	£329,000
IC	IC	R & P	Disc/disc	235/40-18/ 295/35-18	176	3541	196 (Est)	4.8	12.9	£138,000
ITrL	IC	Worm	Drum/drum	125-12	116	1036	51	N/A	31.0	£556
ITrL	IC	Worm	Drum/drum	125-12	116	1113	57	N/A	29.0	£556
ITrL	IC	Worm	Drum/drum	125-12	116	1106	60	N/A	26.6	£483
ITrL	IC	Worm	Drum/drum	125-12	125	1246	59	N/A	27.7	£585
ITor	Beam1/4E/C	Worm	Drum/drum	5.90-14	176	2680	90 (Est)	N/A	N/A	£1475
ITor	Beam1/2E	Worm	Disc/disc	5.90-14	176	2789	90 (Est)	N/A	N/A	£1387
ITor	Beam1/4E/C	Worm	Drum/drum	5.90-14	176	2680	91	15.9	20.0	£1550
ITor	Beam1/2E	Worm	Disc/disc	6.40-14	176	2786	99	12.3	18.5	£1525
ITrL	IC	Worm	Drum/drum	5.50-12	141	1516	76	26.8	22.9	£550
ITrL	IC	Worm	Disc/drum	145-13	141	1520	80	19.0	21.3	£659

Make and model	Production Figures	Years Built	Body Styles	Mechanical Layout	Engine Make (if not own)	Capacity/(cc)/Layout/Valves	BHP/rpm	Torque (lb.ft)/rpm	Transmission gearbox/automatic transmission
850 Coupe	342,873	1965–1973	Cpe	R/R	—	843/4IL/OHV	47/6200	44/3600	4-spd/-
						903/4IL/OHV	52/6500	48/4000	4-spd/-
850 Spider	124,660	1965–1973	Spts	R/R	—	843/4IL/OHV	49/6200	43/4200	4-spd/-
						903/4IL/OHV	52/6500	48/4000	4-spd/-
124/124S/124ST	1,543,000 (Approx)	1966–1974	Sal Est	F/R	—	1197/4IL/OHV	60/5600	64/3400	4-spd/-
						1438/4IL/OHV	70/5400	81/3300	4-spd/-
						1438/4IL/2OHC	80/5800	81/4000	4-spd/-
						1592/4IL/2OHC	95/6000	93/4000	4-spd/5-spd/-
124 Coupe	279,672	1967–1975	Cpe	F/R	—	1438/4IL/2OHC	90/6000	80/3600	4-spd/5-spd/-
						1592/4IL/2OHC	108/6000	101/4200	4-spd/5-spd/-
						1608/4IL/2OHC	110/6400	101/3800	4-spd/5-spd/-
						1756/4IL/2OHC	118/6000	113/4000	4-spd/5-spd/-
124 Spider	178,439	1966–1982	Spts	F/R	—	1438/4IL/2OHC	90/6000	80/3600	5-spd/-
						1592/4IL/2OHC	108/6000	101/4200	5-spd/-
						1608/4IL/2OHC	110/6400	101/3800	5-spd/-
						1756/4IL/2OHC	118/6000	113/4000	4-spd/5-spd/-
125/125S	603,870	1967–1972	Sal	F/R	—	1608/4IL/2OHC	90/5600 100/6000	94/3400 96/4000	4-spd/- 5-spd/-
Dino 2000/2400 Coupe	6,068	1967–1973	Cpe	F/R	Ferrari	1987/V6/2OHC	160/7200	126/6000	5-spd/-
						2418/V6/2OHC	180/6600	159/4600	5-spd/-
Dino 2000/2400 Spider	1,583	1966–1973	Spts	F/R	Ferrari	1987/V6/2OHC	160/7200	126/6000	5-spd/-
						2418/V6/2OHC	180/6600	159/4600	5-spd/-
128	2,776,000 (Est)	1969–1984	Sal Est	F(Tr)/F	—	1116/4IL/OHC	55/6000	57/3000	4-spd/-
						1290/4IL/OHC	61/6000	66/3000	4-spd/-
128 Coupe/3P	330,897	1971–1978	Cpe/Htch	F(Tr)/F	—	1116/4IL/OHC	64/6000 65/6000	61/4000 64/4100	4-spd/-
						1290/4IL/OHC	75/6600 73/6000	68/3600 74/3900	4-spd/-
130	15,000	1969–1976	Sal	F/R	—	3235/V6/OHC	165/5600	184/3400	Auto/-
130 Coupe	4,491	1971–1977	Cpe	F/R	—	3235/V6/OHC	165/5600	184/3400	5-spd/Auto
127	3,730,000 (Est)	1971–1983	Sal Htch	F(Tr)/F	—	903/4IL/OHV	47/6200	46/3500	4-spd/-
						1049/4IL/OHC	50/5600 70/6500	57/3000 62/4500	4-spd/5-spd/- 4-spd/5-spd/-
						1301/4IL/OHC	75/5750	76/3500	5-spd/-
132/Argenta	975,970	1972–1984	Sal	F/R	—	1585/4IL/2OHC	98/6000	98/4000	5-spd/Auto
						1592/4IL/2OHC	98/6000	95/4000	4-spd/5-spd/Auto
						1756/4IL/2OHC	105/6000 107/6000	104/4200 104/4200	4-spd/5-spd/Auto 4-spd/5-spd/Auto
						1995/4IL/2OHC	112/5600 113/5600	116/3000 123/3700	5-spd/Auto 5-spd/Auto
126	1,970,000	1972–1987	Sal	R/R	—	594/2IL/OHV AirC	23/4800	29/3400	4-spd/-
						652/2IL/OHV AirC	24/4500	30/3000	4-spd/-
126 BIS	In prod	1987–Date	Htch	R/R	—	704/2IL/OHV	26/4500	19/2000	4-spd/-
133 (Seat)	N/A	1974–1980	Sal	R/R	—	843/4IL/OHV	37/5000	40/3200	4-spd/-
131 Mirafiori	1,850,500	1974–1984	Sal Est	F/R	—	1297/4IL/OHV	65/5400	75/3000	4-spd/-
						1367/4IL/OHC	70/5500	80/3000	4-spd/5-spd/-

Suspension Front	Rear	Steering	Brakes (Front/rear)	Wheels/Tyres	Length (in)	Weight (lb, unladen)	Top speed (mph)	0–60mph (sec)	Standing 1/4-mile (sec)	UK Total Price (£: at Launch)
ITrL	IC	Worm	Disc/drum	5.20-13	144	1607	87	18.2	21.0	£850
ITrL	IC	Worm	Disc/drum	155-13	146	1609	91	15.6	20.4	£825
ITrL	IC	Worm	Disc/drum	5.20-13	149	1620	92	N/A	N/A	£1000
ITrL	IC	Worm	Disc/drum	155-13	149	1620	96 (Est)	N/A	N/A	£1089
IC	BeamC	Worm	Disc/disc	155-13	159	1800	83	15.9	20.1	£774
IC	BeamC	Worm	Disc/disc	155-13	159	2040	96	12.8	19.0	£968
IC	BeamC	Worm	Disc/disc	155-13	159	2020	102	12.0	18.4	£1240
IC	BeamC	Worm	Disc/disc	155-13	159	2041	100	10.1	17.6	£1427
IC	BeamC	Worm	Disc/disc	165-13	162	2116	102	12.6	18.8	£1298
IC	BeamC	Worm	Disc/disc	165-13	162	2194	106 (Est)	N/A	N/A	£1942
IC	BeamC	Worm	Disc/disc	165-13	162	2194	109	10.7	17.8	£1797
IC	BeamC	Worm	Disc/disc	165-13	162	2194	107	10.5	17.4	£2047
IC	BeamC	Worm	Disc/disc	165-13	156	2083	106	11.9	18.3	Special order
IC	BeamC	Worm	Disc/disc	165-13	156	2201	110 (Est)	N/A	N/A	Special order
IC	BeamC	Worm	Disc/disc	165-13	156	2201	112	12.2	18.6	Special order
IC	BeamC	Worm	Disc/disc	165-13	156	2201	115 (Est)	N/A	N/A	Special order
IC	Beam1/2E	Worm	Disc/disc	175-13	166	2191	99	13.4	19.0	£1007
IC	Beam1/2E	Worm	Disc/disc	175-13	166	2218	104	11.9	18.1	£1203
IC	Beam1/2E	Worm	Disc/disc	185-14	178	3042	127	8.1	16.0	£3493
IC	IC	Worm	Disc/disc	205/70-14	178	3042	130	8.7	16.1	Special order
IC	Beam1/2E	Worm	Disc/disc	185-14	162	2535	127	8.1	16.0	Special order
IC	IC	Worm	Disc/disc	205/70-14	162	2800	130 (Est)	N/A	N/A	Special order
IC	ITrL	R & P	Disc/drum	145-13	151	1802	86	16.3	19.8	£871
IC	ITrL	R & P	Disc/drum	145-13	151	1842	91	12.9	18.8	£1111
IC	ITrL	R & P	Disc/drum	145-13	150	1787 / 1875	93 (Claimed)	N/A	N/A	£1359
IC	ITrL	R & P	Disc/drum	145-13	150	1797	99	13.1	18.8	£1398
IC	ITrL	R & P	Disc/drum	145-13	150	1875	98	11.7	18.4	£2146
ITor	IC	Worm	Disc/disc	205/70-14	187	3574	113	11.4	18.4	£3818
ITor	IC	Worm	Disc/disc	205/70-14	191	3530	116	10.6	17.7	£6165
IC	ITrL	R & P	Disc/drum	135-13	142	1550	83	17.4	19.7	£799
IC	ITrL	R & P	Disc/drum	135-13	142	1687	84	17.6	20.8	£2239
IC	ITrL	R & P	Disc/drum	135-13	142	1699	95	13.8	19.2	£2775
IC	ITrL	R & P	Disc/drum	135-13	142	1709	103 (Claimed)	N/A	N/A	£4250
IC	BeamC	Worm	Disc/drum	185/70-13	173	2381	103 (Est)	N/A	N/A	£2276
IC	BeamC	Worm	Disc/drum	175-13	172	2359	102	11.6	18.2	£1533
IC	BeamC	Worm	Disc/drum	175-13	172	2397	105	10.4	17.9	£1722
IC	BeamC	Worm	Disc/drum	185/70-13	172	2352	106	10.8	17.0	£1889
IC	BeamC	Worm	Disc/drum	175/70-14	172	2513	104	10.0	18.1	£3950
IC	BeamC	Worm	Disc/drum	175/70-14	175	2601	104 (Est)	N/A	N/A	£6345
ITrL	IC	Worm	Drum/drum	135-12	120	1271	63	42.3	24.8	£698
ITrL	IC	Worm	Drum/drum	135-12	120	1271	64	42.1	24.8	£1424
ITrL	IC	R & P	Drum/drum	135/70-13	122	1367	72 (Claimed)	N/A	N/A	£2688
ITrL	IC	Worm	Disc/drum	5.50-12	139	1576	75	21.7	22.1	£1293
IC	BeamC	R & P	Disc/drum	155-13	168	2095	91	16.1	20.4	£1619
IC	BeamC	R & P	Disc/drum	165-13	168	2154	90	14.5	20.5	£4495

Make and model	Production Figures	Years Built	Body Styles	Mechanical Layout	Engine Make (if not own)	Capacity/(cc)/Layout/Valves	BHP/rpm	Torque (lb.ft)/rpm	Transmission gearbox/automatic transmission
						1585/4IL/OHV	75/5400	91/3000	4-spd/Auto
						1585/4IL/OHC	85/5600	93/3000	4-spd/5-spd/Auto
						1585/4IL/2OHC	96/6000	94/3800	5-spd/Auto
						1995/4IL/2OHC	115/5800	123/3600	5-spd/Auto
X1/9	Est 180,000	1972–1989	Targa	M (Tr)/R	—	1290/4IL/OHC	75/6000	72/3400	4-spd/-
						1498/4IL/OHC	85/6000	87/3200	5-spd/-
Strada	1,790,000 (Approx) (Incl. Cabrio)	1978–1988	Htch	F(Tr)/F	—	1116/4IL/OHC	60/6000 55/5600	60/3500 65/2900	4-spd/- 5-spd/-
						1301/4IL/OHC	65/5800 68/5700	72/3500 74/2900	5-spd/Auto 5-spd/-
						1498/4IL/OHC	75/5800 85/5800	87/3000 87/3800	5-spd/Auto 5-spd/Auto
						1585/4IL/2OHC	105/6100 98/6100	98/4000 98/4000	5-spd/- 5-spd/-
						1995/4IL/2OHC	130/5900	130/3600	5-spd/-
Strada Cabrio	N/A	1983–1985	Conv	F(Tr)/F	—	1498/4IL OHC	85/5800	87/3800	5-spd/-
Regata	1,970,000 (Approx)	1984–1990	Sal Est	F(Tr)/F	—	1299/4IL/OHC	65/5800 68/5700	74/2900 74/2900	5-spd/- 4-spd/-
						1498/4IL/OHC	82/5500	91/2900	Auto/-
						1585/4IL/2OHC	82/5500 100/5900	91/2900 98/3800	5-spd/- 5-spd/-
						1929/4IL/OHC Diesel	65/4600 80/4200	88/2000 127/2400	5-spd/- 5-spd/-
Panda	In prod (Incl. 4x4)	1980–Date	Htch	F(Tr)/F	—	769/4IL/OHC	34/5250	42/3000	4-spd/-
						903/4IL/OHV	45/5600 45/5600	47/3000 49/3000	4-spd/5-spd/- 5-spd/5-spd/-
						999/4IL/OHC	45/5000	59/2750	5-spd/Auto
						1108/4IL/OHC	50/5250	62/3000	Auto/-
Panda 4x4	In prod	1984–Date	Htch	F(Tr)/4	—	965/4IL/OHV	48/5800	51/3500	5-spd/-
						999/4IL/OHC	50/5500	58/3000	5-spd/-
Uno	In prod	1983–Date	Htch	F(Tr)/F	—	903/4IL/OHV	45/5600	50/3000	4-spd/5-spd/-
						999/4IL/OHC	45/5000	59/2750	4-spd/5-spd/-
						1108/4IL/OHC	57/5500	64/2900	5-spd/-
						1116/4IL/OHC	55/5600	64/2900	5-spd/Auto
						1301/4IL/OHC	70/5700 105/5750	74/2900 108/3200	5-spd/- 5-spd/-
						1372/4IL/OHC	71/6000 118/6000	80/3000 119/3500	5-spd/- 5-spd/-
						1697/4IL/OHC Diesel	60/4500	76/3000	5-spd/-
Tipo	N/A	1988–1995	Htch	F(Tr)/F	—	1372/4IL/OHC	72/6000	78/2900	5-spd/-
						1580/4IL/OHC	83/6000	96/2900	5-spd/Auto
						1756/4IL/2OHC	110/6000	105/2500	5-spd/-
						1995/4IL/2OHC	115/5750 142/6000 148/6250	117/3300 135/4500 131/5000	5-spd/Auto 5-spd/- 5-spd/-
						1697/4IL/OHC Diesel			
						1929/4IL/OHC Diesel	92/4100	136/2400	5-spd/-
Croma	In prod	1986–Date	Htch	F(Tr)/F	—	1995/4IL/2OHC	90/5500 98/5250 120/5250 155/5250	124/2800 123/2750 123/3300 173/2350	5-spd/- 5-spd/- 5-spd/Auto 5-spd/-
Tempra	In prod	1990–Date	Sal Est	F(Tr)/F	—	1372/4IL/OHC	76/6000	78/2900	5-spd/-
						1581/4IL/OHC	86/6000	96/2900	5-spd/Auto
						1756/4IL/	110/6000	103/2500	5-spd/-

Suspension Front	Rear	Steering	Brakes (Front/rear)	Wheels/Tyres	Length (in)	Weight (lb,unladen)	Top speed (mph)	0–60mph (sec)	Standing 1/4-mile (sec)	UK Total Price (£: at Launch)
IC	BeamC	R & P	Disc/drum	155-13	168	2127	96	13.2	19.0	£1860
IC	BeamC	R & P	Disc/drum	165-13	168	2308	99 (Claimed)	N/A	N/A	£4450
IC	BeamC	R & P	Disc/drum	165-13	168	2330	105	11.9	18.8	£3595
IC	BeamC	R & P	Disc/drum	185/60-14	168	2520	108	10.7	17.5	£4636
IC	IC	R & P	Disc/disc	165/70-13	151	2010	99	12.7	18.8	£2997
IC	IC	R & P	Disc/disc	165/70-13	156	2010	110	10.8	17.0	£4575
IC	ITrL	R & P	Disc/drum	145-13	155	1807	N/A	N/A	N/A	£3990
IC	ITrL	R & P	Disc/drum	145-13	158	1807	93	14.7	19.7	£3990
IC	ITrL	R & P	Disc/drum	165/70-13	155	2000	87	15.6	19.8	£3198
IC	ITrL	R & P	Disc/drum	165/70-13	158	1915	93	12.1	18.9	£3845
IC	ITrL	R & P	Disc/drum	165/70-13	155	2025	95	13.3	18.9	£3637
IC	ITrL	R & P	Disc/drum	165/65-14	155	2083	100	10.9	18.0	£4772
IC	ITrL	R & P	Disc/drum	185/60-14	158	2051	104	9.7	17.5	£5195
IC	ITrL	R & P	Disc/drum	185/60-14	158	2144	103	10.4	17.9	£5495
IC	ITrL	R & P	Disc/drum	185/60-14	158	2168	122	8.1	16.3	£7800
IC	ITrL	R & P	Disc/drum	165/65-14	158	1994	100	10.1	17.6	£7539
IC	ITrL	R & P	Disc/drum	155-13	168	2002	97	13.2	18.7	£4990
IC	ITrL	R & P	Disc/drum	155-13	168	2002	96 (Claimed)	N/A	N/A	£6289
IC	ITrL	R & P	Disc/drum	165/70-13	168	2028	106 (Est)	N/A	N/A	£5490
IC	ITrL	R & P	Disc/drum	165/65-14	168	2268	111	9.9	17.6	£6491
IC	ITrL	R & P	Disc/drum	165/65-14	168	2282	94	15.6	19.9	£6860
IC	ITrL	R & P	Disc/drum	165/65-14	168	2338	103	12.9	19.4	£7890
IC	BeamC	R & P	Disc/drum	135-13	134	1663	79	20.6	22.1	£3490
IC	Beam1/2E	R & P	Disc/drum	135-13	133	1546	86	16.2	20.6	£2860
IC	Beam1/2E	R & P	Disc/drum	135-13	133	1445	84	17.1	20.3	£3189
IC	BeamC	R & P	Disc/drum	135-13	134	1663	88	16.0	20.2	£3939
IC	BeamC	R & P	Disc/drum	135-13	134	1576	87	N/A	N/A	£6090
IC	Beam1/2E	R & P	Disc/drum	145-13	143	1642	83	16.8	21.2	£4390
IC	Beam1/2E	R & P	Disc/drum	135-13	143	1984	84	N/A	N/A	£4872
IC	IC	R & P	Disc/drum	135-13	144	1543	87 (Claimed)	N/A	N/A	£3300
IC	IC	R & P	Disc/drum	135-13	144	1708	84	18.0	20.4	£3990
IC	IC	R & P	Disc/drum	155/70-13	145	1768	94	14.2	19.6	£7140
IC	IC	R & P	Disc/drum	155/70-13	144	1708	93	14.1	19.4	£3690
IC	IC	R & P	Disc/drum	155/70-13	144	1730	104	11.3	18.5	£4321
IC	IC	R & P	Disc/disc	175/60-13	144	1724	120	9.1	16.7	£6889
IC	IC	R & P	Disc/drum	155/70-13	145	2272	102	12.3	18.8	£8772
IC	IC	R & P	Disc/drum	175/60-13	145	2079	126	8.3	16.4	£9936
IC	IC	R & P	Disc/drum	155/70-13	144	1917	94	15.8	20.2	£6541
IC	IC	R & P	Disc/drum	165/70-13	156	2082	99	13.1	19.1	£7150
IC	IC	R & P	Disc/drum	165/70-13	156	2313	106	11.3	18.4	£8090
IC	IC	R & P	Disc/drum	185/60-14	156	2621	120	10.5	17.9	£10,403
IC	IC	R & P	Disc/disc	185/60-14	156	2426	118 (Est)	10.5	N/A	£11,950
IC	IC	R & P	Disc/disc	185/55-15	156	2558	127	8.5	16.5	£13,695
IC	IC	R & P	Disc/disc	185/55-15	156	2602	128 (Est)	N/A	N/A	£13,945
IC	IC	R & P	Disc/drum	175/60-14	156	2690	111	10.8	18.0	£9890
IC	IC	R & P	Disc/drum	175/70-14	177	2390	113	12.1	18.3	£8849
IC	IC	R & P	Disc/disc	175/70-14	177	2592	112	11.6	18.2	£11,750
IC	IC	R & P	Disc/disc	175/70-14	177	2649	121	9.9	17.3	£10,150
IC	IC	R & P	Disc/disc	195/60-14	177	2778	131	8.2	15.9	£13,500
IC	IC	R & P	Disc/drum	165/65-14	174	2271	107 (Claimed)	N/A	N/A	£8650
IC	IC	R & P	Disc/drum	165/65-14	174	2277	111	12.2	18.7	£9750
IC	IC	R & P	Disc/drum	185/60-14	174	2694	122	10.6	17.8	£11,750

Make and model	Production Figures	Years Built	Body Styles	Mechanical Layout	Engine Make (if not own)	Capacity/(cc)/Layout/Valves	BHP/rpm	Torque (lb.ft)/rpm	Transmission gearbox/automatic transmission
						2OHC			
						1995/4IL/ 2OHC	115/5750	115/3300	5-spd/Auto
						1929/4IL/ OHC Diesel	65/4600	87/2000	5-spd/-
							92/4100	140/2400	5-spd/-
Cinquecento	In prod	1991–Date	Htch	F(Tr)/F	—	903/4IL/ OHV	41/5500	48/3000	5-spd/-
						1108/4IL/ OHC	54/5500	63/3250	5-spd/-
Punto	In prod	1993–Date	Htch	F(Tr)/F	—	1108/4IL/ OHC	55/5500	63/3500	6-spd/-
						1242/4IL/ OHC	60/5500	71/3000	5-spd/Auto
							75/6000	78/4000	5-spd/-
						1372/4IL/ OHC	136/5750	150/3000	5-spd/-
						1581/4IL/ OHC	88/5750	94/2750	5-spd/-
						1698/4IL/ OHC Diesel	72/4500	99/2500	5-spd/-
Coupe	In prod	1994–Date	Cpe	F(Tr)/F	—	1995/4IL/ 2OHC	142/6000	135/4500	5-spd/-
							195/5500	214/3400	5-spd/-
Ulysse	In prod	1994–Date	Est	F(Tr)/F	Peugeot	1998/4IL/ OHC	121/5750	128/2650	5-spd/-
						1905/4IL/ OHC Diesel	92/4000	148/2250	5-spd/-
Barchetta	In prod	1995–Date	Spts	F(Tr)/F	—	1747/4IL/ 2OHC	130/6300	121/4300	5-spd/-
Bravo/Brava	In prod	1995–Date	Htch	F(Tr)/F	—	1370/4IL/ OHC	80/6000	83/2750	5-spd/-
						1581/4IL/ 2OHC	103/5750	106/4000	5-spd/Auto
						1747/4IL/ 2OHC	113/5800	113/4400	5-spd/-
						1998/5IL/ 2OHC	147/6100	137/4500	5-spd/-
						1929/4IL/ OHC Diesel	65/4600	88/2000	5-spd/-
Ford (UK and Europe)									
Zephyr/ Zodiac Mk IV	149,263	1966–1971	Sal Est	F/R	—	1996/V4/ OHV	88/4750	116/2750	4-spd/Auto
						2495/V6/ OHV	112/4750	137/3000	4-spd/Auto
						2994/V6/ OHV	136/4750	181/3000	4-spd/Auto
Escort I	1,082,472	1967–1974	Sal Est	F/R	—	1098/4IL/ OHV	50/5500	59/3000	4-spd/-
							48/6000	54/3000	
						1298/4IL/ OHV	58/5000	72/2500	4-spd/-
							71/6000	70/4300	4-spd/-
							57/5500	67/3000	4-spd/Auto
							72/6000	68/4000	4-spd/-
Escort TC	1,263	1968–1971	Sal	F/R	Lotus	1558/4IL/ 2OHC	110/6000	107/4500	4-spd/-
Escort RS1600	Est 1,000	1970–1974	Sal	F/R	—	1599/4IL/ 2OHC	120/6500	112/4000	4-spd/-
Escort Mexico	9,382	1970–1974	Sal	F/R	—	1599/4IL/ OHV	86/5500	92/4000	4-spd/-
Escort RS2000	4,324	1973–1974	Sal	F/R	—	1993/4IL/ OHC	100/5750	108/3500	4-spd/-
Capri I	374,700 (UK prod)	1968–1973	Cpe	F/R	—	1298/4IL/ OHV	52/5000	66/2500	4-spd/-
							64/6000	65/4000	4-spd/-
							57/5500	67/3000	4-spd/-
							72/6000	68/4000	4-spd/-
						1593/4IL/ OHC	72/5500	87/2700	4-spd/Auto
							88/5700	92/4000	4-spd/Auto
						1599/4IL/ OHV	64/4800	85/2500	4-spd/Auto
							82/5400	92/3600	4-spd/Auto
							68/5200	85/2600	4-spd/Auto
							86/5000	92/4000	4-spd/Auto
						1996/V4/ OHV	93/5500	104/3600	4-spd/Auto
						2994/V6/ OHV	128/4750	173/3000	4-spd/Auto
							138/4750	191/3000	4-spd/Auto
Capri RS3100	Est. 200	1973–1974	Cpe	F/R	—	3093/V6/ OHV	148/5000	187/3000	4-spd/-
Capri II	403,612 (Incl. German build)	1974–1978	Spts Htch	F/R	—	1298/4IL/ OHV	57/5500	67/3000	4-spd/-
							50/5000	64/3000	4-spd/-
						1593/4IL/ OHC	72/5200	87/2700	4-spd/Auto
							88/5700	92/4000	4-spd/Auto

Suspension Front	Rear	Steering	Brakes (Front/rear)	Wheels/ Tyres	Length (in)	Weight (lb,unladen)	Performance Top speed (mph)	0–60mph (sec)	Standing 1/4-mile (sec)	UK Total Price (£: at Launch)
IC	IC	R & P	Disc/disc	185/60-14	174	2514	121 (Claimed)	10.0	N/A	£12,845
IC	IC	R & P	Disc/drum	165/65-14	174	2492	101 (Est)	16.9	N/A	£10,500
IC	IC	R & P	Disc/drum	165/65-14	174	2558	111 (Est)	12.1	N/A	£11,990
IC	IC	R & P	Disc/drum	145/70-13	127	1562	83	20.3	21.8	£5416
IC	IC	R & P	Disc/drum	165/55-13	127	1612	93	13.5	19.3	£6195
IC	IC	R & P	Disc/drum	165/65-14	148	1852	93 (Claimed)	16.5	N/A	£6350
IC	IC	R & P	Disc/drum	165/65-14	148	1907	99 (Est)	N/A	N/A	£8449
IC	IC	R & P	Disc/drum	165/65-14	148	2062	95	11.9	18.6	£7589
IC	IC	R & P	Disc/disc	185/55-14	148	2161	127	8.1	16.4	£10,995
IC	IC	R & P	Disc/drum	175/60-14	148	2198	110	10.5	16.9	£9228
IC	IC	R & P	Disc/drum	165/65-14	148	2205	101 (Claimed)	N/A	N/A	£7350
IC	IC	R & P	Disc/disc	195/55-15	167	2743	124	9.5	17.1	£17,349
IC	IC	R & P	Disc/disc	205/50-16	167	2822	140	6.8	15.3	£19,248
IC	IC	R & P	Disc/drum	195/65-15	175	3330	106	13.9	19.6	£15,895
IC	IC	R & P	Disc/drum	195/65-15	175	3451	100 (Claimed)	15.1	N/A	£16,645
IC	IC	R & P	Disc/disc	195/55-15	154	2335	118	8.7	16.6	£13995
IC	IC	R & P	Disc/drum	165/65-14	158/165	2293	106 (Claimed)	13.6	N/A	£9608
IC	IC	R & P	Disc/drum	185/60-14	158/165	2403	112 (Claimed)	11.2	N/A	£11,424
IC	IC	R & P	Disc/drum	185/55-15	158/165	2567	114	10.5	17.9	£12,580
IC	IC	R & P	Disc/disc	195/55-15	158/165	2624	130 (Claimed)	8.2	N/A	£N/A
IC	IC	R & P	Disc/drum	175/65-14	158/165	2426	96 (Claimed)	17.3	N/A	£N/A
IC	IC	Worm	Disc/disc	6.40-13 185-14	185	2828	95	17.7	20.3	£933
IC	IC	Worm	Disc/disc	6.70-13 185-14	185	2884	96	14.6	19.6	£1005
IC	IC	Worm	Disc/disc	6.70-13 185-14	185	2912	103	11.0	17.9	£1220
IC	Beam1/2E	R & P	Drum/drum	5.50-12	157	1641	79	22.3	22.1	£666
IC	Beam1/2E	R & P	Disc/drum	155-12	157	1704	79	19.8	21.6	£853
IC	Beam1/2E	R & P	Drum/drum	5.50-12	157	1674	83	20.6	21.3	£691
IC	Beam1/2E	R & P	Disc/drum	155-12	157	1716	94	14.8	19.5	£765
IC	Beam1/2E	R & P	Drum/drum	5.50-12	157	1674	87	16.9	20.4	£863
IC	Beam1/2E	R & P	Disc/drum	155-12	157	1716	94	13.1	19.2	£966
IC	Beam1/2E	R & P	Disc/drum	165-13	157	1730	113	9.9	17.2	£1171
IC	Beam1/2E	R & P	Disc/drum	165-13	157	1920	113	8.9	16.7	£1447
IC	Beam1/2E	R & P	Disc/drum	165-13	157	1965	99	10.7	18.0	£1150
IC	Beam1/2E	R & P	Disc/drum	165-13	160	1978	108	9.0	17.1	£1568
IC	Beam1/2E	R & P	Disc/drum	6.00-13	168	1940	86 (Est)	N/A	N/A	£890
IC	Beam1/2E	R & P	Disc/drum	165-13	168	1985	96	14.6	19.5	£986
IC	Beam1/2E	R & P	Disc/drum	165-13	168	1982	84	18.8	21.4	£1004
IC	Beam1/2E	R & P	Disc/drum	165-13	168	1985	98 (Est)	N/A	N/A	£1123
IC	Beam1/2E	R & P	Disc/drum	165-13	168	2121	98	12.9	18.9	£1260
IC	Beam1/2E	R & P	Disc/drum	165-13	168	2030	104	11.1	18.4	£1370
IC	Beam1/2E	R & P	Disc/drum	6.00-13	168	1985	92 (Est)	N/A	N/A	£936
IC	Beam1/2E	R & P	Disc/drum	165-13	168	2030	100	12.7	18.8	£1042
IC	Beam1/2E	R & P	Disc/drum	165-13	168	1985	94 (Est)	N/A	N/A	£1074
IC	Beam1/2E	R & P	Disc/drum	165-13	168	2072	99	12.4	18.7	£1042
IC	Beam1/2E	R & P	Disc/drum	165-13	168	2115	106	10.6	18.2	£1088
IC	Beam1/2E	R & P	Disc/drum	185-13	168	2380	113	10.3	17.6	£1291
IC	Beam1/2E	R & P	Disc/drum	185-13	168	2430	122	8.4	16.2	£1484
IC	Beam1/2E	R & P	Disc/drum	185-13	168	2315	123	7.2	15.7	£2450
IC	Beam1/2E	R & P	Disc/drum	165-13	171	2227	89 (Est)	N/A	N/A	£1336
IC	beam1/2E	R & P	Disc/drum	165-13	171	2178	86	18.8	21.0	£1717
IC	Beam1/2E	R & P	Disc/drum	165-13	171	2293	94	13.1	19.2	£1416
IC	Beam1/2E	R & P	Disc/drum	165-13	171	2326	104	11.4	18.2	£1633

Make and model	Production Figures	Years Built	Body Styles	Mechanical Layout	Engine Make (if not own)	Capacity/(cc)/Layout/Valves	BHP/rpm	Torque (lb.ft)/rpm	Transmission gearbox/automatic transmission
						1993/4IL/ OHC	98/5200	111/3500	4-spd/Auto
						2994/V6/ OHV	138/5000	174/3000	4-spd/Auto
Capri III	324,045 (Incl. German build)	1978–1986	Spts Htch	F/R	—	1298/4IL/ OHV	57/5500	67/3000	4-spd/-
						1593/4IL/ OHC	72/5200	87/2700	4-spd/Auto
							88/5700	92/4000	4-spd/Auto
						1993/4IL/ OHC	98/5200	111/3500	4-spd/Auto
						2994/V6/ OHV	138/5000	174/3000	4-spd/Auto
Capri 2.8i/ 280	N/A	1981–1986	Spts Htch	F/R	—	2792/V6/ OHV	160/5700	162/4200	4-spd/5-spd/-
Escort II	960,007 (UK prod)	1975–1980	Sal Est	F/R	—	1097/4IL/ OHV	48/5500	54/3000	4-spd/-
							41/5300	52/3000	4-spd/-
						1297/4IL/ OHV	57/5500	67/3000	4-spd/-
							70/5500	68/4000	4-spd/-
						1598/4IL/ OHV	84/5500	92/3500	4-spd/Auto
Escort RS1800	N/A	1975–1977	Sal	F/R	—	1835/4IL/ 2OHC	115/6000	120/4000	4-spd/-
Escort RS Mexico	1,442	1976–1978	Sal	F/R	—	1593/4IL/ OHC	95/5750	92/4000	4-spd/-
Escort RS2000 Mk II	25,638	1976–1980	Sal	F/R	—	1993/4IL/ OHC	110/5500	119/4000	4-spd/-
Cortina Mk III	1,126,559	1970–1976	Sal Est	F/R	—	1298/4IL/ OHV	57/5500	67/3000	4-spd/Auto
							50/5000	64/3000	4-spd/-
						1599/4IL/ OHV	68/5200	85/2600	4-spd/Auto
						1593/4IL/ OHC	86/5500	92/4000	4-spd/Auto
							72/5500	87/3000	4-spd/Auto
						1993/4IL/ OHC	98/5500	111/3500	4-spd/Auto
Cortina Mk IV/Mk V	1,131,850	1976–1982	Sal Est	F/R	—	1297/4IL/ OHV	50/5000	64/3000	4-spd/-
							61/6000	68/3000	4-spd/-
						1593/4IL/ OHC	59/4500	82/2600	4-spd/-
							72/5000	87/2700	4-spd/-
							76/5500	88/2800	4-spd/Auto
							93/5900	93/4000	4-spd/Auto
						1993/4IL/ OHC	98/5200	111/3500	4-spd/Auto
							102/5400	114/4000	4-spd/Auto
						2293/V6/ OHV	108/5000	130/3000	4-spd/Auto
							116/5500	132/3000	4-spd/Auto
Consul/ Granada Mk I	123,368 (UK prod)	1972–1977	Sal Est	F/R	—	1993/4IL/ OHV	75/5000	106/3000	4-spd/-
							98/5200	111/3000	4-spd/Auto
						1996/V4/ OHV	82/5000	106/3000	4-spd/Auto
						2494/V6/ OHV	120/5300	132/3800	4-spd/Auto
						2994/V6/ OHV	138/5000	174/3000	4-spd/Auto
Granada Coupe	N/A (German-built)	1973–1977	Cpe	F/R	—	1993/4IL/ OHC	98/5500	111/3500	4-spd/Auto
						2994/V6/ OHC	138/5000	174/3000	4-spd/Auto
Granada Mk II	639,440	1977–1985	Sal Est	F/R	—	1993/4IL/ OHC	99/5200	111/4000	4-spd/5-spd/Auto
						2293/V6/ OHV	108/5000	130/3000	4-spd/5-spd/Auto
							114/5300	130/3000	4-spd/5-spd/Auto
						2792/V6/ OHV	135/5200	159/3000	4-spd/5-spd/Auto
							160/5700	162/4300	4-spd/5-spd/Auto
					Peugeot	2112/4IL/ OHV Diesel	63/4500	90/2000	4-spd/-
					Peugeot	2498/4IL/ OHV Diesel	69/4200	109/2000	5-spd/-
Fiesta Mk I	1,750,000 (Incl. Spanish and German build, all types)	1976–1983	Htch	F(Tr)/F	—	957/4IL/ OHV	40/5500	47/2700	4-spd/-
						1117/4IL/ OHV	53/6000	59/3000	4-spd/-
							57/5700	61/3000	4-spd/-
						1298/4IL/ OHV	66/5600	68/3250	4-spd/-
Fiesta XR2	(Incl. in overall Fiesta figures)	1981–1983	Htch	F(Tr)/F	—	1598/4IL/ OHV	84/5500	91/2800	4-spd/-
Fiesta (Facelift)	1,980,100 (Incl. Spanish and German build, all types)	1983–1989	Htch	F(Tr)/F	—	957/4IL/ OHV	45/5700	50/3700	4-spd/-
						1117/4IL/ OHV	50/5000	61/2700	4-spd/5-spd/Auto
						1297/4IL/	69/6000	74/4000	5-spd/-

| Suspension | | Steering | Brakes | Wheels/ | Length (in) | Weight | Performance | | Standing | UK Total |
Front	Rear		(Front/rear)	Tyres		(lb,unladen)	Top speed (mph)	0–60mph (sec)	1/4-mile (sec)	Price (£: at Launch)
IC	Beam1/2E	R & P	Disc/drum	165-13	171	2348	106	10.4	17.9	£1687
IC	Beam1/2E	R & P	Disc/drum	185/70-13	171	2580	117	9.0	17.0	£1932
IC	Beam1/2E	R & P	Disc/drum	165-13	171	2172	89 (Est)	N/A	N/A	£2792
IC	Beam1/2E	R & P	Disc/drum	165-13	171	2195	96	13.7	19.2	£3101
IC	Beam1/2E	R & P	Disc/drum	165-13	171	2293	99	12.7	19.0	£3822
IC	Beam1/2E	R & P	Disc/drum	165-13	171	2273	106	10.8	17.7	£3560
IC	Beam1/2E	R & P	Disc/drum	185/70-13	171	2646	117	8.6	16.6	£4422
IC	Beam1/2E	R & P	Disc/drum	205/60-13	171	2620	127	7.9	16.2	£7995
IC	Beam1/2E	R & P	Drum/drum	155-12	157	1844	80	18.5	20.8	£1440
IC	Beam1/2E	R & P	Drum/drum	6.00-12	157	1845	79	20.8	21.3	£1299
IC	Beam1/2E	R & P	Disc/drum	155-13	157	1872	86	16.4	20.7	£1502
IC	Beam1/2E	R & P	Disc/drum	155-13	157	1872	93	13.5	19.9	£1803
IC	Beam1/2E	R & P	Disc/drum	155-13	157	1987	100	10.3	17.9	£1860
IC	Beam1/2E	R & P	Disc/drum	175/70-13	157	2015	111	9.0	16.9	£2825
IC	Beam1/2E	R & P	Disc/drum	175/70-13	157	1990	106 (Est)	11.1	17.8	£2444
IC	Beam1/2E	R & P	Disc/drum	175/70-13	163	2075	109	8.6	16.7	£2857
IC	BeamC	R & P	Disc/drum	5.60-13	168	2083	84	18.1	21.0	£914
IC	BeamC	R & P	Disc/drum	165-13	168	2183	80 (Est)	N/A	N/A	£1732
IC	BeamC	R & P	Disc/drum	5.60-13	168	2115	92	14.7	19.7	£961
IC	BeamC	R & P	Disc/drum	175-13	168	2182	98	13.3	19.0	£1112
IC	BeamC	R & P	Disc/drum	165-13	168	2240	93	15.1	19.9	£1141
IC	BeamC	R & P	Disc/drum	175-13	168	2346	105	10.7	18.1	£1027
IC	BeamC	R & P	Disc/drum	165-13	170	2128	88 (Est)	N/A	N/A	£1950
IC	BeamC	R & P	Disc/drum	165-13	170	2128	88 (Est)	N/A	N/A	£3346
IC	BeamC	R & P	Disc/drum	165-13	170	2139	94 (Est)	N/A	N/A	£2153
IC	BeamC	R & P	Disc/drum	165-13	170	2325	93	13.7	19.4	£2291
IC	BeamC	R & P	Disc/drum	165-13	170	2140	91	13.6	18.9	£4006
IC	BeamC	R & P	Disc/drum	165-13	170	2161	100	N/A	N/A	£5380
IC	BeamC	R & P	Disc/drum	165-13	170	2307	100	11.0	17.9	£2696
IC	BeamC	R & P	Disc/drum	165-13	170	2274	103	10.3	17.4	£4634
IC	BeamC	R & P	Disc/drum	185/70-13	170	2507	99 (Auto)	12.2	18.8	£3901
IC	BeamC	R & P	Disc/drum	185/70-13	170	2472	103	10.5	18.0	£6084
IC	IC	R & P	Disc/disc	175-14	184	2673	90 (Est)	N/A	N/A	£2429
IC	IC	R & P	Disc/disc	175-14	184	2756	95	14.7	20.5	£2313
IC	IC	R & P	Disc/disc	175-14	184	2352	96	14.1	19.2	£1255
IC	IC	R & P	Disc/disc	185-14	184	2934	109	10.4	17.5	£1357
IC	IC	R & P	Disc/disc	175-14	184	3073	113	9.1	16.8	£1659
IC	IC	R & P	Disc/disc	175-14	180	2753	95 (Est)	N/A	N/A	£3901
IC	IC	R & P	Disc/disc	185-14	180	3051	110	10.3	17.8	£3878
IC	IC	R & P	Disc/drum	175-14	192	2735	102	11.9	18.5	£4144
IC	IC	R & P	Disc/drum	185-14	182	2932	100	13.5	N/A	£4391
IC	IC	R & P	Disc/drum	175-14	182	2923	105	11.4	18.3	£9615
IC	IC	R & P	Disc/drum	185-14	182	3009	111	9.9	17.8	£5636
IC	IC	R & P	Disc/drum	185-14	182	3009	117	8.9	16.7	£5863
IC	IC	R & P	Disc/drum	175-14	182	2935	85	27.2	23.4	£4668
IC	IC	R & P	Disc/drum	185-14	182	2745	87	17.5	20.7	£8020
IC	BeamC	R & P	Disc/drum	145-12	141	1635	79	19.0	21.0	£1856
IC	BeamC	R & P	Disc/drum	145-12	141	1691	86	15.7	20.0	£2179
IC	BeamC	R & P	Disc/drum	145-12	141	1568	85	14.5	19.5	£4162
IC	BeamC	R & P	Disc/drum	155-12	141	1764	94	13.7	19.3	£2844
IC	BeamC	R & P	Disc/drum	185/60-13	146	1848	104	9.4	17.4	£5500
IC	BeamC	R & P	Disc/drum	135-13	146	1654	85 (Claimed)	N/A	N/A	£3560
IC	BeamC	R & P	Disc/drum	165/70-13	146	1664	88	14.2	19.4	£4155
IC	BeamC	R & P	Disc/drum	155/70-13	144	1720	100	11.2	18.4	£5133

Make and model	Production Figures	Years Built	Body Styles	Mechanical Layout	Engine Make (if not own)	Capacity/(cc)/Layout/Valves	BHP/rpm	Torque (lb.ft)/rpm	Transmission gearbox/automatic transmission
						OHC			
						1392/4IL/	75/5600	80/4000	5-spd/-
						OHC			
						1608/4IL/	54/4800	95/3000	5-spd/-
						OHC Diesel			
Fiesta XR2	(Incl. in overall Fiesta 'facelift' figures)	1984–1989	Htch	F(Tr)/F	—	1596/4IL/	96/6000	98/4000	5-spd/-
						OHC			
Escort Mk III (Incl. European build, all types, and Orion)	1,857,000	1980–1986	Htch Est Conv	F(Tr)/F	—	1117/4IL/	55/5700	61/4000	4-spd/-
						OHV			
						1296/4IL/	69/6000	74/3500	4-spd/5-spd/-
						OHC			
						1596/4IL/	79/5800	92/3000	4-spd/5-spd/Auto
						OHC			
						1608/4IL/	54/4800	70/3000	5-spd/-
						OHC Diesel			
Orion (Mk III)	(See above)	1983–1986	Sal	F(Tr)/F	—	1296/4IL/	69/6000	74/3500	5-spd/-
						OHC			
						1597/4IL/	79/5800	93/3000	5-spd/Auto
						OHC	105/6000	101/4800	5-spd/-
						1608/4IL/	54/4800	70/3000	5-spd/-
						OHC Diesel			
Escort XR3/XR3i	(See above)	1980–1986	Htch	F(Tr)/F	—	1596/4IL/	96/6000	98/4000	4-spd/5-spd/-
						OHC	105/6000	101/4800	5-spd/-
Escort RS1600i	8,659	1982–1984	Htch	F(Tr)/F	—	1596/4IL/	115/6000	109/5250	5-spd/-
						OHC			
Escort RS Turbo	8,604	1984–1986	Htch	F(Tr)/F	—	1596/4IL/	132/6000	133/3000	5-spd/-
						OHC			
Escort Mk IV (Incl. European build, all types, and Orion and XR3i + Turbo)	1,855,000	1986–1990	Htch Est Conv	F(Tr)/F	—	1117/4IL/	50/5000	61/2700	4-spd/5-spd/-
						OHV			
						1297/4IL/	60/5000	74/3000	4-spd/5-spd/-
						OHV	63/5000	75/3000	5-spd/-
						1392/4IL/	75/5600	80/4000	4-spd/5-spd/-
						OHC			
						1597/4IL/	90/5800	98/4000	5-spd/Auto
						OHC	105/6000	104/4800	5-spd/-
							132/5750	133/2750	5-spd/-
						1608/4IL/	54/4800	70/3000	5-spd/-
						OHC Diesel			
Orion (Mk IV)	(See above)	1986–1990	Sal	F(Tr)/F	—	1297/4IL/	60/5000	74/3000	4-spd/5-spd/-
						OHV			
						1392/4IL/	75/5600	80/4000	4-spd/5-spd/-
						OHC			
						1597/4IL/	90/5800	98/4000	5-spd/Auto
						OHC	105/6000	102/4800	5-spd/-
						1608/4IL/	54/4800	70/3000	5-spd/-
						OHC Diesel			
Sierra	3,444,229	1982–1992	Htch Sal Est	F/R	—	1294/4IL/	60/5700	72/3100	4/spd/5-spd/-
						OHC			
						1593/4IL/	75/5300	88/2900	4-spd/5-spd/Auto
						OHC			
						1597/4IL/	75/5300	91/2900	4-spd/5-spd/Auto
						OHC			
						1769/4IL/	90/5250	108/3000	5-spd/Auto
						OHC			
						1796/4IL/	90/5300	100/3300	5-spd/Auto
						OHC			
						1993/4IL/	105/5200	115/4000	5-spd/Auto
						OHC	115/5500	118/4000	5-spd/Auto
						1998/4IL/	109/5600	128/3000	5-spd/Auto
						2OHC	125/5600	128/2500	5-spd/Auto
						2294/V6/	114/5300	130/3000	5-spd/Auto
						OHV			
						1753/4IL/	75/4500	112/2200	5-spd/-
						OHC Diesel			
					Peugeot	2304/4IL/	67/4200	102/2000	5-spd/-
						OHV Diesel			
Sierra XR4i	25,662	1983–1985	Htch	F/R	—	2792/V6/	150/5700	161/3800	5-spd/-
						OHV			
Sierra XR4x4	Incl. in total Sierra figures	1985–1992	Htch Est	F/4	—	1998/4IL/	125/5600	130/3500	5-spd/-
						2OHC			
						2792/V6/	150/5700	159/3800	5-spd/-
						OHV			
						2933/V6/	150/5700	172/3000	5-spd/-
						OHV			
Sierra RS Cosworth	Est 16,000	1986–1990	Htch Sal	F/R	—	1993/4IL/	204/6000	203/4500	5-spd/-
						2OHC			
							224/6000	206/4500	5-spd/-
Sierra Cosworth 4x4	Est 10,000	1990–1992	Sal	F/4	—	1993/4IL/	220/6000	214/3500	5-spd/-
						2OHC			

Suspension Front	Rear	Steering	Brakes (Front/rear)	Wheels/Tyres	Length (in)	Weight (lb,unladen)	Top speed (mph)	0–60mph (sec)	Standing 1/4-mile (sec)	UK Total Price (£: at Launch)
IC	BeamC	R & P	Disc/drum	155/70-13	144	1720	102	11.9	18.1	£5828
IC	BeamC	R & P	Disc/drum	155/70-13	144	1918	91	15.8	19.9	£5110
IC	BeamC	R & P	Disc/drum	185/60-13	146	1851	110	8.7	17.0	£5731
IC	IC	R & P	Disc/drum	145-13	160	1830	92	15.5	20.2	£3374
IC	IC	R & P	Disc/drum	155-13	160	2024	96	12.5	18.9	£3543
IC	IC	R & P	Disc/drum	155-13	160	1904	103	10.7	18.0	£4021
IC	IC	R & P	Disc/drum	155-13	160	1918	91 (Claimed)	N/A	N/A	£5836
IC	IC	R & P	Disc/drum	155-13	165	1929	98 (Claimed)	N/A	N/A	£5905
IC	IC	R & P	Disc/drum	155-13	165	2001	108	10.4	17.8	£6200
IC	IC	R & P	Disc/drum	175/70-13	165	2219	115	9.7	17.2	£7435
IC	IC	R & P	Disc/drum	155-13	165	2062	93 (Claimed)	N/A	N/A	£6108
IC	IC	R & P	Disc/drum	185/60-14	160	2040	113	9.2	17.0	£5123
IC	IC	R & P	Disc/drum	185/60-14	160	2027	116	8.6	16.1	£6030
IC	IC	R & P	Disc/drum	195/50-15	160	2027	116	8.7	16.7	£6700
IC	IC	R & P	Disc/drum	195/50-15	160	2150	125	8.1	16.2	£9720
IC	IC	R & P	Disc/drum	145-13	159	1819	90	N/A (Est)	N/A	£4921
IC	IC	R & P	Disc/drum	145-13	159	1852	94	14.3	19.6	£5137
IC	IC	R & P	Disc/drum	155-13	159	1945	96	14.1	19.8	
IC	IC	R & P	Disc/drum	155-13	159	1918	103	12.4	18.5	£6140
IC	IC	R & P	Disc/drum	155-13	159	1896	110	10.0	17.8	£6712
IC	IC	R & P	Disc/drum	185/60-14	159	2133	116	9.6	17.0	£7854
IC	IC	R & P	Disc/drum	195/50-15	159	2247	124	9.2	16.8	£10,028
IC	IC	R & P	Disc/drum	155-13	159	2006	91 (Claimed)	N/A	N/A	£6079
IC	IC	R & P	Disc/drum	145-13	166	1929	98 (Est)	N/A	N/A	£6245
IC	IC	R & P	Disc/drum	155-13	166	2097	102	12.8	19.1	£6455
IC	IC	R & P	Disc/drum	155-13	166	1962	110 (Est)	N/A	N/A	£6807
IC	IC	R & P	Disc/drum	185/60-14	166	2061	115	9.7	17.2	£8390
IC	IC	R & P	Disc/drum	155-13	166	2061	93 (Claimed)	N/A	N/A	£7186
IC	IC	R & P	Disc/drum	165-13	173	2260	94 (Claimed)	N/A	N/A	£4783
IC	IC	R & P	Disc/drum	165-13	173	2360	101	13.0	19.1	£5071
IC	IC	R & P	Disc/drum	165-13	173	2360	103	12.7	18.9	£5522
IC	IC	R & P	Disc/drum	165-13	173	2540	107 (Claimed)	11.1	N/A	£8605
IC	IC	R & P	Disc/drum	165-13	173	2540	102	12.2	18.0	£6627
IC	IC	R & P	Disc/drum	165-13	173	2458	114	9.3	17.1	£6524
IC	IC	R & P	Disc/drum	195/60-14	173	2141	116	9.2	16.9	£8276
IC	IC	R & P	Disc/drum	185/65-14	173	2337	112 (Est)	N/A	N/A	£10,630
IC	IC	R & P	Disc/drum	195/65-14	173	2692	119	10.0	17.3	£14,950
IC	IC	R & P	Disc/drum	185/70-13	173	2627	112	10.2	17.1	£7382
IC	IC	R & P	Disc/drum	185/65-14	173	2414	99 (Claimed)	15.2	N/A	£9600
IC	IC	R & P	Disc/drum	165-13	173	2677	98	17.1	20.7	£6159
IC	IC	R & P	Disc/drum	195/60-14	176	2656	129	7.8	15.9	£9170
IC	IC	R & P	Disc/disc	195/60-14	176	2720 (Est)	116 (Claimed)	10.0	N/A	£16,000
IC	IC	R & P	Disc/disc	195/60-14	176	2751	125	8.4	16.6	£11,500
IC	IC	R & P	Disc/disc	195/60-14	176	2665	129	8.6	16.6	£15,750
IC	IC	R & P	Disc/disc	205/50-15	176	2688	145	6.2	15.5	£15,950
						2750	142	5.8	15.4	£19,000
IC	IC	R & P	Disc/disc	205/50-15	176	2651	154	6.1	15.1	£19,950
IC	IC	R & P	Disc/disc	205/50-15	176	2822	146	6.6	14.3	£24,995

Make and model	Production Figures	Years Built	Body Styles	Mechanical Layout	Engine Make (if not own)	Capacity/(cc)/Layout/Valves	BHP/rpm	Torque (lb.ft)/rpm	Transmission gearbox/automatic transmission
Granada (Scorpio)	755,037	1985–1994	Htch Sal Est	F/R	—	1798/4IL/OHC	90/5400	103/3500	5-spd/-
						1993/4IL/OHC	105/5200	116/4000	5-spd/Auto
							115/5500	118/4000	5-spd/Auto
						1998/4IL/2OHC	109/5600	128/3000	5-spd/Auto
							125/5600	128/2500	5-spd/Auto
					Peugeot	2498/4IL/OHV Diesel	92/4150	150/2250	5-spd/-
					VM	2500/4IL/OHC Diesel	115/4200	199/2000	5-spd/Auto
					—	2393/V6/OHV	130/5800	142/3000	5-spd/Auto
						2792/V6/OHV	150/5800	161/3000	5-spd/Auto
						2933/V6/OHV	150/5700	172/3000	Auto/-
						2933/V6/2OHC	195/5750	203/4500	Auto/-
Granada-4x4	Incl. in total Granada/Scorpio figures	1985–1992	Htch	F/4	—	2792/V6/OHV	150/5800	161/3000	5-spd/-
						2933/V6/OHV	150/5700	172/3000	5-spd/-
RS200	200	1985–1986	Spts Cpe	M/4	—	1803/4IL/2OHC	250/6500	215/4000	5-spd/-
Fiesta/ Fiesta Classic	In prod	1989–Date	Htch	F(Tr)/F	—	999/4IL/OHV	45/5000	54/3000	4-spd/-
						1118/4IL/OHV	55/5200	63/2700	5-spd/Auto
						1298/4IL/OHV	59/5000	74/2500	5-spd/Auto
						1392/4IL/OHV	75/5600	80/4000	5-spd/Auto
						1596/4IL/OHC	90/5800	98/4000	5-spd/-
						1596/4IL/2OHC	90/5250	95/4000	5-spd/-
						1753/4IL/OHC Diesel	60/4800	81/2500	5-spd/-
Fiesta XR2i	Incl. in total Fiesta figures	1989–1994	Htch	F(Tr)/F	—	1596/4IL/OHC	110/6000	102/2800	5-spd/-
						1796/4IL/2OHC	105/5500	113/4000	5-spd/-
Fiesta RS Turbo	Incl. in total Fiesta figures	1990–1992	Htch	F(Tr)/F	—	1596/4IL/OHC	133/5500	135/2400	5-spd/-
Fiesta RS1800	Incl. in total Fiesta figures	1992–1995	Htch	F(Tr)/F	—	1796/4IL/2OHC	128/6250	119/4500	5-spd/-
Escort (Mk V) (Incl. all Orion, renamed Escort saloon for 1993)	2,471,401	1990–1994	Htch Est Sal Conv	F(Tr)/F	—	1297/4IL/OHV	60/5000	74/3000	5-spd/-
						1392/4IL/OHC	73/5500	80/4000	5-spd/-
						1597/4IL/2OHC	88/5500	99/3000	5-spd/-
						1596/4IL/OHC	108/6000	104/4500	5-spd/-
						1796/4IL/2OHC	105/5500	113/4000	5-spd/-
							130/6250	119/4000	5-spd/-
						1753/4IL/OHC Diesel	60/4800	81/2500	5-spd/-
Escort RS2000	Incl. in above total figures	1991–1994	Htch	F(Tr)/F	—	1998/4IL/2OHC	150/6000	140/4500	5-spd/-
				F(Tr)/4	—	1998/4IL/2OHC	148/6000	140/4500	5-spd/-
Escort RS Cosworth	7,000	1992–1996	Htch	F/4	—	1993/4IL/2OHC	227/6250	224/3500	5-spd/-
							224/5750	220/2500	
Mondeo	In prod	1993–Date	Sal Htch Est	F(Tr)/F and F(Tr)/4	—	1598/4IL/2OHC	90/5250	102/3500	5-spd/-
						1796/4IL 2OHC	113/5750	116/3750	5-spd/Auto
						1998/4IL/2OHC	134/6000	133/4000	5-spd/Auto
						1753/4IL/OHC Diesel	87/4500	131/2000	5-spd/-
						2544/V6/2OHC	168/6250	162/4250	5-spd/Auto
Maverick	In prod	1993–Date	Ute	F/4	Nissan	2389/4IL/OHC	123/5200	145/4000	5-spd/-
						2663/4IL/OHV Diesel	100/4000	163/2200	5-spd/-

Suspension Front	Rear	Steering	Brakes (Front/rear)	Wheels/ Tyres	Length (in)	Weight (lb, unladen)	Top speed (mph)	0–60mph (sec)	Standing 1/4-mile (sec)	UK Total Price (£: at Launch)
IC	IC	R & P	Disc/disc	175-14	184	2700	111 (Claimed)	N/A	N/A	£8514
IC	IC	R & P	Disc/disc	175-14	184	2767	109 (Auto)	13.4	19.3	£8877
IC	IC	R & P	Disc/disc	185/70-14	184	2789	116	10.2	17.6	£9276
IC	IC	R & P	Disc/disc	185/70-14	184	2723	115 (Est)	N/A	N/A	£13,300
IC	IC	R & P	Disc/disc	185/70-14	184	2745	119 (Est)	N/A	N/A	£13,895
IC	IC	R & P	Disc/disc	185/70-14	184	3065	106	13.4	19.2	£15,320
IC	IC	R & P	Disc/disc	185/70-14	184	3164	121 (Claimed)	N/A	N/A	£18,670
IC	IC	R & P	Disc/disc	185/70-14	184	2955	122	9.5	17.4	£12,709
IC	IC	R & P	Disc/disc	185/70-14	184	2976	125	9.5	16.9	£12,706
IC	IC	R & P	Disc/disc	195/65-15	184	2952	123	9.5	17.3	£14,879
IC	IC	R & P	Disc/disc	205/50-16	184	3140	136	8.5	16.6	£27,383
IC	IC	R & P	Disc/disc	205/60-15	184	3187	125	9.4	16.9	£18,109
IC	IC	R & P	Disc/disc	205/60-15	184	3187	126 (Claimed)	N/A	N/A	£17,478
IC	IC	R & P	Disc/disc	225/50-16	157	2835	140	6.1	15.0	£49,995
IC	IC	R & P	Disc/drum	135-13	147	1751	85	19.9	21.8	£5199
IC	IC	R & P	Disc/drum	155/70-13	147	1927	90	15.3	20.0	£6645
IC	IC	R & P	Disc/drum	165/65-13	147	1940	87	15.5	20.2	£8025
IC	IC	R & P	Disc/drum	155/70-13	147	1960	98	13.4	19.1	£7992
IC	IC	R & P	Disc/drum	165/65-13	147	1947	109	10.2	18.0	£7865
IC	IC	R & P	Disc/drum	185/55-14	147	2123	109	11.7	18.4	£9594
IC	IC	R & P	Disc/drum	145-13	147	1918	94 (Claimed)	14.1	N/A	£7005
IC	IC	R & P	Disc/drum	185/60-13	150	2024	118	8.9	16.7	£9995
IC	IC	R & P	Disc/drum	185/55-14	147	2148	116	9.4	17.1	£11,533
IC	IC	R & P	Disc/drum	185/55-14	150	2004	129	7.9	16.1	£11,950
IC	IC	R & P	Disc/disc	185/55-14	150	2104	123	8.3	16.5	£12,940
IC	IC	R & P	Disc/drum	175/70-13	159	1985	96 (Claimed)	N/A	N/A	£8220
IC	IC	R & P	Disc/drum	175/70-13	159	2224	105	12.8	18.8	£9470
IC	IC	R & P	Disc/drum	185/60-14	159	2514	111	11.9	18.6	£10,512
IC	IC	R & P	Disc/drum	185/60-14	159	2392	119	10.0	17.6	£12,272
IC	IC	R & P	Disc/disc	175/70-13	159	2304	118	9.9	17.4	£12,160
IC	IC	R & P	Disc/disc	185/60-14	159	2401	125	8.6	16.7	£13,990
IC	IC	R & P	Disc/drum	175/70-13	159	2216	94 (Claimed)	N/A	N/A	£8290
IC	IC	R & P	Disc/disc	195/50-15	159	2477	131	8.3	16.4	£15,995
IC	IC	R & P	Disc/disc	195/50-15	159	2756	128	9.4	17.8	£16,675
IC	IC	R & P	Disc/disc	245/45-16	166	2882	137	6.2	14.9	23,500
IC	IC	R & P	Disc/disc	225/45-16	166	2882	138	6.3	15.0	25,825
IC	IC	R & P	Disc/drum	185/65-14	176	2676	112 (Claimed)	12.6	N/A	£11,200
IC	IC	R & P	Disc/drum	185/65-14	176	2775	122	10.4	18.0	£12,070
IC	IC	R & P	Disc/disc	195/60-14	176	2844	126	9.8	17.3	£13,680
IC	IC	R & P	Disc/drum	185/65-14	176	2988	109	14.7	20.2	£13,550
IC	IC	R & P	Disc/disc	205/55-15	176	2994	139	7.9	16.1	£15,970
ITor	BeamC	Worm	Disc/drum	215-15	162/181	3616/3859	(SWB) 99	12.3	N/A	£15,000
ITor	BeamC	Worm	Disc/drum	215-15	162/181	3616/3859	90 (Claimed)	19.0	N/A	£15,500

Make and model	Production Figures	Years Built	Body Styles	Mechanical Layout	Engine Make (if not own)	Capacity/(cc)/Layout/Valves	BHP/rpm	Torque (lb.ft)/rpm	Transmission gearbox/automatic transmission
Probe	In prod	1992–Date	Cpe	F(Tr)/F	—	1991/4IL/2OHC	115/5500	125/4500	5-spd/-
						2497/V6/2OHC	164/5600	160/4800	5-spd/-
Scorpio	In prod	1994–Date	Sal Est	F/R	—	1998/4IL/2OHC	115/5500	123/2500	5-spd/Auto
						1998/4IL/2OHC	134/6300	129/4200	5-spd/Auto
						2933/V6/OHV	150/5500	168/3500	5-spd/Auto
						2933/V6/2OHC	204/6000	207/4200	Auto/-
Galaxy	In prod	1995–Date	Est	F(Tr)/F	—	1998/4IL/2OHC	115/5500	123/2300	5-spd/Auto
						2792/V6/2OHC	174/5800	174/4200	5-spd/Auto
						1896/4IL/OHC Diesel	90/4000	145/1940	5-spd/-
Escort (Mk VI)	In prod	1995–Date	Sal Htch Est Conv	F(Tr)/F	—	1299/4IL/OHV	60/5000	74/2500	5-spd/-
						1392/4IL/OHV	75/5100	73/2800	5-spd/-
						1597/4IL/2OHC	90/5500	99/4000	5-spd/Auto
						1796/4IL/2OHC	105/5500	115/4000	5-spd/-
							130/6250	119/4500	5-spd/-
							115/5750	118/4500	5-spd/-
						1753/4IL/OHC Diesel	60/4800	81/2500	5-spd/-
							89/4500	132/2200	5-spd/-
Escort RS 2000 (Mk VI)	In prod	1995–1996	Htch	F(Tr)/F F(Tr)/4	—	1998/4IL/2OHC	150/6000	140/4500	5-spd/-
Fiesta	In prod	1995–Date	Htch	F(Tr)/F	—	1299/4IL/OHV	60/5000	76/2500	5-spd/-
						1242/4IL/2OHC	75/5200	81/4000	5-spd/Auto
						1753/4IL/OHC Diesel	60/4800	78/2500	5-spd/-

(Ford (USA, Canada and Australia)

Make and model	Production Figures	Years Built	Body Styles	Mechanical Layout	Engine Make (if not own)	Capacity/(cc)/Layout/Valves	BHP/rpm	Torque (lb.ft)/rpm	Transmission gearbox/automatic transmission
Mustang **	—	1973 model	Cpe	F/R	—	4945/V8/OHV	143/4000	243/2000	Auto
Mustang II **	—	1974 model	Cpe	F/R	—	2798/V6/OHV	105/4600	140/3200	Auto
Mustang ** II V8	—	1975 model	Cpe	F/R	—	4945/V8/OHV	131/4000	213/2000	Auto
Fairmont **	—	1975 model	Est	F/R	—	4945/V8/OHV	230/5000	300/2600	Auto
Mustang Ghia Turbo **	—	1979 model	Cpe	F/R	—	2301/4IL/OHC	120/5400	135/3200	4-spd

FSO (Earlier named Polski-Fiat)

Make and model	Production Figures	Years Built	Body Styles	Mechanical Layout	Engine Make (if not own)	Capacity/(cc)/Layout/Valves	BHP/rpm	Torque (lb.ft)/rpm	Transmission gearbox/automatic transmission
125p	N/A	1968–1991	Sal Est	F/R	—	1481/4IL/OHV	70/5400	83/3200	4-spd/-
Polonez	N/A	1978–Date	Htch	F/R	—	1295/4IL/OHV	65/5200	69/3400	4-spd/5-spd/-
						1481/4IL/OHV	76/5250	85/3300	4-spd/5-spd/-
							82/5200	84/3400	4-spd/5-spd/-
Caro	In prod	1993–Date	Htch	F/R	Fiat	1481/4IL/OHV	74/5300	77/3800	5-spd/-
					Citroen	1905/4IL/OHC Diesel	69/4600	87/2000	5-spd/-

Gilbern

Make and model	Production Figures	Years Built	Body Styles	Mechanical Layout	Engine Make (if not own)	Capacity/(cc)/Layout/Valves	BHP/rpm	Torque (lb.ft)/rpm	Transmission gearbox/automatic transmission
Genie/Invader	Est 800	1966–1974	Cpe Est	F/R	Ford	2994/V6 OHV	141/4750	181/3000	4-spd/-

Ginetta

Make and model	Production Figures	Years Built	Body Styles	Mechanical Layout	Engine Make (if not own)	Capacity/(cc)/Layout/Valves	BHP/rpm	Torque (lb.ft)/rpm	Transmission gearbox/automatic transmission
G4	Est 500	1961–1969	Spts	F/R	Ford	997/4IL/OHV	40/5000	53/2700	4-spd/-
	N/A	1981–1984	Spts	F/R	Ford	1993/4IL/OHC	98/5200	111/3500	4-spd/-
G15	Est 800	1968–1974	Spts Cpe	R/R	Rootes/Sunbeam	875/4IL/OHC	50/5800	49/4500	4-spd/-
G21	180	1973–1978	Spts Cpe	F/R	Rootes/Sunbeam	1725/4IL/OHV	85/5200	107/4000	4-spd (+O/D)/-
							93/5200	106/4000	4-spd (+O/D)/-

Suspension Front	Rear	Steering	Brakes (Front/rear)	Wheels/ Tyres	Length (in)	Weight (lb, unladen)	Top speed (mph)	0–60mph (sec)	Standing ¼-mile (sec)	UK Total Price (£: at Launch)
IC	IC	R & P	Disc/disc	205/55-16	181	2676	118 (Claimed)	10.4	N/A	£15,995
IC	IC	R & P	Disc/disc	225/50-16	179	2808	134	7.9	16.2	£19,350
IC	IC	R & P	Disc/disc	195/65-15	190	3164	120 (Claimed)	12.0	N/A	£16,600
IC	IC	R & P	Disc/disc	195/65-15	190	3285	122	10.3	17.6	£17,215
IC	IC	R & P	Disc/disc	195/65-15	190	3285	124 (Claimed)	12.5	N/A	£18,185
IC	IC	R & P	Disc/disc	205/65-15	190	3515	138	9.0	16.9	£26,275
IC	IC	R & P	Disc/disc	195/65 to 215/60-15	182	3781	110	12.8	19.0	£15,995
IC	IC	R & P	Disc/disc	205/60 to 215/60-15	182	3770	124 (Claimed)	10.0	N/A	£20,550
IC	IC	R & P	Disc/disc	195/65 to 215/60-15	182	3638	99 (Claimed)	N/A	N/A	£16,995
IC	IC	R & P	Disc/drum	175/70-13	162	2223	95 (Claimed)	16.4	N/A	£9495
IC	IC	R & P	Disc/drum	175/70-13	162	2313	101 (Claimed)	14.4	N/A	£9760
IC	IC	R & P	Disc/drum	185/60-14	162	2388	106	12.1	18.6	£11,995
IC	IC	R & P	Disc/drum	185/60-14	162	2388	112 (Est)	10.0	N/A	£12,255
IC	IC	R & P	Disc/disc	185/60-14	162	2388	123 (Est)	N/A	N/A	£17,165
IC	IC	R & P	Disc/drum	185/60-14	162	2392	122 (Est)	9.2	N/A	£13,150
IC	IC	R & P	Disc/drum	175/70-13	162	2426	95 (Est)	16.7	N/A	£9760
IC	IC	R & P	Disc/drum	175/70-13	162	2511	107 (Est)	10.8	N/A	£10,735
IC	IC	R & P	Disc/disc	195/50-15	162	2569	131	8.3	16.4	£16,315
						2734	128	9.4	17.8	£17,370
IC	IC	R & P	Disc/drum	155/70-13	151	2093	96 (Claimed)	14.8	N/A	£7595
IC	IC	R & P	Disc/drum	165/70-13	151	2073	102	11.2	18.3	£8895
IC	IC	R & P	Disc/drum	165/70-13	151	2254	96 (Claimed)	16.2	N/A	£8300
IC	Beam1/2E	Worm	Disc/drum	E70-14	190	3260	108	10.4	17.7	£3483
IC	Beam1/2E	R & P	Disc/drum	185-13	177	3073	97	13.0	19.0	£2980
IC	Beam1/2E	R & P	Disc/drum	195/70-13	175	3069	107	10.1	17.5	£3952
IC	Beam1/2E	Worm	Disc/drum	185-14	196	3550	106	10.0	17.8	£4147
IC	BeamC	R & P	Disc/drum	190/65-390	179	2776	109	11.2	17.8	£7757
IC	Beam1/2E	Worm	Disc/disc	165-13	167	2285	93	14.4	19.5	£1249
IC	Beam1/2E	Worm	Disc/disc	165-13	168	2249	90 (Claimed)	N/A	N/A	£2449
IC	Beam1/2E	Worm	Disc/disc	175-13	168	2250	91	17.0	20.8	£2999
IC	Beam1/2E	Worm	Disc/disc	175-13	168	2481	96 (Claimed)	N/A	N/A	£5149
IC	Beam1/2E	Worm	Disc/disc	175-13	170	2459	93 (Claimed)	18.8	N/A	£5999
IC	Beam1/2E	Worm	Disc/disc	175-13	170	2503	87 (Claimed)	21.8	N/A	£6999
IC	BeamC	R & P	Disc/drum	165-15	159	1990	115	10.7	17.8	£1752
IC	BeamC	R & P	Disc/drum	5.20-13	140	1080	85 (Est)	N/A	N/A	£697
IC	BeamC	R & P	Disc/drum	165-13	140	1456	115	7.6	16.0	£2064
IC	IC	R & P	Disc/drum	5.20-13	144	1105	94	12.9	18.8	£1024
IC	BeamC	R & P	Disc/drum	165-13	156	1740	112	9.7	N/A	£1875
IC	BeamC	R & P	Disc/drum	165-13	156	1740	117	9.2	17.0	£2598

Make and model	Production Figures	Years Built	Body Styles	Mechanical Layout	Engine Make (if not own)	Capacity/ (cc)/Layout/ Valves	BHP/ rpm	Torque (lb.ft)/rpm	Transmission gearbox/automatic transmission
					Ford	2994/V6/ OHV	138/5000	174/3000	4-spd/Auto
G32	N/A	1988–1992	Spts Cpe Spts	M(Tr)/R	Ford	1598/4IL/ OHC	110/6000	102/2800	5-spd/-
G33	N/A	1991–Date	Spts	F/R	Rover	3946/V8/ OHV	198/5280	220/3500	5-spd/-
							294/5500	300/4150	5-spd/-
					Ford	1993/4IL/ 2OHC	220/6000	214/3500	5-spd/-
					Ford	1796/4IL/ 2OHC	128/6250	120/4500	5-spd/-

Hillman

Make and model	Production Figures	Years Built	Body Styles	Mechanical Layout	Engine Make (if not own)	Capacity/ (cc)/Layout/ Valves	BHP/ rpm	Torque (lb.ft)/rpm	Transmission gearbox/automatic transmission
Imp	440,032 (All Imp types)	1963–1976	Sal	R/R	—	875/4IL/ OHC	37/4800	49/2600	4-spd/-
Hunter	Est 470,000 (All Hunter and Minx)	1966–1977	Sal Est	F/R	—	1496/4IL/ OHV	54/4600	73/2500	4-spd/-
						1725/4IL/ OHV	61/4700	85/2600	4-spd (+O/D)/Auto
							72/5000	90/3000	4-spd (+O/D)/Auto
Hillman GT/ Hunter GT/GLS	Incl. in total Hunter figures	1969–1976	Sal	F/R	—	1725/4IL/ OHV	79/5100	93/3300	4-spd (+O/D)/-
							93/5200	106/4000	
Avenger	638,631	1970–1976	Sal Est	F/R	—	1248/4IL/ OHV	53/5000	66/3000	4-spd/-
						1295/4IL/ OHV	57/5000	69/2800	4-spd/-
							69/5800	68/4000	4-spd/-
						1498/4IL/ OHV	63/5000	80/3000	4-spd/Auto
							75/5400	81/3750	
						1599/4IL/ OHV	69/5000	87/2900	4-spd/Auto
							81/5500	86/3400	4-spd/Auto

Note: All surviving Hillman Avengers were renamed Chryslers from September 1976.

Hindustan

Make and model	Production Figures	Years Built	Body Styles	Mechanical Layout	Engine Make (if not own)	Capacity/ (cc)/Layout/ Valves	BHP/ rpm	Torque (lb.ft)/rpm	Transmission gearbox/automatic transmission
Ambassador	In prod.	1959–Date	Sal	F/R	Isuzu	1818/4IL/ OHC	74/5000	N/Q	5-spd/-

Honda

Make and model	Production Figures	Years Built	Body Styles	Mechanical Layout	Engine Make (if not own)	Capacity/ (cc)/Layout/ Valves	BHP/ rpm	Torque (lb.ft)/rpm	Transmission gearbox/automatic transmission
S600/S800	25,853	1966–1971	Spts Spts Cpe	F/R	—	791/4IL/ 2OHC	70/8000	49/6000	4-spd/-
N360/N600	1,165,441	1966–1971	Sal	F(Tr)/F	—	354/2IL/ OHC AirC	27/8500	24/5500	4-spd/Auto
						599/2IL/ OHC AirC	42/6600	40/5000	4-spd/Auto
Z Coupe	N/A	1970–1975	Htch	F(Tr)/F	—	599/2IL/ OHC AirC	32/6600	32/4000	4-spd/Auto
Civic	2,000,000 (Approx)	1972–1979	Sal Htch	F(Tr)/F	—	1169/4IL/ OHC	60/5500	58/3500	4-spd/Auto
						1238/4IL/ OHC	60/5500	62/3000	4-spd/Auto
						1488/4IL/ OHC	70/5500	76/4000	4-spd/Auto
Accord	N/A	1976–1981	Sal Htch	F(Tr)/F	—	1599/4IL/ OHC	80/5300	89/3000	4-spd/Auto
						1602/4IL/ OHC	80/5300	93/3500	4-spd/Auto
Prelude	264,842	1978–1981	Cpe	F(Tr)/F	—	1602/4IL/ OHC	80/5300	127/3500	5-spd/-
Civic	3,336,983	1980–1983	Htch	F(Tr)/F	—	1335/4IL/ OHC	60/5000	69/3500	5-spd/Auto
							70/5750	74/3400	5-spd/-
Quintet Included in Accord figures		1980–1985	Htch	F(Tr)/F	—	1602/4IL OHC	79/5300	93/3500	5-spd/Auto
Civic	1,573,907 (Incl. Shuttle)	1983–1987	Htch	F(Tr)/F	—	1342/4IL/ OHC	71/6000	77/3500	5-spd/Auto
						1488/4IL/ OHC	100/5750	96/4500	5-spd/-
Civic	2,016,669 (Incl. Shuttle)	1987–1991	Htch Sal	F(Tr)/F	—	1343/4IL/ OHC	75/6300	75/3100	5-spd/Auto
						1396/4IL/ OHC	90/6300	83/4500	5-spd/Auto
						1590/4IL/ 2OHC	120/6800	100/5700	5-spd/Auto
						1595/4IL/ 2OHC	150/7600	106/7100	5-spd/-
Civic Shuttle	Incl. in Civic figures	1983–1988	Est	F(Tr)/F	—	1488/4IL/ OHC	85/6000	93/3500	5-spd/Auto
				F(Tr)/4	—	1488/4IL/	85/6000	93/3500	5-spd/-

Suspension Front	Rear	Steering	Brakes (Front/rear)	Wheels/ Tyres	Length (in)	Weight (lb,unladen)	Performance Top speed (mph)	0–60mph (sec)	Standing ¼-mile (sec)	UK Total Price (£: at Launch)
IC	IC (or BeamC)	R & P	Disc/drum	195-13	156	1920	127 (Claimed)	N/A	N/A	£2564
IC	IC	R & P	Disc/disc	185/60-14	148	1938	112	9.0	16.8	£10,495
IC	IC	R & P	Disc/disc	215/50-15	154	1927	137	5.3	14.1	£18,187
IC	IC	R & P	Disc/disc	215/50-15	154	1927	155 (Est)	N/A	N/A	£27,225
IC	IC	R & P	Disc/disc	215/50-15	154	1927	150 (Claimed)	N/A	N/A	£27,795
IC	IC	R & P	Disc/disc	195/60-15	154	1927	125 (Claimed)	N/A	N/A	£16,895
IC	IC	R & P	Drum/drum	5.50-12	139	1530	78	25.4	22.8	£508
IC	Beam1/2E	Worm	Disc/drum	5.60-13	168	2035	83	17.8	20.9	£838
IC	Beam1/2E	Worm	Disc/drum	5.60-13	168	2035	90	14.6	19.6	£989
IC	Beam1/2E	Worm	Disc/drum	155-13	168	2000	92	14.3	19.7	£838
IC	Beam1/2E	Worm	Disc/drum	155-13	168	2105	96	13.9	19.4	£962
				165-13	168	2114	108	10.5	17.4	£1293
IC	BeamC	R & P	Disc/drum	5.60-13	161	1895	81	19.8	21.4	£822
IC	BeamC	R & P	Disc/drum	5.60-13	161	1895	85	17.5	20.9	£807
IC	BeamC	R & P	Disc/drum	155-13	161	1882	92	14.4	19.9	£1202
IC	BeamC	R & P	Disc/drum	5.60-13	161	1895	91	15.6	20.1	£942
				155-13	161	1941	96	12.5	18.5	£1073
IC	BeamC	R & P	Disc/drum	155-13	161	1895	96	13.2	19.4	£1051
IC	BeamC	R & P	Disc/drum	155-13	161	1971	100	12.2	19.0	£1156
ITor	Beam1/2E	R & P	Drum/drum	5.90-15	170	2569	87 (Claimed)	N/A	N/A	£5895
ITor	BeamC	R & P	Disc/drum	145-13	131	1694	94	13.4	18.8	£779
IC	Beam1/2E	R & P	Drum/drum	5.20-10	118	1119	72	29.3	22.9	£536
IC	Beam1/2E	R & P	Drum/drum Disc/drum	5.20-10	121	1198	85	17.3	19.6	£589
IC	Beam1/2E	R & P	Disc/drum	5.20-10	123	1301	73	32.6	23.6	£755
IC	IC	R & P	Disc/drum	6.00-12	140	1449	88	14.1	19.3	£999
IC	IC	R & P	Disc/drum	155-12	140	1613	87	14.5	19.4	£1809
IC	IC	R & P	Disc/drum	155-12	140	1623	90	12.8	18.9	£1636
IC	IC	R & P	Disc/drum	155-13	163	1962	94	13.3	19.3	£2895
IC	IC	R & P	Disc/drum	155-13	171	2232	91 (Auto)	15.0	20.2	£3915
IC	IC	R & P	Disc/drum	175/70-13	161	2030	98	11.3	18.6	£4950
IC	IC	R & P	Disc/drum	155-13	151	1627	90	13.5	18.9	£2990
IC	IC	R & P	Disc/drum	165/70-13	151	1821	93	12.1	18.7	£4495
IC	IC	R & P	Disc/drum	155-13	162	2058	93	12.2	18.7	£4990
ITor	BeamC	R & P	Disc/drum	155-13	150	1806	95	10.7	18.0	£4840
ITor	IC	R & P	Disc/disc	175/70-13	150	1874	108	9.9	17.5	£6595
IC	IC	R & P	Disc/drum	155-13	156	1764	105	10.5	18.0	£6395
IC	IC	R & P	Disc/drum	165/70-13	156	1993	106	9.7	17.4	£8150
IC	IC	R & P	Disc/disc	185/60-14	156	2051	124 (Est)	N/A	N/A	£10,800
IC	IC	R & P	Disc/disc	195/60-14	156	2290	127	7.6	16.1	£13,195
IC	ITor	R & P	Disc/drum	155-13	157	1978	100	11.2	18.1	£5690
IC	BeamC	R & P	Disc/drum	165-13	159	2130	94	12.6	18.8	£6495

Make and model	Production Figures	Years Built	Body Styles	Mechanical Layout	Engine Make (if not own)	Capacity/(cc)/Layout/Valves	BHP/rpm	Torque (lb.ft)/rpm	Transmission gearbox/automatic transmission
Civic Shuttle	Incl. in Civic figures	1988–1991	Est	F(Tr)/F	—	1396/4IL/ OHC	90/6300	83/4500	5-spd/Auto
				F(Tr)/4	—	1590/4IL/ 2OHC	116/6300	104/5300	5-spd/-
Jazz	26,419	1983–1985	Htch	F(Tr)/F	—	1231/4IL/ OHC	56/5000	69/3500	5-spd/-
Civic CRX	269,719	1983–1987	Spts Cpe	F(Tr)/F	—	1488/4IL/ OHC	100/5750	96/4500	5-spd/-
					—	1590/4IL/ OHC	125/6500	103/5500	5-spd/-
Civic CRX	420,741	1987–1991	Spts Cpe	F(Tr)/F	—	1590/4IL/ OHC	130/6800	105/5700	5-spd/-
						1595/4IL/ 2OHC	150/7600	106/7100	5-spd/-
Accord	1,510,932	1981–1985	Sal Htch	F(Tr)/F	—	1598/4IL/ OHC	90/5000	98/3500	5-spd/Auto
						1602/4IL/ OHC	80/5000	93/3500	5-spd/Auto
						1829/4IL/ OHC	100/5800	108/3500	5-spd/Auto
Accord	1,799,382 (Incl. Aerodeck)	1985–1989	Sal Cpe Htch Est	F(Tr)/F	—	1955/4IL/ OHC	122/5500	122/5000	5-spd/Auto
							106/5500	113/3500	5-spd/Auto
						1958/4IL/ 2OHC	137/6000	125/5000	5-spd/-
Accord	1,717,208 (Incl. Aerodeck)	1989–1993	Sal Coupe	F(Tr)/F	—	1997/4IL/ OHC	133/5300	132/5000	5-spd/Auto
							110/5700	117/3700	5-spd/Auto
						2156/4IL/ OHC	148/5900	148/5000	5-spd/Auto
Integra	1,027,180	1985–1989	Sal Cpe Htch	F(Tr)/F	—	1488/4IL/ OHC	85/6000	87/3750	5-spd/Auto
						1590/4IL/ 2OHC	125/6500	103/5500	5-spd/Auto
Ballade	73,842	1983–1987	Sal	F(Tr)/F	—	1488/4IL/ OHC	85/6000	87/3750	5-spd/Auto
							99/5750	96/4500	5-spd/Auto
Concerto	In prod	1988–Date	Sal Htch	F(Tr)/F	—	1396/4IL/ OHC	90/6300	81/4500	5-spd/Auto
						1493/4IL/ OHC	89/6000	87/5000	5-spd/Auto
						1590/4IL/ OHC	106/6300	96/4500	5-spd/Auto
						1590/4IL/ 2OHC	130/6800	105/5700	5-spd/Auto
Prelude	623,620	1982–1987	Cpe	F(Tr)/F	—	1829/4IL/ OHC	106/5500	114/3500	5-spd/Auto
						1958/4IL/ 2OHC	137/6000	125/5000	5-spd/-
						2OHC	158/6300	137/5000	5-spd/-
Prelude	637,132	1987–1991	Cpe	F(Tr)/F	—	1958/4IL/ OHC	114/5800	116/4500	5-spd/Auto
						1958/4IL/ 2OHC	150/6000	133/5500	5-spd/Auto
Legend	538,611	1985–1990	Sal Cpe	F(Tr)/F	—	2493/V6/ 2OHC	173/6000	160/5000	5-spd/-
							165/6000	163/4000	Auto/-
						2675/V6/ 2OHC	177/6000	165/4500	Auto/-
Civic	3,000,000 (Incl. Shuttle – approx)	1991–1994	Htch Est Sal Est	F(Tr)/F	—	1343/4IL/ OHC	74/6300	75/3100	5-spd/-
						1493/4IL/ OHC	90/6000	88/4700	5-spd/Auto
							90/5500	95/4500	5-spd/-
							102/5900	98/4900	5-spd/-
						1590/4IL/ OHC	123/6500	105/5200	5-spd/Auto
						1595/4IL/ 2OHC	158/7500	111/7000	5-spd/-
Civic	In prod	1994–Date	Sal Htch Cpe	F(Tr)/F	—	1343/4IL/ OHC	74/6300	75/3100	
						1396/4IL/ OHC	89/6100	86/5000	5-spd/Auto
						1493/4IL/ OHC	89/5500	97/4500	5-spd/-
							113/6300	97/5200	5-spd/-
						1590/4IL/ OHC	111/6200	103/5100	5-spd/Auto
							124/6500	103/5100	5-spd/Auto
						1595/4IL/ 2OHC	158/7600	113/7000	5-spd/Auto
CRX	In prod	1992–Date	Cpe	F(Tr)/F	—	1590/4IL/ OHC	125/6500	105/5200	5-spd/-
						1595/4IL/ 2OHC	158/7600	111/7000	5-spd/-
Prelude	In prod	1991–Date	Cpe	F(Tr)/F	—	1997/4IL/ 2OHC	131/5300	132/5000	5-spd/Auto

Suspension Front	Rear	Steering	Brakes (Front/rear)	Wheels/Tyres	Length (in)	Weight (lb, unladen)	Top speed (mph)	0–60mph (sec)	Standing 1/4-mile (sec)	UK Total Price (£: at Launch)
IC	IC	R & P	Disc/drum	165/70-13	162	2101	95 (Est)	N/A	N/A	£8350
IC	IC	R & P	Disc/drum	165/70-13	162	2420	104	10.0	17.1	£10,250
IC	IC	R & P	Disc/drum	145-12	133	1556	89	12.7	18.9	£4315
ITor	BeamC	R & P	Disc/drum	175/70-13	145	1869	115	8.7	16.7	£6950
ITor	BeamC	R & P	Disc/drum	185/60-14	148	1984	122	8.0	16.2	£7950
IC	IC	R & P	Disc/disc	185/60-14	148	2006	121	8.0	16.2	£9600
IC	IC	R & P	Disc/disc	195/60-14	149	2258	130	8.0	16.4	£13,900
IC	IC	R & P	Disc/drum	165-13	166	2040	106 (Claimed)	N/A	N/A	£4835
IC	IC	R & P	Disc/drum	165-13	166	2093	96	11.8	18.5	£5101
IC	IC	R & P	Disc/drum	165-13	175	2352	103	10.5	17.8	£6995
IC	IC	R & P	Disc/disc	185/70-13	179	2527	114	9.9	17.2	£9990
IC	IC	R & P	Disc/drum	185/70-13	179	2417	106	10.7	18.3	£8290
IC	IC	R & P	Disc/disc	185/70-13	179	2623	121	8.2	16.8	£13,900
IC	IC	R & P	Disc/drum	185/70-14	184	2797	123	9.9	17.5	£15,050
IC	IC	R & P	Disc/drum	185/70-14	184	2934	114 (Est)	N/A	N/A	£12,150
IC	IC	R & P	Disc/disc	195/60-15	185	3097	132 (Est)	N/A	N/A	£18,900
IC	IC	R & P	Disc/drum	185/70-13	171	2232	100	11.8	18.2	£7150
IC	IC	R & P	Disc/disc	185/60-14	171	2247	117	8.6	17.0	£8980
IC	IC	R & P	Disc/drum	165-13	163	2044	97	11.1	18.5	£7330
IC	IC	R & P	Disc/drum	175/70-13	163	2083	107	9.6	17.3	£8280
IC	IC	R & P	Disc/drum	175/65-14	168	2095	106 (Claimed)	N/A	N/A	£8995
IC	IC	R & P	Disc/drum	175/65-14	168	2346	103	11.8	18.6	£10,895
IC	IC	R & P	Disc/disc	175/65-14	168	2183	112 (Est)	N/A	N/A	£10,950
IC	IC	R & P	Disc/disc	185/60-14	168	2511	120	9.3	17.2	£11,998
IC	IC	R & P	Disc/disc	185/70-13	169	2323	109	9.9	16.8	£8040
IC	IC	R & P	Disc/disc	195/60-14	169	2315	116	8.4	16.2	£11,200
IC	IC	R & P	Disc/disc	195/60-14	169	2330	121	8.2	16.5	£11,200
IC	IC	R & P	Disc/disc	185/70-13	176	2409	118 (Claimed)	N/A	N/A	£11,090
IC	IC	R & P	Disc/disc	185/70-13	176	2419	128	8.5	16.4	£14,100
IC	IC	R & P	Disc/disc	205/60-15	189	3050	126	8.0	16.5	£14,700
IC	IC	R & P	Disc/disc	205/60-15	189	3050	123 (Est)	N/A	N/A	£15,350
IC	IC	R & P	Disc/disc	205/60-15	189	3075	132	8.0	16.4	£20,300
IC	IC	R & P	Disc/drum	165/70-13	160	2028	106 (Claimed)	N/A	N/A	£9295
IC	IC	R & P	Disc/drum	175/70-13	160	2192	110 (Est)	9.6	N/A	£10,795
IC	IC	R & P	Disc/drum	175/70-13	160	2126	111	11.2	17.8	£11,750
IC	IC	R & P	Disc/drum	175/70-13	160	2227	117	9.7	17.3	10,995
IC	IC	R & P	Disc/drum	185/60-14	160	2205	116	8.6	16.7	£11,995
IC	IC	R & P	Disc/drum	195/55-15	160	2293	134 (Claimed)	7.5	N/A	£14,495
IC	IC	R & P	Disc/drum	175/65-14	160	2040	106 (Claimed)	11.2	N/A	£9495
IC	IC	R & P	Disc/drum	175/65-14	170	2370	107 (Claimed)	13.1	N/A	£11,495
IC	IC	R & P	Disc/drum	175/65-14	160	2414	108	11.7	18.7	£11,795
IC	IC	R & P	Disc/drum	175/65-14	160	2690	114	9.7	17.5	£10,995
IC	IC	R & P	Disc/disc	185/60-14	160	2481	107	9.3	17.2	£10,995
IC	IC	R & P	Disc/disc	195/55-15	160	2533	121 (Est)	8.7	N/A	£12,845
IC	IC	R & P	Disc/disc	195/55-15	160	2591	129 (Claimed)	7.4	N/A	£15,485
IC	IC	R & P	Disc/disc	185/60-14	158	2315	118 (Claimed)	N/A	N/A	£14,595
IC	IC	R & P	Disc/disc	195/60-14	158	2437	132	8.0	16.0	£16,416
IC	IC	R & P	Disc/disc	195/65-14	158	2772	125 (Claimed)	9.2	N/A	£16,495

Make and model	Production Figures	Years Built	Body Styles	Mechanical Layout	Engine Make (if not own)	Capacity/(cc)/Layout/Valves	BHP/rpm	Torque (lb.ft)/rpm	Transmission gearbox/automatic transmission
						2157/4IL/2OHC	183/6800	156/5300	5-spd/Auto
						2259/4IL/2OHC	160/5800	156/4500	5-spd/Auto
Accord	In prod	1992–Date	Sal Cpe Est	F(Tr)/F	—	1850/4IL/2OHC	115/5500	117/4200	5-spd/-
						1997/4IL/OHC	115/5300	127/4200	5-spd/-
							131/5300	131/4800	5-spd/Auto
						2157/4IL/2OHC	150/5600	146/5500	5-spd/Auto
							150/5600	148/4600	5-spd/Auto
						2259/4IL/2OHC	158/5800	152/4500	5-spd/Auto
					Rover	1994/4IL/OHC Diesel	105/4200	155/2000	5-spd/-
Legend	N/A	1990–1996	Sal	F(Tr)/F	—	3206/V6/2OHC	205/5500	216/4400	Auto/-
Legend Coupe	In prod	1990–Date	Cpe	F(Tr)/F	—	3206/V6/2OHC	205/5500	216/4400	Auto/-
NSX	In prod	1990–Date	Spts Cpe Targa	M/R	—	2977/V6/2OHC	274/7000	210/5300	5-spd/Auto
Shuttle	In prod	1994–Date	Est	F(Tr)/F	—	2156/4IL/OHC	148/5600	146/4600	Auto/-

Humber

Make and model	Production Figures	Years Built	Body Styles	Mechanical Layout	Engine Make (if not own)	Capacity/(cc)/Layout/Valves	BHP/rpm	Torque (lb.ft)/rpm	Transmission gearbox/automatic transmission
Sceptre Mk III	43,951	1967–1976	Sal Est	F/R	—	1725/4IL/OHV	79/5100	93/3300	4-spd (+O/D)/Auto

Hyundai

Make and model	Production Figures	Years Built	Body Styles	Mechanical Layout	Engine Make (if not own)	Capacity/(cc)/Layout/Valves	BHP/rpm	Torque (lb.ft)/rpm	Transmission gearbox/automatic transmission
Pony	3,230,378 (Incl. 1985–1989)	1976–1985	Sal Htch	F/R	Mitsubishi	1238/4IL/OHC	54/5000	62/3000	4-spd/Auto
						1439/4IL/OHC	67/5000	77/3000	4-spd/Auto
Pony	See above	1985–1989	Sal Htch	F(Tr)/F	Mitsubishi	1298/4IL/OHC	66/5500	71/3500	5-spd/-
						1468/4IL/OHC	71/5500	82/3500	5-spd/Auto
Stellar	405,459	1984–1991	Sal	F/R	Mitsubishi	1597/4IL/OHC	73/5200	101/4000	4-spd/5-spd/Auto
Scoupe	In prod	1989–Date	Cpe	F(Tr)/F	Mitsubishi	1468/4IL/OHC	82/5500	89/4000	5-spd/-
						1495/4IL/OHC	87/5600	95/4000	5-spd/-
							114/5500	126/4300	5-spd/-
Sonata	In prod	1988–Date	Sal	F(Tr)/F	Mitsubishi	1795/4IL/	99/5000	108/4000	5-spd/Auto
						1997/4IL/2OHC	100/5000	121/3500	5-spd/Auto
							136/5800	132/4000	5-spd/Auto
						2351/IL/OHC	115/4500	142/3500	5-spd/Auto
						2972/V6/OHC	143/5000	170/2400	5-spd/Auto
Pony (X2)	In prod	1989–Date	Sal Htch	F(Tr)/F	Mitsubishi	1298/4IL/OHC	72/5500	83/3700	5-spd/-
						1468/4IL/OHC	83/5500	89/4000	5-spd/Auto
Lantra	N/A	1990–1995	Sal	F(Tr)/F	Mitsubishi	1468/4IL/OHC	84/5500	91/4000	5-spd/Auto
						1596/4IL/2OHC	112/6200	103/4500	5-spd/Auto
						1836/4IL/2OHC	124/6000	119/4400	5-spd/Auto
Lantra	In prod	1995–Date	Sal	F(Tr)/F	—	1596/4IL/2OHC	111/6100	105/3000	5-spd/Auto
						1795/4IL/2OHC	125/6100	119/3000	5-spd/Auto
Accent	In prod	1994–Date	Sal Htch Cpe	F(Tr)/F	—	1341/4IL/OHC	83/5700	87/3100	5-spd/-
						1495/4IL/OHC	87/5600	97/3050	5-spd/-

Iso

Make and model	Production Figures	Years Built	Body Styles	Mechanical Layout	Engine Make (if not own)	Capacity/(cc)/Layout/Valves	BHP/rpm	Torque (lb.ft)/rpm	Transmission gearbox/automatic transmission
Grifo	504	1963–1974	Cpe	F/R	Chevrolet	5359/V8/OHV	350/5800	360/3600	4-spd/-
							365/6200	360/4000	4-spd/-
					Chevrolet	6998/V8/OHV	400/5400	460/3600	4-spd/-
Fidia	192	1967–1974	Cpe	F/R	Chevrolet	5359/V8/OHV	300/5800	360/3200	4-spd/Auto
					Ford-USA	5768/V8/	325/5800	360/3800	5-spd/Auto

Suspension Front	Rear	Steering	Brakes (Front/rear)	Wheels/Tyres	Length (in)	Weight (lb,unladen)	Top speed (mph)	0–60mph (sec)	Standing 1/4-mile (sec)	UK Total Price (£: at Launch)
IC	IC	R & P	Disc/disc	205/55-15	175	3109	139	7.5	15.3	£20,750
IC	IC	R & P	Disc/disc	205/55-15	175	2866	133	8.1	16.2	£18,221
IC	IC	R & P	Disc/drum	185/65-15	184	2811	121 (Claimed)	11.3	N/A	£13,695
IC	IC	R & P	Disc/drum	185/70-14	184	2734	122	10.8	N/A	£13,795
IC	IC	R & P	Disc/drum	185/65-15	184	2943	122	9.2	17.0	£15,145
IC	IC	R & P	Disc/disc	185/65-15	184	2867	123 (Est)	8.8	N/A	£16,995
IC	IC	R & P	Disc/disc	195/60-15	184	2911	128	8.8	16.7	£20,995
IC	IC	R & P	Disc/disc	195/60-15	184	2911	132 (Claimed)	8.4	N/A	£19,975
IC	IC	R & P	Disc/disc	185/65-15	184	2966	115 (Claimed)	N/A	N/A	£17,750
IC	IC	R & P	Disc/disc	205/65-15	195	3546	141	8.2	16.5	£27,695
IC	IC	R & P	Disc/disc	205/65-15	192	3436	141	8.1	16.3	£29,695
IC	IC	R & P	Disc/disc	205/50-15/ 225/50-16	173	3020	162	5.2	14.2	£52,000
IC	IC	R & P	Disc/disc	205/65-15	187	3378	109	11.0	18.2	£22,995
IC	Beam1/2E	Worm	Disc/drum	6.00-13	170	2185	98	13.1	19.3	£1139
IC	Beam1/2E	Worm	Disc/drum	155-13	156	2133	96 (Claimed)	N/A	N/A	£3177
IC	Beam1/2E	Worm	Disc/drum	155-13	156	2133	92	15.3	19.6	£3625
IC	IC	R & P	Disc/drum	155-13	157	1918	96	13.3	19.2	£4500
IC	IC	R & P	Disc/drum	175/70-13	157	2058	96	13.4	19.5	£5499
IC	BeamC	R & P	Disc/drum	165-13	173	2231	98	14.7	19.6	£4497
IC	IC	R & P	Disc/drum	185/60-14	166	2158	104	12.5	18.5	£9649
IC	IC	R & P	Disc/drum	185/60-14	166	2164	112 (Est)	11.1	N/A	£9999
IC	IC	R & P	Disc/drum	185/60-14	166	2164	120	9.1	17.0	£10,998
IC	IC	R & P	Disc/drum	185/70-14	184	2646	106 (Claimed)	N/A	N/A	£9499
IC	IC	R & P	Disc/drum	185/70-14	184	2692	107	11.7	18.9	£10,999
IC	IC	R & P	Disc/drum	195/70-14	184	2902	120 (Est)	10.2	N/A	£12,999
IC	IC	R & P	Disc/drum	195/70-14	184	2867	112	12.3	19.0	£13,399
IC	IC	R&P	Disc/disc	205/60-15	184	3100	116	10.2	17.8	£17,999
IC	IC	R & P	Disc/drum	175/70-13	161	2007	102 (Claimed)	N/A	N/A	£5499
IC	IC	R & P	Disc/drum	175/70-13	161	2233	97	13.7	19.1	£7998
IC	IC	R & P	Disc/drum	175/70-13	172	2260	103 (Claimed)	N/A	N/A	£8999
IC	IC	R & P	Disc/drum	185/60-14	172	2451	110	10.9	18.1	£9999
IC	IC	R & P	Disc/drum	185/60-14	172	2448	118 (Claimed)	N/A	N/A	£11,998
IC	IC	R & P	Disc/drum	175/65-14	174	2448	120 (Claimed)	10.9	N/A	£9999
IC	IC	R & P	Disc/drum	195/60-14	174	2633	124	9.6	17.3	£12,299
IC	IC	R & P	Disc/drum	175/70-13	162	2062	109 (Claimed)	12.6	N/A	£6599
IC	IC	R & P	Disc/drum	175/70-13	162	2156	106	11.0	18.1	£8799
IC	DDC	Worm	Disc/disc	205-15	175	2826	163	6.4	14.5	£7280
IC	DDC	Worm	Disc/disc	205-15	175	3177	161	7.4	14.9	£5950
IC	DDC	Worm	Disc/disc	205-15	175	3000	170 (Est)	N/A	N/A	£8700
IC	DDC	Worm	Disc/disc	215/70-15	197	3943	130 (Est)	N/A	N/A	£7225
IC	DDC	Worm	Disc/disc	215/70-15	197	3943	133 (Est)	8.1	16.2	£11868

Make and model	Production Figures	Years Built	Body Styles	Mechanical Layout	Engine Make (if not own)	Capacity/(cc)/Layout/Valves	BHP/rpm	Torque (lb.ft)/rpm	Transmission gearbox/automatic transmission
Lele	317	1969–1974	Sal	F/R	Chevrolet	5359/V8/OHV	350/5800	360/3600	4-spd/5-spd/Auto
					Ford	5768/V8/OHV	325/5800	360/380	4-spd/5-spd/Auto
Isuzu									
Piazza	114,000	1981–1991	Cpe	F/R	—	1996/4IL/OHC	150/5400	167/3000	5-spd/-
Trooper	577,000	1981–1991	Ute	F/4	—	2254/4IL/OHC	108/4600	123/2600	5-spd/-
						2238/4IL/OHC Diesel	74/4000	114/2500	5-spd/-
						2559/4IL/OHC	111/5000	138/2500	5-spd/-
						2771/4IL/OHC Diesel	95/3800	153/2100	5-spd/-
Trooper	In prod	1991–Date	Ute	F/4	Chevrolet	3165/V6/2OHC	174/5200	192/3750	5-spd/Auto
						3059/4IL/OHV Diesel	125/3600	202/2000	5-spd/Auto
Jaguar									
E-Type 3.8/4.2	46,300	1961–1971	Spts Spts Cpe	F/R	—	3781/6IL/2OHC	265/5500	260/4000	4-spd/-
						4235/6IL/2OHC	265/5400	283/4000	4-spd/-
E-Type 2+2	10,930	1966–1971	Spts Cpe	F/R	—	4235/6IL/2OHC	265/5400	283/4000	4-spd/Auto
E-Type SIII vee-12	15,290	1971–1975	Spts Spts Cpe	F/R	—	5343/V12/OHC	272/5850	304/3600	4-spd/Auto
XJ6 SI/SII	152,219	1968–1979	Sal	F/R	—	2792/6IL/2OHC	140/5150	150/4250	4-spd (+O/D)/Auto
						3442/6IL/2OHC	160/5000	189/3500	4-spd (+O/D)/Auto
						4235/6IL/2OHC	173/4750	227/3000	4-spd (+O/D)/5-spd/Auto
XJC 4.2/5.3C	8,378	1975–1977	Cpe	F/R	—	4235/6IL/2OHC	173/4750	227/3000	4-spd (+O/D)/Auto
						5343/V12/OHC	285/5750	294/3500	Auto/-
XJ6 SIII	122,452	1979–1988	Sal	F/R	—	3442/6IL/2OHC	160/5000	189/5000	5-spd/Auto
						4235/6IL/2OHC	205/5000	236/3700	5-spd/Auto
XJ12 SI/SII	17,461	1972–1979	Sal	F/R	—	5343/V12/OHC	265/5850	304/3500	Auto/-
							285/5750	294/3500	Auto/-
XJ12 SIII	14,229	1979–1993	Sal	F/R	—	5343/V12/OHC	299/5500	318/3000	Auto/-
XJ-S (V12)	115,413 all types	1975–1996	Cpe Conv	F/R	—	5343/V12/OHC	285/5500	294/3500	4-spd/Auto
							296/5400	318/3900	Auto/-
							299/5500	318/3000	Auto/-
						5994/V12/OHC	308/5350	355/2850	Auto/-
XJ-S (6-cyl)	Incl. in above figures	1983–1996	Cpe Conv	F/R	—	3690/6IL/2OHC	225/5300	240/4000	5-spd/Auto
						3980/6IL/2OHC	223/4750	277/3650	5-spd/Auto
							241/4700	282/4000	5-spd/Auto
XJ6	204,474	1986–1994	Sal	F/R	—	2919/6IL/2OHC	165/5600	176/4000	5-spd/Auto
						3239/6IL/2OHC	200/5250	220/4000	5-spd/Auto
						3590/6IL/2OHC	221/5000	248/4000	5-spd/Auto
						3980/6IL/2OHC	223/4750	278/3650	Auto/-
							235/4750	285/3750	Auto/-
XJR	N/A	1988–1994	Sal	F/R	—	3980/6IL/2OHC	251/5250	278/4000	Auto/-
XJR-S	448/389	1988–1994	Cpe Conv	F/R	—	5993/V12/OHC	318/5250	362/3750	Auto/-
							333/5250	365/3650	Auto/-
XJ6	In prod	1994–Date	Sal	F/R	—	3239/6IL/2OHC	216/5100	232/4500	5-spd/Auto
						3980/6IL/2OHC	245/4800	289/4000	5-spd/Auto
							321/5000	378/3050	5-spd/Auto
– Long-wheelbase versions, weighing 50lb. extra, also available									
XJ12	3,992	1993–1994	Sal	F/R	—	5994/V12/OHC	313/5350	353/2850	Auto/-
XJ12	In prod	1994–Date	Sal	F/R	—	5994/V12/	318/5350	353/2850	Auto/-

Suspension Front	Rear	Steering	Brakes (Front/rear)	Wheels/ Tyres	Length (in)	Weight (lb,unladen)	Top speed (mph)	0–60mph (sec)	Standing ¼-mile (sec)	UK Total Price (£: at Launch)
IC	DDC	Worm	Disc/disc	205-15	185	3042	135 (Est)	N/A	N/A	£7725
IC	DDC	Worm	Disc/disc	215/70-15	185	3707	132 (Est)	7.3	15.5	£9945
IC	BeamC	R & P	Disc/drum	195/60-14	171	2810	127	8.4	16.0	£11,950
ITor	Beam1/2E	Worm	Disc/drum	215-15	160	3325	85	18.7	21.3	£9999
ITor	Beam1/2E	Worm	Disc/drum	215-15	160	3641	78	26.1	22.4	£10,998
ITor	Beam1/2E	Worm	Disc/disc	235/75-15	162	3439	90 (Est)	N/A	N/A	£9999
ITor	Beam1/2E	Worm	Disc/disc	235/75-15	176	4002	86	18.2	21.0	£10,998
IC	BeamC	Worm	Disc/disc	245/70-16	163	4300	102	10.9	18.0	£15,148
IC	BeamC	Worm	Disc/disc	245/70-16	163	4080	94 (Claimed)	16.6	N/A	£15,148
ITor	IC	R & P	Disc/disc	6.40-15	176	2688	149	7.1	15.0	£2098
ITor	IC	R & P	Disc/disc	6.40-15	176	2856	149	7.4	15.0	£1896
ITor	IC	R & P	Disc/disc	185-15	184	3108	139	7.4	15.4	£2245
ITor	IC	R & P	Disc/disc	E70-15	185	3304	146	6.4	14.2	£3123
IC	IC	R & P	Disc/disc	205-15	190	3388	117 (Claimed)	11.0	18.1	£1797
IC	IC	R & P	Disc/disc	205-15	195	3708	117	10.9	18.0	£4795
IC	IC	R & P	Disc/disc	205-15	190	3703	124	8.8	16.5	£2253
IC	IC	R & P	Disc/disc	205-15	190	3724	124	8.8	16.5	£5480
IC	IC	R & P	Disc/disc	205-15	190	3885	148	7.6	15.7	£6850
IC	IC	R & P	Disc/disc	205/70-15	195	4033	117	10.9	18.0	£11,189
IC	IC	R & P	Disc/disc	205/70-15	195	3875	131	8.6	17.2	£12,326
IC	IC	R & P	Disc/disc	205-15	190/195	3881	146	7.4	15.7	£3726
IC	IC	R & P	Disc/disc	205-15	195	4116	147	7.8	15.7	£6794
IC	IC	R & P	Disc/disc	205-15	195	4234	150	8.1	16.2	£15,015
IC	IC	R & P	Disc/disc	205/70-15	182	3902	153	6.9	15.2	£8900
IC	IC	R & P	Disc/disc	205/70-15	182	3890	151	6.6	14.9	£19,187
IC	IC	R & P	Disc/disc	215/70-15	182	3824	153	6.5	14.9	£18,950
IC	IC	R & P	Disc/disc	225/55-16	190	4377	161 (Claimed)	N/A	N/A	£45,100
IC	IC	R & P	Disc/disc	215/70-15	188	3660	141	7.4	15.9	£19,249
IC	IC	R & P	Disc/disc	235/60-15	188	3551	136	8.7	16.7	£33,400
IC	IC	R & P	Disc/disc	235/60-15	188	3583	143	8.2	16.3	£36,800
IC	IC	R & P	Disc/disc	220/65-390	196	3793	117	9.9	17.5	£16,495
IC	IC	R & P	Disc/disc	225/55-16	196	3674	135	8.3	16.1	£23,750
IC	IC	R & P	Disc/disc	220/65-390	196	3719	137	7.4	15.8	£18,495
IC	IC	R & P	Disc/disc	225/55-16	196	3991	141	8.2	16.3	£25,200
IC	IC	R & P	Disc/disc	225/65-15	196	3855	140	8.3	16.0	£32,500
IC	IC	R & P	Disc/disc	225/55-16	196	3938	142	8.3	16.6	£39,450
IC	IC	R & P	Disc/disc	225/50-16/	190	3965	157	7.0	15.3	£45,500
IC	IC	R & P	Disc/disc	245/55-16	190	3987	155	6.3	14.7	£49,950
IC	IC	R & P	Disc/disc	225/60-16	198/203	3968	137	8.6	16.7	£28,950
IC	IC	R & P	Disc/disc	225/60-16	198/203	3968	143	6.9	15.3	£42,950
IC	IC	R & P	Disc/disc	255/45-17	198	3859	153	5.7	14.5	£45,450
IC	IC	R & P	Disc/disc	225/55-16	196/203	4376	155 (Claimed)	6.8	N/A	£51,700
IC	IC	R & P	Disc/disc	225/55-16	198/203	4350/	155	6.8	N/A	£53,450

Make and model	Production Figures	Years Built	Body Styles	Mechanical Layout	Engine Make (if not own)	Capacity/ (cc)/Layout/ Valves	BHP/ rpm	Torque (lb.ft)/rpm	Transmission gearbox/automatic transmission
XJ220	271	1992–1994	Spts Cpe	M/R	—	OHC 3498/V6/ 2OHC	542/7200	475/4500	5-spd/-

Jeep

Make and model	Production Figures	Years Built	Body Styles	Mechanical Layout	Engine Make (if not own)	Capacity/ (cc)/Layout/ Valves	BHP/ rpm	Torque (lb.ft)/rpm	Transmission gearbox/automatic transmission
CJ-5 **	—	1974 model	Ute	F/4	—	3803/6IL/ OHV	100/3600	185/1800	3-spd
CJ-6 **	—	1975 model	Ute	F/4	—	3803/6IL/ OHV	100/3600	185/1800	3-spd
Cherokee **	—	1978 model	Ute	F/4	—	5896/V8/ OHV	175/4000	280/2800	Auto
CJ-7	379,354	1975–1986	Ute	F/4	—	4226/6IL/ OHV	110/3500	195/2000	3-spd/4-spd/Auto
						4980/V8/ OHV	150/4200	245/2500	3-spd/4-spd/Auto
Cherokee	In prod	1984–Date	Ute	F/4	—	2464/4IL/ OHV	122/5300	148/3200	5-spd/Auto
						3930/6IL/ OHV	184/4750	214/3950	Auto/-
				VM		2499/4IL/ OHC Diesel	116/4000	207/2000	5-spd/Auto
Wrangler	In prod	1986–Date	Ute	F/4	GM	2464/4IL/ OHV	117/5000	135/3500	4-spd/5-spd/Auto
					—	3956/6IL/ OHV	184/4750	220/4000	4-spd/5-spd/Auto
Grand Cherokee	In prod	1993–Date	Ute	F/4	—	3960/6IL/ OHC	174/4600	222/2400	Auto/-
						5216/V8/ OHV	212/4750	285/3050	Auto/-

Jensen

Make and model	Production Figures	Years Built	Body Styles	Mechanical Layout	Engine Make (if not own)	Capacity/ (cc)/Layout/ Valves	BHP/ rpm	Torque (lb.ft)/rpm	Transmission gearbox/automatic transmission
Interceptor/ SP	6,639	1966–1976	Sal Conv Cpe	F/R	Chrysler	6276/V8/ OHV 7212/V8/ OHV	325/4600 300/4800 330/5000 385/5000 287/4800	425/2800 380/3200 425/2800 490/3200 383/3200	Auto/- Auto/- Auto/- Auto/-
FF	320	1966–1971	Sal	F/4	Chrysler	6276/V8/ OHV	325/4600	425/2800	Auto/-
Jensen GT	507	1975–1976	Spts Est	F/R	Lotus	1973/4IL/ 2OHC	144/6500	134/5000	5-spd/-
Interceptor IV	18	1984–1991	Sal Conv	F/R	Chrysler	5898/V8/ OHV	243/4400	302/2000	Auto/-

Jensen-Healey

Make and model	Production Figures	Years Built	Body Styles	Mechanical Layout	Engine Make (if not own)	Capacity/ (cc)/Layout/ Valves	BHP/ rpm	Torque (lb.ft)/rpm	Transmission gearbox/automatic transmission
Sports	10,504	1972–1976	Spts	F/R	Lotus	1973/4IL/ 2OHC	144/6500	134/5000	4-spd/- 5-spd/-

Kia

Make and model	Production Figures	Years Built	Body Styles	Mechanical Layout	Engine Make (if not own)	Capacity/ (cc)/Layout/ Valves	BHP/ rpm	Torque (lb.ft)/rpm	Transmission gearbox/automatic transmission
Pride	In prod	1991–Date	Sal Htch	F(Tr)/F	Mazda	1139/4IL/ OHC 1324/4IL/ OHC	53/5500 60/5500 64/5500	74/3500 87/3500 72/3000	4-spd/- 5-spd/- 5-spd/-
Mentor	In prod	1994–Date	Sal	F(Tr)/F	Mazda	1598/4IL/ OHC	79/5000	91/3500	5-spd/Auto
Sportage	In prod	1994–Date	Ute	F/4	—	1998/4IL/ 2OHC	126/5300	129/4700	5-spd/-

Lada

Make and model	Production Figures	Years Built	Body Styles	Mechanical Layout	Engine Make (if not own)	Capacity/ (cc)/Layout/ Valves	BHP/ rpm	Torque (lb.ft)/rpm	Transmission gearbox/automatic transmission
1200/1300	N/A	1970–Date	Sal Est	F/R	—	1198/4IL/ OHC 1294/4IL/ OHC	62/5600 67/5600	64/3400 69/3400	4-spd/- 4-spd/-
1500/1600	N/A	1976–1984	Sal Est	F/R	—	1452/4IL/ OHC 1569/4IL/ OHC	75/5600 78/5400	78/3500 88/3000	4-spd/- 4-spd/-
Riva	N/A	1984–Date	Sal Est	F/R	—	1198/4IL/ OHC 1294/4IL/ OHC 1452/4IL/ OHC	62/5600 65/5600 75/5600	64/3400 68/3400 78/3400	4-spd/- 4-spd/- 4-spd/5-spd/-
Niva 4x4	In prod	1975–Date	Ute	F/4	—	1569/4IL/ OHC	78/5400	88/3000	4-spd/5-spd/-
Samara	In prod	1986-date	Sal	F(Tr)/F	—	1100/4IL/	55/5600	57/3400	5-spd/-

Suspension Front	Rear	Steering	Brakes (Front/rear)	Wheels/ Tyres	Length (in)	Weight (lb,unladen)	Performance Top speed (mph)	0–60mph (sec)	Standing ¼-mile (sec)	UK Total Price (£: at Launch)
						4400	(Claimed)			
IC	IC	R & P	Disc/disc	255/45-17/ 345/45-18	194	3210	213	3.6	11.7	£403,000
Beam1/2E	Beam1/2E	Worm	Drum/drum	E78-15	141	2934	79	14.3	19.2	£1572
Beam1/2E	Beam1/2E	Worm	Drum/drum	E78-15	159	2961	82	16.5	20.3	£2130
Beam1/2E	Beam1/2E	Worm	Disc/drum	H78-15	184	4515	89	12.2	18.7	£9749
Beam1/2E	Beam1/2E	Worm	Drum/drum	F78-15	148	2650	87 (Claimed)	N/A	N/A	Special order
Beam1/2E	Beam1/2E	Worm	Drum/drum	F78-15	148	2650	90 (Est)	N/A	N/A	Special order
BeamC	Beam1/2E	Worm	Disc/drum	225/70-15	167	3241	99	12.2	N/A	£15,995
BeamC	Beam1/2E	Worm	Disc/drum	225/70-15	167	3709	105	9.5	17.4	£18,245
BeamC	Beam1/2E	Worm	Disc/drum	225/70-15	167	3709	98	12.0	18.7	£18,195
Beam1/2E	Beam1/2E	Worm	Disc/drum	215/75-15	152	3100	93 (Claimed)	13.6	N/A	£12,995
Beam1/2E	Beam1/2E	Worm	Disc/drum	215/75-15	152	3100	105 (Est)	8.8	N/A	£14,395
BeamC	BeamC	Worm	Disc/disc	225/70-16	181	4024	105	10.6	18.1	£28,995
BeamC	BeamC	Worm	Disc/drum	225/70-15	181	3797	111	6.8	17.1	£27,995
IC	Beam1/2E	R & P	Disc/disc	6.70-15	185	3500	133	7.3	15.7	£3743
IC	Beam1/2E	R & P	Disc/disc	ER70-15	185	3635	126	7.6	15.8	£6744
IC	Beam1/2E	R & P	Disc/disc	ER70-15	185	3950	143	6.9	14.8	£6977
IC	Beam1/2E	R & P	Disc/disc	ER70-15	185	3898	129	7.7	15.9	£8334
IC	Beam1/2E	R & P	Disc/disc	ER70-15	191	4030	130	8.4	15.9	£5340
IC	BeamC	R & P	Disc/drum	185/70-13	166	2417	119	8.7	16.7	£4178
IC	Beam1/2E	R & P	Disc/disc	225/70-15	186	3950	135	7.5	N/A	£40,000
IC	BeamC	R & P	Disc/drum	185/70-13	166	2340	119	7.8	16.2	£1810
IC	BeamC	R & P	Disc/drum	185/70-13	166	2128	116	8.3	16.3	£2952
IC	IC	R & P	Disc/drum	145/70-12	140	1661	90 (Claimed)	N/A	N/A	£5799
IC	IC	R & P	Disc/drum	145/70-12	140	1784	92	12.8	19.1	£6399
IC	IC	R & P	Disc/drum	145/70-12	140	1705	93	14.5	19.9	£6749
IC	IC	R & P	Disc/drum	175/70-13	169	2271	107 (Claimed)	11.8	N/A	£8950
IC	BeamC	Worm	Disc/drum	205/70-15	167	3193	103	11.8	18.4	£13250
IC	BeamC	Worm	Disc/drum	155-13	158	2082	90	14.7	19.9	£981
IC	BeamC	Worm	Disc/drum	155-13	158	2100	86	16.6	20.7	£2148
IC	BeamC	Worm	Disc/drum	165-13	158	2271	94	13.8	19.4	£1676
IC	BeamC	Worm	Disc/drum	165-13	158	2230	92	13.1	19.1	£2881
IC	BeamC	Worm	Disc/drum	155-13	163	2106	84 (Claimed)	N/A	N/A	£2499
IC	BeamC	Worm	Disc/drum	165-13	163	2131	84	16.9	20.8	£3158
IC	BeamC	Worm	Disc/drum	165-13	163	2181	87	16.1	19.9	£3475
IC	BeamC	Worm	Disc/drum	6.00-16 or 185-15	146	2604	77	22.4	22.2	£4098
IC	IC	R & P	Disc/drum	155-13	158	1989	85	14.1	N/A	£4245

Make and model	Production Figures	Years Built	Body Styles	Mechanical Layout	Engine Make (if not own)	Capacity/(cc)/Layout/Valves	BHP/rpm	Torque (lb.ft)/rpm	Transmission gearbox/automatic transmission
			Htch			OHC			
			Conv			1288/4IL/	65/5600	71/3600	5-spd/-
						OHC			
						1499/4IL/	75/5600	78/3500	5-spd/-
						OHC			

Lamborghini

Make and model	Production Figures	Years Built	Body Styles	Mechanical Layout	Engine Make (if not own)	Capacity/(cc)/Layout/Valves	BHP/rpm	Torque (lb.ft)/rpm	Transmission gearbox/automatic transmission
Miura	775	1966–1972	Spts Cpe	M(Tr)/R	—	3929/V12/	350/7000	278/5000	5-spd/-
						2OHC	370/7700	286/5500	5-spd/-
							385/7850	294/5750	5-spd/-
Espada	1,217	1968–1978	Sal	F/R	—	3929/V12/	325/6500	276/4500	5-spd/-
						2OHC	350/7500	290/5500	5-spd/-
							365/7500	300/5500	5-spd/Auto
Jarama	327	1970–1978	Sal	F/R	—	3929/V12/	350/7500	289/5500	5-spd/-
						2OHC	365/7500	300/5500	5-spd/Auto
Urraco	776	1970–1978	Cpe	M(Tr)/R	—	2463/V8/	220/7500	166/5750	5-spd/-
						OHC			
						2995/V8/	250/7500	195/5750	5-spd/-
						2OHC			
Countach	1,111 (All types)	1974–1990	Spts Cpe	M/R	—	3929/V12/ 2OHC	375/8000	268/5000	5-spd/-
							375/8000	268/5000	5-spd/-
						4754/V12/ 2OHC	375/7000	302/4500	5-spd/-
						5167/V12/ 2OHC	455/7000	369/5200	5-spd/-
Silhouette	52	1976–1977	Cpe	M(Tr)/R	—	2995/V8/ 2OHC	260/7500	202/3500	5-spd/-
Jalpa	410	1981–1991	Cpe	M(Tr)/R	—	3485/V8/ 2OHC	250/7000	235/3250	5-spd/-
Diablo	In prod	1990–Date	Spts Cpe Spts	M/R	—	5707/V12/ 2OHC	492/7000	428/5200	5-spd/-
							525/7100	428/5900	5-spd/-
							590/6850	448/5200	5-spd/-
				M/4	—	5707/V12/ 2OHC	492/6850	428/5200	5-spd/-

Lancia

Make and model	Production Figures	Years Built	Body Styles	Mechanical Layout	Engine Make (if not own)	Capacity/(cc)/Layout/Valves	BHP/rpm	Torque (lb.ft)/rpm	Transmission gearbox/automatic transmission
Flavia/ 2000	79,764	1961–1974	Sal	F/F	—	1488/4HO/ OHV	78/5200	82/3500	4-spd/-
						1800/4HO/ OHV	102/5200	113/3500	4-spd/-
						1991/4HO/ OHV	114/5400	118/4300	4-spd/5-spd/-
							125/5800	127/3700	5-spd/-
Flavia Coupe	26,084	1962–1973	Cpe	F/F	—	1500/4HO/ OHV	90/4500	85/4500	4-spd/-
						1800/4HO/ OHV	92/5200	108/3000	4-spd/-
							102/5200	113/3500	
						1991/4HO/ OHV	114/5400	118/4300	4-spd/5-spd/-
							125/5800	127/3700	
Flavia Zagato Sport	N/A	1962–1969	Spts Cpe	F/F	—	1800/4HO/ OHV	100/5200	120/3000	4-spd/-
Fulvia	192,097	1963–1972	Sal	F/F	—	1091/V4/ 2OHC	58/5800	62/4000	4-spd/-
							71/6000	68/4300	4-spd/-
						1216/V4/ 2OHC	80/6000	77/4000	4-spd/-
						1298/V4/ 2OHC	87/6000	83/4500	4-spd/-
Fulvia Coupe	139,817	1965–1976	Cpe	F/F	—	1216/V4/ 2OHC	80/6000	77/4000	4-spd/-
							88/6000	80/5000	
						1298/V4/ 2OHC	87/6000	83/4500	4-spd/-
							90/6200	84/5000	4-spd/-
							101/6400	96/4750,	4-spd/-
						1584/V4/ 2OHC	115/6000	113/4500	5-spd/-
Stratos	492	1973–1975	Spts Cpe	M(Tr)/R	Ferrari	2418/V6/ 2OHC	190/7000	166/4000	5-spd/-
Beta	194,916	1972–1981	Sal	F(Tr)/F	—	1297/4IL/ 2OHC	82/6200	80/3300	5-spd/-
						1438/4IL/ 2OHC	90/6000	85/3800	5-spd/-
						1585/4IL/ 2OHC	100/5800	99/3000	5-spd/-
						1592/4IL/	100/6000	95/3000	5-spd/-

Suspension Front	Rear	Steering	Brakes (Front/rear)	Wheels/ Tyres	Length (in)	Weight (lb,unladen)	Top speed (mph)	0–60mph (sec)	Standing ¼-mile (sec)	UK Total Price (£: at Launch)
							(Claimed)			
IC	IC	R & P	Disc/drum	165-13	158	1989	94	14.0	19.6	£4795
IC	IC	R & P	Disc/drum	165/70-13	158	1989	100	12.0	N/A	£5445
							(Claimed)			
IC	IC	R & P	Disc/disc	GR70-15	172	2850	170 (Est)	N/A	N/A	£8050
IC	IC	R & P	Disc/disc	GR70-15	172	2850	172	6.7	14.5	£10,860
IC	IC	R & P	Disc/disc	FR70-15	172	2877	177	N/A	N/A	£10,250
							(Claimed)			
IC	IC	Worm	Disc/disc	205-15	187	3740	150 (Est)	N/A	N/A	£10,295
IC	IC	Worm	Disc/disc	205-15	187	3740	150	7.8	15.7	£9500
IC	IC	Worm	Disc/disc	205-15	187	3740	155 (Est)	N/A	N/A	
IC	IC	Worm	Disc/disc	215/70-15	177	2960	162	6.8	14.9	£9800
IC	IC	Worm	Disc/disc	215/70-15	177	2960	162 (Est)	N/A	N/A	
IC	IC	R & P	Disc/disc	205-14	167	2885	143	8.5	16.6	£5950
IC	IC	R & P	Disc/disc	195/70-14/ 205/70-14	167	2990	158	7.6	15.6	£9975
IC	IC	R & P	Disc/disc	205/70-14/ 215/70-14	163	3020	175 (Est)	5.6	14.1	£17,285
IC	IC	R & P	Disc/disc	205/50-15/ 345/35-15	163	2915	175 (Est)	5.9	14.6	£25,960
IC	IC	R & P	Disc/disc	205/50-15/ 345/35-15	163	2915	164	4.8	13.2	£49,500
IC	IC	R & P	Disc/disc	225/50-15/ 345/35-15	163	3188	178	4.9	13.0	£65,901
IC	IC	R & P	Disc/disc	195/50-15/ 285/40-15	176	2734	155 (Claimed)	N/A	N/A	£13,684
IC	IC	R & P	Disc/disc	205/55-16/ 225/50-16	190	2972	148	5.8	14.3	£26,001
IC	IC	R & P	Disc/disc	245/40-17/ 335/35-17	176	3474	205	4.2	12.3	£152,614
IC	IC	R & P	Disc/disc	235/40-17/ 335/30-18	176	3197	210 (Claimed)	4.2	12.6	£175,000
IC	IC	R & P	Disc/disc	235/40-18/ 335/30-18	176	3219	211 (Claimed)	3.8	N/A	£192,200
IC	IC	R & P	Disc/disc	235/40-17/ 335/35-17	176	3575	202	5.1	13.6	£160,000
ITrL	Beam1/2E	Worm	Disc/disc	165-15	180	2624	93	18.7	22.0	£2188
ITrL	Beam1/2E	Worm	Disc/disc	165-15	180	2643	103	14.3	19.9	£2075
ITrL	Beam1/2E	Worm	Disc/disc	165-15	180	2756	109 (Est)	N/A	N/A	£2158
ITrL	Beam1/2E	Worm	Disc/disc	175-14	182	2715	115	10.4	17.9	£2121
ITrL	Beam1/2E	Worm	Disc/disc	165-15	176	2558	103 (Claimed)	N/A	N/A	£2275
ITrL	Beam1/2E	Worm	Disc/disc	165-15	176	2492	109	13.4	18.9	£2497
ITrL	Beam1/2E	Worm	Disc/disc	165-15	178	2621	109	12.4	18.9	£2989
ITrL	Beam1/2E	Worm	Disc/disc	165-15	174	2310	113	11.9	18.3	£2736
ITrL	Beam1/2E	Worm	Disc/disc	155-14	163	2170	85	23.5	22.9	£1389
ITrL	Beam1/2E	Worm	Disc/disc	155-14	163	2170	93	18.2	21.1	£1379
ITrL	Beam1/2E	Worm	Disc/disc	155-14	163	2307	95	15.7	20.0	£1251
ITrL	Beam1/2E	Worm	Disc/disc	155-14	163	2318	96	13.9	19.1	£1438
ITrL	Beam1/2E	Worm	Disc/disc	145-14	156	2073	100	15.8	20.0	£1490
ITrL	Beam1/2E	Worm	Disc/disc	145-14	156	1971	103	11.9	18.9	£1548
ITrL	Beam1/2E	Worm	Disc/disc	145-14	156	1971	106	12.7	18.7	£1745
ITrL	Beam1/2E	Worm	Disc/disc	145-14	156	1819	108 (Est)	N/A	N/A	£1812
ITrL	Beam1/2E	Worm	Disc/disc	175-13/ 175-14	156	1874	103	9.4	17.3	£2526
IC	IC	R & P	Disc/disc	205/70-14	146	2161	143 (Est)	6.8	N/A	£7000
IC	IC	R & P	Disc/disc	155-14	169	2370	96	13.8	19.6	£2153
IC	IC	R & P	Disc/disc	155-14	169	2370	103 (Claimed)	N/A	N/A	£1594
IC	IC	R & P	Disc/disc	175/70-14	169	2426	106 (Claimed)	N/A	N/A	£2785
IC	IC	R & P	Disc/disc	175/70-14	169	2392	106 (Est)	10.8	18.2	£1792

217

Make and model	Production Figures	Years Built	Body Styles	Mechanical Layout	Engine Make (if not own)	Capacity/(cc)/Layout/Valves	BHP/rpm	Torque (lb.ft)/rpm	Transmission gearbox/automatic transmission
						2OHC			
						1756/4IL/	110/6000	106/3000	5-spd/-
						2OHC			
						1995/4IL/	119/5500	128/2800	5-spd/-
						2OHC	115/5500	129/2800	5-spd/Auto
Beta Coupe & Spider	111,801/ 9,390 (All types)	1973–1985 1975–1983	Cpe Conv	F(Tr)/F	—	1297/4IL/ 2OHC	82/6200	80/3300	5-spd/-
						1585/4IL/ 2OHC	100/5800	99/3000	5-spd/-
						1592/4IL/ 2OHC	108/6000	100/4500	5-spd/-
						1995/4IL/ 2OHC	119/5500	128/2800	5-spd/-
							122/5500	129/2800	5-spd/Auto
							135/5500	152/3000	5-spd/-
Beta HPE	71,258 (All types)	1975–1984	Spts Est	F(Tr)/F	—	1585/4IL/ 2OHC	100/5800	99/3000	5-spd/-
						1995/4IL/ 2OHC	119/5500	128/2800	5-spd/-
							122/5500	129/2800	5-spd/-
							135/5500	152/3000	5-spd/-
Monte Carlo	7,595	1975–1984	Spts Cpe Targa	M(Tr)/R	—	1995/4IL/ 2OHC	120/6000	121/3400	5-spd/-
							120/6000	126/3400	5-spd/-
Gamma	15,296	1976–1984	Sal	F/F	—	2484/4HO/ OHC	140/5400	153/3000	5-spd/Auto
Gamma Coupe	6,789	1976–1984	Cpe	F/F	—	2484/4HO/ OHC	140/5400	153/3000	5-spd/Auto
Trevi	40,628	1980–1984	Sal	F(Tr)/F	—	1585/4IL/ 2OHC	100/5800	99/3000	5-spd/-
						1995/4IL/ 2OHC	115/5500	129/2800	5-spd/Auto
Delta	193,473	1979–1990	Htch	F(Tr)/F	—	1301/4IL/ OHC	78/5800	77/3400	5-spd/-
						1498/4IL/ OHC	85/6200	90/3500	5-spd/Auto
						1585/4IL/ 2OHC	130/5600	140/3700	5-spd/-
							140/5500	141/3500	5-spd/-
Prisma	150,577	1983–1990	Sal	F(Tr)/F	—	1498/4IL/ OHC	85/6200	90/3500	5-spd/Auto
						1585/4IL/ 2OHC	105/5800	100/3300	5-spd/-
							108/5900	135/3500	5-spd/-
Delta HF 4x4/Integrale	N/A	1986–1994	Htch	F/4	—	1995/4IL/ 2OHC	165/5250	210/2750	5-spd/-
							185/5300	224/3500	5-spd/-
							200/5500	200/3000	5-spd/-
							210/5750	220/3500	5-spd/-
Y10	In prod	1985–Date	Htch	F(Tr)/F	—	999/4IL/ OHC	45/5000	59/2750	5-spd/-
						1049/4IL/ OHC	55/5850	60/3000	5-spd/-
							85/5750	90/2750	
						1108/4IL/ OHC	57/5500	67/3000	5-spd/Auto
						1301/4IL/ OHC	78/5750	75/3250	5-spd/-
Thema	N/A	1984–1994	Sal	F(Tr)/F	—	1995/4IL/ 2OHC	120/5250	113/3300	5-spd/Auto
							165/5750	208/2750	5-spd/-
							150/6000	136/4000	5-spd/Auto
							155/6500	131/3500	5-spd/-
							185/5500	236/3500	5-spd/Auto
Thema V6/ 8.32	4,888/2,370	1985–1990	Sal	F(Tr)/F	Peugeot/ Renault	2849/V6/ OHC	150/5750	117/2700	5-spd/Auto
					Ferrari	2926/V8/ 2OHC	215/6750	209/4500	5-spd/-
Dedra	In prod	1989–Date	Sal	F(Tr)/F	—	1581/4IL/ 2OHC	90/5500	94/3500	5-spd/-
						1756/4IL/ 2OHC	110/6000	105/3000	5-spd/-
						1995/4IL/ 2OHC	120/5750	117/3300	5-spd/Auto
							165/5500	201/3000	5-spd/-
Land-Rover									
SII/IIA		1958–1971	Ute	F/4	—	2286/4IL/ OHV	77/4250	124/2500	4-spd/-
						2052/4IL/ OHV Diesel	51/3500	87/2000	4-spd/-
						2286/4IL/ OHV Diesel	62/4000	103/1800	4-spd/-
						2625/6IL/ IOEV	83/4500	128/1500	4-spd/-
Series III	(Total: SI to SIII 1,400,000+)	1971–1985	Ute	F/4	—	2286/4IL/	70/4000	120/1500	4-spd/-

Suspension Front	Rear	Steering	Brakes (Front/rear)	Wheels/Tyres	Length (in)	Weight (lb, unladen)	Top speed (mph)	0–60mph (sec)	Standing 1/4-mile (sec)	UK Total Price (£: at Launch)
IC	IC	R & P	Disc/disc	175/70-14	169	2414	109	10.7	17.9	£1989
IC	IC	R & P	Disc/disc	175/70-14	169	2426	110	10.1	17.5	£2985
IC	IC	R & P	Disc/disc	155-14	157	2161	100	12.3	18.2	£2153
IC	IC	R & P	Disc/disc	175/70-14	157/159	2183	111 (Claimed)	N/A	N/A	£3218
IC	IC	R & P	Disc/disc	175/70-14	157/159	2183	113	10.4	17.3	£2884
IC	IC	R & P	Disc/disc	175/70-14	157/159	2183	112	9.8	17.3	£3495
IC	IC	R & P	Disc/disc	185/65-14	157	2359	112	9.2	17.1	£6191
IC	IC	R & P	Disc/disc	185/65-14	157	2414	122	10.3	16.7	£7995
IC	IC	R & P	Disc/disc	175/70-14	169	2338	102	11.3	18.0	£3688
IC	IC	R & P	Disc/disc	175/70-14	169	2338	116	10.6	17.7	£3896
IC	IC	R & P	Disc/disc	175/70-14	169	2448	113	9.2	16.7	£7691
IC	IC	R & P	Disc/disc	185/65-14	169	2503	122	9.2	16.9	£8500
IC	IC	R & P	Disc/disc	185/65-13	150	2293	119	9.8	16.0	£5927
IC	IC	R & P	Disc/disc	185/65-14	150	2195	118	8.6	16.4	£8100
IC	IC	R & P	Disc/disc	185/70-14	180	3052	118	10.1	17.5	£7136
IC	IC	R & P	Disc/disc	185/70-14	177	2800	125	9.2	17.0	£9186
IC	IC	R & P	Disc/disc	185/65-14	171	2525	106 (Claimed)	N/A	N/A	£6090
IC	IC	R & P	Disc/disc	185/65-14	171	2569	113	11.1	17.7	£6490
IC	IC	R & P	Disc/drum	165/70-13	153	2062	99 (Claimed)	N/A	N/A	£4950
IC	IC	R & P	Disc/drum	165/70-13	153	2176	99	12.2	18.4	£5429
IC	IC	R & P	Disc/disc	170/65-340	153	2387	121	8.2	16.4	£7990
IC	IC	R & P	Disc/disc	165/65-14	153	2352	119	8.5	16.1	£8790
IC	IC	R & P	Disc/drum	165/70-13	165	2027	104	11.2	18.0	£5550
IC	IC	R & P	Disc/disc	165/65-14	165	2218	108	10.8	17.8	£6150
IC	IC	R & P	Disc/disc	165/65-14	165	2338	116	9.5	17.3	£8295
IC	IC	R & P	Disc/disc	185/60-14	154	2740	128	6.6	15.2	£13,980
IC	IC	R & P	Disc/disc	195/55-15	154	2793	128	6.4	14.8	£15,455
IC	IC	R & P	Disc/disc	205/50-15	153	2846	129	6.3	14.9	£19,625
IC	IC	R & P	Disc/disc	205/50-15	154	2977	134	6.0	14.7	£23,249
IC	BeamC	R & P	Disc/drum	135-13	134	1717	88	16.7	20.6	£4330
IC	BeamC	R & P	Disc/drum	135-13	134	1654	94	15.5	20.3	£4995
IC	BeamC	R & P	Disc/drum	155/70-13	134	1738	111	11.8	N/A	£5795
IC	IC	R & P	Disc/drum	155/70-13	134	1782	96 (Claimed)	N/A	N/A	£6300
IC	IC	R & P	Disc/drum	155/70-13	134	1916	106	11.5	18.1	£7420
IC	IC	R & P	Disc/disc	175/70-14	181	2464	115	10.3	17.3	£11,000
IC	IC	R & P	Disc/disc	195/60-14	181	2686	139	7.6	16.0	£15,500
IC	IC	R & P	Disc/disc	195/60-14	181	2867	124	8.8	16.7	£15,995
IC	IC	R & P	Disc/disc	195/60-14	181	2860	127 (Est)	10.1	N/A	£16,512
IC	IC	R & P	Disc/disc	195/60-15	181	3029	142	6.8	15.2	£20,512
IC	IC	R & P	Disc/disc	185/70-14	181	2552	127 (Claimed)	N/A	N/A	£14,300
IC	IC	R & P	Disc/disc	205/55-15	181	3130	139	7.2	15.2	£37,500
IC	IC	R & P	Disc/drum	175/65-14	171	2337	112 (Claimed)	12.1	N/A	£10,695
IC	IC	R & P	Disc/disc	175/65-14	171	2731	117	11.5	18.1	£11,635
IC	IC	R & P	Disc/disc	185/60-14	171	2772	125	10.0	17.6	£13,300
IC	IC	R & P	Disc/disc	195/50-15	171	2709	132	7.4	15.9	£18,034
Beam1/2E	Beam1/2E	Worm	Drum/drum	6.00-16	142/175	2900/3886	67	36.1	24.0	£640
Beam1/2E	Beam1/2E	Worm	Drum/drum	6.00-16	142/175	3095/4081	55 (Est)	N/A	N/A	£740
Beam1/2E	Beam1/2E	Worm	Drum/drum	6.00-16	142/175	3044/4030	60 (Est)	N/A	N/A	£N/A
Beam1/2E	Beam1/2E	Worm	Drum/drum	6.00-16	175	3459	73	29.0	23.6	£873
Beam1/2E	Beam1/2E	Worm	Drum/drum	6.00-16	143/175	2953/3301	68	29.1	22.6	£1002

Make and model	Production Figures	Years Built	Body Styles	Mechanical Layout	Engine Make (if not own)	Capacity/(cc)/Layout/Valves	BHP/rpm	Torque (lb.ft)/rpm	Transmission gearbox/automatic transmission
						OHV			
						2286/4IL/	62/4000	103/1800	4-spd/-
						OHV Diesel			
						2625/6IL/	86/4500	132/1500	4-spd/-
						OIEV			
						3528/V8/	91/3500	166/2000	4-spd/-
						OHV			
90/110 Defender	In prod	1983–Date	Ute	F/4	—	2286/4IL/	74/4000	120/2000	5-spd/-
						OHV			
						2495/4IL/	83/4000	133/2000	5-spd/-
						OHV			
						2286/4IL/	60/4000	103/1800	5-spd/-
						OHV Diesel			
						2495/4IL/	67/4000	114/1800	5-spd/-
						OHV Diesel	85/4000	150/1800	5-spd/-
							109/3800	188/1800	
						3528/V8/	114/4000	185/2500	4-spd/5-spd/-
						OHV	134/5000	187/2500	5-spd/-
Discovery	In prod	1989–Date	Est	F/4	—	1994/4IL/	136/6000	140/3600	5-spd/-
						2OHC			
						2495/4IL/	111/4000	195/1800	5-spd/Auto
						OHC Diesel			
						3528/V8/	145/5000	192/2800	5-spd/-
						OHV	164/4750	212/2600	5-spd/Auto
						3947/V8/	180/4750	230/3100	5-spd/Auto
						OHV			

Lexus

Make and model	Production Figures	Years Built	Body Styles	Mechanical Layout	Engine Make (if not own)	Capacity/(cc)/Layout/Valves	BHP/rpm	Torque (lb.ft)/rpm	Transmission gearbox/automatic transmission
LS400	N/A	1991–1994	Sal Cpe	F/R	—	3969/V8/ 2OHC	241/5400	258/4400	Auto/-
GS300	In prod	1992–Date	Sal	F/R	—	2997/6IL/ 2OHC	209/5800	202/4800	Auto/-
LS400	In prod	1994–Date	Sal	F/R	—	3969/V8/ 2OHC	260/5400	269/4600	Auto/-

Lister

Make and model	Production Figures	Years Built	Body Styles	Mechanical Layout	Engine Make (if not own)	Capacity/(cc)/Layout/Valves	BHP/rpm	Torque (lb.ft)/rpm	Transmission gearbox/automatic transmission
Storm	In prod	1994–Date	Spts Cpe	F/R	Jaguar	6997/V12/ OHC	594/6100	580/3450	6-spd/-

Lonsdale (Note: These cars were re-badged, Australian-built, Mitsubishi Colt Galant types)

Make and model	Production Figures	Years Built	Body Styles	Mechanical Layout	Engine Make (if not own)	Capacity/(cc)/Layout/Valves	BHP/rpm	Torque (lb.ft)/rpm	Transmission gearbox/automatic transmission
Lonsdale	N/A	1983–1984	Sal Est	F/R	—	1597/4IL/ OHC	81/5600	87/3200	4-spd/-
						1995/4IL/ OHC	94/5600	112/2400	5-spd/Auto
						2555/4IL/ OHC	102/4800	142/2400	5-spd/Auto

Lotus

Make and model	Production Figures	Years Built	Body Styles	Mechanical Layout	Engine Make (if not own)	Capacity/(cc)/Layout/Valves	BHP/rpm	Torque (lb.ft)/rpm	Transmission gearbox/automatic transmission
Seven S4	1,000	1969–1973	Spts	F/R	Ford	1598/4IL/ OHV	84/6500	96/3600	4-spd/-
					—	1558/4IL/ 2OHC	115/5500	108/4000	4-spd/-
[Note: Several very limited edition Seven models with different engines were also built]									
Elan (Incl. Sprint model)	Est 12,200	1962–1971	Spts	F/R	—	1499/4IL/ 2OHC	100/5700	102/4500	4-spd/-
						1558/4IL/ 2OHC	105/5500	108/4000	4-spd/-
							115/6000	108/4000	4-spd/-
Elan Sprint	(See above)	1971–1973	Spts	F/R	—	1558/4IL/ 2OHC	126/6500	113/5500	4-spd/-
Elan Plus 2 (Incl. Plus 2S 130)	5,200	1969–1971	Spts Cpe	F/R	—	1558/4IL/ 2OHC	118/6250	112/4600	4-spd/-
Elan Plus 2S/130	(See above)	1971–1974	Spts Cpe	F/R	—	1558/4IL/ 2OHC	126/6500	113/5500	4-spd/- 5-spd/-
Europa (All Europa types)	9,230	1967–1971	Spts Cpe	M/R	—	1470/4IL/ OHV	78/6500	76/4000	4-spd/-
Europa TC/Special	(See above)	1971–1975	Spts Cpe	M/R	—	1558/4IL/ 2OHC	105/6000	103/4500	4-spd/-
							126/6500	113/5500	5-spd/-
Elite SI/ S2.2	2,535	1974–1983	Spts Htch	F/R	—	1973/4IL/ 2OHC	160/6200	140/4900	5-spd//Auto
						2174/4IL/ 2OHC	160/6500	160/5000	5-spd/-
Eclat S1/S2.2	1,519	1975–1982	Spts Cpe	F/R	—	1973/4IL/ 2OHC	160/6200	140/4900	4-spd/5-spd/Auto
						2174/4IL/ 2OHC	160/6500	160/5000	5-spd/-
Esprit I/II/									

Suspension Front	Rear	Steering	Brakes (Front/rear)	Wheels/ Tyres	Length (in)	Weight (lb,unladen)	Top speed (mph)	0–60mph (sec)	Standing ¹/₄-mile (sec)	UK Total Price (£: at Launch)
Beam1/2E	Beam1/2E	Worm	Drum/drum	6.00-16	143/175	3097/3445	60 (Est)	N/A	N/A	See above
Beam1/2E	Beam1/2E	Worm	Drum/drum	6.00-16	175	3459	69	31.7	22.9	See above
Beam1/2E	Beam1/2E	Worm	Drum/drum	7.50-16	175	4300	81	26.1	23.2	See above
BeamC	BeamC	Worm	Disc/drum	6.00-16 7.50-16	147/175	3540/3799	70 (Est)	N/A	N/A	£8606 (From)
BeamC	BeamC	Worm	Disc/drum	6.00-16 7.50-16	147/175	3540/3799	75 (Est)	N/A	N/A	See above
BeamC	BeamC	Worm	Disc/drum	6.00-16 7.50-16	147/175	3540/3799	60 (Est)	N/A	N/A	See above
BeamC	BeamC	Worm	Disc/drum	6.00-16	147/175	3540/3799	65 (Est)	N/A	N/A	£16,995
BeamC	BeamC	Worm	Disc/drum	205-16	153	3767	74	22.3	22.1	£12,783
BeamC	BeamC	Worm	Disc/drum	6.00-16	147/175	3540/3799	84	14.7	19.5	See above
BeamC	BeamC	Worm	Disc/drum	205-16	147/175	3540/3799	90 (SWB)	13.6	18.8	See above
BeamC	BeamC	Worm	Disc/drum	205-16	178	4167	98 (Claimed)	15.3	N/A	£16,995
BeamC	BeamC	Worm	Disc/disc	205-16	178	4427	92	17.1	20.5	£15,750
BeamC	BeamC	Worm	Disc/disc	205-16	178	4145	97	12.8	18.8	£15,500
BeamC	BeamC	Worm	Disc/disc	205-16	178	4152	105	11.7	17.7	£17,985
BeamC	BeamC	Worm	Disc/disc	225/70-16	178	4249	105	12.9	N/A	£21,494
IC	IC	R & P	Disc/disc	205/65-15	197	3888	147	8.3	16.3	£34,250
IC	IC	R & P	Disc/disc	225/55-16	195	3594	139	9.4	17.1	£31,950
IC	IC	R & P	Disc/disc	225/60-16	197	3663	155	8.5	16.4	£42,863
IC	IC	R & P	Disc/disc	245/40-18/ 325/30-18	179	3665	200 (Claimed)	4.7	N/A	£219,725
IC	BeamC	Worm	Disc/drum	185-14	176	2421	101	12.0	N/A	£5699
IC	BeamC	Worm	Disc/disc	185-14	176	2571	103	11.9	18.3	£6599
IC	BeamC	Worm	Disc/disc	185-14	176	2588	107	10.8	17.8	£7499
IC	BeamC	R & P	Disc/drum	165-13	145	1276	100	8.8	16.0	£895
IC	BeamC	R & P	Disc/drum	165-13	145	1276	116	8.7	15.8	£1245
IC	IC	R & P	Disc/disc	5.20-13	145	1290	110 (Est)	N/A	N/A	£1499
IC	IC	R & P	Disc/disc	5.20-13	145	1516	114	8.7	16.4	£1312
IC	IC	R & P	Disc/disc	145-13	145	1574	122	7.6	15.7	
IC	IC	R & P	Disc/disc	155-13	145	1590	121	6.7	15.2	£1706
IC	IC	R & P	Disc/disc	165-13	168	1882	123	8.2	16.6	£1923
IC	IC	R & P	Disc/disc	165-13	168	1954	121	7.4	15.4	£2676
IC	IC	R & P	Disc/disc	165-13	168	1960	120	7.5	16.0	£2716
IC	IC	R & P	Disc/drum	155-13	157	1375	109	10.7	17.3	£1667
IC	IC	R & P	Disc/drum	185/70-13	157	1557	117	7.0	15.6	£1996
IC	IC	R & P	Disc/drum	185/70-13	157	1588	121	7.7	15.7	£2370
IC	IC	R & P	Disc/disc	205/60-14	176	2440	124	7.8	16.4	£5445
IC	IC	R & P	Disc/disc	205/70-14	176	2645	127	7.5	16.1	£16,142
IC	IC	R & P	Disc/disc	185/70-13/ 205/70-14	176	2440	129	7.9	16.3	£5729
IC	IC	R & P	Disc/disc	205/70-14	176	2645	127	7.5	16.1	£15,842

Make and model	Production Figures	Years Built	Body Styles	Mechanical Layout	Engine Make (if not own)	Capacity/ (cc)/Layout/ Valves	BHP/ rpm	Torque (lb.ft)/rpm	Transmission gearbox/automatic transmission
2.2/III (Figures include 'X180' cars)	2,919	1976–1990	Spts Cpe	M/R	—	1973/4IL/ 2OHC	160/6200	140/4900	5-spd/-
						2174/4IL/ 2OHC	160/6500	160/5000	5-spd/-
Excel	1,327	1982–1992	Spts Cpe	F/R	—	2174/4IL/ 2OHC	160/6500	160/5000	5-spd/Auto
							180/6500	165/5000	5-spd/Auto
Esprit Turbo	In prod	1980–1987	Spts Cpe	M/R	—	2174/4IL/ 2OHC	210/6000	200/4000	5-spd/-
							215/6000	220/4250	5-spd/-
Esprit (X180)	(See above)	1987–1990	Spts Cpe	M/R	—	2174/4IL/ 2OHC	172/6500	163/5000	5-spd/-
Esprit Turbo (X180)	In prod	1987–Date	Spts Cpe	M/R	—	2174/4IL/ 2OHC	215/6500	220/4250	5-spd/-
							228/6500	218/4000	
							264/6500	261/3900	5-spd/-
							302/6400	287/4400	5-spd/-
							285/6400	290/4100	5-spd/-
Elan FWD	4,555	1989–1994	Spts	F(Tr)/F	Isuzu	1588/4IL/ 2OHC	130/7200	105/4200	5-spd/-
							165/6600	148/4200	5-spd/-
							155/6000	146/4600	5-spd/-
Elise	In prod	1995–Date	Spts	M/R	Rover	1796/4IL/ 2OHC	118/5500	122/3000	5-spd/-

Mahindra

Make and model	Production Figures	Years Built	Body Styles	Mechanical Layout	Engine Make (if not own)	Capacity/ (cc)/Layout/ Valves	BHP/ rpm	Torque (lb.ft)/rpm	Transmission gearbox/automatic transmission
Indian Brave/Chief	In prod	N/A–Date	Ute	F/4	Peugeot	2112/4IL/ OHV Diesel	62/4500	88/2000	4-spd/-

Marcos

Make and model	Production Figures	Years Built	Body Styles	Mechanical Layout	Engine Make (if not own)	Capacity/ (cc)/Layout/ Valves	BHP/ rpm	Torque (lb.ft)/rpm	Transmission gearbox/automatic transmission
2-litre/ 2.5-litre/ 3.0-litre/ Volvo	N/A	1968–1971/ 1981–1987	Cpe	F/R	Ford	1996/V4/ OHV	83/4750	123/2750	4-spd/-
					Ford	2994/V6/ OHV	136/4750	193/3000	4-spd (+O/D)/-
					Volvo	2979/6IL/ OHV	130/5000	152/2500	4-spd/Auto
Mantis	32	1970–1971	Spts Cpe	F/R	Triumph	2498/6IL/ OHV	150/5700	158/3000	4-spd (+O/D)/-
Mantula/ Mantara	In prod	1987–Date	Spts Cpe Conv	F/R	Rover	3528/V8/ OHV	190/5280	220/4000	5-spd/Auto
						3946/V8/ OHV	190/4750	235/4000	5-spd/Auto
						4441/V8/ OHV	300/5250	N/A	5-spd/Auto
						4998/V8/ OHV	320/5250	330/4000	5-spd/Auto
LM500	In prod	1994–Date	Spts Cpe	F/R	Rover	4998/V8/ OHV	320/5250	330/3900	5-spd/Auto
						3946/V8/ OHV	190/4750	235/4000	5-spd/Auto

Maserati

Make and model	Production Figures	Years Built	Body Styles	Mechanical Layout	Engine Make (if not own)	Capacity/ (cc)/Layout/ Valves	BHP/ rpm	Torque (lb.ft)/rpm	Transmission gearbox/automatic transmission
Mexico	468	1966–1972	Cpe	F/R	—	4136/V8/ 2OHC	260/5800	268/4000	5-spd/Auto
						4719/V8/ 2OHC	330/5000	290/4000	5-spd/Auto
Ghibli	1,274	1967–1973	Cpe Spts Conv	F/R	—	4719/V8/ 2OHC	330/5000	290/4000	5-spd/Auto
						4930/V8/ 2OHC	355/5500	340/4000	5-spd/Auto
Indy	1,136	1969–1974	Cpe	F/R	—	4136/V8/ 2OHC	260/5800	268/4000	5-spd/Auto
						4719/V8/ 2OHC	330/5000	290/4000	5-spd/Auto
						4930/V8/ 2OHC	335/5500	354/4000	5-spd/Auto
Bora	495	1971–1978	Spts Cpe	M/R	—	4719/V8/ 2OHC	310/6000	340/4200	5-spd/-
						4930/V8/ 2OHC	335/6000	354/4000	5-spd/-
Merak	1,699	1972–1983	Spts Cpe	M/R	—	2965/V6/ 2OHC	190/6000	188/4000	5-spd/-
							220/6500	200/4500	5-spd/-
							208/5800	188/4500	5-spd/-
Khamsin	421	1973–1982	Cpe	F/R	—	4930/V8/ 2OHC	320/5500	354/4000	5-spd/Auto
Kyalami	187	1976–1983	Sal	F/R	—	4136/V8/	270/6000	289/3800	5-spd/Auto

Suspension Front	Rear	Steering	Brakes (Front/rear)	Wheels/ Tyres	Length (in)	Weight (lb,unladen)	Top speed (mph)	0–60mph (sec)	Standing ¼-mile (sec)	UK Total Price (£: at Launch)
IC	IC	R & P	Disc/disc	205/70-14	165	2218	135 (Est)	8.4	16.3	£7883
IC	IC	R & P	Disc/disc	205/70-14 195/60-15/ 235/60-15	165	2218	135	6.5	15.0	£13,461
IC	IC	R & P	Disc/disc	205/60-14/	172	2503	130	7.1	15.4	£13,787
IC	IC	R & P	Disc/disc	215/50-15	172	2581	131	6.8	15.3	£17,980
IC	IC	R & P	Disc/disc	195/60-15/	165	2653	148	6.1	14.6	£16,982
IC	IC	R & P	Disc/disc	235/60-15	165	2530	141	5.6	14.4	£25,980
IC	IC	R & P	Disc/disc	195/60-15/ 235/60-15	171	2590	135 (Est)	N/A	N/A	£22,950
IC	IC	R & P	Disc/disc	195/60-15/ 235/60-15	171	2800	150	5.4	13.7	£28,900
IC	IC	R & P	Disc/disc	215/40-17/ 245/45-17	171	2929	159	4.9	13.5	£46,995
IC	IC	R & P	Disc/disc	245/45-16/ 315/35-17	173	2738	165 (Est)	4.5	N/A	£64,995
IC	IC	R & P	Disc/disc	235/40-17/ 285/35-18	174	2966	160 (Claimed)	4.7	N/A	£53,995
IC	IC	R & P	Disc/disc	205/50-15	150	2276	N/A	N/A	N/A	£17,850
IC	IC	R & P	Disc/disc	205/50-15	150	2392	136	6.5	15.0	£19,850
IC	IC	R & P	Disc/disc	205/45-16	150	2335	131	7.3	15.8	£24,500
IC	IC	R & P	Disc/disc	185/55-16/ 205/50-16	147	1485	124	5.5	14.4	£18,950
Beam1/2E	Beam1/2E	Worm	Drum/drum	235/75-15	147	2951	65 (Est)	N/A	N/A	£8234
IC	BeamC	R & P	Disc/drum	165-13	161	1950	106 (Est)	N/A	N/A	£2114
IC	BeamC	R & P	Disc/drum	175-13	161	1949	125 (Est)	7.8	15.8	£2350
IC	BeamC	R & P	Disc/drum	175-13	161	2028	125	7.2	15.6	£2574
IC	BeamC	R & P	Disc/drum	185-13	187	2300	125 (Est)	N/A	N/A	£3185
IC	BeamC	R & P	Disc/disc	225/60-14	158	2077	133	5.4	14.1	£16,694
IC	IC	R & P	Disc/disc	205/55-15/ 225/50-15	158	2249	131	6.0	14.7	£20,803
IC	IC	R & P	Disc/disc	205/55-15/ 225/50-15	158	2249	160 (Est)	N/A	N/A	£29,251
IC	IC	R & P	Disc/disc	205/55-15/ 225/50-15	158	2249	165 (Est)	N/A	N/A	£33,123
IC	IC	R & P	Disc/disc	245/45-16	158	2428	168 (Est)	4.6	13.5	£44,650
IC	IC	R & P	Disc/disc	245/45-16	158	2428	143	5.4	N/A	£31,695
IC	Beam1/2E	Worm	Disc/disc	205-15	187	3640	143 (Claimed)	N/A	N/A	£7216
IC	Beam1/2E	Worm	Disc/disc	205-15	187	3640	155 (Claimed)	N/A	N/A	£7893
IC	Beam1/2E	Worm	Disc/disc	205-15	181	2980	154	7.5	15.1	£10,180
IC	Beam1/2E	Worm	Disc/disc	205-15	181	2980	160 (Est)	N/A	N/A	£9849
IC	Beam1/2E	Worm	Disc/disc	205-14 205-15	192	3640	140	7.2	15.7	£8320
IC	Beam1/2E	Worm	Disc/disc	205-14	192	3638	156	7.5	15.6	£8890
IC	Beam1/2E	Worm	Disc/disc	205-14	192	3638	165 (Claimed)	N/A	N/A	Special order
IC	IC	R & P	Disc/disc	215/70-15	170	3210	162	6.5	14.6	£9832
IC	IC	R & P	Disc/disc	215/70-15	170	3484	174 (Claimed)	N/A	N/A	£17,960
IC	IC	R & P	Disc/disc	195/70-15/	170	3085	135	8.2	16.0	£7966
IC	IC	R & P	Disc/disc	215/70-15	170	3024	154	7.8	16.0	£12,390
IC	IC	R & P	Disc/disc	205/70-15/ 215/70-15	170	3062	143	7.7	15.8	
IC	IC	R & P	Disc/disc	215/70-15	173	3620	160	8.1	14.8	£13,999
IC	IC	R & P	Disc/disc	215/70-15	180	3836	147 (Est)	7.6	15.8	£16,673

Make and model	Production Figures	Years Built	Body Styles	Mechanical Layout	Engine Make (if not own)	Capacity/(cc)/Layout/Valves	BHP/rpm	Torque (lb.ft)/rpm	Transmission gearbox/automatic transmission
						2OHC			
						4930/V8/ 2OHC	280/5600	354/4000	5-spd/Auto
Biturbo	In prod	1981–Date	Sal	F/R	—	1996/V6/ OHC	180/6000	188/3500	5-spd/Auto
			Cpe						
			Conv			2491/V6/ OHC	192/5500	220/3000	5-spd/-
						1996/V6/ 2OHC	245/6200	218/5000	5-spd/-
Ghibli	In prod	1993–Date	Cpe	F/R	—	2790/V6/ 2OHC	280/5500	317/3750	5-spd/-
Shamal	In prod	1990–Date	Cpe	F/R	—	3217/V6/ 2OHC	326/6000	321/2800	6-spd/-
Quattroporte	In prod	1994–Date	Sal	F/R	—	2790/V6/ 2OHC	284/6000	305/3500	6-spd/Auto
Matra (-Simca)									
M530A	9,609	1967–1973	Spts Cpe	M/R	Ford-Germany	1699/V4/ OHV	73/4800	98/2800	4-spd/-
Bagheera	N/A	1973–1980	Spts Cpe	M(Tr)/R	Simca	1294/4IL/ OHV	84/6000	78/4400	4-spd/-
						1442/4IL/ OHV	84/5600	92/3200	4-spd/-
							90/5800	88/3200	4-spd/-
Rancho	N/A	1977–1984	Ute	F(Tr)/F	—	1442/4IL/ OHV	80/5600	89/3000	4-spd/-
Murena	N/A	1980–1984	Spts Cpe	M(Tr)/R	Talbot/Simca	1592/4IL/ OHV	92/5600	102/3200	5-spd/-
						2155/4IL/ OHC	118/5800	139/3200	5-spd/-
Mazda									
1000/ 1200/1300	980,968	1968–1977	Sal	F/R	—	985/4IL/ OHC	65/6000	60/4000	4-spd/-
			Cpe						
			Est			1169/4IL/ OHC	73/6000	72/3000	4-spd/-
						1272/4IL/ OHC	69/6200	68/4000	4-spd/-
1500/1800	121,804	1966–1972	Sal	F/R	—	1490/4IL/ OHC	78/5500	85/2500	4-spd/-
			Est			1796/4IL/ OHC	100/5500	112/2500	4-spd/-
110S Cosmo Wankel	1,176	1967–1972	Cpe	F/R	—	1964/2Rotor/ Wankel	110/7000	96/3500	4-spd/-
R100 Wankel	95,706	1968–1973	Sal	F/R	—	1964/2Rotor/ Wankel	100/7000	98/3500	4-spd/-
			Cpe						
Capella 616	254,919	1970–1978	Sal	F/R	—	1586/4IL/ OHC	75/6000	85/3500	4-spd/-
			Cpe						
RX2 Wankel	225,004	1970–1978	Sal	F/R	—	2292/2Rotor/ Wankel	120/7000	100/4000	4-spd/-
			Cpe						
818	625,439	1971–1978	Sal	F/R	—	1272/4IL/ OHC	81/6200	78/4000	4-spd/-
			Cpe						
			Est						
RX3 Wankel	286,685	1971–1978	Sal	F/R	—	1964/2Rotor/ Wankel	110/7000	100/4000	4-spd/Auto
			Cpe						
			Est						
RX4 Wankel	213,998	1972–1978	Sal	F/R	—	2292/2Rotor/ Wankel	130/7000	115/4000	4-spd/Auto
			Cpe						
			Est						
929	Incl. in later 2000/929 figure	1973–1979	Sal	F/R	—	1769/4IL/ OHC	83/5000	99/3000	4-spd/-
			Cpe						
			Est						
323	904,573	1976–1986	Htch	F/R	—	985/4IL/ OHV	45/5500	51/3000	4-spd/-
			Est			1272/4IL/ OHV	60/5500	69/3500	4-spd/-
						1415/4IL/ OHC	70/5700	82/3200	5-spd/-
						1490/4IL/ OHC	88/6000	88/3200	5-spd/-
626 'Montrose'	723,709	1978–1982	Sal	F/R	—	1586/4IL/ OHC	75/5500	88/3500	4-spd/Auto
			Cpe			1970/4IL/ OHC	90/4800	114/2500	5-spd/Auto
2000/929L	103,426	1979–1988	Est	F/R	—	1970/4IL/ OHC	90/4800o	114/2500	5-spd/Auto
RX7 Coupe	570,500	1978–1985	Spts Htch	F/R	—	2292/2 Rotor/	105/6000	106/4000	4-spd/5-spd/Auto

Suspension Front	Rear	Steering	Brakes (Front/rear)	Wheels/Tyres	Length (in)	Weight (lb, unladen)	Performance Top speed (mph)	0–60mph (sec)	Standing ¼-mile (sec)	UK Total Price (£: at Launch)
IC	IC	R & P	Disc/disc	215/70-15	180	3836	170 (Claimed)	N/A	N/A	Special Order
IC	IC	R & P	Disc/disc	195/60-14	164	2591	133 (Claimed)	N/A	N/A	Special Order
IC	IC	R & P	Disc/disc	205/55-14	159	2739	126	7.2	16.0	£28,795
IC	IC	R & P	Disc/disc	205/55/15	164	2591	140 (Est)	N/A	N/A	Special Order
IC	IC	R & P	Disc/disc	205/45-16/ 225/45-16	166	3009	153	5.6	14.2	£42,813
IC	IC	R & P	Disc/disc	225/45-16/ 245/45-16	161	3120	169 (Claimed)	5.1	N/A	£63,450
IC	IC	R & P	Disc/disc	205/55-16/ 225/50-16	179	3432	158	5.9	N/A	£56,912
IC	IC	R & P	Disc/disc	145-14/ 165-14	165	1930	95	15.6	19.9	£2160
ITor	ITor	R & P	Disc/disc	155-13/ 185-13	161	2157	101	12.3	18.7	Special Order
ITor	ITor	R & P	Disc/disc	155-13/ 185-13	161	2139	110	11.6	18.3	£5370
ITor	ITor	R & P	Disc/drum	185/70-14	170	2620	89	14.9	20.0	£5650
ITor	IC	R & P	Disc/disc	175/70-13/ 195/70-13	160	2200	N/A	N/A	N/A	Special order
ITor	IC	R & P	Disc/disc	185/60-14/ 195/60-14	160	2310	121	9.4	16.8	Special Order
IC	Beam1/2E	Worm	Disc/drum	6.15-13	150	1654	76	20.0	22.5	£999
IC	Beam1/2E	Worm	Disc/drum	6.15-13	150	1780	86	17.2	20.3	£879
IC	Beam1/2E	Worm	Disc/drum	155-13	152	1806	93	15.1	19.8	£949
IC	Beam1/2E	Worm	Disc/drum	6.45-14	172	2396	91	18.0	20.7	£994
IC	Beam1/2E	Worm	Disc/drum	6.45-14	172	2330	98	13.4	19.3	£1189
IC	DD1/2E	R & P	Disc/drum	165-14	163	2111	115	10.2	17.7	£2607
IC	Beam1/2E	Worm	Disc/drum	145-14	152	1926	105	10.9	18.0	£1650
IC	BeamC	Worm	Disc/drum	165-13	168	2135	102 (Claimed)	N/A	N/A	£1699
IC	BeamC	Worm	Disc/drum	165-13	163	2182	113	9.9	17.0	£1633
IC	Beam1/2E	Worm	Disc/drum	155-13	160	1720	93	15.2	19.9	£1199
IC	Beam1/2E	Worm	Disc/drum	155-13	160	1875	108	10.2	17.5	£1525
IC	Beam1/2E	Worm	Disc/drum	195/70-13	167	2356	106	10.8	17.8	£2000
IC	Beam1/2E	Worm	Disc/drum	175-13	167	2587	92	14.0	19.6	£1649
IC	BeamC	Worm	Disc/drum	155-13	154	1790	N/A	N/A	N/A	£2033
IC	BeamC	Worm	Disc/drum	155-13	154	1862	86	14.7	19.6	£2323
IC	BeamC	Worm	Disc/drum	175/70-13	154	1896	86	14.4	19.5	£3299
IC	BeamC	Worm	Disc/drum	155-13	161	1985	87 (Claimed)	N/A	N/A	£4449
IC	BeamC	Worm	Disc/drum	165-13	170	2307	98	13.6	19.6	£3649
IC	BeamC	Worm	Disc/drum	185/70-13	170	2389	106	11.7	18.0	£4149
IC	Beam1/2E	Worm	Disc/drum	175-14	183	2613	103 (Claimed)	N/A	N/A	£5330
IC	BeamC	Worm	Disc/drum	185/70-13	169	2258	117	9.9	17.2	£8549

Make and model	Production Figures	Years Built	Body Styles	Mechanical Layout	Engine Make (if not own)	Capacity/(cc)/Layout/Valves	BHP/rpm	Torque (lb.ft)/rpm	Transmission gearbox/automatic transmission
Wankel						Wankel	115/6000	112/4000	5-spd/-
121	222,398	1988–1991	Htch	F(Tr)/F	—	1138/4IL/ OHC	56/5880	65/3600	5-spd/-
			Sal			1324/4IL/ OHC	65/5600	76/3600	5-spd/-
323	2,567,162	1980–1985	Htch	F(Tr)/F	—	1071/4IL/ OHC	55/6000	58/4000	4-spd/-
			Sal			1296/4IL/ OHC	68/6000 75/5500	70/3500 85/3000	4-spd/5-spd/- Auto/-
			Est			1490/4IL/ OHC	88/6000	88/3200	4-spd/5-spd/-
323	1,578,755 (Incl. 4x4 Turbo)	1985–1989	Htch	F(Tr)/F	—	1071/4IL/ OHC	55/6000	58/4000	4-spd/-
			Sal			1296/4IL/ OHC	68/5800	70/3800	4-spd/5-spd/Auto
			Est			1323/4IL/ OHC	68/6000	70/3800	4-spd/5-spd/Auto
						1488/4IL/ OHC	75/5500	85/3500	5-spd/Auto
						1498/4IL/ OHC	72/5700	82/2200	5-spd/Auto
						1597/4IL/ OHC	104/6000	101/4200	5-spd/-
323 1600 Turbo 4x4	—	1985–1989	Htch	F(Tr)/4	—	1597/4IL/ 2OHC	148/6000	144/5000	5-spd/-
323	N/A	1989–1994	Sal	F(Tr)/F	—	1323/4IL/ OHC	76/6500	75/4000	4-spd/Auto
			Htch						
			Est			1498/4IL/ OHC	91/6500	90/4000	5-spd/Auto
						1597/4IL/ OHC	130/7000 87/6000	101/5500 92/3100	4-spd/Auto 5-spd/Auto
						1840/4IL/ 2OHC	140/6500	121/4700	5-spd/-
				F(Tr)/4	—	1840/4IL/ 2OHC	180/6000	175/3000	5-spd/-
626	1,373,766	1982–1987	Sal	F(Tr)/F	—	1586/4IL/ OHC	81/5500	88/4000	5-spd/-
			Htch						
			Cpe			1998/4IL/ OHC	102/5600 117/5000	116/3700 126/4000	5-spd/Auto 5-spd/Auto
626	N/A	1987–1991	Sal	F(Tr)/F	—	1789/4IL/ OHC	90/5500	103/3400	5-spd/-
			Htch						
			Est			1998/4IL/ OHC	109/5500	122/3300	5-spd/Auto
			Cpe			1998/4IL/ 2OHC	148/6000	134/4000	5-spd/-
				F(Tr)/4	—	2184/4IL/ 2OHC	114/5000	132/3000	5-spd/-
RX-7	N/A	1985–1991	Spts Cpe	F/R	—	2616/2Rotor/ Wankel	150/6500 200/6500	135/3000 195/3500	5-spd/- 5-spd/-
MX-5	In prod	1989–Date	Spts	F/R	—	1598/4IL/ 2OHC	114/6500 88/6000	100/5500 95/4000	5-spd/- 5-spd/-
						1839/4IL/ 2OHC	128/6500	110/5000	5-spd/-
121	In prod	1990–Date	Sal	F(Tr)/F	—	1324/4IL/ OHC	73/6000	78/3700	5-spd/Auto
MX-3	In prod	1991–Date	Cpe	F(Tr)/F	—	1598/4IL/ OHC	88/5300	99/4000	Auto/-
						1845/V6/ 2OHC	134/6800	118/5300	5-spd/-
MX-6	In prod	1991–Date	Cpe	F(Tr)/F	—	2497/V6/ 2OHC	165/5600	163/4800	5-spd/-
626	In prod	1991–Date	Sal	F(Tr)/F	—	1840/V6/ 2OHC	105/5500	116/4300	5-spd/Auto
			Cpe						
			Htch			1991/V6/ 2OHC	115/5000	127/4500	5-spd/Auto
			Est			2497/V6/ 2OHC	165/5600	163/4800	5-spd/Auto
						1998/4IL/ OHC Diesel	75/4000	127/2000	5-spd/-
Xedos 6	In prod	1991–Date	Sal	F(Tr)/F	—	1598/4IL/ 2OHC	114/6500	100/5500	5-spd/Auto
						1995/4IL/ 2OHC	144/6000	129/5000	5-spd/Auto
Xedos 9	In prod	1993–Date	Sal	F(Tr)/F	—	2497/V6/ 2OHC	168/6000	159/4900	Auto/-
RX-7	In prod	1991–Date	Spts Cpe	F/R	—	2616/2 Rotor/ Wankel	237/6500	218/5000	5-spd/-
323	In prod	1994–Date	Sal	F(Tr)/F	—	1324/4IL/ OHC	75/5500	79/4000	5-spd/-
			Htch						
						1489/4IL/	90/5500	99/4000	5-spd/Auto

| Suspension | | Steering | Brakes | Wheels/ | Length (in) | Weight | Performance | | Standing | UK Total |
Front	Rear		(Front/rear)	Tyres		(lb,unladen)	Top speed (mph)	0–60mph (sec)	1/4-mile (sec)	Price (£: at Launch)
IC	BeamC	Worm	Disc/disc	185/70-13	170	2352	125	8.6	16.3	£8699
IC	IC	R & P	Disc/drum	145-12	137	1598	93 (Claimed)	N/A	N/A	£5499
IC	IC	R & P	Disc/drum	165/70-12	137	1664	88	11.0	18.1	£6149
IC	IC	R & P	Disc/drum	155-13	156	1819	87 (Claimed)	N/A	N/A	£3399
IC	IC	R & P	Disc/drum	155-13	156	1869	93	13.1	18.9	£3649
IC	IC	R & P	Disc/drum	155-13	156	1869	99 (Est)	N/A	N/A	£5049
IC	IC	R & P	Disc/drum	155-13	156	1740	101	10.7	17.8	£5399
IC	IC	R & P	Disc/drum	155-13	165	1786	87 (Est)	N/A	N/A	£4749
IC	IC	R & P	Disc/drum	155-13	165	1786	91 (Claimed)	N/A	N/A	£5299
IC	IC	R & P	Disc/drum	155-13	165	1786	96	12.2	18.9	£6149
IC	IC	R & P	Disc/drum	155-13	165	2063	96	13.0	19.2	£6099
IC	IC	R & P	Disc/drum	155-13	165	2094	100	11.1	18.2	£7449
IC	IC	R & P	Disc/disc	175/70-13	157	2166	116	8.8	16.7	£6799
IC	IC	R & P	Disc/disc	185/60-14	157	2447	123	7.8	15.9	£11,750
IC	IC	R & P	Disc/drum	175/70-13	157	2006	98 (Claimed)	N/A	N/A	£7849
IC	IC	R & P	Disc/drum	175/70-13	157	2029	105 (Est)	N/A	N/A	£9229
IC	IC	R & P	Disc/drum	185/60-14	157	2227	124 (Est)	N/A	N/A	£9649
IC	IC	R & P	Disc/drum	175/70-13	157	2051	110 (Est)	N/A	N/A	£9649
IC	IC	R & P	Disc/disc	185/60-14	157	2288	125	8.6	16.8	£12,299
IC	IC	R & P	Disc/disc	195/60-14	157	2557	131 (Claimed)	N/A	N/A	Special Order
IC	IC	R & P	Disc/drum	165-13	174	2304	102	12.3	18.9	£4799
IC	IC	R & P	Disc/drum	185/70-14	174	2386	109	10.0	17.3	£5499
IC	IC	R & P	Disc/disc	185/70-14	174	2379	116	9.8	17.8	£9124
IC	IC	R & P	Disc/drum	185/70-14	178	2539	105	11.5	18.7	£8399
IC	IC	R & P	Disc/drum	195/60-15	178	2638	111	10.4	17.9	£10,829
IC	IC	R & P	Disc/disc	195/60-15	178	2904	122	9.4	17.3	£13,129
IC	IC	R & P	Disc/disc	195/60-15	178	2866	114 (Claimed)	9.7	N/A	£16,899
IC	IC	R & P	Disc/disc	205/60-15	171	2691	134	8.5	16.2	£13,995
IC	IC	R & P	Disc/disc	205/60-16	171	2756	148	6.7	14.9	£21,999
IC	IC	R & P	Disc/disc	185/60-14	156	2182	114	9.1	17.4	£14,249
IC	IC	R & P	Disc/disc	185/60-14	156	2249	109 (Est)	10.6	N/A	£12,995
IC	IC	R & P	Disc/disc	185/60-14	156	2249	115	10.1	17.6	£14,495
IC	IC	R & P	Disc/drum	165/70-13	150	1866	90	15.3	20.4	£8499
IC	IC	R & P	Disc/disc	185/65-14	166	2401	101	13.4	19.6	£13,449
IC	IC	R & P	Disc/disc	205/55-15	166	2447	124	8.9	16.9	£15,445
IC	IC	R & P	Disc/disc	205/55-15	182	2634	134	7.5	16.0	£17,499
IC	IC	R & P	Disc/disc	185/65-14	185	2628	119	9.5	17.2	£14,614
IC	IC	R & P	Disc/disc	195/65-14	185	2750	124 (Claimed)	10.4	N/A	£14,133
IC	IC	R & P	Disc/disc	205/55-15	185	2822	137 (Claimed)	N/A	N/A	£17,909
IC	IC	R & P	Disc/disc	195/65-14	185	2774	104	14.7	20.0	£13,395
IC	IC	R & P	Disc/disc	195/60-15	180	2558	110 (Est)	10.3	N/A	£15,995
IC	IC	R & P	Disc/disc	195/60-15	180	2686	132	8.2	16.4	£17,200
IC	IC	R & P	Disc/disc	205/65-15	190	3120	127	10.8	18.3	£24,399
IC	IC	R & P	Disc/disc	225/50-16	169	2888	156	6.0	14.6	£34,000
IC	IC	R & P	Disc/drum	175/70-13	159	2227	101 (Claimed)	13.3	N/A	£9995
IC	IC	R & P	Disc/drum	175/70-13	159	2227	108	11.9	N/A	£11,995

Make and model	Production Figures	Years Built	Body Styles	Mechanical Layout	Engine Make (if not own)	Capacity/(cc)/Layout/Valves	BHP/rpm	Torque (lb.ft)/rpm	Transmission gearbox/automatic transmission
						2OHC			
						1839/4IL/ 2OHC	115/6000	118/4000	5-spd/Auto
						1995/V6/ 2OHC	147/7000	135/5500	5-spd/-

McLaren

Make and model	Production Figures	Years Built	Body Styles	Mechanical Layout	Engine Make (if not own)	Capacity/(cc)/Layout/Valves	BHP/rpm	Torque (lb.ft)/rpm	Transmission gearbox/automatic transmission
F1	In prod	1993–Date	Spts Cpe	M/R	BMW	6064/V12/ 2OHC	627/7400	479/4000	6-spd/-
							668/7800	520/4500	6-spd/-

Mercedes-Benz

Make and model	Production Figures	Years Built	Body Styles	Mechanical Layout	Engine Make (if not own)	Capacity/(cc)/Layout/Valves	BHP/rpm	Torque (lb.ft)/rpm	Transmission gearbox/automatic transmission
220SE Cpe 'Fintail'	28,302	1960–1971	Cpe Conv	F/R	—	2195/6IL/ OHC	120/4800	152/4100	4-spd/Auto
						2496/6IL/ OHC	150/5500	159/4200	4-spd/Auto
						2778/6IL/ OHC	160/5500	177/4250	4-spd/5-spd/Auto
						3499/V8/ OHC	200/5800	211/4000	4-spd/5-spd/Auto
230SL/250SL/ 280SL	48,912	1963–1971	Spts Cpe	F/R	—	2308/6IL/ OHC	170/5600	159/4500	4-spd/Auto
						2496/6IL/ OHC	150/5500	174/4500	4-spd/Auto
						2778/6IL/ OHC	170/5750	177/4500	4-spd/Auto
600	2,677	1963–1981	Limo Land	F/R	—	6332/V8/ OHC	250/4000	369/2800	Auto/-
250S family Series (W108)	325,562	1965–1972	Sal Cpe	F/R	—	2496/6IL/ OHC	130/5400	143/4000	4-spd/Auto
							146/5600	157/4200	4-spd/Auto
							170/5600	174/4500	4-spd/Auto
						2778/6IL/ OHC	140/5400	166/3600	4-spd/Auto
							160/5500	177/4250	4-spd/Auto
200 family Series (W115) (4-cyl)	1,450,298	1967–1976	Sal	F/R	—	1988/4IL/ OHC	95/5000	115/2800	4-spd/Auto
						2197/4IL/ OHC	105/5000	132/2800	4-spd/Auto
						2197/4IL/ OHC Diesel	60/4200	93/2400	4-spd/-
						2307/4IL/ OHC	110/4800	137/2500	4-spd/Auto
						2404/4IL/ OHC Diesel	65/4200	97/2400	4-spd/-
230 family Series (W114) (6-cyl)	412,968	1967–1976	Sal	F/R	—	2292/6IL/ OHC	120/5300	132/3600	4-spd/Auto
						2496/6IL/ OHC	130/5300	147/3600	4-spd/Auto
						2778/6IL/ OHC	130/5200	159/3200	4-spd/Auto
						2746/6IL/ 2OHC	185/6000	176/4500	4-spd/Auto
250C/280CE	55,530	1968–1976	Cpe	F/R	—	2496/6IL/ OHC	150/5500	170/4650	4-spd/5-spd/Auto
						2746/6IL/ 2OHC	185/6000	175/4500	4-spd/5-spd/Auto
							185/6000	175/4500	
280SE 3.5	33,960	1971–1972	Sal	F/R	—	3499/V8/ OHC	200/5500	211/4000	Auto/-
300SEL 3.5/4.5	12,136	1969–1972	Sal	F/R	—	3499/V8/ OHC	200/5500	211/4000	Auto/-
300SEL 6.3	6,526	1968–1972	Sal	F/R	—	6332/V8/ OHC	250/4000	369/2800	Auto/-
350SL family	300,175	1971–1989	Conv	F/R	—	2746/6IL/ 2OHC	185/5800	171/4500	4-spd/5-spd/Auto
						2962/6IL/ OHC	190/5600	192/4250	Auto/-
						3499/V8/ OHC	200/5800	211/4000	4-spd/Auto
						3818/V8/ OHC	218/5500	224/4000	Auto/-
						3839/V8/ OHC	204/5250	225/3250	Auto/-
						4196/V8/ OHC	218/5200	236/3750	Auto/-
						4520/V8/ OHC	225/5000	278/3000	Auto/-
							217/5000	257/3250	
							225/5000	263/3250	
						4973/V8/	240/5000	298/3200	Auto/-

Suspension Front	Rear	Steering	Brakes (Front/rear)	Wheels/Tyres	Length (in)	Weight (lb, unladen)	Top speed (mph)	0–60mph (sec)	Standing 1/4-mile (sec)	UK Total Price (£: at Launch)
IC	IC	R & P	Disc/disc	185/65-14	159	2448	118 (Claimed)	10.0	N/A	£13,995
IC	IC	R & P	Disc/disc	205/50-16	159	2734	126 (Claimed)	8.1	16.4	£17,495
IC	IC	R & P	Disc/disc	235/45-17/315/45-17	169	2509	230 +	3.2	11.1	£540,000
IC	IC	R & P	Disc/disc	275/35-18/345/35-18	169	2336	220 (Est)	N/A	N/A	£799,000
IC	IC	Worm	Disc/drum	7.25-13	192	3190	106	12.4	18.5	£4288
IC	IC	Worm	Disc/disc	185-14	192	3278	110 (Auto)	14.8	20.7	£3859
IC	IC	Worm	Disc/disc	185-14	192	3388	115	11.2	17.8	£4947
IC	IC	Worm	Disc/disc	185-14	193	3586	125	9.3	17.2	£6995
IC	IC	Worm	Disc/drum	185-14	169	2800	120	10.7	17.5	£3595
IC	IC	Worm	Disc/drum	185-14	169	2855	120 (Est)	N/A	N/A	£3611
IC	IC	Worm	Disc/disc	185-14	169	3000	121	9.3	17.0	£3850
IAir	IAir	Worm	Disc/disc	9.00-15	218	5445	130	9.7	17.3	£8752
					246	5820	130 (Est)	N/A	N/A	£9796
IC	IC	Worm	Disc/disc	7.35-14	193	3175	106	12.6	19.3	£2575
IC	IC	Worm	Disc/disc	7.35-14	193	3175	114	10.8	17.9	£2575
IC	IC	Worm	Disc/disc	7.35-14	193	3263	120 (Est)	N/A	N/A	£2865
IC	IC	Worm	Disc/disc	7.35-14	193	3175	108	11.2	18.4	£3116
IC	IC	Worm	Disc/disc	7.35-14	193	3270	115	11.2	17.8	£3410
IC	IC	Worm	Disc/disc	6.95-14	185	2890	95	13.7	19.2	£3475
IC	IC	Worm	Disc/disc	6.95-14	185	2890	102	13.6	19.0	£2388
IC	IC	Worm	Disc/disc	6.95-14	185	2950	84	24.2	22.4	£2438
IC	IC	Worm	Disc/disc	175-14	185	2978	110	13.4	19.2	£3846
IC	IC	Worm	Disc/disc	175-14	185	3058	83	21.3	22.2	£4179
IC	IC	Worm	Disc/disc	6.95-14	185	2945	109 (Claimed)	N/A	N/A	£4753
IC	IC	Worm	Disc/disc	6.95-14	185	3000	108	12.7	19.0	£2804
IC	IC	Worm	Disc/disc	6.95-14	185	3063	112 (Claimed)	N/A	N/A	£3495
IC	IC	Worm	Disc/disc	205/70-14	185	3169	124	8.5	16.5	£3995
IC	IC	Worm	Disc/disc	185-14	184	3003	118 (Claimed)	N/A	N/A	£3475
IC	IC	Worm	Disc/disc	205/70-14	184	3200	124	8.9	16.9	£4275
IC	IC	Worm	Disc/disc	185-14	193	3821	125	9.3	17.2	£5158
					197	3876	128	8.4	16.4	
IC	IC	Worm	Disc/disc	185-14	197	3680	131 (Claimed)	N/A	N/A	£6795
IC	IC	Worm	Disc/disc	FR70-14	197	3828	134	7.1	15.5	£7743
IC	IC	Worm	Disc/disc	195/70-14	172	3307	124 (Claimed)	N/A	N/A	£16,599
IC	IC	Worm	Disc/disc	205/65-14	172	3322	123	8.4	16.5	£24,840
IC	IC	Worm	Disc/disc	205/70-14	172	3405	126	9.3	17.0	£7395
IC	IC	Worm	Disc/disc	205/70-14	172	3392	134 (Claimed)	N/A	N/A	£18,300
IC	IC	Worm	Disc/disc	205/70-14	172	3392	132 (Claimed)	N/A	N/A	£18,300
IC	IC	Worm	Disc/disc	205/70-14	172	3520	132 (Claimed)	N/A	N/A	£29,150
IC	IC	Worm	Disc/disc	205/70-14	172	3487	134 (Claimed)	N/A	N/A	£8598
IC	IC	Worm	Disc/disc	205/70-14	172	3395	142	7.2	15.6	£20,300

Make and model	Production Figures	Years Built	Body Styles	Mechanical Layout	Engine Make (if not own)	Capacity/(cc)/Layout/Valves	BHP/rpm	Torque (lb.ft)/rpm	Transmission gearbox/automatic transmission
						OHC			
350SLC family	40,963	1972–1981	Cpe	F/R	—	2746/6IL/ 2OHC	185/6000	170/4500	4-spd/5-spd/Auto
						3499/V8/ OHC	200/5800	211/4000	4-spd/Auto
						3818/V8/ OHC	218/5500	224/4000	Auto/-
						4520/V8/ OHC	225/5000	278/3000	Auto/-
S-Class (W116) (Incl. 450SEL 6.9 figs)	473,035	1972–1980	Sal	F/R	—	2746/6IL/ 2OHC	156/5500 160/5500 185/6000	159/4000 166/4000 176/4500	4-spd/5-spd/Auto 4-spd/5-spd/Auto
						3499/V8/ OHC	200/5800	204/4000	4-spd/Auto
						4520/V8/ OHC	225/5000 225/5000	279/3000 279/3000	Auto/- Auto/-
450SEL 6.9	7,380	1975–1980	Sal	F/R	—	6834/V8/ OHC	286/4250	405/3000	Auto/-
200/230TE (W123) (4-cyl + Diesels)	1,850,456	1975–1982	Sal Est	F/R	—	1988/4IL/ OHC	94/4800	113/3000	4-spd/Auto
						1997/4IL/ OHC	109/5200	121/3000	4-spd/Auto
						1988/4IL/ OHC Diesel	55/4200 60/4200	80/2400	4-spd/5-spd/Auto
						2299/4IL/ OHC	136/5100	148/3500	4-spd/Auto
						2307/4IL/ OHC	109/4800	132/3000	4-spd/Auto
						2399/4IL/ OHC Diesel	72/4400	101/2400	4-spd/Auto
						2404/4IL/ OHC Diesel	65/4200 74/4400	98/2400	4-spd/Auto
						2998/5IL/ OHC Diesel	80/4000 88/4400	127/2400 127/2400	4-spd/Auto
230C/280CE Coupe (W123)	79,147	1977–1982	Cpe	F/R	—	2299/4IL/ OHC	136/5100	148/3500	4-spd/Auto
						2307/4IL/ OHC	109/4800	132/3000	4-spd/Auto
						2746/6IL/ 2OHC	177/6000 185/5800	164/4500 168/4500	4-spd/5-spd/Auto 4-spd/5-spd/Auto
250/280E (W123) (6-cyl)	280,768	1975–1982	Sal Est	F/R	—	2525/6IL/ OHC	129/5500 140/5500	137/3500 140/3500	4-spd/Auto
						2746/6IL/ 2OHC	177/6000 185/5800	164/4500 168/4500	4-spd/5-spd/Auto
G-Wagon	In prod	1979–Date	Est Ute	F/4	—	2299/4IL/ OHC	125/5000	140/4000	4-spd/5-spd/-
						2746/6IL/ 2OHC	156/5250	169/4250	4-spd/5-spd/Auto
						2960/6IL/ OHC	170/5500	173/4500	5-spd/Auto
						2998/5IL/ OHC Diesel	88/4400	126/2400	4-spd/Auto
						2996/6IL/ OHC Diesel	113/4600	141/2900	5-spd/Auto
S-Class (W126)	666,986	1979–1991	Sal	F/R	—	2746/6IL/ 2OHC	185/5800	177/4500	4-spd/5-spd/Auto
						2962/6IL/ OHC	190/5600	192/4250	4-spd/5-spd/Auto
						3818/V8/ OHC	218/5500	225/4000	Auto/-
						3839/V8/ OHC	204/5250	225/3250	Auto/-
						4196/V8/ OHC	218/5200	236/3750	Auto/-
500SE/ 560SEL (W126)	74,062	1980–1991	Sal	F/R	—	4973/V8/ OHC	240/4750 231/4750 245/4750	297/3200 298/3000 286/3750	Auto/- Auto/-
						5547/V8/ OHC	300/5000	335/3750	Auto/-
380SEC/ 560SEC (W126)	147,764	1979–1992	Cpe	F/R	—	3839/V8/ OHC	204/5250	225/3250	Auto/-
						4196/V8/ OHC	218/5200	236/3750	Auto/-
						4973/V8/ OHC	231/4750 245/4750	298/3000 286/3750	Auto/-
						5547/V8/ OHC	300/5000	325/3750	Auto/-
190 family (W201) (Incl. 16V figures)	1,879.630	1982–1992	Sal Est	F/R	—	1797/4IL/ OHC	109/5500	110/3700	5-spd/Auto
						1997/4IL/	90/5500	122/2500	4-spd/5-spd/Auto

Suspension Front	Rear	Steering	Brakes (Front/rear)	Wheels/Tyres	Length (in)	Weight (lb,unladen)	Top speed (mph)	0–60mph (sec)	Standing 1/4-mile (sec)	UK Total Price (£: at Launch)
IC	IC	Worm	Disc/disc	185-14	187	3415	124 (Claimed)	N/A	N/A	£17,600
IC	IC	Worm	Disc/disc	205/70-14	187	3597	126 (Claimed)	N/A	N/A	£7875
IC	IC	Worm	Disc/disc	205/70-14	187	3435	133	8.4	16.5	£21,531
IC	IC	Worm	Disc/disc	205/70-14	187	3586	136	9.0	16.9	£10,435
IC	IC	Worm	Disc/disc	185-14	195	3542	118 (Claimed)	N/A	N/A	£5597
IC	IC	Worm	Disc/disc	185-14	195/199	3542/3619	124 (Est)	N/A	N/A	£5995
IC	IC	Worm	Disc/disc	205/70-14	195/199	3685/3740	122	10.4	17.6	£6995
IC	IC	Worm	Disc/disc	205/70-14	195	3828	134 (Est)	N/A	N/A	£8597
IC	IC	Worm	Disc/disc	205/70-14	199	3904	134	9.1	16.7	£9582
IHP	IHP	Worm	Disc/disc	215/70-14	199	4060	140	7.3	15.4	£21,995
IC	IC	Worm	Disc/disc	175-14	186	2954	100	15.1	N/A	£4940
IC	IC	Worm	Disc/disc	175-14	186	2954	104 (Claimed)	N/A	N/A	£8394
IC	IC	Worm	Disc/disc	175-14	186	3146	81 (Claimed)	N/A	N/A	£5166
IC	IC	Worm	Disc/disc	175-14	186	2975	112	10.3	18.0	£9450
IC	IC	Worm	Disc/disc	175-14	186	2975	106 (Claimed)	N/A	N/A	£6375
IC	IC	Worm	Disc/disc	175-14	186	3054	89 (Claimed)	N/A	N/A	£7995
IC	IC	Worm	Disc/disc	175-14	186	3075	86 (Claimed)	N/A	N/A	£6565
IC	IC	Worm	Disc/disc	175-14	186	3197	90	20.8	21.7	£7600
IC	IC	Worm	Disc/disc	195/70-14	183	3080	109	10.3	17.3	£8951
IC	IC	Worm	Disc/disc	195/70-14	183	3080	99	14.0	19.2	£11,550
IC	IC	Worm	Disc/disc	195/70-14	183	3322	124 (Est)	N/A	N/A	£10,990
IC	IC	Worm	Disc/disc	185-14	183	3324	124	8.9	16.9	£11,361
IC	IC	Worm	Disc/disc	175-14	186	2998	112 (Claimed)	N/A	N/A	£5789
IC	IC	Worm	Disc/disc	195/70-14	186	3322	116	11.0	18.0	£7990
BeamC	BeamC	Worm	Disc/drum	205-16	165/184	3788	89	15.6	20.1	£14,195
BeamC	BeamC	Worm	Disc/drum	215-16	165/184	4267	92	14.4	19.5	£13,910
BeamC	BeamC	Worm	Disc/drum	215-16	165/184	4608	103 (Claimed)	N/A	N/A	£31,300
BeamC	BeamC	Worm	Disc/drum	215-16	165/184	4267	79 (Claimed)	N/A	N/A	£13,560
BeamC	BeamC	Worm	Disc/drum	255/75-15	173	5051	84	25.4	23.4	£31,890
IC	IC	Worm	Disc/disc	195/70-14	197	3432	126	8.7	16.9	£15,300
IC	IC	Worm	Disc/disc	205/65-15	197	3352	131 (Claimed)	N/A	N/A	£20,800
IC	IC	Worm	Disc/disc	205/70-14	197	3509	133	8.4	16.6	£18,400
IC	IC	Worm	Disc/disc	205/70-14	197	3515	130	9.4	16.7	£18,800
IC	IC	Worm	Disc/disc	205/65-15	197	3527	135	7.6	16.1	£26,680
IC	IC	Worm	Disc/disc	205/70-14	197	3,570	145	7.5	15.5	£20,950
IC	IC	Worm	Disc/disc	205/70-14	202	3,864	131	8.0	16.3	£20,950
IC	IC	Worm	Disc/disc	215/65-15	202	3,990	147	7.1	15.8	£45,850
IC	IC	Worm	Disc/disc	205/70-14	193	3494	131	9.1	16.6	£25,700
IC	IC	Worm	Disc/disc	205/65-15	193	3572	138 (Claimed)	N/A	N/A	£36,255
IC	IC	Worm	Disc/disc	205/70-14	193	3606	142	7.9	16.2	£28,700
IC	IC	Worm	Disc/disc	205/65-15	193	3858	155 (Claimed)	N/A	N/A	£52,185
IC	IC	Worm	Disc/disc	185/65-15	174	2425	118	12.3	19.1	£15,190
IC	IC	Worm	Disc/disc	175/70-14	174	2425	107	13.4	19.5	£9685

Make and model	Production Figures	Years Built	Body Styles	Mechanical Layout	Engine Make (if not own)	Capacity/(cc)/Layout/Valves	BHP/rpm	Torque (lb.ft)/rpm	Transmission gearbox/automatic transmission
						OHC	105/5200	125/2500	4-spd/5-spd/Auto
							122/5100	128/3500	4-spd/5-spd/Auto
						2599/6IL/ OHC	166/5800	168/4600	5-spd/Auto
						1997/4IL/ OHC Diesel	72/4600	88/2800	4-spd/5-spd/Auto
190E 2.3/ 2.5-16V	26,128	1983–1992	Sal	F/R	—	2299/4IL/ 2OHC	185/6200	173/4500	5-spd/Auto
						2498/4IL/ 2OHC	204/6750	173/5000	5-spd/Auto
						2463/4IL/ 2OHC	235/7200	180/5500	5-spd/-
200 family (W124) (later renamed E-Class)	2,718,366	1984–1995	Sal Est	F/R	—	1997/4IL/ OHC	109/5200	126/2500	5-spd/Auto
							122/5100	128/3500	5-spd/Auto
						1997/4IL/ 2OHC	136/5500	140/4000	5-spd/Auto
						2199/4IL/ 2OHC	150/5500	155/4000	5-spd/Auto
						2299/4IL/ OHC	136/5100	152/3500	5-spd/Auto
						2599/6IL/ OHC	166/5800	170/4250	5-spd/Auto
						2799/6IL/ 2OHC	197/6000	199/3750	Auto/-
						2962/6IL/ OHC	190/5600	192/4250	Auto/-
						2962/6IL/ 2OHC	231/6300	200/4600	5-spd/Auto
						3199/6IL/ 2OHC	220/5500	229/3750	Auto/-
						3606/6IL/ 2OHC	280/5750	284/4000	Auto/-
						2497/5IL/ OHC Diesel	90/4600	114/2800	5-spd/Auto
						2996/6IL/ OHC Diesel	109/4600	136/2800	5-spd/Auto
						2994/6IL/ 2OHC Diesel	136/5000	156/2200	5-spd/Auto
				F/4	—	2962/6IL/ OHC	188/5700	191/4400	Auto/-
200 Coupes/ Cabriolets (W124) (later renamed E-Coupes)	Figs incl. above	1987–Date	Cpe Conv	F/R	—	2299/4IL/ OHC	136/5100	151/3500	5-spd/Auto
						2199/4IL/ 2OHC	150/5500	155/4000	5-spd/Auto
						2962/6IL/ OHC	188/5700	191/4400	5-spd/Auto
						2960/6IL/ 2OHC	220/6400	195/4600	5-spd/Auto
						3199/6IL/ 2OHC	220/5500	229/3750	5-spd/Auto
						3606/6IL/ 2OHC	280/5750	284/4000	Auto/-
500E	10,479	1990–1995	Sal	F/R	—	4973/V8/ 2OHC	326/5700	354/3900	Auto/-
SL300/ SL500/SL600	In prod	1989–Date	Conv	F/R	—	2799/6IL/ 2OHC	193/5500	199/3750	5-spd/Auto
						2960/6IL/ OHC	190/5700	192/4500	5-spd/Auto
						2960/6IL/ 2OHC	231/6300	201/4600	5-spd/Auto
						3199/6IL/ 2OHC	231/5600	232/3750	Auto/-
						4973/V8/ 2OHC	326/5500	332/4000	Auto/-
						5956/V8/ 2OHC	375/5500	427/3750	Auto/-
						5987/V12/ 2OHC	395/5200	420/3800	Auto/-
C-Class	In prod	1993–Date	Sal	F/R	—	1799/4IL/ 2OHC	120/5500	125/4200	5-spd/Auto
						1998/4IL/ 2OHC	136/5500	140/4200	5-spd/Auto
						2199/4IL/ 2OHC	150/5500	155/4000	5-spd/Auto
						2295/4IL/ 2OHC	193/5300	206/2500	5-spd/-
						2799/6IL/ 2OHC	193/5500	199/3750	5-spd/Auto
						3606/6IL/ 2OHC	280/5750	284/4000	Auto/-

Suspension Front	Rear	Steering	Brakes (Front/rear)	Wheels/ Tyres	Length (in)	Weight (lb,unladen)	Top speed (mph)	0–60mph (sec)	Standing 1/4-mile (sec)	UK Total Price (£: at Launch)
IC	IC	Worm	Disc/disc	175/70-14	174	2425	117	11.2	17.8	£10,575
IC	IC	Worm	Disc/disc	175-70-14	174	2425	121	9.7	17.4	£10,640
IC	IC	Worm	Disc/disc	185/65-15	174	2662	130	8.3	16.5	£18,000
IC	IC	Worm	Disc/disc	185/65-15	174	2425	98	15.9	20.0	£10,600
IC	IC	Worm	Disc/disc	205/55-15	174	2954	143	8.0	16.0	£21,045
IC	IC	Worm	Disc/disc	205/55-16	174	2954	142	7.2	15.1	£29,900
IC	IC	R & P	Disc/disc	245/40-17	178	2948	155 (Est)	7.1	N/A	£55,200
IC	IC	Worm	Disc/disc	185/65-15	187	2910	117	13.0	19.1	£12,500
IC	IC	Worm	Disc/disc	195/65-15	187	3062	120	12.3	18.5	£17,150
IC	IC	Worm	Disc/disc	195/65-15	187	2999	124 (Claimed)	N/A	N/A	£20,740
IC	IC	Worm	Disc/disc	195/65-15	187	3021	131 (Claimed)	N/A	N/A	£23,820
IC	IC	Worm	Disc/disc	195/65-15	187	3087	125	9.9	17.4	£13,665
IC	IC	Worm	Disc/disc	195/65-15	187	3021	132	8.8	16.9	£16,980
IC	IC	Worm	Disc/disc	195/65-15	187	3244	138	8.1	16.3	£27,360
IC	IC	Worm	Disc/disc	195/65-15	187	3234	136	8.4	17.1	£17,840
IC	IC	Worm	Disc/disc	195/65-15	187	3396	146	7.8	16.0	£30,950
IC	IC	Worm	Disc/disc	195/65-15	187	3285	142	7.0	15.4	£33,600
IC	IC	Worm	Disc/disc	225/45-17	187	3308	155 (Claimed)	N/A	N/A	£44,700
IC	IC	Worm	Disc/disc	195/65-15	187	2977	109 (Claimed)	N/A	N/A	£13,790
IC	IC	Worm	Disc/disc	195/65-14	187	3293	113	15.5	20.5	£24,130
IC	IC	Worm	Disc/disc	195/65-14	187	3241	124 (Claimed)	N/A	N/A	£27,650
IC	IC	Worm	Disc/disc	195/65-15	187	3443	134	8.3	16.3	£30,150
IC	IC	Worm	Disc/disc	195/65-15	183	3050	122	9.8	17.1	£23,800
IC	IC	Worm	Disc/disc	195/65-15	183	3065	131 (Claimed)	N/A	N/A	£30,900
IC	IC	Worm	Disc/disc	195/65-15	183	3238	139	7.5	16.0	£30,100
IC	IC	Worm	Disc/disc	195/65-15	183	3262	147 (Claimed)	N/A	N/A	£31,600
IC	IC	Worm	Disc/disc	195/65-15	183	3285	146 (Claimed)	N/A	N/A	£36,691
IC	IC	Worm	Disc/disc	225/45-17	183	3308	155 (Claimed)	N/A	N/A	£48,700
IC	IC	Worm	Disc/disc	225/55-16	187	3810	156	6.3	14.7	£57,220
IC	IC	Worm	Disc/disc	225/55-16	176	3881	140 (Claimed)	9.5	N/A	£53,200
IC	IC	Worm	Disc/disc	225/65-16	176	3630	142 (Claimed)	N/A	N/A	£42,130
IC	IC	Worm	Disc/disc	225/55-16	176	3954	134	8.6	16.7	£46,270
IC	IC	Worm	Disc/disc	225/55-16	176	3925	149 (Claimed)	8.1	N/A	£58,000
IC	IC	Worm	Disc/disc	225/55-16	176	4167	157	5.9	14.4	£58,000
IC	IC	Worm	Disc/disc	235/45-17	176	3960	155 (Claimed)	5.6	N/A	£89,950
IC	IC	Worm	Disc/disc	225/55-16	176	4356	159	6.0	14.5	£88,707
IC	IC	Worm	Disc/disc	185/65-15	177	2694	120	11.2	18.0	£17,600
IC	IC	Worm	Disc/disc	195/65-15	177	3010	123 (Claimed)	11.1	N/A	£19,500
IC	IC	Worm	Disc/disc	195/65-15	177	2928	130	9.5	17.5	£21,500
IC	IC	Worm	Disc/disc	195/65-15	177	3131	143 (Claimed)	8.2	N/A	£25,300
IC	IC	Worm	Disc/disc	195/65-15	177	3250	140	8.0	16.4	£27,400
IC	IC	Worm	Disc/disc	225/45-17/ 245/40-17	177	3345	152	6.0	14.5	£38,250

Make and model	Production Figures	Years Built	Body Styles	Mechanical Layout	Engine Make (if not own)	Capacity/(cc)/Layout/Valves	BHP/rpm	Torque (lb.ft)/rpm	Transmission gearbox/automatic transmission
						2155/4IL/ 2OHC Diesel	95/4800	111/3100	5-spd/Auto
						2497/5IL/ 2OHC Diesel	113/5000	125/2800	5-spd/Auto
S-Class	In prod	1991–Date	Sal	F/R	—	2799/6IL/ 2OHC	193/5500	199/3750	Auto/-
						3199/6IL/ 2OHC	231/5800	228/4100	Auto/-
						4196/V8/ 2OHC	286/5700	302/3900	Auto/-
						4973/V8/ 2OHC	326/5700	354/3900	Auto/-
						5987/V12/ 2OHC	408/5200	428/3800	Auto/-
S-Class Coupes	In prod	1992–Date	Cpe	F/R	—	4973/V8/ 2OHC	304/5500	347/3900	Auto/-
						5987/V12/ 2OHC	394/5200	420/3800	Auto/-
E-Class	In prod	1995–Date	Sal	F/R	—	1998/4IL/ 2OHC	136/5500	140/4000	5-spd/Auto
						2295/4IL/ 2OHC	150/5400	162/3700	5-spd/Auto
						2799/6IL/ 2OHC	193/5500	199/3850	5-spd/Auto
						3199/6IL/ 2OHC	220/5500	232/3850	5-spd/Auto
						2497/5IL/ 2OHC Diesel	113/5000	125/3200	5-spd/Auto
						2996/6IL/ 2OHC Diesel	136/5000	155/2200	5-spd/Auto

Mercury

Make and model	Production Figures	Years Built	Body Styles	Mechanical Layout	Engine Make (if not own)	Capacity/(cc)/Layout/Valves	BHP/rpm	Torque (lb.ft)/rpm	Transmission gearbox/automatic transmission
Monarch **	—	1977 model	Cpe	F/R	—	4942/V8/ OHV	134/3600	245/1600	Auto

MG

Make and model	Production Figures	Years Built	Body Styles	Mechanical Layout	Engine Make (if not own)	Capacity/(cc)/Layout/Valves	BHP/rpm	Torque (lb.ft)/rpm	Transmission gearbox/automatic transmission
Midget I to IV/1500	226,526	1961–1979	Spts	F/R	—	948/4IL/ OHV	46/5500	53/3000	4-spd/-
						1098/4IL/ OHV	56/5500 59/5750	62/3250 65/3500	4-spd/-
						1275/4IL/ OHV	65/6000	72/3000	4-spd/-
						1493/4IL/ OHV	66/5500	77/3000	4-spd/-
1100/1300	189,958	1962–1973	Sal	F(Tr)/F	—	1098/4IL/ OHV	55/5500	61/2500	4-spd/Auto
						1275/4IL/ OHV	58/5250 65/5750 70/6000	69/3500 71/3000 77/3000	4-spd/Auto 4-spd/Auto 4-spd/Auto
MGB	513,272	1962–1980	Spts Spts Cpe	F/R	—	1798/4IL/ OHV	95/5400	110/3000	4-spd (+O/D)/Auto
MGB GT V8	2,591	1973–1976	Spts Cpe	F/R	—	3528/V8/ OHV	137/5000	193/2900	4-spd+O/D/-
Metro/Turbo	120,206/ 21,969	1982–1990	Htch	F(Tr)/F	—	1275/4IL/ OHV	72/6000 93/6130	73/4000 85/2650	4-spd/- 4-spd/-
Maestro	39,714	1983–1991	Htch	F(Tr)/F	—	1598/4IL/ OHC	103/6000	100/4000	5-spd/-
						1994/4IL/ OHC	115/5500	134/2800	5-spd/-
Maestro Turbo	501	1989–1991	Htch	F(Tr)/F	—	1994/4IL/ OHC	152/5100	169/3500	5-spd/-
Montego	37,925	1984–1991	Sal	F(Tr)/F	—	1994/4IL/ OHC	117/5500	134/2800	5-spd/-
Montego Turbo	7,352	1985–1991	Sal	F(Tr)/F	—	1994/4IL/ OHC	150/5100	169/3500	5-spd/-
RV8	2,000	1992–1995	Spts	F/R	—	3946/V8/ OHV	190/4750	234/3200	5-spd/-
MGF	In prod	1995–Date	Spts	M(Tr)/R	—	1796/4IL/ 2OHC	118/5500 143/7000	122/3000 128/4500	5-spd/- 5-spd/-

Middlebridge

Make and model	Production Figures	Years Built	Body Styles	Mechanical Layout	Engine Make (if not own)	Capacity/(cc)/Layout/Valves	BHP/rpm	Torque (lb.ft)/rpm	Transmission gearbox/automatic transmission
Scimitar GTE	Est. 80	1988–1990	Spts Htch	F/R	Ford	2792/V6/ OHV	150/5700	157/3000	5-spd/Auto

Mini

Suspension Front	Rear	Steering	Brakes (Front/rear)	Wheels/ Tyres	Length (in)	Weight (lb,unladen)	Top speed (mph)	0–60mph (sec)	Standing ¼-mile (sec)	UK Total Price (£: at Launch)
IC	IC	Worm	Disc/disc	185/65-15	177	3087	108 (Claimed)	16.3	N/A	£18,900
IC	IC	Worm	Disc/disc	185/65-15	177	2967	118 (Claimed)	14.3	N/A	£21,100
IC	IC	Worm	Disc/disc	235/60-16	201	4163	130 (Claimed)	10.5	N/A	£37,500
IC	IC	Worm	Disc/disc	225/60-16	201	4117	143 (Claimed)	8.9	N/A	£43,700
IC	IC	Worm	Disc/disc	235/60-16	201	4670	144	8.4	16.5	£55,450
IC	IC	Worm	Disc/disc	235/60-16	205	4431	155 (Claimed)	7.0	N/A	£64,450
IC	IC	Worm	Disc/disc	235/60-16	201	4818	159	6.7	15.1	£89,600
IC	IC	Worm	Disc/disc	255/45-18	199	4564	153	7.9	16.1	£74,600
IC	IC	Worm	Disc/disc	255/45-18	199	4938	155 (Claimed)	6.6	N/A	£93,500
IC	IC	R & P	Disc/disc	195/65-15	189	3003	126 (Claimed)	11.3	N/A	£23,500
IC	IC	R & P	Disc/disc	195/65-15	189	3025	131	8.8	16.9	£26,000
IC	IC	R & P	Disc/disc	215/55-16	189	3289	143 (Claimed)	9.1	N/A	£29,600
IC	IC	R & P	Disc/disc	215/55-16	189	3355	142	7.5	16.0	£34,200
IC	IC	R & P	Disc/disc	195/65-15	189	3330	120 (Claimed)	15.3	N/A	£24,800
IC	IC	R & P	Disc/disc	205/65-15	189	3267	127 (Claimed)	13.1	N/A	£26,900
IC	Beam1/2E	Worm	Disc/drum	ER70-14	200	3514	100	11.3	17.9	£N/Q
IC	Beam1/4E	R & P	Drum/drum	5.20-13	138	1525	86	20.0	22.0	£670
IC	Beam1/4E	R & P	Disc/drum	5.20-13	138	1525	89	16.9	21.0	£682
IC	Beam1/2E	R & P	Disc/drum	5.20-13	138	1566	92	14.7	19.8	£623
IC	Beam1/2E	R & P	Disc/drum	5.20-13	138	1575	94	14.1	19.6	£684
IC	Beam1/2E	R & P	Disc/drum	145-13	141	1700	101	12.3	18.5	£1351
IHydroL	IHydroL	R & P	Disc/drum	5.50-12	147	1820	85	18.4	21.3	£799
IHydroL	IHydroL	R & P	Disc/drum	5.50-12	147	1820	88	17.3	20.7	£813
IHydroL	IHydroL	R & P	Disc/drum	145-12	147	1850	93	15.6	20.0	£845
IHydroL	IHydroL	R & P	Disc/drum	145-12	147	1765	97	14.1	19.6	£911
IC	Beam1/2E	R & P	Disc/drum	5.60-14/ 155-165-14	153/158	2030 to 2260	103	12.2	18.7	£834
IC	Beam1/2E	R & P	Disc/drum	175-14	153/158	2387	124	8.6	16.4	£2294
IHydraG	IHydraG	R & P	Disc/drum	155/70-12	134	1785	100	12.2	18.6	£4799
IHydraG	IHydraG	R & P	Disc/drum	165/60-13	134	1826	111	9.4	17.1	£5650
IC	IC	R & P	Disc/drum	175/65-14	160	2127	111	9.6	17.1	£6245
IC	IC	R & P	Disc/drum	175/65-14	160	2150	116	8.7	16.9	£7279
IC	IC	R & P	Disc/drum	185/55-15	158	2379	129	6.9	15.4	£12,999
IC	IC	R & P	Disc/drum	185/65-365	176	2271	114	9.6	17.0	£8165
IC	IC	R & P	Disc/drum	190/65-365	176	2380	125	7.5	15.9	£10,301
IC	Beam1/2E	R & P	Disc/drum	205/65-15	158	2428	136	6.9	15.2	£26,500
IHydraG	IHydraG	R & P	Disc/disc	185/55-15/	154	2366	123	8.7	16.6	£15,995
IHydraG	IHydraG	R & P	Disc/disc	205/50-15	154	2337	131	7.6	N/A	£17,995
IC	BeamC	R & P	Disc/drum	195/65-15	175	2792	130 (Est)	N/A	N/A	£25,000

Make and model	Production Figures	Years Built	Body Styles	Mechanical Layout	Engine Make (if not own)	Capacity/(cc)/Layout/Valves	BHP/rpm	Torque (lb.ft)/rpm	Transmission gearbox/automatic transmission
Mini 850/ 1000 (Total sales over 5 million)	In prod.	1959–Date	Sal Est	F(Tr)/F	—	848/4IL/ OHV	34/5500	44/2900	4-spd/Auto
						998/4IL/ OHV	38/5250	52/2700	4-spd/Auto
							40/5000	50/2500	4-spd/Auto
							42/5250	58/2600	4-spd/Auto
						1275/4IL/ OHV	50/5000	66/2600	4-spd/Auto
Cooper S	45,629	1963–1971	Sal	F(Tr)/F	—	970/4IL/ OHV	65/6500	55/3500	4-spd/-
						1071/4IL/ OHV	70/6000	62/4500	4-spd/-
						1275/4IL/ OHV	76/5800	79/3000	4-spd/-
Clubman	331,675	1969–1980	Sal Est	F(Tr)/F	—	998/4IL/ OHV	38/5250	52/2700	4-spd/-
					—		41/4850	52/2750	-/Auto
					—	1098/4IL/ OHV	45/5250	56/2700	4-spd/-
1275GT	117,949	1969–1980	Sal	F(Tr)/F	—	1275/4IL/ OHV	59/5300	65/2550	4-spd/-
Cooper/S	In prod	1990–Date	Sal Conv	F(Tr)/F	—	1275/4IL/ OHV	61/5550	61/3000	4-spd/-
							78/6000	78/3250	4-spd/-
							63/5700	70/3900	4-spd/-

Mitsubishi (This marque was badged **Colt** in the UK until 1984 – for earlier models, see **Colt** above)

[If sold in the UK before 1984, the following models bore **Colt** badges]

Make and model	Production Figures	Years Built	Body Styles	Mechanical Layout	Engine Make (if not own)	Capacity/(cc)/Layout/Valves	BHP/rpm	Torque (lb.ft)/rpm	Transmission gearbox/automatic transmission
Sapporo	N/A	1976–1985	Cpe Sal	F/R	—	1995/4IL/ OHC	98/5500	105/3500	5-spd/-
							90/5250	102/3000	Auto/-
						1997/4IL/ OHC	109/5800	114/4000	5-spd/-
							170/5500	180/3500	5-spd/-
Mirage	N/A	1978–1984	Htch	F(Tr)/F	—	1244/4IL/ OHC	55/5000	67/3500	4-spd/-
						1410/4IL/ OHC	70/5000	78/3500	4-spd (x2)/-
							104/5000	114/3500	4-spd (x2)/-
Colt	N/A	1983–1987	Htch	F(Tr)/F	—	1198/4IL/ OHC	54/5000	67/3500	5-spd/-
						1468/4IL/ OHC	74/5500	83/4000	5-spd/Auto
						1598/4IL/ OHC	120/5500	127/3000	5-spd/-
						1796/4IL/ OHC Diesel	58/4500	80/2500	5-spd/-
Colt	N/A	1987–1991	Htch	F(Tr)/F	—	1298/4IL/ OHC	68/6000	75/4000	5-spd/-
						1468/4IL/ OHC	74/5500	87/4000	5-spd/Auto
						1596/4IL/ 2OHC	125/6500	105/5000	5-spd/-
						1836/4IL/ 2OHC	134/6500	119/4500	5-spd/-
Tredia	N/A	1981–1989	Sal	F(Tr)/F	—	1410/4IL/ OHC	70/5000	78/3500	4-spd (x2)/-
						1597/4IL/ OHC	75/5500	86/3500	4-spd (x2)/Auto
							115/5500	125/3500	4-spd (x2)/-
Cordia	N/A	1981–1989	Cpe	F(Tr)/F	—	1597/4IL/ OHC	75/5500	86/3500	4-spd (x2)/Auto
							115/5500	125/3500	4-spd (x2)/-
						1795/4IL/ OHC	134/6000	144/3500	5-spd/-
Lancer	N/A	1983–1987	Sal Est	F(Tr)/F	—	1198/4IL/ OHC	54/5000	67/3500	5-spd/-
						1468/4IL/ OHC	74/5500	83/4000	5-spd/Auto
						1795/4IL/ OHC Diesel	58/4500	80/2500	5-spd/-
Lancer	N/A	1987–1991	Sal Htch Est	F(Tr)/F	—	1468/4IL/ OHC	74/5500	87/3500	5-spd/Auto
						1596/4IL/ 2OHC	123/6500	104/5000	5-spd/-
						1755/4IL/ OHC	95/5500	104/4000	5-spd/Auto
						1836/4IL/ 2OHC	134/6500	119/4500	5-spd/-
Galant	N/A	1983–1987	Sal	F(Tr)/F	—	1597/4IL OHC	75/5500	90/3500	5-spd/-
						1997/4IL/ OHC	102/5500	118/3500	5-spd/Auto
							147/5500	180/3500	5-spd/-
						1795/4IL/ OHC Diesel	82/4500	121/2250	5-spd/-
Galant	N/A	1987–1992	Sal	F(Tr)/F	—	1755/4IL/	88/5500	101/3500	5-spd/Auto

Suspension Front	Rear	Steering	Brakes (Front/rear)	Wheels/Tyres	Length (in)	Weight (lb,unladen)	Top speed (mph)	0–60mph (sec)	Standing ¼-mile (sec)	UK Total Price (£: at Launch)
IRubber	IRubber	R & P	Drum/drum	5.20-10	120/130	1380	72	27.1	23.6	£497
IHydroL	IHydroL									
IHydroL	IHydroL	R & P	Drum/drum	5.20-10	120/130	1400	75	26.2	22.7	£635
IRubber	IRubber	R & P	Disc/drum	145-10	120	1498	78	22.0	21.8	£5457
IRubber	IRubber	R & P	Disc/drum	145-12	120/130	1375	84	19.7	N/A	£4465
IRubber	IRubber	R & P	Disc/drum	145/70-12	120	1375	87	13.4	N/A	£5753
IHydroL	IHydroL	R & P	Disc/drum	5.20-10 145-10	120	1440	92 (Est)	N/A	N/A	£671
IRubber	IRubber	R & P	Disc/drum	145-10	120	1440	95	12.9	18.9	£695
IRubber	IRubber	R & P	Disc/drum	145-10	120	1440	97	10.9	18.2	£756
IHydroL	IHydroL			145-10						
IHydroL	IHydroL	R & P	Drum/drum	5.20-10	125	1406	75	21.0	N/A	£720
IRubber	IRubber			145-10						
IRubber	IRubber	R & P	Drum/drum	5.20-10 145-10	125	1424	82	17.9	N/A	£1643
IHydroL	IHydroL	R & P	Disc/drum	145-10 145-12	125	1555	90	13.3	19.0	£834
IRubber	IRubber									
IRubber	IRubber	R & P	Disc/drum	165/60-12	120	1530	92	13.1	19.0	£6995
IRubber	IRubber	R & P	Disc/drum	165/60-12	120	1556	97	11.0	18.1	£8826
IRubber	IRubber	R & P	Disc/drum	145/70-12	120	1530	92	11.5	N/A	£7845
IC	BeamC	Worm	Disc/disc	185/70-13	174	2525	102	12.7	18.8	£5241
IC	BeamC	Worm	Disc/disc	185/70-13	174	2525				
IC	IC	Worm	Disc/disc	195/70-14	178	2587	111	10.3	17.7	£6999
IC	IC	Worm	Disc/disc	195/70-14	178	2646	124 (Est)	N/A	N/A	£10,158
IC	IC	R & P	Disc/drum	155-13	149	1772	91 (Claimed)	N/A	N/A	£4099
IC	IC	R & P	Disc/drum	155-13	149	1772	92	13.8	19.3	£3488
IC	IC	R & P	Disc/drum	175/70-13	149	1880	105	9.9	17.2	£5959
IC	IC	R & P	Disc/drum	155-13	152	1709	80 (Est)	N/A	N/A	£4749
IC	IC	R & P	Disc/drum	155-13	152	1742	99 (Claimed)	N/A	N/A	£5299
IC	IC	R & P	Disc/drum	185/60-14	152	2156	121	8.5	16.6	£7749
IC	IC	R & P	Disc/drum	155-13	152	2007	90 (Claimed)	N/A	N/A	£5999
IC	IC	R & P	Disc/drum	155-13	156	2024	98	12.3	19.3	£6769
IC	IC	R & P	Disc/drum	155-13	156	2046	94	12.2	18.9	£7399
IC	IC	R & P	Disc/disc	195/60-14	156	2183	115	8.9	16.8	£10,169
IC	IC	R & P	Disc/disc	195/60-14	156	2183	125 (Claimed)	N/A	N/A	£10,779
IC	IC	R & P	Disc/drum	165-13	172	1896	90 (Claimed)	N/A	N/A	£5500
IC	IC	R & P	Disc/drum	165-13	172	2073	96 (Est)	N/A	N/A	£6150
IC	IC	R & P	Disc/drum	185/70-13	172	2073	120 (Est)	N/A	N/A	£7500
IC	IC	R & P	Disc/drum	165-13	168	1995	99 (Est)	N/A	N/A	£6650
IC	IC	R & P	Disc/drum	185/70-13	168	2149	111	9.2	17.2	£7750
IC	IC	R & P	Disc/drum	195/60-14	168	2238	124	7.7	16.0	£9399
IC	IC	R & P	Disc/drum	155-13	162	1764	80 (Est)	N/A	N/A	£5499
IC	IC	R & P	Disc/drum	155-13	162	1808	95	12.7	19.4	£6250
IC	IC	R & P	Disc/drum	155-13	162	2007	85 (Est)	N/A	N/A	£6500
IC	IC	R & P	Disc/drum	155-13	167	2230	100 (Claimed)	12.9	N/A	£10,129
IC	IC	R & P	Disc/disc	195/60-14	167	2367	112	9.0	17.1	£11,379
IC	IC	R & P	Disc/drum	175/70-13	167	2668	103	11.7	18.3	£11,499
IC	IC	R & P	Disc/disc	195/60-14	167	2564	120	8.5	16.7	£12,069
IC	IC	R & P	Disc/drum	165-13	180	2381	101	12.8	18.7	£6899
IC	IC	R & P	Disc/disc	185/70-14	180	2520	108	11.0	18.0	£8749
IC	IC	R & P	Disc/disc	195/60-14	180	2670	125	8.6	16.5	£9979
IC	IC	R & P	Disc/drum	165-13	180	2470	103	N/A	N/A	£8639
IC	IC	R & P	Disc/drum	165-14	179	2381	106	N/A	N/A	£9399

Make and model	Production Figures	Years Built	Body Styles	Mechanical Layout	Engine Make (if not own)	Capacity/(cc)/Layout/Valves	BHP/rpm	Torque (lb.ft)/rpm	Transmission gearbox/automatic transmission
			Cpe			OHC			
						1997/4IL/OHC	101/6000	114/3500	5-spd/Auto
							111/5500	118/4500	5-spd/Auto
						1997/4IL/2OHC	144/6500	126/5000	5-spd/-
						1795/4IL/Diesel	74/4500	112/2500	5-spd/-
				F(Tr)/4	—	1997/4IL/2OHC	147/6750	129/5500	5-spd/Auto
Galant Sapporo	N/A	1987–1993	Sal	F(Tr)/F	—	2351/4IL/OHC	127/5000	142/4000	5-spd/Auto
Starion	N/A	1982–1989	Cpe	F/R	—	1997/4IL/OHC	168/5500	181/3500	5-spd/-
							177/6000	214/3500	5-spd/-
							177/6000	214/3500	5-spd/-
						2555/4IL/OHC	153/5000	209/2500	5-spd/-
Space Wagon	N/A	1983–1991	Est	F(Tr)/F	—	1755/4IL/OHC	90/5500	97/4000	5-spd/Auto
						1795/4IL/OHC Diesel	75/4500	112/2500	5-spd/-
Shogun	N/A	1983–1991	Ute	F/4	—	2555/4IL/OHC	102/4500	143/2500	5-spd/-
						2346/4IL/OHC Diesel	84/4200	81/2500	5-spd/-
						2477/4IL/OHC Diesel	94/4200	173/2000	5-spd/-
							84/4500	148/2000	5-spd/Auto
						2972/V6/OHC	141/5000	166/3000	5-spd/Auto
Shogun	N/A	1991–Date	Ute	F/4	—	2972/V6/OHC	147/5000	174/4000	5-spd/Auto
						3497/V6/2OHC	205/5000	221/3000	5-spd/Auto
						2477/4IL/OHC Diesel	105/4200	177/2000	5-spd/Auto
						2835/4IL/OHC Diesel	123/4000	215/2000	5-spd/Auto
Colt	In prod	1991–Date	Htch	F(Tr)/F	—	1298/4IL/OHC	74/6000	79/3000	5-spd/-
						1597/4IL/OHC	111/6000	101/5000	5-spd/Auto
						1834/4IL/2OHC	138/6500	123/5500	5-spd/-
Lancer	In prod	1991–Date	Htch Sal	F(Tr)/F	—	1597/4IL/OHC	111/6000	101/5000	5-spd/Auto
						1834/4IL/2OHC	138/6500	123/5500	5-spd/-
Galant	In prod	1992–Date	Sal Cpe	F(Tr)/F	—	1834/4IL/OHC	125/6000	119/4500	5-spd/Auto
						1997/4IL/OHC	135/6000	130/4750	5-spd/Auto
						1999/V6/2OHC	147/6750	132/4000	5-spd/Auto
						2497/V6/2OHC	168/6000	159/4000	5-spd/Auto
Sigma	In prod	1990–Date	Sal Est	F(Tr)/F	—	2972/V6/2OHC	202/6000	199/3000	Auto/-
Space Runner/Space Wagon	In prod	1991–Date	Sal Est	F(Tr)/F	—	1834/4IL/OHC	121/6000	119/4500	4-spd/Auto
							121/6000	119/4500	4-spd/Auto
						1997/4IL/OHC	131/6000	130/4750	5-spd/Auto
						1998/4IL/OHC Diesel	80/4500	127/2500	5-spd/Auto
3000GT Coupe	In prod	1990–Date	Spts Cpe Spts	F/4	—	2972/V6/2OHC	282/6000	300/3000	5-spd/-
Carisma	In prod	1995–Date	Htch Sal	F/F	—	1597/4IL/OHC	90/5500	101/4000	5-spd/Auto
						1834/4IL/OHC	115/5500	119/4500	5-spd/Auto
Monteverdi									
High Speed 375	N/A	1967–1977	Cpe Conv	F/R	Chrysler	7206/V8/OHV	375/4600	480/3200	Auto/-
375L	N/A	1967–1977	Cpe	F/R	Chrysler	7206/V8/OHV	380/4600	480/3200	Auto/-
375/4 Limousine	N/A	1971–1977	Limo	F/R	Chrysler	7206/V8/OHV	380/4600	480/3200	Auto/-

Suspension Front	Rear	Steering	Brakes (Front/rear)	Wheels/ Tyres	Length (in)	Weight (lb, unladen)	Top speed (mph)	0–60mph (sec)	Standing 1/4-mile (sec)	UK Total Price (£: at Launch)
IC	IC	R & P	Disc/disc	185/70-14	179	2513	102 (Auto) (Claimed)	13.1	19.6	£10,899
IC	IC	R & P	Disc/disc	185/65-14	179	2749	112	10.4	17.9	£11,549
IC	IC	R & P	Disc/disc	195/60-15	179	2558	121	8.7	16.6	£13,199
IC	IC	R & P	Disc/drum	185/70-14	179	2492	101 (Claimed)	N/A	N/A	£10,799
IC	IC	R & P	Disc/disc	195/60-15	179	2976	118	9.4	16.8	£16,969
IC	IC	R & P	Disc/disc	195/60-15	184	2714	115	10.2	17.7	£12,999
IC	IC	Worm	Disc/disc	205/70-14	174	2698	133	7.5	16.1	£11,734
IC	IC	Worm	Disc/disc	215/60-15	174	2710	138	6.6	15.5	£13,066
IC	IC	Worm	Disc/disc	205/55-16/ 225/50-16	174	2885	133	6.9	16.0	£16,149
IC	IC	Worm	Disc/disc	205/55-16/ 225/50-16	174	3032	129	7.8	15.9	£16,969
IC	IC	R & P	Disc/drum	165-13	169	2430	97	12.5	19.2	£7750
IC	IC	R & P	Disc/drum	165-13	169	2430	96 (Claimed)	N/A	N/A	£9292
ITor	Beam1/2E	Worm	Disc/drum	215-15	155	3171	87	14.5	19.8	£9449
ITor	Beam1/2E	Worm	Disc/drum	215-15	155	3346	83	15.1	20.2	£10,500
ITor	Beam1/2E	Worm	Disc/drum	215R-15	181	3913	85	18.8	21.1	£16,999
ITor	Beam1/2E	Worm	Disc/drum	215-15	181	3825	83	17.8	20.6	£14,099
ITor	BeamC	Worm	Disc/drum	215R-15	181	4185	97	12.8	18.8	£18,499
ITor	BeamC	Worm	Disc/disc	215-15	163/186	4222/4526	104	13.1	19.7	£18,319
ITor	BeamC	Worm	Disc/disc	265/70-15	186	4675	107	10.7	17.7	£35,199
ITor	BeamC	Worm	Disc/disc	215-15	163/186	3748	91 (Claimed)	18.1	N/A	£17,989
ITor	BeamC	Worm	Disc/disc	235/75-15	186	4344	94 (Claimed)	17.3	N/A	£25,499
IC	IC	R & P	Disc/drum	155-13	156	2040	106 (Claimed)	12.5	N/A	£8779
IC	IC	R & P	Disc/drum	175/70-13	156	2271	112	9.6	17.5	£10,145
IC	IC	R & P	Disc/disc	195/60-14	156	2359	128	8.4	16.6	£10,989
IC	IC	R & P	Disc/disc	175/70-13	167	2381	115 (Claimed)	N/A	N/A	£11,279
IC	IC	R & P	Disc/disc	195/60-14	167	2469	127 (Claimed)	8.3	N/A	£14,449
IC	IC	R & P	Disc/drum	165-14	182	2492	125 (Claimed)	10.0	N/A	£12,999
IC	IC	R & P	Disc/disc	165-14	182	2492	128 (Claimed)	9.7	N/A	£14,529
IC	IC	R & P	Disc/disc	195/60-15	182	2778	128	8.7	16.7	£17,399
IC	IC	R & P	Disc/disc	205/60-15	182	3019	134 (Claimed)	N/A	N/A	£20,299
IC	IC	R & P	Disc/disc	205/65-15	187	3581	128	9.3	17.2	£24,789
IC	IC	R & P	Disc/drum	185/70-14	169	2612	113	10.6	18.1	£11,499
IC	IC	R & P	Disc/drum	185/70-14	178	2745	113 (Est)	N/A	N/A	£12,499
IC	IC	R & P	Disc/drum	185/70-14	178	2855	112	9.3	17.2	£13,319
IC	IC	R & P	Disc/drum	185/70-14	178	2799	97 (Claimed)	17.8	N/A	£16,449
IC	IC	R & P	Disc/disc	245/45-17	179	3771	153	5.8	14.5	£35,500
IC	IC	R & P	Disc/drum	175/65-14	175	2437	113 (Claimed)	12.0	N/A	£10,999
IC	IC	R & P	Disc/drum	185/65-14	175	2503	121	9.8	17.4	£13,499
IC	DDC	Worm	Disc/disc	GR70-15	181	3344	155 (Claimed)	N/A	N/A	£9250
IC	DDC	Worm	Disc/disc	GR70-15	189	3665	152	6.3	14.6	£9250
IC	DDC	Worm	Disc/disc	GR70-15	209	3637	146 (Claimed)	N/A	N/A	Special Order

Make and model	Production Figures	Years Built	Body Styles	Mechanical Layout	Engine Make (if not own)	Capacity/(cc)/Layout/Valves	BHP/rpm	Torque (lb.ft)/rpm	Transmission gearbox/automatic transmission
Morgan									
4/4 1600	3,708	1968–1981	Spts	F/R	Ford	1599/4IL/ OHV	74/4750	98/2500	4-spd/-
							88/5400	96/3600	4-spd/-
Plus 8	In prod	1968–Date	Spts	F/R	Rover	3528/V8/ OHV	161/5200	210/3000	4-spd/-
							155/5250	198/2500	5-spd/-
							190/5280	220/4000	5-spd/-
						3946/V8/ OHV	190/4750	235/2600	5-spd/-
4/4 – 1600/1800	In prod	1981–Date	Spts	F/R	Ford	1596/4IL/ OHC	96/6000	98/4000	4-spd/5-spd/-
						1796/4IL/ 2OHC	121/6000	115/4500	5-spd/-
					Fiat	1585/4IL/ 2OHC	96/6000	94/3800	5-spd/-
Plus 4	In prod	1985–Date	Spts	F/R	Fiat	1995/4IL/ 2OHC	122/5300	127/3500	5-spd/-
					Rover	1994/4IL/ 2OHC	140/6000	131/4500	5-spd/-
Morris									
Minor	1,303,331	1948–1971	Sal Est Conv	F/R	—	918/4IL/ SV	27/4400	42/2400	4-spd/-
						803/4IL/ OHV	30/4800	40/2400	4-spd/-
						948/4IL/ OHV	37/4750	50/2500	4-spd/-
						1098/4IL/ OHV	48/5100	60/2500	4-spd/-
Oxford	296,255	1959–1971	Sal Est	F/R	—	1489/4IL/ OHV	52/4350	82/2100	4-spd/-
						1622/4IL/ OHV	61/4500	90/2100	4-spd/Auto
						1489/4IL/ OHV/Diesel	40/4000	64/1900	4-spd/-
Mini – see 'Mini' marque									
1100/1300	743,000 (Approx)	1962–1973	Sal Est	F(Tr)/F	—	1098/4IL/ OHV	48/5100	60/2500	4-spd/Auto
						1275/4IL/ OHV	58/5250	69/3000	4-spd/Auto
							70/6000	74/3250	4-spd/-
1800	95,271	1966–1975	Sal	F(Tr)/F	—	1798/4IL/ OHV	80/5000	100/2100	4-spd/-
							86/5300	101/3000	4-spd/Auto
							96/5700	106/3000	4-spd/-
2200	Incl. in Austin 2200 figures	1972–1975	Sal	F(Tr)/F	—	2227/6IL/ OHC	110/5250	126/3500	4-spd/Auto
Marina	659,852	1971–1980	Sal Est	F/R	—	1275/4IL/ OHV	60/5250	69/2500	4-spd/Auto
						1695/4IL/ OHC	78/5150	93/3400	4-spd/Auto
						1798/4IL/ OHV	77/5100	98/2900	4-spd/Auto
							95/5500	105/2500	4-spd/-
1800/ 2200	19,000 (Incl. Austin and Wolseley figures)	1975 only	Sal	F(Tr)/F	—	1798/4IL/ OHV	82/5200	102/2750	4-spd/Auto
						2227/6IL/ OHC	110/5250	125/3520	4-spd/Auto
Ital	175,276	1980–1984	Sal Est	F/R	—	1275/4IL/ OHV	61/5300	69/2950	4-spd/Auto
						1695/4IL/ OHC	78/5150	93/3400	4-spd/Auto
						1993/4IL/ OHC	90/4750	114/3250	-/Auto
Moskvich									
408/426	N/A	1964–1971	Sal Est	F/R	—	1358/4IL/ OHV	61/4500	80/2750	4-spd/-
412/427	N/A	1969–1975	Sal Est	F/R	—	1478/4IL/ OHC	80/5800	85/3400	4-spd/-
Naylor									
TF1700	Approx 100	1985–1986	Spts	F/R	British Leyland	1695/4IL/ OHC	77/5180	99/3700	4-spd/-
Nissan									

[If sold in the UK before 1984, the following models bore **Datsun** badges]

Suspension Front	Rear	Steering	Brakes (Front/rear)	Wheels/ Tyres	Length (in)	Weight (lb,unladen)	Performance Top speed (mph)	0–60mph (sec)	Standing ¼-mile (sec)	UK Total Price (£: at Launch)
IC	Beam1/2E	Worm	Disc/drum	5.60-15	144	1516	100 (Est)	N/A	N/A	£858
IC	Beam1/2E	Worm	Disc/drum	5.60-15	144	1516	102	9.8	17.2	£890
IC	Beam1/2E	Worm	Disc/drum	185-15	147	1979	124	6.7	15.1	£1478
IC	Beam1/2E	Worm	Disc/drum	185/70-14	147	2128	123	6.5	15.1	£5417
IC	Beam1/2E	R & P	Disc/drum	205/60-15	147	2022	120	5.6	14.4	£12,999
IC	Beam1/2E	R & P	Disc/drum	205/60-15	156	2059	121	6.1	15.1	£22,363
IC	Beam1/2E	Worm (Later R & P)	Disc/drum	165-15	144	1702	103	10.0	17.3	£7245
IC	Beam1/2E	R & P	Disc/drum	165-15	144	1850	111	7.8	16.1	£19152
IC	Beam1/2E	Worm (Later R & P)	Disc/drum	165-15	144	1850	115 (Claimed)	N/A	N/A	£7413
IC	Beam1/2E	Worm	Disc/drum	195/60-15	144	1786	111	9.0	16.9	£10,901
IC	Beam1/2E	R & P	Disc/drum	195/60-15	144	2042	109	7.7	15.2	£13,500
ITor	Beam1/2E	R & P	Drum/drum	5.00-14	148	1652	62	36.5	26.3	£359
ITor	Beam1/2E	R & P	Drum/drum	5.00-14	148	1652	62	N/A	26.9	£582
ITor	Beam1/2E	R & P	Drum/drum	5.00-14	148	1652	73	25.9	23.4	£603
ITor	Beam1/2E	R & P	Drum/drum	5.00-14	148	1652	74	24.8	22.8	£587
IC	Beam1/2E	Worm	Drum/drum	5.90-14	178	2473	78	23.6	22.5	£816
IC	Beam1/2E	Worm	Drum/drum	5.90-14	175	2473	81	21.4	21.8	£869
IC	Beam1/2E	Worm	Drum/drum	5.90-14	175	2520	66	39.4	25.9	£868
IHydroL	IHydroL	R & P	Disc/drum	5.50-12	147	1780	78	22.2	22.7	£661
IHydroL	IHydroL	R & P	Disc/drum	5.50-12	147	1780	88	17.3	20.7	£672
IHydroL	IHydroL	R & P	Disc/drum	145-12	147	1900	93	15.6	20.0	£910
IHydroL	IHydroL	R & P	Disc/drum	175-13	164	2645	90	17.1	20.5	£873
IHydroL	IHydroL	R & P	Disc/drum	165-14	164	2645	93	16.3	19.9	£999
IHydroL	IHydroL	R & P	Disc/drum	165-14	164	2645	99	13.7	19.4	£1056
IHydroL	IHydroL	R & P	Disc/drum	165-14	167	2620	104	13.1	18.7	£1325
ITor	Beam1/2E	R & P	Drum/drum Disc/drum	5.20-13	167	1949	86	16.8	20.2	£923
ITor	Beam1/2E	R & P	Disc/drum	155-13	167	2117	98	12.5	18.7	£3029
ITor	Beam1/2E	R & P	Disc/drum	145-13	167	2050	95	12.2	18.5	£995
ITor	Beam1/2E	R & P	Disc/drum	165/70-13	167	2070	100	12.1	18.7	£1138
IHydraG	IHydraG	R & P	Disc/drum	185/70-14	175	2557	96	14.9	20.1	£2117
IHydraG	IHydraG	R & P	Disc/drum	185/70-14	175	2600	104	13.5	19.2	£2424
ITor	Beam1/2E	R & P	Disc/drum	155-13	171	2070	91	15.2	19.6	£3736
ITor	Beam1/2E	R & P	Disc/drum	155-13	171	2139	98	12.5	18.7	£3962
ITor	Beam1/2E	R & P	Disc/drum	155-13	171	2163	101	11.7	18.8	£5533
IC	Beam1/2E	Worm	Drum/drum	6.00-13	161	2178	80	23.1	22.0	£667
IC	Beam1/2E	Worm	Drum/drum Disc/drum	6.45-13	162	2005	93	14.5	19.7	£749
IC	BeamC	R & P	Disc/drum	165-15	147	1932	89	12.5	19.5	£13,950

Make and model	Production Figures	Years Built	Body Styles	Mechanical Layout	Engine Make (if not own)	Capacity/(cc)/Layout/Valves	BHP/rpm	Torque (lb.ft)/rpm	Transmission gearbox/automatic transmission
Laurel Mk 2	670,900	1981–1985	Sal	F/R	—	1998/6IL/OHC	97/5600	99/3600	5-spd/-
						2393/6IL/OHC	113/5200	128/3200	5-spd/Auto
Laurel	Figs. incl. above	1985–1989	Sal	F/R	—	2393/6IL/OHC	128/5600	135/4400	5-spd/Auto
Cherry	1,450,300	1982–1986	Htch	F(Tr)/F	—	988/4IL/OHC	50/6000	55/4000	4-spd/-
						1270/4IL/OHC	60/5600	74/3600	4-spd/5-spd/-
						1488/4IL/OHC	75/5600 114/5600	89/3600 121/3200	Auto/- 5-spd/-
Cherry/ GTI Europe	27,900	1983–1984	Htch	F/F	—	1186/4HO/OHC	62/6000	66/3200	5-spd/-
						1490/4HO/OHC	93/5800	96/4000	5-spd/-
Sunny	1,857,200	1981–1986	Sal Est Cpe Htch	F(Tr)/F	—	1270/4IL/OHC	60/5600	74/3600	5-spd/-
						1488/4IL/OHC	75/5600	91/2800	5-spd/Auto
Sunny	N/A	1986–1991	Htch Sal Est Cpe	F(Tr)/F	—	1270/4IL/OHC	60/5600	74/3600	5-spd/-
						1392/4IL/OHC	83/6200	82/4000	5-spd/-
						1597/4IL/OHC	94/5600	97/3200	5-spd/Auto
						1809/4IL/OHC	128/6400	116/4800	5-spd/-
						1681/4IL/OHC Diesel	55/4800	77/2800	5-spd/-
Sunny ZX	1,990,000 (Check the above)	1987–1991	Cpe	F(Tr)/F	—	1598/4IL/2OHC	120/6600	102/5200	5-spd/-
						1809/4IL/OHC	128/6400	116/4800	5-spd/-
						1809/4IL/2OHC	128/6400	116/4800	5-spd/-
280C	975,500	1980–1984	Sal Est	F/R	—	2753/6IL/OHC	125/4800	144/3200	5-spd/Auto
300C	640,470	1984–1987	Sal Est	F/R	—	2960/V6/OHC	155/5200 150/5200	175/3600 171/3600	Auto/- 5-spd/-
Prairie	1,079,000	1983–1988	Est	F(Tr)/F	—	1488/4IL/OHC	75/5600	90/3200	5-spd/-
						1809/4IL/OHC	90/5200	112/3200	5-spd/-
Prairie	750,000	1988–1991	Est	F(Tr)/F	—	1974/4IL/OHC	98/5600	116/3200	5-spd/Auto
				F(Tr)/4	—	1974/4IL/OHC	98/5600	116/3200	5-spd/-
Micra	2,079,900	1982–1992	Htch	F(Tr)/F	—	988/4IL/OHC	50/6000 55/6000	54/3600 55/3600	4-spd/- 5-spd/-
						1235/4IL/OHC	60/5600	69/3200	5-spd/-
Stanza	720,830	1981–1986	Sal Htch	F(Tr)/F	—	1598/4IL/OHC	81/5200	96/3200	4-spd/5-spd/-
						1809/4IL/OHC	88/5200	105/3200	5-spd/- Auto/-
Bluebird	1,850,700	1980–1984	Sal Est Cpe	F/R	—	1770/4IL/OHC	88/5600	98/3600	4-spd/5-spd/Auto
Bluebird	1,250,500	1984–1986	Sal Htch Est	F(Tr)/F	—	1598/4IL/OHC	82/5000	96/3200	5-spd/Auto
						1809/4IL/OHC	90/5200 135/6000 137/6400	111/2800 121/3600 148/4000	5-spd/- 5-spd/- 5-spd/-
						1973/4IL/OHC	105/5200	119/3600	5-spd/Auto
						1952/4IL/OHC Diesel	67/4600	95/2400	5-spd/-
Bluebird	167,671 (British built)	1986–1990	Sal Est Htch	F(Tr)/F	—	1598/4IL/OHC	82/5200	98/3200	5-spd/-
						1809/4IL/OHC	90/5200	112/2800	5-spd/Auto
						1809/4IL/OHC	135/6000	142/4000	5-spd/-
						1973/4IL/OHC	105/5200	115/4000	5-spd/Auto
						1952/4IL/OHC Diesel	67/4600	95/2400	5-spd/-

Suspension Front	Rear	Steering	Brakes (Front/rear)	Wheels/Tyres	Length (in)	Weight (lb, unladen)	Top speed (mph)	0–60mph (sec)	Standing 1/4-mile (sec)	UK Total Price (£: at Launch)
IC	BeamC	Worm	Disc/drum	185/70-14	183	2480	103 (Est)	N/A	N/A	£5736
IC	BeamC	Worm	Disc/drum	185/70-14	183	2546	112 (Claimed)	N/A	N/A	£6635
IC	BeamC	R & P	Disc/drum	185/70-14	183	2911	99 (Auto)	11.6	18.4	£10,201
IC	IC									£11,799
IC	IC	R & P	Disc/drum	155-13	156	1720	87 (Est)	N/A	N/A	£3697
IC	IC	R & P	Disc/drum	155-13	156	1731	93	12.8	19.0	£3833
IC	IC	R & P	Disc/drum	155-13	156	1841	96 (Est)	N/A	N/A	£4496
IC	IC	R & P	Disc/drum	175/70-13	156	1781	114	8.0	16.3	£6400
IC	IC	R & P	Disc/drum	145-13	158	1874	93 (Claimed)	N/A	N/A	£4185
IC	IC	R & P	Disc/drum	165/70-13	158	1874	106 (Claimed)	N/A	N/A	£5350
IC	IC	R & P	Disc/drum	155-13	159	1808	90 (Est)	N/A	N/A	£3866
IC	IC	R & P	Disc/drum	155-13	159	1828	95	11.0	18.2	£4188
IC	IC	R & P	Disc/drum	155-13	159	2070	92	13.7	19.7	£5595
IC	IC	R & P	Disc/drum	155-13	159	2132	103	12.0	18.5	£8199
IC	IC	R & P	Disc/drum	155-13	159	2178	103	11.6	18.2	£7790
IC	IC	R & P	Disc/disc	185/60-14	159	2249	128 (Claimed)	8.3	N/A	£11,985
IC	IC	R & P	Disc/drum	155-13	159	2139	94 (Claimed)	17.5	N/A	£7395
IC	IC	R & P	Disc/disc	185/60-14	167	2381	115	9.2	17.2	£10,500
IC	IC	R & P	Disc/disc	185/60-14	167	2381	128 (Claimed)	8.3	N/A	£11,695
IC	IC	R & P	Disc/disc	185/60-14	167	2359	128 (Claimed)	N/A	N/A	£11,696
IC	BeamC	Worm	Disc/disc	195/70-14	190	3031	104	11.9	18.9	£8036
IC	BeamC	Worm	Disc/disc	195/70-14	185	3197	115 (Est)	N/A	N/A	£10,750
IC	BeamC (Beam1/2E on Estate)	Worm	Disc/disc	195/70-14	185	3197	110 (Est)	N/A	N/A	£10,750
IC	ITor	R & P	Disc/drum	165-13	161	2352	83	16.3	20.2	£6000
IC	IC	R & P	Disc/drum	185/70-13	161	2455	95	12.6	18.8	£8395
IC	IC	R & P	Disc/drum	195/65-14	172	2890	97	14.4	19.4	£13,996
IC	IC	R & P	Disc/drum	195/65-14	172	2907	95 (Est)	N/A	N/A	£15,585
IC	BeamC	R & P	Disc/drum	145-12	144	1465	85 (Est)	N/A	N/A	£3750
IC	BeamC	R & P	Disc/drum	145-12	144	1465	88	14.5	19.6	£4150
IC	BeamC	R & P	Disc/drum	155/70-13	144	1755	92	14.0	19.6	£7099
IC	IC	R & P	Disc/drum	165-13	169	2114	98	12.0	18.4	£4485
IC	IC	R & P	Disc/drum	185/70-13	169	2029	106 (Est)	N/A	N/A	£5693
IC	IC	R & P	Disc/drum	185/70-13	169	2029	99 (Est)	N/A	N/A	£6263
IC	IC	R & P	Disc/drum	165-14	171	2451	100	11.9	18.5	£4098
IC	IC	R & P	Disc/drum	165-13	172	2095	96	12.9	18.9	£6499
IC	IC	R & P	Disc/drum	165-13	172	2183	106 (Est)	N/A	N/A	£6095
IC	IC	R & P	Disc/disc	195/60-15	172	2674	120	8.8	16.3	£8250
IC	IC	R & P	Disc/disc	195/60-15	172	2381	115	8.6	16.5	£9675
IC	IC	R & P	Disc/drum	185/70-14	172	2430	108	10.0	17.6	£8199
IC	IC	R & P	Disc/drum	165-13	172	2403	87 (Claimed)	N/A	N/A	£7595
IC	IC	R & P	Disc/drum	165-13	173	2359	96	12.9	18.9	£6499
IC	IC	R & P	Disc/drum	165-13	173	2293	106 (Claimed)	N/A	N/A	£7195
IC	IC	R & P	Disc/disc	195/60-15	173	2710	115	8.6	16.5	£9675
IC	IC	R & P	Disc/drum	185/70-14	173	2558	103	10.5	18.0	£8199
IC	IC	R & P	Disc/drum	165-14	173	2734	87 (Claimed)	N/A	N/A	£7596

Make and model	Production Figures	Years Built	Body Styles	Mechanical Layout	Engine Make (if not own)	Capacity/(cc)/Layout/Valves	BHP/rpm	Torque (lb.ft)/rpm	Transmission gearbox/automatic transmission
Patrol	850,900	1981–Date	Ute	F/4	—	2753/4IL/ OHC	120/4800	149/3200	4-spd/-
						4169/6IL/ OHC	170/4000	230/2800	5-spd/-
						2826/6IL/ OHC Diesel	115/4400	174/2400	5-spd/-
						3246/6IL/ OHC Diesel	95/3600	160/1800	5-spd/-
						4169/6IL/ OHC Diesel	124/4000	201/2000	5-spd/Auto
300ZX	798,450	1984–1989	Spts Cpe	F/R	—	2960/V6/ 2OHC	170/5600	175/4400	5-spd/Auto
							228/5400	242/4000	5-spd/Auto
							225/5400	240/4400	5-spd/Auto
Silvia ZX	524,680	1984–1988	Spts Cpe	F/R	—	1809/4IL/ OHC	137/6000	142/4000	5-spd/Auto
						1990/4IL/ 2OHC	145/6400	129/5000	5-spd/-
200SX	196,225	1989–1993	Spts Cpe	F/R	—	1809/4IL/ 2OHC	171/6400	168/4000	5-spd/-
							164/6400	163/4000	5-spd/-
Maxima	752,676	1988–1994	Sal	F(Tr)/F	—	2960/V6/ OHC	168/5600	183/2800	Auto/-
Micra	In prod	1992–Date	Htch	F(Tr)/F	—	998/4IL/ 2OHC	55/6000	58/4000	5-spd/-
						1275/4IL/ 2OHC	75/6000	76/4000	5-spd/Auto
Sunny	N/A	1990–1994	Htch Sal Est	F(Tr)/F	—	1392/4IL/ OHC	83/6200	82/4000	5-spd/-
						1597/4IL/ 2OHC	95/6000	99/4000	5-spd/Auto
						1998/4IL/ 2OHC	143/6400	131/4800	5-spd/-
						1974/4IL/ OHC Diesel	74/4800	97/2800	5-spd/-
Sunny GTi-R	N/A	1990–1994	Htch	F/4	—	1998/4IL/ 2OHC	220/6400	196/4800	5-spd/-
Primera	In prod	1990–Date	Sal Htch Est	F(Tr)/F	—	1597/4IL/ 2OHC	95/6000	100/4000	5-spd/-
						1998/4IL/ 2OHC	121/6000	124/4000	5-spd/Auto
							150/6400	133/4800	5-spd/Auto
						1974/4IL/ OHC Diesel	74/4800	97/2800	5-spd/-
100NX	In prod	1990–Date	Spts Cpe	F(Tr)/F	—	1597/4IL/ 2OHC	95/6000	99/4000	5-spd/Auto
							102/6000	100/4000	5-spd/Auto
Serena	In prod	1992–Date	Est	M/R	—	1596/4IL/ 2OHC	97/5600	97/3600	5-spd/-
						1998/4IL/ 2OHC	124/6000	125/4800	5-spd/-
						1952/4IL/ OHC Diesel	67/4600	94/2400	5-spd/-
						2283/4IL/ OHC Diesel	75/4300	107/2300	5-spd/-
200SX	In prod	1993–Date	Spts Cpe	F/R	—	1998/4IL/ 2OHC	197/6400	195/4800	5-spd/Auto
Terrano II	In prod	1993–Date	Ute	F/R	—	2389/4IL/ OHC	123/5200	145/4000	5-spd/-
						2663/4IL/ OHV Diesel	100/4000	163/2200	5-spd/-
300ZX	In prod	1989–Date	Spts Cpe Spts	F/R	—	2960/V6/ 2OHC	280/6400	274/3600	5-spd/Auto
Almera	In prod	1994–Date	Sal Htch	F(Tr)/F	—	1392/4IL/ 2OHC	87/6000	86/4000	5-spd/-
						1596/4IL/ 2OHC	98/6000	100/4000	5-spd/Auto
						1974/4IL/ Diesel	76/4800	98/2800	5-spd/-
QX	In prod	1994–Date	Sal	F(Tr)F	—	1995/V6/ 2OHC	138/6400	131/4000	5-spd/Auto
						2988/V6/ 2OHC	190/6400	188/4000	5-spd/Auto
NSU									
Prinz 4	570,000	1961–1973	Sal	R(Tr)/R	—	598/2IL/ OHC AirC	30/5700	33/3250	4-spd/-
1000/TT/TTS	261,691	1964–1972	Sal	R(Tr)/R	—	996/4IL/ OHC AirC	43/5500	53/2000	4-spd/-
							55/5800	59/2500	4-spd/-
							70/6150	62/4500	4-spd/-
110/110S/	230,688	1965–1973	Sal	R(Tr)/R	—	1085/4IL/	53/5000	58/2500	4-spd/-

Suspension Front	Rear	Steering	Brakes (Front/rear)	Wheels/Tyres	Length (in)	Weight (lb,unladen)	Performance Top speed (mph)	0–60mph (sec)	Standing 1/4-mile (sec)	UK Total Price (£: at Launch)
Beam1/2E	Beam1/2E	Worm	Disc/drum	205-16	185	3881	93 (Claimed)	N/A	N/A	£8994
BeamC	BeamC	Worm	Disc/disc	265/70-16	167/189	4608	106 (Claimed)	14.3	N/A	£20,553
BeamC	BeamC	Worm	Disc/disc	215-16	167/189	4046/4156	90 (Claimed)	N/A	N/A	£14,278
Beam1/2E	Beam1/2E	Worm	Disc/drum	205-16	185	4450	80	N/A	N/A	£9747
BeamC	BeamC	Worm	Disc/disc	205-16	167/189	4234/4432	87 (Claimed)	20.7	N/A	£17,995
IC	IC	R & P	Disc/disc	195/70-14	179	3055	137 (Est)	N/A	N/A	£13,349
IC	IC	R & P	Disc/disc	205/55-16/ 225/55-16	179	3200	141	6.8	15.4	£16,996
IC	IC	R & P	Disc/disc	225/50-16	181	3266	143	7.0	15.5	£20,875
IC	IC	R & P	Disc/disc	195/60-15	174	2453	124	7.9	16.2	£8994
IC	IC	R & P	Disc/disc	195/60-15	174	2536	127 (Est)	N/A	N/A	£9395
IC	IC	R & P	Disc/disc	195/60-15	179	2703	140	7.2	15.3	£16,996
IC	IC	R & P	Disc/disc	195/60-15	179	2752	140	6.8	15.3	£17,500
IC	IC	R & P	Disc/disc	205/65-15	188	3042	119	9.4	16.8	£20,500
IC	BeamC	R & P	Disc/drum	155/70-13	145	1852	88	15.0	20.0	£6695
IC	BeamC	R & P	Disc/drum	155/70-13	145	1874	99	12.7	19.2	£7970
IC	IC	R & P	Disc/drum	155-13	157	2051	105 (Claimed)	N/A	N/A	£8849
IC	IC	R & P	Disc/drum	175/65-14	157	2335	112	10.5	17.9	£12,634
IC	IC	R & P	Disc/disc	195/55-14	157	2447	131	7.5	16.0	£14,950
IC	IC	R & P	Disc/drum	175/65-14	157	2249	99 (Claimed)	N/A	N/A	£10595
IC	IC	R & P	Disc/disc	199/55-14	151	2756	134	6.1	15.1	£20,553
IC	IC	R & P	Disc/drum	165-13	173	2508	112	12.4	18.3	£9995
IC	IC	R & P	Disc/disc	185/60-14	173	2370	121	8.9	16.9	£11,790
IC	IC	R & P	Disc/disc	195/60-14	173	2797	130	8.7	17.9	£16,997
IC	IC	R & P	Disc/drum	165-13	173	2546	103 (Claimed)	16.8 (Claimed)	N/A	£12,130
IC	IC	R & P	Disc/drum	175/65-14	163	2269	114	10.1	17.7	£15,023
IC	IC	R & P	Disc/drum	175/65-14	163	2390	114	9.8	17.5	£12,995
IC	IC	R & P	Disc/drum	175/65-14	170	3043	93 (Claimed)	18.0	N/A	£13,225
IC	IC	R & P	Disc/drum	195/70-14	170	3307	104	11.3	18.7	£17,750
IC	IC	R & P	Disc/drum	195/70-14	170	2955	81 (Claimed)	N/A	N/A	£13,225
IC	IC	R & P	Disc/drum	195/70-14	170	2955	84 (Claimed)	26.5	N/A	£13,415
IC	IC	R & P	Disc/disc	205/55-16	178	2734	146	6.4	15.0	£19,250
ITor	BeamC	R & P	Disc/drum	215-15	162/ 181	3616/ 3859	(SWB) 99	12.3	N/A	£18,275
ITor	BeamC	R & P	Disc/drum	215-15	162/ 181	3616/ 3859	90 (Claimed)	19.0	N/A	£15,175
IC	IC	R & P	Disc/disc	225/50-16/	178	3485	155	5.6	14.4	£34,600
IC	IC	R & P	Disc/drum	175/70-13	162	2459	103	11.8	18.5	£9,295
IC	IC	R & P	Disc/disc	185/65-14	162	2461	113	11.1	18.2	£11,495
IC	IC	R & P	Disc/drum	185/65-14	162	2359	99 (Claimed)	N/A	N/A	£11,495
IC	IC	R & P	Disc/disc	205/65-15	188	3005	120	9.9	17.5	£16,495
IC	IC	R & P	Disc/disc	205/65-15	188	3228	127	8.4	16.5	£21,995
IC	IC	R & P	Drum/drum	4.80-12	135	1246	71	32.2	23.7	£729
IC	IC	R & P	Drum/drum	5.50-12	149	1365	80	20.5	21.2	£673
IC	IC	R & P	Disc/disc	135-13	149	1365	95	15.1	19.5	£824
IC	IC	R & P	Disc/drum	135-13	149	1465	95 (Est)	12.8	18.7	£1036
IC	IC	R & P	Disc/drum	155-13	158	1584	87	18.4	21.0	£770

Make and model	Production Figures	Years Built	Body Styles	Mechanical Layout	Engine Make (if not own)	Capacity/(cc)/Layout/Valves	BHP/rpm	Torque (lb.ft)/rpm	Transmission gearbox/automatic transmission
1200C						OHC AirC			
						1177/4IL/ OHC AirC	55/5200	61/3500	4-spd/-
Ro80	37,204	1968–1977	Sal	F/F	—	1990/2Rotor Wankel	115/5500	121/4500	3-spd/-
Opel									
Kadett	2,311,389	1962–1973	Sal	F/R	—	1078/4IL/ OHV	45/5000	55/2800	4-spd/Auto
			Est				55/5400	60/2400	4-spd/Auto
			Cpe				60/5200	62/3800	4-spd/Auto
						1196/4IL/ OHV	60/5400	70/3900	4-spd/Auto
						1897/4IL/ OHC	90/5100	108/2800	4-spd/-
Rekord	1,280,000	1966–1971	Sal	F/R	—	1492/4IL/ OHC	58/4800	76/2500	3-spd/4-spd/-
			Cpe						
			Est			1698/4IL/ OHC	75/5200	94/2500	3-spd/4-spd/Auto
							60/4600	85/2300	
						1897/4IL/ OHC	90/5100	108/2800	4-spd/Auto
							106/5800	116/3500	4-spd/Auto
Commodore	156,330	1967–1971	Sal	F/R	—	2490/6IL/ OHC	115/5200	128/3800	4-spd/Auto
			Cpe				130/5300	138/4000	4-spd/Auto
GT 1900	103,373	1968–1973	Cpe	F/R	—	1897/4IL/ OHC	90/5100	108/2800	4-spd/-
Manta	498,553	1970–1975	Cpe	F/R	—	1584/4IL/ OHC	80/5200	95/4200	4-spd/Auto
						1897/4IL/ OHC	90/5100	108/2800	4-spd/Auto
							156/5500	174/4000	4-spd/Auto
Ascona	641,438	1970–1975	Sal	F/R	—	1584/4IL/ OHC	80/5200	95/4200	4-spd/Auto
			Est						
						1897/4IL/ OHC	90/5100	108/2800	4-spd/Auto
Rekord II	1,128,196	1972–1977	Sal	F/R	—	1897/4IL/ OHC	97/5200	124/3800	4-spd/Auto
			Est						
						1979/4IL/ OHC	100/5200	109/3800	4-spd/Auto
						2068/4IL/ OHV Diesel	60/4400	87/2500	4-spd/-
Commodore	140,827	1972–1977	Sal	F/R	—	2490/6IL/ OHC	115/5200	128/3800	4-spd/Auto
			Cpe				130/5300	138/4000	4-spd/Auto
						2784/6IL/ OHC	142/5200	159/3400	4-spd/Auto
							160/5400	168/4200	Auto/-
Kadett	1,701,075	1973–1979	Sal	F/R	—	993/4IL/ OHV	40/5400	56/3400	4-spd/-
			Cpe						
			Htch			1196/4IL/ OHV	52/5600	58/3400	4-spd/Auto
			Est				60/5600	63/3400	4-spd/Auto
						1897/4IL/ OHC	105/5400	122/4200	5-spd/-
						1979/4IL/ OHC	110/5400	112/3000	4-spd/-
Ascona	1,512,971	1975–1981	Sal	F/R	—	1584/4IL/ OHC	60/5000	76/3000	4-spd/Auto
							75/5000	95/4200	4-spd/Auto
						1897/4IL/ OHC	90/4800	105/3800	4-spd/Auto
						1979/4IL/ OHC	100/5400	114/3800	4-spd/Auto
Manta	603,000	1975–1988	Cpe	F/R	—	1584/4IL/ OHC	75/5000	95/4200	4-spd/Auto
			Htch			1796/4IL/ OHC	90/5400	105/3000	5-spd/Auto
						1897/4IL/ OHC	90/4800	105/3800	4-spd/Auto
						1979/4IL/ OHC	100/5400	114/3800	4-spd/Auto
							110/5400	120/3400	5-spd/-
Ascona 400/Manta 400	448/236	1979–1980 1981–1983	Sal Spts Cpe	F/R	—	2410/4IL/ 2OHC	144/5200	155/3800	5-spd/-
Kadett	2,092,140	1979–1984	Sal	F(Tr)/F	—	1196/4IL/ OHV	53/5400	61/3600	4-spd/-
			Htch			1297/4IL/ OHC	60/5800	69/3600	4-spd/-
			Est				75/5800	75/4600	4-spd/-
						1598/4IL/ OHC			
Rekord	1,362,000	1977–1986	Sal	F/R	—	1979/4IL/ OHC	100/5200	109/3800	4-spd/Auto
			Est			2068/4IL/ OHV Diesel	60/4400	87/2500	4-spd/-
						2260/4IL/ OHV Diesel	65/4200	93/2500	4-spd/Auto
Senator	118,500	1978–1987	Sal	F/R	—	2490/6IL/	136/5600	137/4600	5-spd/Auto

Suspension Front	Rear	Steering	Brakes (Front/rear)	Wheels/Tyres	Length (in)	Weight (lb, unladen)	Top speed (mph)	0–60mph (sec)	Standing 1/4-mile (sec)	UK Total Price (£: at Launch)
IC	IC	R & P	Disc/drum	155-13	158	1579	93	14.8	19.5	£799
IC	IC	R & P	Disc/disc	175-14	190	2688	110	13.1	19.1	£2249
ITrL	BeamC	R & P	Drum/drum	6.00-12	165	1653	75	20.6	21.9	£708
ITrL	BeamC	R & P	Disc/drum	155-13	165	1653	86 (Est)	N/A	N/A	Special Order
ITrL	BeamC	R & P	Disc/drum	155-13	165	1653	88	15.5	20.0	£999
ITrL	BeamC	R & P	Disc/drum	155-13	165	1697	88 (Est)	N/A	N/A	£979
ITrL	BeamC	R & P	Disc/drum	155-13	165	1962	104 (Claimed)	N/A	N/A	£999
IC	BeamC	Worm	Disc/drum	6.40-13	180	2304	83 (Claimed)	N/A	N/A	£1035
IC	BeamC	Worm	Disc/drum	6.40-13	180	2304	92 (Claimed)	N/A	N/A	£N/A
IC	BeamC	Worm	Disc/drum	6.40-13	180	2380	99	12.3	18.6	£N/A
IC	BeamC	Worm	Disc/drum	165-14	180	2436	105	10.9	17.9	£N/A
IC	BeamC	Worm	Disc/drum	165-14	181	2491	104	11.4	18.5	£1380
IC	BeamC	Worm	Disc/drum	165-14	181	2579	115	12.8	18.6	£N/A
ITrL	BeamC	R & P	Disc/drum	165-13	162	2107	115	12.0	18.6	£1882
IC	BeamC	R & P	Disc/drum	165-13	169	2130	101	12.7	18.9	£1327
IC	BeamC	R & P	Disc/drum	185-13	169	2111	105	12.2	18.2	£1475
IC	BeamC	R & P	Disc/drum	185/70-13	171	2111	125	7.6	15.7	£3500
IC	BeamC	R & P	Disc/drum	165-13	164	2083	93	13.0	18.9	£1263
IC	BeamC	R & P	Disc/drum	185/70-13	164	2135	98	12.5	18.3	£1297
IC	BeamC	Worm	Disc/drum	175-14	180	2403	99	12.3	18.6	£1540
IC	BeamC	Worm	Disc/drum	185/70-14	180	2403	106 (Claimed)	N/A	N/A	£3239
IC	BeamC	Worm	Disc/drum	175-14	180	2773	81	27.4	24.0	£3021
IC	BeamC	Worm	Disc/drum	175-14	180	2645	108 (Est)	N/A	N/A	£1803
IC	BeamC	Worm	Disc/drum	175-14	180	2673	107	12.0	18.6	£1980
IC	BeamC	Worm	Disc/drum	175-14	180	2690	109	10.9	18.3	£2699
IC	BeamC	Worm	Disc/disc	195/70-14	180	2914	115	10.7	17.6	£4288
IC	BeamC	R & P	Drum/drum	6.00-12	162	1687	74	23.3	22.2	£1425
IC	BeamC	R & P	Disc/drum	175-13	162	1697	80	17.0	20.5	£1239
IC	BeamC	R & P	Disc/drum	175-13	162	1775	89	13.0	19.1	£N/A
IC	BeamC	R & P	Disc/drum	175/70-13	162	1877	111	9.6	17.3	£3166
IC	BeamC	R & P	Disc/drum	175/70-13	162	2028	118 (Claimed)	N/A	N/A	£3546
IC	BeamC	R & P	Disc/drum	165-13	173	2138	90 (Est)	N/A	N/A	£1922
IC	BeamC	R & P	Disc/drum	165-13	173	2205	96	13.4	19.1	£2133
IC	BeamC	R & P	Disc/drum	165-13	173	2174	103	11.6	18.3	£2188
IC	BeamC	R & P	Disc/drum	165-13	173	2205	108 (Claimed)	N/A	N/A	£3769
IC	BeamC	R & P	Disc/drum	165-13	173	2138	101 (Claimed)	N/A	N/A	£2370
IC	BeamC	R & P	Disc/drum	185/70-13	175	2352	110	10.2	17.2	£5919
IC	BeamC	R & P	Disc/drum	185/70-13	173	2205	101	12.0	18.7	£2425
IC	BeamC	R & P	Disc/drum	185/70-13	173	2249	112	10.7	N/A	£4517
IC	BeamC	R & P	Disc/drum	195/60-14	175	2305	120	8.5	16.5	£6444
IC	BeamC	R & P	Disc/disc	205/50-15	175	2430	120	7.4	15.5	£10,603
IC	IC	R & P	Disc/drum	145-13	157	1797	89 (Claimed)	N/A	N/A	£3501
IC	IC	R & P	Disc/drum	155-13	157	1819	93 (Est)	N/A	N/A	£3330
IC	IC	R & P	Disc/drum	175/60-13	157	1895	101	14.2	19.6	£3544
IC	BeamC	Worm	Disc/drum	185-14	171	2497	104	11.0	18.2	£4061
IC	BeamC	Worm	Disc/drum	175-14	171	2497	85 (Claimed)	N/A	N/A	£4382
IC	BeamC	Worm	Disc/drum	175-14	171	2767	87 (Claimed)	N/A	N/A	£5382
IC	IC	Worm	Disc/disc	195/70-14	189	3076	122	9.6	17.4	£10,374

Make and model	Production Figures	Years Built	Body Styles	Mechanical Layout	Engine Make (if not own)	Capacity/ (cc)/Layout/ Valves	BHP/ rpm	Torque (lb.ft)/rpm	Transmission gearbox/automatic transmission
						OHC			
						2786/6IL/	140/5200	158/3600	4-spd/Auto
						OHC			
						2968/6IL/	150/5200	170/3400	4-spd/Auto
						OHC	180/5800	179/4800	Auto/-
Monza	43,500	1978–1987	Cpe	F/R	—	2968/6IL/	180/5800	179/4800	4-spd/5-spd/Auto
						OHC			
Commodore	N/A	1978–1983	Sal	F/R	—	2490/6IL/	115/5200	130/4000	4-spd/Auto
						OHC			

Panther

Make and model	Production Figures	Years Built	Body Styles	Mechanical Layout	Engine Make (if not own)	Capacity/ (cc)/Layout/ Valves	BHP/ rpm	Torque (lb.ft)/rpm	Transmission gearbox/automatic transmission
J72/ Brooklands	300	1972–1981	Spts	F/R	Jaguar	3781/6IL/ 2OHC	190/5000	200/3000	4-spd (+O/D)/-
						4235/6IL/ 2OHC	190/5000	200/2000	4-spd (+O/D)/Auto
						5343/V12/ OHC	266/5750	304/3500	4-spd (+O/D)/Auto
FF	12	1974–1975	Spts	F/R	Ferrari	3967/V12/ OHC	300/7000	288/5000	5-spd/-
Deville	60	1974–1985	Sal Conv	F/R	Jaguar	4235/6IL/ 2OHC	190/5000	200/2000	4-spd (+O/D)/Auto
						5343/V12/ 2OHC	266/5750	304/3500	Auto/-
Lima	897	1976–1982	Spts	F/R	Vauxhall	1759/4IL/ OHC	96/5200	99/3500	4-spd/Auto
						2279/4IL/ OHC	108/5000	138/3000	4-spd/Auto
Kallista	N/A	1982–1990	Spts	F/R	Ford	1596/4IL/ OHC	96/6000	98/4000	4-spd/5-spd/-
						2792/V6/ OHV	135/5200	162/3000	5-spd/-
							150/5700	159/4000	5-spd/-
						2933/V6/ OHV	150/5700	171/3000	5-spd/-
Solo	12	1989–1990	Spts Cpe	M/4	—	1993/4IL/ 2OHC	204/6000	198/4500	5-spd/-

Peugeot

Make and model	Production Figures	Years Built	Body Styles	Mechanical Layout	Engine Make (if not own)	Capacity/ (cc)/Layout/ Valves	BHP/ rpm	Torque (lb.ft)/rpm	Transmission gearbox/automatic transmission
404	2,416,733 (Incl. Coupe/ Cabriolet)	1960–1975	Sal Est	F/R	—	1618/4IL/ OHV	72/5400	94/2250	4-spd/-
							88/5500	101/2800	4-spd/-
							80/5400	94/2250	4-spd/-
						1948/4IL/ OHV Diesel	55/4500	88/2250	4-spd/-
204	1,604,296 (Incl. Coupe/ Cabriolet)	1965–1977	Sal Est	F(Tr)/F	—	1130/4IL/ OHC	53/5800	61/3000	4-spd/-
204/304 Coupe/Cabriolet	60,937	1966–1975	Cpe Conv	F(Tr)/F	—	1130/4IL/ OHC	53/5800	61/3000	4-spd/-
						1288/4IL/ OHC	65/5750	69/3750	4-spd/-
							69/5800	78/3750	4-spd/-
							74/6000	74/4500	4-spd/-
304	1,178,425	1969–1980	Sal Est Cpe	F(Tr)/F	—	1288/4IL/ OHC	65/6000	69/3750	4-spd/-
							69/5800	78/3750	4-spd/-
504	3,173,191	1968–1989	Sal Est Cpe Conv	F/R	—	1796/4IL/ OHV	82/5500	108/3000	4-spd/Auto
							97/5600	114/3000	4-spd/Auto
							79/5100	105/2500	4-spd/Auto
						1971/4IL/ OHV	87/5000	118/3000	4-spd/Auto
							93/5200	118/3000	4-spd/Auto
							97/5000	124/3000	4-spd/Auto
							106/5200	124/3000	4-spd/Auto
						1948/4IL/ OHV Diesel	56/4500	80/2000	4-spd/-
						2112/4IL/ OHV Diesel	59/4500	86/2500	4-spd/-
						2304/4IL/ OHV Diesel	64/4500	95/2000	4-spd/-
504 V6 Coupe/ Cabriolet	(Incl. in 504 figs)	1974–1983	Cpe Conv	F/R	—	2664/V6/ OHC	136/5750	153/3500	4-spd/Auto
							144/5500	159/3750	4-spd/Auto
104	1,731,186	1972–1988	Sal Htch	F(Tr)/F	—	954/4IL/ OHC	50/6250	54/3000	4-spd/-
						1124/4IL/ OHC	57/6000	59/3000	4-spd/5-spd/-
						1219/4IL/ OHC	57/5500	68/2750	4-spd/-
						1360/4IL/ OHC	72/6000	70/3000	4-spd/5-spd/-
104ZS/ 104ZL	(Incl. in 104 figs)	1975–1985	Cpe	F(Tr)/F	—	954/4IL/ OHC	44/6000	45/3000	4-spd/-

Suspension Front	Rear	Steering	Brakes (Front/rear)	Wheels/ Tyres	Length (in)	Weight (lb, unladen)	Top speed (mph)	0–60mph (sec)	Standing ¼-mile (sec)	UK Total Price (£: at Launch)
IC	IC	Worm	Disc/disc	175-14	189	3021	118 (Claimed)	N/A	N/A	£8887
IC	IC	Worm	Disc/disc	195/70-14	189	2923	116	9.7	16.9	£10,021
IC	IC	Worm	Disc/disc	195/70-14	189	3080	119	9.2	17.0	£9500
IC	IC	Worm	Disc/disc	205/60-15	185	3025	133	8.5	16.5	£9762
IC	IC	Worm	Disc/drum	195/70-14	181	2640	109	12.2	18.7	£7714
BeamC	BeamC	Worm	Disc/disc	E70-15	160	2504	114	6.4	15.3	£4380
BeamC	BeamC (Later IC)	Worm	Disc/disc	E70-15	160	2504	114	6.4	N/A	£5285
BeamC	BeamC (Later IC)	Worm	Disc/disc	ER70-15	160	2504	136 (Claimed)	N/A	N/A	£9500
IC	BeamC	R & P	Disc/disc	205-14	154	2100	N/A	N/A	N/A	Special Order
IC	IC	R & P	Disc/disc	235/70-15	204	4264	127 (Claimed)	N/A	N/A	£21,965
IC	IC	R & P	Disc/disc	235/70-15	204	4368	137 (Claimed)	N/A	N/A	£17,650
IC	BeamC	R & P	Disc/drum	165-13	142	1800	107 (Est)	N/A	N/A	£8997
IC	BeamC	R & P	Disc/drum	185/70-13	142	1950	115	6.7	15.1	£4998
IC	BeamC	R & P	Disc/drum	165-13	154	1962	92	12.6	18.0	£5850
IC	BeamC	R & P	Disc/drum	195/60-14	154	2035	111	7.9	15.9	£6995
IC	BeamC	R & P	Disc/drum	195/60-14	154	2061	109	7.7	16.3	£9625
IC	BeamC	R & P	Disc/drum	175/70-14	154	2061	112	7.6	15.8	£11,950
IC	IC	R & P	Disc/disc	195/50-15/ 205/50-15	171	2723	144	6.8	15.3	£39,850
IC	BeamC	R & P	Drum/drum	165-380	174	2296	84	22.0	21.9	£1297
IC	BeamC	R & P	Drum/drum	165-380	174	2415	100	13.9	18.8	£1495
IC	BeamC	R & P	Drum/drum	6.40-14	174	2300	92 (Est)	N/A	N/A	£1112
IC	BeamC	R & P	Drum/drum	165-380	174	2420	81	25.4	23.1	£1396
IC	IC	R & P	Disc/drum	145-14	156	1874	86	18.1	21.1	£992
IC	IC	R & P	Disc/drum	145-14	148	1960	88	19.9	21.5	£983
IC	IC	R & P	Disc/drum	145-14	148	2015	94 (Est)	N/A	N/A	£1496
IC	IC	R & P	Disc/drum	145-14	148	2052	98	14.7	19.5	£1638
IC	IC	R & P	Disc/drum	145-14	148	2052	100 (Est)	N/A	N/A	£2218
IC	IC	R & P	Disc/drum	145-14	163	2017	93	14.9	20.0	£1195
IC	IC	R & P	Disc/drum	145-14	163	2017	96	14.5	19.6	£1466
IC	IC	R & P	Disc/disc	175-14	177	2645	95	13.2	19.0	£1500
IC	IC	R & P	Disc/disc	175-14	177	2600	106	12.6	18.7	£1676
IC	BeamC	R & P	Disc/drum	165-14	177	2469	96	13.4	18.9	£2609
IC	IC	R & P	Disc/disc	175-14	177	2722	99	12.7	19.1	£1594
IC	IC	R & P	Disc/disc	175-14	177	2667	100	12.0	18.7	£1926
IC	IC	R & P	Disc/disc	175-14	177	2722	103	12.4	18.9	£1705
IC	IC	R & P	Disc/disc	175-14	177	2666	104	11.4	18.3	£2115
IC	BeamC	R & P	Disc/drum	165-14	177	2607	84	21.7	22.4	£2361
IC	BeamC	R & P	Disc/drum	185-14	177	2866	78 (Claimed)	N/A	N/A	£4550
IC	IC	R & P	Disc/drum	175-14	177	2866	87 (Claimed)	N/A	N/A	£4472
IC	IC	R & P	Disc/disc	175-14	172	3065	110 (Est)	N/A	N/A	Special order
IC	IC	R & P	Disc/disc	175-14	172	3065	115 (Est)	N/A	N/A	Special order
IC	IC	R & P	Disc/drum	135-13	141	1674	84	18.5	20.3	£1194
IC	IC	R & P	Disc/drum	145-13	141	1781	89	14.0	19.3	£2189
IC	IC	R & P	Disc/drum	145-13	142	1834	89	14.1	19.4	£3491
IC	IC	R & P	Disc/drum	165/70-13	142	1860	100 (Est)	N/A	N/A	£3934
IC	IC	R & P	Disc/drum	135-13	130	1631	84	17.1	20.3	£2259

Make and model	Production Figures	Years Built	Body Styles	Mechanical Layout	Engine Make (if not own)	Capacity/ (cc)/Layout/ Valves	BHP/ rpm	Torque (lb.ft)/rpm	Transmission gearbox/automatic transmission
						1124/4IL/ OHC	66/6200	62/4000	4-spd/-
						1360/4IL/ OHC	72/6000	70/3000	4-spd/5-spd/-
604	165,243	1975–1986	Sal	F/R	—	2664/V6/ OHC	136/5750 144/5500	153/3500 159/3750	4-spd/Auto 5-spd/Auto
						2849/V6/ OHC	155/5750	175/3000	Auto/-
						2304/4IL/ OHV Diesel	80/4150	136/2000	5-spd/Auto
						2498/4IL/ OHV Diesel	94/4150	152/2000	5-spd/-
305	N/A	1977–1988	Sal Est	F(Tr)/F	—	1290/4IL/ OHC	65/6000	69/3750	4-spd/-
						1472/4IL/ OHC	74/5700 89/6000	83/3000 92/3000	4-spd/- 4-spd/Auto
						1580/4IL/ OHC	93/6000	99/3750	5-spd/Auto
						1905/4IL/ OHC	105/5600	119/3000	5-spd/-
						1548/4IL/ OHC Diesel	49/5000	62/2500	5-spd/-
						1905/4IL/ OHC Diesel	64/4600	88/2000	4-spd/5-spd/-
505	In prod	1979–Date	Sal Est	F/R	—	1796/4IL/ OHV	90/5250	106/2750	5-spd/-
						1971/4IL/ OHV	96/5200 99/5000	119/3000 119/3000	4-spd/5-spd/Auto 4-spd/5-spd/Auto
						1995/4IL/ OHC	110/5250	126/4000	5-spd/Auto
						2165/4IL/ OHC	125/5750	139/4250	5-spd/Auto
						2849/V6/ OHC	170/6000	174/4250	5-spd/Auto
						2304/4IL/ OHV Diesel	70/4500	97/2000	4-spd/-
						2498/4IL/ OHV Diesel	76/4500	15.3/2000	5-spd/-
205	In prod	1983–Date	Htch Conv	F(Tr)/F	—	954/4IL/ OHC	45/6000	51/2750	4-spd/-
						1124/4IL/ OHC	50/4800 55/5800	63/2800 66/3200	4-spd/- 4-spd/-
						1360/4IL/ OHC	60/5000 65/5400 80/5800 85/6400	79/2500 83/3000 81/2800 85/4000	5-spd/- 5-spd/- 5-spd/- 5-spd/-
						1580/4IL/ OHC	105/6250 115/6250	99/4000 98/4000	5-spd/- 5-spd/-
						1905/4IL/ OHC	130/6000	119/4750	5-spd/-
						1769/4IL/ OHC Diesel	60/4600 78/4300	80/2000 116/2100	4-spd/5-spd/- 5-spd/-
309	837,520	1986–1993	Htch	F(Tr)/F	—	1118/4IL/ OHC	55/6000	65/3000	4-spd/5-spd/-
						1124/4IL/ OHC	60/5800	65/3200	5-spd/-
						1294/4IL/ OHC	65/5600	76/2800	5-spd/-
						1580/4IL/ OHC	80/5600 115/6250	98/2800 98/4000	5-spd/- 5-spd/-
						1905/4IL/ OHC	130/6000	119/4750	5-spd/-
						1769/4IL/ OHC Diesel	78/4300	116/2100	5-spd/-
						1905/4IL/ OHC Diesel	65/4600	88/2000	5-spd/-
405	In prod	1987–Date	Sal Est	F(Tr)/F	—	1580/4IL/ OHC	92/6000	99/2600	5-spd/-
						1761/4IL/ OHC	103/6000	113/3000	5-spd/Auto
						1905/4IL/ OHC	110/6000 125/5500	119/3000 129/4500	5-spd/Auto 5-spd/Auto
						1905/4IL/ 2OHC	160/6500	133/5000	5-spd/-
				F(Tr)/4	—	1905/4IL/ OHC	110/6000	119/3000	5-spd/Auto
				F(Tr)/4	—	1905/4IL/ 2OHC	160/6500	133/5000	5-spd/-
				F(Tr)/F	—	1998/4IL/ OHC	123/5750	132/2750	5-spd/Auto

Suspension Front	Suspension Rear	Steering	Brakes (Front/rear)	Wheels/Tyres	Length (in)	Weight (lb, unladen)	Top speed (mph)	0–60mph (sec)	Standing 1/4-mile (sec)	UK Total Price (£: at Launch)
IC	IC	R & P	Disc/drum	145-13	130	1709	96	13.6	19.2	£2259
IC	IC	R & P	Disc/drum	165/70-13	133	1932	96	11.8	18.4	£3939
IC	IC	R & P	Disc/disc	175-14	186	3111	113	9.4	17.1	£4600
IC	IC	R & P	Disc/disc	175-14	186	3252	115 (Est)	N/A	N/A	£8522
IC	IC	R & P	Disc/disc	205/60-15	186	3131	118 (Claimed)	N/A	N/A	£12,495
IC	IC	R & P	Disc/disc	175-14	186	3168	94	17.0	20.9	£9508
IC	IC	R & P	Disc/disc	205/60-15	186	3230	102 (Claimed)	N/A	N/A	£11,695
IC	IC	R & P	Disc/drum	145-14	167	2039	90	14.4	19.8	£2999
IC	IC	R & P	Disc/drum	145-14	167	2100	100	12.7	18.8	£3599
IC	IC	R & P	Disc/drum	165/70-14	167	2156	95	12.8	18.5	£5495
IC	IC	R & P	Disc/drum	165/70-14	167	2150	101	11.1	18.1	£6145
IC	IC	R & P	Disc/drum	185/60-14	167	2166	110	9.5	17.1	£7445
IC	IC	R & P	Disc/drum	145-14	167	2039	83	21.4	21.9	£4251
IC	IC	R & P	Disc/drum	155-14	167	2227	93	16.8	20.9	£5495
IC	IC	R & P	Disc/disc	175-14	180	2679	100 (Claimed)	N/A	N/A	£8485
IC	IC	R & P	Disc/disc	175-14	180	2600	102 (Est)	N/A	N/A	£5781
IC	IC	R & P	Disc/disc	175-14	180	2646	104 (Est)	N/A	N/A	£6995
IC	IC	R & P	Disc/disc	185-14	180	2737	105	10.8	17.3	£6820
IC	IC	R & P	Disc/disc	190/65-390	180	2905	111	10.1	17.6	£9595
IC	IC	R & P	Disc/disc	195/60-15	180	3049	121	9.3	17.0	£15,150
IC	IC	R & P	Disc/disc	175-14	180	2800	88 (Claimed)	N/A	N/A	£7013
IC	IC	R & P	Disc/disc	175-14	180	2855	93 (Est)	N/A	N/A	£7879
IC	ITor	R & P	Disc/drum	135-13	146	1628	83 (Claimed)	N/A	N/A	£3895
IC	ITor	R & P	Disc/drum	135-13	146	1639	85	16.1	20.3	£4395
IC	ITor	R & P	Disc/drum	145-13	146	1742	97	13.3	19.4	£6625
IC	ITor	R & P	Disc/drum	165/70-13	146	1759	96	12.5	19.0	£4995
IC	ITor	R & P	Disc/drum	165/70-13	146	1918	100	11.7	18.4	£7045
IC	ITor	R & P	Disc/drum	165/70-13	146	1828	98	11.3	17.9	£5395
IC	ITor	R & P	Disc/drum	165/70-13	146	1797	106	9.4	17.2	£7195
IC	ITor	R & P	Disc/drum	165/70-13	146	2004	116	8.6	16.6	£6295
IC	ITor	R & P	Disc/drum	185/60-14	146	1953	122	8.7	17.4	£7490
IC	ITor	R & P	Disc/disc	185/55-15	146	2006	120	7.8	16.3	£9295
IC	ITor	R & P	Disc/drum	145-13	146	1973	94	14.6	19.7	£4,745
IC	ITor	R & P	Disc/drum	165/70-13	146	2093	103	12.3	18.9	£10,475
IC	ITor	R & P	Disc/drum	145-13	159	1874	89	16.6	20.7	£4995
IC	ITor	R & P	Disc/drum	165/70-13	159	1841	94 (Claimed)	N/A	N/A	£7850
IC	ITor	R & P	Disc/drum	165/70-13	159	1938	93	16.5	20.6	£5715
IC	ITor	R & P	Disc/drum	165/70-13	159	1980	96	12.9	19.0	£6835
IC	ITor	R & P	Disc/drum	175/65-14	159	2026	116	9.7	17.9	£8495
IC	ITor	R & P	Disc/disc	185/55-15	159	2166	122	8.8	16.5	£9595
IC	ITor	R & P	Disc/drum	175/65-14	159	2183	104	12.8	19.2	£11,125
IC	ITor	R & P	Disc/drum	165/70-13	159	2071	99	14.8	19.7	£7435
IC	IC	R & P	Disc/drum	165/70-14	174	2244	108	10.9	18.1	£8245
IC	IC	R & P	Disc/drum	175/70-14	174	2445	112	10.6	18.0	£13,190
IC	IC	R & P	Disc/drum	175/70-14	174	2244	115	10.9	18.0	£8695
IC	IC	R & P	Disc/drum	185/65-14	174	2288	116	10.3	17.9	£10455
IC	IC	R & P	Disc/disc	195/60-14	174	2533	132	8.0	16.3	£14,995
IC	IC	R & P	Disc/drum	185/65-14	174	2288	119 (Auto)	11.9	18.8	£11,740
IC	IC	R & P	Disc/disc	195/55-15	174	2844	127	9.5	17.1	£17,995
IC	IC	R & P	Disc/drum	185/65-14	174	2492	123	9.6	17.2	£12,960

Make and model	Production Figures	Years Built	Body Styles	Mechanical Layout	Engine Make (if not own)	Capacity/(cc)/Layout/Valves	BHP/rpm	Torque (lb.ft)/rpm	Transmission gearbox/automatic transmission
						1998/4IL/2OHC	150/6500	135/3500	5-spd/Auto
							200/6500	212/4500	5-spd/-
						1769/4IL/OHC Diesel	92/4300	132/2200	5-spd/-
						1905/4IL/OHC Diesel	70/4600	88/2000	5-spd/-
605	In prod	1989–Date	Sal	F(Tr)/F	—	1998/4IL/OHC	123/5600	126/4000	5-spd/Auto
							130/5600	128/4800	5-spd/Auto
							150/5300	177/2500	5-spd/Auto
						2975/V6/OHC	170/5600	173/4650	5-spd/Auto
							200/6000	191/3600	5-spd/-
						2088/4IL/OHC Diesel	110/4300	177/2000	5-spd/-
106	In prod	1991–Date	Htch	F(Tr)/F	—	954/4IL/OHC	45/5200	52/3200	4/spd/-
						1124/4IL/OHC	60/5800	65/3200	4-spd/5-spd/-
						1294/4IL/OHC	100/7200	80/5400	5-spd/-
						1360/4IL/OHC	75/5800	84/3800	5-spd/-
							100/6800	89/4200	5-spd/-
						1580/4IL/OHC	105/6200	101/3500	5-spd/-
						1360/4IL/OHC Diesel	50/5000	61/2500	5-spd/-
						1527/4IL/OHC Diesel	57/5000	70/2500	5-spd/-
306	In prod	1993–Date	Htch Sal Conv	F(Tr)/F	—	1360/4IL/OHC	75/5800	80/3400	5-spd/-
						1587/4IL/OHC	90/5600	98/3000	5-spd/-
						1761/4IL/OHC	102/6000	111/3000	5-spd/Auto
						1998/4IL/OHC	123/5750	130/2750	5-spd/-
						1998/4IL/2OHC	155/6500	134/3500	5-spd/-
						1905/4IL/OHC Diesel	92/4000	145/2250	5-spd/-
806	In prod	1995–Date	Est	F(Tr)/F	—	1998/4IL/Petrol	69/4600	88/2000	5-spd/-
							123/5750	127/2650	5-spd/-
						1905/4IL/OHC Diesel	92/4000	145/2250	5-spd/-
406	In prod	1995–Date	Sal	F(Tr)/F	—	1761/4IL/2OHC	112/5500	116/4250	5-spd/-
						1998/4IL/2OHC	135/5500	135/4200	5-spd/-
						1905/4IL/OHC Diesel	90/4000	148/2250	5-spd/-
						2088/4IL/OHC Diesel	110/4300	188/2000	5-spd/-

Polski-Fiat, See **FSO**, above

Pontiac

Make and model	Production Figures	Years Built	Body Styles	Mechanical Layout	Engine Make (if not own)	Capacity/(cc)/Layout/Valves	BHP/rpm	Torque (lb.ft)/rpm	Transmission gearbox/automatic transmission
Firebird **	—	1971 model	Cpe	F/R	—	6560/V8/OHV	330/4800	430/3000	Auto
Firebird ** Trans-Am	—	1978 model	Cpe	F/R	—	6609/V8/OHV	185/3600	320/2200	Auto

Porsche

Make and model	Production Figures	Years Built	Body Styles	Mechanical Layout	Engine Make (if not own)	Capacity/(cc)/Layout/Valves	BHP/rpm	Torque (lb.ft)/rpm	Transmission gearbox/automatic transmission
911	305,395	1964–1989	Cpe Targa Conv	R/R	—	1991/6HO/OHC AirC	110/5800	115/4200	5-spd/-
							130/6100	130/4200	5-spd/-
							140/6500	130/4500	5-spd/-
							160/6600	133/5200	5-spd/-
							170/6800	135/5500	5-spd/-
						2195/6HO/OHC AirC	125/5800	131/4200	5-spd/SemiAuto
							155/6200	141/4500	5-spd/SemiAuto
							180/6500	147/5200	5-spd/SemiAuto
						2341/6HO/OHC AirC	130/5600	145/4000	5-spd/SemiAuto
							165/6200	152/4500	5-spd/SemiAuto
							190/6500	159/5200	5-spd/SemiAuto
						2687/6HO/OHC AirC	150/5700	174/3800	5-spd/SemiAuto
							165/5800	166/4000	5-spd/SemiAuto
							175/5800	174/4000	5-spd/SemiAuto
							210/6300	188/5100	5-spd/SemiAuto
						2994/6HO/OHC AirC	165/5800	174/4000	5-spd/SemiAuto
							188/5500	195/4300	5-spd/SemiAuto

Suspension Front	Rear	Steering	Brakes (Front/rear)	Wheels/ Tyres	Length (in)	Weight (lb, unladen)	Performance Top speed (mph)	0–60mph (sec)	Standing ¼-mile (sec)	UK Total Price (£: at Launch)
IC	IC	R & P	Disc/disc	195/55-15	174	2596	134 (Est)	N/A	N/A	£16,315
IC	IC	R & P	Disc/disc	205/50-16	174	2948	146 (Est)	N/A	N/A	£22,500
IC	IC	R & P	Disc/drum	185/65-14	174	2948	108	12.2	18.6	£13,195
IC	IC	R & P	Disc/drum	165/70-14	174	2486	99	15.4	20.8	£9945
IC	IC	R & P	Disc/disc	195/65-15	186	3077	121	11.8	18.2	£16,660
IC	IC	R & P	Disc/disc	195/65-15	186	2919	126 (Est)	10.9	N/A	£18,420
IC	IC	R & P	Disc/disc	205/60-15	186	3274	132 (Est)	10.8	N/A	£19,565
IC	IC	R & P	Disc/disc	205/60-15	186	3117	131	10.6	17.5	£22,500
IC	IC	R & P	Disc/disc	205/55-16	186	3491	142	7.9	16.3	£27,097
IC	IC	R & P	Disc/disc	205/60-15	186	3289	114	12.8	19.3	£19,820
IC	ITor	R & P	Disc/drum	155/70-13	140	1676	93 (Claimed)	19.0	N/A	£6195
IC	ITor	R & P	Disc/drum	145/70-13	140	1740	97	13.8	19.5	£6800
IC	ITor	R & P	Disc/drum	195/55-15	140	1786	118 (Claimed)	9.3	N/A	£9095
IC	ITor	R & P	Disc/drum	155/70-13	140	1804	109	11.0	18.5	£9150
IC	ITor	R & P	Disc/drum	175/60-14	140	1892	117	9.7	17.5	£10,395
IC	ITor	R & P	Disc/drum	175/60-14	140	1985	117	9.7	17.3	£10,995
IC	ITor	R & P	Disc/drum	155/70-13	140	1857	85	17.9	21.2	£7595
IC	ITor	R & P	Disc/drum	155/70-13	140	1940	96 (Claimed)	16.9	N/A	£7645
IC	ITor	R & P	Disc/drum	165/70-13	157	2249	103	12.9	19.1	£9995
IC	ITor	R & P	Disc/drum	175/50-13	157	2337	112	11.5	18.3	£10,245
IC	ITor	R & P	Disc/drum	175/65-14	157	2381	114	10.2	17.5	£12,500
IC	ITor	R & P	Disc/disc	195/55-15	157	2557	119	9.8	17.4	£12,695
IC	ITor	R & P	Disc/disc	195/55-15	157	2557	129	8.1	16.3	£15,090
IC	ITor	R & P	Disc/drum	175/65-14	157	2535	106	11.2	18.2	£12,145
IC	ITor	R & P	Disc/drum	165/70-13	157	2381	101 (Est)	16.9	N/A	£9345
IC	IC	R & P	Disc/drum	195/65-15	175	3330	110 (Claimed)	13.7	N/A	£16,450
IC	IC	R & P	Disc/drum	195/65-15	175	3451	99 (Claimed)	15.5	N/A	£17,450
IC	IC	R & P	Disc/disc	185/70-14	179	2677	117	11.5	18.4	£12,595
IC	IC	R & P	Disc/disc	195/65-15	179	3110	121	10.7	18.1	£13,995
IC	IC	R & P	Disc/drum	195/65-15	179	2944	111 (Claimed)	N/A	N/A	£14,345
IC	IC	R & P	Disc/disc	195/65-15	179	3120	118 (Claimed)	N/A	N/A	£N/A
IC	Beam1/2E	Worm	Disc/drum	F70-14	191	3685	131	6.5	14.8	£3817
IC	Beam1/2E	Worm	Disc/drum	GR70-15	197	3812	118	9.4	16.4	£8014
ITor	ITor	R & P	Disc/disc	165-15	164	2200	124 (Est)	N/A	N/A	£2745
ITor	ITor	R & P	Disc/disc	165-15	164	2200	130	8.3	16.1	£2996
ITor	ITor	R & P	Disc/disc	165-15	164	2200	130	9.8	17.0	£3992
ITor	ITor	R & P	Disc/disc	165-15	164	2309	137	8.0	15.8	£3556
ITor	ITor	R & P	Disc/disc	165-15	164	2309	137	7.3	15.8	£4663
ITor	ITor	R & P	Disc/disc	165-15	164	2250	129	8.1	16.0	£3671
ITor	ITor	R & P	Disc/disc	165-15	164	2307	137	7.0	15.4	£4585
ITor	ITor	R & P	Disc/disc	165-15	164	2350	143 (Est)	N/A	N/A	£5211
ITor	ITor	R & P	Disc/disc	165-15	164	2250	127	7.6	15.7	£3971
ITor	ITor	R & P	Disc/disc	185/70-15	164	2394	139	6.4	14.4	£4827
ITor	ITor	R & P	Disc/disc	185/70-15	164	2436	145	6.2	14.7	£5402
ITor	ITor	R & P	Disc/disc	185/70-15	169	2370	130 (Est)	7.8	15.8	£6135
ITor	ITor	R & P	Disc/disc	185/70-15	169	2475	135	7.2	15.7	£6249
ITor	ITor	R & P	Disc/disc	185/70-15	169	2443	142	6.1	15.0	£6993
ITor	ITor	R & P	Disc/disc	215/60-15	164	2398	149	5.5	14.1	£5825
ITor	ITor	R & P	Disc/disc	205/55-16/	169	2716	130 (Est)	N/A	N/A	£9999
ITor	ITor	R & P	Disc/disc	225/50-16	169	2716	141	6.5	15.1	£14,100

Make and model	Production Figures	Years Built	Body Styles	Mechanical Layout	Engine Make (if not own)	Capacity/(cc)/Layout/Valves	BHP/rpm	Torque (lb.ft)/rpm	Transmission gearbox/automatic transmission
							200/6000	188/4200	5-spd/SemiAuto
							204/5900	195/4300	5-spd/-
						3164/6HO/	231/5900	210/4800	5-spd/-
914/6	3,107	1969–1972	Spts Cpe	M/R	—	1991/6HO/ OHC AirC	110/5800	116/4200	5-spd/SemiAuto
911 Turbo	20,652	1975–1990	Cpe Conv Targa	R/R	—	2994/6HO/ OHC AirC	260/5500	253/4000	4-spd/-
						3299/6HO/ OHC AirC	300/5500	304/4000	4-spd/5-spd/-
							300/5500	318/4000	5-spd/-
							330/5750	344/4540	5-spd/-
924	122,304	1975–1985	Spts Cpe	F/R	Audi	1984/4IL/ OHC	125/5800	122/3500	4-spd/Auto 5-spd/Auto
924 Turbo	12,385	1978–1982	Spts Cpe	F/R	Audi	1984/4IL/ OHC	170/5500	181/3500	5-spd/-
924 Carrera GT	406/59	1980/1981	Spts Cpe	F/R	Audi	1984/4IL/ OHC	210/6000	206/3500	5-spd/-
928 family	61,054	1977–1995	Cpe	F/R	—	4474/V8/ OHC	240/5250	267/3600	5-spd/Auto
						4664/V8/ OHC	300/5900	283/4500	5-spd/Auto
							310/5900	295/4500	5-spd/Auto
						4957/V8/ 2OHC	320/6200	317/4100	5-spd/Auto
							330/6200	317/4100	5-spd/Auto
						5397/V8/ 2OHC	350/5700	369/4250	5-spd/Auto
911 Carrera 2/Carrera 4	N/A	1988–1993	Cpe/ Conv	R/R	—	3600/6HO/ 2OHC AirC	250/6100	228/4800	5-spd/Auto
							260/6100	232/4800	5-spd/-
				R/4	—	3600/6HO/ 2OHC AirC	250/6100	228/4800	5-spd/-
911 Turbo	N/A	1990–1995	Cpe	R/R	—	3299/6HO/ OHC AirC	320/5750	332/4500	5-spd/-
						3600/6HO/ 2OHC AirC	360/5500	384/4200	5-spd/-
924S	16,282	1985–1988	Spts Cpe	F/R	—	2479/4IL/ OHC	150/5800	144/3000	5-spd/Auto
							160/5900	155/4500	5-spd/Auto
944/944S/ 944S2	112,550	1982–1993	Spts Cpe Spts	F/R	—	2479/4IL/ OHC	163/5800	151/3500	5-spd/Auto
							160/5900	155/4500	
						2681/4IL/ OHC	165/5800	166/4200	5-spd/Auto
						2479/4IL/ 2OHC	190/6000	170/4300	5-spd/-
						2990/4IL/ 2OHC	211/5800	207/4000	5-spd/-
944 Turbo	51,270	1985–1991	Spts Cpe	F/R	—	2479/4IL/ OHC	220/5800	243/3500	5-spd/-
							250/6500	258/4000	5-spd/-
959	250	1987–1988	Spts Cpe	R/4	—	2849/6HO/ 2OHC	450/6500	369/5500	6-spd/-
968	11,602	1991–1995	Spts Cpe Spts Conv	F/R	—	2990/4IL/ 2OHC	240/6200	225/4100	6-spd/Auto
968 Turbo	Incl. in total 968 figures	1993–1995	Spts Cpe	F/R	—	2990/4IL/ 2OHC	305/5600	368/3000	6-spd/-
911 Carrera 2/Carrera 4	In prod	1993–Date	Spts Cpe Conv	R/R	—	3600/6HO/ 2OHC AirC	272/6100	252/5000	6-spd/Auto
							285/6100	251/5250	6-spd/Auto
							430/5750	398/4500	6-spd/-
						3746/6HO/ 2OHC AirC	300/6500	262/5400	6-spd/-
				R/4	—	3600/6HO/ 2OHC AirC	272/6100	243/5000	6-spd/-
911 Turbo 4WD	In prod	1995–Date	Cpe	R/R	—	3600/6HO/ 2OHC AirC	408/4750	398/4500	6-spd/-

Princess

Make and model	Production Figures	Years Built	Body Styles	Mechanical Layout	Engine Make (if not own)	Capacity/(cc)/Layout/Valves	BHP/rpm	Torque (lb.ft)/rpm	Transmission gearbox/automatic transmission
1800/2200/ 1700/2000	224,942	1975–1982	Sal	F(Tr)/F	—	1695/4IL/ OHC	87/5200	87/3800	4-spd/Auto
						1798/4IL/ OHV	82/5200	102/2750	4-spd/Auto
						1993/4IL/ OHC	93/4900	113/3400	5-spd/Auto

Suspension Front	Rear	Steering	Brakes (Front/rear)	Wheels/Tyres	Length (in)	Weight (lb, unladen)	Top speed (mph)	0–60mph (sec)	Standing ¼-mile (sec)	UK Total Price (£: at Launch)
ITor	ITor	R & P	Disc/disc	185/70-15/ 215/60-15	169	2475	143	N/A	N/A	£10,996
ITor	ITor	R & P	Disc/disc	185/70/15/ 215/60-15	169	2688	148	5.7	14.3	£16,731
ITor	ITor	R & P	Disc/disc	205/55-16/ 225/50-16	169	2780	151	5.2	13.9	£23,366
ITor	IC	R & P	Disc/disc	165-15	157	2070	125	8.3	16.2	£3475
ITor	ITor	R & P	Disc/disc	205/50-15/ 225/50-15	168	2703	153	6.1	14.7	£14,749
ITor	ITor	R & P	Disc/disc	205/55-16/ 225/50-16	168	2884	160	5.3	13.4	£23,200
ITor	ITor	R & P	Disc/disc	205/55-16/ 245/45-16	169	3051	162	5.1	13.4	£57,851
ITor	ITor	R & P	Disc/disc	205/55-16/ 245/55-16	169	3051	165 (Est)	N/A	N/A	£42,444
IC	ITor	R & P	Disc/drum	185/70-14	167	2380	126	9.5	17.2	£6,999
IC	ITor	R & P	Disc/drum	185/70-14	167	2450	126	9.5	17.1	£7,799
IC	ITor	R & P	Disc/disc	185/70-15	167	2602	142	6.9	15.0	£13,629
IC	IC	R & P	Disc/disc	205/55-16/ 225/50-16	167	2602	150	6.5	15.1	£19,210
IC	IC	R & P	Disc/disc	225/60-16	175	3200	142	7.5	15.7	£19,499
IC	IC	R & P	Disc/disc	225/50-16	175	3390	152	6.2	14.3	£25,251
IC	IC	R & P	Disc/disc	225/50-16	175	3390	158	6.2	14.5	£30,679
IC	IC	R & P	Disc/disc	225/50-16/	178	3449	165	5.6	13.8	£46,534
IC	IC	R & P	Disc/disc	245/45-16	178	3450	171 (Est)	N/A	N/A	£55,441
IC	IC	R & P	Disc/disc	225/45-17/ 255/40-17	178	3570	168	5.4	14.1	£62,398
IC	IC	R & P	Disc/disc	205/55-16/ 225/50-16	168	2985	158	5.1	13.6	£41,504
IC	IC	R & P	Disc/disc	205/50-17/ 255/40-17	168	2976	161	4.9	13.4	£63,544
IC	IC	R & P	Disc/disc	205/55-16/ 225/50-16	168	3197	156	5.2	13.9	£47,699
IC	IC	R & P	Disc/disc	205/50-17/ 255/50-17	167	3216	167	4.7	13.3	£72,993
IC	IC	R & P	Disc/disc	225/40-18/ 265/35-18	168	3234	174 (Claimed)	4.6	N/A	£80,499
IC	ITor	R & P	Disc/disc	195/65-15	167	2567	133	8.2	16.1	£21,031
IC	ITor	R & P	Disc/disc	195/65-15	167	2641	137	7.4	15.7	£21,031
IC	ITor	R & P	Disc/disc	185/70-15	165	2635	137	7.4	15.6	£12,999
IC	ITor	R & P	Disc/disc	195/65-15	165	2911	136	7.0	15.7	£25,990
IC	ITor	R & P	Disc/disc	195/65-15	165	2822	140	6.7	15.1	£23,977
IC	ITor	R & P	Disc/disc	205/55-16/ 225/50-16	165	2889	146	6.0	14.4	£31,304
IC	ITor	R & P	Disc/disc	205/55-16/ 225/50-16	165	2977	153	6.0	14.8	£25,311
IC	ITor	R & P	Disc/disc	225/50-16	165	2699	152	5.7	14.2	£39,893
IC	IC	R & P	Disc/disc	235/45-17/ 255/40-17	168	2977	197	N/A	N/A	£150,251
IC	ITor	R & P	Disc/disc	225/45-17/ 255/40-17	170	3131	153	6.1	14.7	£34,945
IC	IC	R & P	Disc/disc	235/40-18/ 265/35-18	170	2863	175 (Claimed)	N/A	N/A	£70,000
IC	IC	R & P	Disc/disc	205/55-16/ 245/45-16	167	3020	160	5.2	13.8	£53,995
IC	IC	R & P	Disc/disc	205/50-17/ 255/40-17	167	3091	171 (Claimed)	5.3	13.9	£58,995
IC	IC	R & P	Disc/disc	235/40-18/ 285/35-18	167	2679	183	N/A	N/A	£131,000
IC	IC	R & P	Disc/disc	225/40-18/ 265/35/18	167	2800	159	5.0	13.6	£65,245
IC	IC	R & P	Disc/disc	205/55-16/ 245/45-16	167	3018	155	5.0	13.7	£58,245
IC	IC	R & P	Disc/disc	225/40-18/ 285/30-18	167	3323	180 (Est)	3.7	12.3	£91,950
IHydraG	IHydraG	R & P	Disc/drum	185/70-14	175	2510	99 (Claimed)	N/A	N/A	£3725
IHydraG	IHydraG	R & P	Disc/drum	185/70-14	175	2557	96	14.9	20.1	£2237
IHydraG	IHydraG	R & P	Disc/drum	185/70-14	175	2540	98	14.6	19.4	£4060

Make and model	Production Figures	Years Built	Body Styles	Mechanical Layout	Engine Make (if not own)	Capacity/(cc)/Layout/Valves	BHP/rpm	Torque (lb.ft)/rpm	Transmission gearbox/automatic transmission
						2227/6IL/OHC	110/5250	125/3520	4-spd/Auto
Proton									
1300/1500	In prod	1988–Date	Sal Htch	F(Tr)/F	Mitsubishi	1299/4IL/OHC	68/6000 75/6000	75/4000 80/3000	5-spd/- 5-spd/-
						1468/4IL/OHC	75/5500 86/6000	87/3500 87/4000	5-spd/Auto 5-spd/Auto
Persona	In prod	1993–Date	Sal	F(Tr)/F	Mitsubishi	1299/4IL/OHC	74/6000	80/3000	5-spd/-
						1468/4IL/OHC	89/6000	93/3000	5-spd/Auto
						1597/4IL/OHC	111/6000	101/5000	5-spd/Auto
Range Rover									
Range Rover/Classic	317,615	1970–1996	Est	F/4	VM	2393/4IL/OHV Diesel	112/4200	183/2400	5-spd/Auto
					—	2497/4IL/OHC Diesel	113/4000 119/4200	195/1800 209/1950	5-spd/Auto 5-spd/Auto
						3528/V8/OHV	135/4750 125/4000 127/4000 165/4750	205/3000 185/2500 194/2500 206/3200	4-spd (+O/D)/- 4-spd/5-spd/Auto 5-spd/Auto 5-spd/Auto
						3947/V8/OHV	185/4750 178/4750	235/2600 220/3250	5-spd/Auto 5-spd/Auto
						4278/V8/OHV	200/4850	250/3250	Auto/-
Range Rover	In prod	1994–Date	Est	F/4	BMW	2497/6IL/OHC Diesel	134/4400	199/2300	5-spd/Auto
					—	3950/V8/OHV	190/4750	236/3000	5-spd/Auto
					—	4554/V8/OHV	225/4750	277/3000	5-spd/Auto
Reliant									
Rebel	700	1965–1972	Sal Est	F/R	—	598/4IL/OHV	25/5250	31/3000	4-spd/-
						700/4IL/OHV	31/5000	38/2500	4-spd/-
						748/4IL/OHV	35/5500	38/3000	4-spd/-
Scimitar GTE	5,127	1968–1975	Spts Htch	F/R	Ford	2994/V6/OHV	138/5000	172/3000	4-spd (+O/D)/Auto
Scimitar GTE (SE6/SE8)	5,298	1975–1986	Spts Htch Conv	F/R	Ford	2994/V6/OHV	135/5000	172/3000	4-spd (+O/D)/Auto
						2792/V6/OHV	135/5200	159/3000	4-spd (+O/D)/Auto
Kitten	4,074	1975–1982	Sal Est	F/R	—	848/4IL/OHV	40/5500	46/3500	4-spd/-
Scimitar SS1/SST	N/A	1984–1990	Spts	F/R	Ford	1296/4IL/OHC	69/6000	74/3500	4-spd/-
						1392/4IL/OHC	72/5600	80/4000	5-spd/-
						1596/4IL/OHC	96/6000	98/4000	5-spd/-
					Nissan	1809/4IL/OHC	135/6000	143/4000	5-spd/-
Scimitar Sabre	In prod	1992–Date	Spts	F/R	Rover	1396/4IL/2OHC	103/6000	94/5000	5-spd/-
					Nissan	1809/4IL/OHC	135/6000	141/4000	5-spd/-
Renault									
4	8,135,424	1961–1992	Est	F/F	—	747/4IL/OHV	27/4500	41/2000	3-spd/-
						845/4IL/OHV	28/4700 30/4700 34/5000	49/2300 48/2300 42/2500	3-spd/- 4-spd/- 4-spd/-
						1108/4IL/OHV	34/4000	55/2500	4-spd/-
8/8S	1,316,134	1962–1971	Sal	R/R	—	956/4IL/OHV	42/5200	55/2500	4-spd/Auto
						1108/4IL/OHV	45/4900 57/5500	65/2500 70/3000	4-spd/Auto 4-spd/Auto
10	687,675	1969–1971	Sal	R/R	—	1289/4IL/	48/4800	72/2500	4-spd/-

Suspension Front	Rear	Steering	Brakes (Front/rear)	Wheels/ Tyres	Length (in)	Weight (lb,unladen)	Top speed (mph)	0–60mph (sec)	Standing 1/4-mile (sec)	UK Total Price (£: at Launch)
IHydraG	IHydraG	R & P	Disc/drum	185/70-14	175	2638	104	13.5	19.2	£2562
IC	IC	R & P	Disc/drum	175/60-13	163	2029	96 (Est)	N/A	N/A	£5999
IC	IC	R & P	Disc/drum	175/60-13	163	2029	95 (Est)	13.8	N/A	£6799
IC	IC	R & P	Disc/drum	175/70-13	163	2044	95	14.4	19.8	£6449
IC	IC	R & P	Disc/drum	175/70-13	163	2181	98	12.4	17.9	£7350
IC	IC	R & P	Disc/drum	155-13	172	2051	103 (Claimed)	13.6	N/A	£7799
IC	IC	R & P	Disc/disc	175/70-13	172	2262	108 (Claimed)	12.1	N/A	£8990
IC	IC	R & P	Disc/disc	185/60-14	172	2362	113	10.4	17.8	£9990
BeamC	BeamC	Worm	Disc/disc	205-16	176	3880	92	16.5	20.6	£18,109
BeamC	BeamC	Worm	Disc/disc	205-16	176	4525	94 (Est)	16.6	N/A	£27,889
BeamC	BeamC	Worm	Disc/disc	205-16	176	4525	95 (Est)	15.8	N/A	£25,905
BeamC	BeamC	Worm	Disc/disc	205-16	176	3880	99	12.9	18.7	£1998
BeamC	BeamC	Worm	Disc/disc	205-16	176	4249	96	14.4	19.5	£13,505
BeamC	BeamC	Worm	Disc/disc	205-16	176	4300	97 (Est)	N/A	N/A	£13,632
BeamC	BeamC	Worm	Disc/disc	205-16	176	4334	105	11.9	18.4	£18,696
BeamC	BeamC	Worm	Disc/disc	205R-16	176	4379	108	11.3	18.5	£25,506
BeamC	BeamC	Worm	Disc/disc	205R-16	176	4427	107	10.8	18.2	£28,055
BeamAir	BeamAir	Worm	Disc/disc	205R-16	183	4593	110	10.8	18.1	£39,995
BeamAir	BeamAir	Worm	Disc/disc	255/65-16	186	4664	101	15.1	20.5	£31,950
BeamAir	BeamAir	Worm	Disc/disc	235/70-16	186	4549	116	11.1	18.4	£31,950
BeamAir	BeamAir	Worm	Disc/disc	235/70-16	186	4498	119	10.5	18.0	£43,950
IC	Beam1/2E	Worm	Drum/drum	5.20-12	138	1178	63	N/A	24.6	£525
IC	Beam1/2E	Worm	Drum/drum	5.50-12	138	1211	68	35.9	23.7	£592
IC	Beam1/2E	Worm	Drum/drum	5.50-12	138	1211	72 (Est)	N/A	N/A	£845
IC	BeamC	R & P	Disc/drum	185-14	170	2500	117	10.7	17.4	£1759
IC	BeamC	R & P	Disc/drum	185-14	175	2770	119	10.0	17.6	£4368
IC	BeamC	R & P	Disc/drum	185-14	175	2421	119	10.0	17.6	£10,324
IC	Beam1/2E	R & P	Drum/drum	145-10	133	1159	78	19.6	21.2	£1499
IC	IC	R & P	Disc/drum	175/70-13	153	1852	99 (Claimed)	N/A	N/A	£6995
IC	IC	R & P	Disc/drum	185/60-14	153	1996	100	12.0	18.6	£10,950
IC	IC	R & P	Disc/drum	175/70-13	153	1939	108	11.5	18.1	£7795
IC	IC	R & P	Disc/drum	185/60-14	153	1966	124	7.2	15.5	£9750
IC	IC	R & P	Disc/drum	195/50-15	153	1996	120 (Claimed)	8.5	N/A	£13,995
IC	IC	R & P	Disc/drum	195/50-15	153	1850	126 (Claimed)	7.6	N/A	£14,900
ITor	ITor	R & P	Drum/drum	145-13	142	1275	60	N/A	27.1	£583
ITor	ITor	R & P	Drum/drum	145-13	144	1323	68	40.5	24.3	£539
ITor	ITor	R & P	Drum/drum	5.00-13	144	1393	66	38.1	24.6	£544
ITor	ITor	R & P	Drum/drum	135-13	144	1532	72 (Est)	N/A	N/A	£2624
ITor	ITor	R & P	Drum/drum Disc/drum	135-13	144	1626	72	25.7	22.6	£3050
IC	IC	R & P	Disc/disc	145-15	158	1568	82	21.9	21.8	£764
IC	IC	R & P	Disc/disc	135-380	158	1652	82	20.6	21.9	£675
IC	IC	R & P	Disc/disc	135-15	158	1652	90	16.5	20.7	£778
IC	IC	R & P	Disc/disc	135-15	165	1758	86	17.0	20.5	£776

Make and model	Production Figures	Years Built	Body Styles	Mechanical Layout	Engine Make (if not own)	Capacity/(cc)/Layout/Valves	BHP/rpm	Torque (lb.ft)/rpm	Transmission gearbox/automatic transmission
						OHV			
						1108/4IL/ OHV	43/4600	57/3000	Auto/-
6	1,773,304	1968–1979	Htch	F/F	—	845/4IL/ OHV	34/5000	42/3000	4-spd/-
						1108/4IL/ OHV	45/5300	58/3000	4-spd/-
16	1,846,000	1965–1979	Htch	F/F	—	OHV	47/5500	56/5000	4-spd/-
						1470/4IL/ OHV	59/5000	78/2800	4-spd/-
						1565/4IL/ OHV	67/5000	84/3000	4-spd/Auto
							83/5750	87/3500	4-spd/Auto
							65/5100	83/3000	4-spd/Auto
							83/5750	88/3500	4-spd/Auto
						1647/4IL/ OHV	93/6000	95/4000	5-spd/Auto
12	2,865,079	1969–1980	Sal Est	F/F	—	1289/4IL/ OHV	54/5250	69/3000	4-spd/-
							60/5800	71/3500	4-spd/-
15/17 Coupe	207,854/ 92,589	1971–1979	Cpe	F/F	—	1289/4IL/ OHV	60/5800	71/3500	4-spd/Auto
						1565/4IL/ OHV	90/5500	90/2500	4-spd/Auto
							108/6000	98/5500	5-spd/-
						1605/4IL/ OHV	108/6000	99/5500	5-spd/-
						1647/4IL/ OHV	98/5750	98/3500	5-spd/Auto
5 range	5,471,709 (Incl. Gordini production figs)	1972–1984	Htch	F/F	—	845/4IL/ OHV	36/5500	41/3000	4-spd/-
						956/4IL/ OHV	43/5500	46/3500	4-spd/-
						1108/4IL/ OHV	45/4400	63/2000	4-spd/-
						1289/4IL/ OHV	64/6000	69/3500	4-spd/-
							44/5000	62/2000	4-spd/-
							55/5750	69/2500	Auto/-
						1397/4IL/ OHV	63/5250	76/3000	5-spd/-
							58/5000	75/3000	Auto/-
5 Gordini	See above	1976–1981	Htch	F/F	—	1397/4IL/ OHV	93/6400	85/4000	5-spd/-
5 Gordini Turbo	See above	1982–1984	Htch	F/F	—	1397/4IL/ OHV	110/6000	109/4000	5-spd/-
5 Turbo	N/A	1980–1986	Htch	M/R	—	1397/4IL/ OHV	160/6000	155/3250	5-spd/-
20/30	622,314/ 160,265	1975–1984	Htch	F/F	—	1647/4IL/ OHV	90/5750	97/3500	4-spd/-
						1995/4IL/ OHC	110/5500	128/3000	4-spd/Auto
						2165/4IL/ OHC	115/5500	133/3000	5-spd/Auto
						2664/V6/ OHC	131/5500	148/2500	4-spd/Auto
							125/5000	150/2500	4-spd/Auto
							142/5500	161/3000	5-spd/Auto
						2068/4IL/ OHC Diesel	64/4500	94/2250	5-spd/-
14	999,093	1976–1982	Htch	F(Tr)/F	Peugeot	1218/4IL/ OHC	57/6000	68/3000	4-spd/-
						1360/4IL/ OHC	70/6000	78/3000	4-spd/5-spd/-
18	2,173,100	1978–1986	Sal Est	F/F	—	1397/4IL/ OHV	64/5000	74/3000	4-spd/-
						1565/4IL/ OHV	110/5000	134/2250	5-spd/-
							125/5500	134/2250	5-spd/-
						1647/4IL/ OHV	79/5500	89/3000	4-spd/5-spd/Auto
							96/5750	98/3500	5-spd/-
							74/5000	96/3000	5-spd/-
						1995/4IL/ OHC	104/5500	118/3250	5-spd/-
						2068/4IL/ OHC Diesel	67/4500	93/2250	5-spd/-
5 Supercinque	In prod	1984–Date	Htch	F(Tr)/F	—	956/4IL/ OHV	42/5750	48/3000	4-spd/-
						1108/4IL/ OHV	47/5250	59/2500	4-spd/5-spd
						1237/4IL/ OHV	55/5250	65/3000	5-spd/-
						1390/4IL/ OHC	59/4750	75/3000	5-spd/-
						1397/4IL/ OHV	60/5250	77/2500	5-spd/-
							72/5750	78/3500	5-spd/-
							68/5250	78/3000	Auto/-
						1721/4IL/	90/5500	102/3500	5-spd/-

Suspension Front	Rear	Steering	Brakes (Front/rear)	Wheels/ Tyres	Length (in)	Weight (lb,unladen)	Top speed (mph)	0–60mph (sec)	Standing 1/4-mile (sec)	UK Total Price (£: at Launch)
IC	IC	R & P	Disc/disc	135-15	165	1758	80 (Est)	N/A	N/A	£871
ITor	ITor	R & P	Drum/drum	135-330	152	1610	73	29.8	23.8	£735
ITor	ITor	R & P	Disc/drum	135-13	152	1770	81	18.9	21.4	£869
ITor	ITor	R & P	Disc/drum	145-13	152	1636	84	17.2	21.0	£1207
ITor	ITor	R & P	Disc/drum	145-14	167	2156	88	16.7	20.8	£949
ITor	ITor	R & P	Disc/drum	145-14	167	2229	90	15.7	20.5	£1159
ITor	ITor	R & P	Disc/drum	155-14	167	2271	101	12.3	19.2	£1085
ITor	ITor	R & P	Disc/drum	145-14	167	2229	90 (Est)	N/A	N/A	£1269
ITor	ITor	R & P	Disc/drum	155-14	167	2337	101 (Est)	N/A	N/A	£1487
ITor	ITor	R & P	Disc/drum	155-14	167	2237	104	12.4	18.6	£1895
IC	BeamC	R & P	Disc/drum	145-13	171	1940	89	16.5	20.6	£870
IC	BeamC	R & P	Disc/drum	145-13	171	2006	94	12.9	19.3	£1199
IC	BeamC	R & P	Disc/drum	155-13	168	2130	97	15.1	20.0	£1325
IC	BeamC	R & P	Disc/drum	155-13	168	2216	104	10.9	18.1	£1458
IC	BeamC	R & P	Disc/disc	165-13	168	2326	111	9.9	17.3	£1998
IC	BeamC	R & P	Disc/disc	165-13	168	2326	112 (Claimed)	N/A	N/A	£2149
IC	BeamC	R & P	Disc/disc	155-13	168	2293	106 (Claimed)	N/A	N/A	£3138
ITor	ITor	R & P	Disc/drum	135-13	138	1609	78 (Est)	N/A	N/A	£854
ITor	ITor	R & P	Disc/drum	135-13	138	1731	86	20.6	21.8	£929
ITor	ITor	R & P	Disc/drum	135-13	138	1644	82	15.7	21.2	£3218
ITor	ITor	R & P	Disc/drum	145-13	138	1793	94	13.4	19.2	£1720
ITor	ITor	R & P	Disc/drum	145-13	138	1668	83	17.6	20.7	£1952
ITor	ITor	R & P	Disc/drum	145-13	138	1778	84	20.1	22.1	£3050
ITor	ITor	R & P	Disc/drum	145-13	138	1812	96	12.2	18.8	£4291
ITor	ITor	R & P	Disc/drum	145-13	138	1786	87 (Est)	N/A	N/A	£4530
ITor	ITor	R & P	Disc/drum	155/70-13	140	1813	107	10.7	17.8	£4149
ITor	ITor	R & P	Disc/disc	155/70-13	140	1876	113	9.8	16.9	£5752
ITor	IC	R & P	Disc/disc	190/55-340/ 220/55-365	140	2072	124	7.8	15.8	Special order
IC	IC	R & P	Disc/drum	165-13	178	2510	98	12.6	18.5	£3299
IC	IC	R & P	Disc/drum	165-14	178	2754	104	12.2	19.0	£4724
IC	IC	R & P	Disc/drum	190-14	178	2863	106	10.5	18.0	£7677
IC	IC	R & P	Disc/disc	175-14	178	2853	114	9.2	16.9	£3952
IC	IC	R & P	Disc/disc	175-14	178	2844	117	9.8	17.6	£6125
IC	IC	R & P	Disc/disc	175-14	178	2840	115	10.3	17.1	£8218
IC	IC	R & P	Disc/disc	175-14	178	2778	91 (Claimed)	N/A	N/A	£7090
IC	ITor	R & P	Disc/drum	145-13	159	1906	89	15.3	19.9	£2562
IC	ITor	R & P	Disc/drum	145-13	159	1942	97	12.5	19.0	£4246
IC	BeamC	R & P	Disc/drum	145-13	172	1837	91	14.4	19.5	£3313
IC	BeamC	R & P	Disc/drum	185/65-14	172	2355	112	10.8	17.5	£6589
IC	BeamC	R & P	Disc/drum	185/70-13	172	2293	121 (Est)	N/A	N/A	£7464
IC	BeamC	R & P	Disc/drum	155-13	172	2128	96	13.4	19.1	£3313
IC	BeamC	R & P	Disc/drum	155-13	172	2128	107 (Est)	N/A	N/A	£4233
IC	BeamC	R & P	Disc/drum	165-13	172	2072	96	13.4	19.5	£5363
IC	BeamC	R & P	Disc/drum	185/65-14	172	2128	108	10.1	17.6	£6301
IC	BeamC	R & P	Disc/drum	165-13	172	2297	97	14.3	19.7	£5490
IC	ITor	R & P	Disc/drum	145/70-13	141	1532	85 (Claimed)	N/A	N/A	£3845
IC	ITor	R & P	Disc/drum	145/70-13	141	1652	90	16.3	19.5	£4300
IC	ITor	R & P	Disc/drum	145/70-13	141	1621	96 (Claimed)	N/A	N/A	£5550
IC	ITor	R & P	Disc/drum	145/70-13	141	1713	96	13.7	19.3	£8655
IC	ITor	R & P	Disc/drum	145/70-13	141	1731	97	14.8	19.5	£4900
IC	ITor	R & P	Disc/drum	155/70-13	141	1731	104	11.4	18.2	£5095
IC	ITor	R & P	Disc/drum	155/70-13	141	1731	102 (Est)	N/A	N/A	£5545
IC	ITor	R & P	Disc/drum	165/65-13	141	1823	109	9.5	17.0	£7130

Make and model	Production Figures	Years Built	Body Styles	Mechanical Layout	Engine Make (if not own)	Capacity/(cc)/Layout/Valves	BHP/rpm	Torque (lb.ft)/rpm	Transmission gearbox/automatic transmission
						OHC			
						1595/4IL/ OHC Diesel	55/4800	74/2250	5-spd/-
5 GT Turbo	See above	1986–1991	Htch	F(Tr)/F	—	1397/4IL/ OHV	115/5750	121/3000	5-spd/-
							120/5750	122/3750	5-spd/-
Fuego	83,725	1980–1986	Cpe	F/F	—	1397/4IL/ OHV	64/5500	76/3300	4-spd/-
						1565/4IL/ OHV	132/5500	147/3000	5-spd/-
						1647/4IL/ OHV	96/5750	98/3500	5-spd/Auto
						1995/4IL/ OHC	110/5500	120/3000	5-spd/-
9	1,109,300	1982–1989	Sal	F(Tr)/F	—	1108/4IL/ OHV	48/5250	59/2500	4-spd/-
						1237/4IL/ OHV	55/5250	66/3000	5-spd/-
						1397/4IL/ OHV	60/5250	75/3000	4-spd/5-spd/-
							68/5250	78/3000	Auto/-
							72/5750	78/3500	5-spd/-
							105/5500	119/2500	5-spd/-
							115/5750	121/3000	5-spd/-
						1721/4IL/ OHC	82/5000	100/3250	5-spd/-
							90/5500	100/3500	5-spd/-
						1595/4IL/ OHC Diesel	54/4800	75/2250	5-spd/-
11	973,740	1983–1989	Htch	F(Tr)/F	—	1108/4IL/ OHC	48/5250	59/2500	4-spd/-
						1237/4IL/ OHC	55/5250	66/3000	5-spd/-
						1397/4IL/ OHV	60/5250	75/3000	5-spd/-
							68/5250	78/3000	5-spd/Auto
							72/5750	78/3500	5-spd/-
							105/5500	119/2500	5-spd/-
							115/5750	121/3000	5-spd/-
						1721/4IL/ OHC	80/5000	100/3250	5-spd/-
							90/5500	100/3500	5-spd/-
						1595/4IL/ OHC Diesel	54/4800	75/2250	5-spd/-
25	173,685	1984–1992	Htch	F/F	—	1995/4IL/ OHC	104/5550	119/3250	5-spd/Auto
							120/5500	124/4500	5-spd/Auto
							140/6000	130/4300	5-spd/-
						2165/4IL/ OHC	123/5250	134/2750	5-spd/Auto
							126/5250	141/2750	5-spd/Auto
						2664/V6/ OHC	142/5500	142/2500	5-spd/Auto
						2458/V6/ OHC	182/5500	207/3000	5-spd/-
						2849/V6/ OHC	160/5400	170/2500	Auto/-
25 Limousine	800	1985–1986	Limo	F/F	—	2664/V6/ OHC	142/5500	142/2500	5-spd/Auto
Espace	In prod	1984–Date	Est	F/F	—	1995/4IL/ OHC	103/5500	119/3000	5-spd/-
							110/5500	120/3000	5-spd/-
							120/5500	124/4500	5-spd/-
						2165/4IL/ OHC	110/5000	128/3500	Auto/-
						2849/V6/ OHC	153/5400	163/2500	5-spd/Auto
						2068/4IL/ OHC Diesel	88/4250	134/2000	5-spd/-
				F/4	—	1995/4IL/ OHC	120/5500	124/4500	5-spd/-
GTA Alpine (was Alpine-Renault)	17,450	1985–1991	Spts Cpe	R/R	—	2849/V6/ OHC	160/5750	166/3500	5-spd/-
						2458/V6/ OHC	200/5750	214/2500	5-spd/-
21	In prod	1985–1995	Sal Est Htch	F/F	—	1721/4IL/ OHC	76/5000	95/3250	4-spd/-
							90/5500	102/3500	5-spd/-
						1995/4IL/ OHC	120/5500	124/4500	5-spd/Auto
							140/6000	130/2250	5-spd/-
							175/5200	199/3000	5-spd/-
						1870/4IL/ OHC Diesel	65/4500	87/2250	5-spd/Auto
						2068/4IL/ OHC Diesel	67/4500	93/2250	5-spd/-
							88/4250	134/2000	5-spd/-
21 Quadra	Incl. in above 21 figures	1989–Date	Sal	F/4	—	1995/4IL/ OHC	175/5200	199/3000	5-spd/-
							140/6000	130/2250	5-spd/-
19	In prod	1988–Date	Sal Htch	F(Tr)/F	—	1390/4IL/ OHC	80/5750	78/2750	5-spd/Auto

Suspension Front	Rear	Steering	Brakes (Front/rear)	Wheels/Tyres	Length (in)	Weight (lb,unladen)	Top speed (mph)	0–60mph (sec)	Standing ¼-mile (sec)	UK Total Price (£: at Launch)
IC	ITor	R & P	Disc/drum	165/65-13	141	1753	91	15.3	20.2	£6395
IC	ITor	R & P	Disc/disc	195/55-13	141	1749	125	7.1	15.7	£7360
IC	ITor	R & P	Disc/disc	195/55-13	141	1889	120	7.3	16.0	£8405
IC	BeamC	R & P	Disc/drum	155-13	172	2223	98 (Claimed)	N/A	N/A	£4489
IC	BeamC	R & P	Disc/disc	185/65-14	172	2317	121	8.4	16.4	£8700
IC	BeamC	R & P	Disc/drum	175/70-13	172	2278	107	11.2	18.1	£4941
IC	BeamC	R & P	Disc/drum	185/65-14	172	2317	114	9.20	16.8	£6660
IC	ITor	R & P	Disc/drum	145-13	160	1709	84	18.3	21.1	£4100
IC	ITor	R & P	Disc/drum	155-13	160	1885	90 (Claimed)	N/A	N/A	£5275
IC	ITor	R & P	Disc/drum	145-13	160	1786	94	14.2	19.2	£4649
IC	ITor	R & P	Disc/drum	155-13	160	1923	90	17.2	21.3	£5378
IC	ITor	R & P	Disc/drum	155-13	160	1898	98	11.7	18.4	£5378
IC	ITor	R & P	Disc/drum	175/65-14	160	2043	111	9.0	16.6	£8130
IC	ITor	R & P	Disc/disc	175/65-14	160	1996	118 (Est)	N/A	N/A	£9710
IC	ITor	R & P	Disc/drum	175/70-13	160	1985	105 (Est)	N/A	N/A	£5750
IC	ITor	R & P	Disc/drum	175/70-13	160	1973	112 (Est)	N/A	N/A	£7440
IC	ITor	R & P	Disc/drum	155-13	160	1915	89	17.2	20.1	£4990
IC	ITor	R & P	Disc/drum	145-13	157	1830	86 (Claimed)	N/A	N/A	£4350
IC	ITor	R & P	Disc/drum	155-13	157	1918	90 (Claimed)	N/A	N/A	£5405
IC	ITor	R & P	Disc/drum	155-13	157	1781	92	13.2	19.0	£4900
IC	ITor	R & P	Disc/drum	155-13	157	1918	99	12.7	18.1	£5870
IC	ITor	R & P	Disc/drum	175/70-13	157	1907	95	12.8	18.8	£5975
IC	ITor	R & P	Disc/drum	175/65-14	157	2015	116	8.7	16.8	£6800
IC	ITor	R & P	Disc/drum	175/65-14	157	2068	119	7.9	16.4	£8155
IC	ITor	R & P	Disc/drum	175/70-13	157	1944	102	10.6	17.8	£5500
IC	ITor	R & P	Disc/drum	175/70-13	157	1973	112 (Est)	N/A	N/A	£7510
IC	ITor	R & P	Disc/drum	155-13	157	2040	92 (Claimed)	N/A	N/A	£5800
IC	IC	R & P	Disc/disc	195/60-15	183	2650	116	11.2	17.9	£7950
IC	IC	R & P	Disc/disc	195/65-15	183	2568	121	10.2	17.5	£11,700
IC	IC	R & P	Disc/disc	195/60-15	186	3029	126	10.0	17.3	£14,995
IC	IC	R & P	Disc/disc	195/60-15	183	2613	122	10.1	17.5	£9995
IC	IC	R & P	Disc/disc	195/60-15	183	2613	122 (Est)	N/A	N/A	£11,750
IC	IC	R & P	Disc/disc	195/60-15	183	2861	126	9.0	16.5	£13,440
IC	IC	R & P	Disc/disc	205/60-15	183	2965	137	8.1	15.9	£18,700
IC	IC	R & P	Disc/disc	195/60-15	186	3098	128	9.5	17.4	£17,520
IC	IC	R & P	Disc/disc	195/60-15	194	2911	125 (Claimed)	N/A	N/A	£18,900
IC	IC	R & P	Disc/drum	185/65-14	172	2624	103	12.9	19.1	£12,100
IC	IC	R & P	Disc/drum	185/65-14	172	2602	105	12.1	18.2	£10,145
IC	IC	R & P	Disc/disc	195/65-14	172	2751	106	10.8	18.0	£16,990
IC	IC	R & P	Disc/disc	195/65-14	172	2679	106 (Claimed)	12.8	N/A	£19,430
IC	IC	R & P	Disc/disc	195/65-15	174	3238	116	9.4	17.2	£21,460
IC	IC	R & P	Disc/drum	195/65-14	174	3131	100	14.1	19.5	£17,795
IC	BeamC	R & P	Disc/disc	195/65-14	174	2844	107	11.2	18.2	£18,785
IC	IC	R & P	Disc/disc	190/55-365/ 220/55-365	171	2535	139	7.5	16.0	£19,040
IC	IC	R & P	Disc/disc	195/50-15/ 255/45-15	171	2618	149	6.3	15.3	£23,635
IC	ITor	R & P	Disc/drum	155-13	176	2105	109 (Est)	N/A	N/A	£6485
IC	ITor	R & P	Disc/drum	175/70-13	176	2187	113	10.9	17.8	£6845
IC	ITor	R & P	Disc/drum	185/65-14	176	2441	120	10.3	17.7	£8885
IC	ITor	R & P	Disc/disc	185/55-15	176	2731	125	9.8	17.1	£13,995
IC	ITor	R & P	Disc/disc	195/55-15	176	2623	137	7.9	15.5	£16,500
IC	ITor	R & P	Disc/drum	175/70-13	176	2293	96 (Est)	N/A	N/A	£9170
IC	ITor	R & P	Disc/drum	175/70-13	176	2370	105 (Est)	N/A	N/A	£8395
IC	ITor	R & P	Disc/drum	185/70-13	176	2502	110 (Est)	N/A	N/A	£9630
IC	IC	R & P	Disc/disc	195/55-15	178	3160	138	7.8	15.4	£20,785
IC	IC	R & P	Disc/disc	185/55-15	178	2877	123 (Est)	N/A	N/A	£18,080
IC	ITor	R & P	Disc/drum	165/70-13	164	2172	106	12.8	18.7	£7740

Make and model	Production Figures	Years Built	Body Styles	Mechanical Layout	Engine Make (if not own)	Capacity/(cc)/Layout/Valves	BHP/rpm	Torque (lb.ft)/rpm	Transmission gearbox/automatic transmission
			Conv			1397/4IL/OHV	60/5250	76/2750	4-spd/-
						1721/4IL/OHC	92/5750	99/3000	5-spd/-
						1764/4IL/2OHC	137/6500	119/4250	5-spd/-
						1794/4IL/OHC	95/5750	104/2750	5-spd/-
						1870/4IL/OHC Diesel	65/4500 / 93/4500	87/2250 / 129/2250	5-spd/- / 5-spd/-
Clio	In prod	1990–Date	Htch	F(Tr)/F	—	1108/4IL/OHV	48/5250	58/2500	4-spd/5-spd/-
						1171/4IL/OHC	60/6000	63/3500	4-spd/5-spd/-
						1390/4IL/OHC	80/5750	79/3500	5-spd/Auto
						1764/4IL/2OHC	137/6500	119/4250	5-spd/-
						1794/4IL/OHC	110/5500	114/4250	5-spd/-
						1870/4IL/OHC Diesel	65/4500	87/2250	5-spd/-
Clio Williams	In prod	1993–Date	Htch	F(Tr)/F	—	1998/4IL/2OHC	150/6100	129/4500	5-spd/-
Laguna	In prod	1993–Date	Sal Est	F/(Tr)/F	—	1794/4IL/OHC	95/5750	104/2750	5-spd/-
						1998/4IL/OHC	115/5250	127/3500	5-spd/-
						1998/4IL/2OHC	140/6000	134/4500	5-spd/-
						2963/V6/OHC	170/5500	173/4500	Auto/-
						2188/4IL/OHC Diesel	85/4500	107/2250	5-spd/-
Safrane	In prod	1992–Date	Htch	F(Tr)/F	—	1995/4IL/OHC	105/5000 / 135/6000	114/2500 / 128/4500	5-spd/- / 5-spd/-
						2165/4IL/OHC	140/5750	137/4500	5-spd/Auto
						2963/V6 OHC	170/5500	173/4500	Auto/-
						2499/4IL/OHC Diesel	115/4200	177/2400	5-spd/Auto
GTA (A610) Alpine	In prod	1991–Date	Spts Cpe	R/R	—	2963/V6/OHC	250/5750	258/2900	5-spd/-
Sport Spider	In prod	1995–Date	Spts	M/R	—	1998/4IL/2OHC	150/6000	137/5400	5-spd/-
Megane	In prod	1995–Date	Sal Htch Conv Cpe Est	F(Tr)/F	—	1390/4IL/OHC	70/6000 / 75/6000	79/4000 / 80/4000	5-spd/- / 5-spd/-
						1598/4IL/OHC	90/5000	98/4000	5-spd/Auto
						1998/4IL/OHC	115/5400	126/4250	5-spd/Auto
						1998/4IL/2OHC	150/6000	136/4500	5-spd/-
						1870/4IL/OHC Diesel	65/4500 / 95/4500	87/2250 / 132/2000	5-spd/- / 5-spd/-

Rocket

Make and model	Production Figures	Years Built	Body Styles	Mechanical Layout	Engine Make (if not own)	Capacity/(cc)/Layout/Valves	BHP/rpm	Torque (lb.ft)/rpm	Transmission gearbox/automatic transmission
Rocket	In prod	1992–Date	Spts	M(Tr)/R	Yamaha	1002/4IL/2OHC	143/10,500	77/8500	5-spd/-

Rolls-Royce

Make and model	Production Figures	Years Built	Body Styles	Mechanical Layout	Engine Make (if not own)	Capacity/(cc)/Layout/Valves	BHP/rpm	Torque (lb.ft)/rpm	Transmission gearbox/automatic transmission
Phantom V/VI	1,241	1959–1992	Limo	F/R		6230/V8/OHV	N/Q	N/Q	Auto/-
						6750/V8/OHV	N/Q	N/Q	Auto/-
Silver Shadow I/II	27,915	1965–1980	Sal	F/R	—	6230/V8/OHV	N/Q	N/Q	Auto/-
						6750/V8/OHV	N/Q	N/Q	Auto/-
Silver Shadow Coupe/Corniche	7,355	1966–1994	Cpe Conv	F/R	—	6230/V8/OHV	N/Q	N/Q	Auto/-
						6750/V8/OHV	N/Q	N/Q	Auto/-
Silver Wraith II (1977)	2,144	1977–1980	Sal Limo	F/R	—	6750/V8/OHV	N/Q	N/Q	Auto/-

Suspension Front	Rear	Steering	Brakes (Front/rear)	Wheels/Tyres	Length (in)	Weight (lb, unladen)	Top speed (mph)	0–60mph (sec)	Standing 1/4-mile (sec)	UK Total Price (£: at Launch)
IC	ITor	R & P	Disc/drum	145-13	164	1985	108 (Claimed)	15.0	N/A	£6520
IC	ITor	R & P	Disc/drum	175/70-13	164	2293	110	11.7	18.4	£9520
IC	ITor	R & P	Disc/disc	195/50-15	164	2489	130	9.1	17.0	£11,995
IC	ITor	R & P	Disc/drum	175/70-13	164	2304	114 (Est)	N/A	N/A	£11,565
IC	ITor	R & P	Disc/drum	165/70-13	164	2280	97	16.0	20.6	£9285
IC	ITor	R & P	Disc/drum	165/70-13	164	2381	114 (Est)	11.3	N/A	£11,935
IC	ITor	R & P	Disc/drum	145/70-13	146	1786	90 (Claimed)	N/A	N/A	£6715
IC	ITor	R & P	Disc/drum	145/70-13	146	1866	99	14.0	19.7	£7190
IC	ITor	R & P	Disc/drum	165/65-13	146	1872	106	12.0	18.7	£8695
IC	ITor	R & P	Disc/disc	185/55-15	146	2247	126	8.6	16.7	£12,000
IC	ITor	R & P	Disc/disc	175/60-14	146	2017	117	9.3	17.0	£10,695
IC	ITor	R & P	Disc/drum	165/65-13	146	2048	97	13.9	19.6	£7561
IC	ITor	R & P	Disc/disc	185/55-15	146	2181	130	7.7	16.1	£13,275
IC	ITor	R & P	Disc/drum	185/65-14	177	2816	112	12.3	18.8	£10570
IC	ITor	R & P	Disc/drum	185/65-14	177	2745	117	10.7	17.9	£12925
IC	ITor	R & P	Disc/disc	195/65-15	177	3008	127	10.1	17.5	£14810
IC	ITor	R & P	Disc/disc	205/60-15	177	3065	128	9.8	17.5	£18565
IC	ITor	R & P	Disc/drum	185/65-14	177	2944	109 (Claimed)	15.3	N/A	£11995
IC	IC	R & P	Disc/drum	185/70-14	177	3021	117 (Est)	12.5	N/A	£16,320
IC	IC	R & P	Disc/disc	195/65-15	177	3087	126 (Est)	N/A	N/A	£16,295
IC	IC	R & P	Disc/disc	195/65-15	177	3109	128 (Claimed)	10.2	N/A	£18,200
IC	IC	R & P	Disc/disc	195/65-15	177	3384	129	9.9	17.6	£20,995
IC	IC	R & P	Disc/disc	195/65-15	177	3451	118 (Claimed)	18.7	N/A	£19,910
IC	IC	R & P	Disc/disc	205/45-16/ 245/45-16	174	3043	159	5.8	14.7	£37,980
IC	IC	R & P	Disc/disc	205/50-16/ 225/50-16	150	1740	131 (Claimed)	6.5	N/A	£N/A
IC	ITor	R & P	Disc/drum	165/70-13	155	2238	103 (Est)	N/A	N/A	£N/A
IC	ITor	R & P	Disc/drum	175/70-13	155	2238	106 (Est)	14.3	N/A	£10,690
IC	ITor	R & P	Disc/drum	175/70-13	155	2392	110	11.4	18.3	£11,855
IC	ITor	R & P	Disc/drum	175/65-14	155	2392	122 (Est)	N/A	N/A	£14.320
IC	ITor	R & P	Disc/disc	195/50-16	155	2412	131	7.8	16.2	£15,700
IC	ITor	R & P	Disc/drum	175/70-13	155	2448	99 (Est)	N/A	N/A	£11,110
IC	ITor	R & P	Disc/drum	175/65-14	155	2492	112	N/A	N/A	£12,780
IC	IC	R & P	Disc/disc	195/50-15	144	882	131	5.0	13.7	£38,000
IC	Beam1/2E	Worm	Drum/drum	8.90-15	238	5600	101	13.8	19.4	£8905
IC	Beam1/2E	Worm	Drum/drum	8.90-15	238	6000	105 (Est)	N/A	N/A	Special Order
IC	IC	Worm	Disc/disc	8.45-15	204	4660	115	10.9	17.6	£6670
IC	IC	Worm R & P (from 1977)	Disc/disc	8.45-15 205-15	204	4660	117	10.2	17.5	£9272
				235/70-15	204	4930	119	9.4	17.7	£22,809
IC	IC	Worm	Disc/disc	8.45-15	204	4978	115 (Est)	N/A	N/A	£9849
IC	IC	Worm R & P (from 1977)	Disc/disc	8.45-15 205-15	204	4816	120	9.6	17.1	£11,556
				235/70-15			126	9.7	17.1	£73,168
IC	IC	R & P	Disc/disc	235/70-15	208	5010	119	10.4	17.3	£26,887

Make and model	Production Figures	Years Built	Body Styles	Mechanical Layout	Engine Make (if not own)	Capacity/ (cc)/Layout/ Valves	BHP/ rpm	Torque (lb.ft)/rpm	Transmission gearbox/automatic transmission
Camargue	530	1975–1986	Cpe	F/R	—	6750/V8/ OHV	N/Q	N/Q	Auto/-
Silver Spirit/ Silver Spur	With latest cars, still In Prod	1980–1993	Sal	F/R	—	6750/V8/ OHV	N/Q	N/Q	Auto/-
						6750/V8/ OHV	N/Q	N/Q	Auto/-
Silver Spirit III/Spur II	In prod	1993–Date	Sal	F/R	—	6750/V8/ OHV	N/Q	N/Q	Auto/-
Flying Spur	In prod	1994–1995	Sal	F/R	—	6750/V8/ OHV	N/Q	N/Q	Auto/-
Limousine/ Stretch saloon	In prod	1984–Date	Limo Sal	F/R	—	6750/V8/ OHV	N/Q	N/Q	Auto/-
Rover									
2000/TC	213,890 (Incl. 2200/TC)	1963–1973	Sal	F/R	—	1978/4IL/ OHC	89/5000 110/5500	108/2500 124/2750	4-spd/Auto 4-spd/-
2200/TC	—	1974–1977	Sal	F/R	—	2205/4IL/ OHC	98/5000 115/5000	126/2500 135/3000	4-spd/Auto 4-spd/-
3.5-litre (P5B)	20,600	1967–1973	Sal Cpe	F/R	—	3528/V8/ OHV	151/5200	201/2750	-/Auto
3500/3500S	79,057	1968–1976	Sal	F/R	—	3528/V8/ OHV	144/5000 143/5000 150/5000	197/2700 202/2700 204/2700	-/Auto 4-spd/-
3500 SDI/ Vitesse	303,345 (Incl. 2000/2300 figs)	1976–1986	Htch	F/R	—	3528/V8/ OHV	155/5250 190/5280	198/2500 220/4000	5-spd/Auto 5-spd/Auto
2000/2300 2600	See above	1977–1986	Htch	F/R	—	1994/4IL/ OHC	101/5250	120/3250	5-spd/Auto
						2350/6IL/ OHC	123/5000	134/4000	4-spd/5-spd/Auto
						2597/6IL/ OHC	136/5000	152/3750	5-spd/Auto
					VM	2393/4IL/ OHV Diesel	90/4200	142/2350	5-spd/-
200 series	408,521	1984–1989	Sal	F(Tr)/F	Honda	1342/4IL/ OHC	70/6000	77/3500	5-spd/Auto
					—	1598/4IL/ OHC	85/5600 103/6000	97/3500 102/3500	5-spd/Auto 5-spd/Auto
200	In Prod	1989–Date	Htch Conv	F(Tr)/F	—	1396/4IL/ OHC	75/5700 95/6250 103/6000	84/3500 91/4000 92/3500	5-spd/- 5-spd/- 5-spd/-
					Honda	1590/4IL/ OHC	114/6300 130/6800 111/6300	104/5200 105/5700 101/5200	5-spd/Auto 5-spd/Auto 5-spd/Auto
						1994/4IL/ 2OHC	140/6000 136/6000 197/6000	132/4500 136/2500 174/2100	5-spd/- 5-spd/- 5-spd/-
					Peugeot	1769/4IL/ OHC Diesel	87/4300	133/2500	5-spd/-
					Peugeot	1905/4IL/ OHC Diesel	66/4600	89/2500	5-spd/-
800 series	221,227	1986–1991	Htch Sal	F(Tr)/F	—	1994/4IL/ OHC	100/5400	120/3000	5-spd/Auto
						1994/4IL/ 2OHC	120/5600 138/5300 180/6100	119/3500 131/4500 216/2000	5-spd/Auto 5-spd/Auto 5-spd/-
						2494/V6/ 2OHC	173/6000 167/6000	160/5000 163/4000	5-spd/- Auto/-
						2675/V6/ 2OHC	177/6000	168/4500	5-spd/Auto
					VM	2500/4IL/ OHC	118/4200	197/2100	5-spd/-
400	In Prod	1990–Date	Sal Est	F(Tr)/F	—	1396/4IL/ 2OHC	95/6250 103/6000	91/4000 92/3500	5-spd/- 5-spd/-
					Honda	1590/4IL/ OHC	116/6300 111/6300	104/5200 101/5200	5-spd/Auto 5-spd/Auto
					Honda	1590/4IL/ 2OHC	130/6800	105/5700	5-spd/Auto
					—	1994/4IL/ 2OHC	140/6000 136/6000 197/6000	132/4500 136/2500 174/2100	5-spd/Auto 5-spd/Auto 5-spd/-
					Peugeot	1769/4IL/ OHC Diesel	87/4300	133/2500	5-spd/-
					Peugeot	1905/4IL/ OHC Diesel	66/4600	89/2500	5-spd/-

Metro : For details of 1980–1990 models, see the **Austin** entry.

Suspension Front	Rear	Steering	Brakes (Front/rear)	Wheels/ Tyres	Length (in)	Weight (lb, unladen)	Top speed (mph)	0–60mph (sec)	Standing 1/4-mile (sec)	UK Total Price (£: at Launch)
IC	IC	Worm R & P	Disc/disc	235/70-15	204	5175	118 (Claimed)	N/A	N/A	£29,250
IC	IC	R & P	Disc/disc	235/70-15	207	4907	119	10.0	17.1	£49,629
IC	IC	R & P	Disc/disc	235/70-15	207	5038	126	10.4	17.4	£85,609
IC	IC	R & P	Disc/disc	235/70-15	207	5358	133 (Claimed)	9.5	N/A	£98,194
IC	IC	R & P	Disc/disc	255/65-15	211	5263	130	6.9	15.5	£148,545
IC	IC	R & P	Disc/disc	235/70-15	244	5821	124 (Claimed)	N/A	N/A	£140,000
IC	DDC	Worm	Disc/disc	165-14	179	2760	104	14.6	19.4	£1264
IC	DDC	Worm	Disc/disc	165-14	179	2810	108	11.9	18.4	£1415
IC	DDC	Worm	Disc/disc	165-14	179	2822	101	13.4	19.4	£2019
IC	DDC	Worm	Disc/disc	165-14	181	2829	108	11.5	18.3	£2139
IC	Beam1/2E	Worm	Disc/drum	6.70-15	187	3498	108	12.4	18.3	£2009
IC	DDC	Worm	Disc/disc	185-14	180	2862	117	9.5	17.6	£1801
IC	DDC	Worm	Disc/disc	185-14	180	2868	122	9.1	16.8	£1988
IC	BeamC	R & P	Disc/drum	185-14	185	2989	123	8.4	16.6	£4750
IC	BeamC	R & P	Disc/drum	205/60-15	185	3136	132	7.1	15.8	£14,950
IC	BeamC	R & P	Disc/drum	175-14	185	2947	103	12.4	18.6	£7450
IC	BeamC	R & P	Disc/drum	175-14	185	2787	111	11.9	18.7	£5645
IC	BeamC	R & P	Disc/drum	175-14	185	2866	117	10.7	17.7	£5800
IC	BeamC	R & P	Disc/drum	175-14	185	3241	104	14.3	19.7	£10,500
IC	IC	R & P	Disc/drum	155-13	164	1895	96	13.0	18.7	£5545
IC	IC	R & P	Disc/drum	165-13	164	1994	104	10.0	N/A	£6490
IC	IC	R & P	Disc/drum	175/65-14	164	2084	107	9.4	17.4	£7899
IC	IC	R & P	Disc/drum	155-13	166	2260	99	13.3	19.3	£9335
IC	IC	R & P	Disc/drum	175/65-14	166	2423	106	11.7	18.3	£8775
IC	IC	R & P	Disc/drum	175/65-14	166	2423	112 (Est)	N/A	N/A	£9595
IC	IC	R & P	Disc/disc	175/65-14	166	2555	116	10.9	18.2	£10,940
IC	IC	R & P	Disc/disc	185/55-15	166	2533	123	8.8	16.8	£13,750
IC	IC	R & P	Disc/disc	175/65-14	166	2348	118 (Est)	N/A	N/A	£11,587
IC	IC	R & P	Disc/disc	185/55-15	166	2577	124	8.8	16.9	£15,495
IC	IC	R & P	Disc/disc	175/70-14	166	2527	125 (Est)	N/A	N/A	£13,819
IC	IC	R & P	Disc/disc	195/55-15	166	2758	146 (Est)	6.4	N/A	£15,984
IC	IC	R & P	Disc/drum	175/70-14	166	2580	106 (Claimed)	N/A	N/A	£11,966
IC	IC	R & P	Disc/drum	175/70-14	166	2524	94	16.9	20.9	£10,690
IC	IC	R & P	Disc/disc	195/65-15	185	2923	113	11.6	18.4	£12,640
IC	IC	R & P	Disc/disc	195/70-14	185	2800	116	10.2	18.5	£10,750
IC	IC	R & P	Disc/disc	195/70-14	185	2849	125	9.1	17.2	£11,820
IC	IC	R & P	Disc/disc	205/55-16	189	3101	135	9.0	16.9	£23,950
IC	IC	R & P	Disc/disc	195/65-15	185	2998	129	8.0	16.3	£15,871
IC	IC	R & P	Disc/disc	195/65-15	185	2970	125	10.1	17.7	£15,871
IC	IC	R & P	Disc/disc	195/65-15	185	3156	137	8.0	16.6	£16,550
IC	IC	R & P	Disc/disc	195/65-15	189	3240	116	11.7	18.5	£17,930
IC	IC	R & P	Disc/drum	175/65-14	172	2302	103	11.5	18.5	£9565
IC	IC	R & P	Disc/drum	175/65-14	172	2302	112 (Est)	N/A	N/A	£10,363
IC	IC	R & P	Disc/disc	175/65-14	172	2445	118	9.5	16.9	£11,990
IC	IC	R & P	Disc/drum	175/65-14	172	2437	112	9.7	17.4	£11,286
IC	IC	R & P	Disc/disc	185/60-14	172	2489	120	10.0	17.2	£13,795
IC	IC	R & P	Disc/disc	185/60-14	172	2425	126 (Est)	8.1	N/A	£14,110
IC	IC	R & P	Disc/disc	175/70-14	172	2569	124 (Est)	8.4	N/A	£13,170
IC	IC	R & P	Disc/disc	195/55-15	172	2679	146 (Est)	6.4	N/A	£17,232
IC	IC	R & P	Disc/drum	175/70-14	172	2580	107	11.5	18.6	£14,870
IC	IC	R & P	Disc/drum	175/70-14	172	2579	95 (Est)	N/A	N/A	£14,250

Make and model	Production Figures	Years Built	Body Styles	Mechanical Layout	Engine Make (if not own)	Capacity/(cc)/Layout/Valves	BHP/rpm	Torque (lb.ft)/rpm	Transmission gearbox/automatic transmission
Metro	389,024	1990–1994	Htch Conv	F(Tr)/F	—	1120/4IL/OHC	60/6000	66/3500	4-spd/5-spd/-
						1396/4IL/OHC	75/5500	86/3500	5-spd/Auto
						1396/4IL/2OHC	95/6250	91/4000	5-spd/-
							103/6000	94/5000	5-spd/-
					Peugeot	1360/4IL/OHC Diesel	53/5000	62/2500	5-spd/-
200 Coupe	In prod	1992–Date	Cpe	F(Tr)/F	Honda	1590/4IL/2OHC	111/6300	101/5200	5-spd/-
					—	1994/4IL/2OHC	136/6000	136/2500	5-spd/-
						1994/4IL/2OHC	197/6000	174/2100	5-spd/-
600	In prod	1993–Date	Sal	F(Tr)/F	—	1994/4IL/2OHC	197/6000	174/2100	5-spd/-
					Honda	1997/4IL/OHC	113/5300	127/4200	5-spd/-
							129/5400	131/4800	5-spd/Auto
					Honda	2259/4IL/2OHC	156/5800	154/4500	5-spd/Auto
						1994/4IL/OHC Diesel	104/4200	155/2000	5-spd/-
800	In prod	1991–Date	Sal Htch	F(Tr)/F	—	1994/4IL/2OHC	136/6000	136/2500	5-spd/Auto
							197/6000	177/2100	5-spd/-
						2675/V6/2OHC	169/5900	165/4500	5-spd/Auto
							177/6100	159/2000	5-spd/Auto
					VM	2500/4IL/OHC Diesel	118/4200	197/2100	5-spd/-
800 Coupe	In prod	1992–Date	Cpe	F(Tr)/F		2675/V6/2OHC	169/5900	165/4500	5-spd/Auto
100	In prod	1994–Date	Htch Conv	F(Tr)/F	—	1120/4IL/OHC	59/5700	66/3900	5-spd/-
						1396/4IL/OHC	74/5500	86/4000	5-spd/Auto
					Peugeot	1527/4IL/OHC Diesel	57/5000	70/2250	5-spd/-
400	In prod	1995–Date	Htch Sal	F(Tr)/F	—	1396/4IL/2OHC	103/6000	94/3000	5-spd/-
					—	1589/4IL/2OHC	111/6000	107/3000	5-spd/-
					Honda	1590/4IL/OHC	113/6200	103/5100	Auto/-
						2.0/4IL/2OHC			
200	In prod	1995–Date	Htch	F(Tr)/F	—	1396/4IL/OHC	74/5500	86/4000	5-spd/Auto
						1396/4IL/2OHC	103/6000	94/3000	5-spd/-
						1589/4IL/2OHC	111/6000	107/3000	5-spd/Auto
						2.0/4IL/OHC Diesel	86/4500	129/2000	5-spd/-
							105/4200	155/2000	5-spd/-

Saab

Make and model	Production Figures	Years Built	Body Styles	Mechanical Layout	Engine Make (if not own)	Capacity/(cc)/Layout/Valves	BHP/rpm	Torque (lb.ft)/rpm	Transmission gearbox/automatic transmission
96 V4/95 V4	407,500 Est	1966–1979	Sal Est	F/F	—	1498/V4/OHV	65/4700	85/2500	4-spd/-
99/90	614,021	1967–1985	Sal Htch	F/F	Triumph	1709/4IL/OHC	80/5300	95/3200	4-spd/-
					Triumph	1854/4IL/OHC	86/5200	108/3000	4-spd/-
					—	1985/4IL/OHC	95/5200	116/3500	4-spd/-
							110/5500	123/3700	4-spd/Auto
							100/5200	119/3500	4-spd/Auto
							108/5300	121/3300	4-spd/Auto
							118/5500	123/3700	4-spd/Auto
99 Turbo	10,607	1977–1980	Sal Htch	F/F	—	1985/4IL/OHC	145/5000	174/3000	4-spd/-
900	710,163	1978–1993	Sal Htch	F/F	—	1985/4IL/OHC	100/5200	112/3500	4-spd/5-spd/Auto
							118/5500	123/3700	4-spd/5-spd/Auto
							108/5200	121/3300	4-spd/5-spd/Auto
900 Turbo	202,284	1978–1993	Sal Htch	F/F	—	1985/4IL/OHC	145/5000	174/3000	4-spd/5-spd/-
						1985/4IL/2OHC	175/5300	201/3000	5-spd/-
							185/5500	201/2800	5-spd/-
							155/5000	177/3000	5-spd/-
900 Convertible	Incl. in 900 figures	1986–1993	Conv						

Suspension Front	Rear	Steering	Brakes (Front/rear)	Wheels/ Tyres	Length (in)	Weight (lb,unladen)	Top speed (mph)	0–60mph (sec)	Standing ¼-mile (sec)	UK Total Price (£: at Launch)
IHydraG	IHydraG	R & P	Disc/drum	155/65-13	139	1896	97	13.7	19.6	£5985
IHydraG	IHydraG	R & P	Disc/drum	155/65-13	139	1874	104	12.0	18.2	£8295
IHydraG	IHydraG	R & P	Disc/drum	185/55-13	139	1949	113	9.8	17.4	£9500
IHydraG	IHydraG	R & P	Disc/drum	185/55-13	139	1949	115	9.6	N/A	£11,340
IHydraG	IHydraG	R & P	Disc/drum	155/65-13	139	1929	86	19.4	21.5	£8144
IC	IC	R & P	Disc/drum	185/55-15	168	2381	122	9.1	17.0	£14,495
IC	IC	R & P	Disc/disc	185/55-15	168	2547	127 (Claimed)	8.2	N/A	£16,670
IC	IC	R & P	Disc/disc	195/55-15	168	2644	149	6.3	14.9	£18,315
IC	IC	R & P	Disc/disc	205/50-16	184	3010	141	7.8	16.2	£19,995
IC	Ic	R & P	Disc/disc	185/70-15	184	2767	122	10.3	17.7	£13,995
IC	IC	R & P	Disc/disc	185/65-15	184	2867	122	9.6	17.1	£14,995
IC	IC	R & P	Disc/disc	195/65-15	184	2867	128	8.8	16.7	£19,250
IC	IC	R & P	Disc/disc	185/65-15	184	2990	115	11.3	18.3	£17,995
IC	IC	R & P	Disc/disc	195/65-15	192	2985	125	9.2	17.2	£17,495
IC	IC	R & P	Disc/disc	215/45-17	192	3252	142	7.3	15.8	£20,995
IC	IC	R & P	Disc/disc	195/65-15	192	3142	131 (Auto)	9.4	17.4	£23,495
IC	IC	R & P	Disc/disc	205/55-16	192	3142	138	7.8	16.2	£19,845
IC	IC	R & P	Disc/disc	195/65-15	192	3186	118 (Claimed)	10.5	N/A	£19,245
IC	IC	R & P	Disc/disc	205/55-16	192	3263	131	9.9	17.7	£30,770
IHydraG	IHydraG	R & P	Disc/drum	155/65-13	139	1841	91	13.6	19.6	£6495
IHydraG	IHydraG	R & P	Disc/drum	155/65-13	139	1852	103	11.6	18.4	£8195
IHydraG	IHydraG	R & P	Disc/drum	155/65-13	139	1852	96 (Claimed)	15.3	N/A	£7395
IC	IC	R & P	Disc/drum or Disc/disc	175/65-14	170	2470	108	10.6	18.0	£11,795
IC	IC	R & P	Disc/drum or Disc/disc	185/60-14	170	2470	115	10.3	17.6	£12,995
IC	IC	R & P	Disc/drum or Disc/disc	185/60-14	170	2547	118 (Claimed)	10.0	N/A	£14,995
IC	IC	R & P	Disc/drum	175/65-14	149	N/A	101 (Claimed)	12.7	N/A	£9995
IC	IC	R & P	Disc/drum	175/65-14	149	2271	108	10.0	17.8	£11,195
IC	IC	R & P	Disc/drum	175/65-14	149	2260	118 (Claimed)	9.5	N/A	£12,195
IC	IC	R & P	Disc/drum	175/65-14	149	2435	96 (Est)	16.0	N/A	£10,995
IC	IC	R & P	Disc/drum	175/65-14	149	2500	106 (Est)	11.8	N/A	£13,295
IC	BeamC	R & P	Disc/drum	155-15	166	2275	92	16.5	20.0	£801
IC	BeamC	R & P	Disc/disc	155-15	171	2327	94	15.2	20.2	£1288
IC	BeamC	R & P	Disc/disc	155-15	171	2421	94	12.8	18.7	£1479
IC	BeamC	R & P	Disc/disc	155-15	171	2535	101	12.0	18.5	£1738
IC	BeamC	R & P	Disc/disc	155-15	171	2466	106	10.3	17.7	£1999
IC	BeamC	R & P	Disc/disc	165-15	171	2520	102	11.9	18.8	£2186
IC	BeamC	R & P	Disc/disc	165-15	178	2555	100	14.4	19.7	£3475
IC	BeamC	R & P	Disc/disc	175/70-15	171	2475	107	10.6	17.4	£4147
IC	BeamC	R & P	Disc/disc	175/70-15	178	2716	122	8.9	16.9	£7850
IC	BeamC	R & P	Disc/disc	165-15	187	2583	100	13.3	18.2	£5745
IC	BeamC	R & P	Disc/disc	165-15	187	2755	106	11.1	18.1	£5775
IC	BeamC	R & P	Disc/disc	165-15	187	2634	103	13.9	19.0	£5775
IC	BeamC	R & P	Disc/disc	185/65-390	187	2888	118	9.6	17.2	£8675
IC	BeamC	R & P	Disc/disc	195/60-15	185	2963	133	8.6	16.6	£13.490
IC	BeamC	R & P	Disc/disc	195/60-15	185	3036	131	8.8	16.5	£20,495
IC	BeamC	R & P	Disc/disc	185/65-15	185	2763	120	8.9	N/A	£19,995

Make and model	Production Figures	Years Built	Body Styles	Mechanical Layout	Engine Make (if not own)	Capacity/(cc)/Layout/Valves	BHP/rpm	Torque (lb.ft)/rpm	Transmission gearbox/automatic transmission
900 CD	N/A	1981–1988	Sal	F/R	—	1985/4IL/OHC	145/5000	174/3000	Auto/-
9000 and Turbo	In prod	1984–Date	Htch Sal	F/F	—	1985/4IL/2OHC	130/5500	127/3000	5-spd/Auto
							150/5500	155/2500	5-spd/Auto
							175/5300	201/3000	5-spd/-
							204/6000	214/3000	5-spd/-
						2290/4IL/2OHC	150/5500	156/3800	5-spd/Auto
							200/5000	244/2000	5-spd/Auto
							170/5700	192/3200	5-spd/Auto
							220/6500	246/2000	5-spd/-
							225/5500	252/1800	5-spd/-
						2962/V6/2OHC	210/6200	199/3300	5-spd/Auto
900	In prod	1993–Date	Htch Cpe Conv	F(Tr)/F	—	1985/4IL/2OHC	133/6100	132/4300	5-spd/Auto
							185/5500	195/2100	5-spd/-
						2290/4IL/2OHC	150/5700	155/4300	5-spd/Auto
						2498/V6/2OHC	170/4900	167/4200	5-spd/Auto

Sao

Make and model	Production Figures	Years Built	Body Styles	Mechanical Layout	Engine Make (if not own)	Capacity/(cc)/Layout/Valves	BHP/rpm	Torque (lb.ft)/rpm	Transmission gearbox/automatic transmission
Penza	In prod	1990–Date	Sal Htch	F(Tr)/F	Mazda	1324/4IL/OHC	64/5500	77/3600	5-spd/-

Seat

Make and model	Production Figures	Years Built	Body Styles	Mechanical Layout	Engine Make (if not own)	Capacity/(cc)/Layout/Valves	BHP/rpm	Torque (lb.ft)/rpm	Transmission gearbox/automatic transmission
Marbella	In prod	1982–Date	Htch	F(Tr)/F	Fiat	843/4IL/OHV	35/5400	41/2800	4-spd/-
						903/4IL/OHV	40/5800	47/3000	5-spd/-
Malaga	247,300	1985–1992	Sal Htch	F(Tr)/F	—	1193/4IL/OHC	63/5800	65/3500	5-spd/-
						1461/4IL/OHC	85/5600	86/3500	5-spd/-
						1714/4IL/OHC Diesel	55/4500	72/3000	5-spd/-
Ibiza	543,900	1985–1993	Htch	F(Tr)/F	Fiat	903/4IL/OHV	44/5800	47/3000	4-spd/5-spd/-
					—	1193/4IL/OHC	63/5800	65/3000	5-spd/-
						1461/4IL/OHC	85/5600	86/3500	5-spd/-
							100/5900	94/4700	5-spd/-
						1675/4IL/OHC	100/5700	102/3800	5-spd/-
						1714/4IL/OHC Diesel	55/4500	72/3000	5-spd/-
Ibiza	In prod	1993–Date	Htch	F(Tr)/F	VW	1043/4IL/OHC	45/5200	56/2800	5-spd/-
						1272/4IL/OHC	55/5000	70/3200	5-spd/-
						1391/4IL/OHC	60/5200	79/2800	5-spd/-
						1598/4IL/OHC	75/5200	92/2600	5-spd/-
						1781/4IL/OHC	90/5500	107/2900	5-spd/-
						1781/4IL/2OHC	130/6000	122/4500	5-spd/-
						1984/4IL/OHC	115/5400	122/3200	5-spd/-
						1896/4IL/OHC Diesel	68/4400	94/2200	5-spd/-
Cordoba	In prod	1993–Date	Sal	F(Tr)/F	VW	1391/4IL/OHC	60/5200	79/2800	5-spd/-
						1598/4IL/OHC	75/5200	92/2600	5-spd/-
						1984/4IL/OHC	115/5400	122/3200	5-spd/-
						1896/4IL/OHC Diesel	68/4400	94/2200	5-spd/-
							75/4400	103/2200	5-spd/-
Toledo	In prod	1991–Date	Htch	F(Tr)/F	VW	1595/4IL/OHC	75/5200	91/2750	5-spd/-
						1781/4IL/OHC	90/5250	103/3000	5-spd/-
						1781/4IL/2OHC	136/6000	118/4300	5-spd/-
						1984/4IL/OHC	115/5400	122/3200	5-spd/Auto
						1984/4IL/	150/6000	133/4800	5-spd/-

| Suspension | | Steering | Brakes | Wheels/ | Length (in) | Weight | Performance | | Standing | UK Total |
Front	Rear		(Front/rear)	Tyres		(lb,unladen)	Top speed (mph)	0–60mph (sec)	¹/₄-mile (sec)	Price (£: at Launch)
IC	BeamC	R & P	Disc/disc	180/65-350	195	2950 (Est)	118 (Est)	N/A	N/A	£14,995
IC	BeamC	R & P	Disc/disc	195/65-15	188	2940	122	9.3	17.6	£11,995
IC	BeamC	R & P	Disc/disc	195/65-15	188	2940	130 (Est)	N/A	N/A	£19,245
IC	BeamC	R & P	Disc/disc	205/55-15	182	2870	138	8.3	15.9	£15,995
IC	BeamC	R & P	Disc/disc	205/50-16	182	2999	141	7.3	15.8	£24,995
IC	BeamC	R & P	Disc/disc	195/65-15	188	3062	126	9.3	16.9	£16,295
IC	BeamC	R & P	Disc/disc	205/55-15	184	2981	140	7.5	15.5	£22,495
IC	BeamC	R & P	Disc/disc	195/65-15	184	2940	137 (Est)	N/A	N/A	£23,895
IC	BeamC	R & P	Disc/disc	195/65-15	184	3128	141	7.4	15.9	£26,995
IC	BeamC	R & P	Disc/disc	205/55-16	184	3032	149 (Est)	N/A	N/A	£29,995
IC	BeamC	R & P	Disc/disc	195/65-15	188	3179	130	10.6	17.7	£31,995
IC	IC	R & P	Disc/disc	195/60-15	183	2998	121	9.7	17.6	£15,995
IC	IC	R & P	Disc/disc	205/50-16	183	3010	135	7.4	15.9	£21,895
IC	IC	R & P	Disc/disc	185/65-15	183	2966	125	8.7	16.9	£17,495
IC	IC	R & P	Disc/disc	195/60-15	183	3296	140 (Claimed)	8.2	N/A	£21,795
IC	IC	R & P	Disc/drum	155-13	157	1874	99 (Claimed)	N/A	N/A	£7549
IC	Beam1/2E	R & P	Disc/drum	135-13	137	1499	80 (Claimed)	N/A	N/A	£3799
IC	Beam1/2E	R & P	Disc/drum	135-13	137	1569	81	18.7	21.3	£4133
IC	ITrL	R & P	Disc/drum	155-13	161	2057	94	15.7	20.4	£5096
IC	ITrL	R & P	Disc/drum	165-14	161	2119	103	10.5	17.9	£5770
IC	ITrL	R & P	Disc/drum	165/65-14	161	2238	90 (Claimed)	N/A	N/A	£6939
IC	ITrL	R & P	Disc/drum	145-13	143	1803	83	19.2	21.2	£4499
IC	ITrL	R & P	Disc/drum	155-13	143	2015	93	15.0	20.0	£3995
IC	ITrL	R & P	Disc/drum	165/65-14	143	1957	107	10.9	17.7	£5569
IC	ITrL	R & P	Disc/drum	185/60-14	143	2040	107	10.3	17.4	£8299
IC	ITrL	R & P	Disc/drum	185/60-14	143	2095	113 (Claimed)	N/A	N/A	£10,095
IC	ITrL	R & P	Disc/drum	165/65-14	143	2095	92 (Claimed)	N/A	N/A	£6262
IC	IC	R & P	Disc/drum	175/70-13	150	2019	84	19.6	21.8	£6395
IC	IC	R & P	Disc/drum	175/70-13	150	1973	95 (Claimed)	N/A	N/A	£6895
IC	IC	R & P	Disc/drum	175/70-13	150	1973	98 (Claimed)	13.9	N/A	£6767
IC	IC	R & P	Disc/drum	185/60-14	150	2174	106	12.9	19.1	£9645
IC	IC	R & P	Disc/drum	175/70-13	150	2160	110	11.0	18.1	£10,495
IC	IC	R & P	Disc/disc	185/60-14	150	2437	126	7.8	16.2	£13,650
IC	IC	R & P	Disc/disc	175/70-13	150	2379	123 (Claimed)	10.3	N/A	£11,250
IC	IC	R & P	Disc/drum	175/70-13	150	2161	103 (Claimed)	16.0	N/A	£7595
IC	IC	R & P	Disc/drum	175/70-13	162	2249	98 (Claimed)	13.9	N/A	£8595
IC	IC	R & P	Disc/drum	175/70-13	162	2271	106 (Claimed)	12.5	N/A	£8787
IC	IC	R & P	Disc/disc	185/60-14	162	2326	122	9.6	17.2	£11,995
IC	IC	R & P	Disc/drum	175/70-13	162	2205	103 (Est)	16.5	N/A	£8989
IC	IC	R & P	Disc/drum	175/70-13	162	2238	106 (Est)	15.0	N/A	£11,415
IC	IC	R & P	Disc/drum	185/60-14	170	2337	106 (Claimed)	13.2	N/A	£8999
IC	IC	R & P	Disc/drum	185/60-14	170	2328	107	12.5	19.0	£10,695
IC	IC	R & P	Disc/disc	185/60-14	170	2489	129 (Claimed)	8.8	N/A	£15,299
IC	IC	R & P	Disc/disc	185/60-14	170	2984	123	10.6	17.9	£13,499
IC	IC	R & P	Disc/disc	195/50-14	170	2573	132	8.3	18.5	£14,995

Make and model	Production Figures	Years Built	Body Styles	Mechanical Layout	Engine Make (if not own)	Capacity/(cc)/Layout/Valves	BHP/rpm	Torque (lb.ft)/rpm	Transmission gearbox/automatic transmission
						2OHC			
						1896/4IL/	68/4400	94/2400	5-spd/-
						OHC Diesel	75/4400	103/2200	5-spd/-
							90/4000	149/1900	5-spd/-

Simca

Make and model	Production Figures	Years Built	Body Styles	Mechanical Layout	Engine Make (if not own)	Capacity/(cc)/Layout/Valves	BHP/rpm	Torque (lb.ft)/rpm	Transmission gearbox/automatic transmission
1000	1,642,091	1961–1978	Sal	R/R	—	944/4IL/	35/4800	47/2750	4-spd/Auto
(All 1000-type sales)						OHV	52/5400	55/3400	4-spd/Auto
							40/5800	47/2200	4-spd/-
						1118/4IL/	50/5600	61/2600	4-spd/-
						OHV			
						1294/4IL/	60/5400	71/2600	4-spd/-
						OHV			
1200S Coupe	14,741	1967–1971	Cpe	R/R	—	1204/4IL/	80/6000	76/4500	4-spd/-
						OHV			
1300/	1,342,907	1963–1976	Sal	F/R	—	1290/4IL/	62/5200	74/2600	4-spd/-
1500/1501			Est			OHV	70/5400	68/2600	4-spd/-
						1475/4IL/	81/5400	90/3000	4-spd/-
						OHV			
1100/	N/A	1967–1979	Htch	F(Tr)/F	—	1118/4IL/	56/5800	60/3600	4-spd/-
1204S/			Est			OHV	60/6000	62/3200	4-spd/-
1100 Special						1204/4IL/	75/6000	70/3600	4-spd/-
						OHV			
						1294/4IL/	75/6000	76/3000	4-spd/-
						OHV			

Skoda

Make and model	Production Figures	Years Built	Body Styles	Mechanical Layout	Engine Make (if not own)	Capacity/(cc)/Layout/Valves	BHP/rpm	Torque (lb.ft)/rpm	Transmission gearbox/automatic transmission
1000MB/	1,563,175	1964–1977	Sal	R/R	—	988/4IL/	43/4500	52/3000	4-spd/-
S100/						OHV			
S110 series						1107/4IL/	46/4600	60/3000	4-spd/-
						OHV	52/4650	64/3500	4-spd/-
S110R	56,902	1968–1977	Cpe	R/R	—	1107/4IL/	52/4650	64/3500	4-spd/-
						OHV			
Estelle	1,350,250	1977–1990	Sal	R/R	—	1046/4IL/	46/4800	55/3000	4-spd/-
						OHV			
						1174/4IL/	52/5000	63/3000	4-spd/-
						OHV	58/5200	66/3250	4-spd/-
							54/5200	67/3250	5-spd/-
						1289/4IL/	58/5000	72/2850	5-spd/-
						OHV			
130 Rapid	29,500	1982–1990	Cpe	R/R	—	1289/4IL/	58/5000	72/2850	5-spd/-
			Conv			OHV	62/5000	74/3000	5-spd/-
Favorit	In prod	1988–1994	Htch	F(Tr)/F	—	1289/4IL/	62/5000	74/3000	5-spd/-
			Est			OHV			
Felicia	In prod	1994–Date	Htch	F(Tr)/F	—	1289/4IL/	54/5000	69/3250	5-spd/-
			Est			OHV	68/5500	74/3750	5-spd/-

Ssangyong

Make and model	Production Figures	Years Built	Body Styles	Mechanical Layout	Engine Make (if not own)	Capacity/(cc)/Layout/Valves	BHP/rpm	Torque (lb.ft)/rpm	Transmission gearbox/automatic transmission
Musso	In prod	1993–Date	Ute	F/4	Mercedes-Benz	2874/5IL/ OHC	94/4100	135/2500	5-spd/Auto

Subaru

Make and model	Production Figures	Years Built	Body Styles	Mechanical Layout	Engine Make (if not own)	Capacity/(cc)/Layout/Valves	BHP/rpm	Torque (lb.ft)/rpm	Transmission gearbox/automatic transmission
1600 Leone	1,269,000	1970–1979	Sal	F/F	—	1595/4HO/	65/5200	83/2400	4-spd/-
			Cpe	(F/4 on Estate)		OHV	70/5200	83/2400	4-spd/-
			Est				77/5600	83/3600	5-spd/-
Justy	In prod	1984–1988	Htch	F(Tr)/4	—	1189/4IL/	67/5600	71/3600	5-spd/Auto
						OHC			
1600/	3,749,817	1979–1984	Sal	F/F and F/4—		1595/4HO/	70/5200	82/2400	5-spd/-
1800			Htch			OHC	85/6000	83/4000	5-spd/-
			Cpe			1781/4HO/	79/5200	98/2400	5-spd/-
			Est			OHC	82/5200	97/2400	5-spd/Auto
1800	(Incl. above)	1984–1989	Sal	F/F and F/4—		1781/4HO/	108/6000	104/3600	5-spd/-
						OHC	134/5600	144/2800	5-spd/-
XT Coupe	98,911	1985–1990	Cpe	F/4	—	1781/4HO/	134/5600	144/2800	5-spd/Auto
						OHC			
Justy	N/A	1988–Date	Htch	F(Tr)/4	—	1189/4IL/	55/6000	59/3600	5-spd/-
						OHC	68/5600	72/3600	5-spd/-
Legacy	N/A	1989–1993	Sal	F/4	—	1820/4HO/	110/6000	110/3200	5-spd/Auto
			Est			OHC			
						1994/4HO/	150/6800	127/5200	5-spd/Auto
						2OHC			
						1994/4HO/	197/6000	193/3600	5-spd/-
						2OHC			
						2212/4HO/	136/6000	140/4800	5-spd/Auto

| Suspension | | Steering | Brakes | Wheels/ | Length (in) | Weight | Performance | | Standing | UK Total |
Front	Rear		(Front/rear)	Tyres		(lb,unladen)	Top speed (mph)	0–60mph (sec)	¹/₄-mile (sec)	Price (£: at Launch)
IC	IC	R & P	Disc/drum	175/70-13	170	2330	101	15.6	20.4	£9999
IC	IC	R & P	Disc/drum	175/70-13	170	2467	106 (Claimed)	14.9	N/A	£11,999
IC	IC	R & P	Disc/drum	175/70-13	170	2467	114 (Claimed)	12.7	N/A	£12,895
ITrL	IC	Worm	Drum/drum	5.60-12	150	1568	74	27.0	23.5	£758
ITrL	IC	Worm	Drum/drum	5.60-12	150	1631	78	22.5	21.8	£640
ITrL	IC	Worm	Drum/drum	145-13	150	1589	81	21.7	22.1	£599
ITrL	IC	Worm	Drum/drum	145-13	150	1631	84	19.6	21.4	£780
ITrL	IC	Worm	Drum/drum	145-13	150	1752	95 (Claimed)	N/A	N/A	£896
ITrL	IC	Worm	Disc/disc	245-13	155	1965	107	N/A	18.0	£1493
IC	BeamC	Worm	Drum/drum	5.90-13	167	2116	84	23.3	22.9	£799
IC	BeamC	Worm	Disc/drum	165-13	167	2182	96	16.4	20.9	£1135
IC	BeamC	Worm	Disc/drum	5.90-13	167	2194	90	15.6	20.5	£919
ITor	ITor	R & P	Disc/drum	145-13	156	1962	80	19.6	21.7	£718
ITor	ITor	R & P	Disc/drum	145-13	156	2016	85	15.9	20.4	£899
ITor	ITor	R & P	Disc/drum	145-13	155	2070	95	13.6	19.3	£1039
ITor	ITor	R & P	Disc/drum	145-13	155	2070	95	13.2	18.4	£893
IC	IC	Worm	Drum/drum	6.00-14 155-14	163	1596	75	30.8	23.6	£580
IC	IC	Worm	Drum/drum	155-14	163	1800	82	21.8	21.8	£683
IC	IC	Worm	Disc/drum	155-14	163	1844	83	19.6	21.6	£846
IC	IC	Worm	Disc/drum	155-14	163	1847	86	17.7	21.0	£1050
IC	IC	Worm	Disc/drum	155-13	164	1895	81 (Claimed)	N/A	N/A	£1549
IC	IC	Worm	Disc/drum	155-13	164	1940	84	18.9	21.5	£1699
IC	IC	Worm	Disc/drum	155-13	164	1951				
IC	IC	R & P	Disc/drum	165-13	164	1951	87	19.9	21.9	£3399
IC	IC	R & P	Disc/drum	165/80-13	164	1967	88	16.3	21.0	£3511
IC	IC	R & P	Disc/drum	165/80-13	164	1967	88	16.3	21.0	£3751
IC	IC	R & P	Disc/drum	165/70-13	165	2026	91	14.9	19.5	£4198
IC	IC	R & P	Disc/drum	165/70-13	150	2070	92	14.3	19.8	£4697
IC	IC	R & P	Disc/drum	165/70-13	152	2048	90 (Est)	N/A	N/A	£5995
IC	IC	R & P	Disc/drum	165/70-13	152	2048	97	13.5	19.4	£6399
ITor	BeamC	R & P	Disc/disc	235/75-15	183	4130	91	18.4	21.7	£15,999
IC	ITor	R & P	Disc/drum	155-13	159	2184	87	16.7	20.7	£2597
IC	ITor	R & P	Disc/drum	155-13	158	1864	97	13.4	19.3	£2726
IC	ITor	R & P	Disc/drum	155-13	158	1885	97	12.1	18.7	£3101
IC	IC	R & P	Disc/drum	165/65-13	146	1905	87	13.0	19.1	£5999
IC	ITor	R & P	Disc/drum	155-13	163	2220	89	15.2	20.0	£3987
IC	ITor	R & P	Disc/drum	175/70-13	163	1960	96	12.7	18.6	£4485
IC	ITor	R & P	Disc/drum	155-13	163	2040	90	16.3	20.5	£4485
IC	ITor	R & P	Disc/drum	175/70-13	157	2006	92 (Est)	N/A	N/A	£5494
IC	IC	R & P	Disc/drum	175/70-13	172	2184	103	10.1	18.0	£7500
IC	IC	R & P	Disc/disc	175/70-13	172	2326	118	9.9	18.1	£9999
IAir	IAir	R & P	Disc/disc	195/60-14	175	2523	118	9.5	17.0	£12,000
IC	IC	R & P	Disc/drum	145-12	146	1610	91 (Est)	N/A	N/A	£6798
IC	IC	R & P	Disc/drum	165/65-13	146	1680	96 (Est)	13.0	N/A	£7390
IC	IC	R & P	Disc/disc	165-13	178	2337	112 (Claimed)	N/A	N/A	£10,999
IC	IC	R & P	Disc/disc	185/65-14	178	2579	124 (Claimed)	N/A	N/A	£12,499
IC	IC	R & P	Disc/disc	205/60-15	178	3089	136	6.9	15.4	£18,499
IC	IC	R & P	Disc/disc	185/70-14	178	2867	124	N/A	N/A	£13,499

Make and model	Production Figures	Years Built	Body Styles	Mechanical Layout	Engine Make (if not own)	Capacity/(cc)/Layout/Valves	BHP/rpm	Torque (lb.ft)/rpm	Transmission gearbox/automatic transmission
						OHC			
Vivio	In prod	1992–Date	Htch	F(Tr)/F	—	658/4IL/ OHC	43/6400	39/3600	5-spd/-
Impreza	In prod	1992-Date	Sal Cpe	F/4	—	1597/4HO/ OHC	88/5600	95/4000	5-spd/Auto
			Est	F/4	—	1820/4HO/ OHC	101/5600	109/4400	5-spd/Auto
						1994/4HO/ 2OHC	208/6000	201/4800	5-spd/-
Legacy	In prod	1993–Date	Sal Est	F/4	—	1994/4HO/ OHC	113/5600	125/4400	5-spd/Auto
						2212/4HO/ OHC	134/6000	139/4800	5-spd/Auto
SVX	In prod	1991–Date	Spts Cpe	F/4	—	3319/6HO/ 2OHC	226/5600	228/4800	Auto/-
Sunbeam									
Imp Sport	Est 10,000	1967–1976	Sal	R/R	—	875/4IL/ OHC	51/6100	53/4300	4-spd/-
Stiletto	Est 10,000	1967–1973	Cpe	R/R	—	875/4IL/ OHC	51/6100	53/4300	4-spd/-
Rapier/H120/ Alpine	46,204	1967–1976	Cpe	F/R	—	1725/4IL/ OHV	76/5100 93/5200 72/5500	93/3300 106/4000 90/3000	4-spd (+O/D)/Auto 4-spd (+O/D)/- 4-spd (+O/D)/Auto
Suzuki									
LJ80	N/A	1978–1982	Ute	F/4	—	797/4IL/ OHC	41/5500	44/3500	4-spd/-
SC100 Coupe	894,000	1979–1982	Cpe	R(Tr)/R	—	970/4IL/ OHC	47/5000	61/3000	4-spd/-
Alto	743,500	1981–1992	Sal Htch	F(Tr)/F	—	796/3IL/ OHC	40/5500	43/3000	4-spd/Auto
Swift SA310	675,450	1983–1986	Htch	F(Tr)/F	—	993/3IL/ OHC	50/5800	55/3600	5-spd/-
						1324/4IL/ OHC	73/5800	77/4000	5-spd/-
Swift	N/A	1985–1991	Htch	F(Tr)/F	—	1298/4IL/ 2OHC	101/6600	80/5500	5-spd/-
						1324/4IL/ OHC	67/5300	76/3700	5-spd/-
				F(Tr)/4	—	1590/4IL/ 2OHC	92/6000	98/3500	5-spd/-
SJ410 4x4/Santana	104,310	1982–1990	Ute	F/4	—	970/4IL/ OHC	45/5500	54/3000	4-spd/-
SJ413/ Samurai	In prod	1985–Date	Ute	F/4	—	1324/4IL/ OHC	63/6000	73/3500	5-spd/-
Vitara	In prod	1988–Date	Ute	F/4	—	1590/4IL/ OHC	75/5250 80/5400	90/3100 94/3000	5-spd/Auto 5-spd/Auto
				—		1998/V6/ 2OHC	136/6500	126/4000	5-spd/Auto
Swift	In prod	1988–Date	Htch Conv Sal	F(Tr)/F	—	993/3IL/ OHC	52/5700	56/3300	5-spd/-
						1298/4IL/ 2OHC	101/6450 67/6000	83/4950 75/4950	5-spd/- 5-spd/-
				F(Tr)/4	—	1590/4IL/ OHC	92/6000	98/3500	5-spd/-
Cappuccino	In prod	1991–Date	Spts	F/R	—	657/3IL/ 2OHC	63/6500	63/4000	5-spd/-
Baleno	In prod	1994–Date	Htch Sal	F(Tr)/F	—	1590/4IL/ OHC	97/6000	94/3000	5-spd/Auto
Talbot (ex-Chrysler-Europe)									
Sunbeam (Incl. Chrysler versions)	105,847	1979–1981	Htch	F/R	—	928/4IL/ OHC	42/5000	51/2600	4-spd/-
						1295/4IL/ OHV	59/5000	69/2600	4-spd/Auto
						1599/4IL/ OHV	69/4800 80/5400	91/2900 86/4400	4-spd/Auto 4-spd/Auto
Sunbeam 1600TI (Incl. Chrysler models)	10,113	1979–1981	Htch	F/R	—	1599/4IL/ OHV	100/6000	96/4600	4-spd/-
Sunbeam-Lotus	2,308	1979–1981	Htch	F/R	Lotus	2174/4IL/ 2OHC	150/5750	150/4500	5-spd/-
Horizon (UK prodn only)	51,230	1979–1985	Htch	F(Tr)/F	—	1118/4IL/ OHV	59/5600	67/3000	4-spd/-
						1294/4IL/ OHV	68/5600	76/3000	4-spd/5-spd/-
						1442/4IL/	82/5600	91/3000	4-spd/Auto

| Suspension | | Steering | Brakes | Wheels/ | Length (in) | Weight | Performance | | Standing | UK Total |
Front	Rear		(Front/rear)	Tyres		(lb, unladen)	Top speed (mph)	0–60mph (sec)	¼-mile (sec)	Price (£: at Launch)
IC	IC	R & P	Disc/drum	145/70-12	130	1632	(Claimed) 82	17.9	21.1	£6697
IC	IC	R & P	Disc/drum	175/70-14	171	2381	108	12.1	N/A	£12,499
IC	IC	R & P	Disc/drum	175/70-14	171	2635	(Claimed) 106	11.8	18.4	£12,999
IC	IC	R & P	Disc/disc	205/55-15	171	2675	137	5.8	14.7	£17,499
IC	IC	R & P	Disc/Auto	175/70-14	178	2337	118	10.1	N/A	£13,648
IC	IC	R & P	Disc/disc	185/70-14	178	2822	(Claimed) 116	10.8	18.0	£13,499
IC	IC	R & P	Disc/disc	225/60-16	182	3559	144	8.7	16.7	£27,999
IC	IC	R & P	Drum/drum	155-12	141	1640	90	16.3	20.2	£665
IC	IC	R & P	Drum/drum	155-12	141	1625	87	17.6	20.5	£726
IC	Beam1/2E	Worm	Disc/drum	155-13	173	2275	103	12.8	18.7	£1200
IC	Beam1/2E	Worm	Disc/drum	155-13	173	2300	105	10.3	17.7	£1599
IC	Beam1/2E	Worm	Disc/drum	6.00-13	173	2220	91	14.6	19.9	£1086
Beam1/2E	Beam1/2E	Worm	Drum/drum	6.00-16	125	1860	68	N/A	24.6	£2900
IC	IC	R & P	Disc/drum	145/70-12	126	1466	76	21.2	21.7	£2400
IC	Beam1/2E	R & P	Disc/drum	145/70-12	130	1456	82	15.8	20.5	£2675
IC	Beam1/2E	R & P	Disc/drum	145-12	141	1501	90	16.0	20.0	£3999
IC	Beam1/2E	R & P	Disc/drum	145-12	141	1636	102	10.3	17.6	£4999
IC	IC	R & P	Disc/drum	165/65-13	160	1685	109	9.1	16.8	£6750
IC	IC	R & P	Disc/drum	165/65-13	160	1606	99	11.3	18.3	£5750
IC	IC	R & P	Disc/disc	165/65-14	160	2059	104	9.5	17.5	£8999
Beam1/2E	Beam1/2E	Worm	Drum/drum	195-15	136	1870	66	29.5	23.1	£4599
Beam1/2E	Beam1/2E	Worm	Disc/drum	195-15	135	1859	74	19.4	20.5	£5885
IC	BeamC	Worm	Disc/drum	195R-15	143	2250	87	14.5	19.5	£9000
IC	BeamC	Worm	Disc/drum	195R-15	143	2381	88 (Est)	16.0	N/A	£11,250
IC	BeamC	Worm	Disc/drum	215/65-16	143	2712	99	12.5	N/A	£15,475
IC	IC	R & P	Disc/drum	155/70-13	147	1470	(Claimed) 88	17.8	20.7	£5995
IC	IC	R & P	Disc/disc	175/60-14	146	1786	114	8.7	16.8	£7299
IC	IC	R & P	Disc/drum	155/70-13	150	1684	100	11.6	18.5	£6599
IC	IC	R & P	Disc/drum	165/65-14	160	1984	111	N/A	N/A	£8999
IC	IC	R & P	Disc/disc	165/65-14	130	1497	(Claimed) 83	11.3	18.5	£11,995
IC	IC	R & P	Disc/drum	175/70-13	151	2029	112	9.7	17.5	£8795
IC	BeamC	R & P	Disc/drum	145-13	151	1757	77	24.3	22.7	£2953
IC	BeamC	R & P	Disc/drum	155-15	151	2002	92	14.8	21.0	£3193
IC	BeamC	R & P	Disc/drum	155-13	151	1953	95	12.9	19.2	£3623
IC	BeamC	R & P	Disc/drum	155-13	151	2004	100 (Est)	N/A	N/A	£3891
IC	BeamC	R & P	Disc/drum	175/70-13	151	2037	107	10.7	18.5	£4433
IC	BeamC	R & P	Disc/drum	185/70-13	151	2166	121	7.4	15.6	£6995
ITor	IC	R & P	Disc/drum	145-13	156	2081	95	15.3	20.3	£3320
ITor	IC	R & P	Disc/drum	145-13	156	2131	95	15.4	20.0	£3477
ITor	IC	R & P	Disc/drum	155-13	156	2138	97	12.3	18.7	£5220

Make and model	Production Figures	Years Built	Body Styles	Mechanical Layout	Engine Make (if not own)	Capacity/(cc)/Layout/Valves	BHP/rpm	Torque (lb.ft)/rpm	Transmission gearbox/automatic transmission
						OHV			
						1905/4IL/ OHC Diesel	64/4600	88/2000	5-spd/-
Avenger	(See Chrysler figures)	1979–1981	Sal Est	F/R	—	1295/4IL/ OHV	59/5000	69/2600	4-spd/-
						1599/4IL/ OHV	69/4800	91/2900	4-spd/Auto
							80/5400	86/4400	4-spd/Auto
Alpine	185,827 (Incl. Chrysler models)	1979–1985	Htch	F(Tr)/F	—	1294/4IL/ OHV	68/5600	79/2800	4-spd/-
						1442/4IL/ OHV	85/5600	93/3000	4-spd/-
						1592/4IL/ OHV	87/5400	101/3000	4-spd/5-spd/Auto
Solara	98,150	1980–1984	Sal	F(Tr)/F	—	1294/4IL/ OHV	67/5600	79/2800	4-spd/-
						1592/4IL/ OHV	72/5200	96/3000	4-spd/5-spd/Auto
							87/5400	101/3000	5-spd/Auto
Minx/Rapier (Based on Solara/Alpine)	27,250	1984–1986	Sal Htch	F(Tr)/F	—	1592/4IL/ OHV	90/5400	101/3800	5-spd/-
Rancho	N/A	1979–1984	Est	F(Tr)/F	—	1442/4IL/ OHV	80/5600	89/3000	4-spd/-
Tagora	23,400	1981–1984	Sal	F/R	—	2155/4IL/ OHC	113/5400	133/3200	5-spd/Auto
						2664/V6 OHC	163/6000	169/4200	5-spd/Auto
Samba	198,470	1982–1986	Htch Conv	F(Tr)/F	—	954/4IL/ OHC	45/6000	47/3000	4-spd/-
						1124/4IL/ OHC	49/4800	63/2800	4-spd/-
						1360/4IL/ OHC	71/6000	79/3000	4-spd/-
							79/5800	81/2800	5-spd/-

Tata

Gurkha	In prod	N/A	Ute	F/R	Peugeot	1948/4IL/ OHC/Diesel	62/4500	84/2000	5-spd/-

Toyota

Corona	1,788,000 (Incl. 1600S and 1900 Mk II)	1965–1972	Sal Est	F/R	—	1490/4IL/ 0HV	74/5000	85/2600	4-spd/-
Corona 1900 Mk II	See above	1969–1972	Sal Cpe	F/R	—	1858/4IL/ OHC	100/5500 124/6000	108/3600 121/4000	4-spd/- 4-spd/-
Crown	352,882	1969–1972	Sal Est	F/R	—	2253/6IL/ OHC	115/5200	127/3600	Auto/-
Corolla 1200	N/A	1970–1978	Sal Est Cpe	F/R	—	1166/4IL/ OHV	73/6000 83/6600	75/3800 75/4600	4-spd/- 4-spd/-
Corolla '30'	4,532,374	1974–1979	Sal Htch Est Cpe	F/R	—	1166/4IL/ OHV 1588/4IL/ OHV	56/6000 83/6600 75/5200	62/3800 75/4600 84/3800	4-spd/Auto 4-spd/Auto 4-spd/Auto
Carina	1,026,068	1970–1977	Sal Cpe	F/R	—	1588/4IL/ OHV	75/5200	85/3800	4-spd/Auto
Carina	1,927,000	1977–1981	Sal Est Cpe	F/R	—	1588/4IL/ OHV	75/5200	85/3800	4-spd/Auto
Carina	(Incl. in 1977–1981 figures)	1981–1984	Sal Est	F/R	—	1588/4IL/ OHC 1770/4IL/ OHC	73/5200 84/5200	85/3600 103/3400	5-spd/- 5-spd/Auto
Celica	1,210,951	1970–1977	Cpe Cpe Htch	F/R	—	1588/4IL/ OHV 1588/4IL/ 2OHC 1968/4IL/ OHC	105/6000 124/6400 95/5000	101/4200 113/5200 105/3600	4-spd/5-spd/- 5-spd/- 5-spd/Auto
Celica	1,399,520	1977–1981	Cpe Cpe Htch	F/R	—	1588/4IL/ OHV 1968/4IL/ OHC 1968/4IL/ 2OHC	86/5600 89/5000 118/5800	87/4000 107/3600 112/5200	5-spd/- 5-spd/- 5-spd/Auto
Crown 2600	N/A	1971–1974	Sal Cpe Est	F/R	—	2563/6IL/ OHC	140/5400 150/5400	156/3600 164/3800	Auto/- Auto/-
Crown 2600 Mk II	N/A	1974–1979	Sal Cpe Est	F/R	—	2563/6IL/ OHC	150/5400	164/3800	Auto/-

Suspension Front	Rear	Steering	Brakes (Front/rear)	Wheels/ Tyres	Length (in)	Weight (lb, unladen)	Top speed (mph)	0–60mph (sec)	Standing ¼-mile (sec)	UK Total Price (£: at Launch)
ITor	IC	R & P	Disc/drum	145-13	156	2205	96	13.8	19.5	£4995
IC	BeamC	R & P	Disc/drum	155-13	163	1889	90	17.5	20.6	£3324
IC	BeamC	R & P	Disc/drum	155-13	163	1929	94	13.7	19.1	£3456
IC	BeamC	R & P	Disc/drum	155-13	163	2013	100 (Est)	N/A	N/A	£4152
ITor	IC	R & P	Disc/drum	155-13	167	2314	90	16.9	20.5	£3872
ITor	IC	R & P	Disc/drum	155-13	167	2314	100	12.9	19.0	£2375
ITor	IC	R & P	Disc/drum	165-13	170	2520	97 (Auto)	14.5	19.9	£6495
ITor	IC	R & P	Disc/drum	155-13	173	2231	90 (Claimed)	N/A	N/A	£4069
ITor	IC	R & P	Disc/drum	155-13	173	2240	93	13.9	19.4	£4266
ITor	IC	R & P	Disc/drum	155-13	173	2416	100	11.6	18.4	£5642
ITor	IC	R & P	Disc/drum	165-15	173	2360	101	14.6	19.5	£5895
ITor	ITor	R & P	Disc/drum	185/70-14	170	2620	89	14.9	20.0	£6316
IC	IC	R & P	Disc/drum	175-14	182	2797	106	11.3	18.2	£6916
IC	IC	R & P	Disc/disc	215/65-365	182	2965	116	8.3	16.2	£10,251
IC	IC	R & P	Disc/drum	135-13	138	1631	80 (Claimed)	N/A	N/A	£2995
IC	IC	R & P	Disc/drum	145-13	138	1631	87	16.0	20.2	£4017
IC	IC	R & P	Disc/drum	165/70-13	138	1742	93	12.5	18.9	£4767
IC	IC	R & P	Disc/drum	165/70-13	138	1669	103	11.0	18.0	£4990
IC	BeamC	Worm	Disc/drum	215/75-15	173	3197	80 (Claimed)	20.0	N/A	£9995
IC	Beam1/2E	Worm	Drum/drum	5.60-13	161	2156	87	17.2	20.3	£777
IC	Beam1/2E	Worm	Disc/drum	165-13	170	2320	99	13.5	19.2	£1196
IC	Beam1/2E	Worm	Disc/drum	165-13	170	2290	102	12.9	19.0	£1559
IC	BeamC	Worm	Disc/drum	6.95-14	184	2888	96	16.0	20.1	£1458
IC	Beam1/2E	Worm	Disc/drum	6.00-12	155	1655	90 (Est)	N/A	N/A	£949
IC	Beam1/2E	Worm	Disc/drum	155-12	155	1715	95	14.3	19.7	£1109
IC	Beam1/2E	Worm	Disc/drum	155-13	157	1902	87	16.9	20.6	£1529
IC	Beam1/2E	Worm	Disc/drum	155-13	157	1904	90	14.7	19.7	£1646
IC	Beam1/2E	Worm	Disc/drum	165-13	157	2094	95	13.2	18.9	£2878
IC	BeamC	Worm	Disc/drum	165-13	164	2106	98	12.2	19.0	£1185
IC	BeamC	Worm	Disc/drum	165-13	167	2295	96	13.4	19.0	£3180
IC	BeamC	R & P	Disc/drum	165-13	170	2073	103	N/A	N/A	£1183
IC	BeamC	R & P	Disc/drum	165-14	170	2161	106	N/A	N/A	£4871
IC	BeamC	Worm	Disc/drum	165-13	160	2128	105	11.5	18.2	£1362
IC	BeamC	Worm	Disc/drum	165-13	164	2215	113	9.3	17.1	£2345
IC	BeamC	Worm	Disc/drum	165-14	167	2356	103	12.3	18.4	£2780
IC	BeamC	Worm	Disc/drum	165-13	171	2305	106 (Claimed)	N/A	N/A	£3586
IC	BeamC	Worm	Disc/drum	165-14	171	2435	109 (Claimed)	N/A	N/A	£4223
IC	BeamC	Worm	Disc/drum	185/70-14	171	2333	111	8.8	16.8	£3909
IC	BeamC	Worm	Disc/drum	175-14	184	2890	100	12.7	18.9	£1921
IC	BeamC	Worm	Disc/drum	175-14	184	2890	103 (Claimed)	N/A	N/A	£2326
IC	BeamC	Worm	Disc/drum	185-14	181	3243	99	13.3	19.4	£4323

Make and model	Production Figures	Years Built	Body Styles	Mechanical Layout	Engine Make (if not own)	Capacity/(cc)/Layout/Valves	BHP/rpm	Torque (lb.ft)/rpm	Transmission gearbox/automatic transmission
Corona 2000 Mk II	N/A	1972–1975	Sal Cpe Est	F/R	—	1968/4IL/ OHC	105/5500	116/3600	4-spd/Auto
2000	N/A	1973–1978	Sal Cpe	F/R	—	1968/4IL/ OHC	86/5000	105/3600	5-spd/Auto
Cressida	742,650	1977–1980	Sal Cpe Est	F/R	—	1968/4IL/ OHC	89/5000	103/3600	4-spd/Auto
Cressida	1,999,557	1980–1988	Sal Cpe Est	F/R	—	1972/4IL/ OHC	105/5200	116/3600	5-spd/Auto
						2188/4IL/ OHC Diesel	66/4200	98/2400	5-spd/-
Corona	N/A	1978–1982	Sal	F/R	—	1770/4IL/ OHC	86/5400	103/3400	5-spd/-
1000 (Publica)	N/A	1972–1978	Sal Cpe Est	F/R	—	993/4IL/ OHV	47/5800	49/3800	4-spd/-
Starlet	950,691	1978–1984	Htch Est	F/R	—	993/4IL/ OHV	47/5800	47/3800	4-spd/-
						1166/4IL/ OHV	56/6000	61/3800	4-spd/-
						1290/4IL/ OHV	64/5400	72/3600	4-spd/-
Land-Cruiser	N/A	1966–1980	Ute	F/4	—	4230/6IL/ OHV	135/3600	210/1800	4-spd/-
Carina II	2,470,000	1983–1988	Sal Htch	F(Tr)/F	—	1587/4IL/ OHC	84/5600 85/5600	96/3600 100/3600	5-spd/Auto
						1974/4IL/ OHC Diesel	68/4500	89/3000	5-spd/-
Carina	2,617,000	1988–1992	Sal Htch Est	F(Tr)/F	—	1587/4IL/ 2OHC	94/6000	100/3600	5-spd/Auto
						1998/4IL/ 2OHC	126/5600	129/4400	5-spd/Auto
Celica ST/XT	1,794,000	1981–1985	Cpe Cpe Htch	F/R	—	1972/4IL/ OHC	103/5000	116/4000	5-spd/Auto
Celica GT	1,980,000	1985–1990	Cpe Htch Conv	F(Tr)/F	—	1998/4IL/ 2OHC	147/6400	133/4800	5-spd/Auto
Celica GT-Four	26,350	1987–1990	Cpe Htch	F(Tr)/4	—	1998/4IL/ 2OHC	182/6000	184/3600	5-spd/-
Celica Supra	863,700	1982–1986	Cpe	F/R	—	2759/6IL/ 2OHC	168/5600	169/4600	5-spd/Auto
Supra	970,000	1986–1993	Cpe Htch	F/R	—	2954/6IL/ 2OHC	201/6000	187/4000	5-spd/Auto
Supra Turbo	407,950	1988–1992	Cpe Htch	F/R	—	2954/6IL/ 2OHC	232/5600	254/3200	5-spd/Auto
Starlet	1,094,900	1984–1990	Htch	F(Tr)/F	—	999/4IL/ OHV	54/6000	55/3800	5-spd/-
Corolla	4,720,790	1979–1983	Sal Htch Est	F/R	—	1290/4IL/ OHV 1588/4IL/ OHC	59/5600 64/5400 86/5500 74/5400	68/3600 72/3600 89/4000 86/3600	4-spd/Auto 5-spd/Auto 5-spd/- 5-spd/-
Corolla	3,270,000	1983–1987	Sal Cpe Htch Est	F(Tr)/F	—	1295/4IL/ OHC 1588/4IL/ 2OHC	69/6000 74/6200 120/6600	75/3800 76/4200 103/5000	5-spd/Auto 5-spd/Auto 5-spd/-
Corolla GT	958,760	1984–1987	Cpe Htch	F/R	—	1588/4IL/ 2OHC	120/6600	103/5000	5-spd/-
Corolla	4,288,405	1987–1992	Sal Htch Est	F(Tr)/F	—	1295/4IL/ OHC 1587/4IL/ 2OHC	74/6200 94/6000 123/6600	76/4200 100/3600 107/5000	5-spd/Auto 5-spd/Auto 5-spd/-
				F(Tr)/4	—	1587/4IL/ 2OHC	94/6000	100/3600	5-spd/-
Crown	823,000	1980–1983	Sal	F/R	—	2759/6IL/ OHC	145/5000	123/4000	Auto/-
Tercel	1,073,720	1982–1985	Htch Est	F/F	—	1295/4IL/ OHC	64/6000	73/3800	5-spd/Auto
				F/F or F/4	—	1452/4IL/ OHC	70/5600	80/3800	5-spd/-
Camry	1,430,000	1982–1986	Sal Est	F(Tr)/F	—	1832/4IL/ OHC	89/5200	105/3400	5-spd/Auto
						1995/4IL/ OHC	106/5200	122/4000	5-spd/-
						1839/4IL/ OHC Diesel	73/4500	107/2600	5-spd/-
						1974/4IL/ OHC Diesel	83/4500	121/2600	5-spd/-
Camry	1,002,400	1986–1990	Sal Est	F(Tr)/F	—	1998/4IL/ 2OHC	126/5600	132/4400	5-spd/Auto
						1974/4IL/	83/4500	121/2400	5-spd/-

Suspension Front	Rear	Steering	Brakes (Front/rear)	Wheels/ Tyres	Length (in)	Weight (lb,unladen)	Performance Top speed (mph)	0–60mph (sec)	Standing 1/4-mile (sec)	UK Total Price (£: at Launch)
IC	BeamC	Worm	Disc/drum	165-13	170	2540	100	11.4	18.7	£1476
IC	Beam1/2E	Worm	Disc/drum	175-14	168	2392	95	12.3	19.1	£2575
IC	BeamC	Worm	Disc/drum	175-14	178	2386	95	12.9	19.3	£3461
IC	BeamC	R & P	Disc/drum	175-14	183	2403	106	11.3	18.1	£6075
IC	BeamC	R & P	Disc/drum	175-14	183	2590	89	17.1	20.6	£5970
IC	BeamC	Worm	Disc/drum	175-14	169	2445	102	13.2	19.1	£5269
IC	Beam1/2E	Worm	Disc/drum	155-12	146	1585	85	15.9	20.5	£1158
IC	BeamC	R & P	Disc/drum	145-13	147	1652	84	18.1	21.0	£2808
IC	BeamC	R & P	Disc/drum	145-13	147	1652	93 (Claimed)	N/A	N/A	£3073
IC	BeamC	R & P	Disc/drum	145-13	147	1652	99 (Claimed)	N/A	N/A	£4274
Beam1/2E	Beam1/2E	Worm	Drum/drum	7.50-16	183	4301	91	16.3	20.3	£4178
IC	IC	R & P	Disc/drum	165-13	170	2149	101	12.6	18.7	£6295
IC	IC	R & P	Disc/drum	165-13	170	2205	96 (Claimed)	N/A	N/A	£6965
IC	IC	R & P	Disc/disc	165-13	175	2387	106	10.5	17.9	£10,069
IC	IC	R & P	Disc/disc	185/65-14	175	2426	120	9.2	17.1	£13,030
IC	IC	R & P	Disc/drum	185/70-14	171	2576	111	10.4	17.7	£6392
IC	IC	R & P	Disc/disc	195/60-14	172	2805	131	8.2	16.7	£12,000
IC	IC	R & P	Disc/disc	205/60-14	172	3260	135	7.6	15.7	£20,495
IC	IC	R & P	Disc/disc	195/70-14	182	2870	131	8.7	16.7	£9888
IC	IC	R & P	Disc/disc	225/50-16	182	3417	135	7.7	16.0	£15,299
IC	IC	R & P	Disc/disc	225/60-15	182	3469	144	6.9	15.9	£22,060
IC	IC	R & P	Disc/drum	145-13	146	1624	85	14.8	19.7	£4439
IC	BeamC	Worm	Disc/drum	155-13	160	1848	90	14.9	19.3	£3249
IC	BeamC	Worm	Disc/drum	155-13	160	1848	93 (Est)	N/A	N/A	£4103
IC	BeamC	Worm	Disc/drum	185/70-13	162	2240	98	12.1	18.5	£4386
IC	BeamC	Worm	Disc/drum	185/70-13	162	2240	92 (Est)	N/A	N/A	£4886
IC	IC	R & P	Disc/drum	155-13	163	1962	97	12.3	18.7	£5133
IC	IC	R & P	Disc/drum	155-13	156	1962	100 (Est)	N/A	N/A	£5250
IC	IC	R & P	Disc/disc	185/60-14	156	2091	120	8.5	16.2	£7295
IC	BeamC	R & P	Disc/drum	185/70-13	165	2156	118	8.6	16.4	£6995
IC	IC	R & P	Disc/drum	155-13	157	2035	93	12.8	19.0	£6999
IC	IC	R & P	Disc/drum	175/70-13	166	2248	103	11.1	18.0	£9499
IC	IC	R & P	Disc/disc	185/60-14	157	2255	121	9.2	16.8	£9950
IC	BeamC	R & P	Disc/drum	185/70-13	167	2575	96	12.1	18.6	£11,498
IC	BeamC	Worm	Disc/drum	195/70-14	191	3164	113	10.4	17.6	£8500
IC	IC	R & P	Disc/drum	145-13	153	1963	94	13.5	19.9	£4562
IC	IC (BeamC with 4x4)	R & P	Disc/drum	175/70-13	153	2219	92	14.2	19.4	£5892
IC	IC	R & P	Disc/drum	165-13	174	2299	102	10.5	18.2	£6070
IC	IC	R & P	Disc/drum	185/70-13	174	2318	105	10.6	17.6	£7795
IC	IC	R & P	Disc/drum	185/70-13	174	2559	99	13.5	19.2	£7922
IC	IC	R & P	Disc/drum	185/70-13	174	2359	103 (Claimed)	N/A	N/A	£7679
IC	IC	R & P	Disc/drum	185/70-14	178	2637	114	9.0	16.9	£10,390
IC	IC	R & P	Disc/drum	185/70-14	178	2536	106	N/A	N/A	£10,700

Make and model	Production Figures	Years Built	Body Styles	Mechanical Layout	Engine Make (if not own)	Capacity/(cc)/Layout/Valves	BHP/rpm	Torque (lb.ft)/rpm	Transmission gearbox/automatic transmission
						OHC Diesel			
				F(Tr)/4	—	1998/4IL/ 2OHC	126/5600	132/4400	5-spd/-
Camry V6	457,900	1988–1990	Sal	F(Tr)/F	—	2507/V6/ 2OHC	158/5800	152/4600	Auto/-
MR-2	166,104	1984–1989	Cpe	M(Tr)/R	—	1588/4IL/ 2OHC	122/6600	105/5000	5-spd/-
MR-2	In prod	1989–Date	Cpe	M(Tr)/R	—	1998/4IL/ 2OHC	119/5600	130/4400	5-spd/-
							158/6600	140/4800	5-spd/-
							173/7000	137/4800	5-spd/-
Space Cruiser	225,700	1983–1990	Est	F/R	—	1812/4IL/ OHV	78/4800	103/3400	5-spd/Auto
						1998/4IL/ OHV	87/4600	120/2600	5-spd/Auto
Land Cruiser	471,150	1980–1989	Est	F/4	—	3980/6IL/ OHC Diesel	103/3500	177/2300	4-spd/5-spd/Auto
Starlet	In prod	1989–Date	Htch	F(Tr)/F	—	999/4IL/ OHC	54/6000	55/3800	5-spd/-
						1331/4IL/ 2OHC	74/6000	81/3600	5-spd/Auto
Corolla	In prod	1992–Date	Htch Sal Est Cpe	F(Tr)/F	—	1331/4IL/ 2OHC	87/6000	82/4800	5-spd/Auto
						1587/4IL/ 2OHC	113/6000	107/4800	5-spd/Auto
						1762/4IL/ 2OHC	118/5800	114/4400	5-spd/Auto
						1975/4IL/ OHC Diesel	72/4600	95/2750	5-spd/Auto
Carina E	In prod	1992–Date	Sal Htch Est	F(Tr)/F	—	1587/4IL/ 2OHC	115/6000	108/4000	5-spd/Auto
						2OHC	106/6000	101/4800	5-spd/Auto
						1838/4IL/ 2OHC	106/5600	111/2800	5-spd/-
						1998/4IL/ 2OHC	131/5800	135/4600	5-spd/Auto
						2OHC	155/6400	137/4400	5-spd/Auto
							173/7000	137/4800	5-spd/-
						1974/4IL/ OHC Diesel	72/4600	97/2800	5-spd/-
Camry	In prod	1991–Date	Sal Est Cpe	F(Tr)/F	—	2164/4IL/ 2OHC	134/5400	145/4000	5-spd/Auto
						2959/V6/ 2OHC	185/5400	188/4400	Auto/-
Celica/ GT-Four	425,628	1989–1993	Cpe	F(Tr)/F	—	1998/4IL/ 2OHC	158/6600	138/4800	5-spd/-
						2OHC	154/6600	137/4800	5-spd/-
				F(Tr)/4	—	1998/4IL/ 2OHC	200/6000	199/3200	5-spd/-
						2OHC	205/6000	203/4000	5-spd/-
Celica/ GT-Four	In prod	1993–Date	Cpe	F(Tr)/F	—	1762/4IL/ 2OHC	115/5800	113/4400	5-spd/-
						1998/4IL/ 2OHC	173/7000	137/4800	5-spd/-
				F(Tr)/4	—	1998/4IL/ 2OHC	239/6000	223/4000	5-spd/-
Supra	In prod	1993–Date	Spts Cpe	F/R	—	2997/6IL/ 2OHC	320/5600	315/4000	6-spd/-
Previa	In prod	1990–Date	Est	M/R	—	2438/4IL/ 2OHC	133/5000	152/4000	5-spd/Auto
Land- cruiser II	In prod	1988–Date	Ute	F/4	—	2446/4IL/ OHC Diesel	84/4000	138/2400	5-spd/-
						2982/4IL/ OHC Diesel	123/3600	218/2000	5-spd/-
Land- cruiser	In prod	1989–Date	Ute	F/4	—	4163/6IL/ OHC Diesel	137/4000	206/2200	5-spd/Auto
							165/3600	266/1800	5-spd/Auto
						4477/6IL/ OHC	202/4400	266/3200	Auto
4 Runner	In prod	1993–Date	Ute	F/R	—	2959/V6/ OHC	141/6000	177/3400	5-spd/-
						2982/4IL/ OHC Diesel	123/3600	218/2000	5-spd/-
RAV-4	In prod	1993–Date	Ute	F/4	—	1998/4IL/ 2OHC	133/6000	134/4400	5-spd/Auto
						2OHC	129/5600	129/4600	5-spd/Auto

Transcat

| Transcat | N/A | N/A | Ute | F/4 | Peugeot | 2304/4IL/ OHV Diesel | 67/4500 | 99/2200 | 4-spd (+O/D)/- |

Trident

Suspension Front	Rear	Steering	Brakes (Front/rear)	Wheels/Tyres	Length (in)	Weight (lb, unladen)	Top speed (mph)	0–60mph (sec)	Standing 1/4-mile (sec)	UK Total Price (£: at Launch)
							(Claimed)			
IC	IC	R & P	Disc/disc	185/70-14	181	3098	111	11.8	18.5	£16,695
IC	IC	R & P	Disc/disc	195/60-15	178	3139	116	11.1	N/A	£16,991
IC	IC	R & P	Disc/disc	185/60-14	152	2319	121	7.7	16.0	£9295
IC	IC	R & P	Disc/disc	195/60-14/ 205/60-14	165	2786	121	9.3	17.0	£14,001
IC	IC	R & P	Disc/disc	195/60-14/ 205/60-14	165	2786	137	6.7	15.2	£15,441
IC	IC	R & P	Disc/disc	195/55-15/ 225/50-15	165	2833	129	7.9	17.1	£19,275
ITor	BeamC	Worm	Disc/drum	175-14	167	2910	80 (Est)	N/A	N/A	£7981
ITor	BeamC	Worm	Disc/drum	175-14	167	2933	87	16.1	19.9	£8995
Beam1/2E	Beam1/2E	Worm	Disc/drum	205-13	184	4267	85	19.3	21.3	£10,659
IC	IC	R & P	Disc/drum	145-13	129	1786	87	14.7	20.1	£7600
IC	IC	R & P	Disc/drum	155-13	129	1720	106 (Est)	10.3	N/A	£8750
IC	IC	R & P	Disc/drum	175/65-14	161	2194	106	11.8	18.6	£9456
IC	IC	R & P	Disc/drum	175/65-14	169	2377	117	9.8	17.5	£11,434
IC	IC	R & P	Disc/drum	175/65-14	169	2377	120 (Est)	N/A	N/A	£13,299
IC	IC	R & P	Disc/drum	175/65-14	169	2293	103	13.9	N/A	£10,280
							(Claimed)			
IC	IC	R & P	Disc/drum	175/70-14	178	2238	117	10.7	18.0	£12,145
IC	IC	R & P	Disc/drum	175/70-14	178	2238	117	10.7	18.0	£12,145
IC	IC	R & P	Disc/drum	175/70-14	178	2293	118 (Est)	11.9	N/A	£15,820
IC	IC	R & P	Disc/disc	185/65-14	178	2734	127	8.9	16.9	£14,028
IC	IC	R & P	Disc/disc	195/60-15	178	2822	134 (Est)	8.2	N/A	£16,980
IC	IC	R & P	Disc/disc	195/60-15	178	2822	134 (Est)	8.2	N/A	£17,745
IC	IC	R & P	Disc/drum	175/70-14	178	2470	103	16.2	N/A	£12,488
							(Claimed)			
IC	IC	R & P	Disc/disc	195/70-15	186	2907	125	9.7	17.4	£17,520
IC	IC	R & P	Disc/disc	205/65-15	186	3337	131	9.2	17.4	£22,325
IC	IC	R & P	Disc/disc	205/60-14	174	2888	132	8.1	16.5	£17,301
IC	IC	R & P	Disc/disc	205/55-15	174	2778	137 (Est)	8.4	N/A	£18,392
IC	IC	R & P	Disc/disc	205/60-14	175	3351	143 (Est)	N/A	N/A	£22,380
IC	IC	R & P	Disc/disc	215/50-15	173	3058	143 (Est)	N/A	N/A	£24001
IC	IC	R & P	Disc/disc	195/65-14	174	2514	124	10.0	N/A	£16,995
							(Claimed)			
IC	IC	R & P	Disc/disc	205/55-15	174	2602	131	7.1	15.6	£20,617
IC	IC	R & P	Disc/disc	215/50-16	174	3043	140	5.9	14.6	£29,235
IC	IC	R & P	Disc/disc	235/45-17/ 255/40-17	178	3450	156	5.1	13.7	£37,500
IC	IC	R & P	Disc/disc	215/65-15	187	3792	109	12.9	19.1	£18,099
BeamC	BeamC	Worm	Disc/drum	215-15	160	3930	78	23.5	22.3	£15,259
BeamC	BeamC	Worm	Disc/drum	205-16	160	4057	93	N/A	N/A	£19,690
							(Claimed)			
BeamC	BeamC	Worm	Disc/drum	215/80-16	190	4971	95 (Est)	N/A	N/A	£27,431
BeamC	BeamC	Worm	Disc/drum	265/70-15	190	4971	103	12.6	19.2	£32,274
BeamC	BeamC	Worm	Disc/disc	275/70-16	190	5049	110	11.1	18.2	£38,689
ITor	BeamC	Worm	Disc/drum	265/70-15	177	3969	103	15.0	N/A	£22,292
							(Claimed)			
ITor	BeamC	Worm	Disc/drum	265/70-15	177	4189	93	16.4	N/A	£23,211
							(Claimed)			
IC	IC	R & P	Disc/drum	215/70-16	145	2533	110	8.8	16.7	£13,995
IC	IC	R & P	Disc/drum	215/70-15	162	2728	107	10.1	17.5	£15,945
Beam1/2E	Beam1/2E	Worm	Drum/drum	7.00-16	152	3638	71	N/A	N/A	£8610
							(Claimed)			

Make and model	Production Figures	Years Built	Body Styles	Mechanical Layout	Engine Make (if not own)	Capacity/ (cc)/Layout/ Valves	BHP/ rpm	Torque (lb.ft)/rpm	Transmission gearbox/automatic transmission
Clipper/ Venturer/ Tycoon	Approx 225	1967–1978	Spts Cpe Conv	F/R	Ford	2994/V6/ OHV	138/5000	174/3000	4-spd (+O/D)/Auto
					Triumph	2498/6IL/ OHV	152/5500	158/3000	Auto/-
					Chrysler	5562/V8/ OHV	243/4800	290/3600	Auto/-
Triumph									
TR6	91,850	1968–1976	Spts	F/R	—	2498/6IL/ OHV	150/5500 124/5000	164/3500 143/3500	4-spd (+O/D)/-
Herald 12/50/ 13/60	135,917	1962–1971	Sal Conv Est	F/R	—	1147/4IL/ OHV 1296/4IL/ OHV	51/5200 61/5000	63/2600 73/3000	4-spd/- 4-spd/-
Vitesse 2-litre Mk II	9,121	1968–1971	Sal Conv	F/R	—	1998/6IL/ OHV	104/5300	117/3000	4-spd (+O/D)/-
Spitfire Mk IV/1500	165,850	1970–1980	Spts	F/R	—	1296/4IL/ OHV 1493/4IL/ OHV	63/6000 71/5500	69/3500 82/3000	4-spd (+O/D)/- 4-spd (+O/D)/-
2000 Mk II/ 2500TC/S	139,524	1969–1977	Sal Est	F/R	—	1998/6IL/ OHV 2498/6IL/ OHV	84/5000 91/4750 99/4700 106/4700	100/2900 110/3300 133/3000 139/3000	4-spd (+O/D)/Auto 4-spd (+O/D)/Auto 4-spd (+O/D)/Auto
2.5 PI Mk 2	47,455	1969–1975	Sal Est	F/R	—	2498/6IL/ OHV	132/5500	153/2000	4-spd (+O/D)/Auto
1300/1300 TC/1500	214,703	1965–1973	Sal	F/F	—	1296/4IL/ OHV 1493/4IL/ OHV	61/5000 75/6000 61/5000 65/5000	73/3000 75/4000 81/2700 80/3000	4-spd/- 4-spd/- 4-spd/- 4-spd/-
GT6 Mk III	13,042	1970–1973	Spts Cpe	F/R	—	1998/6IL/ OHV	104/5300	117/3000	4-spd (+O/D)/-
Toledo 1300/ 1500	119,182	1970–1976	Sal	F/R	—	1296/4IL/ OHV	58/5300	70/3000	4-spd/-
1500TC	25,549	1973–1976	Sal	F/R	—	1493/4IL/ OHV	64/5000 71/5500	78/3000 84/3000	4-spd/Auto 4-spd/Auto
Stag	25,939	1970–1977	Conv Cpe	F/R	—	2997/V8/ OHC	145/5500	170/3500	4-spd + O/D/Auto
Dolomite 1300/1500	127,860	1976–1980	Sal	F/R	—	1296/4IL/ OHV 1493/4IL/ OHV	58/5300 71/5500	70/3000 84/3000	4-spd/Auto 4-spd/Auto
Dolomite 1850	79,010	1972–1980	Sal	F/R	—	1854/4IL/ OHC	91/5200	105/3500	4-spd (+O/D)/Auto
Dolomite Sprint	22,941	1973–1980	Sal	F/R	—	1998/4IL/ OHC	127/5700	124/4500	4-spd (+O/D)/Auto
TR7	112,375	1975–1981	Spts	F/R	—	1998/4IL/ OHC	105/5500	119/3500	4-spd/5-spd/Auto
Acclaim	133,626	1981–1984	Sal	F(Tr)/F	Honda	1335/4IL/ OHC	70/5750	74/3500	5-spd/Auto
TVR									
Vixen S1/S2/S3	723	1967–1972	Spts Cpe	F/R	Ford	1599/4IL/ OHV	88/5400	96/3600	4-spd/-
Tuscan V6	101	1969–1971	Spts Cpe	F/R	Ford	2994/V6/ OHV	128/4750	173/3000	4-spd (+O/D)/-
Vixen S4/1300	38	1972–1973	Spts Cpe	F/R	Triumph	1296/4IL/ OHV	63/6000	69/3500	4-spd/-
					Ford	1599/4IL/ OHV	86/5500	92/4000	4-spd/-
2500	385	1970–1973	Spts Cpe	F/R	Triumph	2498/6IL/ OHV	106/4900	133/3000	4-spd (+O/D)/-
1600M/ 2500M/3000M	1,749	1971–1979	Spts Cpe	F/R	Ford	1599/4IL/ OHV	86/5500	92/4000	4-spd/-
					Triumph	2498/6IL/ OHV	106/4900	133/3000	4-spd (+O/D)/-
					Ford	2994/V6/ OHV	138/5000	174/3000	4-spd/-
Taimar	395	1976–1979	Spts Htch	F/R	Ford	2994/V6/ OHV	142/5000	174/3000	4-spd/-
Convertible	258	1978–1979	Spts	F/R	Ford	2994/V6/ OHV	142/5000	174/3000	4-spd/-
Turbo	63	1975–1979	Spts Spts Htch Spts Cpe	F/R	Ford	2994/V6/ OHV	230/5500	273/3500	4-spd/-
Tasmin	2,563	1980–1990	Spts	F/R	Ford	1993/4IL/	101/5200	112/3500	4-spd/-

Suspension Front	Rear	Steering	Brakes (Front/rear)	Wheels/Tyres	Length (in)	Weight (lb,unladen)	Top speed (mph)	0–60mph (sec)	Standing 1/4-mile (sec)	UK Total Price (£: at Launch)
IC	IC	R & P	Disc/drum	185-15	165	N/Q	120 (Est)	N/A	N/A	£2400
IC	IC	R & P	Disc/drum	185-15	165	N/Q	125 (Est)	N/A	N/A	£3232
IC	IC	R & P	Disc/drum	205-15	165	N/Q	137 (Est)	N/A	N/A	£3456
IC	IC	R & P	Disc/drum	165-15	159	2473	119	8.2	16.3	£1334
IC	ITrL	R & P	Disc/drum	5.20-13	153	1855 to 1988	78	25.2	22.1	£635
IC	ITrL	R & P	Disc/drum	5.20-13	153	1876	84	17.7	20.9	£700
IC	ITrL	R & P	Disc/drum	155-13	153	2044	101	11.3	18.1	£951
IC	ITrL	R & P	Disc/drum	145-13	149	1717	90	16.2	20.6	£985
IC	ITrL	R & P	Disc/drum	155-13	149	1750	100	13.2	19.1	£1360
IC	IC	R & P	Disc/drum	175-13 to 175-14	182	2620 to 2842	96	14.9	19.7	£1412
IC	IC	R & P	Disc/drum	185-13	182	2681	104	11.8	18.7	£2352
IC	IC	R & P	Disc/drum	175-14	182	2609	105	10.4	17.8	£3271
IC	IC	R & P	Disc/drum	185-13	182	2760	106	11.5	18.1	£1595
IC	IC	R & P	Disc/drum	5.60-13	155	2016	84	19.0	21.3	£797
IC	IC	R & P	Disc/drum	5.60-13	155	2016	93	15.9	20.2	£874
IC	BeamC	R & P	Disc/drum	5.60-13	162	2128	85	17.1	20.7	£1113
IC	ITrL	R & P	Disc/drum	155-13	149	2030	112	10.1	17.4	£1287
IC	BeamC	R & P	Drum/drum Disc/drum	5.20-13 to 155-13	157	1905	85	17.1	20.9	£889
IC	BeamC	R & P	Disc/drum	155-13	162	2061	91	13.2	19.4	£1295
IC	BeamC	R & P	Disc/drum	155-13	162	2061	91	N/A	N/A	£1934
IC	IC	R & P	Disc/drum	185-14	174	2807	117	9.7	17.3	£1996
IC	BeamC	R & P	Disc/drum	155-13	162	2079	83	20.1	21.3	£2070
IC	BeamC	R & P	Disc/drum	155-13	162	2161	91	14.2	19.2	£2441
IC	BeamC	R & P	Disc/drum	155-13	162	2127	100	11.6	18.4	£1399
IC	BeamC	R & P	Disc/drum	175-13	162	2214	115	8.7	16.7	£1740
IC	BeamC	R & P	Disc/drum	185/70-13	160	2205/2311	109	9.1	17.0	£3000
IC	IC	R & P	Disc/drum	165/70-13	161	1784	92	12.9	18.6	£4688
IC	IC	R & P	Disc/drum	165-15	138/145	1680/1735	109	10.5	17.2	£1387
IC	IC	R & P	Disc/drum	165-15	145	2000	125 (Est)	8.3	16.2	£1930
IC	IC	R & P	Disc/drum	165-15	145	1625	90 (Est)	N/A	N/A	£1558
IC	IC	R & P	Disc/drum	165-15	145	1970	109	10.5	17.2	£1723
IC	IC	R & P	Disc/drum	165-15	145	1960	111	10.6	17.7	£1927
IC	IC	R & P	Disc/drum	165-15	154	2000	105	10.4	17.6	£1886
IC	IC	R & P	Disc/drum	165-15 185-14	154	2240	109	9.3	17.3	£2049
IC	IC	R & P	Disc/drum	165-15 185-14	154	2240	121	7.7	16.0	£2170
IC	IC	R & P	Disc/drum	185-14	154	2260	121	7.7	16.0	£4260
IC	IC	R & P	Disc/drum	185-14	154	2420	125 (Est)	7.7	16.6	£6390
IC	IC	R & P	Disc/drum	195/70-14	154	2260/2420	139	5.8	14.5	£6903
IC	IC	R & P	Disc/disc	195/60-14	158	2138	110 (Est)	N/A	N/A	£9885

Make and model	Production Figures	Years Built	Body Styles	Mechanical Layout	Engine Make (if not own)	Capacity/(cc)/Layout/Valves	BHP/rpm	Torque (lb.ft)/rpm	Transmission gearbox/automatic transmission
			Spts Htch			OHC			
					Ford	2792/V6/ OHV	150/5700	162/4300	4-spd/5-spd/Auto
					Rover	3528/V8/ OHV	190/5280	220/4000	5-spd/Auto
						OHV	197/5280	220/4000	5-spd/-
						3905/V8/ OHV	275/5500	270/3500	5-spd/Auto
						3948/V8/ OHV	275/5500	270/3500	5-spd/-
						4441/V8/ OHV	320/5700	310/4000	5-spd/-
420SEAC/ 450SEAC	55	1986–1989	Spts	F/R	Rover	4228/V8/ OHV	300/5500	290/4500	5-spd/-
						4441/V8/ OHV	324/5700	310/4000	5-spd/-
S family	In prod	1987–Date	Spts	F/R	Ford	2792/V6/ OHV	160/6000	162/4300	5-spd/-
						2933/V6/ OHV	170/5700	172/3000	5-spd/-
							168/5400	191/3745	5-spd/-
					Rover	3948/V8/ OHV	240/5750	275/4200	5-spd/-
Griffith	In prod	1991–Date	Spts	F/R	Rover	3948/V8/ OHV	240/5750	275/4200	5-spd/-
						4280/V8/ OHV	280/5500	305/4000	5-spd/-
						4988/V8/ OHV	340/5500	350/4000	5-spd/-
Chimaera	In prod	1993–Date	Spts	F/R	Rover	3948/V8/ OHV	240/5750	275/4200	5-spd/-
							275/5750	305/4000	
						4280/V8/ OHV	280/5500	305/4000	5-spd/-
						4988/V8/ OHV	340/5500	350/4000	5-spd/-
Cerbera	In prod	1995–Date	Spts Cpe	F/R	—	4185/V8 OHC	350/6500	320/4500	5-spd/-

Vanden Plas

Make and model	Production Figures	Years Built	Body Styles	Mechanical Layout	Engine Make (if not own)	Capacity/(cc)/Layout/Valves	BHP/rpm	Torque (lb.ft)/rpm	Transmission gearbox/automatic transmission
Princess 1100/1300	39,381	1963–1974	Sal	F(Tr)/F	—	1098/4IL/ OHV	55/5500	61/2500	4-spd/Auto
						1275/4IL/ OHV	58/5250	69/3500	4-spd/Auto
							60/5250	69/2500	Auto/-
							65/5750	71/3000	4-spd/-
Princess 1500/1750	11,842	1974–1980	Sal	F(Tr)/F	—	1485/4IL/ OHC	69/5600	80/3100	5-spd/Auto
							77/5750	84/3250	
						1748/4IL/ OHC	84/5000	97/2600	-/Auto

Vauxhall

Make and model	Production Figures	Years Built	Body Styles	Mechanical Layout	Engine Make (if not own)	Capacity/(cc)/Layout/Valves	BHP/rpm	Torque (lb.ft)/rpm	Transmission gearbox/automatic transmission
Victor (FD)	198,085 (Incl. Ventora)	1967–1972	Sal Est	F/R	—	1599/4IL/ OHC	72/5600	90/3200	3-spd/4-spd/Auto
						1975/4IL/ OHC	88/5500	116/3200	3-spd/4-spd/Auto
VX 4/90	14,277	1969–1972	Sal	F/R	—	1975/4IL/ OHC	104/5600	117/3400	4-spd (+O/D)/Auto
Ventora/ Victor 3300	—	1968–1972	Sal Est	F/R	—	3294/6IL/ OHV	123/4600	176/2400	4-spd (+O/D)/Auto
Velox/Cresta/ Viscount	60,937	1965–1972	Sal Est	F/R	—	3294/6IL/ OHV	123/4600	176/2400	3-spd (+O/D)/ 4-spd/Auto
Firenza	18,352	1971–1973	Cpe	F/R	—	1159/4IL/ OHV	62/5500	65/3800	4-spd/Auto
						1256/4IL/ OHV	53/5200	65/2600	4-spd/Auto
						1599/4IL/ OHC	70/5100	92/2500	4-spd/Auto
						1759/4IL/ OHC	77/5200	104/3000	4-spd/Auto
						1975/4IL/ OHC	104/5600	117/3400	4-spd/Auto
						2279/4IL/ OHC	110/5200	150/3200	4-spd/Auto
Viva (HC)	640,863	1970–1979	Sal Est Cpe	F/R	—	1159/4IL/ OHV	49/5300	63/2900	4-spd/Auto
							62/5500	65/3800	4-spd/Auto
						1256/4IL/ OHV	53/5200	65/2600	4-spd/Auto
							68/5750	72/4000	4-spd/Auto
							59/5600	68/2600	4-spd/Auto
						1599/4IL/ OHC	70/5100	90/2500	4-spd/Auto
						1759/4IL/	77/5200	104/3000	4-spd/Auto

Suspension Front	Rear	Steering	Brakes (Front/rear)	Wheels/ Tyres	Length (in)	Weight (lb,unladen)	Top speed (mph)	0–60mph (sec)	Standing ¼-mile (sec)	UK Total Price (£: at Launch)
IC	IC	R & P	Disc/disc	205/60-14	158/161	2365	130	8.2	16.4	£12,800
IC	IC	R & P	Disc/disc	205/60-15	161	2536	136	6.6	14.8	£14,800
IC	IC	R & P	Disc/disc	205/60-15	161	2520	134	6.5	15.1	£15,540
IC	IC	R & P	Disc/disc	225/60-15	161	2536	143	5.7	14.2	£19,700
IC	IC	R & P	Disc/disc	225/60-15	161	2536	145 (Est)	N/A	N/A	£24,995
IC	IC	R & P	Disc/disc	225/50-15 245/45-16	161	2536	155 (Est)	N/A	N/A	£27,995
IC	IC	R & P	Disc/disc	225/50-15 245/45-16	161	2492	150 (Est)	N/A	N/A	£29,500
IC	IC	R & P	Disc/disc	225/50-15 245/45-16	161	2492	155 (Est)	N/A	N/A	£33,950
IC	IC	R & P	Disc/drum	205/60-15	156	2175	128	7.6	15.9	£12,995
IC	IC	R & P	Disc/drum	205/60-15	156	2175	136 (Est)	N/A	N/A	£15,450
IC	IC	R & P	Disc/disc	205/60-15	156	2175	136	6.8	15.3	£16,645
IC	IC	R & P	Disc/disc	205/60-15	156	2247	146	5.2	14.0	£23,595
IC	IC	R & P	Disc/disc	205/55-15/ 225/50-16	156	2304	158 (Est)	N/A	N/A	£25,795
IC	IC	R & P	Disc/disc	205/55-15/ 225/50-16	156	2304	161	4.7	13.2	£28,295
IC	IC	R & P	Disc/disc	205/55-15/ 235/50-16	153	2370	161	4.2	12.8	£32,995
IC	IC	R & P	Disc/disc	205/60-15/ 225/55-16	158	2337	158	5.2	13.8	£26,250
IC	IC	R & P	Disc/disc	215/50-15/ 225/55-16	158	2337	160 (Est)	N/A	N/A	£28,950
IC	IC	R & P	Disc/disc	205/55-15/ 235/50-16	158	2337	165 (Est)	4.4	N/A	£31,600
IC	IC	R & P	Disc/disc	225/45-16/ 235/50-16	169	2595	185	4.0	12.4	£37,000
IHydroL	IHydroL	R & P	Disc/drum	5.50-12	147	1950	85	21.1	21.7	£895
IHydroL	IHydroL	R & P	Disc/drum	5.50-12	147	2015	88	17.3	20.7	£1000
IHydroL	IHydroL	R & P	Disc/drum	5.50-12	147	2015	87 (Est)	N/A	N/A	£1185
IHydroL	IHydroL	R & P	Disc/drum	5.50-12	147	2015	97	14.1	19.6	£1087
IHydraG	IHydraG	R & P	Disc/drum	155-13	154	2000	90	16.7	20.9	£1951
IHydraG	IHydraG	R & P	Disc/drum	155-13	154	2016	97 (Est)	N/A	N/A	£5706
IC	BeamC	R & P	Drum/drum Disc/drum	5.60-13	177	2321	90	19.3	21.2	£819
IC	BeamC	R & P	Disc/drum	6.20-13	177	2350	95	14.0	19.5	£910
IC	BeamC	R & P	Disc/drum	6.90-13	177	2396	98	13.2	19.2	£1203
IC	BeamC	R & P	Disc/drum	165-13	177	2553	103	11.8	18.4	£1102
IC	Beam1/2E	Worm	Disc/drum	5.90-14 7.00-14	187	2796	103	12.5	18.3	£956
IC	BeamC	R & P	Disc/drum	6.20-13	162	1821	83 (Est)	N/A	N/A	£1017
IC	BeamC	R & P	Disc/drum	6.20-13	162	1821	83	17.0	20.6	£1052
IC	BeamC	R & P	Disc/drum	6.20-13	162	1888	91 (Claimed)	N/A	N/A	£1052
IC	BeamC	R & P	Disc/drum	155-13	162	2080	99 (Claimed)	N/A	N/A	£1037
IC	BeamC	R & P	Disc/drum	155-13	162	2126	100	10.6	17.8	£1282
IC	BeamC	R & P	Disc/drum	175-13	162	2130	103	11.4	18.0	£1299
IC	BeamC	R & P	Drum/drum	5.20-13	162	1859	78	20.6	21.8	£783
IC	BeamC	R & P	Disc/drum	6.20-13	162	1844	83 (Est)	N/A	N/A	£823
IC	BeamC	R & P	Drum/drum	5.20-13	162	1800	84	17.6	20.3	£802
IC	BeamC	R & P	Disc/drum	155-13	162	1887	84	18.1	21.2	£1174
IC	BeamC	R & P	Disc/drum	155-13	162	1837	87	15.8	20.1	£1174
IC	BeamC	R & P	Disc/drum	6.20-13	162	2088	86	17.1	20.6	£994
IC	BeamC	R & P	Disc/drum	155-13	162	2085	94	13.1	18.7	£969

Make and model	Production Figures	Years Built	Body Styles	Mechanical Layout	Engine Make (if not own)	Capacity/ (cc)/Layout/ Valves	BHP/ rpm	Torque (lb.ft)/rpm	Transmission gearbox/automatic transmission
						OHC	88/5800	99/3500	4-spd/Auto
						2279/4IL/ OHC	110/5200	140/3200	4-spd/Auto
Firenza (Droopsnoot)	204	1973–1975	Cpe	F/R	—	2279/4IL/ OHC	131/5500	144/3500	5-spd/-
Magnum	20,300	1973–1977	Sal	F/R	—	1759/4IL/ OHC	77/5200	97/3000	4-spd/Auto
			Cpe				88/5800	99/3500	4-spd/Auto
			Est			2279/4IL/ OHC	110/5000	140/3000	4-spd/Auto
Victor (FE)	44,078	1972–1976	Sal	F/R	—	1759/4IL/ OHC	77/5200	97/3000	4-spd (+O/D)/Auto
			Est						
						2279/4IL/ OHC	100/5200	138/3000	4-spd (+O/D)/Auto
VX4/90 (FE)	N/A	1972–1978	Sal	F/R	—	2279/4IL/ OHV	110/5200	140/3000	4-spd (+O/D)/Auto
							116/5000	145/3000	4-spd/5-spd/Auto
Ventora Victor 3300	7,984	1972–1976	Sal Est	F/R	—	3294/6IL/ OHV	124/4600	174/2400	4-spd (+O/D)/Auto
VX1800/ VX2300	25,185	1976–1978	Sal Est	F/R	—	1759/4IL/ OHC	88/5800	99/3500	4-spd/Auto
						2279/4IL/ OHC	108/5000	138/3000	4-spd/Auto
Chevette	415,608	1975–1984	Htch Sal Est	F/R	—	1256/4IL/ OHV	59/5600	68/2600	4-spd/-
Chevette HS/HSR	450	1976–1980	Htch	F/R	—	2279/4IL/ 2OHC	135/5500	134/4500	5-spd/-
Cavalier	238,980 (Incl. all types)	1975–1981	Sal Cpe Htch	F/R	—	1256/4IL/ OHV	58/5400	66/2600	4-spd/-
						1584/4IL/ OHC	75/5000	81/3800	4-spd/Auto
						1897/4IL/ OHC	89/4800	105/3800	4-spd/Auto
						1979/4IL/ OHC	100/5400	113/3800	4-spd/Auto
Carlton	Est 80,000	1978–1986	Sal Est	F/R	—	1796/4IL/ OHC	90/5400	106/4000	5-spd/Auto
						1979/4IL/ OHC	100/5200	117/3600	4-spd/5-spd/Auto
							110/5400	119/3400	5-spd/Auto
						2197/4IL/ OHC	115/4800	134/2800	5-spd/Auto
						2260/4IL/ OHC Diesel	65/4200	94/2500	4-spd/5-spd/Auto
Viceroy	N/A	1980–1982	Sal	F/R	—	2490/6IL/ OHC	114/5200	132/3800	4-spd/Auto
Royale	7,119	1978–1982	Sal Cpe	F/R	—	2784/6IL/ OHC	140/5200	161/3400	4-spd/Auto
Astra	1,117,662 (Incl. Mk II, below)	1980–1984	Htch Est Sal	F(Tr)/F	—	1196/4IL/ OHV	60/5800	65/3600	4-spd/-
						1297/4IL/ OHC	75/5800	70/3800	4-spd/-
						1598/4IL/ OHC	90/5800	93/4000	4-spd/Auto
						1796/4IL/ OHC	113/5800	111/4800	5-spd/-
						1598/4IL/ OHC Diesel	54/4600	71/2400	4-spd/-
Astra II	—	1984–1991	Htch Est Conv	F(Tr)/F	—	1196/4IL/ OHV	55/5600	62/3600	4-spd/-
						1297/4IL/ OHC	75/5800	70/3800	4-spd/Auto
						1389/4IL/ OHC	60/5600	76/2600	4-spd/5-spd/-
						1598/4IL/ OHC	90/5800	93/4000	5-spd/Auto
							82/5400	96/2600	5-spd/Auto
						1796/4IL/ OHC	115/5800	111/4800	5-spd/-
						1998/4IL/ OHC	115/5400	125/2600	5-spd/Auto
							124/5600	128/2600	5-spd/-
						1998/4IL/ 2OHC	156/5600	150/4800	5-spd/-
						1598/4IL/ OHC Diesel	55/4600	71/2400	4-spd/5-spd/Auto
						1699/4IL/ OHC Diesel	57/4600	77/2400	5-spd/-
Belmont	—	1986–1991	Sal	F(Tr)/F	—	1297/4IL/ OHC	75/5800	70/3800	5-spd/Auto
						1598/4IL/ OHC	90/5800	93/4000	5-spd/Auto
							82/5400	96/2600	5-spd/Auto
						1796/4IL/ OHC	115/5800	111/4800	5-spd/Auto

| Suspension | | Steering | Brakes | Wheels/ | Length (in) | Weight | Performance | | Standing | UK Total |
Front	Rear		(Front/rear)	Tyres		(lb, unladen)	Top speed (mph)	0–60mph (sec)	¼-mile (sec)	Price (£: at Launch)
IC	BeamC	R & P	Disc/drum	165-13	162	2273	97 (Est)	N/A	N/A	£1305
IC	BeamC	R & P	Disc/drum	155-13	162	2085	99	11.5	17.9	£1182
IC	BeamC	R & P	Disc/drum	185/70-13	169	2296	117	8.5	16.6	£2625
IC	BeamC	R & P	Disc/drum	155-13	163	2135	93	15.6	20.3	£1305
IC	BeamC	R & P	Disc/drum	175/70-13	163	2184	99	11.7	18.4	£2021
IC	BeamC	R & P	Disc/drum	175-13	163	2155	103	10.0	17.5	£1410
IC	BeamC	R & P	Disc/drum	6.40-13	179	2495	92	15.9	19.9	£1217
IC	BeamC	R & P	Disc/drum	175-13	179	2519	96	12.4	18.2	£1344
IC	BeamC	R & P	Disc/drum	185-14	179	2590	99	12.0	18.4	£1479
IC	BeamC	R & P	Disc/drum	185/70-14	179	2765	102	11.1	17.9	£2115
IC	BeamC	R & P	Disc/drum	185/70-14	179	2651	104	12.6	18.6	£1763
IC	BeamC	R & P	Disc/drum	175-13	180	2569	100	13.7	19.2	£2592
IC	BeamC	R & P	Disc/drum	175-13	180	2604	104	11.3	18.3	£2709
IC	BeamC	R & P	Disc/drum	155-13	157	1879	91	14.5	19.6	£1650
IC	BeamC	R & P	Disc/drum	205/60-13	157	2235	115	8.5	16.5	£5107 (HS) £7146 (HSR)
IC	BeamC	R & P	Disc/drum	165-13	174	2005	87	17.8	20.9	£2746
IC	BeamC	R & P	Disc/drum	165-13	174	2092	98	14.8	19.0	£1975
IC	BeamC	R & P	Disc/drum	185/70-13	174	2265	106	11.2	18.0	£2307
IC	BeamC	R & P	Disc/drum	185/70-13	174	2144	111	9.2	17.5	£3128
IC	BeamC	Worm	Disc/drum	175-14	187	2430	104	13.1	18.7	£6496
IC	BeamC	Worm	Disc/drum	175-14	187	2568	112	10.0	17.6	£4600
IC	BeamC	Worm	Disc/drum	175-14	187	2568	118 (Est)	N/A	N/A	£8607
IC	BeamC	Worm	Disc/drum	175/70-14	187	2661	117	10.3	17.5	£9795
IC	BeamC	Worm	Disc/drum	175-14	187	2745	104 (Claimed)	N/A	N/A	£7056
IC	BeamC	Worm	Disc/drum	175-14	188	2712	109	12.2	18.7	£7864
IC	IC	Worm	Disc/disc	195/70-14	187	3085	115	12.1	18.5	£7956
IC	IC	R & P	Disc/drum	155-13	157	1814	91	15.5	19.9	£3404
IC	IC	R & P	Disc/drum	155-13	157	1885	99	12.6	18.7	£4602
IC	IC	R & P	Disc/drum	155-13	157	2166	105	10.8	18.2	£5507
IC	IC	R & P	Disc/drum	185/60-14	157	2175	116	8.5	16.5	£6412
IC	IC	R & P	Disc/drum	155-13	157	2095	89 (Claimed)	N/A	N/A	£5145
IC	IC	R & P	Disc/drum	155-13	157	1852	96 (Claimed)	N/A	N/A	£4494
IC	IC	R & P	Disc/drum	155-13	157	2020	103	12.1	19.0	£5485
IC	IC	R & P	Disc/drum	155-13	157	1907	99 (Claimed)	N/A	N/A	£7236
IC	IC	R & P	Disc/drum	185/60-14	157	2096	104	11.8	18.7	£6400
IC	Ic	R & P	Disc/drum	155-13	157	1960	106	10.7	18.1	£7516
IC	IC	R & P	Disc/drum	185/60-14	157	2199	120	9.0	16.8	£7344
IC	IC	R & P	Disc/drum	175/65-14	157	2128	124 (Est)	N/A	N/A	£9499
IC	IC	R & P	Disc/drum	185/60-14	157	2148	123	8.4	16.5	£9499
IC	IC	R & P	Disc/disc	185/65-14	157	2220	132	7.6	15.7	£11,776
IC	IC	R & P	Disc/drum	155-13	157	2073	93 (Claimed)	N/A	N/A	£6177
IC	IC	R & P	Disc/drum	175/70-13	157	2193	95	15.1	19.8	£8569
IC	IC	R & P	Disc/drum	155-13	166	1962	106 (Claimed)	N/A	N/A	£6455
IC	IC	R & P	Disc/drum	155-13	166	2117	108	10.5	18.1	£6833
IC	IC	R & P	Disc/drum	155-13	166	2116	110	10.6	18.3	£7274
IC	IC	R & P	Disc/drum	175/70-13	166	2182	119	9.2	17.4	£8095

Make and model	Production Figures	Years Built	Body Styles	Mechanical Layout	Engine Make (if not own)	Capacity/ (cc)/Layout/ Valves	BHP/ rpm	Torque (lb.ft)/rpm	Transmission gearbox/automatic transmission
						1598/4IL/ OHC Diesel	55/4600	71/2400	4-spd/5-spd/Auto
						1699/4IL/ OHC Diesel	57/4600	77/2400	5-spd/-
Nova	446,462	1983–1993	Htch Sal	F(Tr)/F	—	993/4IL/ OHV	45/5400	50/2600	4-spd/-
						1196/4IL/ OHC	55/5600	66/2200	5-spd/-
						1297/4IL/ OHC	70/5800	74/3800	5-spd/-
						1598/4IL/ OHC	100/5600	100/3400	5-spd/-
						1488/4IL/ OHC Diesel	67/4600 50/4800	97/2600 66/3000	5-spd/- 5-spd/-
Cavalier II	806,359	1981–1988	Htch Sal Conv Est	F(Tr)/F	—	1297/4IL/ OHC	75/5800	74/3000	4-spd/-
						1598/4IL/ OHC	90/5800	93/4000	4-spd/5-spd/Auto
						1796/4IL/ OHC	115/5800	112/4800	5-spd/Auto
						1998/4IL/ OHC	115/5600 130/5600	129/3000 133/4600	5-spd/Auto 5-spd/-
						1598/4IL/ OHC Diesel	54/4600	71/2400	4-spd/5-spd/-
Cavalier III	In prod	1988–1995	Sal Htch	F(Tr)/F	—	1396/4IL/ OHC	75/5600	80/3000	5-spd/Auto
						1598/4IL/ OHC	82/5200	94/2600	5-spd/Auto
						1796/4IL/ OHC	90/5400	107/3000	5-spd/Auto
						1998/4IL/ OHC	115/5600 130/5600	129/3000 133/4600	5-spd/Auto 5-spd/Auto
						1998/4IL/ 2OHC	156/6000 136/4000	150/4800 144/4600	5-spd/- 5-spd/-
						2498/V6/ 2OHC	168/6000	166/4200	5-spd/-
				F(Tr)/4	—	1998/4IL/ OHC	130/5600	133/4600	5-spd/-
						1998/4IL/ 2OHC	150/6000 204/5600	145/4800 206/2400	5-spd/- 6-spd/-
				F(Tr)/F	—	1699/4IL/ OHC Diesel	57/4600	77/2500	5-spd/Auto
						1699/4IL/ OHC Diesel	82/4400	124/2400	5-spd/-
Calibra	In prod	1990–Date	Cpe	F(Tr)/F	—	1998/4IL/ OHC	115/5200	125/2600	5-spd/Auto
						1998/4IL 2OHC	150/6000 136/5600	145/4800 136/4000	5-spd/Auto 5-spd/Auto
				F(Tr)/4	—	1998/4IL/ 2OHC	150/6000 201/5600	145/4800 207/2400	5-spd/- 6-spd/-
				F(Tr)/F	—	2498/V6/ 2OHC	167/6000	167/4200	5-spd/Auto
Carlton II	241,051	1986–1993	Sal Est	F/R	—	1796/4IL/ OHC	90/5200 115/5600	109/3400 111/4600	5-spd/Auto 5-spd/Auto
						1998/4IL/ OHC	122/5400	129/2600	5-spd/Auto
						2594/6IL/ OHC	150/5600	162/3600	5-spd/Auto
						2260/4IL/ OHC Diesel	73/4400	102/2400	5-spd/-
Carlton GSi 3000	1,463	1987–1993	Sal Est	F/R	—	2969/6IL/ OHC	177/5600	183/4800	5-spd/-
						2969/6IL/ 2OHC	204/6000	199/3600	5-spd/Auto
Lotus-Carlton	440	1989–1993	Sal	F/R	—	3615/6IL/ 2OHC	377/5200	419/4200	6-spd/-
Senator	33,125 (*Incl. later model)	1984–1987	Sal	F/R	—	2490/6IL/ OHC	140/5200	151/4000	5-spd/Auto
						2969/6IL/ OHC	180/5800	179/4800	5-spd/Auto
Senator	—	1987–1993	Sal	F/R	—	2490/6IL/ OHC	140/5200	151/4200	5-spd/Auto
						2594/6IL/ OHC	150/5600	162/3600	5-spd/Auto
						2969/6IL/ OHC	177/5600	177/4400	5-spd/Auto
						2969/6IL/ 2OHC	204/6000	199/3600	Auto/-
Corsa	In prod	1993–Date	Htch	F(Tr)/F	—	1195/4IL/	44/5000	65/2800	5-spd/-

Suspension Front	Rear	Steering	Brakes (Front/rear)	Wheels/ Tyres	Length (in)	Weight (lb, unladen)	Top speed (mph)	0–60mph (sec)	Standing ¼-mile (sec)	UK Total Price (£: at Launch)
IC	IC	R & P	Disc/drum	155-13	166	2117	93 (Claimed)	N/A	N/A	£7008
IC	IC	R & P	Disc/drum	155-13	166	2117	95 (Claimed)	N/A	N/A	£8698
IC	IC	R & P	Disc/drum	135-13	143	1652	91	15.7	20.3	£3496
IC	IC	R & P	Disc/drum	145-13	143	1758	94	14.2	19.6	£4125
IC	IC	R & P	Disc/drum	145-13	143	1691	103	10.6	17.9	£4975
IC	IC	R & P	Disc/drum	175/65-14	143	1935	117	9.1	17.0	£8185
IC	IC	R & P	Disc/drum	145-13	143	1806	101	12.2	18.9	£7906
IC	IC	R & P	Disc/drum	145-13	143	1905	92	15.4	20.1	£8600
IC	IC	R & P	Disc/drum	155-13	172	2116	95	12.9	19.1	£4165
IC	IC	R & P	Disc/drum	165-13	172	2209	107	12.0	18.8	£4864
IC	IC	R & P	Disc/drum	185/70-13	172	2330	114	9.4	16.7	£6588
IC	IC	R & P	Disc/drum	185/70-13	172	2431	111	9.3	17.5	£10,446
IC	IC	R & P	Disc/drum	195/60-14	172	2320	117	8.2	16.2	£9999
IC	IC	R & P	Disc/drum	165-13	172	2299	88	17.8	20.5	£5414
IC	IC	R & P	Disc/drum	165-13	172	2347	107	12.9	19.1	£7889
IC	IC	R & P	Disc/drum	165-13	172	2334	109	12.1	18.5	£8289
IC	IC	R & P	Disc/drum	195/60-14	177	2492	110	12.2	18.6	£11,100
IC	IC	R & P	Disc/disc	165-13	177	2392	123 (Est)	N/A	N/A	£9485
IC	IC	R & P	Disc/disc	195/60-14	177	2335	125	8.9	16.4	£12,888
IC	IC	R & P	Disc/disc	195/60-15	177	2591	135 (Est)	N/A	N/A	£15,999
IC	IC	R & P	Disc/disc	195/60-14	177	2646	130 (Est)	N/A	N/A	£14,985
IC	IC	R & P	Disc/disc	195/60-15	177	2955	141	7.2	15.8	£16,085
IC	IC	R & P	Disc/disc	175/70-14	177	2789	123	8.6	16.5	£11,499
IC	IC	R & P	Disc/disc	205/55-15	177	2964	133	7.9	16.2	£17,567
IC	IC	R & P	Disc/disc	205/50-16	177	3078	144	6.5	15.4	£19,539
IC	IC	R & P	Disc/drum	175/70-14	177	2359	94 (Claimed)	N/A	N/A	£9494
IC	IC	R & P	Disc/drum	175/70-14	177	2591	111	12.8	19.2	£13,476
IC	IC	R & P	Disc/disc	195/60-14	177	2654	126	9.5	17.4	£14,750
IC	IC	R & P	Disc/disc	205/55-15	177	2700	137	8.1	16.4	£17,250
IC	IC	R & P	Disc/disc	205/55-15	177	2700	133 (Claimed)	8.0	N/A	£17,635
IC	IC	R & P	Disc/disc	205/55-15	177	2991	132	9.0	16.8	£19,820
IC	IC	R & P	Disc/disc	205/50-16	177	3098	150	6.2	14.6	£20,950
IC	IC	R & P	Disc/disc	195/60-15	177	2822	143	8.2	16.5	£19,870
IC	IC	Worm	Disc/drum	185/70-14	185	2598	114 (Est)	N/A	N/A	£9250
IC	IC	Worm	Disc/drum	185/70-14	185	2673	121	10.8	18.1	£9681
IC	IC	Worm	Disc/disc	185/70-14	185	2810	120	10.4	17.3	£10,790
IC	IC	Worm	Disc/disc	205/65-15	185	3120	134 (Claimed)	N/A	N/A	£21,425
IC	IC	Worm	Disc/drum	185/70-14	185	2844	101	16.2	21.0	£9980
IC	IC	Worm	Disc/disc	205/65-15	185	3160	134	8.2	16.4	£16,999
IC	IC	Worm	Disc/disc	205/65-15	187	3271	146	7.0	15.4	£21,689
IC	IC	R & P	Disc/disc	235/45-17/ 265/40-17	188	3641	176 (Est)	5.1	13.5	£48,000
IC	IC	Worm	Disc/disc	195/70-14	189	3021	123 (Claimed)	N/A	N/A	£10,923
IC	IC	Worm	Disc/disc	195/70-14	189	3080	119	9.2	17.0	£12,896
IC	IC	Worm	Disc/disc	205/65-15	191	3227	127	9.3	17.2	£14,830
IC	IC	Worm	Disc/disc	205/65-15	191	3208	132 (Claimed)	N/A	N/A	£19,920
IC	IC	Worm	Disc/disc	205/65-15	191	3374	132	9.3	17.2	£16,500
IC	IC	Worm	Disc/disc	205/65-15	191	3458	139	9.1	17.0	£24,879
IC	IC	R & P	Disc/drum	165/70-13	147	1861	79	19.6	21.6	£6630

Make and model	Production Figures	Years Built	Body Styles	Mechanical Layout	Engine Make (if not own)	Capacity/(cc)/Layout/Valves	BHP/rpm	Torque (lb.ft)/rpm	Transmission gearbox/automatic transmission
						OHC			
						1389/4IL/ OHC	59/5200	76/2800	5-spd/Auto
							82/5800	84/3400	5-spd/-
							89/6000	92/4000	5-spd/-
						1598/4IL/ 2OHC	108/6000	111/3800	5-spd/-
						1488/4IL/ OHC Diesel	49/4800	66/2400	5-spd/-
							66/4600	97/2600	5-spd/-
Tigra Coupe	In prod	1994–Date	Cpe	F(Tr)/F	—	1389/4IL/ 2OHC	89/6000	92/4000	5-spd/Auto
						1598/4IL/ 2OHC	105/6000	109/4000	5-spd/-
Astra III	In prod	1991–Date	Htch Sal Est	F(Tr)/F	—	1388/4IL/ OHC	60/5200	76/2800	5-spd/Auto
							82/4400	83/3400	5-spd/Auto
						1598/4IL/ OHC	100/5600	100/3400	5-spd/Auto
						1598/4IL/ 2OHC	100/6200	109/3500	5-spd/Auto
						1799/4IL/ 2OHC	115/5400	124/4000	5-spd/-
						1998/4IL/ OHC	115/5400	125/2600	5-spd/Auto
							136/5600	136/4000	5-spd/Auto
						1998/4IL/ 2OHC	150/6000	145/4800	5-spd/-
							134/6000	137/4000	5-spd/Auto
						1686/4IL/ OHC Diesel	82/4400	124/2400	5-spd/-
							68/4500	92/2400	5-spd/-
						1699/4IL/ OHC Diesel	57/4600	77/2400	5-spd/-
							67/4500	98/2400	5-spd/-
Frontera	In prod	1991–Date	Ute	F/4	—	1998/4IL/ OHC	115/5200	125/2600	5-spd/-
						2198/4IL/ OHC	136/5200	149/2600	5-spd/-
						2260/4IL/ OHC Diesel	100/4200	158/2200	5-spd/-
						2410/4IL/ OHC	125/4800	144/2600	5-spd/-
						2771/4IL/ OHC Diesel	111/3600	178/2100	5-spd/-
Monterey	In prod	1994–Date	Ute	F/4	—	3165/V6/ 2OHC	177/5200	192/3750	5-spd/Auto
						3059/4IL/ OHC Diesel	112/3600	192/2000	5-spd/-
Omega	In prod	1993–Date	Sal Est	F/R	—	1998/4IL/ OHC	115/5400	131/2800	5-spd/Auto
						1998/4IL/ 2OHC	133/5600	136/4000	5-spd/Auto
						2498/V6/ 2OHC	168/6000	167/3200	5-spd/Auto
						2962/V6/ 2OHC	210/6200	199/3600	5-spd/Auto
					BMW	2498/6IL/ OHC Diesel	128/4500	184/2200	5-spd/Auto
Vectra	In prod	1995–Date	Sal Htch Est	F(Tr)/F	—	1598/4IL/ OHC	74/5200	94/2800	5-spd/-
						1598/4IL/ 2OHC	99/6200	110/3200	5-spd/Auto
						1796/4IL/ 2OHC	113/5400	125/3600	5-spd/Auto
						1998/4IL/ 2OHC	134/5600	139/3200	5-spd/Auto
						2498/V6/ 2OHC	168/6000	170/3200	5-spd/Auto
						1686/4IL/ OHC Diesel	82/4400	124/2400	5-spd/-
Venturi									
MVS 210/ 260	N/A	1986–Date	Spts Cpe	R/R	Renault	2458/V6/ OHC	200/5750	214/2500	5-spd/-
Volga									
M21/M22	N/A	1955–1972	Sal Est	F/R	—	2445/4IL/ OHV	80/4000	130/2000	3-spd/-
M24	N/A	1969-N/A	Sal	F/R	—	2445/4IL/	112/4700	148/2400	4-spd/-

Suspension Front	Rear	Steering	Brakes (Front/rear)	Wheels/Tyres	Length (in)	Weight (lb,unladen)	Top speed (mph)	0–60mph (sec)	Standing ¼-mile (sec)	UK Total Price (£: at Launch)
IC	IC	R & P	Disc/drum	165/70-13	147	1947	96 (Claimed)	14.0	N/A	£7715
IC	IC	R & P	Disc/drum	165/65-14	147	1947	106	11.5	18.4	£8900
IC	IC	R & P	Disc/drum	167/70-13	147	2130	109	10.1	17.6	£9750
IC	IC	R & P	Disc/drum	185/60-14	147	2161	118	8.7	16.8	£10,975
IC	IC	R & P	Disc/drum	165/70-13	147	2084	93 (Claimed)	18.0	N/A	£6865
IC	IC	R & P	Disc/drum	165/70-13	147	2084	104	13.1	19.3	£8060
IC	IC	R & P	Disc/drum	175/65-14	154	2326	111	10.4	17.7	£10,995
IC	IC	R & P	Disc/drum	185/55-15	154	2326	126 (Claimed)	9.5	N/A	£12,995
IC	IC	R & P	Disc/drum	175/70-13	167	2046	99 (Claimed)	15.5	N/A	£8499
IC	IC	R & P	Disc/drum	175/65-14	167	2280	106	12.8	19.0	£9999
IC	IC	R & P	Disc/drum	185/60-14	167	2183	112	10.3	17.8	£11,173
IC	IC	R & P	Disc/disc	175/65-14	160	2381	113	10.5	17.8	£12,565
IC	IC	R & P	Disc/drum	175/65-14	160	2381	124	N/A	N/A	£16,845
IC	IC	R & P	Disc/drum	195/60-14	160	2310	121	8.9	N/A	£12,350
IC	IC	R & P	Disc/disc	195/55-15	160	2469	126 (Claimed)	9.0	N/A	£13,995
IC	IC	R & P	Disc/disc	195/60-14	160	2469	134	7.5	15.9	£15,780
IC	IC	R & P	Disc/disc	195/55-15	160	2469	130 (Est)	N/A	N/A	£13,995
IC	IC	R & P	Disc/drum	175/55-14	160	2514	103	11.9	18.6	£10,599
IC	IC	R & P	Disc/drum	175/65-14	160	2315	102 (Claimed)	14.5	N/A	£13,095
IC	IC	R & P	Disc/drum	175/70-13	160	2368	96	17.5	21.0	£9450
IC	IC	R & P	Disc/drum	175/70-13	160	2315	102 (Est)	14.5	N/A	£13,095
ITor	Beam1/4E	Worm	Disc/drum	225/75-15	167	3497	97	13.6	N/A	£12,920
	BeamC		Disc/disc	235/70-16						
ITor	BeamC	Worm	Disc/disc	235/70-16	176	3980	100 (Claimed)	12.7	N/A	£18,075
ITor	Beam1/4E	Worm	Disc/disc	225/75-15	176	4141	83	18.1	20.9	£16,830
ITor	Beam1/4E	Worm	Disc/drum	225/75-15	176	3790	90 (Claimed)	19.3	N/A	£15,740
ITor	BeamC	Worm	Disc/disc	255/65-16	165	4097	92	13.5	19.1	£16245
ITor	BeamC	Worm	Disc/disc	245/70-16	179	3958	106 (Claimed)	11.5	N/A	£23,290
ITor	BeamC	Worm	Disc/disc	245/70-16	179	3714	94	16.6	N/A	£23,290
IC	IC	Worm	Disc/disc	195/65-15	189	3087	121 (Claimed)	12.0	N/A	£15,995
IC	IC	Worm	Disc/disc	195/65-15	189	3142	130	9.3	17.1	£16,600
IC	IC	Worm	Disc/disc	205/65-15	189	3263	132	9.3	17.2	£19,450
IC	IC	Worm	Disc/disc	205/65-15	189	3139	136	9.1	16.9	£26,950
IC	IC	Worm	Disc/disc	205/65-15	189	3363	124 (Claimed)	11.0	N/A	£18,500
IC	IC	R & P	Disc/drum	175/70-14	176	2556	108 (Claimed)	14.5	N/A	£12,235
IC	IC	R & P	Disc/disc	185/70-14	176	2800	115	11.6	18.4	£12,235
IC	IC	R & P	Disc/disc	185/70-14	176	2775	126 (Claimed)	10.8	N/A	£13,435
IC	IC	R & P	Disc/disc	195/65-15	176	3042	129	8.7	16.8	£15,630
IC	IC	R & P	Disc/disc	195/65-15	176	2778	144 (Claimed)	7.8	N/A	£16,630
IC	IC	R & P	Disc/disc	185/70-14	176	2862	105	13.2	19.2	£13,135
IC	IC	R & P	Disc/disc	205/55-16/ 245/45-16	161	2602	155 (Claimed)	N/A	N/A	£37,000
IC	Beam1/2E	Worm	Drum/drum	6.70-15	190	3224	78	30.3	24.1	£1113
IC	Beam1/2E	Worm	Drum/drum	7.35-14	188	3090	90	N/A	N/A	Special Order

Make and model	Production Figures	Years Built	Body Styles	Mechanical Layout	Engine Make (if not own)	Capacity/(cc)/Layout/Valves	BHP/rpm	Torque (lb.ft)/rpm	Transmission gearbox/automatic transmission
			Est			OHV			
Volkswagen									
Beetle (Incl. all Beetle models)	21 million +	1945–Date	Sal Conv	R/R	—	1131/4HO/ OHV AirC	25/3300	49/2000	4-spd/-
						1192/4HO/ OHV AirC	30/3400 34/3600	56/2000 65/2400	4-spd/- 4-spd/-
						1285/4HO/ OHV AirC	40/4000 44/4100	64/2000 69/3500	4-spd/SemiAuto 4-spd/SemiAuto
						1493/4HO/ OHV AirC	44/4000	74/2000	4-spd/SemiAuto
						1584/4HO/ OHV AirC	50/4000	78/2800	4-spd/SemiAuto
Karmann-Ghia	Incl. in Beetle statistics	1957–1974	Cpe Conv	R/R	—	1192/4HO/ OHV AirC	30/3400 34/3600	56/2000 61/2000	4-spd/- 4-spd/-
						1285/4HO/ OHV AirC	40/4000 44/4100	64/2000 69/3500	4-spd/SemiAuto 4-spd/SemiAuto
						1493/4HO/ OHV AirC	44/4000	74/2000	4-spd/SemiAuto
						1584/4HO/ OHV AirC	50/4000	78/2800	4-spd/SemiAuto
1600TL/ 1600TE	1,813,600	1965–1973	Sal Est	R/R	—	1584/4HO/ OHV AirC	54/4000 65/4600	81/2200 87/2800	4-spd/Auto 4-spd/Auto
411/412	355,200	1968–1974	Sal Est	R/R	—	1679/4HO/ OHV AirC	68/4500 80/4900	92/2800 98/2700	4-spd/Auto 4-spd/Auto
1302/1302S/ 1303/1303S	Incl. in Beetle statistics	1970–1975	Sal Conv	R/R	—	1584/4HO/ OHV AirC	50/4000	82/3000	4-spd/SemiAuto
181 'The Thing'	Incl. in Beetle statistics	1969–1978	Conv	R/R	—	1584/4HO/ OHV AirC	50/4000	82/3000	4-spd/-
K70	211,100	1970–1975	Sal	F/F	—	1605/4IL/ OHC	75/5200 90/5200	90/3500 99/4000	4-spd/- 4-spd/-
						1807/4IL/ OHC	100/5300	112/3750	4-spd/-
Passat	1,769,700	1973–1980	Sal Htch Est	F/F	—	1296/4IL/ OHC	60/5800	68/2500	4-spd/-
						1470/4IL/ OHC	75/5800 85/5800	84/3500 88/4000	4-spd/Auto 4-spd/Auto
						1588/4IL/ OHC	75/5600 85/5600	83/3200 88/3200	4-spd/Auto 4-spd/Auto
Golf	App. 6,000,000 (Incl. all types, and 400,871 Cabriolets)	1974–1983 (Cabriolet ended 1993)	Htch Conv	F(Tr)/F	—	1093/4IL/ OHC	50/6000 50/5600	57/3000 61/3300	4-spd/-
						1272/4IL/ OHC	60/5600	70/3500	4-spd/-
						1457/4IL/ OHC	70/5600	76/3500	4-spd/-
						1470/4IL/ OHC	70/5800	82/3000	4-spd/-
						1588/4IL/ OHC	75/5600	86/3200	4-spd/Auto
						1595/4IL/ OHC	75/5000	92/2500	5-spd/Auto
						1781/4IL/ OHC	90/5200	107/3300	5-spd/Auto
						1470/4IL/ OHC Diesel	50/5000	57/3000	4-spd/-
						1588/4IL/ OHC Diesel	54/4800	73/3000	4-spd/5-spd/-
Golf GTi	—	1975–1983 (Conv. to 1993)	Htch Conv	F(Tr)/F	—	1588/4IL/ OHC	110/6100	101/5000	4-spd/-
						1781/4IL/ OHC	112/5800	109/3500	5-spd/-
Jetta	1,700,000	1979–1984	Sal	F(Tr)/F	—	1093/4IL/ OHC	50/5600	61/3300	4-spd/-
						1272/4IL/ OHC	60/5600	65/3400	4-spd/-
						1457/4IL/ OHC	70/5600	81/3500	4-spd/-
						1588/4IL/ OHC	110/6100 85/5600	97/3500 92/3800	4-spd/- 4-spd/Auto
						1588/4IL/ OHC Diesel	54/4800	73/3000	4-spd/-
Scirocco	504,200	1974–1981	Cpe Htch	F(Tr)/F	—	1471/4IL/ OHC	85/5800	89/3200	4-spd/-
						1588/4IL/ OHC	85/5600 110/6100	92/3800 97/3500	4-spd/Auto 4-spd/-
Polo	768,200	1975–1981	Htch	F(Tr)/F	—	895/4IL/ OHC	40/5900	45/3500	4-spd/-
						1093/4IL/ OHC	50/6000	53/3500	4-spd/-

Suspension Front	Rear	Steering	Brakes (Front/rear)	Wheels/ Tyres	Length (in)	Weight (lb, unladen)	Top speed (mph) (Claimed)	0–60mph (sec)	Standing 1/4-mile (sec)	UK Total Price (£: at Launch)
ITor	ITor	Worm	Drum/drum	5.60-15	160	1652	63	N/A	24.6	£690
ITor	ITor	Worm	Drum/drum	5.60-15	160	1568	66	47.6	24.2	£690
ITor	ITor	Worm	Drum/drum	5.60-15	160	1669	72	32.1	23.4	£617
ITor	ITor	Worm	Drum/drum	5.60-15	160	1669	75	23.0	22.1	£650
ITor	ITor	Worm	Drum/drum	5.60-15	160	1669	78 (Est)	N/A	N/A	£799
ITor	ITor	Worm	Disc/drum	5.60-15	160	1736	81	21.9	21.9	£697
IC	ITor	Worm	Disc/drum	5.60-15	161	1850	80	18.3	20.7	£875
ITor	ITor	Worm	Drum/drum	5.60-15	163	1915	72 (Est)	N/A	N/A	£1235
ITor	ITor	Worm	Drum/drum	5.60-15	163	1915	77	26.5	26.5	£1196
ITor	ITor	Worm	Disc/drum	5.60-15	163	1915	80 (Est)	N/A	N/A	£1101
ITor	ITor	Worm	Disc/drum	5.60-15	163	1915	85 (Est)	N/A	N/A	Special order
ITor	ITor	Worm	Disc/drum	5.60-15	163	1915	85 (Est)	N/A	N/A	£1098
ITor	ITor	Worm	Disc/drum	5.60-15	163	1915	85 (Est)	N/A	N/A	Special order
ITor	ITor	Worm	Disc/drum	6.00-15	167	2035	83	20.3	21.3	£998
ITor	ITor	Worm	Disc/drum	6.00-15	167	2227	78 (Est)	N/A	N/A	£1112
IC	IC	Worm	Disc/drum	145-15	178	2249	86	16.5	20.4	£1290
IC	IC	Worm	Disc/drum	155-15	179	2341	97	13.8	19.5	£1308
IC	ITor	Worm	Disc/drum	5.60-15	161	1905	80	18.3	20.7	£875
ITor	ITor	Worm	Drum/drum	165-15	149	1985	68	N/A	N/A	£1996
IC	IC	R & P	Disc/drum	165-14	172	2322	92 (Est)	N/A	N/A	£1570
IC	IC	R & P	Disc/drum	165-14	172	2360	93	12.9	18.8	£1571
IC	IC	R & P	Disc/drum	165-14	172	2322	100 (Est)	N/A	N/A	£1790
IC	IC	R & P	Disc/drum	155-13	165	1900	92 (Est)	N/A	N/A	£1495
IC	IC	R & P	Disc/drum	155-13	165	1900	98	12.4	18.8	£1729
IC	IC	R & P	Disc/drum	155-13	165	1900	106 (Est)	N/A	N/A	£1729
IC	IC	R & P	Disc/drum	155-13	165	1994	100	11.9	18.0	£2466
IC	IC	R & P	Disc/drum	175-13	165	2016	99	11.8	18.4	£3367
IC	IC	R & P	Drum/drum	6.15-13	147	1808	86	15.5	20.0	£1349
IC	IC	R & P	Disc/drum	155-13	147	1758	92	13.2	18.9	£3875
IC	IC	R & P	Disc/drum	155-13	147	1768	99	11.4	18.4	£3199
IC	IC	R & P	Disc/drum	155-13	147	1719	98	12.5	18.8	£1654
IC	IC	R & P	Disc/drum	155-13	147	1720	101 (Claimed)	N/A	N/A	£2713
IC	IC	R & P	Disc/drum	175/70-13	147	2051	96 (Claimed)	N/A	N/A	£7886
IC	IC	R & P	Disc/drum	175/70-13	147	2091	106	10.5	17.8	£7296
IC	IC	R & P	Disc/drum	145-13	147	1918	83	18.2	21.0	£3543
IC	IC	R & P	Disc/drum	155-13	147	1863	89	N/A	N/A	£4896
IC	IC	R & P	Disc/drum	175/70-13	147	1862	111 (Claimed)	9.0	16.9	£3707
IC	IC	R & P	Disc/drum	175/70-13	152	1921	113	8.3	16.2	£6500
IC	IC	R & P	Disc/drum	155-13	165	1731	88	N/A	N/A	£4425
IC	IC	R & P	Disc/drum	155-13	165	1731	92 (Claimed)	N/A	N/A	£4080
IC	IC	R & P	Disc/drum	175/70-13	165	1820	97	13.0	18.3	£4603
IC	IC	R & P	Disc/drum	175/70-13	165	1885	110	8.6	16.3	£5988
IC	IC	R & P	Disc/drum	175/70-13	165	1863	103 (Est)	N/A	N/A	£5789
IC	IC	R & P	Disc/drum	155-13	147	1938	88	17.2	20.7	£5005
IC	IC	R & P	Disc/drum	175/70-13	153	1866	104	11.1	18.3	£1995
IC	IC	R & P	Disc/drum	175/70-13	153	1800	100	10.4	17.5	£2694
IC	IC	R & P	Disc/drum	175/70-13	153	1960	115	8.8	16.9	£3665
IC	IC	R & P	Disc/drum	135-13	138	1522	80	18.0	20.8	£1798
IC	IC	R & P	Disc/drum	145-13	138	1568	85	16.0	20.3	£2499

Make and model	Production Figures	Years Built	Body Styles	Mechanical Layout	Engine Make (if not own)	Capacity/(cc)/Layout/Valves	BHP/rpm	Torque (lb.ft)/rpm	Transmission gearbox/automatic transmission
Derby	303,900	1977–1981	Sal	F(Tr)/F	—	1093/4IL/ OHC	50/6000	57/3000	4-spd/-
						1272/4IL/ OHC	60/5600	59/3400	4-spd/-
Passat II	1,978,200	1980–1988	Sal Htch	F/F	—	1588/4IL/ OHC	75/5600	88/3200	5-spd/Auto
			Est			1595/4IL/ OHC	75/5000	92/2500	5-spd/Auto
						1781/4IL/ OHC	90/5200	107/3300	5-spd/Auto
						1921/5IL/ OHC	115/5900	111/3700	5-spd/Auto
						1994/5IL/ OHC	115/5400	121/3200	5-spd/Auto
						1588/4IL/ OHC Diesel	54/4800	74/2000	5-spd/-
Santana (Renamed Passat saloon from 1985)	193,540	1981–1985	Sal	F/F	—	1585/4IL/ OHC	75/5000	92/2500	5-spd/Auto
						1781/4IL/ OHC	90/5200	107/3300	5-spd/Auto
						1921/5IL/ OHC	115/5900	113/3700	5-spd/Auto
						1994/5IL/ OHC	115/5400	121/3200	5-spd/Auto
Passat III	In prod	1988–Date	Sal Htch	F (Tr)/F	—	1781/4IL/ OHC	90/5500 112/5400	105/3000 117/4000	5-spd/- 5-spd/-
						1781/4IL/ 2OHC	136/6300	119/4800	5-spd/-
						1984/4IL/ OHC	115/5400	122/3200	5-spd/Auto
						1984/4IL/ 2OHC	136/5800	133/4400	5-spd/-
						2792/V6/ OHC	174/4800	177/4200	5-spd/-
						1588/4IL/ OHC Diesel	80/4500	114/2500	5-spd/-
						1896/4IL/ OHC Diesel	75/4400 90/4000	103/2400 149/1900	5-spd/- 5-spd/-
				F(Tr)/4	—	1781/4IL/ OHC	160/5600	166/3600	5-spd/-
Golf II	App. 7,000,000 (Incl. all types)	1983–1991	Htch	F(Tr)/F	—	1043/4IL/ OHC	45/4200	56/2800	4-spd/-
						1272/4IL/ OHC	55/5400	71/3300	4-spd/-
						1595/4IL/ OHC	75/5000 72/5200	92/2500 92/2700	5-spd/Auto 5-spd/Auto
						1781/4IL/ OHC	160/6800	165/3800	5-spd/-
						1781/4IL/ OHC	90/5200 112/5500	107/3300 114/3100	5-spd/Auto 5-spd/-
						1588/4IL/ OHC Diesel	54/4800 70/4500	74/2300 98/2600	4-spd/Auto 5-spd/-
Golf GTI II	(See above)	1983–1991	Htch	F(Tr)/F	—	1781/4IL/ OHC	112/5500	114/3100	5-spd/-
						1781/4IL/ 2OHC	139/6100	124/4600	5-spd/-
Golf Synchro	N/A	1985–1991	Htch	F(Tr)/4	—	1781/4IL/ OHC	90/5200	107/3300	5-spd/-
Golf Rallye	9,780	1989–1992	Htch	F(Tr)/4	—	1781/4IL/ OHC	160/6000	165/3800	5-spd/-
Scirocco	340,700	1981–1992	Cpe	F(Tr)/F	—	1457/4IL/ OHC	70/5600	81/2500	5-spd/Auto
						1588/4IL/ OHC	85/5600 110/6100	93/3200 103/5000	5-spd/Auto 5-spd/-
						1595/4IL/ OHC	75/5000	92/2500	5-spd/Auto
						1781/4IL/ OHC	112/5800 90/5200	109/3500 107/3300	5-spd/- 5-spd/-
						1781/4IL/ 2OHC	139/6300	118/4500	5-spd/-
Polo and Classic	App. 4,500,000 (Incl. Classic)	1981–1994	Cpe Htch	F(Tr)/F	—	1043/4IL/ OHC	45/5200 40/5300	56/2800 54/2700	4-spd/5-spd/ 4-spd/-
						1093/4IL/ OHC	50/5600	60/3300	5-spd/-
						1272/4IL/ OHC	75/5900 55/5200 60/5600	73/3600 72/3000 70/3500	5-spd/- 5-spd/- 4-spd/-
						1272/4IL/ OHC	113/6000	111/4400	5-spd/-
Jetta II	4,390,790	1984–1992	Sal	F(Tr)/F	—	1272/4IL/	55/5400	71/3300	5-spd/-

Suspension Front	Rear	Steering	Brakes (Front/rear)	Wheels/ Tyres	Length (in)	Weight (lb, unladen)	Top speed (mph)	0–60mph (sec)	Standing 1/4-mile (sec)	UK Total Price (£: at Launch)
IC	IC	R & P	Disc/drum	155-13	148	1580	85	16.1	20.3	£2850
IC	IC	R & P	Disc/drum	155-13	148	1580	93	13.6	19.2	£3099
IC	IC	R & P	Disc/drum	165-13	175	2048	102	11.9	18.7	£5351
IC	IC	R & P	Disc/drum	165-13	175	2117	102 (Est)	N/A	N/A	£5833
IC	IC	R & P	Disc/drum	195/60-14	175	2336	101	10.9	18.8	£6532
IC	IC	R & P	Disc/drum	185/70-13	175	2312	117 (Claimed)	N/A	N/A	£6447
IC	IC	R & P	Disc/drum	185/70-13	175	2392	113 (Claimed)	N/A	N/A	£8308
IC	IC	R & P	Disc/drum	165-13	175	2106	89 (Claimed)	N/A	N/A	£6197
IC	IC	R & P	Disc/drum	165-13	179	2106	99 (Claimed)	N/A	N/A	£5883
IC	IC	R & P	Disc/drum	185/70-13	179	2139	106	11.4	17.7	£6789
IC	IC	R & P	Disc/drum	185/70-13	179	2443	111	10.8	18.0	£8358
IC	IC	R & P	Disc/drum	185/70-13	179	2392	114 (Claimed)	N/A	N/A	£8358
IC	IC	R & P	Disc/drum	185/65-14	180	2481	110 (Est)	14.4	N/A	£9690
IC	IC	R & P	Disc/drum	185/65-14	180	2555	120	10.3	18.1	£13,636
IC	IC	R & P	Disc/disc	195/60-14	180	2811	127	8.8	17.3	£15,420
IC	IC	R & P	Disc/disc	185/65-14	180	2547	121 (Claimed)	11.8	N/A	£12,499
IC	IC	R & P	Disc/drum	185/65-14	180	2668	132 (Est)	9.7	N/A	£16,732
IC	IC	R & P	Disc/disc	205/50-15	180	2860	139 (Claimed)	8.7	N/A	£22,175
IC	IC	R & P	Disc/drum	185/65-14	180	2624	107 (Claimed)	N/A	N/A	£11,483
IC	IC	R & P	Disc/drum	185/65-14	180	2701	102 (Est)	N/A	N/A	£13,838
IC	IC	R & P	Disc/drum	185/65-14	180	2789	102 (Est)	18.0	N/A	£15,949
IC	IC	R & P	Disc/disc	195/55-15	180	2907	134 (Claimed)	N/A	N/A	Special order
IC	IC	R & P	Disc/drum	155-13	157	1810	85 (Claimed)	N/A	N/A	£4597
IC	IC	R & P	Disc/drum	155-13	157	1863	93	15.1	19.7	£4971
IC	IC	R & P	Disc/drum	175/70-13	157	1918	102	10.9	18.1	£6696
IC	IC	R & P	Disc/drum	175/70-13	157	2070	99	11.5	18.4	£8688
IC	IC	R & P	Disc/disc	185/55-15	159	2376	134 (Claimed)	8.3	N/A	£15,967
IC	IC	R & P	Disc/drum	175/70-13	157	1984	111	9.8	17.5	£7296
IC	IC	R & P	Disc/drum	175/70-13	157	2028	119 (Est)	N/A	N/A	£7867
IC	IC	R & P	Disc/drum	155-13	157	1984	92 (Est)	N/A	N/A	£6310
IC	IC	R & P	Disc/drum	155-13	157	2028	100	12.4	18.8	£7495
IC	IC	R & P	Disc/disc	185/60-14	157	2028	114	8.6	16.6	£7867
IC	IC	R & P	Disc/disc	185/60-14	157	2226	123	8.0	16.2	£10,636
IC	IC	R & P	Disc/drum	175/70-13	157	2365	111 (Est)	N/A	N/A	£11,340
IC	IC	R & P	Disc/disc	205/50-15	157	2635	130 (Claimed)	N/A	N/A	£16,940
IC	IC	R & P	Disc/drum	175/70-13	159	1885	102 (Claimed)	N/A	N/A	£5424
IC	IC	R & P	Disc/drum	175/70-13	159	2009	106	10.3	17.6	£6497
IC	IC	R & P	Disc/drum	175/70-13	159	2027	112	9.8	17.6	£7125
IC	IC	R & P	Disc/drum	175/70-13	159	1895	104 (Claimed)	N/A	N/A	£5921
IC	IC	R & P	Disc/drum	175/70-13	159	2093	116	9.0	16.9	£8005
IC	IC	R & P	Disc/drum	175/70-13	159	2044	111	9.5	17.1	£9295
IC	IC	R & P	Disc/drum	185/60-14	159	2166	130	8.4	16.3	£10,960
IC	IC	R & P	Disc/drum	145-13	144	1718	84	21.4	22.4	£3799
IC	IC	R & P	Disc/drum	135-13	144	1544	84 (Est)	N/A	N/A	£3799
IC	IC	R & P	Disc/drum	145-13	144	1603	94	13.8	19.5	£3975
IC	IC	R & P	Disc/drum	165/70-13	147	1771	104	11.7	18.7	£8989
IC	IC	R & P	Disc/drum	145-13	148	1696	95	13.5	19.4	£7545
IC	IC	R & P	Disc/drum	145-13	148	1630	97	12.9	19.0	£4799
IC	IC	R & P	Disc/drum	175/60-13	148	1828	119	8.4	16.5	£11,568
IC	IC	R & P	Disc/drum	175/70-13	170	2027	95	15.4	19.9	£5269

Make and model	Production Figures	Years Built	Body Styles	Mechanical Layout	Engine Make (if not own)	Capacity/ (cc)/Layout/ Valves	BHP/ rpm	Torque (lb.ft)/rpm	Transmission gearbox/automatic transmission
						OHC			
						1595/4IL/	75/5000	92/2500	5-spd/Auto
						OHC			
						1781/4IL/	90/5200	107/3300	5-spd/Auto
						OHC	112/5500	114/3100	5-spd/-
						1781/4IL/	139/6100	124/4600	5-spd/-
						2OHC			
						1588/4IL/	54/4800	73/3000	4-spd/5-spd/-
						OHC Diesel	70/4500	98/2600	5-spd/-
				F(Tr)/4	—	1781/4IL/	90/5200	107/3300	5-spd/-
						OHC			
Corrado	102,444	1988–1995	Htch Cpe	F(Tr)/F	—	1781/4IL	136/6300	119/4800	5-spd/-
						2OHC	160/5600	166/4000	5-spd/-
						1984/4IL/	115/5400	122/3200	5-spd/Auto
						OHC			
						1984/4IL/	136/5800	132/4400	5-spd/-
						2OHC	150/6000	133/4800	5-spd/-
						2861/V6/	190/5800	181/4200	5-spd/Auto
						OHC			
Polo	In prod	1994–Date	Htch	F(Tr)/F	—	1043/4IL/	45/5200	56/2800	5-spd/-
						OHC			
						1295/4IL/	55/5200	74/3400	5-spd/-
						OHC			
						1390/4IL/	60/4700	86/3200	5-spd/-
						OHC			
						1598/4IL/	75/5200	94/2800	5-spd/-
						OHC			
						1896/4IL/	64/4400	91/2500	5-spd/-
						OHC Diesel			
Golf III	In prod	1991–Date	Htch	F(Tr)/F	—	1391/4IL/	60/5200	79/2800	4-spd/5-spd/-
			Est			OHC			
			Conv			1598/4IL/	75/5200	95/2600	5-spd/Auto
						OHC			
						1781/4IL/	75/5000	103/2500	5-spd/Auto
						OHC	90/5500	107/2500	5-spd/Auto
						1984/4IL/	115/5400	122/3200	5-spd/Auto
						OHC			
						1984/4IL/	150/6000	133/4800	5-spd/-
						2OHC			
						2792/V6/	174/5800	173/4200	5-spd/Auto
						OHC			
						1896/4IL/	64/4400	91/2000	5-spd/-
						OHC Diesel	75/4200	111/2400	5-spd/-
							90/4000	149/1900	5-spd/-
Vento	In prod	1992–Date	Sal	F(Tr)/F	—	1598/4IL/	75/5200	95/2600	5-spd/-
						OHC			
						1781/4IL/	90/5500	107/2500	5-spd/-
						OHC			
						1984/4IL/	115/5400	123/3200	5-spd/Auto
						OHC			
						2792/V6/	174/5800	173/2400	5-spd/Auto
						OHC			
						1896/4IL/	75/4200	111/2400	5-spd/-
						OHC Diesel	64/4400	91/2000	5-spd/-
Sharan	In prod	1995–Date	Est	F(Tr)/F	—	1984/4IL/	115/5000	125/2400	5-spd/Auto
						OHC			
						2792/V6/	174/5800	174/4200	5-spd/Auto
						OHC			
						1896/4IL/	90/4000	145/1940	5-spd/-
						OHC Diesel			

Volkswagen-Porsche

Make and model	Production Figures	Years Built	Body Styles	Mechanical Layout	Engine Make (if not own)	Capacity/ (cc)/Layout/ Valves	BHP/ rpm	Torque (lb.ft)/rpm	Transmission gearbox/automatic transmission
914S/914SC	115,600	1969–1975	Spts Cpe	M/R	—	1679/4HO/	80/4900	98/2700	5-spd/SemiAuto
						OHV AirC			
						1971/4HO/	100/5000	116/3500	5-spd/SemiAuto
						OHV AirC			

Volvo

Make and model	Production Figures	Years Built	Body Styles	Mechanical Layout	Engine Make (if not own)	Capacity/ (cc)/Layout/ Valves	BHP/ rpm	Torque (lb.ft)/rpm	Transmission gearbox/automatic transmission
1800E/ 1800ES	47,600	1969–1973	Cpe Cpe Est	F/R	—	1986/4IL/ OHV	120/6000	123/3500	4-spd (+O/D)/Auto
140 Series	1,205,111	1966–1974	Sal Est	F/R	—	1778/4IL/ OHV	75/4700	108/3000	4-spd/Auto
							100/5600	107/3500	4-spd(+O/D)/-
						1986/4IL/ OHV	82/4700	119/3000	4-spd/Auto
							100/5600	123/3500	4-spd (+O/D)/-
							120/6000	123/3500	4-spd/Auto
164 Family	155,068	1968–1975	Sal	F/R	—	2979/6IL/ OHV	130/5000	152/2500	4-spd (+O/D)/Auto
							160/5500	170/2500	4-spd (+O/D)/Auto

Suspension Front	Rear	Steering	Brakes (Front/rear)	Wheels/Tyres	Length (in)	Weight (lb,unladen)	Top speed (mph)	0–60mph (sec)	Standing 1/4-mile (sec)	UK Total Price (£: at Launch)
IC	IC	R & P	Disc/drum	175/70-13	170	1985	102 (Claimed)	N/A	N/A	£6759
IC	IC	R & P	Disc/drum	175/70-13	170	2210	112	10.3	17.8	£7900
IC	IC	R & P	Disc/drum	185/60-14	170	2282	117	8.5	16.9	£8497
IC	IC	R & P	Disc/disc	185/60-14	170	2232	128	7.1	15.9	£10,998
IC	IC	R & P	Disc/drum	155-13	170	1918	91 (Est)	N/A	N/A	£6666
IC	IC	R & P	Disc/drum	175/70-13	170	2161	101	12.9	19.3	£7538
IC	Ic	R & P	Disc/drum	175/70-13	170	2511	106	11.3	18.5	£11,574
IC	IC	R & P	Disc/disc	185/55-15	159	2456	131	8.7	16.5	£16,699
IC	IC	R & P	Disc/disc	185/55-15	159	2456	140	8.1	16.2	£19,907
IC	IC	R & P	Disc/disc	195/50-15	159	2503	124 (Claimed)	N/A	N/A	£16,574
IC	IC	R & P	Disc/disc	195/50-15	159	2615	126	10.2	17.8	£17,192
IC	IC	R & P	Disc/disc	195/50-15	159	2615	133 (Est)	N/A	N/A	£18,100
IC	IC	R & P	Disc/disc	205/50-15	159	2734	145	6.4	15.1	£19,895
IC	IC	R & P	Disc/drum	155/70-13	146	2018	88	17.6	21.0	£6950
IC	IC	R & P	Disc/drum	155/70-13	146	2128	92	14.0	19.6	£7699
IC	IC	R & P	Disc/drum	175/65-13	146	2059	100	12.6	18.8	£8145
IC	IC	R & P	Disc/drum	175/65-13	146	2090	107	13.0	18.7	£9750
IC	IC	R & P	Disc/drum	155/70-13	146	2051	100 (Claimed)	15.7	N/A	£8499
IC	IC	R & P	Disc/drum	175/70-13	158	2116	94	15.3	20.3	£9010
IC	IC	R & P	Disc/drum	175/70-13	158	2238	104 (Claimed)	14.0	N/A	£11,099
IC	IC	R & P	Disc/drum	175/70-13	158	2390	103	12.0	21.8	£10,989
IC	IC	R & P	Disc/drum	175/70-13	158	2390	107	12.7	19.2	£12,868
IC	IC	R & P	Disc/drum	195/50-15	158	2536	121	9.9	17.5	£13,981
IC	IC	R & P	Disc/disc	205/50-15	158	2557	134	8.1	16.4	£13,998
IC	IC	R & P	Disc/disc	205/50-15	158	2687	138	7.1	15.7	£17,971
IC	IC	R & P	Disc/drum	175/70-13	158	2238	102	17.6	21.1	£10,199
IC	IC	R & P	Disc/drum	185/60-14	158	2254	103	13.1	19.2	£11,851
IC	IC	R & P	Disc/drum	185/60-14	158	2525	105	11.5	18.4	£14,149
IC	IC	R & P	Disc/drum	185/60-14	172	2437	104 (Claimed)	14.6	N/A	£11,598
IC	IC	R & P	Disc/drum	185/60-14	172	2470	111	12.2	18.8	£12,258
IC	IC	R & P	Disc/disc	185/60-14	172	2423	121	10.0	17.5	£14,545
IC	IC	R & P	Disc/disc	205/50-15	172	2789	140 (Claimed)	7.8	N/A	£19,995
IC	IC	R & P	Disc/drum	185/60-14	172	2558	103 (Est)	15.7	N/A	£13,594
IC	IC	R & P	Disc/drum	185/60-14	172	2536	97 (Est)	N/A	N/A	£11,399
IC	IC	R & P	Disc/disc	205/60-15	182	3806	110	14.9	20.0	£15,899
IC	IC	R & P	Disc/disc	205/60-15	182	3770	124 (Claimed)	11.3	N/A	£21,299
IC	IC	R & P	Disc/disc	195/65-15	182	3638	100 (Claimed)	19.3	N/A	£16,648
ITor	IC	R & P	Disc/disc	155-15	157	1900	102	14.8	19.9	£2261
ITor	IC	R & P	Disc/disc	165-15	157	1900	119	10.3	17.8	£2799
IC	BeamC	Worm	Disc/disc	165-15	170	2492	108	9.6	17.4	£2026
IC	BeamC	Worm	Disc/disc	165-15	183	2735	96 (Est)	N/A	N/A	£1354
IC	BeamC	Worm	Disc/disc	165-15	183	2735	101	12.6	18.6	£1415
IC	BeamC	Worm	Disc/disc	165-15	183	2625	90	13.9	19.8	£1465
IC	BeamC	Worm	Disc/disc	165-15	183	2548	99	12.9	18.8	£1569
IC	BeamC	Worm	Disc/disc	165-15	183	2640	105	11.6	18.3	£1974
IC	BeamC	Worm	Disc/disc	165-15	186	2856	106	11.3	18.5	£1791
IC	BeamC	Worm	Disc/disc	165-15	186	3013	113	8.8	16.9	£2488

Make and model	Production Figures	Years Built	Body Styles	Mechanical Layout	Engine Make (if not own)	Capacity/(cc)/Layout/Valves	BHP/rpm	Torque (lb.ft)/rpm	Transmission gearbox/automatic transmission
240 Family	N/A	1974–1993	Sal Est	F/R	—	1986/4IL/ OHV	82/4700	116/2300	4-spd/5-spd/Auto
						2127/4IL/ OHC	100/5250	125/3000	4-spd/5-spd/-
							123/5500	130/3500	4-spd (+O/D)/Auto
							107/5500	125/2500	4-spd/5-spd/Auto
						2315/4IL/ OHC	112/5000	137/2500	4-spd (+O/D)/Auto
							140/5750	140/4500	4-spd (+O/D)/Auto
264	169,127	1974–1985	Sal Est	F/R	—	2664/V6/ OHC	145/6000	150/3000	4-spd/5-spd/Auto
262C Coupe	5,622	1977–1981	Cpe	F/R	—	2664/V6/ OHC	148/5700	218/3000	Auto/-
66	106,137	1975–1980	Sal Est	F/R	Renault	1289/4IL/ OHV	57/5200	69/2800	Auto/-
340 Series (Incl. 360 series)	1,086,405	1976–1987	Sal Htch	F/R	Renault	1397/4IL/ OHV	70/5500	80/3500	4-spd/5-spd/Auto
					Renault	1721/4IL/ OHC	80/5400	96/3000	5-spd/-
360 Series	—	1982–1991	Sal Htch	F/R	—	1986/4IL/ OHC	115/6000	118/3600	5-spd/-
							92/5400	112/3300	5-spd/-
740/760	1,237,200	1982–1990	Sal Est	F/R	—	1986/4IL/ OHC	121/5500	116/3500	4-spd (+O/D)/ 5-spd/Auto
						2316/4IL/ OHC	114/5200	142/2500	5-spd/-
							131/5400	140/3600	4-spd (+O/D)/-
							173/5700	184/3400	4-spd(+O/D)/-
							182/5800	192/3400	4-spd(+O/D)/-
						2316/4IL/ 2OHC	155/5700	150/4450	4-spd (+O/D)/-
						2849/V6/ OHC	156/5700	173/3000	5-spd/Auto
							170/5400	177/4250	5-spd/Auto
					VW	2383/6IL/ OHC Diesel	109/4800	140/3000	4-spd (+O/D)/Auto
							122/4800	174/2400	4-spd (+O/D)/Auto
480	N/A	1985–1995	Cpe Htch	F(Tr)/F	—	1721/4IL/ OHC	109/5800	103/4000	5-spd/Auto
							120/5400	129/4600	5-spd/Auto
440	In prod	1988–Date	Htch	F(Tr)/F	Renault	1596/4IL/ OHC	83/5500	92/4400	5-spd/-
						1721/4IL/ OHC	88/5800	97/3600	5-spd/-
							109/5800	103/4100	5-spd/-
							118/5800	129/4600	5-spd/-
						1794/4IL/ OHC	89/6000	103/2500	5-spd/Auto
						1998/4IL/ OHC	110/5500	121/3500	5-spd/Auto
						1870/4IL/ OHC Diesel	90/4250	132/2250	5-spd/-
460	In prod	1989–Date	Sal	F(Tr)/F	Renault	1596/4IL/ OHC	83/5500	92/4000	5-spd/-
						1721/4IL/ OHC	87/5700	96/3600	5-spd/Auto
							102/5600	105/3900	5-spd/Auto
							122/5400	129/3300	5-spd/Auto
						1794/4IL/ OHC	89/6000	103/2500	5-spd/Auto
						1998/4IL/ OHC	110/5500	121/3500	5-spd/Auto
						1870/4IL/ OHC Diesel	90/4250	132/2250	5-spd/-
850	In prod	1991–Date	Sal	F(Tr)/F	—	1984/5IL/ 2OHC	126/6250	125/4800	5-spd/Auto
							143/6500	130/3800	5-spd/Auto
						2319/5IL/ 2OHC	240/5600	221/2000	5-spd/Auto
							170/6000	162/3300	5-spd/Auto
							250/5400	258/2400	5-spd/Auto
						2435/5IL/ 2OHC	140/5400	152/3600	5-spd/Auto
							170/6200	162/3300	5-spd/Auto
						2435/5IL/ 2OHC	225/5300	221/2000	5-spd/Auto
940/960	In prod	1990–Date	Sal Est	F/R	—	1986/4IL/ OHC	111/5700	116/2400	5-spd/Auto
							155/5600	169/3600	4-spd (+O/D)/Auto
						2316/4IL/	130/5500	137/2950	4-spd (+O/D)/ 5-spd/Auto
						OHC	165/4800	194/3450	4-spd (+O/D)/Auto
						2316/4IL/ 2OHC	155/5700	150/4450	4-spd (+O/D)/Auto
						2383/6IL/ OHC Diesel	122/4800	173/2400	4-spd (+O/D)/Auto
						2473/6IL/ 2OHC	170/5700	169/4400	5-spd/Auto
						2922/6IL/ 2OHC	204/6000	197/4300	Auto/-
S40/V40	In prod	1995–Date	Sal	F(Tr)/F	—	1731/4IL/ 2OHC	115/5500	122/4100	5-spd/Auto

Suspension Front	Rear	Steering	Brakes (Front/rear)	Wheels/Tyres	Length (in)	Weight (lb, unladen)	Top speed (mph)	0–60mph (sec)	Standing ¼-mile (sec)	UK Total Price (£: at Launch)
IC	BeamC	R & P	Disc/disc	175-14	193	2756	93 (Claimed)	N/A	N/A	£2494
IC	BeamC	R & P	Disc/disc	175-14	193	2822	98	12.6	18.4	£2155
IC	BeamC	R & P	Disc/disc	185/70-14	193	2950	106	11.4	18.0	£3175
IC	BeamC	R & P	Disc/disc	175-14	193	2822	100	12.7	18.4	£6656
IC	BeamC	R & P	Disc/disc	175-14	192	2811	105	11.2	18.2	£8767
IC	BeamC	R & P	Disc/disc	195/60-15	192	2877	111	9.7	17.1	£8696
IC	BeamC	R & P	Disc/disc	175-14	193	3058	104	12.5	18.7	£3799
IC	BeamC	R & P	Disc/disc	185/70-14	192	3197	115 (Claimed)	N/A	N/A	£13,000
ITor	DD1/2E	R & P	Disc/drum	155-13	153	1875	84	19.4	21.3	£1945
IC	DD1/2E	R & P	Disc/drum	155-13	166	2184	94	15.0	19.6	£3455
IC	DD1/2E	R & P	Disc/drum	175/70-13	166	2268	99	13.4	18.8	£6159
IC	DD1/2E	R & P	Disc/drum	185/60-14	169	2517	111	9.5	17.1	£6548
IC	DD1/2E	R & P	Disc/drum	175/70-13	169	2381	106 (Est)	N/A	N/A	£5645
IC	BeamC	R & P	Disc/disc	185/70-14	189	2710	110 (Est)	N/A	N/A	£11,910
IC	BeamC	R & P	Disc/disc	185/70-14	189	2710	110	10.6	17.7	£9249
IC	BeamC	R & P	Disc/disc	185/70-14	189	2812	114	9.4	16.8	£12,499
IC	BeamC	R & P	Disc/disc	195/60-15	189	3230	120	9.5	17.0	£13,249
IC	BeamC	R & P	Disc/disc	195/60-15	189	3021	124	8.3	16.4	£15,455
IC	BeamC	R & P	Disc/disc	185/65-15	189	2955	116	N/A	N/A	£17,495
IC	BeamC	R & P	Disc/disc	195/60-14	188	3024	114 (Auto)	10.1	17.5	£12,041
IC	IC	R & P	Disc/disc	195/60-15	188	3181	115	10.2	17.9	£19,495
IC	BeamC	R & P	Disc/disc	185/65-15	188	3131	106 (Est)	N/A	N/A	£13,950
IC	IC	R & P	Disc/disc	195/65-15	188	3308	112 (Est)	N/A	N/A	£14,590
IC	BeamC	R & P	Disc/disc	185/60-14	168	2254	110	10.3	17.7	£10,850
IC	BeamC	R & P	Disc/drum	185/60-14	168	2313	123	8.6	16.6	£14,950
IC	BeamC	R & P	Disc/drum	175/65-14	170	2161	109 (Claimed)	12.8	N/A	£9495
IC	BeamC	R & P	Disc/drum	175/65-14	170	2260	107	12.4	18.9	£9495
IC	BeamC	R & P	Disc/drum	175/65-14	170	2260	115 (Est)	N/A	N/A	£10,810
IC	BeamC	R & P	Disc/drum	185/60-14	170	2357	123	9.6	17.1	£14,595
IC	BeamC	R & P	Disc/drum	175/65-14	170	2161	112 (Claimed)	11.8	N/A	£10,995
IC	BeamC	R & P	Disc/disc	175/65-14	170	2271	116 (Claimed)	10.0	N/A	£12,495
IC	BeamC	R & P	Disc/drum	175/65-14	173	2161	114 (Claimed)	12.1	N/A	£11,445
IC	BeamC	R & P	Disc/drum	175/65-14	173	2161	109 (Claimed)	12.8	N/A	£10,495
IC	BeamC	R & P	Disc/drum	175/65-14	173	2167	109 (Est)	11.7	N/A	£11,925
IC	BeamC	R & P	Disc/drum	175/65-14	173	2244	109	11.1	18.1	£12,190
IC	BeamC	R & P	Disc/disc	185/60-14	173	2288	125	8.9	16.7	£15,995
IC	BeamC	R & P	Disc/drum	175/65-14	173	2161	109 (Claimed)	11.8	N/A	£9795
IC	BeamC	R & P	Disc/disc	175/65-14	173	2271	116 (Claimed)	10.0	N/A	£12,495
IC	BeamC	R & P	Disc/drum	175/65-14	173	2161	114 (Claimed)	12.1	N/A	£11,695
IC	IC	R & P	Disc/disc	195/60-15	183	3087	125 (Est)	10.8	N/A	£17,700
IC	IC	R & P	Disc/disc	195/60-15	183	2983	120 (Claimed)	10.1	17.5	£18,695
IC	IC	R & P	Disc/disc	205/45-17	185	3304	149	7.4	N/A	£26,995
IC	IC	R & P	Disc/disc	195/60-15	183	3181	127	9.7	17.3	£21,795
IC	IC	R & P	Disc/disc	205/45-17	185	3304	144	7.8	16.3	£32,000
IC	IC	R & P	Disc/disc	185/65-15	185	3021	126 (Est)	10.3	N/A	£17,795
IC	IC	R & P	Disc/disc	195/60-15	185	3021	131 (Est)	9.3	N/A	£21,795
IC	IC	R & P	Disc/disc	205/50-16	183	3131	149 (Est)	N/A	N/A	£24,795
IC	BeamC	R & P	Disc/disc	185/65-15	192	3021	107 (Est)	N/A	N/A	£15,900
IC	BeamC	R & P	Disc/disc	185/65-15	192	3058	122	9.3	17.2	£18,345
IC	BeamC	R & P	Disc/disc	185/65-15	192	3021	118 (Est)	10.3	N/A	£20,200
IC	BeamC	R & P	Disc/disc	195/60-15	192	3087	127 (Est)	9.3	N/A	£21,850
IC	BeamC	R & P	Disc/disc	195/60-15	192	3043	124	115	11.6	£20,100
IC	IC	R & P	Disc/disc	195/65-15	192	3307	112 (Claimed)	N/A	N/A	£19,500
IC	IC	R & P	Disc/disc	205/55-16	191	3524	123	9.0	16.8	£23,795
IC	IC	R & P	Disc/disc	195/65-15	192	3436	128	9.3	16.6	£26,950
IC	IC	R & P	Disc/disc	195/55-15	176	2640	112	10.6	17.8	£13,800

297

Make and model	Production Figures	Years Built	Body Styles	Mechanical Layout	Engine Make (if not own)	Capacity/ (cc)/Layout/ Valves	BHP/ rpm	Torque (lb.ft)/rpm	Transmission gearbox/automatic transmission
						1978/4IL/ 2OHC	137/6100	135/4500	5-spd/Auto
					Renault	1870/4IL/ OHC Diesel	90/4250	130/2250	5-spd/-

Wartburg

Make and model	Production Figures	Years Built	Body Styles	Mechanical Layout	Engine Make (if not own)	Capacity/ (cc)/Layout/ Valves	BHP/ rpm	Torque (lb.ft)/rpm	Transmission gearbox/automatic transmission
353 Knight/ Tourist	N/A	1966–1988	Sal Est	F/F	—	991/3IL/ 2str	45/4200 50/4250	71/2200 69/3000	4-spd/- 4-spd/-

Westfield

Make and model	Production Figures	Years Built	Body Styles	Mechanical Layout	Engine Make (if not own)	Capacity/ (cc)/Layout/ Valves	BHP/ rpm	Torque (lb.ft)/rpm	Transmission gearbox/automatic transmission
SE	In prod	1988–Date	Spts	F/R	Ford	1596/4IL/ OHC	108/5600	104/4500	5-spd/-
					Ford	1796/4IL/ 2OHC	128/6250	119/4250	5-spd/-
					Ford	1993IL/ 2OHC	217/6250	214/4250	5-spd/-
					Rover	3946/V8/ OHV	190/5280	220/4000	5-spd/-

– other engines/engine tunes available to special order

William

Make and model	Production Figures	Years Built	Body Styles	Mechanical Layout	Engine Make (if not own)	Capacity/ (cc)/Layout/ Valves	BHP/ rpm	Torque (lb.ft)/rpm	Transmission gearbox/automatic transmission
Farmer	N/A	1969–1974	Ute	F/R	—	246/2IL/ 2-Str	12/4400	N/A	4-spd/-

Wolseley

Make and model	Production Figures	Years Built	Body Styles	Mechanical Layout	Engine Make (if not own)	Capacity/ (cc)/Layout/ Valves	BHP/ rpm	Torque (lb.ft)/rpm	Transmission gearbox/automatic transmission
15/60 and 16/60	87,661	1958–1971	Sal	F/R	—	1489/4IL/ OHV	52/4350	82/2100	4-spd/-
						1622/4IL/ OHV	61/4500	90/2100	4-spd/Auto
1100/1300	44,867	1965–1973	Sal	F(Tr)/F	—	1098/4IL/ OHV	55/5500	61/2500	4-spd/-
						1275/4IL/ OHV	58/5250 60/5250 65/5750	69/3500 69/2500 71/3000	4-spd/Auto Auto/- 4-spd/-
18/85 and 18/85S	35,597	1967–1972	Sal	F(Tr)/F	—	1798/4IL/ OHV	85/5300 86/5300	99/2100 101/3000	4-spd/Auto 4-spd/Auto
2200 Six	25,214	1972–1975	Sal	F(Tr)/F	—	2227/6IL/ OHC	110/5250	126/3500	4-spd/Auto
Six (18-22)	19,000 (Incl. Austin and Morris figures)	1975 Only	Sal	F(Tr)/F	—	2227/6IL/ OHC	110/5250	126/3500	4-spd/Auto

Zastava

Make and model	Production Figures	Years Built	Body Styles	Mechanical Layout	Engine Make (if not own)	Capacity/ (cc)/Layout/ Valves	BHP/ rpm	Torque (lb.ft)/rpm	Transmission gearbox/automatic transmission
Yugo 3/4/5	N/A	1971–Date	Htch	F(Tr)/F	Fiat	1116/4IL/ OHC	55/6000	57/3000	4-spd/-
						1301/4IL/ OHC	65/5800	97/3900	4-spd/-
Yugo 45/55/ 65	N/A	1980–Date	Htch	F(Tr)/F	Fiat	903/4IL/ OHV	45/5800	46/3300	4-spd/-
						1116/4IL/ OHC	55/6000	57/3000	4-spd/-
						1301/4IL/ OHC	65/5800	72/3500	5-spd/-
Yugo Sana	N/A	1989–Date	Htch	F(Tr)/F	Fiat	1372/4IL/ OHC	70/6000	78/2900	5-spd/-

Suspension Front	Rear	Steering	Brakes (Front/rear)	Wheels/ Tyres	Length (in)	Weight (lb, unladen)	Top speed (mph)	0–60mph (sec)	Standing ¼-mile (sec)	UK Total Price (£: at Launch)
IC	IC	R & P	Disc/disc	195/55-15	176	2640	131 (Claimed)	9.1	N/A	£14,800
IC	IC	R & P	Disc/disc	195/55-15	176	2640	113 (Claimed)	N/A	N/A	£N/A
IC	IC	R & P	Drum/drum	165-13	167	1952	74	22.8	22.0	£612
IC	IC	R & P	Drum/drum	165-13	167	1952	84	18.7	21.0	
IC	IC	R & P	Disc/disc	185/60-14	146	1499	109	7.3	16.0	£11,750
IC	IC	R & P	Disc/disc	205/50-15	146	1499	107	7.0	15.7	£14,687
IC	IC	R & P	Disc/disc	205/50-15	146	N/Q	130 (Claimed)	5.0	N/A	£19,950
IC	IC	R & P	Disc/disc	205/50-15	146	N/Q	150 (Claimed)	3.5	N/A	£16,218
ITrL	Beam1/2E	R & P	Drum/drum	4.00-10	82	728	45	N/A	30.6	£794
IC	Beam1/2E	Worm	Drum/drum	5.90-14	178	2473	77	24.3	22.6	£991
IC	Beam1/2E	Worm	Drum/drum	5.90-14	175	2473	81	21.4	21.8	£993
IHydroL	IHydroL	R & P	Disc/drum	5.50-12	147	1820	85	18.4	21.3	£754
IHydroL	IHydroL	R & P	Disc/drum	5.50-12	147	1820	88	17.3	20.7	£825
IHydroL	IHydroL	R & P	Disc/drum	5.50-12	147	1820	87 (Est)	N/A	N/A	£999
IHydroL	IHydroL	R & P	Disc/drum	5.50-12	147	1850	97	14.1	19.6	£903
IHydroL	IHydroL	R & P	Disc/drum	175-13	166	2576	90	18.0	21.2	£1040
IHydroL	IHydroL	R & P	Disc/drum	165-14	166	2576	97	15.2	20.4	£1273
IHydroL	IHydroL	R & P	Disc/drum	165-14	167	2620	104	13.1	18.7	£1470
IHydraG	IHydraG	R & P	Disc/drum	185/70-14	175	2638	104	13.5	19.2	£2838
IC	ITrL	R & P	Disc/drum	145-13	149	1830	84 (Claimed)	N/A	N/A	£2499
IC	ITrL	R & P	Disc/drum	145-13	149	1925	84	16.0	20.3	£3262
IC	ITrL	R & P	Disc/drum	155/70-13	137	1701	79	21.6	22.1	£2749
IC	ITrL	R & P	Disc/drum	155/70-13	137	1768	89	16.8	21.0	£3349
IC	ITrL	R & P	Disc/drum	155/70-13	137	1775	95	11.7	18.1	£4495
IC	IC	R & P	Disc/drum	165/70-13	155	2007	97	13.2	19.2	£5495

APPENDIX C

Ownership of British marques after 1970

Although the British motor industry was already dominated by the large corporations by 1970, there was still plenty of space for individual enterprise to flourish:

AC: The Thames Ditton company had been rescued from receivership by the Hurlock brothers, Charles and Derek, in 1930. By 1945 they had rebuilt the company, taking in some public capital, and eventually sold out in the 1980s.

Aston Martin: Until finally taken over by Ford-UK in 1987, this marque had effectively been a rich-man's toy, kept afloat by a variety of benefactors. In 1945 it was still owned by R G Sutherland, but in 1947 it was bought by David Brown (whose Yorkshire-based business was famous for building tractors and transmissions). Having merged Aston Martin with Lagonda a few months later, Brown ultimately sold the business to Company Developments Ltd in 1972. There was a period of receivership in 1974/75, then a decade of sometimes confused ownership culminating in control by Victor Gauntlett, followed by Ford's rescue in 1987.

Austin: The Austin Motor Co Ltd, founded in 1906, had become Britain's second-largest car-maker by 1945, though the founder, Lord Austin, had died in 1941. Austin merged with the Nuffield Organisation (manufacturers of the Morris, MG, Riley and Wolseley marques) in 1952 to form the British Motor Corporation (BMC).

BMC bought the Jaguar Group in 1966 to found BMH, but in 1968 all were subsumed into British Leyland when BMH joined forces with Leyland. Austin remained alive as a marque until the late 1980s.

Bentley: Set up by W O Bentley in 1919, the several-times bankrupt maker of sportscars had been rescued from the receiver by Rolls-Royce in 1931. By 1945 it was a completely integrated part of Rolls-Royce, the cars being ever more closely derived from Rolls-Royce designs. That situation persisted into the 1990s, even though the car-making side of Rolls-Royce had been separated from the larger aircraft engine-making colossus in 1973. Like Rolls-Royce, Bentley was taken over by the Vickers Group in 1980.

Bristol: The prestigious Bristol Aeroplane Co Ltd started building cars in 1947, using designs 'liberated' from BMW as unofficial war reparations. Later, in 1960, the car-making business was hived off to Sir George White and Anthony Crook (both of whom had been connected with Bristol for some time), and a few years later Anthony Crook became the sole proprietor, which he remained in the 1990s.

Caterham: Originally set up as a car dealership in Caterham, Surrey, in 1959, the company took over the manufacturing rights to the Lotus Seven in 1973, rebadging the cars as Caterhams. To provide more manufacturing space, assembly was moved to Dartford, Kent, at the end of 1987.

Chrysler: Following the takeover of the Rootes Group by Chrysler, the company was renamed Chrysler United Kingdom in 1970. Cars originally badged as Hillmans (or, in France, as Simcas) were rebadged in mid-1976, without technical change. This, though, was a short-lived change, for after Peugeot took over the businesses in 1978, surviving models were speedily rebadged as Talbots.

Clan: This tiny company, which produced cars in County Durham in the 1970s, was set up by ex-Lotus development engineer Paul Haussauer. After it had struck financial trouble there were two separate attempts to revive the marque – one by a Cyprus consortium, which failed, the other (equally short-lived) by a Northern Ireland-based concern.

Daimler: After a turbulent corporate beginning in the 1890s, Daimler had been absorbed by the BSA Group in 1910, who added Lanchester to its clutch of concerns in 1931. Both marques continued in production in Coventry after 1945. BSA then sold the Daimler/Lanchester business to Sir William Lyons of Jaguar in 1960. Although the Lanchester marque was already moribund, the Daimler marque prospered under Jaguar ownership.

Jaguar, of course, merged with BMC in 1966, became a part of British Leyland in 1968, was sold back into private ownership in 1984, and was then taken over by Ford in 1989. Daimler therefore became a Ford-owned marque at that time.

Enfield: Sponsored by the British Electricity Council, these battery-powered runabouts were built in London by the Enfield Automotive Company, which finally was bought by a Greek entrepreneur, who moved the business to Cowes, Isle-of-Wight, without success.

Evante: This was an offshoot of the Lincolnshire-based engine tuning firm Vegantune. The design was different (but not that much!) from that of the front-engined rear-drive Lotus Elan. It was a short-lived enterprise, for the expense of getting the car Type Approved and into a reliable state was too much, and attempts to revive the company in the early 1990s failed.

Fairthorpe: The brainchild of Second World War hero Air Vice-Marshal Donald Bennett, these were originally kit-cars, but later fully built-up cars also, at first built in Chalfont St Peter, later in Gerrards Cross and finally in Denham. The AVM handed control to his son Torix in the 1970s, but the business died in the late 1970s.

Ford-UK: Set up as a personally owned subsidiary of the Henry Ford-controlled Ford Motor Company of Detroit, Ford-UK was always family controlled, especially after minor shareholdings were repurchased in the early 1960s. Over the years, share ownership widened considerably, but Ford (as one of the world's largest car-makers) never linked up with any other major group.

Gilbern: This Welsh company, based on Llantwit, near Pontypridd, was set up by Giles Smith and Bernard Frieze, who held control until financial problems struck in the early 1970s. There was an attempt to restart production under new ownership, but this came to nothing.

Ginetta: Founded by the Walklett family – no fewer than four brothers were involved in running the company – Ginetta cars were first made at Woodbridge in Suffolk, and later at Witham (Essex) and Sudbury (Suffolk). The Walkletts sold out to businessman Martin Pfaff in the late 1980s, but financial problems followed during the early 1990s. In the mid-1990s Pfaff was still in control, but Ginetta was now producing cars in the North of England.

Hillman: Hillman of Coventry had been absorbed by the Rootes Group in the 1930s and was the most important marque in that multi-headed business from 1945. Rootes eventually sold out to Chrysler of Detroit in the 1960s, after which the Hillman marque was overshadowed by Chrysler, and surviving Hillmans took Chrysler badges from the mid-1970s.

Honda: This Japanese manufacturer began making cars in 1962, first became involved with BL for the launch of the Honda-based Triumph Acclaim in 1981, then began manufacturing complete Honda cars at a factory close to Swindon in 1992.

Humber: Like Hillman, Humber of Coventry had been taken into the Rootes Group in the early 1930s, and

was still a most important part of Rootes until the 1960s, the cars latterly being little more than 'badge-engineered' Hillmans. Humber sales were buoyant until Chrysler took over the Rootes business, and in fact the last Humber of all, a Sceptre, was not made until 1976.

Jaguar: Jaguar of Coventry had been a public limited company since the mid-1930s, but the founder, William Lyons, had always held majority control. Jaguar bought up Daimler (and Lanchester) in 1960, then speedily added Coventry Climax, Guy Motors and Henry Meadows. In 1966, though, Sir William merged his company with BMC, the new holding company being BMH (see *Austin*, *above*).

Jaguar became a part of British Leyland in 1968, then a part of the nationalized concern, only to be privatized in 1984. After five years of independence, it was taken over by Ford and by the mid-1990s was controlled by Ford-USA.

Jensen: The Jensen brothers had set up their own company in the 1930s, but after a financially troubled postwar period they partly sold out to the Norcros Group in 1959. By the late 1960s all had ceded control to the merchant bank, Wm Brandt, but in 1970 a consortium headed by the American motor dealer Kjell Qvale, with Donald Healey alongside him, took over the company. Qvale's company then held control until series production ended in 1976. Attempts to restart Interceptor production in the late 1980s, by an offshoot of the old service and parts business, were only barely successful.

Jensen-Healey: This marque was produced by the Jensen company, which had been reformulated in 1970, with ex-manufacturer Donald Healey as the company chairman.

Lagonda: Rescued from receivership in 1935 by Alan Good, Lagonda was in the doldrums in 1945, despite having W O Bentley as technical director and a promising new car design. David Brown (see *Aston Martin*, *above*) bought the much reduced business in 1947, and speedily merged it with Aston Martin. By the 1970s, Lagonda had been reduced to little more than an Aston Martin model name, and was therefore acquired by Ford in 1987.

Land Rover: Rover was a public limited company which found itself with an under-used factory at Solihull in 1945. The Land-Rover 4x4 marque was therefore developed to flesh-out the Rover range. Land Rover always went along with Rover in the corporate manoeuvrings of the 1960s (see *Rover*, *below*), which meant that it was owned by Leyland from 1967, British Leyland from 1968, and finally by the Rover Group. From 1988, therefore, it was owned by British Aerospace, and from 1994 by BMW.

Lotus: Colin Chapman and his wife-to-be, Hazel, founded Lotus Engineering in 1952, and with a single change of name the marque prospered under the Chapman family's control until the 1980s. By that time it had expanded mightily, 'gone public' and moved to Norfolk. After Chapman's untimely death in 1982, when much of the family shareholding had to be sold off and there was scandal in connection with DeLorean, there was a troubled four-year period for the limited company before General Motors took control in 1986. GM persevered until 1993, when it sold Lotus to Bugatti. By 1995, Bugatti was in deep financial trouble, but Lotus somehow survived.

Marcos: Jem Marsh and Frank Costin got together in the 1950s to produce specials based on marine-ply chassis, and although Costin soon withdrew, Marsh continued with Marcos until the 1970s, when financial trouble struck. The business was then sold in 1971 to the Rob Walker Group, but stopped making Marcos cars in the 1970s. Eventually Jem Marsh bought back the rights to his original company, revived manufacture of the sportscars and carried on into the 1990s.

MG: Originally set up in William Morris' Morris Garages premises in Oxford, and developed from there, it was handed over by Morris (who by then had become Lord Nuffield) to the Nuffield Organisation. From then on it followed the fortunes of Morris, then BMC (see *Austin*, *above*, or *Morris*, *below*), becoming a part of BMC, then BMH, then British Leyland and finally the Rover Group. This means that it was controlled by British Aerospace from 1988 to 1994, after which it became one of BMW's clutch of marques, there being a brand-new MGF model in 1995.

Middlebridge: This car was no more than a lightly-redeveloped Reliant Scimitar GTE, the manufacturing rights having been bought by the Middlebridge Group, which was financed from Japan. When the Japanese concern struck major financial problems, the sportscar project died with it, and every item in the factory was sold at auction.

Mini: Originally, in 1959, there were Austin Minis and Morris Minis, but from 1969 British Leyland repositioned Mini to be a marque of its own. Mini, therefore, was controlled by British Leyland and its successors, including the Rover Group, until 1988, thereafter by British Aerospace, and from 1994 by BMW. Some publicists later liked to call this the Rover Mini, but true enthusiasts would have none of this.

Morgan: The Morgan car has always been made by a company based in Malvern Link and controlled by the Morgan family. That was the situation in 1935 when the very first Morgan four-seater was announced and was still the situation 60 years later.

Morris: Morris had been set up by William Morris in 1913, and the Cowley (Oxford)-built cars were always the most important marque in the Nuffield Organisation which was founded in 1935. By 1945, Morris also controlled MG, Riley and Wolseley. When Nuffield merged with Austin in 1952, Morris became a constituent of BMC (see Austin, above). Over the years, therefore, it became a member of BMH and British Leyland, but the last Morris cars were produced in 1984 before the Rover Group was officially inaugurated.

Naylor: Naylor Brothers of Shipley, Yorkshire, prospered in the 1970s by restoring MGs, then remanufacturing complete bodyshells for the cars. The Naylor sportscar was made by the same company, but after the project hit financial troubles, it was closed down and sold to the Hutson company, who made a handful of the TF1700 models.

Nissan: This Japanese concern began making the ancestor of Datsun cars in 1912, but the first Nissan-badged machine followed in 1937. Nissan set up a manufacturing base in the UK, close to Sunderland, in County Durham, the first British-built cars (Bluebirds) being delivered in 1986.

Panther: The Brooklands-based company was set up by Robert Jankel and thrived for some years in the 1970s, using the ex-Cooper F1 premises. After Jankel's business collapsed, it was rescued by a Korean concern, which continued to control it into the 1990s.

Peugeot: The big Peugeot group took over the ex-Chrysler United Kingdom businesses in 1978, imposing a new marque name of Talbot on the cars they had inherited in 1979. From the mid-1980s Peugeot cars were also being assembled and later manufactured at the ex-Rootes/Chrysler UK factories in Coventry.

Princess: This marque was 'invented' by British Leyland in 1975, producing front-wheel-drive saloons which had originally been badged as Austin, Morris or Wolseley types. When these cars were dropped in 1982, the marque disappeared.

Range Rover: The new-style '100 inch Land-Rover' (see Land Rover, above) was named Range Rover when launched in 1970, establishing what has been a separate marque ever since under the ownership of British Leyland, then Rover, which was ultimately controlled by British Aerospace from 1988 and by BMW from 1994.

Reliant: Established by Tom Williams in 1935, the company first built three-wheelers, then progressed into the manufacture of four-seater sportscars in 1962. By that time Reliant had been taken over by the Welsh-based Hodge Group, but although the Bond marque (see Bond, above) was added to the assets in 1969, there was no lasting financial stability. Hodge sold Reliant to Nash Securities, of Kettering, in 1977. Reliant finally descended into major financial chaos in 1990, but was rescued by Beans Industries in 1991, which carried on making cars and three-wheelers.

This should not be confused with the sale of Scimitar GTE manufacturing rights to the Middlebridge concern in the late 1980s, for this arrangement did not include the Reliant company itelf.

Rocket: The Rocket Light Car Company, based at Cambridge, was a tiny firm in which McLaren Cars technical director Gordon Murray was involved, along with ex-racing driver Chris Craft.

Rolls-Royce: Originated by Charles Rolls and Henry Royce in 1904, the company grew enormously into the manufacture of cars and aero-engines, taking in Bentley along the way in 1931 (see Bentley, above), by which time it was a large public limited company. After hitting financial trouble in 1971 (spiralling aero-engine development costs were the culprits) it was rescued by the British Government, and the car-making subsidiary was privatized in 1973. Vickers, the engineering giant, took over in 1980 and have controlled Rolls-Royce (and therefore Bentley) ever since.

Rover: First pedal cycles, then motorcycles, then cars had all been produced by Rover in its early days, this public limited company then expanding strongly after the Second World War by developing the Land-Rover. Rover bought Alvis in 1965, but was then absorbed into Leyland in 1967. Thereafter, Rover became a component of British Leyland and part of the nationalized remains of that group, but then gave its name to the retitled Rover Group in the late 1980s. British Aerospace took control from the Government in 1988, after which BMW bought Rover in 1994.

Sunbeam: Once an independent carmaker, Sunbeam had been rescued from receivership by the Rootes Group in 1935. Killed off in favour of a new Sunbeam-Talbot marque, Sunbeam was then revived in 1954, and was thereafter an important Rootes, later Chrysler UK, marque. The last Sunbeam car was produced under Chrysler control in 1976, after which Sunbeam became a model badge for Chrysler and Talbot. The residual rights are now owned by Peugeot.

Talbot: This one-time independent British name was revived by Peugeot as a new marque badge in 1979 after Peugeot had taken over the ex-Rootes, ex-Chrysler-Europe businesses in 1978, but the last British Talbot was produced in 1986. Talbot cars were also built in France in the same period.

Toyota: This Japanese firm began building cars in 1936. A new British factory, south-east of Derby, started to assemble the Carina E model in 1992 and promised to add a second model line during the late 1990s.

Trident: Bill Last was a Woodbridge (Suffolk)-based TVR dealer, who somehow emerged with the ex-TVR Trident prototype design when the Blackpool firm went through one of its periodic financial crises in 1965. Trident redeveloped the style and applied it to a proprietary Austin-Healey 3000 chassis with various engines. The enterprise failed in the late 1970s.

Triumph: Proud and independent from 1923 to 1939, Triumph lapsed into receivership and was eventually bought by Standard in 1944. Henceforth, Triumph became an upmarket Standard badge. The TR3A, and latterly the Herald, were so successful that Triumph strangled its Standard parent in 1963. In the meantime, Leyland had taken over management, so Triumph followed Leyland into alliances with Rover, then into British Leyland. The last Triumph car was a Japanese-inspired Honda, and was built in 1984. In theory, BMW could build new-generation Triumphs in future, for it now owns all the rights.

TVR: The original TVR sportscar was produced by Trevor Wilkinson's Layton Engineering in Blackpool in 1954. In the next decade, financial turmoil was ever-present and there were several changes of company name and entrepreneurial ownership before the TVR dealership-owning Lilley family – father Arthur and son Martin – bought the business in 1965. Recovery followed, and the Lilleys eventually sold out to self-made millionaire Peter Wheeler in 1981. In the mid-1990s Wheeler was still the sole proprietor of what had become a much larger operation.

Vanden Plas: Having started as a car body coachbuilding concern in northwest London (it supplied sporting shells to companies like Bentley and Alvis), VDP was acquired by Austin immediately after the Second World War. Thereafter it provided bodies for upmarket Austin, later BMC, cars, eventually becoming a marque badge of its own on the front of much-modified mass-market BMC, BMH and British Leyland cars. Vanden Plas also produced the Daimler DS420 Limousine for some years (see *Daimler, above*), but the business was closed down as part of British Leyland's rationalization in 1980.

Vauxhall: Once an independent carmaker, Vauxhall had been absorbed by General Motors of the USA in 1925, and is still a subsidiary of that carmaking colossus. During the 1960s and 1970s its operations were ever more closely merged with those of Opel of West Germany (another GM subsidiary) so that by the 1980s Vauxhalls had become no more than rebadged and mildly facelifted Opels, though still manufactured in the UK.

Westfield: Founded by Chris Smith in the West Midlands, the company began producing cars almost identical to the Caterham Super Seven in the 1980s, but was forced to modify its designs after Caterham took legal action. 'Own-brand' Westfields followed in the late 1980s, the company remaining independent of other concerns.

William: Briefly imported from France and rebadged, this was an Italian Lawil design, which was marketed in the UK by Crayford, who had already become noted in the UK for producing factory-approved convertible conversions of cars like the Mini, Ford Cortina and Ford Corsair.

Wolseley: William Morris had bought up the Wolseley car-making business in 1927 and (as Lord Nuffield) had bequeathed it to the new Nuffield Organisation in 1935. From then on it became one of various upmarket relations of the Morris marque, following Morris into BMC, then BMH and finally British Leyland. As part of the neverending rationalization of BL, Wolseley was killed off in 1975, the surviving cars being rebadged as Princess.

In Memoriam:

A similar survey of all British marques which existed between 1945 and 1970, including marques which did not survive into this period, is included in Volume 1.

The following marques did not survive beyond the years indicated:

Allard	(1960)
Alvis	(1967)
Armstrong Siddeley	(1960)
Austin-Healey	(1970)
Bedford	(1973)
Berkeley	(1961)
Bond	(1970)
Dellow	(1957)
Elva	(1959)
Frazer Nash	(1956)
Gordon-Keeble	(1966)
GSM	(1964)
Healey	(1954)
HRG	(1956)
Invicta	(1950)
Jowett	(1954)
Lanchester	(1956)
Lea-Francis	(1960)
Lloyd (UK)	(1951)
Marauder	(1952)
Meadows	(1962)
Metropolitan	(1961)
Ogle	(1962)
Oppermann	(1959)
Paramount	(1956)
Peerless	(1960)
Riley	(1969)
Singer	(1970)
Standard	(1963)
Sunbeam-Talbot	(1954)
Swallow	(1955)
Tornado	(1962)
Turner	(1966)
Unipower	(1970)
Warwick	(1962)

APPENDIX D

Production figures, registrations, exports and imports, 1970 to 1995

(With grateful thanks to the SMMT for permission to quote official figures.)

Year	Sales of cars in the UK	Private car production in the UK	Car exports from the UK	Car imports into the UK
1970	1,126,824	1,640,966	690,339	157,956
1971	1,334,685	1,741,940	741,788	281,037
1972	1,702,211	1,921,311	640,763	450,314
1973	1,688,322	1,747,321	632,090	504,619
1974	1,273,814	1,534,119	568,205	375,421
1975	1,211,658	1,267,695	537,967	448,749
1976	1,307,873	1,333,449	548,185	533,901
1977	1,335,311	1,327,820	590,875	698,464
1978	1,618,193	1,222,949	487,151	800,772
1979	1,731,882	1,070,452	374,673	1,060,645
1980	1,536,243	923,744	314,519	863,080
1981	1,513,875	954,650	300,623	805,327
1982	1,639,121	887,679	231,898	934,141
1983	1,870,556	1,044,597	233,658	1,075,834
1984	1,827,883	908,906	201,207	1,020,494
1985	1,908,704	1,047,973	226,471	1,071,892
1986	1,943,745	1,019,519	186,158	1,071,747
1987	2,078,711	1,143,045	219,940	1,047,413
1988	2,277,306	1,226,835	212,534	1,356,902
1989	2,373,391	1,299,082	280,863	1,370,589
1990	2,076,051	1,295,611	393,164	1,190,420
1991	1,592,326	1,236,900	594,903	820,436
1992	1,593,601	1,291,880	587,919	942,020
1993	1,778,426	1,375,523	561,351	985,505
1994	1,910,933	1,466,823	612,699	1,089,692
1995	1,945,366	1,532,084	744,608	1,146,602

A similar table covering the years 1945 to 1970 is published as an Appendix to Volume 1.

NOTES:

These figures have been assembled from two separate statistical charts, which explains why it is not possible to correlate every figure exactly. Where the home market is concerned, because of the 'pipeline effect' there is always a significant difference between 'cars delivered' and 'cars sold'.

Production

It took a long time to recover from the war. The prewar UK production record of 379,310 (achieved in 1937) was not beaten until 1949.

The first 'one million' year was 1958.

The nearest to a 'two million' year would be reached in 1972 – 1,921,311.

Imports

The market share of imported cars did not exceed 1 per cent for the first time until 1949. The market share of imports first exceeded 10 per cent in 1969, then rose rapidly – to 25 per cent in 1972 – and would reach 50 per cent in 1977. The peak import penetration figure recorded so far has been 61 per cent in 1979. In recent years many of those imports have been cars such as the Ford Sierra or Vauxhall Nova, which are usually seen as 'domestic' products.

Only 27,206 cars were imported during the first 10 postwar years. It took a total of 25 postwar years (until 1971) for the first million to be reached – a figure that was exceeded almost every year in the 1980s!

Exports

Britain's exports were high in the 1940s and early 1950s due to Government policies and supply restrictions. The figure peaked at no less than 77 per cent in 1951. This figure dropped below 50 per cent two years later, below 40 per cent in 1961, and reached a low of 17.3 per cent in 1988.

In the early 1990s the big new surge in exports was due to the opening of three major new plants for the manufacture of Japanese cars in the United Kingdom. These were located as follows: Nissan (in Washington, Tyne and Wear), Honda (at Swindon) and Toyota (near Derby) – many of these cars being exported to European and other territories.